The Cultural Politics of Opera, 1720–1742

Music in Britain, 1600–2000

ISSN 2053-3217

Series Editors:
BYRON ADAMS, RACHEL COWGILL AND PETER HOLMAN

This series provides a forum for the best new work in the field of British music studies, placing music from the early seventeenth to the late twentieth centuries in its social, cultural, and historical contexts. Its approach is deliberately inclusive, covering immigrants and emigrants as well as native musicians, and explores Britain's musical links both within and beyond Europe. The series celebrates the vitality and diversity of music-making across Britain in whatever form it took and wherever it was found, exploring its aesthetic dimensions alongside its meaning for contemporaries, its place in the global market, and its use in the promotion of political and social agendas.

Proposals or queries should be sent in the first instance to Professors Byron Adams, Rachel Cowgill, Peter Holman or Boydell & Brewer at the addresses shown below. All submissions will receive prompt and informed consideration.

Professor Byron Adams,
Department of Music – 061, University of California, Riverside, CA 92521–0325
email: byronadams@earthlink.net

Professor Rachel Cowgill,
Department of Music, University of York
Heslington, York, YO10 5DD
email: rachel.cowgill@york.ac.uk

Emeritus Professor Peter Holman MBE,
119 Maldon Road, Colchester, Essex, CO3 3AX
email: peter@parley.org.uk

Boydell & Brewer, PO Box 9, Woodbridge, Suffolk, IP12 3DF
email: editorial@boydell.co.uk

Previously published volumes in this series are listed at the back of this volume.

The Cultural Politics of Opera, 1720–1742

The Era of Walpole,
Pope, and Handel

Thomas McGeary

THE BOYDELL PRESS

© Thomas McGeary 2024

All rights reserved. Except as permitted under current legislation
no part of this work may be photocopied, stored in a retrieval system,
published, performed in public, adapted, broadcast,
transmitted, recorded or reproduced in any form or by any means,
without the prior permission of the copyright owner

The right of Thomas McGeary to be identified as
the author of this work has been asserted in accordance with
sections 77 and 78 of the Copyright, Designs and Patents Act 1988

First published 2024
The Boydell Press, Woodbridge

ISBN 978 1 83765 169 6

The Boydell Press is an imprint of Boydell & Brewer Ltd
PO Box 9, Woodbridge, Suffolk IP12 3DF, UK
and of Boydell & Brewer Inc.
668 Mt Hope Avenue, Rochester, NY 14620–2731, USA
website: www.boydellandbrewer.com

The publisher has no responsibility for the continued existence or accuracy of URLs for
external or third-party internet websites referred to in this book, and does not guarantee
that any content on such websites is, or will remain, accurate or appropriate

A CIP catalogue record for this book is available
from the British Library

*To keep in memory the work of
Howard Weinbrot, Maynard Mack, and Robert Hume –
three learned, generous, and humane scholars*

The Theatre is a Kind of Political *Touchstone*; for nothing sooner discovers a *sound* or *sickly* State, than the *Taste* of its People at the Theatrical Assemblies.

—*The True Briton*, no. 56 (13 December 1723)

We may read the Genius of a Nation, or an Age, in those publick Entertainments they frequent and encourage.

—*Fog's Weekly Journal*, no. 98 (8 August 1730)

The Stage is the Representation of the World, and certainly a Man may know the Humours and Inclinations of the People, by what is liked or disliked upon the stage.

—*Common Sense*, no. 19 (11 June 1737)

We have elsewhere observ'd, that there is a Kind of Sympathy betwixt Politics and Musick.

—*Common Sense*, no. 101 (6 January 1739)

Contents

	List of Plates	x
	List of Tables	xii
	Preface	xiii
	Acknowledgments	xv
	Note to the Reader	xvi
	Introduction: Opera and Cultural Politics	1
1	Rise of Walpole and the Whig Oligarchy	10
2	The Royal Academy of Music and Its Audience	22
3	Bolingbroke and the Political Opposition	44
4	Opera and the Luxury Debate	75
5	Excise and the Patriot Opposition	99
6	Opera of the Nobility and the *Furor Farinellicus*	113
7	From Excise to the War of Jenkins' Ear	131
8	A Patriot Vision for Dramatic Music	141
9	Opera and the Politics of Taste	162
10	Opera in Formal Verse Satire	239
11	War of Jenkins' Ear and the Fall of Walpole	271
12	*The New Dunciad*: Opera and the Triumph of Dulness	279
	Coda: The Cultural Work of Opera	303
	Bibliography	315
	Index	343

Plates

6.1 [After William Hogarth], *The Opera House or the Italian Eunuch's Glory* (1735). Etching 10¾ × 7⅞ in. / 25 × 28.9 cm. Courtesy of the Lewis Walpole Library, Yale University.   123

Stephens, *Prints and Drawings in the British Museum*, no. 2148
Paulson, *Hogarth's Graphic Works* (1965), no. 276 (Plate 320)
Paulson, *Hogarth's Graphic Works* (1989), no. 277/6

7.1 *Slavery* (1738). Etching, 19.8 × 28.4 cm. Courtesy of the Lewis Walpole Library, Yale University.   138

Stephens, *Prints and Drawings in the British Museum*, no. 2355

9.1 William Hogarth, *Masquerades and Operas* (*The Bad Taste of the Town*) (1724). Etching 5 × 6¹¹⁄₁₆ in. / 12.7 × 17.2 cm; first state. Courtesy of the Lewis Walpole Library, Yale University.   182

Stephens, *Prints and Drawings in the British Museum*, no. 1742
Paulson, *Hogarth's Graphic Works* (1965), no. 34 (Plate 37, first state "Could new dumb Faustus")
Paulson, *Hogarth's Graphic Works* (1989), no. 44

9.2 *Berenstadt, Cuzzoni, and Senesino* (1724). Etching/engraving, 7¹⁄₁₆ × 10 in. / 19.3 × 26.2 cm [not first state that has a visible vertical line on back flat]. Courtesy of the Lewis Walpole Library, Yale University.   185

Stephens, *Prints and Drawings in the British Museum*, no. 1768
Paulson, *Hogarth's Graphic Works* (1965), no. 266 (Plate 310)
Paulson, *Hogarth's Graphic Works* (1989), p. 34 (omitted)

9.3 *Pasquin, "Vivetur Stultitia"* (c. 1736). Etching, 7 × 8¾ in. / 21 × 24 cm. © The Trustees of the British Museum.   194

Stephens, *Prints and Drawings in the British Museum*, no. 2466
Paulson, *Hogarth's Graphic Works* (1965), p. 317 (Plate 344)
Paulson, *Hogarth's Graphic Works* (1989), p. 317 (forgery)

9.4 Gerard van der Gucht, Frontispiece to James Bramston, *The Man of Taste* (1733). Engraving, 12.7 × 9.3 cm. Hanna Holborn Gray Special Collections Research Center, University of Chicago Library.   204

PLATES   xi

9.5 *Taste, or Burlington Gate* (1732). Etching, 23 × 16.3 cm.
Courtesy of the Lewis Walpole Library, Yale University.   207

Stephens, *Prints and Drawings in the British Museum*, no. 1873
Paulson, *Hogarth's Graphic Works* (1965), no. 277 (Plate 321)
Paulson, *Hogarth's Graphic Works* (1989), p. 35 (omitted: forgery)

9.6 William Hogarth, "The Countess's Levee," *Marriage à la Mode*,
Plate 4 (1745). Etching/engraving, 38.5 × 46 cm; second state.
Courtesy of the Lewis Walpole Library, Yale University.   217

Stephens, *Prints and Drawings in the British Museum*, no. 2731
Paulson, *Hogarth's Graphic Works* (1965), no. 231 (Plate 271)
Paulson, *Hogarth's Graphic Works* (1989), 161

9.7 William Hogarth, "The Rake's Levee," *A Rake's Progress*, Plate 2
(1735). Etching/engraving 12⅜ × 15¼ in. / 35 × 40.3 cm; third
state. Courtesy of the Lewis Walpole Library, Yale University.   220

Stephens, *Prints and Drawings in the British Museum*, no. 2173
Paulson, *Hogarth's Graphic Works* (1965), no. 133 (Plate 140, second state)
Paulson, *Hogarth's Graphic Works* (1989), 133b

12.1 George Bickham, *The Late Premier Minister* (1743).
Engraving, 35.8 × 25.1 cm. Courtesy of the Lewis Walpole
Library, Yale University.   290

Stephens, *Prints and Drawings in the British Museum,* no. 2607

Frederick G. Stephens, *Catalogue of Prints and Drawings in the British
Museum*. Division I. *Political and Personal Satires*, 3 vols. (London:
British Museum, 1877)
Ronald Paulson, *Hogarth's Graphic Works*, 2 vols. (New Haven, Conn.: Yale
University Press, 1965)
Ronald Paulson, *Hogarth's Graphic Works*, 3rd, rev. ed. (London: Print
Room, 1989)

Tables

2.1	Finances of Heidegger's Opera Company, 1713–14 to 1716–17 Seasons	23
2.2	Two-hundred-pound Shareholders in the Royal Academy of Music, 1719	28
2.3	Summary of Productions of the Royal Academy of Music and the Handel-Heidegger Partnership	37
2.4	Two-hundred-pound Sponsors of a Projected 1728–29 Season of the Royal Academy of Music, with Their Previous Opera Company Participation	39
6.1	Directors of the Opera of the Nobility, June 1733, with Their Previous Opera Company Participation	115
6.2	Summary of 1733–34 to 1743–44 Opera Seasons	116
6.3	Two-hundred-pound Subscribers to Middlesex's Opera Company, 1742, with Their Previous Opera Company Participation	128
12.1	Prince Frederick's Patronage of Handel's Operas, Odes, and Oratorios	294

Preface

"Of making books there is no end" we learn from *Ecclesiastes*. This is the third of what decades ago was to be a single book that explored opera and politics in early eighteenth-century Britain. Previously, in response to interest at the time in matters of sex and sexuality, I had explored the relation of opera to issues of gender, the castrato, and sexuality. It seemed the next topic should be politics. In this study, I am interested in what is now called "cultural politics." In a sense, it is about the pursuit of power (the essence of politics) and hegemony in the cultural realm; it is the contest over what cultural product(s) should be dominant or valued in Britain; what art(s) are beneficial or detrimental for the people of Britain. In another sense, it is how a cultural product was put to use in the pursuit of political power; how politics was carried out using a cultural product. In this instance, the focus is on a bivalent Italian opera at the intersection of literature, music and theatre history, social criticism, political polemic, and partisan politics during the ministry of Sir Robert Walpole from 1722 to 1742. In a modern sense, we are talking about the "culture wars" of the Walpole era.

The focus of the book is discourse about the institution of opera as found in a variety of poems, verse satires, political pamphlets, newspaper lead essays, plays, and satiric prints. Most of the writings examined are literary, moralistic, or political works espousing antagonism to the reign of Walpole and that use the institution of opera (embracing the operas, composers, singers, patrons, and audience) for partisan purposes. Opera – with its exploitable associations with court and ministry, the *beau monde*, and Whig social-political oligarchy – was a means for writers to delegitimize Walpole. Polemicists framed opera as a consequence of the corruption, luxury, and False Taste that were spawned by the Robinocracy. The very presence of opera was a sign of the ills generated by Walpole's ministry and visible evidence of the need to remove him from office. Needless to say here and elsewhere, it is doubtful that the institution of opera as reified by political writers had the actual consequences or effects they imagined or feared for it (and were disregarded by opera's patrons).

This book overlaps chronologically with *The Politics of Opera in Handel's Britain* (Cambridge University Press, 2013). It deals at the broad, general level of cultural and ideological contest, whereas the earlier book focused on the day-to-day contest for political place and power. That book examines how specific events at the Haymarket opera theatre – involving its singers, composers, and management personnel – were satirized and allegorized with reference to specific political events of the 1720s, 1730s, and early 1740s as part of the campaign to drive Walpole from office. A major purpose of the book was to debunk the notion that the politics of opera is to be found in topical political allegories and allusions in the operas themselves or in the directors of the opera. That

xiii

book shows that partisan politics can be at work in writings that draw parallels or allegories involving the opera theatre with events of domestic or European politics. A final chapter shows how the political content of individual operas could be read in the manner of the traditional *ars historica*, containing exempla and precepts of political wisdom and civic virtue that could be applied by the audience to the politics of their own time.

The second book, *Opera and Politics in Queen Anne's Britain, 1705–1714* (Boydell, 2022), examines how Italian singing and Italian-style opera intersected with Tory-Whig party politics in the era of Queen Anne. It deals with the political in the sense of topical, day-to-day partisan politics. Even before all-sung, Italian-style opera was produced in London in 1705, Italian and English singing had been politicized around the singers Margarita de l'Epine and Catherine Tofts, respectively. The contrasted features of Italian and English singing were used by Whig writers to deride Tory ministers and admirals and to define British national identity.

That book shows that Whigs were the primary promoters of the introduction of opera. The early responses to Italian opera – denunciatory or satiric – by the Whigs Richard Steele, Joseph Addison, and John Dennis are well known and have often been taken to characterize English response as a whole. These Whigs had different motives and points of view for their writings about opera, which are often not distinguished. Steele, Dennis, and the Earl of Shaftesbury consider the effect of opera using the trope of the Machiavellian moment as elaborated by J. G. A. Pocock. Addison presents a case for correcting opera in accord with the principles of Politeness. After 1710, opera in London was (with only rare exceptions) an Italian institution, sung all in Italian, by mostly Italian singers, to Italian librettos set by Italians. A final chapter shows how several early promoters of opera sung in English continued to produce works that embodied an English aesthetic for dramatic music, and how Handel became involved in politics due to the War of the Spanish Succession.

All three books explore the many ways opera and politics were entwined in early eighteenth-century Britain; all show in some way how attacks on opera had targets other than opera itself or the musical taste of Britons.

This and the first book close in 1742, a year marked by the triple conjunction of final events in the narrative arcs of opera, politics, and satire. The previous year, Handel produced the last of his Italian operas; Robert Walpole fell from power; and Alexander Pope published the last book of his *Dunciad* project, bringing to a close a great era of satire in the intellectual life of Hanoverian Britain.

Acknowledgments

Throughout the course of researching and writing these three books, for providing the time and access to primary materials, especially in the years before ECCO, I am grateful for residential fellowships at the Newberry Library, Chicago; the William Andrews Clark Memorial Library, Los Angeles; the Henry E. Huntington Library and Museum, San Marino, California; and the Harvard University Houghton Library. The Lewis Walpole Library, Farmington, Connecticut, and the Newberry Library-British Academy provided travel grants.

While researching this project, I have benefited from the assistance, learning, and encouragement of Olive Baldwin and Thelma Wilson, Lorenzo Bianconi, Jeremy Black, Robert Bucholz, Xavier Cervantes, Alison DeSimone, Anne Desler, John Dussinger, Andrew Hanham, Peter Holman, (the late) Robert Hume, David Hunter, Harry Johnston, (the late) Maynard Mack, Bill Mann, (the late) Fred Nash, Valerie Rumbold, Carole Taylor, Jennifer Thorp, William Weber, (the late) Howard Weinbrot, Bryan White, and Calhoun Winton. I owe the term *furor Farinellicus* to Carlo Vitali.

I have been guided by the literary scholarship of Howard Weinbrot and Robert Hume (what he calls "archaeo-historicism"); their writings always set high standards to emulate and imbue humility at one's own efforts. The works of Howard Weinbrot and Maynard Mack have been invaluable guides to satire and for Pope, while Robert Hume, Judith Milhous, and Carole Taylor have laid essential foundations for opera history and the prosopography of its audiences.

Helpful have been several archivists: Anna Louise Mason, Archives and Documentation Manager, Castle Howard; Crispin Powell, Boughton House; Emma Floyd, Paul Mellon Center for British Art, London; Christopher Hunwick, Archives of the Duke of Northumberland, Alnwick Castle; and Peter Foden and Victoria Perry, Belvoir Castle.

As well, I am grateful to the College of Agricultural, Consumer and Environmental Sciences (ACES), the Illinois State Geological Survey, and the College of Engineering at the University of Illinois, Urbana-Champaign for providing, if not sinecures, at least means of support that allowed me to conduct the research and writing of these books.

Note to the Reader

During the years of research, many before the availability of Eighteenth-Century Collections Online (ECCO), I consulted original printed editions, in many cases multiple copies. Most primary texts cited are now accessible via ECCO or other online sources, but consulting original exemplars, where possible, is still optimal, for they may contain significant contemporary manuscript annotations or textual differences. Moreover, the single copy of an edition available through ECCO may be defective, may have non-original tipped-in material, or may not be the best edition to consult.

For newspapers, in most cases, the original folio half-sheet issues have been consulted where they exist, in preference to the subsequent collected reprint editions. Some scholars seem not aware that the collected reprint editions or microfilmed sets often do not contain the whole run of the periodical, and collected editions often omit editorial comment or briefer items (especially advertisements).

Further bibliographic information about most printed works can be found in the English Short-Title Catalogue, and, for poetry, David F. Foxon, *English Verse 1701–1750: A Catalogue of Separately Printed Poems with Notes on Contemporary Collected Editions*, 2 vols. (London: Cambridge University Press, 1975).

London is the place of publication for pre-1800 items, unless noted. Before 25 March 1752, Britain still used the Julian (Old Style) calendar, whereas the Continent used the Gregorian (New Style) calendar, which ran 10 or 11 days ahead of the Old Style calendar. The New Year began on 1 January in the New Style, but on Lady Day (or 25 March) for the Old Style. However, all years are given as if beginning on 1 January. For England, this leaves an ambiguity of the year for dates between 1 January and 25 March (before the calendar reconciliation in 1752). Dates in England are presumed to be Old Style (o.s.), and dates on the Continent as New Style (n.s.); however, to avoid confusion some dates on the Continent are given in both Old and New Style.

Where possible I have consulted original sources for manuscripts, even when available in modern editions (which are often unsatisfactory). Transcriptions observe original spelling, capitalization (though original letter forms are often indeterminate), and punctuation. Some punctuation is added in brackets for clarity. Common abbreviations are not expanded; unusual abbreviations are expanded in square brackets.

To avoid awkward locutions, I have occasionally used the term 'Englishmen' realizing women would also have been included. For the convenience of readers, peers are usually referred to by their more familiar titles (not always their ultimate title) rather than family name.

Where possible to reduce footnotes, page, line, or act and scene numbers are given within sentences in parentheses; to avoid ambiguity, numbers that refer to line numbers are indicated as such. Such internal citations always refer to the source immediately mentioned.

To avoid encumbering the notes with routine citations to reference works, readers may consult the following, which will not be cited, except to document extremely pertinent information or to correct details: the print edition and online version of *The Oxford Dictionary of National Biography* (Oxford: Oxford University Press, 2004); and the second edition of *The New Grove Dictionary of Music and Musicians*, ed. Stanley Sadie and John Tyrrell (London: Macmillan, 2001), and its online version as *Oxford Music Online*. Biographies of many politicians can be found in *The History of Parliament: The House of Commons, 1690–1715*, ed. Eveline Cruickshanks, Stuart Handley, and D. W. Hayton, 5 vols. (Cambridge: Cambridge University Press, 2002); and *The History of Parliament. The House of Lords, 1660–1715*, ed. Ruth Paley, 5 vols. (Cambridge: Cambridge University Press, 2016). Biographies of MPs can also be found at the *History of Parliament* website.

* * *

The period covered by this book roughly coincides with that of my *The Politics of Opera in Handel's Britain* (Cambridge University Press, 2013). A common background of political history and history of the opera companies is a necessary context for both books. Readers of the earlier book will forbear if – for the convenience of new readers of this book – episodes in political history and the formation of the opera companies are also briefly reviewed and documented here for the sake of providing narrative continuity and context for this book. However, some episodes are presented here more fully as appropriate.

The material in common to the two books is shaped by and directed to different ends. In *The Politics of Opera in Handel's Britain*, the focus of political history was on Whigs and Tories and then on the Walpole ministry and opposition to it as background for the possible politics at work in opera allegories and the directorship and founding of the opera companies. There, European history is narrated more fully as background for the use of singers and events at the Haymarket theatre in political allegories. The feuds within the royal family receive greater attention for their effect on the founding and rivalry between the opera companies. Farinelli receives attention due to his use in the propaganda leading to the War of Jenkins' Ear.

In this book, the emphasis is less on daily political events and controversies than on the ideological conflict of the era and its cultural consequences: that between the ministry of Robert Walpole and the oppositions to it. The ideological justification for opposition to Walpole underlies much of the motive for Patriot drama and formal verse satire. To help explain why opera was such an attractive target for partisan satire and as an example of False Taste and Dulness, this book elaborates on the social status of the founders of the opera companies, their audience, and their overlap with politicians, the Court, and the Walpole ministry. Farinelli receives attention for his role as a symbol for opera. Political events relevant to the Patriot allegories and formal satires are foregrounded.

The fall of Walpole, Handel's abandonment of opera, and the final book of Pope's *Dunciad* project bring this book to a close.

Introduction: Opera and Cultural Politics

After its introduction to London in 1705, all-sung, Italian-style opera quickly became the most prestigious theatrical entertainment of London's cultural elite and a focus of its social life. Just as quickly, as an expensive, visually spectacular, and polite entertainment, Italian opera and its singers (but especially the foreign castrato) became a powerful symbol in the domain of cultural politics, the occasion for articulating and debating a wide range of British moral, aesthetic, and political concerns.

The early objections to Italian opera became a constant refrain for critics for the rest of the century and beyond.[1] Critiques and attacks came from all quarters – many with no musical concern at all. Social and literary critics claimed opera was an irrational, feminizing, sensuous art form; sung in a foreign language, it violated verisimilitude and the traditional aims of serious literature and theatre. Dramatists and advocates of British theatre objected to the money lavished on opera and the singers to the detriment of native authors, actors, and dramatic traditions. Religious reformers and moralists condemned opera as an expensive offspring of luxury that led to immorality, sensuality, and effeminacy; *castrati* were said to pose a sexual threat to women and gender norms.[2] Nationalists and patriots objected to the presence of a foreign art form on the London stage and its effect on (what was called) Publick Spirit. After 1734, the castrato Farinelli became a proxy for the institution of Italian opera and all it stood for.

These objections to opera in the written and graphic record have distorted modern impressions of the role and place of opera in British culture – which

---

[1] For sources of this (generally hostile) reception of Italian opera and castrati in London, see Xavier Cervantes, "'Tuneful Monsters': The Castrati and the London Operatic Public, 1667–1737," *Restoration and Eighteenth-Century Theatre Research*, 2nd ser., 13 (1998), 1–24; Todd S. Gilman, "The Italian (Castrato) in London," pp. 49–70 in *The Work of Opera: Genre, Nationhood, and Sexual Difference*, ed. Richard Dellamora and Daniel Fischlin (New York, N.Y.: Columbia University Press, 1997); and Lowell Lindgren, "Critiques of Opera in London, 1705–1719," pp. 145–65 in *Il melodramma italiano in Italia e in Germania nell' età barocca*, Contributi musicologici del Centro Ricerche dell' A.M.I.S.-Como, 9 (Como, 1995).

[2] On violation of gender norms, see my series of articles: "Verse Epistles on Italian Opera Singers, 1724–1736," *Royal Musical Association. Research Chronicle*, 33 (2000), 29–88; "Repressing Female Desire on the London Opera Stage, 1724–1727," *Women and Music: A Journal of Gender and Culture*, 4 (2000), 40–58; "Gendering Opera: Italian Opera as the Feminine 'Other' in England, 1700–42," *Journal of Musicological Research*, 14 (1994), 17–34; and "'Warbling Eunuchs': Opera, Gender, and Sexuality on the London Stage," *Restoration and Eighteenth-Century Theatre Research*, 2nd ser., 7 (1992), 1–22.

2 THE CULTURAL POLITICS OF OPERA, 1720–1742

have ignored the fact that many who consumed, valued, and enjoyed opera apparently felt no great need to defend or promote it in print. Poets, though, found praise of singers an attractive and traditional topic for verse.

This book contextualizes a range of verse, prints, newspaper essays, and other political writings that satirize, condemn, remonstrate, or otherwise object to opera to show their political context and the ulterior intent of their critique of opera and its devotees.

Like any cultural product, Italian opera had a relation to politics: but much depends on how one construes politics. In a broad sense, the politics of opera could be examined by showing how opera (as a genre or individual works) can be related to, seen as a general manifestation of prevailing political, cultural, philosophical, class, and social ideas or the general "spirit" of the time. Such broad connections are explored in, for example, *The Politics of Opera: A History from Monteverdi to Mozart* (Princeton University Press, 2017) by the philosopher Mitchell Cohen.

The book, however, is concerned with politics in a more narrow sense of gaining power in the domain of national governance: who should govern the nation, and shaping the opinion of the political nation that could then influence legislative, ministerial, or royal decisions.[3] More precisely, the focus is on the "cultural politics" of opera: how a cultural product could be used in polemic and literary works for political advantage; how political work could be accomplished by means of cultural products; how those involved in the opposition to Robert Walpole's ministry used the institution of opera in literary and graphic works to discredit his ministry and bring about his removal.

❧ Opera as Cultural Symbol

Opera's potential for use in satire, verse, political essays, and prints for cultural critique and political polemic was enabled by its prestigious and highly visible position in the field of cultural productions of Britain. Like any cultural product, opera could be a proxy for, or associated with, those who patronize and attend it.

Italian opera was a controversial cultural product partly because (in Ian Hacking's sense) it was bivalent: it was suspended between the positive pole of approval and acceptance and the negative pole of social and moral disparagement and disdain.[4]

---

[3] On the reality of the impact of public opinion (even of British middling and lower orders) or out-of-doors politics on administrations; see H. T. Dickinson, *The Politics of the People in Eighteenth-Century Britain* (London: Macmillan, 1994), 8; and Kathleen Wilson, *The Sense of the People: Politics, Culture and Imperialism in England, 1715–1785* (Cambridge: Cambridge University Press, 1995), 124–32, 157–8, and 326–7.

[4] I borrow the concepts of bivalent and cultural polarity from Ian Hacking, *Mad Travelers: Reflections on the Reality of Transient Mental Illness* (Charlottesville, Va: University of Virginia Press, 1998), 81–2.

Opera's devotees could see in its music and star singers the pinnacle of music, taste, and polite culture – a sign of Britain's coming of age as a European power competing with Italy and France in matters of culture and the arts. Opera as a prominent cultural institution was visible in the figure of the tall, squeaky-voiced *castrati* about and around in London and their extravagant salaries. On the evenings of opera performances during the season, the streets around the Haymarket theatre were crowded with coaches, sedan chairs, liveried servants, and finely dressed persons of quality. After the opera, patrons were escorted home by link boys.[5]

On the other hand, a long tradition of outspoken and virulent critics denounced opera as a sensuous, luxurious, irrational, effeminate import with supposedly insidious effects on British moral character, national identity, gender stability, and the survival of native British drama. Its patronage and support by the Ministry, Court, and Britain's political-social elite and *beau monde* made it a convenient, useful target for oppositional political writers and social critics.

What made opera such a powerful symbol was its dominant position in what Pierre Bourdieu calls "the field of cultural production."[6] For Bourdieu, the prestige (dominant position) of a cultural product is inverse to the size of its audience and its commercial profitability.[7] High-prestige works such as opera (at least in the field of theatre productions) have a restricted audience (often limited by price and to its own coterie of fellow artists, connoisseurs, and critics) and poor financial success. By contrast, mass market products (Bartholomew Fair events, comedies, harlequinades, popular theatre) have lower prestige among the cultural cognoscenti or arbiters of taste but great commercial potential.

More so than now, experiencing opera was limited to a small, restricted audience: it was available only to those in London at most only twice a week during the season (for usually no more than about 50 performances). The Haymarket opera theatre's seating capacity was usually about 700 to 900. And judging from financial records, it was rarely filled to capacity and usually not even when attended by the royal family. The thin houses, even for the star Farinelli,

---

[5] Link boys (youths carrying torches) are noted in the accounts of Richard Grenville, second Earl Temple for years 1732–1779; Huntington Library, Stowe Manuscripts, ST 164.

[6] Pierre Bourdieu, *The Field of Cultural Production: Essays on Art and Literature*, ed. and intro. Randal Johnson (New York, N.Y.: Columbia University Press 1993). The concept of fields is explored further in the Coda, "The Cultural Work of Opera." Bourdieu's sociological work is especially pertinent to this topic since he provides an institutional theory of art that shows how cultural products are positioned in hierarchically organized fields; while theoretically complex, his sociology of cultural products is grounded in empirical data. His work's application to opera is discussed further in Chapter 2 and the coda.

[7] On the inverse relationship of prestige (restricted production) and commercial success: see *The Field of Cultural Production*, the chapter "The Field of Cultural Production, or: the Economic World Reversed," esp. pp. 39–40, 46–53, and the chapter "The Market of Symbolic Goods," esp. pp. 112–31.

4   THE CULTURAL POLITICS OF OPERA, 1720–1742

were often noted by contemporaries. So even among the potential audience, only a small portion chose to attend and patronize it regularly. The closest substitute experience of opera at the time might be to hear an aria sung at a private musical entertainment or a public concert, or to sing it oneself. Today by contrast, a wide audience can experience opera via LP, CD, DVD, live television, cinema, or Internet streaming.

THE FORMS OF CAPITAL AND OPERA PATRONAGE

For understanding the prestige and status of participation in the world of opera, useful are Bourdieu's concepts of economic, social, and cultural capital. These forms of capital are needed to enter in and reap the status rewards of participation in the small and elite world of Italian opera.[8] At a minimum of course, economic capital, or accumulated human labor, is necessary to acquire the social and cultural capital to enter the world of opera patronage.

For Bourdieu, social capital is one's participation in a group – whether of kinship, friends, workplace, or association. Such personal relations provide a network of potential resources and support. While accrual of social capital may involve obligations (or even possible violation of them), in return one derives benefits in various forms.[9] The group's members share norms and values, and social capital itself may produce profits in the form of economic or cultural capital.

Cultural capital, a form of symbolic capital, is knowledge, possession of cultural objects (pictures, books, art objects), practices learned through exposure and contacts with experts, or academic qualification; its acquisition is obtained by investment of money and time, and it can be transmitted through family or schooling. Cultural capital produces a disposition to attend the opera, the *savoir faire* of being a member of the opera connoisseurs.

It is difficult to convey the economic capital required to fully participate in this elite world of opera, especially at the most prestigious level. For the first opera company established in London, the chartered Royal Academy of Music founded in 1719, a two-hundred-pound share in the joint-stock corporation (in effect underwriting) marked the most committed opera supporters.[10] For sub-

---

[8] On the types of capital, Pierre Bourdieu, "The Forms of Capital" (published in 1983), trans. Richard Nice, pp. 241–58 in John G. Richardson, *Handbook of Theory and Research for the Sociology of Education* (New York, N.Y.: Greenwood Press, 1986). Also reprinted in *Education, Culture, Economy, and Society*, ed. A. H. Halsey et al. (Oxford: Oxford University Press, 1997), 40–58. See also translator's introduction, *Field of Cultural Production*, 7–8. Bourdieu uses capital close to its strict economic sense: it is labor objectified or embodied; it has "a potential capacity to produce profits and to reproduce itself, in identical or expanded form, [and] contains a tendency to persist in its being" (p. 241). Briefer mentions occur elsewhere in his works cited elsewhere.

[9] For useful expansions and explications of Bourdieu's concept of social capital, see the chapters in Part I of *Knowledge and Social Capital: Foundations and Applications*, ed. Eric L. Lesser (Woburn, Mass.: Butterworth-Heinemann, 2000).

[10] For the Royal Academy, the £200 was supposedly a purchase of shares (only £40 was due immediately) that would pay dividends (attendance may have required season

INTRODUCTION: OPERA AND CULTURAL POLITICS 5

scription attendance to a full season, a twenty-guinea ticket allowed admission to all the season's performances; seats in a box required an additional 1½ to 2 guineas. For the occasional walk-in audience member, ticket prices were twice those of usual playhouse tickets (see further analysis in Chapter 2).

It took more than just a ticket to make an acceptable appearance at the opera house: the attendee needed to have transportation to the theatre (by means of coach or chair), fashionable dress, and liveried servants (to save place in the pit or gallery). As well, some pocket money for a libretto for the opera (1 shilling), refreshments, tips to the box keepers, chair hire home (1 shilling), and hire for link boys (1 shilling) would add to the expense for a single night at the opera.[11]

To top this, devotees competed for social status by giving the singers gifts (see accounts of Farinelli's benefit in Chapter 6), inviting them to perform privately at soirees (with a suitable *douceur*), and inviting them to their country homes for the summer.

Some surviving financial accounts highlight the great sums spent for opera attendance. Robert Walpole's household accounts give the expenses for opera for his family. For the full nine-season run of the Academy (1719 to 1728), he was billed by Heidegger and the Royal Academy of Music a total of £687 15s. This account includes calls for his two-hundred-pound share; incidental expenses for the nine seasons (single tickets, librettos) at the opera theatre were £487 15s.[12]

For the Handel-Heidegger 1732–33 season, Lady Walpole, Lord Burlington, the Duchess of Newcastle, and the Duchess of Buckingham were billed £105, £84, £150, and £42, respectively, for use of their boxes at the opera (at 1½ to 2 guineas per night).[13] The accounts reveal how frequently devoted operagoers attended. For perspective on these amounts, a modern estimate gives each pound at the time to be equivalent of £200 to £400 in today's value.[14]

---

subscriptions or individual tickets). For several later opera companies, the £200 promised at the beginning of a season was more like underwriting to guarantee any losses.

[11] For such additional expenses, see the account book of Richard Grenville, second Earl Temple, for years 1732–1779 (Huntington Library, Stowe Manuscripts, ST 164) and that of the Duchess of Newcastle (British Library, Add. MSS 33,627 and 33,628).

[12] The accounts are analyzed in Thomas McGeary, "The Opera Accounts of Sir Robert Walpole," *Restoration and Eighteenth-Century Theatre Research*, 2nd ser., 7 (1996).

[13] Reported in Judith Milhous and Robert D. Hume, "Handel's Opera Finances in 1732-3," *Musical Times*, 125 (1984), 86–9.

[14] On the problems of converting the value of eighteenth-century money, see Robert D. Hume, "The Value of Money in Eighteenth-Century England: Incomes, Prices, Buying Power – and Some Problems in Cultural Economics," *Huntington Library Quarterly*, 77 (2015), 373–416; David Hunter, "Patronizing Handel, Inventing Audiences: The Intersection of Class, Money, Music and History," *Early Music*, 28 (2000), 32–49; and the essay "Defining Measures of Worth; Most Are Better than the CPI" at the website < MeasuringWorth.com >.
  This book uses the conversion of Robert Hume. MeasuringWorth.com proposes four alternative comparators for converting value.

6   THE CULTURAL POLITICS OF OPERA, 1720–1742

One also needed cultural capital for opera appreciation and disposition to attend. For males (and some few females), having been to Italy or on the Grand Tour gave a first-hand education about opera and singers on its home ground. Also useful were knowing French or Italian to converse with the singers or follow the opera's plot. To make the opera more intelligible, helpful was the cultural capital of familiarity with ancient history and mythology, social practices, or customs. To appear a proper connoisseur, one needed to know the appropriate ways to praise arias and singers.

Persons responding inappropriately to singers (lacking the appropriate cultural capital) are frequent targets of satirists and identified as victims of False Taste (see Chapter 9). A fictional example of a country family being unfamiliar with the expectations of dress and behavior at the opera in London, and the father's ignorance of the ticket pricing, are given in Fanny Burney's *Evelina* (1778).[15]

In addition to economic or cultural capital that restricted access to opera, also affecting attendance was social capital. There was no system of introduction to opera in schools or media, so the disposition or interest to attend had to be acquired through one's social connections: being among opera *cognoscenti* to provide news about singers, invitations to share a box at the opera or to a private soiree featuring a singer, or coaching on fashion and behavior at opera attendance.

It has been claimed by Jürgen Habermas about a public sphere that emerged in late-seventeenth- and eighteenth-century Britain:

> For the first time an audience gathered to listen to music as such – a public of music lovers to which anyone who was propertied and educated was admitted. Released from its functions in the service of social representation, art became an object of free choice and of changing preference. The "taste" to which art was oriented from then on became manifest in the assessments of lay people who claimed no prerogative, since within a public everyone was entitled to judge.[16]

As emerges from this discussion (and below in Chapter 2), opera in eighteenth-century Britain was by no means a popular, public, middling-status, or bourgeois entertainment.[17] As David Hunter states, the experience of opera "was restricted to a minute portion of the population, was not thoroughly

---

[15] Fanny Burney, *Evelina: or the History of a Young Lady's Entrance into the World* (1778), letter no. 21. See also Adam Smith's description: "The coxcomb, who imitates their manner [the politeness of the great], and affects to be eminent by the superior propriety of his ordinary behaviour, is rewarded with a double share of contempt for his folly and presumption"; *The Theory of Moral Sentiments* (1759), 120.

[16] Jürgen Habermas, *Structural Transformation of the Public Sphere: An Inquiry into a Category of Bourgeois Society*, trans. Thomas Burger (Cambridge, Mass.: MIT Press), 39–40.

[17] Richard Leppert, "Imagery, Musical Confrontation and Cultural Difference in Early 18th-Century London," *Early Music*, 14 (1986), 323–45, is quite mistaken that opera was "a popular victory among audiences" and "represented something akin to popular culture; a box office success" (p. 330).

INTRODUCTION: OPERA AND CULTURAL POLITICS   7

diffused among the elite, and could not trickle down easily."[18] He concludes the contrast to modern patterns of attendance and familiarization with opera through media is in "striking contrast."[19] The elite and exclusive world of opera was noted by contemporaries. Johann Mattheson, writing of the commercial opera in Hamburg in 1728, noted that "Opern sind mehr für Könige und Fürsten, als für Kauff- und Handels-leute."[20]

Writers sparring over the acceptability (approval) of Italian opera can be seen as attempting to answer the political question (as posed by E. D. Hirsch), "What sort of culture do we want to foster?" [21] Or, for this study, "What role does (or should) opera play in the type of civic-social culture we want to encourage?" Some contemporaries replied it was one absent Italian opera, a product of luxury and corruption. Some, by their subscriptions, attendance, and patronage, endorsed opera as a fitting addition to the culture of Britain – a sign of politeness and mark of Britain's status as a prosperous commercial society.

✒ Chapter Summaries

Chapter 1, "Rise of Walpole and the Whig Oligarchy," sets the political background for the period 1720–1742: the accession of George I, the rise to political dominance of Whig ministries, the Whig Schism, and the emergence of Robert Walpole as prime minister through his adroit management of the South Sea crisis and the Atterbury plot.

For this period, the pattern of opera production in London was set by the Royal Academy of Music, which by its financing by shareholders, Royal bounty, season subscriptions, and overall high prices established opera as a prestigious elite entertainment. Chapter 2, "The Royal Academy of Music and Its Audience," describes the formation of the Academy and the social status of the shareholders and subscribers to show the opera audience as a very elite group of nobility, gentry, financiers, professionals, and men of politics. This social and political oligarchy made opera a target for moralists' critique and literary satire that could have political utility.

Despite its political dominance, the Whig oligarchy was riven by factions. Chapter 3, "Bolingbroke and the Political Opposition," traces the various dissident Whig oppositions and the rise of the opposition to the Walpole ministry led by Viscount Bolingbroke as its main organizer and theorist. In the wake of the Financial Revolution and Britain's growing commercial prosperity, the

---

[18] David Hunter, "Patronizing Handel, Inventing Audiences: The Intersection of Class, Money, Music and History," *Early Music*, 28 (2000), 32–49 (at p. 38). Cf. Robert D. Hume: "Opera was expensive to produce and expensive to attend. From 1708, it was increasingly aimed at a very small group of potential customers. At times it generated huge cash flows and attracted extravagant patronage, but the beneficiaries were a few principal singers"; "The Economics of Culture in London, 1660–1740," *Huntington Library Quarterly*, 69 (2006), 487–533 (at p. 515).

[19] Hunter, "Patronizing Handel," 34.

[20] Johann Mattheson, *Der musikalische Patriot* (Hamburg, 1728), 199.

[21] E. D. Hirsch, "The Politics of Theories of Interpretation," *Critical Inquiry*, 9 (1982), 244.

8   THE CULTURAL POLITICS OF OPERA, 1720–1742

ministry and those in opposition contested various points of political ideology. The differences can be seen as between an Old Whig or Country ideology in opposition, and one of Modern Whigs in power defending the present state of Britain. One salient point of contention for opera was the effects of commercial prosperity and increasing personal wealth. Chapter 4, "Opera and the Luxury Debate," shows how the ideological contest over commerce, corruption, and luxury was worked out in reference to opera.

Robert Walpole's most serious political miscalculation was introducing the Excise, which aroused country-wide opposition despite its obvious advantages. Chapter 5, "Excise and the Patriot Opposition," presents Walpole's Excise proposal and its consequences. After the Excise, Lord Cobham became the impetus for a new "Patriot" Opposition to Walpole, with Frederick, the Prince of Wales, as its figurehead.

The Royal Academy of Music folded in 1728. Chapter 6, "Opera of the Nobility and the *Furor Farinellicus*," presents the history of the subsequent opera companies of Handel and the Opera of the Nobility. Quite possibly the most celebrated episode for opera was the furor over the reception of the castrato Carlo Broschi (called "Farinelli"), who arrived for the 1734–35 season. He came to represent the institution of opera and heightened the potential for invective and satire of opera and its use as a tool for the Opposition.

Chapter 7, "From Excise to the War of Jenkins' Ear," carries the political history from Walpole's Excise scheme through the Depredations Crisis and the declaration of war against Spain in 1739.

Several poets of the new Patriot Opposition held critical views of opera and articulated an alternative to it. Chapter 8, "A Patriot Vision for Dramatic Music," shows how several of their allegorical poems offered a vision of a reformed dramatic music sung in English, one that would counter the supposed ill effects of opera and serve the ideological ends of the Patriot Opposition – and especially Britain under Frederick as a Patriot King.

A perennial lament of artists and critics has been the decline of the arts of their day. Chapter 9, "Opera and the Politics of Taste," shows how one of the major critical touchstones of the era was Taste; critics railed against the (supposed) pervasiveness of False Taste that was over-running Britain, of which the passion for opera was an example, and for which the Hanoverians, Court, and the Ministry were principal causes. An omnibus attack on False Taste and her companion Dulness was led off by Alexander Pope's *Dunciad* (1728). Most critiques of False Taste had no direct, partisan, political application, but cues in some poems show critique of False Taste had pointed, topical political application.

The major verse form of the era, as exemplified in the works of Pope, was the formal verse satire, often an imitation of Horace or Juvenal. Chapter 10, "Opera in Formal Verse Satire," shows how many formal verse satires of the 1730s served a partisan purpose: they present Italian opera and the castrato Farinelli as symptoms of a Britain oppressed by the luxury and corruption of Walpole's regime and a nation humiliated by Spanish depredations.

British trade with Spain and the West Indies had been guaranteed by treaties since the Peace of Utrecht of 1713. Chapter 11, "War of Jenkins' Ear and the Fall of Walpole," traces how disputes over British trading and Spanish seizures of British ships continued. Failure to settle differences between Spain and Britain led to the Depredations Crisis of 1737 and finally the outbreak of war with Spain two years later. The failure of Walpole's ministry to successfully carry out the war was a major cause for his fall from power in 1742.

In March 1742, two months after the fall of Walpole, Pope published his *The New Dunciad*. Chapter 12, "*The New Dunciad*: Opera and the Triumph of Dulness," explores how this final book of his *Dunciad* project is the culmination of his campaign against Dulness, as well as his final indictment of Walpole and the Hanoverians. The chapter explores the political context of the *Dunciad*'s portrait of Handel as the last bulwark against opera and his banishment to Ireland.

Opera in Britain was a bivalent cultural product. Although it suffered satire and criticism in literary sources, opera was endorsed by patronage of the mostly Whig political-cultural elite. "Coda: The Cultural Work of Opera" suggests the positive "cultural work" that opera might have done despite the widespread opposition voiced to it.

* * *

This book complements four studies that explored the politics of literature in the Walpole era: Maynard Mack, *The Garden and the City*; Bertrand Goldgar, *Walpole and the Wits*; Vincent Carretta, *The Snarling Muse: Verbal and Visual Political Satire from Pope to Churchill*, and Christine Gerrard, *The Patriot Opposition to Walpole*. It expands their scope by focusing on the cultural politics of Italian opera, the most prestigious theatrical entertainment of the era. It also complements my own *The Politics of Opera in Handel's Britain*, by focusing less on opera as it related to daily partisan politics and more on the broader cultural politics of opera and its singers.

CHAPTER 1

Rise of Walpole and the Whig Oligarchy

After the heated Tory-Whig party strife of the last years of Queen Anne's reign, the Protestant Succession came to pass peacefully as Elector Georg Ludwig of Hanover was proclaimed King of Great Britain on 1 August 1714. The Tory ministers' secret schemes to engineer the return of the Pretender were foiled by his refusal to abandon his Catholic faith; nor were needed secret Whig plans to use the army in case of civil war or a French invasion to place James on the throne.[1] With the Hanoverian Succession, Britain entered a period of relative stability guided by the Whig oligarchy.[2]

The Elector and Britain's allies knew of the efforts of the Tory ministers, the Earl of Oxford and Viscount Bolingbroke, to extricate Britain from the War of the Spanish Succession, even though the war was going well for the Allies. Whigs claimed their separate peace with France betrayed the Allies. It was Handel's role in celebrating the "shameful" Peace by writing the Utrecht *Te Deum* and *Jubilate* that caused his temporary dismissal from the Elector's employ.[3]

George knew the Whigs were his true friends (despite their alleged Republican ideals) and despised Oxford and Bolingbroke for making peace with France.[4] The new ministry that formed in September and October had a majority of Whigs and a few Hanoverian Tories. Loyal Whigs were rewarded: Robert Walpole became paymaster-general of the forces, one of the most lucrative of places; William Pulteney (later Earl of Bath), secretary at war; and James (later Viscount, then Earl) Stanhope and Charles Viscount Townshend, secretaries of state (south and north, respectively). The Duke of Marlborough resumed his post as captain-general of the army.

---

[1] For most Tories, the Pretender's refusal to abandon his Catholic faith was a permanent bar to his return; B. W. Hill, *The Growth of Parliamentary Parties, 1689–1742* (London: George Allen and Unwin, 1976), 157.

[2] The case for Britain achieving a period of stability under a Whig oligarchy was made in J. H. Plumb's *The Growth of Political Stability in England, 1675–1725* (1967); title in the United States, *The Origins of Political Stability in England, 1675–1725* (1967). *Aristocratic Government and Society in Eighteenth-Century England: The Foundations of Stability*, ed. and intro. Daniel A. Baugh (New York, N.Y.: Franklin Watts, 1975), provides support for stability. Plumb's thesis was subject to refinement and qualifications by later historians.

[3] See Thomas McGeary, *Opera and Politics in Queen Anne's Britain, 1705–1714* (Woodbridge: Boydell, 2022), 324–7.

[4] On the relations of the Hanoverian electorate and the ministry of Oxford and Bolingbroke, see Edward Gregg, *The Protestant Succession in International Politics, 1710–1716* (New York, N.Y.: Garland Publishing, 1986).

The last months of 1714 saw a fierce and nearly complete purge of Tories from national and local offices. Jonathan Swift describes the sweep of Tories from government offices: the Whigs exercised their power "with the utmost rage and revenge; impeached and banished the chief leaders of the church party, and stripped all their adherents of what employments they had."[5]

Spared were the Tories the Earl of Nottingham (who had deserted Tories over the "No Peace without Spain" motion), who became lord president of the Council, and Thomas Coke, who was retained as vice chamberlain, overseeing the London theatres.

The Tories did survive as a parliamentary faction, but were proscribed from major office for nearly 50 years.[6] Despite the lawful succession of the Hanoverians, for decades there were scattered demonstrations of Jacobite sympathy. Writing from exile in France, Bolingbroke lamented, "The grief of my soul is this, I see plainly that the Tory party is gone."[7]

In the summer's general election of 1715, Whigs raised the specter that a Tory victory would mean a Jacobite restoration and an end to the Church of England. From the throne, George urged voters to favor those who "showed a Firmness to the Protestant Succession when it was most in Danger"[8] – meaning, of course, the Whigs. Tory propagandists vilified the King and Whigs. The High Churchman (and later suspected Jacobite plotter) Bishop Francis Atterbury's *English Advice, to the Freeholders of England* (1714), claiming all England's "Dangers and Miseries ... are entirely owing to the Whigs" (29), was so incendiary, the King offered a reward for the author's discovery.

Tarred with Jacobitism, the Tories suffered a massive loss: Whigs were returned 341 to 217 for Tories. J. H. Plumb describes the outcome: with a majority in the Commons and occupying most court offices, "the Whig leaders went about making the world safe for the Whigs."[9]

After their defeat at the polls, decline of the Tories was hastened by other events. In control of Parliament, Stanhope and Walpole decided to break the Tory leadership by impeaching Bolingbroke, Oxford, Strafford, and Ormonde for their intrigues with the Pretender and role in the Treaty of Utrecht and commercial treaties. Fearing impeachment or worse, Bolingbroke had already fled to France on 6 April 1715; Ormonde followed in July. Bolingbroke briefly entered the service of the Pretender as his secretary of state. In Whig eyes, his

---

[5] Swift's note to "Verses on the Death of Dr Swift, D.S.P.D."; in *Jonathan Swift: The Complete Poems*, ed. Pat Rogers (New Haven, Conn.: Yale University Press, 1983), 855.

[6] On the survival of the Tory party, Linda Colley, *In Defiance of Oligarchy: The Tory Party, 1714–60* (Cambridge: Cambridge University Press, 1982), 21–3.

[7] Henry St. John, Viscount Bolingbroke, 1 or 2 September 1714, to Bishop Francis Atterbury; in James Macpherson, *Original Papers: Containing the Secret History of Great Britain*, 2 vols. (1775), 2:651.

[8] *Journals of the House of Commons*, 18 (1714–1718), 14.

[9] J. H. Plumb, *The Growth of Political Stability in England, 1675–1725* (Harmondsworth: Penguin Books, 1969), 163. On the Whig majority, W. A. Speck, "The General Election of 1715," *English Historical Review*, 90 (1975), 507–22.

THE CULTURAL POLITICS OF OPERA, 1720–1742

flight only confirmed his guilt and furthered the impression that Tories were Jacobites. Oxford stayed behind and was sent to the Tower for two years.[10]

The reality of the Jacobite threat was brought home by the uprising in Scotland (the "Fifteen"). On 6 September 1715, the Earl of Mar, leading some Scottish clans, raised the Pretender's standard at Braemar.[11] A rebel uprising in Northern England was defeated at Preston (12–14 November) by General John Campbell, the Duke of Argyll, with the aid of Dutch troops. The Pretender did not land at Peterhead, Scotland, until 22 December; but by then the cause was lost, and he retreated to France on 4 February.

The failed rebellion showed the nation was still at risk; it enabled the Whigs to justify the Septennial Act of 1716. The Triennial Act of 1694 required a new Parliament to be called at least every three years; frequent Parliaments were one of the cornerstones of Whig orthodoxy meant to assert the supremacy of Parliament over the Crown (although they contributed to political instability). The Septennial Act, although it violated Whig principles, prolonged the present Parliament and prevented the confusion caused by another general election. With political power now firmly in Whig hands, the Tory cause seemed even more hopeless, and in April 1716 began a steady flow of Tories over to the Whig party.[12] Now, British politics – at least for those aspiring to be at the center of power – was no longer primarily one of contest between Tories and Whigs, but one between factions in the Whig party.

❧ Whig Schism

The Whigs, though firmly in the King's favor, were beset by division in the ministry.[13] They disagreed about the King's goals for foreign policy, complicated because of his conflicting interests between Britain and his Hanover electorate.

---

[10] The trials of Strafford and Oxford were delayed by the Jacobite uprising.

[11] David Szechi, 1715: The Great Jacobite Rebellion (New Haven, Conn.: Yale University Press, 2006); Frank McLynn, The Jacobites (London: Routledge and Kegan Paul, 1985); Bruce Lenman, The Jacobite Risings in Britain, 1689–1746 (London: Eyre Methuen, 1980).

[12] Hill, Growth of Parliamentary Parties, 160.

[13] On the Schism, royal feud, and subsequent political history: John M. Beattie, The English Court in the Reign of George I (Cambridge: Cambridge University Press, 1967), 225–40, 262–76; Basil Williams, Stanhope: A Study in Eighteenth-Century War and Diplomacy (Oxford: Clarendon Press, 1932), 230–53, 266–7, 423–5; Ragnhild Hatton, George I: Elector and King (Cambridge: Mass.: Harvard University Press, 1978), 193–210, 244–6; W. A. Speck, "The Whig Schism under George I," Huntington Library Quarterly, 40 (1977), 171–9; Speck, Stability and Strife, 185–202; Jeremy Black, "Parliament and the Political and Diplomatic Crisis of 1717–18," Parliamentary History, 3 (1984), 77–101; Wolfgang Michael, England under George I: The Beginning of the Hanoverian Dynasty, trans and adapted L. B. Namier (London: Macmillan, 1936), 327–31; and Michael, England under George I: The Quadruple Alliance, trans. Annemarie and George MacGregor (London: Macmillan, 1939), 24–9, 304–8. A principal contemporary source is Lady Cowper; Diary of Mary Countess Cowper, Lady of the Bedchamber to the Princess of Wales, ed. Spencer Cower, 2nd ed. (London: John Murray, 1865).

At first, Townshend, as secretary for the north, had the King's confidence. Walpole, his brother-in-law, emerged as the ministry's major spokesman in the Commons, and received additional places as first lord of the treasury and chancellor of the Exchequer in October 1715. Their prominence drew resentment from other Whigs, especially the former Junto member Charles Spencer, Earl of Sunderland.

In the north, as Elector, George wanted to use British naval power during the Great Northern War in the struggle of Baltic powers against the regional ambitions of the King of Sweden; he had eyes on the duchies of Bremen and Verden. The most the ministers would reluctantly agree was sending annual fleets to the Baltic, ostensibly to protect British shipping.

In the south, George as King aimed to use the terms of the Treaty of Utrecht to confirm the peace with France, resolve the rivalry between the Emperor and Philip over the Spanish throne and territories in Italy, and neutralize Spanish ambitions against France and in Italy. This southern strategy meant turning from Britain's traditional allies the Dutch and Austrians, as favored by Townshend and Walpole.

The King went over to Hanover in July 1716 with Stanhope, joined later by Sunderland. The two came to support George's northern policy and intrigued against Walpole and Townshend. In Hanover, Stanhope negotiated with the French ambassador a draft of an urgently needed alliance so the King could focus on countering Sweden and (now) Russia in the Baltic and the removal of the Pretender from Avignon. Stanhope came to learn of Townshend and Walpole's opposition to the treaty and the subordination of British interests to those of Hanover.

Disagreement among the King's ministers coincided with a growing feud in the royal family. George and his son had been on poor terms since they came over from Hanover. Before leaving for Hanover in July 1716, the King made him regent but slighted him by withholding many of the customary powers; he then further humiliated him by forcing him to remove as his chamberlain the Duke of Argyll, who seemed likely to intrigue against the ministry at being passed over for commander-in-chief after Marlborough had a stroke.

With his father away in Hanover, the Prince and Princess held court and entertained at Hampton Court, showing favor toward the Tories and opposition Whigs. As ministers remaining in Britain, Walpole and Townshend, along with other Whigs, attended the Prince. The King received reports that the Prince was courting public popularity and that, abetted by Walpole and Townshend, he was plotting to oppose the ministry in the coming Parliament.

Exasperated by Townshend's disagreement with his Northern policies and deliberate delays in getting the Anglo-French treaty signed, George removed him as secretary for the north on 12 December 1716, replacing him with

---

Issues over Baltic policy: Derek McKay, "The Struggle for Control of George I's Northern Policy, 1718–19," *Journal of Modern History*, 45 (1973), 367–86; and John J. Murray, *George I, the Baltic, and the Whig Split of 1717: A Study in Diplomacy and Propaganda* (London: Routledge and Kegan Paul, 1969).

14   THE CULTURAL POLITICS OF OPERA, 1720–1742

Stanhope the following day. For the sake of Whig unity and swallowing his pride, Townshend accepted the lesser post of lord lieutenant of Ireland, which would remove him from the center of politics. The ministry was now split between the Stanhope-Sunderland and Townshend-Walpole factions, with Stanhope to defend the ministry in Parliament.

To advance the King's goal of stabilizing Europe, in 1717 Stanhope negotiated the Triple Alliance with France and, at Townshend and Walpole's insistence, the Dutch to contain Spain's ambitions against France. Austria joined on 2 August 1718 creating the Quadruple Alliance intended to oppose Spain's designs on France and Italy. After the "little war" with Spain from 1718 to 1720, Spain agreed to the terms of the Quadruple Alliance in 1720.

In spring 1717, the Prince absented himself from Parliament and the cabinet while Walpole and Townshend only mildly supported ministry measures in Parliament. Townshend's vote against the annual Mutiny Bill, essential to maintain a standing army, was the last straw for the King, who dismissed him as lord lieutenant on 9 April 1717. The following day, Walpole led a mass resignation of Whigs from the ministry, including Methuen, Orford, Devonshire, and Pulteney. For their resignations, Walpole and Townshend were vilified as "defectors" and "betrayers" whose resignations showed they were abandoning their Whig principles; their actions proved their only motive was power and self-interest.[14] Walpole's places were taken by Stanhope, who now became chief minister and was raised to the peerage as Viscount Stanhope and shortly after to an earldom; Sunderland assumed Townshend's place as secretary of state (north); and James Craggs the younger succeeded Pulteney as secretary of war. Joseph Addison, who had been active as a ministerial propagandist, became the junior secretary of state (south).[15]

Walpole joined with Tories and members of the Prince's party to lead a program of voting against the ministry, opposing all but the most essential

---

[14] On the controversy of their resignations: attacking them were Matthew Tindal, *The Defection Consider'd, and the Designs of Those, who Divided the Friends of the Government, Set in a True Light* (1717); *An Answer to the Character & Conduct of R—— W——, Esq; with an Exact Account of His Popularity* (1717); *The History of the Rise and Fall of Count Hotspur, with That of His Brother-in-Law, Colonel Headstrong* (1717); *An Epistle to R—— W——, Esq; Occasion'd by a Pamphlet, Entitul'd, The Defection Consider'd* (1718); and *The Defection Farther Consider'd, Wherein the Resigners, as Some Would Have Them Sti'd, Are Really Deserters* (1718).

  Walpole and Townshend were defended in: *The Character & Conduct of R—— W——, Esq; with an Exact Account of His Popularity* (1717); *An Impartial Enquiry into the Conduct of the Right Honourable Charles Lord Viscout T——* (1717); *Some Persons Vindicated against the Author of the Defection, &c. and That Writer Convicted of Malice and Falshood* (1718); *The Defection Detected; or, Faults Laid on the Right Side* (1718); and George Sewell, *The Resigners Vindicated; or, the Defection Re-Considered* [in two parts] (1718).

[15] His periodical *The Freeholder* (1715–1716) is a thorough-going defense of the Hanoverian Succession and exposition of Whig principles; modern edition: Joseph Addison, *The Freeholder*, ed. James Leheny (Oxford: Oxford University Press, 1980).

RISE OF WALPOLE AND THE WHIG OLIGARCHY 15

measures, even those that as a Whig he had previously supported.[16] Walpole was setting a pattern of aggressive, opportunistic politics of faction: abandoning principles and allying with former opponents and often the Prince of Wales against former colleagues for the sake of obstruction and gaining power. Having the Prince as an ally cleared the opposition of the taint of Jacobitism, but Walpole's alliance with Tories earned him the distrust of other Whigs. The breach between ministers was apparent when on 20 May 1717 Stanhope openly attacked Walpole in the Commons.[17]

The Whig Schism – between Stanhope and Sunderland in the ministry and the Parliamentary opposition of Walpole, Townshend, and the Prince's followers – would last six years. The resignations and defections left the King's party weak in the Commons and short of talent in the ministry.

Remaining in England for the summer of 1717 to increase his own popularity and court wavering politicians, the King felt compelled to host a season of drawing rooms, balls, concerts, plays, and social events to rival the Prince's court. In this summer of royal entertainments, the King hosted the water party that was accompanied by Handel's *Water Music* on 17 July 1717.[18] The King kept up his uncharacteristically lively and brilliant court through 1719.

The King and Prince broke completely that December. The King forced the Duke of Newcastle upon the Prince as godfather to his son. Following the christening, the Prince uttered what Newcastle thought was a challenge to a duel. Outraged at the incident, the King expelled the Prince and Princess from St. James's on 2 December 1717, taking charge of the royal children. The King made known that those who attended the Prince's court at Leicester House were unwelcome at St. James's; those who did should resign any places they held from the Prince.

For two years, the rival courts of the King and Prince mirrored the two Whig factions. The Prince's court became the center of the opposition to the ministry. His followers included Tories, members of the Walpole-Townshend faction, Earl Cowper, and the Duke of Wharton.

In the parliamentary sessions of 1719 and 1720, the opposition had mixed success against the ministry. In 1719 Walpole abandoned Whig principles in unsuccessfully opposing repeal of the Occasional Conformity and Schism Acts (intended to lighten restrictions on dissenters, who had been strong supporters of the Whigs) but was successful in defeating the Peerage Bill (designed to limit the number of peers in the House of Lords).[19] For the ministerial Whigs, the Bill would prevent the Prince (when King) from filling the Lords with

[16] On Walpole's campaign of opposition, Plumb, *Making of a Statesman*, 163–78; Hill, *Growth of Parliamentary Parties*, 163–78.

[17] William Cobbett, *The Parliamentary History of England*, 7 (20 May 1717).

[18] Donald Burrows and Robert D. Hume, "George I, the Haymarket Opera Company and Handel's Water Music," *Early Music*, 19 (1991), 334–5 (at p. 334).

[19] Edward Raymond Taylor, "The Peerage Bill of 1719," *English Historical Review*, 28 (1913), 243–59; Clyve Jones, "'Venice Preserv'd; Or a Plot Discovered': The Political and Social Context of the Peerage Bill of 1719," pp. 79–112 in *A Pillar of the Constitution:*

16   THE CULTURAL POLITICS OF OPERA, 1720–1742

his own supporters (though it would limit the King's ability to create future peers). Walpole appealed to country MPs by arguing the bill would deny them and their families the opportunity of entering the peerage. The controversial bill led to the falling out between the former Whig colleagues Joseph Addison and Richard Steele: Addison, recently in the Ministry, supported the bill while Steele opposed it.

In April 1720 Walpole and James Craggs the younger, secretary of state, arranged a reconciliation: the Prince would write an apologetic letter to his father, who would invite him to court, and on St. George's day (23 April), the Prince appeared before the King for a short five-minute interview. The following day, opposition Whigs appeared at court and the King and Prince attended chapel together. Sunderland hosted a dinner on 25 April to symbolize unification of the ministerial factions. The reconciliation, though, did not improve relations between the King and Prince, which remained strained.[20]

Walpole and Townshend rejoined the ministry in June, but as junior partners, with Walpole as paymaster of the forces and Townshend as lord president of the Council. In reality, the Whig Schism was not resolved, and Walpole and Stanhope strove to secure majorities in Parliament and control of the ministry. Pulteney, one of Walpole's loyal followers, resented not being brought into the ministry and would later turn against Walpole.

It has been suggested that the lapse of opera from June 1717 and its revival by the Royal Academy in April 1720 (see following chapter) was related to the royal feud that disrupted the social activities of the *beau monde* and social-political elite, the primary supporters of opera. The reunion was said to be symbolized by the King and Prince attending the premiere of Handel's *Radamisto* on 27 April 1720.[21] Attractive as this narrative might be for putting opera at the center of politics, the timing of the resolution of the royal feud and the revival of opera is most likely just coincidence. The more likely causes for the lapse and then resumption of opera were the economics of opera production and the pent-up demand for opera. The groundwork for the resumption of opera was well underway before the royal feud and political schism were healed, and the opera season had already begun on 2 April.[22]

---

the *House of Lords in British Politics, 1603–1784*, ed. Clyve Jones (London: Hambledon Press, 1989).

[20] The feud at court can be followed in Lady Mary Cowper's *Diary*.

[21] Elizabeth Gibson, *The Royal Academy of Music, 1719–1728: The Institution and Its Directors* (New York, N.Y.: Garland Publishing, 1989), 7–9; Gibson, "The Royal Academy of Music (1719–28) and its Directors," pp. 138–64 in *Handel Tercentenary Collection*, ed. Stanley Sadie and Anthony Hicks (Ann Arbor [Mich.]: UMI Research Press, 1987) (at pp. 139–40); Donald Burrows, *Handel* (New York, N.Y.: Schirmer, 1994), 106–7; and Burrows, *Handel and the English Chapel Royal* (Oxford: Oxford University Press, 2005), 143–4, 167–9.

[22] I have argued this more completely in McGeary, *Politics of Opera in Handel's Britain* (Cambridge: Cambridge University Press, 2013), 61–4.

🕮 Walpole's Rise to Prime Minister

Robert Walpole's rise to prominence as prime minister between April 1720 and April 1722 was achieved despite public scorn for his role in the Schism and alleged abandonment of Whig principles in his opposition to the Sunderland-Stanhope ministry. Two fortuitous events, his handling of the South Sea Bubble crisis and the Atterbury Plot, coupled with the passing of Sunderland and Stanhope from the political scene, ensured his emergence in April 1722 as undisputed first minister – a role he would fill for two decades.

THE SOUTH SEA BUBBLE

By 1720, the nation's debt had swelled to some £50 million, and on 22 January 1720, Stanhope put forward a proposal from the South Sea Company to take over a large portion of the debt. The scheme was to convert £31 million of the debt (in the form of annuities) into South Sea stock; the government would pay interest to the Company.[23]

The Company issued new stock at a par value of £100, but the share values could fluctuate on the market (presumably based on profits from the South Sea trade). The fatal weakness was that the amount of stock issued was not fixed in proportion to the amount of debt. Investors (and company) could make money by buying (or issuing) shares at or below par value and selling when (hopefully) when the market price rose – giving the Company an ulterior motive for manipulating stock value and issuing more stock to raise capital.

To ease passage of the proposal, the Company directors bribed with or issued stock (often at discounted prices) to the King, his mistresses, ministers, and politicians, which they could sell at a profit. Stanhope and Sunderland guided the bill to passage, and on 7 April 1720 it received royal assent.

The country went wild speculating in South Sea stock. Its price rose from 128 on the first of January 1720 to a peak at 1,050 on 24 June, aided greatly by manipulation by the Company.[24] The belated realization that the Company had no trading profits brought a bitter dose of reality, and the Bubble burst in September 1720, its stock dropping to 180. Although some investors (including Walpole) made huge, honest profits, thousands of the nation's elite suffered losses or went bankrupt as the burst bubble plunged the country into a financial crisis.

Parliament sat on 8 December 1720 amid national outrage at the corruption, and demands to punish Company directors and ministers responsible and to confiscate their wealth for the benefit of sufferers. It was expected Walpole's knowledge of finances would be needed to resolve the crisis.[25] In January the Commons selected a Secret Committee of Inquiry to investigate the Bubble.

---

[23] John Carswell, *The South Sea Bubble*, rev. ed. (London: Alan Sutton, 1993), and P. G. M. Dickson, *The Financial Revolution in England: A Study in the Development of Public Credit, 1688–1756* (London: Macmillan, 1967), 90–198.

[24] Carswell, *South Sea Bubble*, 111–13, 118–19.

[25] Hill, *Growth of Parliamentary Parties*, 179.

18   THE CULTURAL POLITICS OF OPERA, 1720–1742

Its report issued late the following month exposed the corruption and bribery, implicating Sunderland, Sir James Craggs the elder (postmaster general), James Craggs the younger, John Aislabie (chancellor of the Exchequer), and Charles Stanhope (secretary of the Treasury).

Walpole knew it was not to the Court's or his ministry's benefit to seek full revenge and exposure of the corruption. Using his mastery of the Commons, Walpole worked to obstruct the investigation and limit the inquiries. Most of all, his rival Sunderland, favorite of the King and mainstay of the ministry, had to be spared. In the Commons trial in March 1721, Walpole spoke in defense of Charles Stanhope and Sunderland, who both escaped conviction. Aislabie was forced to resign and was expelled from the House and sent to the Tower (his post assumed by Walpole).

Resolution of the scandal was aided by the deaths of others implicated. James Stanhope suffered a stroke on 4 February 1721 during a speech in the Lords defending himself and the ministry and died the following day. Craggs junior died of smallpox in February, and Craggs senior died (probably by suicide) the following month.

After his acquittal, but with 172 votes against him, Sunderland had to resign his treasury post on 3 April 1721 (replaced by Walpole, now also chancellor of the Exchequer). But he was still in favor with the King and had his protégé James Lord Carteret appointed to replace Stanhope as secretary of state; Carteret, who spoke German, emerged as a new rival to Walpole.

Walpole is often given credit for rescuing the nation's finances, but they recovered by themselves. He proposed the Engraftment scheme to restore public credit on 21 December 1720. It was not passed until 7 July 1721, receiving royal assent three days later, but never put into effect. It was time that gradually healed the nation's finances.[26]

The South Sea scandal eliminated many of Walpole's political rivals and showed his skill at managing Parliament and protecting the Hanoverian interest. But he was reviled for his role in shielding the Court, ministers, and Company directors for their role in the corruption; henceforth, he would be known as the "screen" or "screen-master."[27] But public opinion and distrust by other Whigs were irrelevant, as long as he retained the King's favor. Through his mastery of the Commons, Walpole checked the demands for vengeance, limited the scope of the investigations, and protected the Court and Ministry from greater scandal.

---

[26] The traditional view (begun with William Coxe) gives credit to Walpole for solving the crisis; William Coxe, *Memoirs of the Life and Administration of Sir Robert Walpole, Earl of Orford*, 3 vols. (1798), 1:157–8. Plumb, *Walpole: The Making of a Statesman*, 293–4, 302–12, 339, 357, suggests his role is overstated, and that financial recovery was slow and was the result of the passage of time; see also Carswell, *South Sea Bubble*, who follows Plumb; and Charles B. Realey, *The Early Opposition to Sir Robert Walpole* (Lawrence, Kans., University of Kansas Press, 1931), 1–67, who anticipated Plumb.

[27] Hill, *Growth of Parliamentary Parties*, 180–6; and in the Lords, A. S. Turberville, *The House of Lords in the XVIIIth Century* (Oxford: Clarendon Press, 1927), 186–249.

Despite exposure of the corruption of the South Sea scandal, the hotly contested March 1722 parliamentary election returned a Whig majority in the Commons, further weakening the Tories. But in the Commons, the Whig party remained divided between a court (or ministerial) party and a country party of backbenchers.

Only with Sunderland's death on 19 April 1722 did the leadership struggle end with a Walpole-Townshend ministry securely in place, as Townshend filled Stanhope's place as secretary of state (north). Walpole consolidated his position and increased control in the Commons by giving government places to family members and MPs.

The passing of Sunderland and Stanhope enabled Walpole to emerge as prime minister. His only remaining rival was Carteret. As Plumb summarizes: "the country enjoyed a stability of government such as it had not known for a hundred years; a pattern of politics came into being which lasted long beyond the century which brought it into being."[28]

THE ATTERBURY PLOT

Public anger over the South Sea scandal brought hope to the Jacobites and with it their best chance for success since the fall of the Tories at the end of Queen Anne's reign. Arthur Onslow, later speaker of the house, thought the rage against the government brought about by the Bubble was so great, "the King being at that time abroad, that could the Pretender then have landed at the Tower, he might have rode to St. James's with very few hands held up against him."[29]

In April 1722, the French government informed the ministry of a plot to restore the Pretender. In the previous spring, leading Tories including the Earl of Strafford, Lord North and Grey, and Francis Atterbury, Bishop of Rochester, began corresponding with the Pretender and his agents abroad, urging them to take advantage of the situation in Britain. Appeals for money and troops were sent abroad, and plans set afoot for a rising in London, a spring invasion, and insurrection.[30]

Walpole used the office of the treasury to intercept the plotters' mail and gained evidence of the plans. The Duke of Ormonde's invasion from Spain was thwarted in April. To calm the public, troops were encamped in Hyde Park,

---

[28] Plumb, *Walpole: Making of a Statesman*, 379.

[29] Diary of Arthur Onslow; in Historical Manuscripts Commission, *The Manuscripts of the Earl of Buckinghamshire* [etc.] (London: Her Majesty's Stationery Office, 1895), 504.

[30] Eveline Cruickshanks and Howard Erskine-Hill, *The Atterbury Plot* (Basingstoke: Palgrave Macmillan, 2004); G. V. Bennett, *The Tory Crisis in Church and State, 1688–1730: The Career of Francis Atterbury, Bishop of Rochester* (Oxford: Clarendon Press, 1975), esp. 223–75; Paul S. Fritz, *The English Ministers and Jacobitism between the Rebellions of 1715 and 1745* (Toronto: University of Toronto Press, 1975), 67–98; and Eveline Cruickshanks, "Lord North, Christopher Layer and the Atterbury Plot: 1720–23," pp. 92–106 in *The Jacobite Challenge*, ed. Eveline Cruickshanks and Jeremy Black (Edinburgh: John Donald, 1988).

20 THE CULTURAL POLITICS OF OPERA, 1720–1742

Townshend announced the plot to the Lord Mayor on 8 May, and the Jacobite threat faded away.

On the basis of evidence provided by Atterbury's secretary Christopher Layer, arrests began the following week and culminated on 24 August with the arrest of Atterbury and his commitment to the Tower for high treason. Lord North and Grey and the Earl of Orrery were arrested in September and followed Atterbury to the Tower. Habeas corpus was suspended when the new Parliament sat on 9 October, leaving the plotters at the mercy of the ministry. To salvage his political future, Walpole now had to prove the conspiracy.

Despite massive amounts of intercepted mail and other documents, Walpole had no legal grounds for charges of treason against Atterbury and two other conspirators, John Plunkett and George Kelly, and had to proceed with a less rigorous Commons bill of Pains and Penalties against them, which circumvented normal protections of the legal process. The trial became a public spectacle that consumed the attention of London. In November, Layer was convicted in court and later executed for treason; Plunkett and Kelley were sent to the Tower.

On 27 May the King assented to Atterbury's exile. Lord North and Grey and Orrery were released on bond, and Atterbury departed for exile in France on 18 June 1723. The trials unified the Whigs, gained Walpole the King's favor, and left the public with the impression that Tories were Jacobite sympathizers. But the arrest of a clergyman and his humiliating confinement in the Tower aroused support for the bishop, and Walpole was attacked for his violation of procedure and rules of evidence in the trials.[31]

Walpole's almost two-year obsession with the Atterbury Plot increased domestic support for the Hanoverians and gave a permanent setback to the Jacobite movement, which would not threaten Britain until 1745. His ruthless persecution of the Atterbury conspirators and Jacobite witch hunt was so successful, he would continually raise the specter of Jacobite plots and tar the political opposition as Tory and Jacobitical.[32]

The significance of the Atterbury Plot for Walpole's consolidation of power was seen early on by Speaker Onslow:

> The pursuing of it and the conduct of the whole were principally the work of Mr. Walpole whose dexterity and skill in it showed him to be equal to the ablest minister that ever unravalled the deepest and darkest contrivance against a State.

---

[31] *True Briton*, no. 5 (17 June 1723). The *True Briton* continued objecting to the methods used in the Atterbury trials. The collected edition of the *True Briton*, 2 vols. (1723–1724), contains Wharton's speech on 15 May 1723 on the third reading of the bill to inflict pains and penalties against Atterbury (2:633–85).

[32] On Walpole's paranoia of Jacobites and exploitation of the Jacobite scare: Diary of Arthur Onslow, 465 ("he deemed a Jacobite who was not a professed and known Whig"); G. V. Bennett, "Jacobitism and the Rise of Walpole," pp. 70–92 in *Historical Perspectives: Studies in English Thought and Society in Honour of J. H. Plumb*, ed. Neil McKendrick (London: Europa Publications, 1974); and Fritz, *English Ministers and Jacobitism*.

... [It] ought therefore to be reckoned one of, if not the, most fortunate and greatest circumstance of Mr. Walpole's life. It fixed him with the King, and united for a time the whole body of Whigs to him, and gave him the universal credit of an able and vigilant Minister.[33]

In 1724, the last remaining threat to the Walpole-Townshend ministry was removed when Walpole engineered Carteret's rustication to Ireland as lord lieutenant on 22 October. Walpole had cleared the field of rivals and now had complete control of government. The next two parliamentary sessions were as quiet and uneventful as any comparable period in English history; Plumb called them "the happiest and most peaceful that Walpole ever knew as the King's first minister."[34]

* * *

By the early 1720s, the Whig oligarchy was now securely in power. But because of the corruption revealed by the South Sea crisis and then outrage at the persecution of the Atterbury plotters, both the Stanhope-Sunderland and Walpole-Townshend ministries faced opposition from Whig factions and attacks in the press.[35] For the next quarter century, politics in Britain was no longer one of Tory-Whig contest as in the reign of Anne, but a series of Whig factions (often stiffened by Tories and followers of the Prince of Wales) trying to gain mastery of government. The series of oppositions to Walpole and their use of opera in their propaganda campaigns to remove him are the subject of following chapters.

---

[33] Diary of Arthur Onslow, 513.
[34] Realey, *Early Opposition to Sir Robert Walpole*, 126–45; Plumb, *Walpole: The King's Minister*, 74–7, 78 (quoted), 112.
[35] Laurence Hanson, *Government and the Press, 1695–1763* (London: Oxford University Press, 1936), 36–83.

CHAPTER 2

The Royal Academy of Music
and Its Audience

The accession of Georg Ludwig, Elector of Hanover, as King of Great Britain might have augured well for opera in London, for of the arts, he seemed most enthusiastic about opera.[1] His father, Elector Ernst August, had established a court theatre at Hanover in 1689. It was the grandest opera house in northern Europe,[2] seating 2,000, with Agostino Steffani as court composer. Due to reduced finances when he succeeded as elector in 1698 and then the outbreak of the War of the Spanish Succession, Georg Ludwig did not reopen the theatre, although he kept a musical establishment along the lines of the French court. The court also maintained boxes at several opera houses in Venice, which as electoral prince, he himself had attended.[3] In London, in the early years of his reign, he attended about half of the operas performed each season and gave generous payments to performers, as much as 50 guineas to Nicolini, and 10 guineas per box for each performance he attended.[4] But this *ad hoc* largesse did little to provide sufficient long-term support for opera.

Opera's highpoint so far had been the 1711–12 season, in which seven operas (among them four new productions) were presented for a total of sixty-two performances. Thereafter, offerings declined, until for the 1716–17 season six operas received only thirty-two performances. John James Heidegger, who managed the opera company at the Haymarket (now called the King's theatre), lost increasing amounts of money each season until, after the disastrous 1716–17 season, he abandoned an unprofitable enterprise.[5] Table 2.1 shows the steadily

[1] Donald Burrows and Robert D. Hume, "George I, the Haymarket Opera Company and Handel's *Water Music*," *Early Music*, 19 (1991), 323–41; and Ragnhild Hatton, *George I: Elector and King* (Cambridge, Mass.: Harvard University Press, 1978), 46–7, 364 n. 53.

[2] John Toland, *An Account of the Courts of Prussia and Hanover* (1705), 52–3, described the opera house at the Hanoverian court as "the best painted and the best contriv'd in all Europe."

[3] Colin Timms, "George I's Venetian Palace and Theatre Boxes in the 1720s," pp. 95–130 in *Music and Theatre: Essays in Honour of Winton Dean*, ed. Nigel Fortune (Cambridge: Cambridge University Press, 1987).

[4] Burrows and Hume, "George I, the Haymarket Opera Company."

[5] Judith Milhous and Robert D. Hume, "Heidegger and the Management of the Haymarket Opera, 1713–17," *Early Music*, 27 (1999), 65–84 (at pp. 74 and 82). Milhous and Hume offer motives for why Heidegger would have continued such a money-losing enterprise.

TABLE 2.1. Finances of Heidegger's Opera Company, 1713–14 to 1716–17 Seasons

Season	Number of Operas	Performances	Income	Expenses	Loss
1713–14	4	31	£4,255	£4,604	£349
1714–15	6	42	5,700(?)	6,700	1,000(?)
1715–16	5	29	na	na	na
1716–17	6	32	2,197+(?)	4,533+(?)	2,336(?)

Figures marked with "?" are estimates.
Sources: Adapted from Judith Milhous and Robert D. Hume, "Heidegger and the Management of the Haymarket Opera, 1713–17," *Early Music*, 17 (1999), 81; and Winton Dean and Merrill Knapp, *Handel's Operas, 1704-1726*, rev. ed. (Oxford: Clarendon Press, 1995), 156.

mounting losses incurred by Heidegger's opera company. For the 1717–18 and 1718–19 seasons, London had no Italian opera.[6]

Milhous and Hume outline conditions for opera to thrive in London. Instead of walk-in ticket purchases and subscriptions to single productions, needed were a large amount of money, a royal subsidy, new operas by major composers, a new supply of major singers from the continent, increased prices, and substantial annual subscriptions.[7]

These conditions were to be met by the Royal Academy of Music, London's first permanent opera company. But even a company established with a new mode of financing and generous royal subsidy could not (as will be seen) put opera in London on a secure footing. As Milhous and Hume, wryly observe, "The lesson of the first decade of Italian opera in London was essentially that it did not pay."[8]

The nine-season life of the Royal Academy of Music established opera as the most prestigious theatrical entertainment in Great Britain. The founding occurred during a critical period in the history of early Hanoverian Britain as sketched in Chapter 1: the consolidation of the Whig oligarchy, the Tory proscription, failed Jacobite invasions, the Whig Schism, the South Sea Bubble, the Atterbury conspiracy and trial, opposition to Whig ministries, and the beginning of the twenty-year ministry of Robert Walpole.

Given the world of politics outside the Haymarket theatre, politics might be expected at work in the Royal Academy, and various hands have attempted to find such politics: either in the directors of the Academy itself or – on the basis of a generic expectation – in the form of allegory and allusion in the opera

---

[6] On the abortive attempts to mount operas for the 1718–19 season, Lowell Lindgren, "La carriera di Gaetano Berenstadt, contralto evirato (*c.* 1690–1735)," *Rivista italiana di musicologia*, 19 (1984), 36–112.

[7] Milhous and Hume, "Heidegger and the Management of the Haymarket Opera," 82.

[8] Milhous and Hume, "Heidegger and the Management of the Haymarket Opera," 82.

24   THE CULTURAL POLITICS OF OPERA, 1720–1742

librettos themselves. Because of the tendency to focus on major composers, the political interpretations of opera all happen to be of Handel operas.

This possibility of politics at work at the Academy was no doubt sanctioned by Charles Burney, who, after noting that oppositions are inherent to popular governments, stated that "political animosities were blended with Musical faction" in the Academy.[9] Yet overall, the governance of the Academy and content of the operas it produced do not show the impact of the world of politics outside the Haymarket theatre, although incidents among the singers and actions of the company personnel were allegorized by the political opposition and used for partisan purposes.[10]

The lull in opera productions between 1717 and their resumption on 2 April 1720 has often been related to the uncertainty and chaos of court life because of the feud between George I and his son, the Prince of Wales, which had a ripple effect on the activities of London's social-political elite.[11] The relationship between the royal feud and its reconciliation and the fortunes of the London opera company – that the Academy began its season once truce had been established among the royal family and Whig politicians – is more likely just coincidence. Briefly, there is no evidence that the early phase of the feud between the King and Prince affected attendance at the opera house. Attendance had already been in decline (see Table 2.1), and Heidegger had already given his last opera performance on 29 June 1717, well before the royal rupture in December 1717.[12]

The more likely causes for opera's lapse and resumption were Heidegger's shutting down the unsustainable opera company, causing a pent-up demand for opera that could only be met by a new approach to organizing and financing opera production.

CHARTERING THE ROYAL ACADEMY

After years of relying on seasons undertaken by individual managers or impresarios, Britain's operagoers must have realized that relying on the present opera system was unreliable and they would have to make a fresh start of their own if they wanted opera.

The usual pattern of financing opera in London was to offer for each new opera a subscription to an initial, limited number of performances (usually six); if successful enough, the opera's run could be extended to additional

---

[9] Charles Burney, "Sketch of the Life of Handel," in *An Account of the Musical Performances in Westminster-Abbey* (1785), 16.

[10] I argue these points in detail in *The Politics of Opera in Handel's Britain* (Cambridge: Cambridge University Press), 79–93.

[11] On the opera lull: Elizabeth Gibson, *The Royal Academy of Music, 1719–1728: The Institution and Its Directors* (New York, N.Y.: Garland Publishing, 1989), 7–9; and Gibson, "The Royal Academy of Music (1719–28) and its Directors," pp. 138–64 in *Handel Tercentenary Collection*, ed. Stanley Sadie and Anthony Hicks (Ann Arbor [Mich.]: UMI Research Press, 1987), on pp. 139–40. Followed by Donald Burrows, *Handel* (New York, N.Y.: Macmillan, 1994), 78, 106–7.

[12] I argue these points in McGeary, *Politics of Opera in Handel's Britain*, 57–61.

performances. The manager or impresario was thus dependent on a supply of (preferably new) foreign singers, new operas, attracting subscribers for each new opera, and a fickle walk-in box office. By contrast, opera at European princely courts and many major cities depended largely on court sponsorship or impresarios backed by a group of patrons or guarantors (in Italy, often academies).[13] The London impresario had been largely dependent upon attracting and pleasing a limited, elite London audience. Even the ten unbroken performances of Handel's *Rinaldo* in the 1714–15 season, called for by the coronation of George I, which is often held up as proof of the opera's popularity, ran at a loss.[14]

The leaders of London's *beau monde* and social-political elite settled upon a novel means of organizing an opera company: a joint-stock company, no doubt inspired by the exuberant financial speculation leading up to the South Sea Bubble that would burst in August-September of 1720. The chartered company would raise a pool of working capital, divide risk, and, it was hoped, even return a dividend to shareholders.[15] By this means, the Royal Academy set a new model for collective patronage of opera in London.

In January 1719 "Severall Gentlemen" petitioned the King to establish opera in London as a joint-stock company.[16] Their goal was to provide London with regular seasons of international-caliber opera befitting such a "great and

---

[13] On types of continental opera sponsorship: William C. Holmes, *Opera Observed: Views of a Florentine Impresario in the Early Eighteenth Century* (Chicago, Ill.: University of Chicago Press, 1993), 8–13; Lorenzo Bianconi, *Music in the Seventeenth Century*, trans. David Bryant (Cambridge: Cambridge University Press, 1987), esp. 161–263; and Lorenzo Bianconi and Thomas Walker, "Production, Consumption and Political Function of Seventeenth-Century Italian Opera," *Early Music History*, 4 (1985), 209–96.

[14] Milhous and Hume, "Heidegger and the Management of the Haymarket Opera," 74. On the fictions relating to Handel's *Rinaldo*, David Hunter, "Bragging on *Rinaldo*: Ten Ways Writers have Trumpeted Handel's Coming to Britain," *Göttinger Händel-Beiträge*, 10 (2004), 113–31; and summarized in Hunter, *The Lives of George Frideric Handel* (Woodbridge: Boydell, 2015), 349–60.

[15] The history and organization of the Royal Academy have been well documented. See Judith Milhous and Robert D. Hume, "The Charter for the Royal Academy of Music," *Music and Letters*, 67 (1986), 50–8; Milhous and Hume, "New Light on Handel and The Royal Academy of Music in 1720," *Theatre Journal*, 35 (1983), 149–67; and Gibson, *Royal Academy of Music*. These supersede earlier and incomplete accounts, such as J. Merrill Knapp, "Handel, the Royal Academy of Music, and Its First Opera Season in London (1720)," *Musical Quarterly*, 45 (1959), 145–67. Many of the primary documents are also reprinted in *George Frideric Handel: Collected Documents*, ed. Donald Burrows, Helen Coffey, John Greenacombe, and Anthony Hicks, 6 vols. (Cambridge: Cambridge University Press, 2013–).

[16] On such companies: William Robert Scott, *The Constitution and Finance of English, Scottish and Irish Joint-Stock Companies to 1720*, 3 vols. (Cambridge: Cambridge University Press, 1910–12). His discussion does not touch on the Royal Academy of Music. Given that most joint-stock companies were raising capital beginning upwards of ten million pounds, the Royal Academy with its unusual project was likely not of interest to serious investors.

26   THE CULTURAL POLITICS OF OPERA, 1720–1742

opulent City" as London.[17] A "Proposall for carrying on Operas by a company and a Joynt Stock" was drafted, probably in April 1719.[18] This document set out the governance, the means of raising the £10,000 capital from shareholders, plans for assigning boxes and hiring musicians, and an (overly) optimistic estimate of the dividends to be paid the shareholders. The projectors gained the participation of several Londoners with acquaintance with opera: John Vanbrugh, builder of the Haymarket theatre, opera manager, and ground landlord of the theatre; Handel, who had international experience composing operas; Heidegger, the former opera impresario; and the Earls of Burlington and Manchester and others who had seen opera and star singers in Italy. Handel was hired as "Master of the Orchester" with a salary of £700.[19]

Like the building of Vanbrugh's Haymarket theatre in 1703–1705, the founding the Royal Academy was largely a project of Britain's powerful Whig socio-political oligarchy.[20] The proposal makes clear the organizers saw the Academy as a patriotic endeavor and matter of national prestige. An opera would affirm Britain's place in Europe as a sponsor of culture to match her growing economic and military power:

> Opera's ... carry along with them some Marks of Publick Magnificence and are the great Entertainment which Strangers share in. Therefore it seems very strange that this great and opulent City hath not been able to support Publick Spectacles of this Sort for any considerable time.[21]

Heidegger made a similar claim in 1713 about opera as "a Diversion which most Foreign States think it their Interest to Support: By these Means we may retrieve the Reputation of our Affairs, and in a short time Rival the Stage of Italy."[22] Charles Burney claimed the patent was "a memorial of our prosperity, good-humour, patronage of polite art, and happiness."[23] Moreover, the organizers believed such a means of financing opera would relieve "People of Quality of the exorbitant Burthen of Subscriptions" to operas.

---

[17] Milhouse and Hume, "New Light on Handel and The Royal Academy of Music," 150.

[18] The "Proposall for carrying on Operas by a Company and a Joynt Stock" is in the records of the Lord Chamberlain, Public Record Office, L.C. 7/3, ff. 46–7. Reprinted in Knapp, "Handel and the Royal Academy of Music," 148; Milhous and Hume, "New Light on Handel and The Royal Academy of Music," and *Handel: Collected Documents*, ed. Burrows et al., 1:421–3.

[19] The salary, hitherto unknown, has been determined in Ellen Harris, "'Master of the Orchester with a Salary': Handel at the Bank of England," *Music and Letters*, 101 (2020), 1–29.

[20] I have presented the Whig promotion of opera in *Opera and Politics in Queen Anne's Britain, 1705–1714* (Woodbridge: Boydell, 2022), Chapter 4, "The Haymarket Theatre: A Whig Project," 125–82.

[21] Milhous and Hume, "New Light on Handel and The Royal Academy of Music," 165.

[22] Preface to *Ernelinda* (1713).

[23] *The Cyclopædia; or, Universal Dictionary of Arts, Sciences, and Literature*, ed. Abraham Rees, 39 vols. (1819), vol. 4, s.v. *Bononcini*. Burney claimed he owned the original deed and covenant, whose present location is unknown.

On 8 May 1719, the King granted his subsidy, and the following day he ordered the Academy incorporated. Five days later the Duke of Newcastle issued Handel a warrant for travel to Europe to gather a company of singers.[24] The Academy would bring to London some of the most prominent singers of the day. Francesco Bernardi (called "Senesino") arrived in September 1720; the composer Giovanni Bononcini arrived the following month. The soprano Francesca Cuzzoni arrived in December 1722; and the mezzo-soprano Faustina Bordoni followed in the spring of 1726. The Academy was never able to obtain the services of the "blazing star" Carlo Broschi, called "Farinelli."

By the terms of the Royal Charter, granted on 27 July 1719, the King granted an annual bounty or subsidy of £1,000 to the Academy for the duration of its twenty-one-year charter.[25] Governance was in the hands of directors, who were elected for each season. The Academy hoped to raise £10,000 in subscribed shares of £200.

Originally, there were fifty-eight shareholders, a number that grew to seventy-six shareholders, who in total pledged in the range of £15,000 to £20,000.[26] Some subscribers bought two or more shares. Each shareholder had to put up only £40 of each share but were liable for further calls; it was not expected that more than 25% of the subscription would be called, but in the event, calls were made for all £200. It is not known how many shareholders actually fulfilled their pledges. Table 2.2 lists those who subscribed for shares in the Royal Academy.

The new model, though, was not financially viable, confirming Bourdieu's argument about the low commercial success of prestige cultural products and their restricted consumption. The Academy quickly ran through the approximately £3,500 in capital from the initial purchase payment of £40 per share, and even before the season began, in November 1719 the directors were making calls on the shareholders.[27] In February, Vanbrugh, who had actual experience managing a company, foresaw that expenses were likely to be about double receipts.[28] At the end of the second season, when the directors made the sixth call on shareholders in July, many were in arrears, and the directors threatened to declare them in default.[29]

---

[24] Warrant to Handel: *Handel: Collected Documents*, ed. Burrows et al., 1:429–30.

[25] The charter and other aspects of the Academy's organization are discussed in Milhous and Hume, "Charter for the Royal Academy"; see also *Handel: Collected Documents*, ed. Burrows et al., 1:435–40. Most important, the charter reveals that the King proposed to settle £1,000 annually upon the Academy for the duration of its twenty-one-year charter, as well as the clumsy and ill-conceived organization of the Academy. The bounty in effect went to whomever was presenting operas at the Haymarket theatre.

[26] Burney, *Cyclopædia*, vol. 4, s.v. *Bononcini*, cites the sum of £50,000, which is implausible.

[27] The subscription calls are recorded in *Handel: Collected Documents*, ed. Burrows et al., beginning at 1:448.

[28] John Vanbrugh, letter of 18 Feb., London, to the publisher Jacob Tonson, Paris; reprinted in *Handel: Collected Documents*, ed. Burrows et al., 1: 467.

[29] *Handel: Collected Documents*, ed. Burrows et al., 1:548.

TABLE 2.2. Two-hundred-pound Shareholders in the Royal Academy of Music, 1719*

Original Fifty-eight Shareholders, 27 July 1719[1]

Henry Grey, first Duke of Kent

Thomas Pelham-Holles, first Duke of Newcastle (five shares)

Charles Fitzroy, second Duke of Grafton

Henry Bentinck, first Earl, then first Duke of Portland (three shares)

James Graham, first Duke of Montrose

Charles Montagu, first Duke of Manchester

James Brydges, first Duke of Chandos (five shares)

Charles Stanhope, third Earl of Sunderland

Henry Hyde, Viscount Cornbury (later fifth Earl of Rochester)

James Berkeley, third Earl of Berkeley

Richard Boyle, third Earl of Burlington (five shares)

George Henry Lee, second Earl of Lichfield

Henry Clinton (Fiennes-Clinton), seventh Earl of Lincoln

Thomas Wentworth, first Earl of Strafford

George Montagu, first Earl of Halifax

Henry O'Brien, eighth Earl of Thomond [I]

Talbot Yelverton, first Earl of Sussex

Charles Cadogan, MP (later second Baron Cadogan, 1726))

David Colyear, first Earl of Portmore

Henry Coote, fifth Earl of Mountrath [I]

Henry Lowther, third Viscount Lonsdale

Richard Child, MP, first Viscount Castlemayne [I](two shares)

James Hamilton, MP, first Viscount Limerick [I]

John Gower, second Baron Gower

Allen Bathurst, first Baron Bathurst

Robert Benson, Baron Bingley

George Granville, first Baron Lansdowne

Henry Boyle, first Baron Carleton

Charles Powlett, third Duke of Bolton

Walter Chetwynd, MP

James Craggs, MP

Richard Hampden, MP

Sir Hungerford Hoskyns, MP, baronet

Sir Matthew Decker, MP, baronet

Sir John Guise, MP, baronet

THE ROYAL ACADEMY OF MUSIC AND ITS AUDIENCE   29

TABLE 2.2. *continued*

Sir Wilfred Lawson, MP, baronet

Sir John Jennings, MP

Sir George Coke

Sir Humphry Howarth

Thomas Coke (Vice Chamberlain)

William Evans

Roger Jones, MP

James Bruce

William Pulteney, MP, later first Earl of Bath (1742)

Thomas Coke, MP (later Lord Lovell, then first Viscount and Earl of Leicester)

Thomas Harrison, MP

Hon. Benjamin Mildmay (later Baron FitzWalter and first Earl Fitzwalter)

George Harrison, MP

General George Wade, MP

Francis Whitworth, MP

William Richard Chetwynd, MP (later third Viscount Castlemayne [I])

Thomas Smith, MP

Martin Bladen, MP

Thomas Gage, MP, first Baron and first Viscount Gage [I]

Francis Negus, MP

Sir William Yonge, MP (later fourth baronet)

Brian Fairfax

Dr. John Arbuthnot

On Undated Roster[2]

Hans Kaspar von Bothmer, Hanoverian minister in London

William North, sixth Baron North and second Earl of Guilford

Christoph Kreienberg, Hanoverian resident in London

Samuel Edwin, MP

John Blith

Additional Shareholders Proposed by Motion, 30 November 1719[3]

Philip Wharton, first Duke of Wharton

John Perceval, MP, first Baron Perceval [I] (later first Viscount, then first Earl Egmont [I])

Sir Robert Child, MP

Sir John Eyles, MP, second baronet

Mr. Burnett

30 THE CULTURAL POLITICS OF OPERA, 1720–1742

TABLE 2.2. *concluded*

Francis Whitworth, MP

Major Boyle Smyth (Smith)

Sir Thomas Samuel, MP (Samwell), second baronet

Additional Shareholders Proposed by Motion, 2 December 1719[4]

Sir William Gordon, MP, baronet

John Proby, MP

Shareholders Known from Other Sources

Sir Godfrey Kneller, baronet[5]

Robert Walpole, MP (later KG)[6]

Edward Harley, MP, styled Lord Harley (later second Earl of Oxford and
Mortimer)[7]

---

[*] Shareholders refers to those who purchased £200 shares, as distinct from those who subscribed £20 to annual seasons.
  Used for identification of persons: Carole Taylor, "Italian Operagoing in London, 1700–1745" (Ph.D. dissertation, Syracuse University, 1991); *The History of Parliament. The House of Commons, 1690–1715*, 5 vols. (London: History of Parliament Trust, 2002); and *The History of Parliament. The House of Commons, 1715–1754*, 2 vols. (London: History of Parliament Trust, 1970) [also available at History of Parliament online].

[1] Original patent roll (NA C66/3531, no. 3); printed in Judith Milhous and Robert D. Hume, "The Charter for the Royal Academy of Music," *Music and Letters* 67 (1986), 50–1; and *Handel: Collected Documents*, ed. Donald Burrows, Helen Coffey, John Greenacombe, and Anthony Hicks, 6 vols. (Cambridge: Cambridge University Press, 2013–), 1:425–7.

[2] Additional names found on NA LC 7/3 ff. 52–3; printed in Elizabeth Gibson, *The Royal Academy of Music, 1719–1728: The Institution and Its Directors* (New York, N.Y.: Garland Publishing, 1989), 319–20. Gibson suggests date of May 1719; however, since this list has five more names than on the patent charter, it is likely to date after July 1719 (unless it is earlier and these persons ultimately decided not to become shareholders).

[3] Judith Milhous and Robert D. Hume, "New Light on Handel and the Royal Academy of Music in 1720," *Theatre Journal*, 35 (1983), 152, and Milhous and Hume, "Charter for the Royal Academy," 57.

[4] Gibson, *Royal Academy of Music*, 24,

[5] For Godfrey Kneller's obligations to the Royal Academy, see J. Douglas Stewart, *Sir Godfrey Kneller* (Oxford: Clarendon Press, 1983), 85 n. 38.

[6] For Robert Walpole's payments, see Thomas McGeary, "The Opera Accounts of Sir Robert Walpole," *Restoration and Eighteenth-Century Theatre Research*, 2nd ser., 7 (1996), 1–9.

[7] Gibson, *Royal Academy of Music*, 22 n. 2.

THE ROYAL ACADEMY OF MUSIC AND ITS AUDIENCE   31

What was intended by operalovers as a way to guarantee an opera in London –
with the added possibility of a share in a profitable company – ultimately
became a subsidy. Milhous and Hume estimate that the Academy lost from
about £5,600 to £6,000 in just the first season.[30] Although a profit was turned
for the 1721–22 season and a dividend of 7% was paid in February 1723,[31] ultimately twenty-one calls on shareholders were made, and the mounting losses
ended up consuming each shareholder's share.

THE OPERA AUDIENCE

It is difficult to convey – even by the number of peers among the shareholders –
the exclusivity and wealth required to participate in this elite world of the Royal
Academy and subsequent opera companies, whether at the level of a £200
shareholder or even the twenty-guinea season subscriber.

Conversion to modern values of eighteenth-century money is notoriously
difficult.[32] But one scholar has proposed £1 to have a modern equivalent in the
range of £200 to £400.[33] Accordingly, each pledged two-hundred-pound share
would be £40,000–£80,000 today; a season subscription (usually at twenty
guineas, which gives a discounted rate), £4,200–£8,400; and single tickets for
boxes or the pit at half a guinea, £105–£210 per night.

The major supporters of the Royal Academy, the shareholders and sea-
sonal subscribers, were an exclusive fraction of London's *beau monde* and
social-political elite. Of the total seventy-six shareholders, almost half (34 or
45%) were peers – or about one-fifth of the peerage being represented in the
Academy.[34] Thirteen (17%) of the shareholders were baronets or knights, and
almost half (34 or 45%) were MPs.[35] Although untitled, MPs were a select group,
requiring a qualification of landed income of £600 (for a knight of the shire)
or £300 (for a burgess of a borough).[36] These land qualifications for an MP do
not include the added costs of contested elections, which could run hundreds
of pounds.[37] Most members of Parliament would have borne the costs of maintaining a residence in London when Parliament sat, if not the whole season.

It was not just the number who potentially *could* invest or attend (based on
disposable income) that is significant, but the number of those who *chose* to.
Probably 310 families (of England's total population of perhaps 5 million) had

---

[30] "New Light on Handel and The Royal Academy of Music," 164.
[31] Gibson, *Royal Academy of Music*, 159; *Handel: Collected Documents*, ed. Burrows et al.,
1:625.
[32] For a discussion of the difficulties in making such conversions, and the conversion
figures used here, see Introduction, note 14.
[33] Hume, "Value of Money in Eighteenth-Century England."
[34] Based on the House of Lords having 190 lords temporal at the time.
[35] Some subscribers may be counted as both baronets or knights and as MPs.
[36] According to the Landed Qualification Act of 1710/11 (9 Anne, c.5). Some exceptions
to the amounts were allowed.
[37] Some election costs are given in J. H. Plumb, *The Growth of Political Stability in
England, 1675–1725* (Harmondsworth: Penguin Books, 1969), 93–9.

32   THE CULTURAL POLITICS OF OPERA, 1720–1742

an average annual income of over £5,388 and conceivably could easily afford such a speculative investment of £200.[38] But only seventy-six persons chose to invest. Few families could afford a season subscription, usually 20 guineas for fifty promised performances. Nation-wide, there were about 53,000 households (3% to 4%) with incomes above £200, of which perhaps 5,000 to 6,000 lived in London for the season and were potential season subscribers.[39] Of these, about 130 to 170 chose to buy a 20-guinea season subscription.[40]

There was indeed a middling social-economic group (comprising only 12% to 13% of the population) between the topmost stratum and the laboring poor. But at about £50 to £200 annual income, even if a couple from this stratum were inclined to see an opera, a pair of tickets for the gallery (5 shillings) would have been quite expensive for regular attendance.

The opera audience was not limited to the elite who subscribed. Even the casual walk-in audience for single performances was small, probably limited to those with cultural or social capital who desired to participate in some way in the world of opera, even if by seeing a single opera. Contemporaries often remarked on the thin houses at the opera. Judith Milhous calculates that the Haymarket theatre could comfortably seat about 670 persons, normally about 763, and at maximum (crowded) 940. The prestigious boxes and pit could comfortably accommodate 400, normally 413, and at maximum 500–540.[41] Judging from financial records, the theatre was rarely filled to capacity, and usually not even for special performances when attended by the royal family. For example, for six Handel opera performances for the seasons from 1731 to 1733 for which reports survive (before competition with a rival opera company), attendance ranged from 262 to 361 (not including footmen admitted free in the second gallery).[42]

As early as 1718, the exclusive nature of operagoing was apparent. The Whig periodical the *Free-Thinker*, devoted to promoting and encouraging a Whig version of politeness, noted in 1718:

> *Operas* are a very elegant Diversion; but more confined in *England*, by reason of the Expense required to support them; and, because the People are not, so universally, prepared to understand the Language of Musick [i.e., Italian], as they are to apprehend Expressions of Wit and Sense [English theatre]: Therefore,

---

[38] Hunter, "Patronizing Handel," 36.

[39] Hunter, "Patronizing Handel," 33.

[40] Hunter, "Patronizing Handel," 35 (Table 4); see also detailed examinations of accounts for seasons in the 1730s: Judith Milhous and Robert D. Hume, "Box Office Reports for Five Operas Mounted by Handel in London, 1732–1734," *Harvard Library Bulletin*, 26 (1978), 245–66; and Milhous and Hume, "Handel's Opera Finances in 1732–3," *Musical Times*, 125 (Feb. 1984), 86–9.

[41] Judith Milhous, "The Capacity of Vanbrugh's Theatre at the Haymarket," *Theatre History Studies*, 4 (1984), 38–46. See also Milhous, "Opera Finances in London, 1674–1738," *Journal of the American Musicological Society*, 37 (1984), 567–92.

[42] Hunter, "Patronizing Handel," 38–9; Milhous and Hume, "Box Office Reports for Five Operas Mounted by Handel"; and Milhous and Hume, "Handel's Opera Finances in 1732–3," (at p. 88).

amongst us, Operas cannot, yet, be so properly accounted publick Shews, as Entertainments for a select Audience.[43]

Johann Mattheson, writing of the commercial opera in Hamburg in 1728, stated that operas are more for kings and princes than merchants and tradespersons.[44]

How the high ticket prices limited those who attended opera was noted by the *Weekly Journal* in March 1723.[45] In one of a pair of essays intending to make London's "Pleasures and Entertainments as elegant as possible," the writer approves the practice of the ancient Greek and Roman patricians to sponsor and present gratis "Shews and Representations." Addressing the directors of the Royal Academy of Music, the author urges that their operas "must deserve our highest Praise, were they carried on with the same Spirit and Design," as were those in Greece and Rome. Unfortunately, anyone admitted pays the same price (per performance) as the subscribers or shareholders; hence, "the far greatest Number of our People are quite excluded from these Entertainments, because of the Expence." For music lovers, the attendance becomes a vice when they otherwise cannot afford the expense.

While it not possible to be exact about the political affiliations of all shareholders, it is possible to extrapolate from the make-up of Parliament. The 1722 House of Commons (of 558 seats) was seventy percent Whig.[46] The Lords was somewhat less Whiggish, at about sixty percent Whig.[47] Since the initial organization of the Royal Academy occurred during the Whig Schism, the shareholders also include a number of Schismatic Whigs allied with Walpole, Townshend, and the Prince of Wales.[48] There was a Tory faction; but by this date, most of those who remained were increasingly shedding their Tory colors and joining the Whigs, and were reconciling themselves to the government and the Hanoverian Succession; they saw themselves, Linda Colley has argued, as a "loyal opposition."[49] Overall, the world of the leadership of the Royal Academy functioned above the fray of partisan politics.[50]

---

[43] *Free-Thinker*, no. 68 (14 Nov. 1718); quoted from the collected reprint edition in 3 vols. (1722), 89.

[44] Johann Mattheson, *Der musikalische Patriot* (Hamburg, 1728), 199 ("Opern sind mehr für Könige und Fürsten, als für Kauff- und Handels-leute").

[45] *Weekly Journal: or, Saturday's Post*, no. 228 (9 March 1723)[quoted]. Probably by Daniel Defoe, since it is included in *A Collection of Miscellany Letters*, 4 vols. (1722, 1727), 3: 269–80. Reprinted in Gibson, *Royal Academy of Music*, 383–5, who reports the item was written by Defoe for Nathaniel Mist.

[46] *The History of Parliament: The House of Commons, 1715–1754*, ed. Romney Sedgwick, 2 vols. (New York, N.Y.: Oxford University Press, 1970), 1:34.

[47] Based on the party affiliations given in Clyve Jones, "The Impeachment of the Earl of Oxford and the Whig Schism of 1717: Four New Lists," *Bulletin of the Institute of Historical Research*, 55 (1982), 66–87.

[48] Further analysis of politics of the Royal Academy subscribers, McGeary, *Politics of Opera in Handel's Britain*, 69–72 and Appendix 1, p. 250.

[49] Linda Colley, *In Defiance of Oligarchy: The Tory Party, 1714–60* (Cambridge: Cambridge University Press).

[50] As argued in McGeary, *Politics of Opera in Handel's Britain*.

34   THE CULTURAL POLITICS OF OPERA, 1720–1742

For describing the operagoers, it is best to see them as part of what Hannah Greig, in her study of London's *beau monde*, called the 'socio-economic elite.'[51] Using such a term as 'elite' is preferable to seeing the opera patrons as members of the aristocracy or upper class. 'Aristocracy' is problematic because, then and now, its boundaries are fluid, its use is often used just for the peerage (not including baronets and knights), and using it overlooks the number of operagoers who were not titled.[52] Beyond the titled and gentry, the operagoing elite also included wealthy financiers and merchants, high-ranking public officials, and members of the worthy professions who also had social and cultural capital.

'Upper class' is to be avoided since it invokes a Marxist division based on economic determination, class struggle, and the notion of a complementary bourgeois middle class – the last two being especially inappropriate for the period.[53] As much as anything, the membership in a social class, status group, aristocracy, or the *beau monde* has both objective and subjective components;

[51] Hannah Greig, *The Beau Monde: Fashionable Society in Georgian London* (New Haven, Conn.: Yale University Press, 2013).

[52] On problems defining the aristocracy, J. V. Beckett, "The English Aristocracy," *Parliamentary History*, 5 (1986), 133–42. Lawrence Stone and Jeanne C. F. Stone avoid the confusing definition of aristocracy by using the term elite for their detailed analysis of what they call the landed elite; *An Open Elite? England 1540–1880* (Oxford: Clarendon Press, 1984). Alternatively, "aristocratic" could be used for standards of taste appropriate to a certain class (which still leaves defining that class problematic).

Roy Porter notes there was contemporary awareness of social strata and the difficulties in defining them; he gives a lively description of what he calls the "English aristocracy" in *English Society in the Eighteenth Century*, rev. ed. (London: Penguin Books, 1991), 52–66. Still valuable is the concise overview in H. J. Habakkuk, "England's Nobility," reprinted on pp. 97–115, in *Aristocratic Government and Society in Eighteenth-Century England: The Foundations of Stability*, ed. Daniel A. Baugh (New York, N.Y.: New Viewpoints, 1975).

M. L. Bush, *The English Aristocracy: A Comparative Synthesis* (Manchester: Manchester University Press, 1984), pertinently notes that what gave coherence and integrity to the aristocratic order was not so much privilege as "its members' subscription to an aristocratic life-style based on rentier landownership, a sense of public duty and the lavish display of wealth" (p. 36).

[53] More useful is Max Weber's departure from Marx with his multi-dimensional approach to social stratification that sees social status as based on class, status, and power (politics). Many factors contribute to status: values, behaviors, and external signs; wealth is only one aspect of status. See Max Weber, "Social Ranks and Social Classes," Chapter 4, in Max Weber, *Economy and Society: A New Translation*, ed. and trans. Keith Tribe (Cambridge, Mass.: Harvard University Press, 2019), 450–7. Importantly, social class is based on objective criteria, whereas rank is subjective, based on claims to privilege based on positive or negative estimation, tradition, and inheritance. See also his widely translated, reprinted, and discussed essay "Class, Status, and Party." J. C. D Clark discusses the many non-economic elements for what he calls "elite hegemony"; *English Society, 1688–1832: Ideology, Social Structure and Political Practice During the Ancien Regime* (Cambridge: Cambridge University Press, 1985), 90–113.

that is, it involves some economic requirements, as well as self-identification or perception of others. Such groups are better defined culturally by a lifestyle marked by willingness and ability to display the requisite signs and behavior.[54]

Cultural differentiation is achieved (created) partly through leisure and material consumption; opera attendance, and the expense required, were one such way of identifying one's social status. Disregarding the moralists' emphasis on frugality and economy, elite social status required a lifestyle of excess on lavish spending, consumption, and outward display, such as maintaining splendid country homes with the necessary household staffs – all of which often ruined families.

Being part of the operagoing social-political elite meant living in London during the Season, with the social and cultural capital to enable attending an exclusive entertainment – all marking operagoing as an essential element of the elusive category of the *beau monde*.[55] Greig's study of the *beau monde* shows how central was operagoing to the world of the *beau monde*, and as well how closely linked were the worlds of the operagoer and political class – a point confirmed by Table 2.2.

ORGANIZATION OF THE ROYAL ACADEMY

The Royal Academy (like Britain's constitution) was a mixed form. Like the commercial opera houses in Hamburg and Venice, it was intended as a profit-oriented enterprise, open to any who could afford a ticket (with constraints of attire, etc.) – but subject to the uncertainties of season subscriptions, walk-in audience, sustained novelty of opera, and availability of favorite singers or new operas. The Royal Academy's collective patronage by means of the joint-stock company and season subscriptions were similar to those that supported the academies of some Italian cities.

And there is an element of the continental court opera because of the royal bounty, frequent royal attendance, royal representative on the board of directors, and governance by courtiers and high-ranking officials. Beyond the King's annual bounty of £1,000, attendance by members of the royal family brought in money for their use of boxes. All totaled, for Handel's 1731–32 season, for

---

[54] Norbert Elias stresses the importance of the outward display of wealth and luxury for establishing status in *The Court Society*, trans. Edmund Jephcott (New York, N.Y.: Pantheon Books, 1983), 37–8, 63–5, 67–77. A point made earlier by Thorstein Veblen in *The Theory of the Leisure Class* (New York, N.Y.: Macmillan, 1899), where he coined the term "conspicuous consumption."

[55] The centrality of opera and music in elite social life and status is set forth most extensively in Greig, *The Beau Monde*, 84–7. See also William Weber, "Musical Culture and the Capital City: The Epoch of the *beau monde* in London, 1700–1870," pp. 71–89 in *Concert Life in Eighteenth-Century Britain*, ed. Susan Wollenberg and Simon McVeigh (Aldershot: Ashgate, 2004), who notes that "cultural life was central to the process by which [the *beau monde*] was formed" (p. 72), and that opera "stood at the centre of the elite public world [and] attendance was presumed as a normal social act for anyone reckoned part of the *beau monde*. Opera became considerably more of an obligation than the spoken theatre" (p. 77).

36   THE CULTURAL POLITICS OF OPERA, 1720–1742

example, the royal family (including the Prince of Wales' own bounty of £250) brought in £1,642, or approximately 20% of the year's income.[56]

The governor of the Academy, the lord chamberlain, was the king's permanent representative on the board and had a veto over the directors' decisions.[57] The Crown presumably had the right to forbid or censor any opera production as it could any other theatre production, but there are few instances of royal involvement in the Academy's operations.[58] Since many shareholders and subscribers had royal or ministerial appointments, the Academy could seem in some sense an extension of the Court, and so at most might be a "quasi-court" opera.[59]

But the Royal Academy was not what Bianconi and Walker call an *instrumentum regni*, a public expression, demonstration, and representation of royal power or authority (as it had been in the operas sponsored by the court of Charles II).[60] For Bianconi and Walker, "the real addressee [of an opera production] is the promoter, and the promoter is the one who pays the deficit."[61] For a genuine princely court opera (such as sponsored by Louis XIV or the Habsburgs), the promoter and addressee is the court – for whom the splendid production (often an allegorical opera) is an *instrumentum regni*. But in the case of operas produced by the Royal Academy (and subsequent companies), the impresario and addressee is the Academy. Financial support came mostly from shareholders and season subscribers, ticket sales, and box rentals; and artistic direction of the Academy was in the hands of a committee elected by shareholders, whose overriding concerns were financial, hiring singers, and choosing operas, not celebration of royal events or dynasties. Hence, the addressee of opera at the Haymarket was the socio-political elite of London, the *beau monde*.[62]

---

[56] See Milhous and Hume, "Handel's Opera Finances in 1732–3," at 88.
[57] The governor for many early seasons was the Duke of Newcastle, who with his Duchess was an avid opera enthusiast (see Tables 2.1, 2.4, and 6.3 and p. 5). Diplomatic dispatches to him often mention matters of opera.
[58] The few direct instances of royal influence on the Academy were when the King made known his wishes about re-engaging Cuzzoni and Faustina (upon which royal subsidy would depend) and settling a dispute among other singers; see McGeary, *Politics of Opera in Handel's Britain*, 111, and notes 72 and 73 in this present chapter.
[59] On Handel's link to the Court and role as court composer, Donald Burrows, "Handel as a Court Musician," *Court Historian*, vol. 3, no. 2 (July 1998) 3–9.
[60] See Andrew Walkling, *English Dramatick Opera, 1661–1706* (London: Routledge, 2019), and *Masque and Opera in England, 1656–1688* (Abingdon: Routledge, 2017).
[61] Bianconi and Walker, "Production, Consumption and Political Function of Seventeenth-Century Italian Opera," 241.
[62] Operas or their prefaces alluding to the monarch are few (for example, *Riccardo Primo* and *Il Muzio Scevola)* as are royal dedications; see McGeary, *Politics of Opera in Handel's Britain* (Appendix 2). Musical-dramatic works that directly address the royal family took other forms (odes, serenatas) and were usually performed at other venues; see McGeary, *Politics of Opera in Handel's Britain* (Appendix 5).

THE ROYAL ACADEMY OF MUSIC AND ITS AUDIENCE   37

TABLE 2.3 Summary of Productions of the Royal Academy
of Music and the Handel-Heidegger Partnership

Season	Operas Produced	Number of Performances
Royal Academy of Music		
1719–20	3	22
1720–21*	5	60
1721–22	6	62
1722–23	8	59
1723–24	7	51
1724–25	6	63
1725–26	6	?55
1726–27	5	38
1727–28	7	?62
Handel-Heidegger Partnership**		
1729–30	5	49
1730–31	7	52
1731–32	12	68
1732–33	9	51

Number of performances may be approximate due to missing issues
of newspapers.
*   Excluding a serenata by A. Scarlatti
**   Includes odes, oratorios, and operas not by Handel
   Source: *Handel: Collected Documents*, ed. Burrows et al., vols. 1 and 2.

SEASONS

The Academy opened late in the 1719–20 season on 2 April 1720. In that initial short season, the Academy offered only twenty-two performances of three operas. In the following eight seasons, the Academy mounted from thirty-nine to about sixty-three performances, in most seasons between fifty-one and about sixty-three (see Table 2.3).[63]

Two London theatrical events during the course of the Royal Academy are widely known: the rivalry between the singers Faustina and Cuzzoni that supposedly led to hisses and catcalls from the singers' partisans in the audience and an on-stage fight that caused an opera performance to be halted,[64] and John

[63] Newspapers are lacking for some days, so a precise calendar of performances is not possible.
[64] The rivalry between the partisans of the two singers was embellished on the basis they supposedly broke out in a hair-pulling fight onstage. The antagonism was the basis for

38   THE CULTURAL POLITICS OF OPERA, 1720–1742

Gay's ballad opera *The Beggar's Opera*, which premiered on 29 January 1728 and ran for an unprecedented sixty-three performances (see further in Chapter 3). Both are said to have led to the demise of the Royal Academy.

These occurrences have overshadowed the Academy's actual success at producing nine seasons of highest-quality opera. From its beginning, the Academy was one of the most important opera companies in Europe, usually presenting a season of upwards of fifty performances, featuring many of Europe's greatest singers (including Faustina, Cuzzoni, and Senesino), and new operas by Bononcini and Handel. Such a long season and generous salary, benefits, and audience gifts was more attractive to singers than the shorter continental seasons at Carnival or Ascension or for court festivities.

Like Heidegger's previous attempts at producing opera, the inherent financial impossibility of producing opera in London on even a break-even basis finally caught up with the Royal Academy. Correspondence of opera enthusiasts in the winter and spring of 1728 mentions divisions and quarrels among the directors, dissatisfaction with singers, their demands for payment, the popularity of the *Beggar's Opera*, and dwindling attendance at the opera: all raising fears the opera would not survive for the following season. Most ominously, as early as November 1727, it was reported that Senesino and Faustina threatened not to return for another season.[65] In June, the Academy directors were meeting to make contingency plans were the Academy to fold.

Despite a royal stipend, pledged capital of more than £15,000, involvement of men experienced in opera, and splendid productions with Europe's greatest singers and composers, expenses always outran income. The Academy was ultimately doomed, in Milhous and Hume's assessment, by its ambitiousness, extravagance, and cumbersome government by amateur committee.[66]

But there was still hope for opera. London's social-political elite was not willing to lose a favorite status-affirming cultural institution. The Royal Academy's patent still ran for another twelve years. By June 1728, thirty-five peers and gentry (twenty-eight of whom had participated in subsidizing or directing the Academy) had each pledged a capital infusion of £7,000 "to the corporation of the Royal Academy of Musick towards carrying on of Operas which are to begin in October 1728" (see Table 2.4).[67]

---

numerous newspaper reports, satires, poems, and an operatic skit. For details of the actual event, Suzanne Aspden, *The Rival Sirens: Performance and Identity on Handel's Opera Stage* (Cambridge: Cambridge University Press, 2013), 47–9; and McGeary, *Politics of Opera in Handel's Britain*, 108–12.

[65] Gibson, *Royal Academy of Music*, 269–71.

[66] Milhous and Hume, "New Light on Handel and The Royal Academy of Music," 153, 155, 164.

[67] Undated lists at the West Sussex Record Office, Goodwood MSS 143 and 144. Gibson, *Royal Academy of Music*, 278–9, prints only one of them. For other reprints with the two lists distinguished, *Handel: Collected Documents*, ed. Burrows et al., 2:225. On such subscription campaigns, see McGeary, "More Light (and Some Speculation)." For further on the winding-down of the Academy, Gibson, *Royal Academy of Music*, 277–9.

TABLE 2.4. Two-hundred-pound Sponsors of a Projected 1728–29 Season of the Royal Academy of Music, with their Previous Opera Company Participation

---

Present on Scribal Copy

Charles Lennox, second Duke of Richmond
Royal Academy of Music: director (1727), subscriber (1723?, 1726)

John Manners, third Duke of Rutland (1696–1779)
Royal Academy of Music: director (1727), subscriber (1723)

James Hamilton, MP, first Viscount Limerick [I]
Royal Academy of Music: shareholder, director (1726, 1727), subscriber (1723)

Charles Cadogan, MP, second Baron Cadogan
Royal Academy of Music: shareholder, director (1727), subscriber (1723)

Henry Davenant
Royal Academy of Music: director (1726, 1727), subscriber (1723)

Charles Edwin, MP
Royal Academy of Music: director (1726), subscriber (1723)

W. Dudley

Philip Dormer Stanhope, fourth Earl of Chesterfield
Royal Academy of Music: director (1720, 1726), subscriber (1723)

Thomas Coke, MP, Lord Lovell (1728), later first Viscount and Earl of Leicester
Royal Academy of Music: shareholder, director (1719, 1720)

Charles Douglas, third Duke of Queensberry
Royal Academy of Music: director (1720), subscriber (1723)

General George Wade, MP
Royal Academy of Music: shareholder, director (1720, 1726. 1727), subscriber (1723)

Charles Bennet, second Earl of Tankerville

Alan Brodrick, MP, Baron Brodrick [I], later first Viscount Midleton [I]

(The Hon.) John St. John, MP (later second Viscount St. John)*

William van Keppel, second Earl of Albemarle
Royal Academy of Music: director (1726, 1727), subscriber (1723)

George Stanley
Royal Academy of Music: director (1727), subscriber (1723)

Sir Conyers Darcy, MP
Royal Academy of Music: director (1720), subscriber (1723)

Sir Thomas Prendergast (Pendergrass), MP, second baronet
Royal Academy of Music: director (1727), subscriber (1723)

Henry Clinton (Fiennes-Clinton), seventh Earl of Lincoln
Royal Academy of Music: shareholder, subscriber (1723)

Thomas Pelham-Holles, first Duke of Newcastle-upon-Tyne
Royal Academy of Music: governor (1719 – before 1726), shareholder, director (1719, 1720), subscriber (1723)

Talbot Yelverton, first Earl of Sussex
Royal Academy of Music: shareholder, subscriber (1723)

40 THE CULTURAL POLITICS OF OPERA, 1720–1742

TABLE 2.4. *continued*

Henry Grey, first Duke of Kent
  Royal Academy of Music: shareholder, director (1719, 1720)

(Hon.) James Brudenell, MP
  Royal Academy of Music: director (1726, 1727), subscriber (1723)

Charles Spencer, fifth Earl of Sunderland (later third Duke of Marlborough)

Henry Pelham (younger brother of Thomas Pelham-Holles)
  Royal Academy of Music: subscriber (1723)

John Fitzwilliam, second Earl Fitzwilliam [I]
  Royal Academy of Music: subscriber (1723)

Daniel Finch, MP, Lord Finch (later third Earl of Nottingham and eighth Earl of
    Winchelsea)
  Royal Academy of Music: director (1727)

Thomas Smith, MP
  Royal Academy of Music: shareholder, director (1719), subscriber (1723)

B. Webb (?= Borlase Richmond Webb, MP)

John Jeffreys, MP

Charles Fitzroy, second Duke of Grafton
  Royal Academy of Music: shareholder, governor (1726, 1727), director (1719,
  1726, 1727)

Added to Scribal Transcript

Sir John Charlton

Charles Beauclerk, third Duke of St. Albans

Henry Furnese, MP
  Royal Academy of Music: subscriber (1723)

Sir Thomas Aston, MP

Present Only on Circulating Pledge Sheet

Sir John Brownlow, MP, baronet (later first Viscount Tyrconnel [I])
  Royal Academy of Music: subscriber (1723)

George Fox, MP (later Baron Bingley)
  Royal Academy of Music: subscriber (1723)

James Hamilton, fifth Duke of Hamilton [S]
  Royal Academy of Music: director (1727)

Source: West Sussex Record Office. Goodwood MS 143 and 144. Papers of the Duke of
Richmond, "We whose names are underwritten promise to Subscribe the summe of
Two hundred pounds to the Corporation of the Royal Academy of Musick towards
carrying on of Operas which are to begin in October 1728." Richmond presumably was a
promoter of the project.
    There are two manuscript copies of the list: the circulating pledge sheet with
autograph signatures of subscribers; the second, a fair copy transcript with some names
omitted and some names added. Gibson, *Royal Academy of Music*, 278–9, prints the
shorter of the two lists (the copy). On such subscription campaigns, see Thomas

THE ROYAL ACADEMY OF MUSIC AND ITS AUDIENCE   41

TABLE 2.4. *concluded*

McGeary, "More Light (and Some Speculation) on Vanbrugh's Haymarket Theatre Project," *Early Music*, 48 (2020), 91–104.

Used for identification of names: Taylor, "Italian Operagoing in London, 1700–1745," where forenames are abbreviated; and Gibson, *Royal Academy of Music*.

* Taylor, "Italian Operagoing," 328, suggests less likely Henry St. John (later Viscount Bolingbroke).

That month Heidegger left for France and Italy to assemble a cast of singers for a coming season.[68] As feared, the principal singers slipped back to Italy: Senesino and Faustina in July 1728; Cuzzoni, a month later.[69]

Optimism for opera turned to disappointment when Heidegger returned in November without singers. Without a star cast, the Royal Academy could not present a season in 1728–1729, even though it had the promised support of the sponsors in June 1728. A newspaper reported, the "Italian Opera's are now entirely laid aside in this Kingdom for the present."[70] Anne, Countess of Albemarle concluded several days later, "so no operas this winter."[71] In reality then, the immediate cause of the demise of the Royal Academy was Heidegger's failure to return with a cast of singers – not the scandal of the Faustina and Cuzzoni rivalry nor success of Gay's *Beggar's Opera*.

❧ *The Handel-Heidegger Partnership*

After Heidegger's return in November, the Academy's directors called a final General Court of shareholders for 18 January 1729 and gave up active management of opera. Since their charter still ran until 1741, they voted to permit Heidegger and Handel to carry on operas for five years and lent them all the

---

[68] As reported in the *London Evening Post*, no. 82 (15–18 June 1728); and the *Craftsman*, no. 103 (22 June 1728); see also *Handel: Collected Documents*, ed. Burrows et al., 2:229.

[69] *Daily Post*, nos. 2740 and 2747 (3 and 11 July 1728); the *Craftsman*, no. 104 (6 July 1728); and *Mist's Weekly Journal*, no. 168 (6 July 1728); see also *Handel: Collected Documents*, 2:236. On Faustina, Senesino, and Cuzzoni in Paris in August, Lowell Lindgren, "Musicians and Librettists in the Correspondence of Gio. Giacomo Zamboni (Oxford Bodleian Library, MSS Rawlison Letters 116–38)," *Royal Musical Association Research Chronicle*, 24 (1991), letters nos. 222 and 223; and "Parisan Patronage of Performers from the Royal Academy of Music (1719–29)," *Music and Letters*, 58 (1977), 4–28.

[70] *London Evening Post*, no. 144 (7–9 Nov. 1728); see also *Handel: Collected Documents*, ed. Burrows et al., 2:258.

[71] Letter from Anne, Countess of Albemarle, 11 Nov. 1728, to the Duke of Richmond; in *A Duke and His Friends: The Life and Letters of the Second Duke of Richmond*, ed. Charles March, Earl of March, 2 vols. (London: Hutchinson, 1911), 1:161. A series of twice-weekly subscription concerts was proposed; Gibson, *Royal Academy of Music*, 280. It is not known whether this subscription series took place.

42   THE CULTURAL POLITICS OF OPERA, 1720–1742

scenery, costumes, instruments, and furniture.[72] Handel set out for Italy on 4 February 1729 to recruit singers.[73] He was unable to engage any of the Royal Academy's previous singers or the rising star Farinelli,[74] but he did assemble a cast and returned on 29 June 1729.[75]

The practical arrangements of the Handel-Heidegger partnership, often called the Second Academy, and its relation to the Royal Academy are uncertain.[76] Heidegger held the lease on the King's (Haymarket) theatre and presumably handled the managerial end, Handel ran the musical department and continued to draw a £700 salary, and the royal bounty continued. In these seasons Handel relied more than usual on revivals of his own works and assembling *pasticci*, through which he was introducing London audiences to the latest Neapolitan style, a style noticeably different from his own.[77]

The royal family took interest in the Handel-Heidegger partnership. Paulo Rolli informed Senesino that Handel's "new plans find favor at Court" and revealed the King's conditions for his royal bounty.[78] At one point a dispute between two singers had to be settled by "royal interpositions."[79] According to recollections of the fourth Earl of Shaftesbury, the subscription for the first

---

[72] As reported by John Perceval (later, Earl of Egmont): Historical Manuscripts Commission, *Manuscripts of the Earl of Egmont. Diary of Viscount Percival afterwards First Earl of Egmont*, 3 vols. (London: His Majesty's Stationery Office (1920–1923), 3:329 (Appendix) (18 Jan. 1729). See also Gibson, *Royal Academy of Music*, 280–4; Donald Burrows, *Handel* (New York, N.Y.: Schirmer, 1994), 126–9; and *Handel: Collected Documents*, ed. Burrows et al., 2:265.

[73] *Handel: Collected Documents*, ed. Burrows et al., 2:270. On Handel in Italy in 1729, the most extensive account is Juliane Riepe, *Händel vor dem Fernrohr: Die Italienreise* (Beeskow: Ortus Musikverlag, 2013); see also Gibson, *Royal Academy of Music*, 280–4; Johann Georg Keyssler, *Travels through Germany, Bohemia, Hungary, Switzerland, Italy, and Lorrain*, 4 vols. (1756–57), 3:263–4; and Burrows, *Handel*, 128–9.

[74] Handel's failure to recruit Farinelli was widely reported; see sources cited in McGeary, "Farinelli's Progress to Albion: The Recruitment and Reception of Opera's 'Blazing Star,'" *British Journal for Eighteenth-Century Studies*, 28 (2005), 339–61.

[75] *Craftsman*, no. 157 (5 July 1729); see also *Handel: Collected Documents*, ed. Burrows et al., 2:299.

[76] The few available details about the partnership are presented in Milhous and Hume, "Box Office Reports for Five Operas Mounted by Handel in London, 1732–1734"; Milhous and Hume, "Handel's Opera Finances in 1732–3"; Robert D. Hume, "Handel and Opera Management in London in the 1730s," *Music and Letters*, 67 (1986), 347–62; Judith Milhous, "Opera Finances in London," *Journal of the American Musicological Society*, 37 (1984), 567–92; Taylor, "Italian Operagoing in London"; and Burrows, *Handel*, 125–8. Ellen Harris, "'Master of the Orchester,'" gives details of Handel's salary.

[77] Reinhard Strohm, *Essays on Handel and Italian Opera* (Cambridge: Cambridge University Press, 1985), 164, 211.

[78] Letter from Paulo Rolli, 25 January and 4 February 1729, to Senesino; *Handel: Collected Documents*, ed. Burrows et al., 2:271–3, 274–5.

[79] Letter from John Lord Hervey, 2 December 1729, to Stephen Fox; in *Lord Hervey and His Friends, 1726–38*, ed. Earl of Ilchester (London: John Murray, 1950), 41; see also *Handel: Collected Documents*, ed. Burrows et al., 2:320–1.

season was conducted under the patronage of Handel's pupil Anne, the Princess Royal.[80]

By the middle of February 1729, the subscription for the coming 1729–30 season was going "very well, to the great satisfaction of all musical folks," according to Handel's friend Mary Delany.[81] The new singers hired by Handel began arriving in September,[82] and as was customary, they performed before the royal family.[83]

After a year-and-a-half interval, opera in London resumed on 2 December 1729 with Handel's *Lothario*. The failure of the castrato Antonio Bernacchi to please London audiences forced Handel to approach Senesino, who was hired in August 1730 for 1,400 guineas to replace Bernacchi.[84] In partnership with Heidegger, Handel produced operas through the 1732–33 season (see Table 2.3).

* * *

Opera was established in 1705 on an *ad hoc* basis, produced by a series of theatre managers and impresarios. Lacking any permanent means of finance, it failed financially, and Heidegger ceased productions in 1717. In 1719, London operagoers established the Royal Academy of Music, which made London a major European center for opera and put opera on a more stable footing with subsidies by London's social-political elite and royal bounty. Nonetheless, it was not financially viable, which, following Bourdieu, is characteristic of prestige cultural products.

It was the exclusivity, wealth, and social and economic capital of London's operagoers, and their intersection with the Court, Ministry, and Parliament that made the institution of opera at the Haymarket such a highly visible proxy for (and target for attack on) the Whig ministry of Walpole and object for critique of Britain's dominant culture.

---

[80] Shaftesbury memoir, as printed in O. E. Deutsch, *Handel: A Documentary Biography* (New York, N.Y.: W. W. Norton, 1955), 845. The role of Anne's participation, though, is not known.

[81] Letter from Mary Delany, 16 February 1729, to her sister Ann Granville; in *Handel: Collected Documents*, ed. Burrows et al., 2:276.

[82] *Craftsman*, no. 168 (20 Sept. 1729); see also *Handel: Collected Documents*, ed. Burrows et al., 2:311–12.

[83] Notice from *Norwich Gazette* (18 Oct. 1729); printed in Burrows, *Handel*, 161 n. 34; and *Handel: Collected Documents*, ed. Burrows et al., 2:315. For other notices of singers at court: In October 1734, Farinelli sang before the royal family when he first arrived in Britain; see *London Evening-Post*, no. 1076 (10–12 Oct. 1734) [and *Handel: Collected Documents*, 3:10–11], and *Daily Advertiser*, no. 1155 (11 Oct. 1734). Domenico Annibali sang at court in October 1736; see *Old Whig*, no. 84 (14 Oct. 1736). In October 1736, Lord Hervey reported that "The Queen is to have all the new singers with her this afternoon"; *Lord Hervey and his Friends*, 252; and for November 1736, see Deutsch, *Handel*, 417. See also, letter from Princess Amelia, 23 October 1729, to Lady Portland; printed in Richard G. King, "Two New Letters from Princess Amelia," *Händel-Jahrbuch*, 40/41 (1994/1995), 169; *Handel: Collected Documents*, ed. Burrows et al., 2:315.

[84] Burrows, *Handel*, 131.

CHAPTER 3

Bolingbroke and the Political Opposition

Although in favor with the King, the Whig ministries of the day – first of Stanhope and Sunderland and then Walpole and Townshend – were beset by opposition from discontented Whigs and attacks in the press. Opposition was carried out in newspapers and pamphlets and in Parliamentary motions, bills, contested elections, and obstructionist procedures.[1] The prizes were places in the ministry. Certain policies of the Stanhope-Sunderland ministry – such as protection of dissenters, repeal of the Septennial Act, the Peerage Bill, and a foreign policy that seemed to favor the interests of Hanover above Britain – proved unpopular even to some in the Whig party.

As early as April 1720, William, first Earl Cowper, the highly respected former Whig Lord Chancellor, organized in the Lords an opposition of dissident Whigs, Hanoverian Tories, and Jacobites.[2] Disgusted at the Whig ministry,

---

[1] On the political press of the period, see Laurence Hanson, *Government and the Press, 1695–1763* (London: Oxford University Press, 1936); Michael Harris, *London Newspapers in the Age of Walpole: A Study of the Origins of the Modern English Press* (Cranbury, N.J.: Associated University Presses, 1987), 102–54; Harris, "Print and Politics in the Age of Walpole," pp. 189–210 in *Britain in the Age of Walpole*, ed. Jeremy Black (London: Macmillan, 1984); Robert Harris, *A Patriot Press: National Politics and the London Press* (Oxford: Clarendon, 1993), esp. 1–103; J. A. Downie, "The Development of the Political Press," pp. 111–27 in *Britain in the First Age of Party, 1680–1750: Essays Presented to Geoffrey Holmes*, ed. Clyve Jones (London: Hambledon Press, 1987); Jeremy Black, *The English Press in the Eighteenth Century* (London: Croom Helm, 1987), 197–243; and David H. Stevens, *Party Politics and English Journalism, 1720–1742* (Menash, Wis.: Collegiate Press, 1916), 104–34.

[2] On Cowper's new opposition: Clyve Jones, "The New Opposition in the House of Lords, 1720–3," *Historical Journal*, 36 (1993), 309–29; Jones, "Jacobitism and the Historian: The Case of William, 1st Earl Cowper," *Albion*, 23 (1991), 681–96; Jones, "Opposition in the House of Lords, Public Opinion, Newspapers and Periodicals," *Journal of Newspaper and Periodical History*, vol. 8, no. 1 (1992), 51–5; and Jones, "William, First Earl Cowper, Country Whiggery, and the Leadership of the Opposition in the House of Lords, 1720–1723," pp. 29–43 in *Lords of Parliament: Studies, 1714–1914*, ed. R. W. Davis (Stanford, Calif.: Stanford University Press, 1995). Jones's work corrects earlier accounts by C. B. Realey, *The Early Opposition to Sir Robert Walpole, 1720–1727* (Lawrence, Kan., University of Kansas, 1931).

   Eveline Cruickshanks's suggestion that Cowper was a Tory or Jacobite ("Lord Cowper, Lord Orrery, the Duke of Wharton, and Jacobitism," *Albion*, 26 [1994], 27–40) has been effectively refuted by Clyve Jones, in "1720–23 and All That: A Reply to Eveline Cruickshanks," *Albion*, 26 (1994), 41–53.

BOLINGBROKE AND THE POLITICAL OPPOSITION

he had refused to join other Whigs in ending the Schism and entering the government. Cowper was motivated by Independent Whig principles of preservation of English liberties, primacy of law over political expediency, integrity in government, administrations that governed for the public good, and opposition to the corruption in the ministry revealed by the South Sea scandal. By means of speeches, motions, and entering and printing Parliamentary protests, Cowper sought to reform the Sunderland-Stanhope and then Walpole-Townshend ministries and effect a change of policies and personnel.[3]

The South Sea crisis of 1720 – revealing the corruption throughout the Court and Ministry, the Company's deceitful practices, and the thousands of sufferers – was the initial focus of a series of letters in the *London Journal* and *British Journal* that called for vengeance upon the South Sea malefactors, denounced betrayal of the public trust by the government, and warned against false and deceitful remedies for the South Sea sufferers.[4] The essays were collected as *Cato's Letters* (1720–1723), after the stoic Roman Republican hero who preferred death to life under the tyrant Julius Caesar, which became canonical statements of true Whig principles that became useful for ministerial opponents for generations to come.[5] Cato's writings, more so

---

On other aspects of Cowper's new opposition: Jeremy Black, "Giving Life to the Honest Part of the City: The Opposition Woo the City in 1721," *Historical Research*, 60 (1987), 116–17; and Andrew Hanham, "Early Whig Opposition to the Walpole Administration: The Evidence of Francis Gwyn's Division List on the Wells Election Case, 1723," *Parliamentary History*, 15 (1996), 333–60.

[3] From January 1721 to May 1723, Cowper organized the publication of forty-seven protests; other Lords protests were entered, but not published. The protests are collected in *A Complete Collection of the Protests of the Lords*, ed. James E. T. Rogers, 2 vols. (Oxford: Clarendon Press, 1875).

[4] Written by the whigs Thomas Gordon and John Trenchard from 5 November 1720 to 27 July 1723, they were at first partially collected and then completely collected in 1724 under the title *Cato's Letters* and thereafter regularly reprinted. A reading edition with modernized text is John Trenchard and Thomas Gordon, *Cato's Letters: or, Essays on Liberty, Civil and Religious, and Other Important Subjects*, ed. and intro. Ronald Hamowy, 2 vols. (Indianapolis, Ind.: Liberty Fund, 1995).

[5] On the letters: Caroline Robbins, *The Eighteenth-Century Commonwealthman: Studies in the Transmission, Development and Circumstances of English Liberal Thought from the Restoration of Charles II until the War with the Thirteen Colonies* (Cambridge, Mass.: Harvard University Press, 1959), 120–5; David L. Jacobson, "Introduction," *The English Libertarian Heritage from the Writings of John Trenchard and Thomas Gordon in "The Independent Whig" and "Cato's Letters,"* ed. David L. Jacobson (Indianapolis, Ind.: Bobbs-Merrill, 1965); Isaac Kramnick, *Bolingbroke and His Circle: The Politics of Nostalgia in the Age of Walpole* (Cambridge, Mass.: Harvard University Press, 1968), 243–52; J. G. A. Pocock, *The Machiavellian Moment: Florentine Political Thought and the Atlantic Republican Tradition* (Princeton, N.J.: Princeton University Press, 1975), 467–77; and Marie P. McMahon, *The Radical Whigs, John Trenchard and Thomas Gordon: Libertarian Loyalists to the New House of Hanover* (Lanham, Md.: University Press of America, 1990).

46   THE CULTURAL POLITICS OF OPERA, 1720–1742

than John Locke's, were the most important source of political ideas in the American colonies.[6]

After castigating the corruption of the South Sea Bubble, in later issues Cato moved on to attack social vices, priests, stock-jobbers, and corrupt ministers. Harking back to the hallowed classical republican ideas of Machiavelli and the martyr Algernon Sidney, Cato drew on the lesson of the Roman Republic and reiterated the necessity to avoid luxury and corruption and to encourage virtue to prevent Britain from falling into decadence and slavery. A central series of essays exposed the consequences of life under tyrants, evil ministers, and arbitrary government and reiterated that liberty was the source of the blessings of the arts, sciences, learning, and commerce. Cato defended the Revolution Principles and advocated the right to resist tyranny. A radical Whig-loyalist, Cato never proposed throwing out the Whig ministers. Rather, he was concerned to preserve the House of Hanover and believed the Financial Revolution had to be accommodated.

The Walpole-Townshend ministry finally had enough of Cato's hectoring and struck back in late 1722. A pamphlet *The Censor Censur'd: or, Cato Turn'd Catiline* (1722)[7] charged that Cato was "mischievously bent, and writ with a Design to perplex the Administration, and distract the publick Affairs." Cato pretends a zeal for liberty and the Protestant religion, yet his "malignant Disposition of vilifying the Administration" only lessens their reputation and support. Cato, the pamphlet claimed, would fault any government, and his raising groundless fears and misrepresentations only encourages Jacobites.[8]

Interpretation of *Cato's Letters* is far from settled. McMahon strongly challenged Pocock's and Kramnick's interpretations that Cato is essentially a Country opposition of a "neo-Harrington" or civic humanist cast. Rather, Cato represents less a strict Country ideology than a strongly Independent or even Radical Whig position: its acceptance of Septennial Parliaments, hostility to High Churchmen (necessary to ensure Whig and Protestant survival), commerce, and of self-interest and passion as men's motivations by were at odds with the Country tradition. Jacobson, Robbins, and McMahon see Cato as a radical Lockean Whig endorsing unpopular ideas of contract and non-resistance theory.

[6] See the classic studies of the influence of British Whig writings: Clinton Rossiter, *The First American Revolution: The American Colonies on the Eve of Independence* (New York, N.Y.: Harcourt, Brace, and World, 1956), 225, and Bernard Bailyn, *The Ideological Origins of the American Revolution* (Cambridge, Mass.: Harvard University Press, 1967), 22–54. Thomas Gordon and *Cato's Letters*, rather than John Locke, were the most important sources of political ideas in the Americas. See also, Trevor Colbourn, *The Lamp of Experience: Whig History and the Intellectual Origins of the American Revolution* (Indianapolis, Ind.: Liberty Fund, 1998).

[7] The pamphlet was excerpted in the ministerial *St. James's Journal*, no. 29 (15 Nov. 1722), which suggests it appeared late in the year.

[8] See also *A Defense of Our Present Happy Establishment: and the Administration Vindicated from … Cato's Letters* (1722), and the *Whitehall Journal* for 6 November 1722.

Also begun in the wake of the South Sea crisis, the *Freeholders Journal* (1722–1723) reviled the Whig ministries on the basis of bedrock Country or Old Whig principles.[9] The Freeholder writes from the position of the independent countryman railing against the corruption at Court and the Ministry. Mostly a political journal, it pays little attention to social manners or polite entertainment. The *Journal* reiterates principles of true Whig ideology: frequent parliaments that are free from placeholders and pensioners, dangers of corruption, the Gothic origin of British liberties, resistance to tyrants, dangers of evil ministers, and exhortations to Publick Spirit.[10] The *Journal* already sets themes of the *Craftsman*'s later Country opposition.

Just before Bishop Atterbury departed for exile on 18 June 1723, the Duke of Wharton launched the *True Briton*. Wharton denounced Walpole's prosecution of the bishop as a violation of the Constitution, legal procedures, and British liberties.[11] Begun on 3 June 1723 and running for eight months despite the government's jailing its printer for publishing libels against the government,[12] the *True Briton* took an Independent Whig approach in attacking the Ministry. Perhaps because of Wharton's mercurial politics, bankruptcy, and later defection to the Pretender,[13] the principled integrity of the *True Briton*'s critique of ministerial politics has often mistakenly been taken as Jacobitical. In its skill in ransacking history for evil ministers along with use of innuendo and historical allegories intended to apply to Walpole (with accompanying ironic assertions that no innuendo or application was intended), the *True Briton* anticipates the techniques and topics of later opposition journals such as the *Craftsman*, *Fog's Weekly Journal*, and *Common Sense*.

With the death of Lord Cowper on 10 October 1723 and Wharton bankrupt and gone to Vienna to enter the Pretender's service in 1725, there was little opposition to the Ministry. At the close of the 1723–24 session, one observer wrote, "There is nothing disposed of here but by the interest of one great man who has made himself so useful to the nation that we cannot be without him."[14]

---

[9] The *Freeholder's Journal* ran from 31 January 1722 to 8 May 1723 for seventy-six issues.

[10] See especially the four letters on Publick Spirit: *Freeholders Journal*, nos. 46, 47, 48, 65 (7, 14, and 21 Nov. 1722, and 6 March 1723).

[11] The *True Briton* ran from 3 June 1723 to 17 February 1724. The collected reprint edition in two volumes (1723–1724) included Wharton's widely printed Lords speech on 15 May 1723 defending Atterbury. In its defense of the church against the encroachments of the Quaker's Bill (see nos. 31 and 32, 16 and 20 Sept. 1723), the *True Briton* is departing from Whig orthodoxy.

[12] On government attempts to suppress the *True Briton* and other opposition papers, Hanson, *Government and the Press*, 36–83. The libelous issues were nos. 3, 4, 5, and 6.

[13] Wharton at first supported Cowper's new opposition in the Lords in 1720–1721, but went over to the ministry between December 1721 and May 1723, and then opposed the ministry over the Atterbury affair (Jones, "1720–23 and All That," 49–52).

[14] G. Malcolm to the Hon. John Molesworth, summer 1724; quoted from the manuscripts of M. L. S. Clements, in Historical Manuscripts Commission, *Reports of Manuscripts in Various Collections*, v. 8 (London: His Majesty's Stationery Office, 1913), 379.

48   THE CULTURAL POLITICS OF OPERA, 1720–1742

To consolidate his position, in April 1724 Walpole engineered the rustication of Stanhope's protégé Secretary of State Carteret to Ireland as lord lieutenant – thus effectively removing from the political center the last of the Sunderland-Stanhope faction and Walpole's only remaining rival.[15] Carteret was replaced by Thomas Pelham-Holles, Duke of Newcastle. A great Whig landowner, Newcastle became one of the ministry's major dispensers of patronage, spending his personal wealth to extend his influence and manage elections to return dozens of loyal candidates to Parliament. As well, he was a major shareholder and the governor of the Royal Academy of Music and subscriber to later companies (see Tables 2.1 and 2.2).

By the end of 1725, Walpole held complete control of Parliament and the Ministry. The King showed his favor by making him a knight of the Bath on 27 May 1725, followed by the order of the Garter on 27 June 1726, the first commoner to be so honored since 1660. The visible sign of the Garter knight was the blue sash, and Walpole's vanity at this honor was ridiculed by his political opponents, who called him "Sir Blue String," and depicting him with the sash was a prominent identifier in political cartoons.[16]

🎵 Bolingbroke's Opposition

Ominously though, meanwhile in the Parliamentary session of 1724–1725, there emerged what would be a sustained, well-organized, and well-financed opposition to Walpole's ministry. Two major figures in this opposition were the Whig MP and former minister William Pulteney and Walpole's arch-nemesis from the reign of Queen Anne: the Tory Henry St. John, Viscount Bolingbroke.

Pulteney was a friend and close ally of Walpole while the two were in opposition to Stanhope. He was a skillful, often intemperate, and witty debater in the Commons with a sharp head for figures. He bore resentment against Walpole at the slow pace of his political advancement, for he had expected to fill Carteret's vacancy as secretary of state, the post given to Newcastle. He openly challenged Walpole in the Commons on 8 April 1725 over his proposal for discharging the Civil List debt; the following day in debate, he brazenly accused him of waste, corruption, and financial mismanagement.[17] Walpole replied to the charges and had the final card to play: he had the King dismiss Pulteney as cofferer of

---

[15] Six years later, he resigned, returned from Ireland, and openly joined the Opposition, acting as one of its important leaders, until it succeeded in forcing Walpole from office in 1742.

[16] On Walpole's vanity over his Star and Garter, and the envy and hostility aroused, see J. H. Plumb, *Sir Robert Walpole: The King's Minister* (London: Cresset, 1960), 101–2.

[17] The debate is recorded in *The Parliamentary Diary of Sir Edward Knatchbull, 1722–1730*, ed. A. N. Newman. *Camden Third Series*, 94 (1963), 43–5; and Cobbett, *The Parliamentary History of England*, 8 (1722–1733), 501–2. Another notorious confrontation occurred during Commons debates on the state of the National Debt, 4, 8, 12 March 1728; see *History of Parliament*, 8:647–50.

BOLINGBROKE AND THE POLITICAL OPPOSITION 49

the household.[18] By the end of the 1724–1725 session, Pulteney was recognized as the leader of a small group of dissident Whigs and Tories in the Commons, numbering at the time as few as seventeen. Pulteney would be a prolific political pamphleteer and major contributor to the *Craftsman*.

The major extra-parliamentary force behind the new opposition was Viscount Bolingbroke – Walpole's foe from the days of Anne's reign when he was sent by the Tories to the Tower in 1713 on trumped-up charges of peculation. After the Hanoverian Succession, expecting his impeachment (or worse) from a Whig Parliament, Bolingbroke fled to France on 27 March 1715, where for a short time he was in the Pretender's service as his secretary of state.[19] Blamed by the Pretender's court for the failure of the Jacobite invasion of March–April 1715, he was dismissed in March 1716. As his enemies never failed to point out, he had now twice colluded with the Pretender and betrayed his country.

During his decade of self-exile, Bolingbroke schemed for a pardon, removal of his attainder, and full restoration of his estates so he could enter the Lords and resume his political career. He tried to make himself useful to the Whig ministers. By diplomatic intrigues at the French court, he had helped Walpole and Townshend gain interest with the new French Regent and worked against Carteret. Also aiding his return was the success of his wife in bribing the King's mistress, the Duchess of Kendal. Fulfilling a promise to reward Bolingbroke for his services to the House of Hanover, the King granted him a pardon on 25 May 1723, which allowed him to return to England.[20] But full restoration of his titles and estates depended on Parliament, to which Walpole, the Whigs, and some Tories objected. Finally, against his better judgment, Walpole yielded. Parliament removed the Act of Attainder in April 1725, and the following month he regained his estates. But at Walpole's insistence, he was not allowed to assume his seat in the Lords, thus preventing him from taking an active role in politics – for which he never forgave Walpole. In June 1725, after some brief visits to Britain, Bolingbroke returned to his family estate at Dawley Farm.

Realizing that Walpole would never allow him to resume his seat in the Lords, Bolingbroke saw his only path to entering government would be with Walpole out of office. At Dawley Farm, the opposition he forged came to include those who had various grievances against Walpole: dissident Whigs, Tories, Jacobites, lesser country gentry, High Church clergy, and London's small merchants and traders.

Without his place in the Lords, he would have to work indirectly. His principal allies in Parliament were the Whigs William and Daniel Pulteney, Carteret, Chesterfield, and Cobham; Sir William Wyndham, the leader of the Tories; William Shippen, leader of the Jacobites; and Samuel Sandys, a Country Whig.

---

[18] Plumb, *Walpole: The King's Minister*, 122–4; Realey, *Early Opposition to Sir Robert Walpole*.

[19] Bolingbroke's flight and time in France, return to England, and obtaining pardon: H. T. Dickinson, *Bolingbroke* (London: Constable, 1970), 134–83.

[20] On the protracted process of arranging the pardon, Henry L. Synder, "The Pardon of Lord Bolingbroke," *Historical Journal*, 14 (1971), 227–40.

50   THE CULTURAL POLITICS OF OPERA, 1720–1742

Bolingbroke also gathered around him the literary wits of the Scriblerus Club, Alexander Pope, Jonathan Swift, Dr. John Arbuthnot, and John Gay, who conducted a literary culture of opposition.[21] Later, another literary opposition developed that was organized by Lord Cobham (see Chapter 5).

While in exile, Bolingbroke took up the study of philosophy and history, and moved in Parisian intellectual and social circles, befriending Voltaire and Montesquieu. Upon seeing him in 1725, Pope wrote to Swift, "Lord B. is the most *Improv'd Mind* since you saw him, that ever was without shifting into a new body or being."[22]

CRAFTSMAN

As a vehicle for political polemic and theory, on 5 December 1726, Bolingbroke and the Pulteney brothers launched the *Craftsman*.[23] The newspaper would carry on a continuous campaign against the Walpole administration through its fall. Its principal contributors were Bolingbroke and the Pulteneys, assisted by Nicholas Amhurst as editor. At its peak in early 1731, the *Craftsman* probably reached a circulation of at least 10,000. More than just a propaganda piece, it was a reputable newspaper: in addition to the front-page political essay, it carried domestic and foreign news and a full range of advertising, from serious theological books to the latest quack medicines. The paper's prominence as an Opposition organ was taken over by *Common Sense* in 1737.

[21] Ashley Marshall, *The Practice of Satire in England, 1658–1770* (Baltimore, Md.: Johns Hopkins Press, 2013), provides a concise summary of their satire, but argues that "scholars assume more commonality than actually exits" among the Scriblerians, and that "a 'Scriblerian mode' of satire is a critical delusion" (pp. 179–80, 215–17). She emphasizes the differences in tone and types of satire they used, and provides a concise summary of their political writings on pp. 212–15.

[22] Pope to Swift, 15 Oct. 1725; in *The Correspondence of Alexander Pope*, ed. George Sherburn, 5 vols. (Oxford: Clarendon Press, 1956), 2:332.

[23] The first single issues were titled *The Craftsman. By Caleb Danvers, of Gray's-Inn, Esq.* At first, the paper appeared on Mondays and Fridays with a circulation of 300. After five months, in May 1727, now with a circulation of 700, it became a once-weekly newspaper published on Saturday and now titled *The Country Journal: or, the Craftsman* (the original title is used here throughout).

On the founding, financing, and circulation of the *Craftsman*, see *Lord Bolingbroke: Contributions to the "Craftsman,"* ed. and intro. Simon Varey (Oxford: Clarendon Press, 1982), and William Arnall, *The Case of Opposition Stated, Between the Craftsman and the People*, ed. and intro. Simon Varey (Lewisburg, Penn.: Bucknell University Press, 2003), Appendix B, 105–42. The *Craftsman* lost its pre-eminence as an Opposition newspaper to *Common Sense* after its founding in 1737; it continued publishing at least through the mid-1740s.

See also Simon Varey, "The Craftsman," *Prose Studies: History, Theory, Criticism*, 16 (1993), 58–77, and the entry in *British Literary Periodicals*, ed. Alvin Sullivan, 4 vols. (Westport, Conn.: Greenwood, 1983–1986), 1:68–72.

BOLINGBROKE AND THE POLITICAL OPPOSITION

The first issue's epigraph from Juvenal captures the "gloom of the Tory satirists"[24] that pervades much Opposition writing:

> Nona ætas agitur, pejoraque sæcula ferri
> Temporibus, quorum sceleri non invenit ipsa
> Nomen, & a nullo posuit natura metallo.
>
> We are living in a ninth age; an age more evil than
> that of iron – one for whose wickedness Nature herself
> can find no name, no metal from which to call it.[25]

Its fictional author was "Caleb D'Anvers, of Gray's Inn, Esquire," whose persona was used to elicit the political sympathy of the reader and engage him as an opponent of Walpole. D'Anvers introduces himself as a member of an ancient, north England landed family, retired from the law, "warmly affected with the interest of my country."[26] His wealth and leisure allow him time to reflect on

> the manifold vices and corruptions, upon that general prostitution of principles and degeneracy of manners, which have by degrees over-run the whole kingdom, and put virtue and honesty almost quite out of countenance.

The design of his paper is

> to detect and animadvert upon all these corruptions ... ; to shew how general the evil is grown, and how *Craft* predominates in all professions. But the mystery of *State-Craft* abounds with such innumerable frauds, prostitutions, and enormities, in all shapes, and under all disguises, that it is an inexhaustible fund, an eternal resource for satire and reprehension; since from this grand fountain of corruption flow all those little streams and rivulets, which have spread themselves through every part of this kingdom, and debauched all ranks and orders of men: it shall therefore be my chief business to unravel the dark secrets of *political Craft*, and trace it through all its various windings and intricate recesses.

On a weekly basis, the *Craftsman* harassed and attacked the Walpole ministry's handling of domestic or foreign issues, justified with essays on political theory and history.

Drawing heavily on classical republican, Old Whig, and Country ideas, Bolingbroke's oppositional rhetoric took the principled line that Walpole was corrupting government and the Ancient Constitution and that his removal was the first step to reversing the nation's decline. The *Craftsman* and other Opposition polemic demonized Walpole as a corrupt and wicked minister who was

---

[24] The phrase is from Louis Bredvold, "The Gloom of the Tory Satirists," the title of his essay in *Pope and His Contemporaries: Essays Presented to George Sherburn*, ed. James L. Clifford and Louis A. Landa (Oxford: Clarendon Press, 1949), 1–19. Isaac Kramnick somewhat more positively describes the period as one of "political nostalgia"; *Bolingbroke and His Circle*, 205–35.

[25] Juvenal, *Satire* XIII.28–30; as trans. by G. G. Ramsay in *Juvenal and Persius*, rev. ed. Loeb Classical Library (Cambridge, Mass.: Harvard University Press, 1950), 249.

[26] *Craftsman*, no. 1 (5 Dec. 1726).

52   THE CULTURAL POLITICS OF OPERA, 1720–1742

responsible for every possible political, social, aesthetic, or moral evil.[27] He diverted public money for his own use; he ruled by bribing MPs with lucrative places or pensions to secure their subservience; his corruption of politics destroyed public spirit and personal morals; he promoted faction to weaken the country and divide the Opposition; he subverted traditional liberties; he was leading Britain into domestic tyranny; he spread rumors of Jacobite threats to justify a standing army; he fostered luxury to divert attention from his misdeeds; his corruption ruined arts, sciences, and morals; and he failed to protect merchants from Spanish depredations, thus ruining trade. The implication always was that solving these issues required the removal of Walpole.

Opposition propaganda conveniently divided the political landscape to its own moral advantage. The Opposition claimed the high ground of standing for virtue, liberty, and patriotism, adhering to strict Whig principles, and protecting the British Constitution.[28] They were the true patriots and lovers of Britain, while the Ministry abused the notion of patriotism.[29] To the Ministry was ceded corruption and self-interest. The moral gulf could be conveyed through the labels Court and Country. If Walpole and corruption were located in London at Court and the Ministry, then British virtue and public spirit could only be preserved through the simplicity of ancient Country values – a theme developed in Pope's major satires of the 1730s and Johnson's *London*.

Other oppositional newspapers had their own viewpoints and motives.[30] Nathaniel Mist's *Weekly Journal, or British Gazette* (1716–1725), followed by *Mist's Weekly Journal* (1725–1728), was crypto-Jacobite.[31] *The Grub-street Journal*

---

[27] The identifying effects of an evil minister are pointed out in *Craftsman*, no. 51 (24 June 1727). Some typical *Craftsman* essays on favorites and evil ministers: nos. 67, 72, 136 (14 Oct. and 18 Nov. 1727; and 8 Feb. 1729).

[28] This claim of standing for "Publick Virtue" was ridiculed in *Free Briton*, no. 275 (13 Feb. 1735).

[29] For a typical example, *Craftsman*, no. 230 (28 Nov. 1730).

[30] The viewpoints of the political papers and their writers are described in *The Bee: or Universal Weekly Pamphlet*, vol. 1, no. 1 (Feb. 1733), 5–30; and *The Gentleman's Magazine*, 3 (Feb. 1733), 91. The writers are surveyed in *An Historical View of the Principles, Characters, Persons, &c. of the Political Writers in Great Britain* (1740), 10–51.

In addition to the pamphlets mentioned in the following notes, John Perceval (second Earl of Egmont), *Faction Detected, by the Evidence of Facts* (1743), provides a full history of the Opposition and its polemics on the various political issues of the Walpole Ministry. A ministerial rebuttal is contained in *A Review of the Whole Political Conduct of a Late Eminent Patriot, and His Friends; for Twenty Years Last Past* (1743).

[31] Nathaniel Mist's *Weekly Journal* (begun 15 Dec. 1716) became *Mist's Weekly Journal* (1 May 1725), and then *Fog's Weekly Journal* (28 Sept. 1728–29 Oct. 1737). On Mist, see Jeremy Black, "An Underrated Journalist: Nathaniel Mist and the Opposition Press During the Whig Ascendancy," *British Journal for Eighteenth-Century Studies*, 10 (1987), 27–42.

(1730–1737) was ostensibly established in defense of Pope.[32] Its accounts of a fictional society of Grub Street writers functioned as satire on Walpole's writers, and its victims were often those ministerial scribblers pilloried in Pope's *Dunciad*. Later, *Common Sense*, the *Champion*, and the *Westminster Journal* were organs of the Patriot Opposition.[33]

Opera and its star singers (and especially Farinelli) appear in Opposition writing, often coupled with masquerades. Singers and opera were the butt of ridicule or satire and held up as examples of the luxury, corruption, and effeminacy that ruined the Roman Republic and now threatened to ruin Britain, if they had not already done so.

The *Craftsman* uses events dealing with singers and personnel at the Haymarket theatre as vehicles for allegorical parallels with domestic and foreign affairs.[34] Irony was a favored technique for *Craftsman* writers, so what may seem a favorable mention in that paper on closer consideration is but part of a larger satire, as in this letter from "Philomath":

---

[32] *The Grub-street Journal*, edited principally by Richard Russel, ran from 8 January 1730 to 1738. On the *Grub-street Journal*: James T. Hillhouse, *The Grub-street Journal* (Durham, N.C.: Duke University Press, 1928); Alexander Pettit, "The *Grub-street Journal* and the Politics of Anachronism," *Philological Quarterly*, 69 (1990), 435–51; Bertrand A. Goldgar, Introduction to facsimile edition, *The Grub Street Journal, 1730-33*, 4 vols. (London: Pickering and Chatto, 2002) [argues Pettit's view of the *Journal* as Carolinism opposition is too simple]; and Goldgar's entry in *British Literary Periodicals*, ed. Sullivan, 1:144–9. Goldgar, "Pope and the *Grub-street Journal*," *Modern Philology*, 74 (1976–1977), 366–80, argues the connection of the *Journal* and Pope, as argued by Hillhouse, is unlikely, as does George Sherburn in his review of Hill's edition, *Modern Philology*, 26 (1928–29), 361–7.

The defense of Pope is suggested by the epigram to the first issue:

> Dullness! whose good old cause I yet defend,
> With whom my Muse began, with whom shall end!
> For thee I dim these eyes, and stuff this head,
> With all such reading as was never read.

Quoted from reprint of selected issues, *Memoirs of the Society of Grub-street*, 2 vols. (1737), 1:1.

[33] On *Common Sense*, Thomas Lockwood, "The Life and Death of *Common Sense*," *Prose Studies: History, Theory, Criticism*, 16 (1993), 78–93; on *The Champion*, Michael Harris, "Literature and Commerce in Eighteenth-Century London: The Making of *The Champion*," *Prose Studies: History, Theory, Criticism*, 16 (1993), 94–115; and the entry in *British Literary Periodicals*, ed. Sullivan, 1:43–6. J. C. D. Clark, *English Society, 1688-1832: Ideology, Social Structure and Political Practice During the Ancien Regime* (Cambridge: Cambridge University Press, 1985), 145–6, unconvincingly suggests *Common Sense* is in the tradition of Jacobitism.

[34] These allegories are presented and explicated in McGeary, *Opera and Politics in Handel's Britain*, 104–16. On only one occasion (see Chapter 4) did the *Craftsman* directly oppose opera. An essay in no. 577 (30 July 1737) routinely denounces it in an essay on the necessity of regulating the stage.

54   THE CULTURAL POLITICS OF OPERA, 1720–1742

Sir,

> … I have always look'd upon it as a laudable inclination in my Countrymen, and therefore have been a constant Advocate for the Importation of *Italian Operas*, and *Singers, Dancing-Posture-Ballance-Masters, Tumblers, Rope-Dancers* and *Harlequins*; all which I could prove to have been of so much Advantage to our *most excellent Ministry.*[35]

With its strongly moralistic social critique, *Mist's Weekly Journal* will directly denounce opera (along with masquerades, pantomimes, rope-dancing, and ballad opera) as an instance of the degeneracy of taste that is driving true drama from the stage.[36] *Fog's Weekly Journal*, of higher literary quality than *Mist's*, indicts opera as an example of luxury and effeminacy over-running Britain.[37] The *Grub-street Journal*, allied in spirit with Pope, will attack opera and its devotees as an instance of the debasement of taste occurring under the Robinocracy. In the wake of Farinelli's three stellar seasons and then departure to Spain in summer 1737, *Common Sense* will pointedly invoke opera and Farinelli's residing in Madrid in its campaign to embarrass and provoke the ministry into war with Spain.[38]

Through their polemic and satire, Opposition writers and the *Craftsman* subjected the Walpole ministry to what J. H. Plumb called "an endless stream of vilification and criticism which made not only England but Europe roar with delight."[39]

OPPOSITION TACTICS

In Parliament, the Opposition seized any issue, legitimate or not, that could embarrass Walpole, obstruct his legislation, and somehow weaken his favor with the King.[40] It opposed addresses to the King, called for papers and military instructions to be laid before the House, and harassed parliamentary management with hostile motions. The Opposition resolutely attacked standing armies, Walpole's alliance with France, the subordination of British interests to those of Hanover, pay for Hessian troops, placemen and pensioners, Walpole's pacific foreign policy (especially toward Spain), and, above all, the effects of his corrupt political methods. The Opposition's proposed reforms were such long-standing

---

[35] *Craftsman*, no. 588 (15 Oct. 1737).

[36] See especially, *Mist's Weekly Journal*, no. 34 (18 Dec. 1725); no. 80 (29 Oct. 1726); no. 87 (17 Dec. 1726); and no. 91 (14 Jan. 1727).

[37] *Fog's Weekly Journal* often indicts opera as effeminacy: see especially, no. 311 (19 Oct. 1734) and nos. 335 and 338 (5 and 26 April 1735).

[38] The print campaign is explained in detail in Thomas McGeary, "Farinelli in Madrid: Opera, Politics, and the War of Jenkins' Ear," *Musical Quarterly*, 82 (1998), 383–421.

[39] Plumb, *Walpole: The King's Minister*, 141.

[40] On the sustained Whig dissatisfaction with Walpole, Andrew H. Hanham, "Whig Opposition to Sir Robert Walpole, 1727–1734 in the House of Commons, 1727–1734," (Ph.D. dissertation, University of Leicester, 1992). Hanham estimates Walpole led a ministerial force of some 180 supporters, while Pultney led eighty malcontent Whigs, stiffened by Tories. Walpole's control of Parliament largely depended on those independent Whigs without a connection to the administration.

Country and Old Whig measures as reinstating Triennial (or even annual) Parliaments, reducing the standing army and taxes, and reforming elections. From 1730 until Walpole's fall in 1742, the Tory leader Samuel Sandys introduced twelve bills outlawing MPs from holding places or pensions.[41]

The Opposition flooded the political nation with pamphlets, satiric verse, newspapers, ballads, engraved and woodcut prints, and illustrated broadsides – all developing anti-ministerial imagery, codes, and themes to inflame public opinions against Walpole: either to affect local parliamentary elections or cause the King to lose faith in his minister's ability to govern.[42]

In print media, Walpole was known by a string of nicknames, epithets, caricatures, and catchwords: the Great Man, Sir Blue String, the Norfolk Steward (site of his country house). His role in the South Sea scandal earned him the name Screen-master. Walpole may be shown screening persons from parliamentary inquiry, controlling MPs like a puppeteer, ignoring Spanish depredations, and riding roughshod over liberty. From these prints and engravings emerged the distinctive British political cartoon.

To the politically attuned, the presence of even one of these names or images could turn the seemingly harmless print or poem into a political satire on Walpole and set off trains of associations and innuendo damning him and the ministry. One epithet or cue placed in a narrative of an historical episode about a corrupt statesman or the downfall of a royal favorite turned it into a warning about the dangers of Walpole as an evil minister.

BOLINGBROKE AS THEORIST

The principal source of ideas underpinning oppositional writing was Viscount Bolingbroke, who until his second exile in 1735 contributed extensively to the *Craftsman* and wrote numerous political pamphlets.[43] Many of his ideas –

---

[41] Simon Targett, "Government and Ideology During the Age of Whig Supremacy: The Political Argument of Sir Robert Walpole's Newspaper Propagandists," *Historical Journal*, 37 (1994), 289–317, 308 n. 144.

[42] For the range of oppositional partisan media: *Political Ballads Illustrating the Administration of Sir Robert Walpole*, ed. Milton Percival. Oxford Historical and Literary Studies, 8 (1916); Paul Langford, *Walpole and the Robinocracy* (Cambridge: Chadwyck-Healey, 1986), 13–14; M. Dorothy George, *English Political Caricature to 1792: A Study of Opinion and Propaganda,* 2 vols. (Oxford: Clarendon Press, 1959), 1:77–94; Thomas Wright, *Caricature History of the Georges; or, Annals of the House of Hanover* (London: Chatto and Windus, 1868), 94–142; Herbert M. Atherton, *Political Prints in the Age of Hogarth* (Oxford: Clarendon Press, 1974); Mark Hallett, *The Spectacle of Difference: Graphic Satire in the Age of Hogarth* (New Haven, Conn.: Yale University Press, 1999), 131–67. Prints are catalogued in Frederick G. Stephens, *Catalogue of Prints and Drawings in the British Museum*. Division I. Political and Personal Satires, 3 vols. (London: British Museum, 1877). The prints are reproduced on the British Museum website.

[43] The following modern editions of Bolingbroke's writings include introductory essays on his political ideas: David Armitage, ed., Bolingbroke, *Political Writings* (Cambridge: Cambridge University Press, 1997) [with exhaustive bibliography]; Simon

56   THE CULTURAL POLITICS OF OPERA, 1720–1742

especially despairing of the transformation of England due to the Financial Revolution and idealizing a precommercial England – also found expression in serious literature, such as by the satirists Swift and Pope and in works of the later Patriot Opposition.

Using his considerable rhetorical skills, he sought, as Simon Varey writes, "to persuade his reader to share a coherent vision of Britain in a condition of dangerous decline."[44] On the philosophical level, Bolingbroke elaborated what H. T. Dickinson calls "important ideas and concepts of opposition, which raised the whole level of the debate above the more obvious and very real contest for power."[45]

Bolingbroke drew heavily on the classical republican and Old Whig or Country ideas from the seventeenth century.[46] He claimed to be truer to Whig

---

Varey, ed., *Lord Bolingbroke: Contributions to the "Craftsman"* (Oxford: Clarendon Press, 1982); Isaac Kramnick, ed., *Lord Bolingbroke: Historical Writings* (Chicago, Ill.: University of Chicago Press, 1972); Kramnick, ed., *Viscount Bolingbroke: Political Writings* (New York, N.Y.: Appleton-Century-Crofts, 1970); and Bernard Cottret, ed., *Bolingbroke's Political Writings: The Conservative Enlightenment* (London: Macmillan, 1997).

Still valuable as a collection of his writings is *The Works of Lord Bolingbroke*, 4 vols. Philadelphia, Penn.: Carey and Hart, 1843). Bolingbroke's political pamphlets are listed in Giles Barber, "Some Uncollected Authors XLI: Henry Saint John, Viscount Bolingbroke, 1678–1751," *The Book Collector*, 14 (1965), 528–37.

[44] Simon Varey, *Henry St. John, Viscount Bolingbroke* (Boston, Mass.: Twayne, 1984), ix.

[45] Dickinson, *Bolingbroke*, 183.

[46] Principal expositions of Bolingbroke's political philosophy include: Isaac Kramnick, *Bolingbroke and His Circle: The Politics of Nostalgia in the Age of Walpole* (Cambridge, Mass.: Harvard University Press, 1968); Varey, *Henry St. John, Viscount Bolingbroke*; H. T. Dickinson, *Bolingbroke*, 184–211; Quentin Skinner, "The Principles and Practice of Opposition: The Case of Bolingbroke versus Walpole," pp. 93–128 in *Historical Perspectives: Studies in English Thought and Society in Honour of J. H. Plumb*, ed. Neil McKendrick (London: Europa Publications, 1974); Shelley Burtt, *Virtue Transformed: Political Argument in England, 1688–1740* (Cambridge: Cambridge University Press, 1992), 87–109; Alexander Pettit, "Propaganda, Public Relations, and the *Remarks on the Craftsman's Vindication of His Two Honble Patrons, in His Paper of May 22, 1731,*" *Huntington Library Quarterly*, 57 (1994), 45–59; R. J. Smith, *The Gothic Bequest: Medieval Institutions in British Modern Thought, 1688–1863* (Cambridge: Cambridge University Press, 1987, 57–70; and Brean S. Hammond, *Pope and Bolingbroke: A Study of Friendship and Influence* (Columbia, Mo.: University of Missouri Press, 1984).

On the opposition to Whig ministries more broadly: Archibald S. Foord, *His Majesty's Opposition, 1714–1830* (Oxford: Clarendon Press, 1964), 55–109, 111–216; J. A. W. Gunn, *Beyond Liberty and Property: The Process of Self-Recognition in Eighteenth-Century Political Thought* (Kingston, Canada: McGill-Queen's University Press, 1983); and Hammond, *Pope and Bolingbroke*, Chapter 8, "The Common Language"; M. M. Goldsmith, "Liberty, Virtue, and the Rule of Law, 1689–1770," pp. 197–232 in *Republicanism, Liberty, and Commercial Society, 1649–1716*, ed. David Wootton (Stanford, Calif.: Stanford University Press, 1994); and Christine Gerrard, *The Patriot Opposition to Walpole: Politics, Poetry, and National Myth, 1725–1742* (Oxford: Clarendon, 1994).

principles than the Modern Whigs at Court and in the Ministry. Many of his principal ideas or rhetorical devices are anticipated in *Cato's Letters*, the *Freeholders Journal*, and the *True Briton*.

He repeatedly charged that Britain's liberties were disappearing under Walpole: he was a wicked minister whose management of government fostered corruption, which bred luxury and destruction of the Ancient Constitution; he fostered a system of men looking after their own short-term self-interest instead of the national interest and safeguarding liberty; he encouraged faction and party division to prevent a unified opposition from removing him from office. Bolingbroke disputed the Ministry's claim that the Opposition was mostly Jacobites and posed a threat to the Hanoverian Succession. Always asserting himself a defender of William and the Revolution Principles, he claimed that the true division of politics was between a Court party and a Country party and that parties were no longer needed.

As a positive program, Bolingbroke urged a return to a constitution consisting of checks and balances, so that King, Lords, and Commons could control one another's possible excesses. This goal required an independent, uncorrupted parliament – free of ministerial or crown influence – that could be obtained only by Triennial Parliaments and elimination of placemen and pensioners. Reductions in the size of the household, ministry, and military were necessary to curb Walpole's ability to corrupt men. Public spirit, personal virtue, and elimination of parties would redeem Britain and lead her out of Walpolean corruption. Later he would argue a virtuous Patriot King who rose above parties could redeem Britain.

Bolingbroke was not a systematic political thinker; rather, his writings consist primarily of weekly, topical essays that often responded to immediate issues of politics that he could use to embarrass the Ministry. Two of Bolingbroke's major political works were collections of his essays published pseudonymously as letters to the *Craftsman*.

Remarks on the History of England, contributed to the *Craftsman* by "Henry Oldcastle" in 1730–1731, surveys English history from the Norman invasion to the reign of Charles I, which he portrays as a perpetual struggle between freedom of the people and tyranny of monarchs.[47] He warns of the dangers of royal favorites and faction and holds up Elizabeth as an ideal monarch.[48] The Ancient Constitution balanced between King, Lords, and Commons was now upset by faction and the growing power of the Court and Ministry. Reviving the spirit of liberty meant concern for national interest, not party or private interest, and a Machiavellian *ricorso* (return) to the principles of the Constitution.

---

[47] The *Remarks on the History of England* was first published in the *Craftsman* as twenty-four essays from 13 June 1730 to May 1731 (nos. 206–55); the essays were collected in 1743. See also Alexander Pettit, "Lord Bolingbroke's *Remarks on the History of England* and the Rhetoric of Political Controversy," *Age of Johnson*, 7 (1996), 365–95.

[48] Especially *Remarks on the History of England*, letters nos. 13, 14, 15, and 16. See also Pat Rogers, "Swift and Bolingbroke on Faction," *Journal of British Studies*, 9, no. 2 (1970), 71–101 ("both attribute every civil vice under the sun to faction"; p. 100).

A Dissertation upon Parties, written in 1733–1734, with its audacious dedication to Walpole, was the most frequently reprinted of Bolingbroke's works.[49] Here the dangers of faction and the case for a united Opposition are most thoroughly worked out. Tories and Whigs joined to accomplish the Glorious Revolution and the Toleration Act of 1689; having done so, Tory-Whig differences were now obsolete and party labels unnecessary. Party divisions merely helped Walpole. The distinction that now mattered was between the corrupt Court party and the virtuous Country party, which preserved Old Whig principles.[50] Only a new Country party that rose above faction could defeat Walpole and revive the spirit of liberty and the British Constitution.

Holding the beliefs that history moved in cycles, that human nature was constant, and that similar causes produced similar effects, Bolingbroke ransacked history for examples of wicked ministers and corrupt court favorites and demonstrated their consequences to the nation. He wrote history with an eye on the present and with intended current application. The reader was to see a similarity between the past and Walpole and so be warned of the dangers of his rule. The *Craftsman*, the ministry complained, was able to show that "the whole of *English History* might be prov'd a Libel upon the *present Government*" by drawing of parallels.[51]

So readers could not miss the intended comparison, Bolingbroke would ironically assert that no present minister resembles any of England's past corrupt and scheming ministers.[52] Not surprisingly, several essays in the *Craftsman*, with their implied parallels between certain past kings and their evil ministers and George II and Walpole, were so incendiary, the printer was jailed for printing them.

BOLINGBROKE'S VIEW OF HISTORY

Bolingbroke wrote history in the classical vein as philosophy teaching by example.[53] His expositions of episodes from Roman, British, and European history

---

[49] *A Dissertation Upon Parties* was first published as nineteen essays in *The Craftsman* from 27 Oct. 1733 to 28 Dec. 1734 (nos. 382–443); the essays were collected in 1735 with its ironic dedication to Walpole. Ministerial writers replied in the *Free Briton*, nos. 262 [*sic*] and 263 (14 and 21 Nov. 1734).

[50] The *Grub-street Journal*, no. 211 (10 Jan. 1734), noted the "distinction of *Court* and *Country party* is propagated throughout the nation, representing the leaders of the latter as the only true *patriots*, and those of the former as a set of corrupt men, carrying on an interest very different from that of their own country."

[51] *Craftsman*, no. 220 (19 Sept. 1730).

[52] The *Craftsman's* gallery of evil kings and favorites included Buckingham (Charles I), Wolsey (Henry VIII), and Sejanus (Tiberius).

[53] History as philosophy teaching by example: George H. Nadel, "Philosophy of History before Historicism," *History and Theory*, 3 (1964), 291–315. On Bolingbroke's own views, see his "Concerning the True Use and Advantages of the Study of History," the second of his *Letters on the Study and Use of History* (written, 1735–1738; published 1752). For an expression of the position, see the *Craftsman*, no. 220 (19 Sept. 1730): the use of the study of history is "to propagate *Political Knowledge*, and to make the

had contemporary applications: he taught Englishmen to be wary of evil ministers, despotic monarchs, and corruption.[54]

Bolingbroke fluctuated between two theories of history.[55] Principally, he believed in a materialist theory that economic change was the determinant of social and political life. This premise underlies his obsession with the corrosive social effects of Britain's new financial order that enabled Walpole's manner of governing.[56]

The increase in public funds available to the Treasury provided new means for public corruption. Credit and paper money were illusory, dependent on the fickleness of public markets and the passions of speculation and avarice. Hence, credit was often gendered as feminine.[57] Money, not land, now became the source of real power, disrupting Britain's traditional social order idealized by Old Whigs and Tories.

The nation-wide spread of private wealth bred greed and envy and made men yield to corruption to amass more wealth and luxury goods; wealth and luxury led to slavery as men pursued self-interest instead of virtue and the public good. Money, fraud, and corruption now brought men power and places in government. This change in the economic realm was at the root of the decline in the morals, manners, and taste of English public life,[58] and is a major theme in his writings.

But Bolingbroke could not shake the classical republican tenet that human nature – personal character, virtue, and Publick Spirit – was also an important factor in history. He stressed the role of great men (and Queen Elizabeth) in shaping human affairs and directly intervening in history and a nation's fate. This humanist philosophy of history helps explain his constantly parading the actions of the heroes and villains of Roman and English history as well as his anxiety about the effect of corruption and luxury on an individual's moral character.

Bolingbroke's belief in the power of a great man of virtue comes to the fore in *The Idea of a Patriot King*, written about 1738.[59] Here Bolingbroke adopts the

---

present Age wiser by the Experience of the *past*; by searching into the great Springs of Action; by examining the true Causes of the Revolutions of Government; and by pointing out the Measures, which have made some Kingdoms flourish and reduc'd others to Slavery and Ruin." On Clarendon's influence on Bolingbroke's *Letters on the Study and Use of History*, Philip Hicks, "Bolingbroke, Clarendon, and the Role of the Classical Historian," *Eighteenth-Century Studies*, 20 (1987), 445–71. See also McGeary, *Politics of Opera in Handel's Britain*, 210–14.

[54] *Bolingbroke: Historical Writings*, ed. Kramnick, xlv.

[55] *Bolingbroke: Historical Writings*, ed. Kramnick, xlviii–l.

[56] Kramnick, *Bolingbroke and His Circle*, 39–55.

[57] Terry Mulcaire, "Public Credit; or, the Feminization of Virtue in the Marketplace," *PMLA*, 114 (1999), 1029–42.

[58] See especially letter no. 6 of the *Letters on the Study and Use of History* and letter no. 19 of the *Dissertation Upon Parties*, although the ideas permeate the *Craftsman*.

[59] Text in *Bolingbroke: Political Writings*, ed. David Armitage (Cambridge: Cambridge University Press, 1997), 217–94. On the Patriot King and the political Opposition: Mabel

60   THE CULTURAL POLITICS OF OPERA, 1720–1742

Machiavellian concern with a person of *virtù* as an agent in history. A moral regeneration is needed to preserve the republic. The treatise assumes a nation at a Machiavellian moment: a fragile republic caught in the contingency of time facing dissolution caused by a decline in virtue.[60] When Parliament and the people are corrupted, the nation needs a Patriot King who, by his own example, will rise above faction, rule without regard for party, and defend liberty and the Constitution. He would restore honor and virtue to government and lead his people from pursuit of self-interest. Bolingbroke foresaw:

> As soon as corruption ceases to be an expedient of government, and it will cease to be such as soon as a Patriot King is raised to the throne, the panacea is applied; the spirit of the constitution revives of course; and, as fast as it revives, the orders and forms of the constitution are restored to their primitive integrity.[61]

The idea of a Patriot King becomes prominent in the later Patriot Opposition's adoption of Prince Frederick as its figurehead (see Chapter 5).

Historians have generally regarded Bolingbroke's ideal of a Patriot King and party that rose above faction impractical. Plumb called it "utterly futile, as ridiculously unrealistic, as was the rest of Bolingbroke's political philosophy."[62]

Bolingbroke seized on the mythology of the Gothic north. His historical touchstone was the Ancient Constitution: the institutions that went back in "time out of mind" in the northern woods when the Saxons and Goths preserved freedom and love of liberty and limited the power of their elective

---

H. Cable, "The Idea of a Patriot King in the Propaganda of the Opposition to Walpole, 1735–1739," *Philological Quarterly*, 18 (1939), 119–30; H. T. Dickinson, "Bolingbroke: 'The Idea of a Patriot King,'" *History Today*, 20 (1970), 13–19; Dickinson, *Bolingbroke*, 260–6; Kramnick, *Bolingbroke and His Circle*, 33–5, 163–9; David Armitage, "A Patriot for Whom? The Afterlives of Bolingbroke's Patriot King," *Journal of British Studies*, 36 (1997), 397–418; and Gerrard, *Patriot Opposition*, 185–229. Clark, *English Society, 1688–1832*, 179–82, sees the Patriot King as an outlet for Divine Right thought. Fannie E. Ratchford's "Pope and the *Patriot King*," *Texas Studies in English*, 6 (1926), 157–77, is not reliable. It has been argued the person Bolingbroke imagined could have been Charles Edward Stuart, the Young Pretender; see Simon Varey, "Hanover, Stuart, and the Patriot King," *British Journal for Eighteenth-Century Studies*, 6 (1983), 163–72.

[60] The classic account is J. G. A. Pocock, *The Machiavellian Moment: Florentine Political Thought and the Atlantic Republican Tradition* (Princeton, N.J.: Princeton University Press, 1975). I have worked out the use of the Machiavellian moment trope in relation to opera in the writings of Richard Steele, John Dennis, and the Earl of Shaftesbury in *Opera and Politics in Queen Anne's Britain*, 241–85.

Clark's controversial revisionist study, *English Society, 1688–1832*, offers an alternative model of England that does not use a humanist and Machiavellian vocabulary (see his Afterword, p. 423).

[61] "The Idea of a Patriot King," in *Bolingbroke: Political Writings*, ed. Armitage, 251.

[62] J. H. Plumb, *The Growth of Political Stability in England, 1675–1725* (Harmondsworth: Penguin Books, 1967), 133. Dickinson, *Bolingbroke*, 210–11, 246; and Kramnick, *Bolingbroke and His Circle*, 168–9. For a fuller, more generous appraisal of Bolingbroke's ideas, Dickinson, *Bolingbroke*, 184–211, and (for his tactics), 212–36.

kings.[63] Traditionally, the Goths, living in the severe northern climate, acquired hardiness and love of liberty, which were lacking in people of the warm climate of the Mediterranean.

The English constitution had been preserved unbroken despite encroachments by occasional rulers who gained arbitrary and absolute power. The mythic free Saxon past was the final stage of the northward *translatio* of liberty from Greece, Rome, and Germany to Britain.[64] This notion will become prominent in the works of the later Patriot Opposition. The *Craftsman* succinctly stated:

> From the earliest Accounts of Time, our Ancestors in *Germany* were a *free People*, and had a Right to assent, or dissent to *all Laws*; that *that Right* was exercis'd, and preserv'd under the *Saxon* and *Norman Kings*; even to our Days; and may an *uninterrupted Exercise* thereof (for the *Right itself* can never be extinguished) continue till Time shall be no more![65]

The unbroken constitution was a point of contention between the Ministry and Opposition (see below).

---

[63] A clear statement by Bolingbroke is letter no. 4 of *Remarks on the History of England*. The classical sources include Tacitus's *Germania* and *Annals*. Early English statements of the myth include: Richard Verstegen, *Restitutions of Decayed Intelligence* (1605; numerous later editions); Nicholas Bacon, *Historical Discourse of the Uniformity of the Government of England* (1647; numerous later editions); Robert Molesworth, *An Account of Denmark as It Was in the Year 1692* (1694), Chapter 6, "Of Their Form of Government" and "The Conclusion" (pp. 264–5); [John Shute, Viscount Barrington], *The Revolution and Anti-Revolution Principles Stated and Compar'd* (1714), 68–9. On the use of Tacitus in British thought, Howard Weinbrot, "Politics, Taste, and National Identity: Some Uses of Tacitism in Eighteenth-Century Britain," pp. 168–84 in *Tacitus and the Tacitean Tradition*, ed. T. J. Luce and A. J. Woodman (Princeton, N.J.: Princeton University Press, 1993).

On the history and survival of the myth of the Ancient Constitution, Saxon origins, and Gothic limited monarchy: J. G. A. Pocock, *The Ancient Constitution and the Feudal Law: A Study of English Historical Thought in the Seventeenth-Century. A Reissue with a Retrospect* (Cambridge: Cambridge University Press, 1987); Pocock, *Virtue, Commerce, and History: Essays on Political Thought and History, Chiefly in the Eighteenth Century* (Cambridge: Cambridge University Press, 1985); Glenn Burgess, *The Politics of the Ancient Constitution: An Introduction to English Political Thought, 1603–1642* (University Park, Pa.: Pennsylvania State University Press, 1993); Samuel Kliger, *The Goths in England: A Study in Seventeenth and Eighteenth Century Thought* (Cambridge, Mass.: Harvard University Press, 1952), esp. 1–3, 31–5; Smith, *The Gothic Bequest*; Quentin Skinner, "History and Ideology in the English Revolution," *Historical Journal*, 8 (1965), 151–78; and Gerrard, *Patriot Opposition*, 108–49 *passim*. See Howard Weinbrot, "The Historiography of Nostalgia," *Age of Johnson*, 7 (1996), 183–7, for uses of myth in later Patriot drama.

[64] On the *translatio* of Liberty: Kliger, *Goths in England*, 33–111. The northward progress of Liberty will figure in Patriot poetry of the 1730s; see Chapter 8.

[65] *Craftsman*, no. 470 (5 July 1735) [stating it is quoting from St. Amand, *Historical Essays on the Legislative Power of England*].

62 THE CULTURAL POLITICS OF OPERA, 1720–1742

Bolingbroke subscribed to a Polybian theory of history occurring in cycles. For him, English history was a series of Machiavellian *occasione*, struggles between the people who maintained the spirit of liberty and rulers who, abetted by their evil ministers and favorites, sowed faction and usurped absolute power. English history was a series of moments when the nation broke free from corruption and by force of virtue restored liberty.

Bolingbroke looked back to certain reigns when the spirit of liberty flourished: Alfred, Edward I and III, Henry V, and, especially Elizabeth. English and Protestant, she promoted the arts and trade, respected the Constitution, based her authority on the gratitude and affection of her people, and whose foreign policy served the national interest.[66] There was no "Norman Yoke" in the Old Whig account; William the Conqueror had adapted his government and preserved the continuity of free English institutions.[67] Landmarks in the heroic struggle were Magna Carta, resistance to the early Stuarts, and the overthrow of James II by the Glorious Revolution. Bolingbroke called for a Machiavellian *ricorso* to Britain's original balanced constitutional model as a way to preserve virtue and Britain's moral character.[68] The Revolution was such a return.

CAVEATS ABOUT OPPOSITION

The Opposition attracted much of the best literary talent of the day: Swift's *Gulliver's Travels*, Pope's major verse satires and the *Dunciad*, and Gay's *Beggar's Opera* and *Fables* have overcome their political topicality to enter the literary canon of the period. But the caveat should be entered against accepting Opposition satire – what Louis Bredvold called "the gloom of the Tory satirists"[69] – at face value as providing a valid portrayal of the social or political conditions of the day or even most of the public's (or literary world's) opinion.[70] Samuel Johnson's comment on Pope and Swift's correspondence would apply to oppositional literature as a whole:

[66] The Ministry could also draw parallels with past ministers, and a series of papers in the *Daily Gazetteer* compared Walpole to Elizabeth's minister, William Cecil, Baron Burghley; collected in Ralph Courteville, *Memoirs of the Life and Administration of William Cecil Baron Burleigh* (1738).

[67] On the Norman Yoke: Christopher Hill, "The Norman Yoke," pp. 50–122 in *Puritanism and Revolution: Studies in Interpretation of the English Revolution of the 17th Century* (New York, N.Y.: Schocken Books, 1964) [also on the origins of the mythology of a golden Saxon past]; Isaac Kramnick, "Augustan Politics and English Historiography: The Debate on the English Past, 1730–35," *History and Theory*, 6 (1967), 35–56; and Kramnick, *Bolingbroke and His Circle*, 177–81.

As Skinner points out, this view of the Norman invasion (the Norman Yoke) is sheer historical fiction; "History and Ideology," 154–60.

[68] Machiavelli, *Discorsi sopra la prima deca di Tito Livio* (*Discourses on the First Ten Books of Titus Livi*; written 1513–1517; pub. 1531), Book 3, section 1.

[69] Bredvold: cited in note 24.

[70] A point also made in J. A. Downie, "Walpole, 'the Poet's Foe'," pp. 117–88 in *Britain in the Age of Walpole*, ed. Jeremy Black (London: Macmillan, 1984), 172–3.

Whosoever should form his opinion of the age from their representation, would suppose them to have lived amidst ignorance and barbarity, unable to find among their contemporaries either virtue or intelligence, and persecuted by those that could not understand them.[71]

Of the mid-1730s, Johnson wrote, "At this time a long course of opposition to Sir Robert Walpole had filled the nation with clamours for liberty, of which no man felt the want, and with care for liberty, which was not in danger."[72]

Simon Varey cautions that although Opposition propaganda certainly helped to stabilize a portion of public opinion against Walpole, reassure the faithful, and lend authority to the Opposition's political view, the Opposition campaign never mobilized public opinion into action, except for local demonstrations and petitions and protests to their MPs.[73] As one contemporary writer on the political press commented, "no Man can be so weak as to think that a People of Good Sense, such as the *English* are, will ever be laughed into an Opposition to the Government."[74]

Despite its wealth of political and literary talent, the Opposition was so fragmented between Hanoverian Tories, high-flying Tories, dissident Whigs, and Jacobite sympathizers that it could not obtain a majority in Parliament. The Opposition was ineffective because its members refused to work together on important issues, nor was an opposition united only by the goal of removing Walpole from office an effective electoral or parliamentary program. Never secure allies of the disaffected Whigs, the Tories even distrusted Bolingbroke (for his past Jacobitism); they were often unwilling to challenge the King's prerogative and resented being dominated by Whigs; and few Tories had any interest in defeating Walpole just to see him replaced by another Whig minister. Despite their motions, bills, and obstructionist parliamentary tactics, Walpole was usually able to pass his legislation, with the exception of the 1733 Excise bill, which he withdrew before it could be voted down.

While George I reigned, the Opposition hoped a new king would bring a new ministry, possibility even a mixed Tory-Whig one. After his accession on 11 June 1727, George II indicated his intention to place at the head of the Treasury Speaker Spencer Compton, who had been his own treasurer as Prince of Wales. But the influence of Queen Caroline, Compton's ineptitude, and Walpole's skill at passing an increase in the Civil List and the Queen's jointure made the King

---

[71] "Life of Pope," in *Lives of the Poets*, ed. George B. Hill, 3 vols. (Oxford: Clarendon, 1905), 3:212.

[72] "Life of Thomson," in *Lives of the Poets*, ed. Hill, 3:289. Cf. *Daily Gazetteer*, no. 120 (15 Nov. 1735): "[At present] Liberty was never in greater Perfection, never stronger guarded, nor ever is less Danger of being lost."

[73] William Arnall, *The Case of Opposition Stated*, ed. and intro. Simon Varey, xix; *An Historical View of the ... Political Writers in Great Britain* (1740), 23–4. Jeremy Black, "Press and Politics in the 1730s," *Durham University Journal*, 77 (1984), 87–93, cautions against overestimating the influence of the *Craftsman*.

[74] *Historical View of the ... Political Writers*, 23.

64   THE CULTURAL POLITICS OF OPERA, 1720–1742

realize Walpole as his prime minister would best serve his interests.[75] Queen Caroline would be Walpole's strongest ally at Court. The later resignation of his brother-in-law Charles Townshend as secretary of state in 1730 left Walpole in control of both financial and foreign policy, and he emerged as a prime minister of unprecedented longevity and power.

It would not be until almost two decades into his ministry, when about to lose his majority in Parliament, did Walpole forestall the inevitable and resign, allowing Pulteney, Carteret, and others of the Opposition to enter the ministry.

❧ Walpole and Modern Whiggery

The attention given to the Opposition's sustained propaganda campaign – enlivened by lively satire, wit, and daring innuendo – should not obscure that the ministry conducted its own continuous, well-coordinated, and well-financed campaign against its opponents. Walpole had certainly learned from Robert Harley's earlier example,[76] and he too gathered a stable of writers who defended him, his ministry, and its policies and attacked the Opposition's politicians and writers. Despite Swift's epithet "Bob, the Poet's Foe," the stream of poems and odes in his praise that filled the pamphlet shops show he also rewarded poets willing to tune their lyre to his praises.[77]

To respond to the attacks in the Opposition press, Walpole subsidized numerous ministerial papers, most importantly the *Daily Courant, British Journal, London Journal, Free Briton, Hyp-doctor, Corn-cutter's Journal,* and later Mary Wortley Montague's *The Nonsense of Common Sense,* many sent free through the Post Office. These were consolidated into the *Daily Gazetteer* on 30 June 1735.[78] Between February 1731 and February 1741, the Treasury paid out £50,077 18s to authors and printers.[79] Walpole also used the power of

---

[75] William Coxe, *Memoirs of Horatio, Lord Walpole* (1802), 152–4, explains Walpole's survival in 1727.

[76] See J. A. Downie, *Robert Harley and the Press: Propaganda and Public Opinion in the Age of Swift and Defoe* (Cambridge: Cambridge University Press, 1979).

[77] Swift's line is from "To Mr. Gay on his being Steward to the Duke of Queensbury," line 4.
    On pro-Walpole poetry, see Tone S. Urstad, *Sir Robert Walpole's Poets: The Use of Literature as Pro-Government Propaganda, 1721–1742* (Newark, Del.: University of Delaware Press, 1999). On Walpole's patronage of writers (including some who later wrote for the Opposition), Downie, "Walpole, 'the Poet's Foe,'"; and Dustin Griffin, *Literary Patronage in England, 1650–1800* (Cambridge: Cambridge University Press, 1996), 51–5.

[78] Origins of the *Daily Gazetteer*: Robert L. Haig, *The Gazetteer, 1735–1797: A Study in the Eighteenth-Century English Newspaper* (Carbondale, Ill.: Southern Illinois University Press, 1960), 3–15.

[79] Hanson, *Government and the Press*, 109, estimates that in 1731 the government spent £20,000 per annum on free mailing, printing, and publishing of newspapers. The *London Journal*, the *Free Briton*, and the *Daily Courant* were sent through the Post Office. On Walpole's employment of the Treasury and the press, Urstad, *Robert Walpole's Poets*, 38–55. The Commons report for expenses throughout his ministry,

BOLINGBROKE AND THE POLITICAL OPPOSITION 65

the Treasury to harass the Opposition press: blocking circulation through the mail, seizing libelous issues, raiding the printers' shops to seize documents, and jailing printers.[80]

William Arnall ("Francis Walsingham"), James Pitt ("Francis Osborne"), and Ralph Courteville ("Ralph Freeman") used their essays to attack the motives and principles of the Opposition. Lord Hervey, Bishop Benjamin Hoadly, Sir William Yonge, and Walpole's brother Horatio also actively wrote pamphlets on the ministry's behalf.

Ministerial writers answered the Opposition's charges head on, point by point, often carrying on controversies responding issue-by-issue for weeks.[81] They accused them of faction and dissent, and encouraging Jacobites; they vigorously pointed out that liberty was in no danger in Britain; economic prosperity and its consequences were benefits to Britain, not evils; they denied they had betrayed true Whig principles and the Constitution. What the Opposition charged as ruling by corruption, was the usual means of managing the

---

A Further Report from the Committee ... into the Conduct of Robert, Earl of Orford ... the 30th of June, 1742 (1742), Appendix 13; and *Journals of the House of Commons*, 24 (1741–1745), 288–331.

[80] Hanson, *Government and the Press*, 67–70; see p. 140 for a list of prosecutions of printers. On both Walpole's commitment to freedom of the press, as well his management of his writers, see Simon Targett, "'The Premier Scribbler Himself': Sir Robert Walpole and the Management of Political Opinion," *Studies in Newspaper and Periodical History: 1994 Annual* (1996), 19–33.

[81] The *Free Britain* was especially diligent in responding within several weeks to attacks in the *Craftsman*. Some principal ministerial pamphlets include: *The Free Briton: or, the Opinion of the People* (1727); William Arnall, *Clodius and Cicero: With Other Examples and Reasonings, in Defense of Just Measures Against Faction and Obloquy, Suited to the Present Conjuncture* (1727); Arnall, *The Case of Opposition Stated, Between the Craftsman and the People* (1731); Arnall, *Remarks on the Craftsman's Vindication of His Two Hon[ble] Patrons, in His Paper of May 22, 1731* (1731); Arnall, *Opposition No Proof of Patriotism: With Some Observations and Advice Concerning Party-Writings* (1735); John Lord Hervey, *Ancient and Modern Liberty Stated and Compar'd* (1734); Hervey, "Dedication" to William Yonge, *Sedition and Defamation Display'd* (1731); Hervey, *Observations on the Writings of the Craftsman* (1730) [reply by William Pulteney, *A Proper Reply to a Later Scurrilous Libel; Intitled Sedition and Defamation Display'd* [1731]); Hervey, *The Conduct of the Opposition* (1734); Hervey, *Miscellaneous Thoughts on the Present Posture both of Our Foreign and Domestic Affairs* (1742); *The Merits of the Crafts-men: or, a Display of the Injuries Offer'd by that Party* (1734); *The Crafts of the Craftsmen; or, a Detection of the Designs of the Coalition* (1736); Joseph Trapp, *The Ministerial Virtue: or, Long Suffering Extolled in a Great Man* (1738); and *The True Principles of the Revolution Revived and Asserted. Being a Defense of the Present Administration* (1741).

A Review of the Whole Political Conduct of the Late Eminent Patriot (1743) defends the Walpole administration by an attack on William Pulteney; J. A. W. Gunn, *Factions No More: Attitudes to Party in Government and Opposition in Eighteenth-Century England* (London: Frank Cass, 1972), provides extracts from ministerial tracts, 110–32.

66 THE CULTURAL POLITICS OF OPERA, 1720–1742

Commons. An exasperated William Arnall asked: "Place and Pensions are an old Cry. Can there be any Government without places?"[82]

Walpole and the ministerial or Modern Whigs were descendants of the radical Whigs of the Exclusion Crisis and Glorious Revolution who wanted to prevent a Catholic monarchy, resisted James's policies, established a limited monarchy, invited William and Mary to assume the throne, and assured the Protestant Succession. The principles of the Old Whigs were frequent Parliaments, no standing army, right of resistance, limited prerogative of the Crown, supremacy of Parliament, toleration of dissent, low taxation, and no rapprochement with France.

It was commonly observed that over the decades, the meanings of the labels 'Tory' and 'Whig', 'Old' and 'Modern' Whigs reversed. Now in power as Modern or Court Whigs and finding themselves needing to adapt to the problem of governing, Whig ministries now shed many of the ideas that served them when in opposition to the Stuarts.[83] As J. A. W. Gunn notes, even in the reign of George I, "Whiggism in power possessed certain Tory features and, indeed, it was a creed fashioned for governors whose revolutions lay behind them."[84] It was noticeable that men out of government were Old Whigs but, when in power,

[82] William Arnall, *Opposition No Proof of Patriotism* (1735), 6.
[83] Important studies of the defense of Modern Whiggery and the Walpole ministry are Targett, "Government and Ideology During the Age of Whig Supremacy"; Thomas A. Horne, "Politics in a Corrupt Society: William Arnall's Defense of Robert Walpole," *Journal of the History of Ideas*, 41 (1980), 601–14; and J. A. W. Gunn, "Court Whiggery – Justifying Innovation," pp. 125–56 in *Politics, Politeness, and Patriotism*, ed. Gordon J. Schochet (Washington, D.C.: The Folger Shakespeare Library, 1993). See also Browning, *Political and Constitutional Ideas;* Burtt, *Virtue Transformed*, 110–27; Urstad, *Robert Walpole's Poets*, 172–215; Hanson, *Government and the Press*, 108–18; M. M. Goldsmith, "Faction Detected: Ideological Consequences of Robert Walpole's Decline and Fall," *History*, 64 (1979), 1–19; Goldsmith, "The Principles of True Liberty: Political Ideology in Eighteenth-Century Britain," *Political Studies*, 27 (1979), 141–6; Goldsmith, *Private Vices, Public Benefits: Bernard Mandeville's Social and Political Thought* (Cambridge: Cambridge University Press, 1985), 131–4; H. T. Dickinson, *Liberty and Property: Political Ideology in Eighteenth-Century Britain* (New York, N.Y.: Holmes and Meier, 1977), 121–62; Kramnick, *Bolingbroke and His Circle*, 111–36; and Nicholas Phillipson, "Politics and Politeness in the Reigns of Anne and the Early Hanoverians," pp. 211–45 in *The Varieties of British Political Thought, 1500–1800*, ed. J. G. A. Pocock, Gordon J. Schochet, and Lois Schwoerer (Cambridge: Cambridge University Press, 1993).

On some of the more specific pamphlet skirmishes or individual tracts: Alexander Pettit, "Propaganda, Public Relations, and the *Remarks on the Craftsman's Vindication of His Two Honble Patrons, in His Paper of May 22, 1731*," *Huntington Library Quarterly*, 57 (1994), 45–59; and H. T. Dickinson, Introduction to John Lord Hervey, *Ancient and Modern Liberty Stated and Compar'd*. Augustan Reprint Society, no. 255–6 (1989).

[84] Gunn, "Court Whiggery – Justifying Innovation," 126.

Modern Whigs. Tories out of power became Old Whigs. The Court party out of power became the Country party.[85]

After the Revolution, the central issue in English political thought, J. G. A. Pocock argues, was not the legitimacy of resistance, but "whether a regime founded on patronage, public debt, and professionalization of the armed forces did not corrupt both governors and governed."[86] The task for Walpole's writers was to legitimize a Modern Whig government that rested on principles hitherto anathema to true Whigs: Septennial Parliaments, a standing army, increased taxation, nonresistance, alliance with France, deference to the Church of England, and Crown influence on Parliament.[87]

Walpole and his ministerial writers argued there was no change of Old and Modern Whig principles; before the Revolution, it was just for Whigs to resist and oppose courts that were "continually carrying on *Designs against the* Liberties of the People. ... The *Country-Interest* of those Times was formed on the Principles of Liberty only." The need for resistance has ceased, and "We *Modern Whigs* fully enjoy what the *Old Whigs* so gloriously contended for; we have the *End*, to which their *Opposition* was the *Means*." Ministry writers argued that "There cannot be a *wise* and *honest Country Party* at this Time, in *Opposition* to the Court" for the simple reason "there is no *Court Party* against the *true Interest* of their *Country*." The "Modern Country" party [of Bolingbroke's Opposition] exists only "to oppose and obstruct all the Measures of an Administration, without Regard to the Peace and Preservation of Mankind."[88]

---

[85] On reversal of the meaning of the labels for Old and Modern Whigs: see the tracts [Charles Davenant], *The True Picture of a Modern Whigg* (1701) [traduces both Old and Modern Whigs], *The Old and Modern Whig Truly Represented* (1702), and *R—'s [Roques] on Both Sides; ... with a True Description of an Old Whig, and a Modern Whig* (1711). In the Walpole era, see for example, *Free Briton*, no. 239 (30 May 1734); *Craftsman*, no. 18 (30 Jan. 1727); *Craftsman*, no. 103 (22 June 1728); *Craftsman*, nos. 379 and 380 (6 and 13 Oct. 1733); and *Craftsman*, no. 366 (7 July 1733).

On the transition and principles of the Whigs, Mark Goldie, "The Roots of True Whiggism, 1688–94," *History of Political Thought*, 1 (1980), 195–236; and J. P. Kenyon, *Revolution Principles: The Politics of Party, 1689–1720* (Cambridge: Cambridge University Press, 1977); and Pocock, "Varieties of Whiggism."

[86] Pocock, *Virtue, Commerce, and History*, 48.

[87] See defense of Septennial Parliaments in the *Free Briton*, nos. 227–9 (7, 14, 21 March 1734). For a ministerial statement of Whig principles, see *Free Briton*, no. 54 (10 Dec. 1730).

When the Whigs were in power, they made no effort to revive radical notions of natural rights or popular sovereignty; they consolidated conservative tendencies and rejected the claim that people had the right to resist any government that didn't serve their interest; see H. T. Dickinson, *The Politics of the People in Eighteenth-Century Britain* (New York, N.Y.: St. Martin's Press, 1995), 271.

[88] Quoting from the *London Journal*, nos. 733–4 (14 and 21 July 1733), and the *Free Briton*, no. 239 (30 May 1734). The *Craftsman* denied the identity of the Old and Court Whigs, arguing the Old Whigs were the Tories of the Walpole era, and vice versa: *Craftsman*, no. 379 (6 Oct. 1733); no. 548 (1 Jan. 1737).

68   THE CULTURAL POLITICS OF OPERA, 1720–1742

The Ministry offered a pragmatic, realistic defense of modern Whiggery and the new commercial realm of Britain.[89] The progress from an agricultural-feudal society to one of credit and commerce, where the arts and sciences flourish, was an advance toward politeness and culture that made obsolete the Country ideology's notions of virtue, public spirit, and ideals of classical republicanism – appropriate to the ancient states of Sparta and republican Rome.[90]

Post-Revolution Britain had progressed beyond those primitive, warlike states and its own Saxon past to a prosperous, commercial, polite society. Modern economic man was naturally motivated by appetites, self-interest, and competition, which were engines for commerce and trade. Faction was the natural condition of men pursuing their own affairs and marked a healthy political system. A society of self-interested men competing in pursuit of private gain required a strong government.

A point of contention between Bolingbroke and the Whig ministry was interpretation of English history. Bolingbroke and Opposition writers dwelt on Saxon liberties, the Ancient Constitution, and the antiquity and continuity of Parliament to highlight Walpole's supposed corruption of the Constitution and betrayal of British liberties.[91]

The ministerial Whigs minimized the supposed liberties and Ancient Constitution of the early Britons, regarding them as mythic.[92] The Norman Conquest was a "yoke" that placed absolute power in a monarch and made the English slaves of a feudal system.[93] Under the Ancient Constitution, the people of England "were *absolute Slaves* to the King, the Barons, or the Church."[94]

---

[89] The relation of Modern Whiggery and the new economic order has been studied extensively by Pocock; see especially his *Virtue, Commerce, and History* and *Machiavellian Moment*. Throughout his writings, Pocock shows the indebtedness of the Old Whig or Country part to classical ideas and Machiavelli, commonly called "civic humanism" or "classical republicanism." Pocock sees the period marked by the paradigm of virtue vs. corruption; the one way to reconcile the two was to redefine virtue in terms of "politeness" and "manners."

[90] Pocock, *Virtue, Commerce, and History*, 68–70, 112–16; Horne, "Politics in a Corrupt Society," 607–9.

[91] On the debate over Ancient Constitutions and Glorious Revolution: see note 64 above; also Isaac Kramnick, "Augustan Politics and English Historiography," 35–56; H. T. Dickinson, "The Eighteenth-Century Debate on the 'Glorious Revolution,'" *History*, 61 (1976), 28–45; Targett, "Government and Ideology," 304–5; and Dickinson, *Liberty and Property*, 140–1.

[92] On the Modern Whig adoption of Tory historiography, see Kramnick, "Augustan Politics and English Historiography"; Kramnick, *Bolingbroke and His Circle*, 128–36; and *Lord Bolingbroke, Historical Writings*, ed. Kramnick, xli–xlv. For a brief Modern Whig view of the history of England, *Free Briton*, nos. 245–6, 248 (11 and 18 July, 1 Aug. 1734).

[93] On the historical validity of this position, Skinner, "History and Ideology," 154–60; this is the position adopted by David Hume, John Millar, and others of the Scottish Enlightenment (p. 155).

[94] *London Journal*, no. 768 (16 March 1734). See also no. 575 (8 Aug. 1730) and no. 739 (25 Aug. 1733).

England had a succession of rulers who were merely different in monarchical, aristocratic, or ecclesiastical tyranny. For Modern Whigs, Britain had evolved from tyranny to freedom; as the *Daily Gazetteer* could confidently assert,

> As to the Constitution in former Ages, how fair soever it may appear when adorned and deck'd out by the Pens of learned and eloquent Men [of the Opposition], yet it was certainly far inferior to ours, or at least absolutely unfit for us in the State we are now in.[95]

"To wish for a Restoration of the *Ancient Constitution*," as did the Opposition, "is wishing for the most *confirm'd* and *abject State* of Slavery, Civil and Ecclesiastical."[96]

Walpole's writers asserted that English liberties were only of recent origin. The Glorious Revolution established for the first time English liberties and the limited (or mixed) constitution, whereas the Opposition saw the Revolution merely as a *ricorso* to the original model from which the Stuarts and James II had departed. For Modern Whigs, all the blessings of Britain are owed to William and the Glorious Revolution.[97] The Revolution was a break in history that rendered irrelevant previous principles of politics and the ideal of a self-sacrificing citizen-soldier.[98] As the party responsible for the blessings of the Glorious Revolution, only Walpole and the Whigs could be trusted to preserve Britain's "mild and just Government" of liberty and prosperity.[99] Liberty, asserted Lord Hervey, has "never flourish'd in such full Vigor as in the happy and prosperous *Reign* of his *present Majesty*."[100] The best proof of this, he added, was the Opposition's freedom to publish false accusations against the Ministry.

CATO VS. CICERO

Reed Browning has shown that the political divide between the Opposition's Old Whig or Country rhetoric and that of the Modern or Court Whigs can be seen as one between the perspectives of the Romans Cato and Cicero.[101] The Catonic viewpoint of the Opposition conflates and inherits the authority of Cato the Censor, the Stoic martyr Cato of Utica, and the canonic *Cato's Letters*. This Catonic perspective accords with the classical republican tradition stressing personal *virtù* or public spirit that put duty to the state above personal self-interest as the essential guarantor of the republic's survival. The charges of corruption and luxury serve the needs of oppositions that aspire to appear principled, patriotic, and concerned with the public welfare.

---

[95] *Daily Gazetteer*, no. 1442 (2 Feb. 1740). Cf. also *Free Briton*, no. 248 (1 Aug. 1734).

[96] *London Journal*, no. 769 (23 March 1734). See also Kramnick, "Augustan Politics and English Historiography," 40–2.

[97] *Free Briton*, no. 262 (7 Nov. 1734).

[98] Horne, "Politics in a Corrupt Society," 607–9.

[99] *Free Briton*, no. 262 (7 Nov. 1734).

[100] Hervey, *Ancient and Modern Liberty*, 5.

[101] Reed Browning, *Political and Constitutional Ideas of the Court Whigs* (Baton Rouge, La.: Louisiana State University Press, 1982).

70   THE CULTURAL POLITICS OF OPERA, 1720–1742

Ministerial writers portrayed Walpole as the embattled Cicero, defending Britain from conspirators. Unlike the martyred Cato, too idealistic to govern, Cicero governed pragmatically on the basis of a realistic assessment of human nature.[102] Compromise, rather than heroic self-sacrifice, was a better political tactic; political action would be impossible were it accountable to virtue. Government needed to be in the hands of professionals, not nostalgic idealists;[103] it no longer required the individual, self-sacrificing citizen. For Ciceronians, government strove to produce happiness and protect liberty and property, not to produce virtuous men.

As following chapters show, these contrasting Old Whig-Country-Catonic versus Modern Whig-Court-Ciceronian standpoints underlie the contested cultural politics of opera. From the Modern Whig-Court-Ciceronian perspective, and no doubt that of members of London's operagoing *beau monde* and social-political elite, opera was a valued product of Britain's new financial-commercial prosperity. London's world-class Italian opera was a product of a polite society, and a sign Britons had acquired taste and connoisseurship on a parity with Italy and France. Such acceptance of opera needed little public affirmation in print.

For the oppositional Old Whig-Country-Catonic perspective, Italian opera was a ready-to-hand and easily demonized sign of the luxury and corruption spawned by Walpole's ministry and useful for indicting the Whig political oligarchy that supported opera. With the Old Whig-Country-Catonic emphasis on the primacy of personal virtue for the maintenance of the republic, a country in the thralls of opera was a country diverted from pursuing civic virtue and the public good, and one in need of redemption and political reformation.

The Old Whig-Country-Catonic perspective appears in 1719 in the midst of the Whig Schism. Thomas Gordon, who would be a major contributor to *Cato's Letters*, proposed a version of true Whiggism in *The Character of an Independent Whig* (1719); its strident anti-clericism and advocacy of unlimited toleration of dissent marks it as a tract outside the mainstream of Whiggery.

In the midst of inveighing about religion and politics and rehearsing issues of the paper wars of the 1690s, the radical Whig Gordon touches on reformation of manners. Motivated only by "Love of publick Virtue" (p. 23), he singles out for condemnation gambling and Heidegger's masquerades at the Haymarket, which he sees as "a dangerous Luxury opposite to Virtue and Liberty" (p. 22). Hearing that the Haymarket would be used by the Royal Academy of Music for operas instead of masquerades, he musters tepid approval, when he reports "that our Understandings were only to be affronted this Winter in that Place with Italian Quavers and Cremona Fiddles; for which I was not sorry, since leaving of Debauchery for the sake of Nonsense, is still some degree of Reformation."

---

[102] On the virtues of the Walpole ministry, see Conyers Middleton, *The History of the Life of Marcus Tullius Cicero*, 2 vols. (1741), which compares Walpole to Cicero.

[103] *Free Briton*, no. 6 (8 Jan. 1730).

THE BEGGAR'S OPERA

We can see these opposing ideological positions played out in responses to John Gay's *The Beggar's Opera*, premiered at Lincoln's Inn Fields theatre on 29 January 1728, the runaway success of the 1727–28 theatre season that ran for sixty-three unbroken performances.[104] The *Craftsman* quickly noted, "The Waggs say it has made *Rich* very *Gay*, and probably will make *Gay* very *Rich*."[105] The ballad opera became a flashpoint in cultural politics. For some, it proved the deplorable taste of the people, encouraged vice and immorality, and drew audiences away from legitimate theatre. For better or worse, it drew people away from Italian opera.

Moralists and social critics reviled the ballad opera for mocking conventional social values and justice by showing its band of highwaymen and thieves as heroes living a life of merriment and ultimately escaping the gallows. The Opposition press encouraged readers to see the opera's depiction of Macheath and his gang and its general reflections on politics and society as the "the most venemous *allegorical Libel* against the G——t [Government] that hath appeared for many Years past."[106] Quickly sensing the political nature of the opera, Colley Cibber, a loyal Whig and patentee of Drury Lane theatre, refused to produce the ballad opera. There was no doubt that the *Beggar's Opera* scored hits against Walpole and the Ministry.[107] Lord Hervey could record with no little understatement that the *Beggar's Opera* "was thought to reflect a little upon the Court."[108]

Aside from the opera's political satire, the popularity of the ballad opera was occasion for the Opposition and Ministry to contest the legitimacy of Italian opera. With its satire and parody of conventions of Italian opera obvious to all (telegraphed in the Beggar's spoken Introduction), the Opposition papers welcomed the *Beggar's Opera* as setting up a subversive entertainment that challenged the cultural legitimacy of Italian opera.

The *Craftsman* cried crocodile tears about the opera at the Haymarket theatre:

---

[104] On *The Beggar's Opera*, most importantly, William E. Schultz, *Gay's Beggar's Opera: Its Content, History and Influence* (New Haven, Conn.: Yale University Press, 1923. Further on the ballad opera, its politics, and relation to Italian opera, McGeary, *Politics of Opera in Handel's Britain*, 116–18.

[105] *Craftsman*, no. 83 (3 Feb. 1728).

[106] *Craftsman*, no. 85 (17 Feb. 1728); reprinted as "A Key to the Beggar's Opera. In a Letter to Caleb Danvers, Esq.," appended to Christopher Bullock, *Woman's Revenge; or, a Match in Newgate*, 2nd ed. (1728), 69–76. See also *Craftsman*, no. 87 (2 March 1728); *Craftsman*, no. 135 (1 Feb. 1729); and *Craftsman*, no. 153 (7 June 1729). These applications to Walpole are summarized in McGeary, *Politics of Opera in Handel's Britain*, 117–18.

[107] Gay's next opera was in fact suppressed by the Ministry; John Loftis, *The Politics of Drama in Augustan England* (Oxford: Clarendon Press, 1963), 88–98.

[108] John Lord Hervey, *Some Materials Towards Memoirs of the Reign of King George II*, ed. Romney Sedgwick, 3 vols. (London: Eyre and Spottiswoode, 1931), 1:98.

72 THE CULTURAL POLITICS OF OPERA, 1720–1742

We have seen it dwindle by Degrees, for a Year or two past, till it is, at *length*, in a Manner, *deserted*, even by its greatest, quondam *Admirers, Subscribers* and *Directors* —— *O! Tempora! O! Mores!* that ever the Theatre in the *Hay-Market* shou'd be obligated to yield to that in *Lincoln's-Inn Fields!* —— that the coarse Ribaldry and vulgar Catches of a *Newgate* Hero shou'd prevail over the melodious Enchantments of *Senesino!* whilst the once celebrated *Cuzzoni* and *Faustina* lay aside their former Emulation, and, with united Resentment, behold the Palm of Precedence given to *pretty* Miss *Polly Peachum* —— with a *P!*[109]

Within a month, its popularity now assured, the *Craftsman* was delighted to observe: "The *British Opera*, commonly called the *Beggars Opera*, continues to be acted, at the Theatre in Lincoln's-Inn Fields with general Applause, to the great Mortification of the Performers and Admirers of the *Outlandish Opera* in the Haymarket."[110]

After the ballad opera opened in Dublin, in his *Intelligencer* paper, Jonathan Swift, no friend of either the Walpole or opera, approved the *Beggar's Opera* because it "exposeth with great Justice, that unnatural Taste for *Italian* Musick among us, which is wholly unsuitable to our Northern *Climat*, and the *genius* of the People, whereby we are over-run with *Italian-Effeminacy*, and *Italian* Nonsense."[111]

The ministerial journals took the occasion to defend opera, obliquely impugning the taste of the populace who prefer the *Beggar's Opera* to Italian opera. Certainly in response to its popularity, a writer to the ministerial *London Journal* on 23 March 1728 regretted the neglect of the Italian opera despite "that excessive Fondness for *Italian* Operas, which has of late Years over-run the Nation."[112] The surprising neglect of Italian opera, playing to near-empty houses despite three splendid new operas, the writer attributes to the fickle taste of the English.

Although they did not invent opera, the English, the correspondent claims, were so converted to the Italian taste (despite the critics) that they accepted nothing but the best talent from Italy and have improved the Italian opera so

---

[109] *Craftsman*, no. 85 (17 Feb. 1728). The tag comment "with a P!" is no doubt meant to both suggest and deny that the character Polly Peachum was modeled on Molly Skerrett, Walpole's mistress.

[110] *Craftsman*, no. 85 (17 Feb. 1728).

[111] *Intelligencer*, no. 3 (25 May 1728); in Jonathan Swift and Thomas Sheridan, *The Intelligencer*, ed. James Woolley (Oxford: Clarendon Press, 1992), 65. Swift's words are echoed in *Thievery-a-la-mode* (June 1728), 12–13, and *Memoirs of the Times; in a Letter to a Friend in the Country* (1737), 44. The *Intelligencer* paper was reprinted in *Mist's Weekly Journal*, no. 168 (6 July 1728). That this squib again opera does not fully reflect Swift's ideas about music (and especially his defense of the dignity of church music), see Joseph McMinn, "'Was Swift a Philistine?': The Evidence of Music," *Swift Studies*, 17 (2002), 59–74.

[112] *London Journal*, no. 451 (March 23, 1728); the complete letter is reprinted in Elizabeth Gibson, *The Royal Academy of Music, 1719–1728: The Institution and Its Directors* (New York, N.Y.: Garland Publishing, 1989), 398–401. The letter is probably not by Dr. Arbuthnot, although often so attributed.

that nothing wants to make it "as compleat as an Entertainment of that sort, in respect of the Musick and Voices, (which are the essential Parts of an Opera,) was capable of being." Nonetheless, all that "Three such Voices [Senesino, Cuzzoni, and Faustina] as have never been equall'd in any Age; and a Composer [Handel], who is able to set each off to the best Advantage;[113] with such a Band of Musicians to accompany them, as is not to be match'd in *Europe*; (to say nothing of the Decorations of the Stage)" have accomplished is to raise disputes and divide the audience into factions quarreling about two perfect, but different voices.

The writer deplores that the *Beggar's Opera's* performance nights conflict with those of the opera, whereby its full houses demonstrate that the British had only a "violent Affection" for it, rather than "a true Taste of good Musick."[114] Manager Rich, he states, has revealed that true British taste and inclination lies in primitive ballads. The writer does, though, find one advantage of smaller houses for Gay's opera: they diminish the number of false friends of the opera who indulge in cat-calling the singers, and so true lovers of music can enjoy opera without interruption.

A week later in the *Weekly Journal; or British Gazetteer*, Dorimant speaks out against the Town's applause for the *Beggar's Opera* and Miss Polly Peachum: such approbation proves the foolishness of the audiences, the stupidity of the kingdom, and "the Degeneracy of Taste" that has prevailed for some years.[115] The rage for Gay's opera has shown the members of the Royal Academy of Music,

> like a Parcel of F——s and As——s, have been at an infinite deal of Pains and Expence in procuring the compleatest Band of Musick, and some of the best Voices that were ever yet together in one Theatre in *Europe*, to no Manner of Purpose at all.

* * *

The historian Sir Lewis Namier proposed that "one has to steep oneself in the political life of a period before one can safely speak, or be sure of understanding its language."[116] In this spirit, we cannot understand and assimilate the full meaning of the period's diverse writings about opera unless we are well steeped in the controversies of its political life. Toward that end, this and later chapters survey the politics of the period and a broad swathe of journalism and pamphleteering that we can plausibly assume politically attuned Britons would have been familiar with, directly or indirectly. These ideas are the deep background behind the defense or denunciation of Italian opera.

---

[113] Handel is certainly meant, since only one opera by the other major composer for the Royal Academy, Bononcini, had been produced in the past four seasons.

[114] That is, as will be seen in Chapter 9, they were demonstrating a False Taste.

[115] *Weekly Journal; or British Gazetteer*, no. 149 (30 March 1728).

[116] Lewis Namier, *The Structure of Politics at the Accession of George III*, 2nd ed. (London: Macmillan, 1957), xi.

74 THE CULTURAL POLITICS OF OPERA, 1720–1742

The oppositional polemic about opera should be seen as rhetorical opportunism, and not taken to reflect widespread views toward opera. The oppositional charges against opera must have been conveniently disregarded by those in the Court-Ministry circle as well as the many members or sympathizers of the Opposition – Lord Bingley, Pulteney, Lords Burlington and Chesterfield, and Frederick, Prince of Wales – who were avid patrons and attendees of opera, and whose actual patronage has been shown elsewhere in this book.[117]

[117] Opposition members and opera: see Table 6.3 and McGeary, *Opera and Politics in Handel's Britain*, Appendix 3, and pp. 152–66 for Frederick's patronage of both Frederick and Handel.

CHAPTER 4

Opera and the Luxury Debate

A constant charge of Opposition polemic was the perniciousness of the corruption of the Walpole regime. All the political, moral, and cultural ills of Britain that could be imagined were laid at the feet of Walpole and his ministry.[1] A sign of corruption was luxury, and since the days of John Dennis, opera has been linked with luxury and excess.[2]

Bolingbroke and the *Craftsman* used corruption in the Machiavellian sense that corruption was both political and moral and that corruption in one domain corrupted the other. For Machiavelli and the classical republican tradition, the greatest threat to the republic was the internal moral or personal corruption that destroyed what the English called "Publick Spirit" – the willingness to set aside personal self-interest and self-indulgence in favor of service and sacrifice to one's country.

Walpole's management of government operated by means of what the Opposition charged was corruption. Money that flowed to the Treasury (such as would accrue from increased Excise revenue) was used by the Ministry to distribute wealth in the form of places, pensions, bribes, and offices. Such ill-gotten wealth bred pursuit of luxury, self-interest, and further corruption in the lust for more money. Corrupt politicians subverted an independent Parliament that would check the Crown and Ministry. Such corruption enslaved men to dependence on the Ministry, and MPs became mere puppets who danced to the puppet master's strings (a common epithet for Walpole); they voted to benefit themselves and the Ministry, not the country's interest.

The debate over luxury maps the great change in social-moral-political attitudes toward commerce during the post-Financial Revolution era. The new era brought an inversion of the traditional relative valorizations of commerce and luxury, vice and virtue. Commerce, consumption, and luxury were no longer seen as inimical to the cultivation of virtue, but a necessary engine for

---

[1] See, for example, the Opposition tract, *A Short History of Prime Ministers in Great Britain* (1733), 3–4: "If therefore at any Time a Free People … should behold Luxury, Sloth, Vice and Corruption breaking in upon them, like a Torrent: and should discover a *Man in high Station* to be the Promoter of this destructive change of Manners; they can no longer doubt that He is engaged in a Design to enslave them." The Ministry replied in *A Review of the Short History of Prime Ministers, in Which the Numerous fallacies … Are Fully Detected* (1733).

[2] See Michael Burden, "Opera, Excess, and the Discourse of Luxury in Eighteenth-Century England," *Revue de la Société d'études anglo-américaines des XVIIe et XVIIIe siècles*, 71 (2014), 232–48.

76 THE CULTURAL POLITICS OF OPERA, 1720–1742

economic and social progress. The development of a full person in civic society depended not on frugality and an ascetic life but on the benefits of a consumer society.

This inversion coincides with the passing of the seventeenth-century Old Whig ethos and the emergence of Modern Whiggism.[3] If anything could readily characterize the Scriblerian oppositional wits Swift and Pope and the political theorist Bolingbroke, it was "nostalgia" (as Isaac Kramnick terms it) for the Country values associated with England before the Financial Revolution, a retrospective view associated with Toryism. It is the social and moral effects on Britain of the new forms of wealth these writers deplored.

The Opposition argument ran that after the Glorious Revolution, the Financial Revolution promoted by Whig financiers of the City created new sources of wealth and forms of money (credit, stocks, bonds, annuities), which undermined the traditional foundations of society, which were based on ownership of land. For the classical republicans, Tories, and Old Whigs, landed wealth provided the stability, independence, and leisure by which a freeholder-citizen could exercise his civic duties.

Britain's new commercial prosperity, the Opposition claimed, was not based on stable land and trade; it was fueled by desire and passion in pursuing mercurial credit and wealth. Now, the citizen's wealth was dependent upon illusory, transient, unstable credit generated from financial speculation. Great new wealth bred luxury – indulgence in material goods and pleasures. Gone was the virtue of the mythic, frugal, independent lifestyle of the Roman citizen-farmer-soldier and English freeholder. It was a received commonplace that the freedom of the Roman Republic was due to poverty and a life of labor.[4] Dangerous to the Republic was the ill-use of wealth (the moral of Pope's *Epistle to Bathurst*).

---

[3] This broad transformation in commerce, society, and political ideas has been widely explored; of pertinence here for this book, with an emphasis on literature and the obsolescence of the classical republican-Old Whig ethos that was superseded by Modern Whiggism: J. A. G. Pocock, *The Machiavellian Moment: Florentine Political Thought and the Atlantic Republican Tradition* (Princeton, N.J.: Princeton University Press, 1975); esp. pp. 423–505; Pocock, *Virtue, Commerce, and History: Essays on Political Thought and History, Chiefly in the Eighteenth Century* (Cambridge: Cambridge University Press, 1985), 94–110; Isaac Kramnick, *Bolingbroke and His Circle: The Politics of Nostalgia in the Age of Walpole* (Cambridge, Mass.: Harvard University Press, 1968); H. T. Dickinson, *Bolingbroke* (London: Constable, 1970), 184–94; and Colin Nicholson, *Writing and the Rise of Finance: Capital Satires of the Early Eighteenth Century* (Cambridge: Cambridge University Press 1994).

The revaluation of virtue throughout the period is traced in Shelly Burtt, *Virtue Transformed: Political Argument in England, 1688–1740* (Cambridge: Cambridge University Press, 1992). This shift is also explored in Thomas McGeary, *Opera and Politics in Queen Anne's Britain, 1705–1714* (Woodbridge: Boydell, 2022), 286–90.

[4] As conveyed in the numerous English translations of Abbé de Vertot's *Histoire des révolutions de la République romaine* (1719), as trans. in the many editions of *The History of the Revolutions that Happened in the Government of the Roman Republic*, 2 vols. (1720), 1:iii–vi.

Selfish men – with money to pursue their own luxuries and effeminate pleasures – would not sacrifice for the greater public good and national defense.[5]

Luxury and corruption were inseparable. There is a sense, writes Paul Langford, in which

> a history of luxury and attitudes to luxury would come very close to being a history of the eighteenth century. ... Politics in this period is about the distribution and representation of this luxury, religion about the attempt to control it, public polemic about generating and regulating it, and social policy about confining it to those who did not produce it.[6]

Concern with luxury is a feature of moral orthodoxy that reaches back to the ascetic Roman Stoics and the Church Fathers who denounced the pursuit of worldly wealth, possessions, and pleasures as evil itself or in its consequences.[7] In the early eighteenth century, as M. M. Goldsmith observes, a great wave of protest against luxury arose, and critique of luxury became ubiquitous:

> Wherever we look in Augustan England (and Britain) – during the reigns of William and Mary, William, Anne, George I and even afterwards – we discover a denunciation of vice, a fear of luxury and corruption. Whether we look at public life or private, the theatre, the press or the pulpit, we find a campaign against the moral degeneration of Britons.[8]

Roman historians of the classical republican tradition repeatedly claimed that only in their early austere, primitive phases did Greece, Sparta, and Rome maintain liberty and achieve their greatness. For the English neo-Harringtonian, Country, and Old Whig tradition, virtue lay in the independent freeholder, free from dependence on the court or patrons (and hence the corrupting influence of wealth and greed). With stable wealth from his land, the citizen had the independence and public spirit to devote himself to his country's good.

Attitudes toward luxury were an expression of the values of social classes. Renunciation of frugality and ostentatious display of luxury (such as participation in the world of opera at the Haymarket theatre) was not a moral failure but an obligation in hierarchical *ancien régime* or court societies – or even the

---

[5] See also *Fog's Weekly Journal*, no. 58 (1 Nov. 1729); and *Craftsman*, nos. 21 and 56 (13–17 Feb. and 29 July 1727). Walpole is directly charged with promoting corruption and luxury in *Craftsman*, no. 51 (24 June 1727).

[6] Paul Langford, *A Polite and Commercial People: England, 1727–1783* (Oxford: Oxford University Press, 1989), 3–4.

[7] For classic and Christian views of luxury: John Sekora, *Luxury: The Concept in Western Thought, Eden to Smollett* (Baltimore, Md.: Johns Hopkins University Press, 1977), 1–51, and Christopher J. Berry, *The Idea of Luxury: A Conceptual and Historical Investigation* (Cambridge: Cambridge University Press, 1994), 45–98. Juvenal had attributed the decline of Rome to luxury in *Satire* VI.287.

[8] M. M. Goldsmith, *Private Vices, Public Benefits: Bernard Mandeville's Social and Political Thought* (Cambridge: Cambridge University Press, 1985), 24; see also Sekora, *Luxury*, 67–77; and Maxine Berg and Elizabeth Eger, "The Rise and Fall of the Luxury Debate," pp. 78–127 in *Luxury in the Eighteenth Century: Debate, Desire and Delectable Goods*, ed. Berg and Eger (Basingstoke: Palgrave Macmillan, 2003).

78   THE CULTURAL POLITICS OF OPERA, 1720–1742

beau monde – where maintaining status, rank, and prestige was a matter of competitive display and outward expression of rank. The resulting ruin of great families in grand building projects and life styles was, in a sense, not a moral failure but a consequence of the pursuit of status. [9]

But the benefits arising in a commercial society such as Britain's – with wealth, comfort, and luxury goods spreading throughout all levels of society – conflicted with the ideals of the classical tradition of condemning luxury and pursuit of self-interest.

As Britain prospered commercially, the reluctance to condemn luxury and defend frugality waned, and outright defenses of luxury, personal gratification, and self-indulgence as good for society appear.[10] The Tory Nicholas Barbon, in *A Discourse of Trade* (1690), argued that previous writers such as Machiavelli had ignored the importance of trade. Man is naturally desirous, and the liberality of the rich and pursuit of vanity, fashion, and luxury are socially useful; they promote trade, employment, and social well-being: "The Promoting of New Fashions, ought to be Encouraged because it provides a Livelihood for a great part of Mankind."[11] The following year Sir Dudley North amplified:

> The main spur to Trade, or rather to Industry and Ingenuity, is the exorbitant Appetites of Men, which they will take pains to gratifie, and so be disposed to work, when nothing else will incline them to it; for did Men content themselves with bare Necessaries, we should have a poor world.[12]

Desire for luxury goods stimulated innovation in technology and products. Luxury aided in civilizing the middling strata; it was part of the process of providing sociability and refined taste in social behavior.

---

[9] See Norbert Elias, *The Court Society* (1969), trans. Edmund Jephcott (New York, N.Y.: Pantheon Books, 1983), 37–8, 63–5, 67–77. The display of luxury was especially necessary where social classes are not easily defined, and where economic criteria are not sufficient. See also E. P. Thompson's discussion of what he calls a "studied and elaborate hegemonic style, a theatrical role in which the great were schooled at infancy and which they maintained until death"; "Patrician Society, Plebeian Culture," *Journal of Social History*, 7 (1974), 382–405 (at p. 389).

[10] Such an outright defense of frugality was given in Sir George Mackenzie's *The Moral History of Frugality with Its Opposite Vices, Covetousness, Niggardliness, Prodigality, and Luxury* (1691); esp. pp. 71–82 against luxury. See also the many editions of J. S., *The Way to be Wise and Wealthy: or the Excellency of Industry and Frugality* (1716); and Erasmus Jones, *Luxury, Pride and Vanity the Bane of the British nation* (1736). Matthew Tindal, *A Defense of Our Present Happy Establishment: and the Administration Vindicated* (1722), 19, points out how trades people would starve and decline if the populace had to live frugally like the ancient Romans. H. T. Dickinson, *Liberty and Property: Political Ideology in Eighteenth-Century Britain* (New York, N.Y.: Holmes and Meier, 1977), 151, points to sources that state luxury may be dangerous, but corruption is not the inevitable result.

[11] Nicholas Barbon, *A Discourse of Trade* (1690), 67. Modern edition with Introduction by Jacob H. Hollander (Baltimore, Md.: Johns Hopkins Press, 1905).

[12] Sir Dudley North, *Discourses upon Trade* (1691), 14. Modern edition with Introduction by Jacob H. Hollander (Baltimore, Md.: Johns Hopkins Press, 1907).

The revaluation of luxury was argued most vigorously and notoriously by Bernard Mandeville, who justified commercial prosperity and luxury in his scandalous paradox "Private Vices, Publick Benefits," which reverses the place of luxury on the balance of vice and virtue.[13] What was formerly a vice is now essential to social progress. Mandeville first presented his ideas in an allegorical poem about bees, *The Grumbling Hive: or, Knaves turn'd Honest* in 1705. As he summarized in "The Moral" to his poem

> Fraud, Luxury and Pride must live,
> While we the Benefits receive.
> …
> So Vice is beneficial found,
> When it's by Justice lopt and bound.[14]

This slight poem seems to have passed without comment, but the paradox drew public outrage with the publication of its enlarged second edition as *The Fable of the Bees* in 1723, which included twenty-three Remarks and the especially provocative "An Enquiry into the Origin of Moral Virtue" and "Essay on Charity and Charity-Schools."

Mandeville pierced the veil of piety and asserted men were motivated by greed and pride; luxury was a result of a human industriousness fueled by desire. He resolved the conflict between virtue and vice by showing that luxury (private vice) is a positive force (virtue) necessary for economic development and prosperity (public benefits). Traditional luxuries, often characterized by effeminacy, excess, and enervation, produce benefits for the public at large; indeed, they are necessary to make states great.

---

[13] On many aspects of Mandeville's thought relating to classical republicanism, Old and Modern Whiggism, and the luxury debate: Thomas A. Horne, *The Social Thought of Bernard Mandeville: Virtue and Commerce in Early Eighteenth-Century England* (New York, N.Y.: Columbia University Press, 1978); E. J. Hundert, *The Enlightenment's "Fable": Bernard Mandeville and the Discovery of Society* (Cambridge: Cambridge University Press, 1994); J. A .W. Gunn, *Beyond Liberty and Property: The Process of Self-Recognition in Eighteenth-Century Political Thought* (Kingston and Montreal: McGill-Queen's University Press, 1983), 96–119; F. B. Kaye, Introduction to Bernard Mandeville, *The Fable of the Bees: or Private Vices, Publick Benefits*, 2 vols. (1924; reprint: Indianapolis, Ind.: Liberty Fund, 1988); M. M. Goldsmith, *Private Vices, Public Benefits: Bernard Mandeville's Social and Political Thought* (Cambridge: Cambridge University Press, 1985); *Luxury in the Eighteenth Century*, ed. Berg and Eger; M. M. Goldsmith, "Liberty, Luxury and the Pursuit of Happiness," pp. 225–51 in *Languages of Political Theory in Early Modern Europe*, ed. A. Pagden; Malcolm Jack, *Corruption and Progress: The Eighteenth-Century Debate* (New York, N.Y.: AMS Press, 1989), 1–62; *Mandeville and Augustan Ideas: New Essays*, ed. Charles W. A. Prior (Victoria, BC: University of Victoria, 2000); Burtt, *Virtue Transformed*, 128–49; M. M. Goldsmith, "Mandeville and the Spirit of Capitalism," *Journal of British Studies*, 17 (Fall 1977), 63–81; Sekora, *Luxury*, esp. 67–77, 83–8, 113–31; and Berry, *Idea of Luxury*, 126–34.

[14] *Fable of the Bees*, Kaye ed., 1:36–7.

80   THE CULTURAL POLITICS OF OPERA, 1720–1742

Most crucially, Mandeville's paradox rejected the moral view that equated the public good with the virtue of the individual, that the health of the state was inseparable from the virtue of its citizens.[15]

Mandeville denied the virtue of luxury's supposed opposite, frugality. The much-vaunted ancient states, such as the Sparta, that endured frugality and maintained their liberty, he argued, did so out of necessity, not "as a general Aversion to Vice and Luxury." Such frugal societies could not support large populations.[16] It was impossible to enjoy "all the most elegant Comforts of Life" as present in an "industrious, wealthy and powerful Nation" such as Britain and yet retain "all the Virtue and Innocence that can be wish'd for in a Golden Age." It would be hypocritical both to decry "the Vices and Inconveniencies" of "an opulent and flourishing People" and yet be "wonderfully greedy" for the benefits of material prosperity.[17]

Mandeville asserts the benefits of luxuries and refutes the objections to them. The supposedly vicious and immoral actions of all those who live a life of "Pride and Luxury" – the "sensual Courtier," the "fickle Strumpet," the "profuse Rake," and "haughty Courtesan" – "sets the Poor to Work, adds Spurs to Industry and encourages the skilful Artificer to search after further Improvements."[18] The effects of luxury, Mandeville claims, are harmless:

> The greatest Excesses of Luxury are shewn in Buildings, Furniture, Equipages and Clothes: Clean linen weakens a Man no more than Flannel; Tapistry, fine Painting or good Wainscot are no more unwholesom than bare Walls; and a rich Couch, or a gilt Chariot are no more enervating than the cold Floor or a Country Cart.[19]

There can be no doubt that on the basis of several decades of British opera criticism, Mandeville and his readers would no doubt include opera among luxuries that (as Mandeville repeatedly states) "effeminate" and "enervate." Opera at the Haymarket burned through thousands of pounds each season spent for Italian star singers, musicians, dancers, house personnel, carpenters, painters, dressmakers, music copyists, and purchases of candles, oil, cloth, lumber, and playbills. It surely was a luxury that was "of immense Use to the Publick" by spreading economic benefits to London's trades- and craftspeople.[20]

Mandeville enthusiastically commended the aesthetics of opera in a dialogue appended to the *Fable*.[21] His character Horace recommends opera to Fulvia for

> the noble Manner and Stateliness beyond Nature, which every thing there is executed with. What gentle Touches, what slight and yet majestic Motions are made

---

[15] Horne, *Social Thought of Mandeville*, 51–75.
[16] *Fable of the Bees*, Remark Q, Kaye ed., 1:181–98 (at 1:189).
[17] Preface, *Fable of the Bees*, Kaye ed., 1:6–7.
[18] *Fable of the Bees*, Remarks F, M; Kaye ed., 1:85, 1:130.
[19] *Fable of the Bees*, Remark L; Kaye ed., 1:119.
[20] *Fable of the Bees*, First Dialogue, Kaye ed., 2:36. For examples of such expenditures for just two operas in 1711, see Judith Milhous and Robert D. Hume, "The Haymarket Opera in 1711," *Early Music*, 17 (1989), 523–37 (esp. 529–33).
[21] *Fable of the Bees*, First Dialogue, Kaye ed., 2:29–61.

OPERA AND THE LUXURY DEBATE   81

use of to express the most boisterous Passions! … [B]eautiful Action joynes with the skilful Voice in setting before us in a transcendent Light, the Heroick Labours we are come to admire, and which the word *Opera* imports. … At the Opera every thing charms and concurs to make Happiness compleat. … Upon Earth there can not be a Pastime more agreeable.[22]

Mandeville's view of the benign effects of luxury – turning self-interest into the virtue that drives commerce and prosperity, and separating personal virtue from the good of the state – is characteristic of the Modern Whigs of the Ministry, beneficiaries of the new Financial Revolution, and defenders of Italian opera.[23] It is precisely the "nostalgic" view of luxury as a civic and moral vice that underlies Bolingbroke's and the Old Whig-Catonic tradition's critique of Italian opera.

Among those incensed at Mandeville's tract, was the staunch Old Whig and arch-foe of opera John Dennis. [24] Dennis focused directly on the issue of luxury in his polemic *Vice and Luxury Publick Mischiefs* published the following year. As in his earlier writings on Italian opera, he reveals yet again his concern for its effect on private moral character and, ultimately, the health of Britain. Dennis argued that Mandeville made "an open Attack upon the Publick Virtue and Publick Spirit of *Great Britain*" (x). The title-page epigraph quotes Archytus of Tarentum on the evils of the lust for sensual pleasure (*voluptatem corporis*) and the vices set in motion by it.[25]

For Dennis, no further proof for the magnitude "of all manner of Vice and Luxury [and] the utmost Profligacy of the Times" was necessary than that they have found a defender in Mandeville (xvi), whose book seems "to encourage Vice and Luxury" (2). Dennis quotes the classical republicans Algernon Sidney and Machiavelli to support his claim that "Vice and Luxury impair the publick Liberties of a nation, and, if they are lasting, destroy them" (6).

Luxury made men venal and prone to sell out their country. Echoing age-old classical republican commonplaces, Dennis claims "Luxury and Corruption of Manners" are inconsistent with Liberty (14), whereas "Virtue and Moderation are necessary for the Preservation of Liberty" (24).[26] He cites Israel, Sparta, Athens, and Rome as states once blest with liberty that were undermined and

---

[22] *Fable of the Bees*, First Dialogue, Kaye ed., 2:38–40.

[23] Gunn, *Beyond Liberty and Property*, 96–119, points out the political role of Mandeville's tract and how his defense of luxury could serve to justify the techniques of rulers and the use of influence, such as during the Walpole era.

[24] For response to the tract, see *Fable of the Bees*, Kaye ed., 2:401–17. Many of the texts (including that of John Dennis) published in response to Mandeville are reprinted in *Private Vices, Publick Benefits?: The Contemporary Reception of Bernard Mandeville*, ed. J. Martin Stafford (Solihull: Ismeron, 1997); for summary, see Stafford, "Mandeville's Contemporary Critics," *1650–1850: Ideas, Aesthetics, and Inquiries in the Early Modern Era*, 7 (2002), 387–401.

[25] Cicero, ostensibly in the person of Cato, reporting a speech by Archytus in *De Senectute*, xii.

[26] Kaye, *Fable of the Bees*, 2:407, points out that Dennis misunderstands Mandeville's logically rigorous use of the term *vice*.

82 THE CULTURAL POLITICS OF OPERA, 1720–1742

overthrown by luxury.[27] These are the same arguments Dennis had made in his *Essay on the Opera's after the Italian Manner* (1706).

After Mandeville, defense of luxury became commonplace and orthodox. In 1741 David Hume argued that luxury refined gratification of the senses. The liberties of Great Britain, he claimed, increased, not decayed with improvements in luxury and refinement, for "luxury nourishes commerce and industry." "How inconsistent, then," Hume argued, "is it to blame so violently luxury, or a refinement in the arts, and to represent it as the bane of liberty and public spirit!"[28] In fact, the music historian Charles Burney declared simply, "The fine arts are children of affluence and luxury."[29]

Samuel Johnson would explain to James Boswell in 1776, that "Many things which are false are transmitted from book to book, and gain credit in the world. One of these is the cry against the evil of luxury. Now the truth is, that luxury produced much good."[30] In the same year, Adam Smith found no need to remark on luxury, quite accepting it as part of economic life.[31]

THE OPPOSITION AND LUXURY

Luxury was contested in the polemics between the Opposition and Walpole's ministerial writers – and needless to say, opera was singled out by Opposition writers as a luxury.[32] For Bolingbroke and the *Craftsman*, luxury and corruption were at the heart of their condemnation of the Walpole ministry. His corrupt administration, the source of all political evil, led to tyranny as men were enslaved to their passions and reliance on the Ministry. Proclaimed the *Craftsman*: "*Luxury, Corruption,* and *secret, unlimited, unaccountable Expences*

---

[27] Pages 16–20. Consistent with his emphasis on the effects of vice and luxury, Dennis, in the continuing controversy about the culpability of the assassins of Julius Caesar, maintained that it was not Caesar who destroyed Roman liberties but the corruptions of the Romans themselves; *Julius Cæsar Acquitted, and His Murderers Condemn'd* (1722).

Dennis makes no indictment, direct or indirect, of the present ministry, though he does cite the public debt and faction as perils to present-day Britain (pp. 24–6). Judging from the Preface to his *Julius Cæsar Acquitted*, Dennis was fully supportive of the Whig establishment (see Gunn, *Liberty and Property*, 108).

[28] David Hume, "Of Luxury," in *Essays, Moral, Political, and Literary*, 2 vols. (1741, 1742). In later editions, the essay is retitled "Of Refinement in the Arts."

[29] Charles Burney, *The Present State of Music in Germany, the Netherlands, and United Provinces*, 2nd ed. (1773), 116. He went on to explain that in Germany one should expect music at the several courts, not in the free imperial cities, which are inhabited by "poor industrious people" (117).

[30] James Boswell, *The Life of Samuel Johnson, LL.D.*, 3 vols. (1791), 2:385. Johnson provides as a typical example of the benefits of luxury when one buys a dish of green peas (which benefits the industrious) instead of giving the money directly to the idle poor.

[31] Adam Smith, *An Inquiry into the Nature and Causes of the Wealth of Nations* (1776), Book V, Chapter 3, "Of Publick Debts." In Book III, Chapter 4, he shows how luxury in the cities spreads out into the improvement of the country at large.

[32] An examples linking luxury and opera, see George Berkeley, *An Essay Toward Preventing the Ruin of Great Britain* (1721), 15.

OPERA AND THE LUXURY DEBATE   83

... are the *Barrels of Powder* which may, one time or other, *blow up the British Constitution.*"[33]

How luxury corrupted the citizen was explained by the *Craftsman* in 1727:

> For when once Luxury has fix'd a deep Root in their [the people's] minds, it will soon get the better of their noble faculties; it will emasculate, soften and melt down all those stubborn virtues, which are the natural Effects of Temperance and frugality; the consequence of which is, that a man thus debauched and effeminated will, in order to support himself in the same vicious manner, fall into any measures, which are dictated to him with a prospect of advantage, and sacrifice the most valuable Rights of his Country for a fashionable Town-house, a splendid Equipage, and an elegant Table.[34]

Fog's Weekly in 1734 explained that indulging in luxury and effeminacy undermines men's fitness to govern the nation:

> Luxury and Effeminacy take the Mind off from every Thing that is Great or Noble, and it is observ'd that the Passions of Men who are tainted with those Vices, are ingaged upon nothing but Trifles. If I should see Persons of an eminent Rank pass their Lives amongst Dancers and Musicians, if I should observe that they are capable of thinking or talking of Nothing else, and that they interested themselves more in an Emulation betwixt two Singers [possibly recalling Faustina and Cuzzoni], than in the Fate of their Country, what Veneration could I have for Laws or Counsels that came from such Fiddling Fellows.[35]

Henry Carey, a consistent critic of opera and its singers, directly links luxury and opera in the subtitle of his poem on the singer Faustina Bordoni: *Faustina: or the Roman Songstress, a Satyr, on the Luxury and Effeminacy of the Age* (1726).[36]

At one point, the *Craftsman* could assert the necessity of "making some good and effectual Laws for restraining of *Luxury*; which, if not speedily prevented, must infallibly ruin this Kingdom." Luxury is found not only among the quality, but now "among *Shop-keepers* and their *Apprentices.*"[37]

---

[33] *Craftsman*, no. 80 (13 Jan. 1728). For some representative explications of the dangers of luxury and corruption leading to effeminacy and loss of liberty: *Craftsman*, no. 303 (22 April 1732); no. 443 (28 Dec. 1734); no. 488 (8 Nov. 1735) ["Whereever *Luxury* is spread amongst the People, and *Corruption* eats into the Constitution of the State, ... [they] debauch the bold, generous and free *Britons* into easy, effeminate and base Slaves."]; no. 523 (10 July 1736), no. 526 (31 July 1736); and no. 702 (22 Dec. 1739).

[34] *Craftsman*, no. 21 (13–17 Feb. 1727).

[35] *Fog's Weekly Journal*, no. 311 (19 Oct. 1734).

[36] Included in Carey's *Occasional Poems* (1729); *Poems on Several Occasions*, 3rd ed. (1743), 28–37; *The Poems of Henry Carey*, ed. Frederick T. Wood (London: Eric Partridge, 1930), 97–101; and Elizabeth Gibson, *The Royal Academy of Music, 1719-1728: The Institution and Its Directors* (New York, N.Y.: Garland Publishing, 1989), 415–18 (but without epigram).

[37] *Craftsman*, no. 178 (29 Nov. 1729) [The passage also appears in *The British Patriot, or a Timely Caveat Against Giving into the Measures of Any Evil and Corrupt Minister* (1731), 20]; and nos. 702 and 704 (22 Dec. 1739 and 5 Jan. 1740). On the role of luxury in Opposition polemic, see Sekora, *Luxury*, 81–9.

84 THE CULTURAL POLITICS OF OPERA, 1720–1742

Corruption spread from the political realm to all parts of British society, even debasing literary and artistic taste. Wrote Bolingbroke:

> The very idea of wit, and all that can be called taste, has been lost among the great; arts and science are scarce alive; luxury has been increased but not refined; corruption has been established, and is avowed. When governments are worn out, thus it is: the decay appears in every instance. Public and private spirit, science and wit, decline all together.[38]

It had been a commonplace since Longinus that the arts and sciences flourished under liberty.[39] By implication, debased taste and arts were a sign of tyranny. When Opposition writers bemoaned the fallen state of the arts in Britain and the quality of Walpole's own writers, this was evidence of the effects of corruption and luxury. The issue of fallen taste in the arts is developed in Chapter 9.

Any complaint or indictment of immorality and corruption in general could be understood as an attack on those at the head of the state: Walpole's ministry and the Court. The moral decline for which Walpole was responsible was publicly visible in his associates: Lord Hervey (Pope's Sporus) and William Yonge. The scandals of the South Sea Bubble, the Charitable Corporation, the York Buildings Company, and the Derwentwater Estates sale all showed how corruption spread from the Court and Ministry.

Opposition newspapers did not need to – but they did so nonetheless – remind their readers what the Roman historians wrote: that it was the introduction of the wealth, luxury, and effeminacy from Asia that marked the decay, decline, and fall of the Roman Republic.[40] On the basis of the principles of the constancy of human nature, that history repeats in cycles, and that like causes produce like results, the caution for Britain was clear.

MINISTERIAL DEFENSE OF CORRUPTION

As the party whose financial innovations laid the foundation for Britain's commercial revolution, Walpole's Modern Whigs found themselves in the position of defending luxury against Opposition claims the Ministry was corrupting Britain's moral and public character.[41] Their defense was carried out in various ways.

---

[38] *Letters on the Study and Use of History*; in *The Works of Lord Bolingbroke*, 4 vols. (Philadelphia, Pa.: Carey and Hart, 1843), 2:333. Another briefer mention of Walpole's causing the decline of arts: *Craftsman*, no. 20 (10–13 Feb. 1727).

[39] Longinus, *On the Sublime*, Chapter 44. For some English statements, see McGeary, *Opera and Politics in Queen Anne's Britain*, 254.

[40] The point is anticipated in the *True Briton*, no. 70 (31 Jan. 1724). Opposition reminders of decline and fall of Greece and Rome from luxury, corruption, and effeminacy include: *Fog's Weekly Journal*, no. 123 (3 April 1731), no. 311 (19 Oct. 1734); *Craftsman*, no. 213 (1 Aug. 1730), no. 325 (23 Sept. 1732); no. 437 (16 Nov. 1737), no. 441 (14 Dec. 1734), and no. 523 (10 July 1736).

[41] See *Craftsman*, no. 114 (7 Sept. 1728), on the ill effects of stock-jobbing and the commercial companies.

OPERA AND THE LUXURY DEBATE   85

What the Opposition called "corruption," the Ministry considered "influence" that was necessary for the proper function of government. We must have governments, and their leaders must have power. Since men are naturally corrupt, a minister must accept men as they are and use whatever rewards or discouragements are necessary to govern.[42] Influence was a means of governing by art rather than brute force; places and pensions were rewards for service to the public. As the ministerial *London Journal* explained:

> To Expect Men in Power and Office should *pursue the Good of the Publick*, without any Regard to *their own particular Interest*, is the most ridiculous Expectation in the World; that 'tis contrary to *Reason and Justice*, and the *Good of the Community* too; 'tis a *Romantick Notion*, and meer *Visionary Virtue*.[43]

The Ministry accepted that men are inherently self-interested. Whigs serving in government cannot be corrupt because they are not being bribed to serve against their own principles.[44] Nor was writing in pay of the government the same as writing in favor of faction, tyranny, and despotism. Governing by influence was not subverting the Constitution. Rather, only by the dispersal of places and pensions does the monarch have a proper counterweight against the growing power of the Commons and its control of the purse. The Opposition's attack on corruption was, in effect, an attempt to overthrow the Constitution by giving all power into the people.

In another tactic, like Bernard Mandeville, the Modern Whigs revalued self-interest as the engine of economic growth and prosperity.[45] They argued luxury – and here, of course, opera was a visible example – was the result of rising general wealth and prosperity since the Revolution. General riches will produce extraordinary expenditure on commodities, which produces escalating emulation of material goods, which become necessities. To argue that "the Consequences of Freedom and of Plenty" are crimes against a government that preserves them would justify "an Impeachment against Providence as well as against Placemen," one ministerial writer resolutely stated.[46]

Another tactic was to attack the motives of the Opposition, charging its members were motivated by envy, disappointment, and self-interested ambition for office.[47] The Ministry charged the Opposition railed against corruption

---

[42] On men corrupting and governing by art: *London Journal*, no. 673 (20 May 1732); *Free Briton*, nos. 163–634 (11 and 18 Jan. 1732); no. 188 (28 June 1733); and *Daily Gazetteer*, no. 216 (6 March 1736).

[43] *London Journal*, no. 639 (25 Sept. 1731); see also *Free Briton*, no. 164 (18 Jan. 1732).

[44] *London Journal*, no. 770 (30 March 1734).

[45] On revaluation of self-interest, Burtt, *Virtue Transformed*, 128–41.

[46] *Daily Gazetteer*, no. 1483 (24 March 1740). Simon Targett, "Government and Ideology During the Age of Whig Supremacy: The Political Argument of Sir Robert Walpole's Newspaper Propagandists," *Historical Journal*, 37 (1994), 289–317, gives date as 1730.

[47] For examples of vigorous ministerial defense against the Opposition's charge of corruption and luxury: *London Journal*, nos. 606 and 609 (13 and 27 March 1731), and no. 832 (14 June 1735); *Daily Gazetteer*, no. 72 (20 Sept. 1735) and no. 120 (15 Nov. 1735); and *Free Briton*, no. 39 (27 Aug. 1730) and no. 188 (28 June 1733).

86   THE CULTURAL POLITICS OF OPERA, 1720–1742

and "a general Vogue of Luxury," not to "reform the People, but to rouze them up to destroy a Minister." It is but "*Cant* and *Malice*" to charge "*a certain Great Man's* being *the Cause* of Corruption."[48] By putting their own self-interest above the nation's, it was the Opposition who were truly corrupt.[49]

Finally, the causes of luxury and corruption are not in the Ministry, but false teaching and wrong notions of life and pleasure. It is "an absurdity," wrote the *Daily Gazetteer*, to imagine that "we had any Laws to encourage Immorality, or if Luxury were promoted by Publick Authority." The Court and Ministry are, in fact, examples of economy and social virtues. The cure of luxury and corruption is industry, frugality, economy, honesty, and temperance; that is, education in "just Notions of *Virtue and Pleasure, Religion and Government*."[50]

Gibraltar, Opera, and the Luxury Debate

Despite the well-worn associations of Italian opera with effeminacy and luxury and claims of its effects on Britons, Bolingbroke and the *Craftsman* leveled only one direct, frontal attack denouncing opera, and that in a time of war. After 1734 other oppositional newspapers did more frequently directly attack opera and its star singer Farinelli.

In January 1727, Britain was veering toward war with Spain over possession of Gibraltar, which Britain claimed by terms of the Treaty of Utrecht of 1713, which concluded the British role in the War of the Spanish Succession. In that war, Britain, the Dutch, Austria, and other Imperial states allied to contain what they saw as French ambitions for Universal Monarchy in Europe, and which Britain viewed as a threat to the Protestant Succession. In Spain, Austria and the allies contested with Bourbon France over whether Louis XIV's grandson Philip or the Habsburg Archduke Charles would succeed to the Spanish throne. The Treaty brought peace but left unresolved many disputes. Despite the Treaty, Spain still hoped to recover Gibraltar, and Spain and Austria had rival claims to territories in Italy.[51]

Issue no. 832 of the *London Journal* is a direct reply to the *Craftsman*, no. 464 (24 May 1735). The pamphlet *Clodius and Cicero* (1727) argues that although there may be some public corruptions, greater evils may arise from the attempt to uproot them; the wealth (or lack of it) of a minister is no measure of his public conduct or integrity.

On the ministerial reply to charges of corruption, luxury, and self-interest: Sekora, *Luxury*, 113–18; Targett, "Government and Ideology During the Age of Whig Supremacy," 300–1, 305–6; Thomas A. Horne, "Politics in a Corrupt Society: William Arnall's Defence of Robert Walpole," *Journal of the History of Ideas*, 41 (1980), 601–14, esp. pp. 603–6, 611–14 (stressing the importance of Mandeville).

[48] *London Journal*, no. 832 (14 June 1735).

[49] For example, *Free Briton*, no. 257 (3 Oct. 1734), and no. 273 (30 Jan. 1735).

[50] *Daily Gazetteer*, no. 1483 (24 March 1740). [Targett gives date as 1730].

[51] I have given a fuller account of the run-up to Gibraltar and related episodes dealing with the Haymarket theatre in *Politics of Opera in Handel's Britain*, Chapter 4, "The Opera House, Allegory, and the Political Opposition." On European politics leading up to Gibraltar: Wolfgang Michael, *England Under George I: The Beginning of the*

OPERA AND THE LUXURY DEBATE   87

George I, with his Hanoverian interest to protect, sought to maintain peace and seek rapproachement with France and settle the Austrian and Spanish claims in Italy. In June 1717, Secretary of State James Stanhope negotiated the Triple Alliance between England, France, and the Dutch to guarantee the terms of the Utrecht Treaty. The Alliance was expanded as the Quadruple Alliance (2 August 1718) with the addition of Austria, who sought to contain Spanish claims in Italy. To induce Spain to join the Alliance, Stanhope had secretly agreed to restore Gibraltar.[52]

Britain and France waged a "little war" (the War of the Quadruple Alliance) against Spain in 1718–1720 that forced Spain to accede to the Alliance (17 February 1720), which brought Austria and Spain to peace. Spain, having signed the Alliance, made repeated demands for restitution of Gibraltar on the basis of Stanhope's promise.[53]

By the 1720s, Britain felt her trade in the West Indies, guaranteed by treaty, was being threatened by Spain's military position and commercial aspirations. Spain, in turn, resented Britain's naval presence in the Mediterranean. On the pretext of guarding the West Indies, the Spanish harassed and seized British shipping in hopes the British would abandon their trade. By May 1726, British merchants could claim damages of £300,000.[54]

Hanoverian Dynasty, trans and adapted by L. B. Namier (London: Macmillan, 1936), 225–83, 311–58; Wolfgang Michael, *England Under George I: The Quadruple Alliance*, trans and adapted by Annemarie MacGregor and George E. MacGregor (London: Macmillan, 1939), 66–138; Basil Williams, *Stanhope: A Study in Eighteenth-Century War and Diplomacy* (Oxford: Clarendon Press, 1932), 200–29, 273–352; Ragnhild Hatton, *George I: Elector and King* (Cambridge, Mass.: Harvard University Press, 1978), 256–79; Jeremy Black, *The Collapse of the Anglo-French Alliance, 1727–1731* (Gloucester: Alan Sutton, 1987); Stetson Conn, *Gibraltar in British Diplomacy in the Eighteenth Century* (New Haven, Conn.: Yale University Press, 1942); James F. Chance, *The Alliance of Hanover: A Study of British Foreign Policy in the Last Years of George I* (London: John Murray, 1923); W. N. Hargreaves-Mawdsley, *Eighteenth-Century Spain 1700–1788: A Political, Diplomatic and Institutional History* (London: Macmillan, 1979); and Arthur M. Wilson, *French Foreign Policy during the Administration of Cardinal Fleury, 1726–1743* (Cambridge, Mass.: Harvard University Press, 1936).

For more specialized treatments: Jeremy Black, "The Anglo-French Alliance 1716–1731: A Study in Eighteenth-Century International Relations," *Francia: Forschungen zur westeuropäischen Geschichte*, 13 (1985), 295–310; Black, *British Foreign Policy in the Age of Walpole* (Edinburgh: John Donald, 1985); Richard Lodge, "The Treaty of Seville (1729)," *Transactions of the Royal Historical Society*, 4th ser., 16 (1933), 1–43; Basil Williams, "The Foreign Policy of England under Walpole," *English Historical Review*, 15 (1900), 251–76, 479–94, 665–8; and Williams, "Foreign Policy," *English Historical Review*, 16 (1901), 67–83, 308–27, 439–51.

[52] Williams, *Stanhope*, 312, 397.

[53] Conn, *Gibraltar in British Diplomacy*, 31–51.

[54] On the subsequent history of Spanish depredations, Philip Woodfine, *Britannia's Glories: The Walpole Ministry and the 1739 War with Spain* (Woodbridge: Boydell & Brewer, 1998), 75–101.

88   THE CULTURAL POLITICS OF OPERA, 1720–1742

A crisis arose on a new front early in 1725. In March, the French infuriated Philip by breaking off the pending marriage of the young Louis XV to the Infanta by returning her to Spain. Affronted, Spain upset the traditional European alliances by withdrawing from the Quadruple Alliance and entering into the Treaties of Vienna with Austria on 30 April and 1 May 1725, which settled territorial disputes between Spain and Austria in Italy; Charles renounced his claim to the Spanish crown. In June 1725, Philip threatened English commercial privileges in the Indies unless Gibraltar was restored; the Ministry then ordered the Gibraltar defenses strengthened and warned Spain any disruption of British trade would be met with force.[55] In response to the unexpected Austrian-Spanish alliance, on 3 September 1725 Britain and France created the Alliance of Hanover, along with Prussia, the Dutch, Portugal, Sweden, and Denmark.[56] The Treaty guaranteed the signatories' possessions against the Vienna Alliance powers.

Charles and Philip reacted to the Treaty by signing secret additions to their treaty on 5 November 1725, by which Austria pledged to help Spain regain Gibraltar. Europe was now ranged between a new set of alliances, and war on the Continent seemed imminent.[57] In response to the Vienna treaties, Britain readied her army and navy and dispatched fleets to the Baltic, the coast of Spain, and the West Indies.[58] Anticipating an outbreak of hostilities, in September 1726 Admiral Hosier blockaded Porto Bello, the fortified Spanish port in Panama.[59] The action at Porto Bello provoked the Spanish into besieging Gibraltar in December 1726, and Britain sent troops and ships to reinforce the fortress. Government policy toward Gibraltar was a flashpoint between the Ministry and Opposition, with Bolingbroke and Opposition writers raising fears the Ministry would restore Gibraltar and calling for war against Spain.[60]

---

[55] Conn, *Gibraltar in British Diplomacy*, 75–8.
[56] On the diplomacy, Chance, *Alliance of Hanover*; and Williams, "Foreign Policy of England," 15 (1900), 687–92.
[57] Conn, *Gibraltar in British Diplomacy*, 84–8.
[58] The naval campaigns are narrated in William Laird Clowes, *The Royal Navy: A History from the Earliest Times to the Present*, 5 vols. (London: Sampson Low, Martson and Co., 1898), 3:42–7.
[59] On Hosier at Porto Bello, Conn, *Gibraltar in British Diplomacy*, 88–9; Herbert Richmond, *The Navy as an Instrument of Policy, 1558–1727* (Cambridge: Cambridge University Press, 1953), 393–5.
[60] Bishop Benjamin Hoadly defended government policies in *An Enquiry into the Reasons of the Conduct of Great Britain, with Relation to the Present State of Affairs in Europe* (1727). An Opposition rejoinder was *Some Queries to the Author of the Enquiry into the Reasons of the Conduct of Great Britain, &c.* (1727). Hoadly is supported in *A Second Enquiry into the Reasons of the Conduct of Great Britain* (1726 [o.s.] = 1727). Arguments against war over Gibraltar are contained in *Reasons Against a War. In a Letter to a Member of Parliament* (1727).

For the Opposition, Bolingbroke, *Occasional Writer. No. 1* (Jan. 1727) with ministerial reply in the *British Journal*, no. 233 (11 March 1727). *The Evident Approach*

OPERA AND THE LUXURY DEBATE 89

On 1 January 1727, the Spanish ambassador broke off relations with Britain with ultimatums for the return of Gibraltar and recall of the British fleets. Without declaration of war, Spain began bombarding Gibraltar on 22 February 1727.[61]

BOLINGBROKE ON OPERA AND LUXURY

With Gibraltar under siege and Britain and Spain heading toward war, in February 1727 the *Craftsman* and the ministerial *British Journal* sparred over Italian opera. The centerpiece of the exchanges was Bolingbroke's *Craftsman* letter on luxury and music, which brings to bear onto opera the debate over luxury. Invoking principles from the classical republican, Old Whig, and Country traditions, as well as examples from ancient history, Bolingbroke drew the government press into defending an entertainment at the center of British political, cultural, and social life. In these partisan writings, we can see the Catonic-Old Whig-Country position ranged against the Ciceronian-Modern Whig-Court viewpoint over opera. The ministerial writers utilized the Modern Whig defense of commerce and prosperity to disarm the charges against luxury and opera.

Bolingbroke' letter on opera and luxury was announced in a brief notice at the end of the *Craftsman* for 17 February 1727: "We have receiv'd several ingenious Letters from our Correspondents; particularly one concerning *Luxury* and *Musick*, which shall be speedily publish'd."[62]

In what may have been a preemptive strike, two weeks later, the *British Journal* carried a letter providing a sophisticated defense of Italian opera.[63] The *Journal*'s correspondent notes that Italian opera is now "the universal Entertainment of the polite Part of the world" and of "Men of the finest Parts and best Understandings": "Every one is delighted with it but the Criticks, who still keep up their antient Enmity against it … and make no Scruple of arraigning the Taste of Persons of the best Sense." The witticisms and raillery at the expense of Italian opera are so trifling and now so trite, that they are now mistaken for the truth. So much so, that a true lover of music is afraid to risk admitting "a love for the *Opera*," one of "the most innocent Gratification[s] of the Mind" because he finds he "runs the risque of forfeiting his Understanding" and

---

of a War; and Something of the Necessity of It, in Order to Establish Peace, and Preserve Trade (1727) argues for a war with Spain.

[61] On events immediately leading up to the bombardment of Gibraltar: Williams, "Foreign Policy of England," 16 (1901), 67–83; Black, *Collapse*, 1–16; Conn, *Gibraltar in British Diplomacy*, 1–89; and Wilson, *French Foreign Policy*, 91–162.

[62] *Craftsman*, no. 21 (13–17 Feb. 1727).

[63] *British Journal*, no. 232 (4 March 1727). The letter is reprinted in Gibson, *Royal Academy of Music*, 392–4. Almost two weeks later, the *British Journal*, no. 235 (25 March 1727) also gave tribute to Italian opera by printing a poem by Henry Carey, "To Mr. *Handel*, on his *Admetus*"; reprinted in Carey's *Poems*, 3rd ed. (1729); in O. E. Deutsch, *Handel: A Documentary Biography* (New York, N.Y.: W. W. Norton, 1955), 206; and in *Handel: Collected Documents*, ed. Donald Burrows, Helen Coffey, John Greenacombe, and Anthony Hicks, 6 vols. (Cambridge: Cambridge University Press, 2013–), 2:112–13.

90   THE CULTURAL POLITICS OF OPERA, 1720–1742

finding himself "stripped of Rationality, and rank'd among the Brutes." Given the great involvement of the court and nation's social-political elite in the Royal Academy, we may see the ulterior motive of the ministerial paper in defending "the Taste of Persons of the best Sense."

The writer offers a many-pronged defense of opera. He points out that the sole pleasure of music does not consist merely of delight in the sense of sound. Rather, pleasure consists in the perception of the harmony, beauty, or symmetry arising from them; and this perception is an act of the mind. It is no more legitimate to dismiss music as a pleasure of the ear, than to call reading a pleasure of the eye.

If, as proof of its irrationality, music is dismissed merely as an amusement, then one renounces the useful refreshment of the spirits and attentiveness and clearness of mind it offers. Since opera does not profess to be a dramatic entertainment, the rules of the critic are misapplied. A good ear is a better judge of opera than a critic steeped in Rapin, Aristotle, or Bossu. The writer concludes there is no reason to degrade music or opera as an irrational pleasure, because it is equally capable of expressing with equal force and delicacy "all the nobler Passions and Affections of the Mind" and offering "proper Employment to the Understanding," as do painting or poetry.

The promised letter from the *Craftsman*'s correspondent, but actually Bolingbroke, duly appeared the following week in the *Craftsman*.[64] Appearing while Gibraltar was being bombarded by Spain, the letter now has considerable topical bite and application. In an introductory note, Caleb D'Anvers, as editor, apologized to the *beau monde* of both sexes that the letter "tends so directly to impugn their most darling Entertainments," but he hopes the polite will excuse his indispensable duty to "correct Vice and Folly of all kinds." In deference to the operalovers, D'Anvers sincerely (but ironically) wishes that Britain may prove "the singular Instance of a Nation, upon whose Morals Luxury, Corruption and unmanly Diversions shall have no Influence."

But D'Anvers presses on. When he challenges "if any Gentleman of the *Academy* thinks that he can refute these objections, and prove that no bad Consequences ought to be justly apprehended from such *Entertainments* in a *warlike* and *Trading* Nation," he has launched the innuendo that Great Britain *is* on the verge of succumbing to luxury, corruption, and unmanly diversions due to opera at the Royal Academy.

Writing while British troops are awaiting attack at Gibraltar, Bolingbroke writes as if Britain were at a classic Machiavellian moment: faced both with a threat abroad as well as the internal corruption caused by luxury and opera.

---

[64] The *Craftsman*'s letter (no. 28, 10–13 March 1727) was included in the collected reprint edition of the *Craftsman* and reprinted as the essay "On Luxury" in Bolingbroke's *A Collection of Political Tracts* (1747), 72–8, and later editions of his collected works (all the reprints lack the introductory epigraph and introduction to the letter found in the original *Craftsman* folio half-sheet newspaper); the essay is therefore not included in *Lord Bolingbroke: Contributions to the Craftsman*, ed. Simon Varey (Oxford: Clarendon Press, 1982), which includes previously unreprinted essays.

OPERA AND THE LUXURY DEBATE   91

Fortuna and *virtù* hang in the balance, and so does Britain's liberty. His letter attempts a causal relation between luxury and political decline, a relation he proves by historical example.

The epigraph Bolingbroke chose for his letter merits reprinting in its entirety, for the passage from Cicero's *De Legibus* is a canonic statement of the classical republican belief about the relation between the arts, public spirit, and health of a polis – but specifically about the corrupting effect of effeminate music on the people.

> Assentior *Platoni*, nihil tam facile in animos teneros atque molles influere quam varios canendi sonos, quorum dici vix potest quanta sit vis in utramque partem, namque et incitat languentes, et languefacit exitatos, et tum remittit animos, tum contrahit: civitatumque hoc multarum in *Græcia* interfuit, antiquum vocum servare modum: quorum mores lapsi ad mollitiem, pariter sunt immutati cum cantibus; aut hac dulcedine, corruptelaque depravati.

> For I agree with Plato that nothing gains an influence so easily over youthful and impressionable minds as the various notes of song, the greatness of whose power both for good and evil can hardly be set forth in words. For it arouses the languid, and calms the excited; now it restrains our desire, now gives them free rein. Many Greek States considered it important to retain their old tunes; but when their songs became less manly, their characters turned to effeminacy at the same time, perhaps because they were corrupted by the sweetness and debilitating seductiveness of the new music.[65]

In the letter proper, Bolingbroke begins by acknowledging the objection that a "Discourse on *Operas* and the gayer pleasures of the Town may seem to be too trifling for the important scene of affairs in which we are at present engaged." But he fears that opera and such gayer pleasures will, in fact, play too great a role in the present engagement at Gibraltar to be dismissed.

His strategy is revealed when he immediately dips into history to offer a general truth that "every Nation has made either a great or inconsiderable figure in the world, as it has fallen into Luxury or resisted its temptations." As examples of once-great peoples who rose with virtue and declined with luxury, Bolingbroke cites the Persians under Cyrus, the Spartans, and the Romans. He hopes future historians may not furnish "more modern Examples" – by which he certainly means Britain.

Bolingbroke restates the commonplace causal connection between luxury and political decline: luxury enervates the mind, fills it with "soft ideas, and wanton delicacies," and a man becomes incapable of "the great and generous sentiments which virtue inspires" – let alone able to put them into action. He bolsters this claim with appeals to history. Bolingbroke claims the republic of Athens was destroyed by the actions of Pericles who "debauched the people's mind with Shews and Festivals, and all the study'd arts of Ease and Luxury" that he might rule more easily. Tiberius refused to restrain luxury when so

---

[65] Cicero, *De Legibus*, 2.15.37 (Loeb Classical Library translation). The mention of Plato refers to the *Republic* 4.424D.

92   THE CULTURAL POLITICS OF OPERA, 1720–1742

requested by the Senate because he knew it was the surest instrument of arbitrary power. And Cyrus, when the Lydians had revolted from his rule, was advised to encourage them to lay down their arms and take up singing, drinking, and debauchery, which broke their spirits and feminized them so they were again easily subjugated.

Direct attacks on a people's liberties are uncertain of success, Bolingbroke believes, and suspicious people can easily be aroused to action. But more dangerous is the statesman ("the darling Son of Machiavel and Tacitus") who disguises threats to liberty with lavish "Baits of Pleasure." The unaware populace becomes the instrument of its own slavery. "Artful Princes," historians teach, have known the effect of luxury and have intentionally introduced or sanctioned it to cause a people to slip into subjection to despots or tyrants. But history can teach us lessons and "bid us be wise in time, before Luxury has made too great a progress among us." Britain in March 1727, in other words, is at a Machiavellian moment, when by a willful exertion of virtue and public spirit, she can stave off the progress of luxury.

Bolingbroke now turns to the present and indicts the "*Operas* and *Masquerades* and all the politer elegancies of a wanton age" for their tendency to corrupt manners, which is of greater concern than their expense. Joining Cicero in endorsing Plato, he asserts that

> Musick has something so peculiar in it, that it exerts a willing Tyranny over the mind, and forms the ductil Soul into whatever shape the melody directs. Wise nations have observ'd its influence, and have therefore kept it under proper regulations.

Realizing music can be used for good or ill, Bolingbroke recalls how it was regulated by the ancients: the Spartans removed the extra strings Timotheus added to the lyre, which lent his music "a degree of Softness inconsistent with their discipline." Noble, manly music can encourage virtue and heroism; the effect of Italian opera is the opposite. Bolingbroke describes how "the soft *Italian* musick relaxes and unnerves the Soul, and sinks it into weakness; so that while we receive their [the Italians'] Musick, we at the same time are adopting their manners."

Bolingbroke closes the letter with his most immediate application to the besieged officers at Gibraltar. He recalls the story of the people of Sybaris, who indulged luxury and the arts to such a degree that they taught their horses to move in formation at the direction of music. Their enemies, the people of Crotona, observed this and during a battle played harps and pipes; the horses began to dance, and the whole army and people were destroyed. Bolingbroke thinks the story a bit fabulous but believes the moral a very good one: "What effect *Italian* Musick might have on our polite Warriors at *Gibraltar*, I can't take upon me to say; but I wish our Luxury at home, may not influence their Courage abroad."

Bolingbroke's fear about the dangers luxury posed to the British success at Gibraltar was echoed by Mary Davys, in the Dedication to her play *The Accomplished Rake: or, Modern Fine Gentleman* (1727). She satirically reported that the *beaux* of Great Britain were likely to stay home to guard their own selves and the ladies by gallantries, rather than engage in a real fight with the Spanish for military valor.

MANDEVILLE AGAINST DENNIS

About the supposed effect of luxury on the soldier, Mandeville and Dennis had different opinions. Mandeville had specifically considered the effect of luxury on the military. In the last war, he said, the *beaux* of Flanders and Spain proved themselves brave soldiers, as did wild rakes. In any case, the common soldier is too poor to be subject to luxury, and the work of soldiers is too arduous for them to be subject to luxury's "effeminating and enervating" effects. The officers are too burdened with the expense of clothes and equipages to have money for luxury, and moreover their love of honor will render them brave and valorous.[66]

On luxury and the military, though, Dennis agrees with Bolingbroke and argues that luxury, especially of officers, is enervating and corrupting, and its effect is especially demoralizing on armies. He uses the examples of Hannibal and Pompey at Pharsalia to show how "Temperate Armies were Victorious over Luxurious ones." Perhaps lest his similar indictment of the corrupt morals during the reign of Queen Anne be brought up to refute the validity of his historical claims, Dennis states, "If in the late War we overthrew the *French*, in spight of all our Luxury, our Victories were partly owning to this, That we had to do with an Enemy, whose Manners were still more corrupt and more abandon'd, and had been longer so, than our own."[67]

In the context of the *Craftsman*, the political implications of a letter on luxury – and with Bolingbroke's theory of history in the background – are clear. A reiterated theme of the *Craftsman* was that Walpole and his administration were corrupting politics with money, which brought with it vice and luxury. Given the commonly accepted parallels of Britain with Rome and other ancient states and the application of the lessons of history, the pervasiveness of corruption and luxury prophesied disaster for contemporary Britain.[68] The unnamed "Statesman form'd for Ruin and Destruction, whose wily head knows how to disguise the fatal hooks with Baits of Pleasure, which his artful Ambition dispenses with a lavish hand" could be none but Walpole. Fortunately, history teaches Bolingbroke to be aware of the danger. With a causal link between Walpole, corruption, and luxury established, the lesson of the innuendo is clear: remove the source of luxury and corruption, and Britain could be saved.

To what extent could operas and masquerades plausibly be believed to be a deliberate program by Walpole or an "Artful Prince" to enslave the people? Contemporaries surely would have known of George I's fondness for opera, his annual bounty to the King's theatre, and Walpole's and other ministers' own roles as operagoers, directors, and shareholders in the Royal Academy of Music.

The *Craftsman* had prepared the ground for Bolingbroke's essay on luxury and opera in numerous essays. Rehearsing commonplaces of the Catonic, Old

---

[66] *Fable of the Bees*, Remark L, Kaye ed., 1:119–23.

[67] Dennis, *Vice and Luxury Publick Mischiefs*, 56–7 (quoted), 60–70, 69, 69–70.

[68] Sekora, *Luxury*, 86–9.

94 THE CULTURAL POLITICS OF OPERA, 1720–1742

Whig, and classical republican tradition, these essays set out a causal connection between political corruption, luxury, and the health of a state. A nation's health, ran the conventional argument, depends on the aggregation of the individual citizens' virtues of temperance and frugality to foster public spirit and preserve the republic.

In the earlier issue announcing Bolingbroke's letter, the *Craftsman* for 17 February 1727 gave an empirical demonstration of how corruption and luxury do their work. The *Craftsman* describes in general how "*Popularity* amongst the *chief Persons* of any nation" is most dangerous when "it is cultivated by *venal* and *corrupt* methods." It is easiest to gain the assent of the persons of a borough, county, or nation "in a vicious and deprav'd Age, ... for when once Luxury has fix'd a deep Root in their minds, ... it will emasculate, soften and melt down all those stubborn virtues, which are the natural Effects of Temperance and frugality." In government, "a man thus debauched and effeminated" is most susceptible to be persuaded by "the Rhetorick of a *thousand pounds a year*" instead of his country's good. Although only an unnamed British example of "a *Great Man*" is cited, the innuendo is that these are the methods the present prime minister uses to maintain power.

In the issue preceding Bolingbroke's letter, the *Craftsman* for 10 March 1727 describes how nothing is more dangerous to a state than "a Political Lethargy" among the people that allows public ministers the discretion and temptation to pursue with impunity their ambitions unnoticed. Political lethargy is caused by "a general Spirit of Luxury and Profusion, or a prevailing Appetite to soft effeminate inventions and wanton Entertainments." Among such entertainments, Italian opera is no doubt in the author's mind. When people are engrossed in voluptuousness and corruption, they attend only to "the pursuits of private pleasure" and divert their "Thoughts from reflecting on other Matters of the utmost Consequence." The *Craftsman* reminds Britons that the Roman Commonwealth was subverted by corruption and luxury, and England nearly was so too "in the luxurious Reign of King *Charles* the Second." With po-faced irony, the *Craftsman* floats a clear innuendo against the Walpole ministry: "But it is the peculiar Blessing of this Nation at present, that we live under an Administration, which does not stand in need of any such Arts to blind the Eyes of the People, or lay us asleep in *Luxury* and *Indolence*."[69]

A later *Craftsman* for 24 June 1727 proposes to the give the reader seven infallible marks by which to discover a wicked, corrupt administration. One is "a general vein of *Luxury*, and a prevailing Fondness for *Effeminate*, *costly* or *Libertine* Entertainments," certainly pointing to opera.[70]

Decrying the effect of corruption and luxury upon public spirit and placing blame squarely on the Walpole ministry was a staple of Opposition newspapers and pamphleteering. Two years later in a tract *Observations on Publick Affairs* (1729), Bolingbroke would again state the causal relation between the

[69] *Craftsman*, no. 27 (6–10 March 1727).
[70] *Craftsman*, no. 51 (24 June 1727).

private vice of luxury and a state's decline.[71] In the same year, the *Craftsman* would warn of luxury, which has spread throughout Britain, and state the need for "good and effectual Laws for restraining of Luxury," which "must infallibly ruin this Kingdom."[72]

MINISTERIAL DEFENSE OF LUXURY

Ministerial writers did not allow the denunciations of luxury (and implicitly opera) to go unanswered.[73] The month following Bolingbroke's letter, a writer to the ministerial *British Journal* offered a defense against blanket attacks on luxury by leveling the usual ministerial charge about the motives of those in opposition: "General Satires and Reflections on whole Societies of Men, made without any manner of Distinction" are the effects of the "Ill-nature," "Spleen and Disgust" of those not in the government; the greater their disappointment, the harsher their denunciations.[74] Especially objectionable to the writer are the "grievous Complaints and Murmurings against the *Age* in which People happen to live, as more vicious, more corrupt, and in every respect inferior to any of the foregoing" – a charge, he says, that has been made in every age. The contrary is true: "the World, at this present Time, is much more advanced, both in Virtue and Knowledge, beyond what it was some Years ago."

Times have changed since the simple, rural ideal of the Roman Republic or rural England and the freeholder before the Financial Revolution – which is the idealized vision of Old Whig ideology. England is reaping the fruits of the rise of trade and commerce. It is such wealth that is the necessary basis for cultivation of arts and science – of which opera is evidence.

The correspondent grants that Britons live "more Expensively," but, reflecting the Modern Whig ideology, says this is due not to a loss in national "Virtue" but to an increase in arts, sciences, trade, riches, and manufactures. Vanity and luxury have occurred in every age, and, as in every age, some people do deserve censure. Luxurious items in themselves are not harmful; luxury becomes a vice when people become too passionately attached to it and pursue it inordinately. The great increase in trade and riches would be of no use, were we to revert to the "plain and frugal Ways of our Forefathers" with their "Innocence and Virtue."

If we Britons were, as the *Craftsman* charges, "in reality so much further gone in Luxury than our Ancestors, we should undoubtedly see the ill Effects of

---

[71] *Observations on the Publick Affairs of Great-Britain. With Some Toughts [sic] on the Treaty Concluded … between His Catholick Majesty and the King of Great-Britain* (1729).

[72] *Craftsman*, no. 178 (29 Nov. 1729).

[73] For example, *Free Briton*, no. 128 (11 May 1732), which replies to *Craftsman*, no. 304 (29 April 1732).

[74] *British Journal*, no. 241 (29 April 1727). On ministerial uses of Mandeville's ideas: J. A. Gunn, "Mandeville: Poverty, Luxury and the Whig Theory of Government," pp. 12–17 in *Political Theory and Political Economy: Papers from the Annual Meeting of the Conference for the Study of Political Thought*, 1974, ed. Crawford M. Macpherson (Toronto, Canada: n.p., [1975].

THE CULTURAL POLITICS OF OPERA, 1720–1742

it in the Decay of Arts and Sciences, of Trade and Industry; or else in the breaking out of Fraud, Rapine, and Violence, to a greater Degree than among our Ancestors." The writer's defense against the charge of rampant luxury in Britain is simple: "We see none of these Things; and, on the contrary, find Learning and Commerce flourishing as much, or more than formerly." Britons, then, ought to look upon Opposition writers as "Enemies and Monsters" when they portray their countrymen as "a Race of profligate abandon'd Creatures, entirely lost to all Sense of Honour, Virute, and Goodness."

FOG'S WEEKLY JOURNAL

Luxury and opera was still a vital topic during the period when London had the two competing opera companies, Handel's and the Opera of the Nobility with its star castrato Farinelli. In April 1735, almost as if engaging in the luxury debate of 1727, *Fog's Weekly Journal* devoted two issues to a vigorous declaration of the dangers of the "extravagant Increase of Luxury in this Nation, which has shewn itself in that furious Passion with which People follow Opera's, Masquerades, Assemblies Ridotto's, &c."[75] The pair of essays are a compendium of all the vitriol against opera as an effeminate pleasure and the degeneracies it leads to, and summary of the historical instances of luxury leading to the destruction of a people's liberty. The second essay lets loose special spite against Farinelli.

The writer to *Fog's* leads off the first essay quoting the Roman satirist Juvenal's notorious Sixth Satire, where he describes the "Depravity of Manners of the Patricians of Rome," who had "lost even the Sense of Liberty":

> Nunc patimur longæ pacis mala – sævior armis
> Luxuria incubuit, victumque ulciscitur orbem.[76]

This he translates as "We now suffer the Miseries of a long Peace, and Luxury, a greater Plague than War, has reveng'd the conquer'd World." The writer to *Fog's* is surely counting on his reader to make the parallel to Britain. As a satirist, Juvenal's lines might be thought extravagant, so the writer supports his point by quoting a tag from Augustine as "a grave Historian" –

> Asiatica luxuria Romam omni hoste pejor inrepsit[77]

– which he translates as "The Luxury of Asia was more destructive to *Rome* than all its Enemies."

With further support from Tacitus and Machiavelli on the destruction caused by luxury,[78] he trembles at the "Height it is risen within a few Years in this Nation." Looking around at Britain to show "we can vie in Luxury with *Rome* itself, even in its most corrupt Days," he parades opera (one of the "effeminate Pleasures of *Italy*"), opera directors, singers, and "squeaking" eunuchs as consequences of corruption and luxury.

---

[75] *Fog's Weekly Journal*, nos. 335 and 338 (5 April and 26 April 1735).
[76] Juvenal, *Satires*, VI.292–3.
[77] Augustine, *De Civitate Dei*, 6.21 (correcting *Fog's*, which has "irrepsit").
[78] The writer seems to have in mind Machiavelli, *Discourses on Livy*, II.19.

OPERA AND THE LUXURY DEBATE   97

Never was there a time when Britain deserved the scourge of the most severe satire of "our *English* Horace," probably intending Alexander Pope. There is an ample field of fashionably dissolute ladies and effeminate men and who can serve as targets for his satire. All share a passion for opera or masquerade, which are instances of "the effeminate Pleasures of *Italy* introduced amongst us, at such an immense Expence." The mention of expenses lavished on *castrati* probably reflects Farinelli's spectacular 1735 benefit concert, which took place the previous month (see Chapter 6).

The writer to *Fog's* says he can represent "Patricians, Place-Men and Pensioners ambitiously aspiring to the Glory of being Directors of a Band of Fiddlers" or "settling the important Point of a proper Trimming for *Cuzzoni's* Tail." Or he can show matrons presenting a rich jewel "to the squeaking Eunuch" or putting a bank note into a gold case and giving it to "the warbling Charmer of her foolish Heart." Recalling the rivalry between Faustina and Cuzzoni, the satirist can "represent the fiddling World breaking out into a Civil war, ready to draw the Sword about the Merit of two Rival Singers," or ministers of state "squandering away the Wages of their Prostitution upon Fiddlers and Singers."

But as with Juvenal, it is against the misplaced adulation for the castrato singer (and here Farinelli is likely in mind) that the satirist must direct most of his ire.[79]

> Let him laugh at the ridiculous Phrenzy of hiring an Eunuch with the Pay of more than ten Centurions ... and of hundreds of the most useful and ingenious Artists; let him represent him [the castrato] as lolling in his gilded Car with his Livery-Slaves about him, or with titled Fools watching at his Gate, vying who shall first have the Honour to entertain him.
>
> Let him paint all the Foppery and Effeminacy of the Coxcombs of both Sexes, their affected Transports, their languishing, their dying away, when the Eunuch opens his wide Mouth, and stretches his Voice till it cracks; in fine, let him render them as ridiculous to the whole World as they are already to Men of Sense.
>
> It is high Time to give back to *Italy* its Eunuchs and its Singers; it is Time to rouse from this Effeminacy, which is the Consequence of such enervating Entertainments; it is Time to resume a little common Sense, and to banish every Thing that may prepare us for Bondage.

If that screed didn't make his point, the second essay more calmly resumes the topic. He reviews the history of the theatre in the Athenian republic to show that "too great an Attention to Theatrical Entertainments enervated the bravest and wisest People of antient *Greece*" and "diverted their Thoughts from the Consideration of the publick Good, which certainly ought to be the principal Object of a brave and free People." The writer grants that, nevertheless, Greek tragedies might have been written to commend virtue and honor so that a moral might insensibly steal into the soul or some instruction be drawn from the comedies. But such a defense cannot be offered for the "effeminate and expensive" operas that contribute to the present corruption of Britain. He

---

[79] Cf. Juvenal: "when a soft eunuch marries, ... it is harder *not* to be writing satires"; *Satires*, I.22 and 29.

challenges anyone to show how opera or hearing Farinelli has improved any-one's life:

> Has he mended their corrupt Hearts? Will the finest Opera that ever was heard make a Man asham'd of his Follies or teach him to leave off some silly Habit that might make him ridiculous? I have seen Hundreds of both Sexes that have become extremely ridiculous, and are almost turn'd to fools, by frequenting Opera's; but never yet of any one Person that was cured of being ridiculous by it.

Not one of the many justifications for tragedy can be found in opera.

* * *

The longstanding and continuing debate over luxury, corruption, vice, and virtue has been related at some length because opera was caught up in such a wide-ranging field of cultural-sociological-political controversy. The contested valuation of opera aligned with the divergent Country-Old Whig-Catonic versus Ciceronian-Modern Whig views of the Opposition and Walpole's ministry.

For Ciceronian Modern Whigs of the Ministry, luxury was no evil, and opera was a benign and welcome consequence of Britain's growing commercial and financial prosperity. For an opportunistic Opposition grounding its rhetoric in Catonic, Old Whig, or Country ideals, opera – expensive, sensuous, irrational, dominated by foreign singers – was easily demonized as a highly visible sign of the rampant ills spawned by the ruling Whig oligarchy and Walpole's ministry. With their emphasis on the primacy of personal virtue for the maintenance of liberty and the republic, oppositional writers could claim a people in the thralls of opera was a nation diverted from pursuing civic virtue and the public good, and one in need of redemption and political reformation.

CHAPTER 5

Excise and the Patriot Opposition

Walpole's greatest ministerial miscalculation was his proposal for reform of the Excise in 1733.[1] The furor over it spilled over into cultural politics when the Opposition press made a comparison between both unpopular measures: Walpole's Excise and Handel's raising tickets for *Deborah*.[2]

The Treasury had been losing revenue because of smuggling, especially of tobacco and wine. Walpole's plan was to recover more revenue by collecting duties on tobacco and wine when they were withdrawn from bonded customs warehouses for retail, rather than applying duties upon import (when they were easily evaded). The proposal would require additional Excise officers who could search the homes and shops of merchants for contraband; a system of judges would be set up to settle disputes between excise officers and merchants. Walpole argued the plan would eliminate fraud, increase revenue, simplify tax collection, encourage trade and manufacture, and benefit the common trader and consumers by lower prices. Ultimately, the plan would benefit the country gentlemen by lowering the land tax.

Even before Walpole disclosed his plan to the Commons on 14 March 1733, the Opposition caught wind of it in October.[3] Walpole's policies were always unpopular with the City commercial interests, and the Excise especially raised their ire and immediately unleashed a torrent of propaganda that vilified Walpole and all aspects of the plan, claiming the Excise meant loss of liberties, tyranny by Excisemen, increased power of the Ministry, a danger to trade, and an increased tax burden on the poorer parts of society.[4] Propagandists raised the

---

[1] On the Excise, Paul Langford, *The Excise Crisis: Society and Politics in the Age of Walpole* (Oxford: Clarendon Press, 1975); *The Historical Register*, 18 (1733), 130–68, 241–5, and 258–336; and William Coxe, *Memoirs of the Life and Administration of Sir Robert Walpole*, 3 vols. (1798), 1:372–407. On the polemical literature about the Excise, E. Raymond Turner, "The Excise Scheme of 1733," *English Historical Review*, 42 (1927), 34–57. For its consequences for the world of opera, the episode is summarized in Thomas McGeary, *The Politics of Opera in Handel's Britain* (Cambridge: Cambridge University Press, 2013), upon which this chapter draws.

[2] The Deborah scandal is described in McGeary, *The Politics of Opera in Handel's Britain*, 135–45.

[3] See *Craftsman*, no. 330 (28 Oct. 1732), and following issues.

[4] On City opposition to Walpole, Nicholas Rogers, *Whigs and Cities: Politics in the Age of Walpole and Pitt* (Oxford: Clarendon, 1989), esp. pp. 46–86; and Rogers, "Resistance to Oligarchy: The City Opposition to Walpole and his Successors, 1725–47," pp. 1–25 in John Stevens, ed., *London in the Age of Reform*, pp. 1–29 (Oxford: Blackwell,

specter of a country overrun by Excise officers and of merchants hauled before commissions appointed by the Treasury. The Excise was seen as a rapacious attempt by Walpole to increase treasury funds, which he could use to corrupt politics and enrich himself.

Historians consider the proposal was a sound way to reform government finances and reduce taxation; they see Opposition polemic as partisan fanning of hysteria and a willful distortion of the proposal, although there was indeed potential for abuse.[5]

The first reading of the bill carried 232 to 176, but support fell on further procedural votes. Faced with mounting public outcry, mob demonstrations, streams of petitions, and dwindling parliamentary support, Walpole knew he faced defeat and allowed the Excise to die by postponing its second reading until a day that Parliament would not sit. Failure of the Excise was due mainly to collapse of support by the independent Whig MPs.

At the news, the country rejoiced with bonfires, illuminations, ringing of bells, and burning Walpole in effigy. Although Walpole survived the Excise crisis, the future Earl of Egmont, Sir John Perceval, a government supporter, foresaw correctly, "Sir Robert Walpole's influence in the House will never again be so great as it has been, ... for the Crown will hardly attempt anything unreasonable for the future."[6]

The summer election of 1734 was highly contested, rancorous, and expensive, but the Opposition was unable to capitalize on a public inflamed by the Excise.[7] In the new Commons, Walpole commanded a more than ninety-five-seat majority, but the house would never again be as compliant as before the Excise.

1977).The proposal was attacked in political prints; see Milton Percival, *Political Ballads Illustrating the Administration of Sir Robert Walpole*. Oxford Historical and Literary Studies, 8 (1916), 61–81; Paul Langford, *Walpole and the Robinocracy. The English Satirical Print 1600–1832* (Cambridge: Chadwyck-Healey, 1986), Plates 22–32; M. Dorothy George, *English Political Caricature to 1792: A Study of Opinion and Propaganda*, 2 vols. (Oxford: Clarendon Press, 1959), 1:81–3; and Herbert Atherton, *Political Prints in the Age of Hogarth: A Study of the Ideographic Representation of Politics* (Oxford: Clarendon, 1974), 153–62, Plates 11–16. Plays touching on the Excise include the ballad operas, *The Honest Electors, Court Legacy, Rome Excis'd, The Sturdy Beggars, The Commodity Excis'd, The State Juggler,* and *Lord Blunder's Confession* (all 1733), and even as late as Henry Fielding's farce *Eurydice* (1737). On the popular oppositions and then celebrations of the defeat, Kathleen Wilson, *The Sense of the People: Politics, Culture and Imperialism in England, 1715–1785* (Cambridge: Cambridge University Press, 1995), 124–32, 157–8, 326–7, 393.

[5] J. H. Plumb, *England in the Eighteenth Century* (Harmondsworth: Penguin, 1950), 65–6.

[6] John Perceval (Earl of Egmont). *Manuscripts of the Earl of Egmont. Diary of Viscount Percival, afterwards First Earl of Egmont*, 3 vols. (London: His Majesty's Stationery Office), 1930, 1:361.

[7] Plumb provides a lively description of the summer election in *Sir Robert Walpole: The King's Minister* (London: Cresset, 1960), 314–24.

As a consequence of the Excise, arose a new opposition, one that can be called the "Patriot Opposition."[8] One of the peers (along with the Duke of Montrose, Earl of Stair, Earl of Marchmont, and Duke of Bolton) suffering retaliation for speaking out against the Excise was Lord Cobham (Richard Temple, later first Viscount), military hero from the Marlborough campaigns.[9] Cobham was dismissed from his regimental command in June 1733, and J. H. Plumb explains Cobham's anger: "This [loss of a command] astounded society. A colonel's regiment, purchased for hard cash, was regarded as his freehold. To be so deprived for a political offence looked like robbery."[10]

The opposition to the Excise by the Earl of Chesterfield, Lord Steward of the Household, led to his dismissal by the King and exchanges between the Opposition *Craftsman* and ministerial *Free Briton* about the justness of the dismissal. That month, Handel dismissed Senesino from his opera company (see Chapter 6), and the *Craftsman* drew a parallel between the two events, and its reporting made propaganda to remind readers of the King's retribution to a statesman who had spoken out again the measure.[11] Chesterfield was followed into the Opposition by Lord Wilmington, the Duke of Dorset, and the Earl of Scarborough. Walpole's retribution alienated many lords and swelled the ranks of the permanent opposition.[12] To reward loyalty, Walpole found places and rewards for the Duke of Argyll, Earl of Islay, Earl of Wilmington, Lord Talbot, Philip York, and Lord Hervey.[13]

---

[8] I limit the term "Patriot" Opposition to this group assembled by Cobham and rallying behind the figurehead of Prince Frederick, as distinct from the earlier "Scriblerian" opposition begun in 1726 led by Bolingbroke and Pulteney in the Commons with the *Craftsman* as its main voice and aided by major satires by Gay, Swift, and Pope. Here I follow Bertrand Goldgar, *Walpole and the Wits: The Relation of Politics to Literature, 1722–1742* (Lincoln, Nebr.: University of Nebraska Press, 1976), who distinguishes the "wits" from the "Patriots." Christine Gerrard, *The Patriot Opposition to Walpole: Politics, Poetry, and National Myth, 1725–1742* (Oxford: Clarendon, 1994), yokes all opposition to Walpole under Patriots, thus in the first half of her book blurring the distinction; see also Goldgar's reservation about her use in his review in *Modern Philology*, 94 (1997), 393–6 (on p. 394).

[9] How Walpole got the King to dismiss the peers who spoke out is recorded by John Perceval; *The Manuscripts of the Earl of Egmont*, 1:357.

[10] *Walpole: The King's Minister*, 281. The following year, Cobham and others opposed a bill in the Lords to prevent officers from being deprived of their commissions other than by court martial or address of a house of Parliament, which further alienated them from the king. See *The Lords Protests in the Late Session of Parliament* (1734), no. 1.

[11] The Senesino/Chesterfield to King/Handel parallel is discussed in McGeary, *The Politics of Opera in Handel's Britain*, 145–6. Further on Chesterfield's dismissal and those who followed him into opposition, *Letters of Philip Dormer Stanhope* [Earl of Chesterfield], ed. and intro. by Bonamy Dobrée, 6 vols. (London: Eyre & Spottiswoode, 1932), 1:68–72:

[12] On the overlooked opposition in the Lords, Clyve Jones, "The House of Lords and the Excise Crisis: The Storm and the Aftermath, 1733–5," *Parliamentary History*, 33 (2014), 160–200.

[13] Plumb, *Walpole: The King's Minister*, 281.

102   THE CULTURAL POLITICS OF OPERA, 1720–1742

In contrast to his earlier quiet parliamentary career, Cobham threw himself into organizing an opposition to Walpole. Using his wealth and influence, he placed his nephews and relations in the Grenville, Lyttelton, and Pitt families in Parliament where they became leading members of the Patriot Opposition.[14]

Cobham's country estate at Stowe became a meeting place for Patriot Opposition politicians, including visits from Alexander Pope and Frederick, Prince of Wales. Even the statuary and monuments in Cobham's Temple of Worthies at Stowe gardens were designed to embody ideas of the Patriots.[15] His extended political family became known (derisively by the Ministry) as "Cobham's Cubs" or the "Boy Patriots." Thomas Pitt, already an MP, followed Cobham, his wife's uncle, into opposition. Richard Grenville was returned in the general election for 1734; William Pitt (Pitt the elder, later Earl of Chatham) and George Lyttelton, both nephews, won seats the following year. George and James Grenville won seats in the 1741 general election. Lyttelton and William Pitt were active and effective speakers in the Commons, with Lyttelton also writing numerous pamphlets and political essays. Lyttelton had been introduced to the Prince of

[14] On Cobham, the formation of his opposition, and the early careers of his nephews and relatives: Goldgar, *Walpole and the Wits*, 132–62; Gerrard, *Patriot Opposition*, 35–44; Matthew Kilburn, "Cobham's Cubs," *Oxford Dictionary of National Biography*, Online ed., October 2016; Archibald S. Foord, *His Majesty's Opposition, 1714–1830* (Oxford: Clarendon Press, 1964), 111–216.

On the individual persons involved: Lewis M. Wiggin, *The Faction of Cousins: A Political Account of the Grenvilles, 1733–1763* (New Haven, Conn.: Yale University Press, 1958), esp. pp. 1–15 and 84–97; Philip Lawson, *George Grenville: A Political Life* (Oxford: Clarendon Press, 1984), 4–7; Basil Williams, *The Life of William Pitt, Earl of Chatham*, 2 vols. (London: Longmans, Green, and Co., 1914), 1:45–71; Jeremy Black, *Pitt the Elder* (Cambridge: Cambridge University Press, 1992), 10–13, 27–8; Peter Douglas Brown, *William Pitt, Earl of Chatham: The Great Commoner* (London: George Allen & Unwin, 1978), 30–45; John B. Owen, *The Rise of the Pelhams* (London: Methuen, 1957); and J. V. Beckett, *The Rise and Fall of the Grenvilles, Duke of Buckingham and Chandos, 1710 to 1921* (Manchester: Manchester University Press, 1994).

[15] The gardens were described by his nephew Gilbert West in *Stowe, the Gardens of ... Viscount Cobham* (1732), dedicated to Pope, an avid gardener, and published by his publisher L. Gilliver; see also William Gilpin, A *Dialogue upon the Gardens ... at Stow [sic]* (1748) [facsimile ed. with intro. by John Dixon Hunt: Augustan Reprint Society, no. 176 (1976)].

On the gardens' political program: George Clarke, "Grecian Taste and Gothic Virtue: Lord Cobham's Gardening Programme and Its Iconography," *Apollo* (June 1973), 566–71; Gerrard, *Patriot Opposition*, 127–9; Francesca Orestano, "Bust Story: Pope at Stowe, or the Politics and Myths of Landscape Gardening," *Studies in the Literary Imagination*, 38 (2005), 39–61; Jonathan Lamb, "The Medium of Publicity and the Garden at Stowe," *Huntington Library Quarterly*, 50 (1987), 374–93.

On Opposition garden political programs in general (including Stowe), Douglas Chambers, *The Planters of the English Landscape Garden: Botany, Trees, and the "Georgics"* (New Haven, Conn.: Yale University Press, 1993), 58–60. (See also Chapter 12, n. 78.)

Wales in 1732 and became an equerry, close adviser, and finally his secretary in August 1737.

A new generation of writers joined the circle now forming around Cobham and Frederick and wrote plays, verse, periodical essays, and pamphlets advancing the Patriot program.[16] Lyttelton seems to have been a catalyst for much of the literary activity.[17] Some writers who gravitated to the new opposition were discouraged by the lack of patronage from the Court or had been turned out of office by Walpole.[18] Although direct personal links to Lyttelton or Frederick cannot always be documented, some writers, such as James Miller and Thomas Gilbert, seem to have had long-standing grievances with Walpole or the government; others were drawn to the Patriot cause by personal associations with the circle of Cobham, Bolingbroke, Frederick, and Pope. By the end of the decade, the group included James Thomson, David Mallet, Richard Glover, Mark Akenside, James Hammond, Paul Whitehead, Miller, and Lyttelton.[19] Pope was sympathetic to the Patriots, and assisted them in various ways, but was not an active member of the circle.

The young politicians recruited by Cobham revived the parliamentary opposition. The ideal of a party motivated by virtue and opposed to corruption provided a more positive ideological center than one of just opposing the Ministry on all points. In this rhetorical garb, the dissident Whigs claimed to be better patriots, interested in the well-being of the nation, offering a vision for Britain's greatness after Walpole and George II passed from the scene. United behind Frederick, Prince of Wales, who became their figurehead, the Opposition could avoid the taint of Jacobitism, although Walpole never gave up raising the charge when opportune.[20]

---

[16] On these Opposition writers and literature, Goldgar, *Walpole and the Wits,* is a detailed study at the level of literary satire and responses by ministerial writers. Gerrard, *Patriot Opposition,* focuses more on the imaginative literature covering the themes of patriotism and the gothic, Elizabethanism, and the mythologized image of a monarch as the Patriot King. Both Goldgar and Gerrard tend to overlook (with the exception of Pope), the formal verse satire as a vehicle of oppositional ideas (see Chapter 10). For a focus on Thomson, James Sambrook, *James Thomson, 1700–1748: A Life* (Oxford: Clarendon, 1991), 128–213.

[17] On Lyttelton as organizer of this literary patronage, Rose Mary Davis, *The Good Lord Lyttelton: A Study in Eighteenth Century Politics and Culture* (Bethlehem, Pa.: Times Publishing Co., 1939), 48–74.

[18] It is not the case that Walpole did not patronize writers. Many of what we recognize as the major writers of the day felt they were not receiving their deserved patronage from the government, as in the era of Queen Anne; this lack of what they felt was their due patronage was a major source of resentment against Walpole by Opposition polemicists; see Goldgar, *Walpole and the Wits, passim.*

[19] The specifics and amounts of patronage for these writers are unclear, although a few instances are known. For David Mallet, Lyttelton procured the place of under secretary to the Prince at £200; James Thomson received a pension of £100 from the Prince in 1737; Richard Glover received a gift of £500.

[20] See Chapter 1, note 32.

104   THE CULTURAL POLITICS OF OPERA, 1720–1742

❧ Frederick: The Patriot King

Frederick's role as figurehead for the Patriots was furthered by his gradual estrangement and then break with his parents.[21] As was the pattern with Hanoverian monarchs, Frederick had strained relations with his father, and Lord Hervey's *Memoirs* record the King and Queen's dislike and disrespect for their eldest son.[22] Frederick resented being left behind in Hanover when his grandfather and father left for Britain in 1714. While Frederick was still in Hanover, the King thwarted his desired marriage with his cousin, the Princess of Prussia.[23]

After his father's accession in June 1727, Frederick remained in Hanover to represent the Electoral interest; his father probably recalled, as in his own case, the mischief an heir at court could cause with Opposition politicians. The ministers, though, prevailed on the King the importance that the heir reside in Britain, and Frederick arrived at St. James's on 4 December 1728, to be invested as Prince of Wales the following month. Frederick chaffed under his parents' control; he was kept short of money and not given his own household. His father and Walpole were no doubt attempting to forestall Frederick from establishing a rival court.

Frederick befriended politicians whose antipathy to Walpole he came to share. As early as February 1729, it was observed that anyone in favor with the Prince "must of consequence be out with the King."[24] By 1733, Frederick's household had become a gathering place of leaders against Walpole: Pulteney, Wyndham, Chesterfield, Cobham, Carteret, and the young Patriots. Although he did not take a direct role in parliamentary politics, Frederick did extend patronage to writers and politicians and spent money backing Opposition candidates in elections, especially his own electoral interest in the Duchy of Cornwall.

A mounting series of crises marked Frederick's worsening relationship with his parents. In June 1733, the King tried to reconcile Frederick and Walpole by offering him one of three princesses to marry, choice of his own servants, and a settlement of £80,000. The Prince politely declined the offer, excusing himself

---

[21] Modern biography: Francis Vivian, *A Life of Frederick, Prince of Wales, 1707–1751: A Connoisseur of the Arts*, ed. Roger White (Lewiston, N.Y.: Edwin Mellen Press, 2006). Most useful of other biographies is Averyl Edwards, *Frederick Louis Prince of Wales, 1707–1751* (London: Staples Press, 1947).

[22] Modern edition of the manuscripts by Romney Sedwick as *Some Materials Towards Memoirs of the Reign of King George II*, 3 vols. (London: Eyre and Spottiswoode, 1931), (hereafter as *Memoirs*). On Hervey's reliability, Vivian, *Frederick, Prince of Wales*, 182–5, 210 and *passim*. On the basis for the dissolution of their friendship, Hannah Smith and Stephen Taylor, "Hephaestion and Alexander: Lord Hervey, Frederick, Prince of Wales, and the Royal Favourite in England in the 1730s," *English Historical Review*, 124, no. 507 (2009), 283–312.

[23] Coxe, *Memoirs of Walpole*, 1: 520–1.

[24] Letter from Anne, Viscountess Irwin, 1 Feb. 1729, to the Earl of Carlisle; in Historical Manuscripts Commission, *Manuscripts of the Earl of Carlisle* (London: Her Majesty's Stationery Office, 1897), 56.

EXCISE AND THE PATRIOT OPPOSITION   105

from reconciling with Walpole.[25] The Princess Royal Anne, his younger sister, was married in March 1734, and received a jointure of £80,000 from Parliament. Frederick considered his sister's marriage before him and the amount of her jointure insults.[26]

In late June 1734, Frederick offended his father when, it was believed on the advice of the Opposition, he burst into his father's presence with three demands: to serve in a campaign in the Rhine; receive an allowance of £100,000, equal to King's when Prince of Wales; and be married. Indignant at the Prince's demands, the King hinted he would consider the second request, but was silent about the others. Walpole urged moderation, the Queen softened the King's anger, and a complete rupture was prevented.[27] Clearly, it was not in the Court's interest to grant, in effect, £100,000 for patronage to support opposition to the Court and Ministry.

Frederick was married on 27 April 1736 to Augusta, Princess of Saxe-Gotha (but not the wife of his choice). The marriage increased Frederick's popularity, but the speeches of William Pitt and George Lyttelton on the motion for an address to the King became political. Pitt and Lyttelton lavished warm panegyric on the Prince; but their cool praise of the King and censure of Walpole made the motion a partisan affair and widened the breach between the King and his son.[28]

Frederick's actions in summer 1737 caused a complete break with his parents and drove him further into opposition. On 31 July, when the Princess began labor while at Hampton Court, Frederick rushed her to St. James's, where she delivered a daughter.[29] Although the Prince justified his action by pointing out that midwives, nurses, and doctors were wanting at Hampton Court, the

---

[25] *Diary of Viscount Percival*, 1:387 (24 June 1733).

[26] Hervey dismissed Frederick's feelings: "One of his wise quarrels with the Princess Royal was her 'daring to be married before him,' and consenting to take a portion from the Parliament, and an establishment from her father, before those honours and favours were conferred upon him. As if her being married prevented his being so, or that the daughter should decline being settled because her father declined the settling of her brother"; Hervey, *Memoirs*, 1:273.

[27] The key account comes from a letter from Mons. de Loss, the Saxon minister to Britain, to his court; reprinted in John Lord Hervey, *Memoirs of the Reign of George the Second*, ed. John W. Croker, 3 vols. (London: Bickers and Son, 1884), 1:319 n. 11; also reported in Coxe, *Memoirs of Walpole*, 1:522.

[28] The speeches on the marriage are given in William Cobbett, *The Parliamentary History of England*, 9 (1733-1737), 1220-5; and Coxe, *Memoirs of Walpole*, 1:524.

[29] On the feud and expulsion from the court's perspective, Hervey, *Memoirs*, 3:756-93, 807-27, 838-9; Philip C. Yorke, *The Life and Correspondence of Philip Yorke, Lord High Chancellor of Great Britain*, 3 vols. (Cambridge: Cambridge University Press, 1913), 1:169-82; and Coxe, *Memoirs of Walpole*, 1:533-46. The feud and expulsion also appear in private correspondence and diaries; see letters to the Countess of Denbigh, in Historical Manuscripts Commission, *Report on the Manuscripts of the Earl of Denbigh* (London: His Majesty's Stationery Office, 1911), 127, 223, 223-4, 225, 226, 228; and Egmont, *Diary of Viscount Percival*, 2:425 ff.

106 THE CULTURAL POLITICS OF OPERA, 1720–1742

King saw the action as dangerous to the Princess and child and a disrespectful act to prevent a potential heir being born at court. Despite Frederick's dutiful submissive and penitential letters, the King would not pardon what he took as defiant contempt of his authority.

Finally, on 10 September, citing the Prince's "undutiful Behaviour" which for so long he had found offensive, the King banished the Prince and his family, and all persons attached to the Prince, from his palace. Seeing Frederick as a tool of the rival politicians, he commanded him to sever all ties with those in the Opposition. As well, the following day, the King announced those with appointments at both courts would have to renounce one of them. The order even affected Handel's relation with the royal family.[30] So strong was the King's desire to humiliate his son that he commanded that copies of his edict and all the letters they exchanged be distributed to members of Parliament, foreign ministers, and courts throughout Europe. They were also reprinted in domestic pamphlets, newspapers, and magazines.[31]

Banished from Court, Frederick established his household at Norfolk House, in St. James's Square, which became a social and political center of the Opposition. London was now divided politically and socially, as in the days of his father. The defection of peers increased as young, ambitious politicians saw that path to power lay with the Opposition and the next King. The death of Queen Caroline on 20 November 1737 deprived Walpole of his greatest supporter at Court and source of influence with the King. The Opposition took some heart, believing he could not govern the King as well as she had.

Frederick served well for a figurehead. He was personable and sociable. An active arts patron, he cultivated his popular appeal, working toward establishing an image as a dutiful and concerned future monarch. His public acts of charity were widely reported in the press.[32] The month of his arrival, when he gave 100 guineas for relief of the poor of St. Martin's Parish, a newspaper reported that "His Royal Highness the Prince of Wales has begun to give a

---

[30] See Thomas McGeary, "Handel and the Feuding Royals," *The Handel Institute Newsletter*, 17 (Autumn 2006), 5–8.

[31] The edict about courtiers quitting one of two places was reported in *Craftsman*, no. 584 (17 Sept. 1737). Due to the edict's not being obeyed, the King reiterated it the following February; see *London Gazette*, no. 7679 (25–28 Feb. 1737/8); and *The Political State of Great-Britain*, 55 (Jan.–June 1738), 243. The letters were published as *Letters ... That Passed between the King, Queen, Prince and Princess of Wales; on Occasion of the Birth of the Young Princess* (1737), and in *The Political State of Great-Britain*, 54 (Nov. 1737), 477–88.

[32] On Frederick and his wife's courting their public image: Christine Gerrard, "Queens-in-waiting: Caroline of Anspach and Augusta of Saxe-Gotha as Princesses of Wales," pp. 143–61 in *Queenship in Britain, 1660–1837*, ed. Clarissa Campbell Orr (Manchester: Manchester University Press, 2002); and John L. Bullion, "'To Play What Game She Pleased without Observation': Princess Augusta and the Political Drama of Succession, 1736–56," pp. 207–35 in *Queenship in Britain*, ed. Orr, 207–15. For a skeptical view of his popularity and patriotism, W. R. Irwin, "Prince Frederick's Mask of Patriotism," *Philological Quarterly*, 27 (1958), 368–84.

Pattern of that Christian Charity which shines in all this Royal Family."[33] Frederick cultivated the small merchants and traders of Bath, Bristol, and London (which were generally opposed to Walpole) and spoke in support of trade and commerce.

On the occasion of his retine of coaches being the first to pass over the newly completed Fulham-Putney bridge, he gave five guineas to the workmen.[34] Newspapers reported his visits to hospitals and his gifts to staff and patients.[35] When fire broke out at the Inner Temple during the night of 4 January 1737, he and several courtiers went to the scene and "by his Presence animated the People, gave Money to the Fireman, &c. and staid till it was quite over." Richard Wilson commemorated the event by a painting.[36] A week later, he presented £500 to release poor freemen from the City of London prison.[37] His progress to Bath and Bristol in October-November 1738 and his popular reception there were widely reported.[38] At Bath, he discharged all the debtors of the city and gave £1,000 to a new hospital. The visit was commemorated by an obelisk (still standing) erected by Beau Nash bearing an inscription by Pope.[39]

Frederick's reputation has suffered from the biased and spiteful accounts of him in Lord Hervey's *Memoirs*, his feud with his parents, his youthful amatory adventures, and his opposition to Handel, which has been greatly exaggerated.[40] His reputation has been rehabilitated by recognition of his serious arts patronage.[41] He was a sincere and knowledgeable connoisseur of the arts, which gained

[33] *La Staffetta Italiana: or, The Italian Post*, no. 7 (30 Jan. 1729).

[34] *Craftsman*, no. 177 (22 Nov. 1729).

[35] For example, during a visit to a hospital near Hyde Park Corner, he gave £50 to the charity and £20 to the servants (*Daily Advertiser*, no. 1149, 4 Oct. 1734); on a visit to Bethlehem Hospital, he gave money to its servants and inmates (*Weekly Register*, no. 296. 1 Nov. 1735).

[36] *London Magazine*, 6 (1737), 50. The Wilson painting, "The Hall of the Inner Temple after the Fire of 4 January 1737" (London, Tate Gallery), is reproduced in *Manners and Morals: Hogarth and British Painting, 1700–1760*, exhib. cat. (London: Tate Gallery, 1987), no. 100.

[37] *London Magazine*, 6 (1737), 50.

[38] Visit to Bath and Bristol: *Gentleman's Magazine*, 8 (Nov. 1738), 602–4; *London Magazine*, 7 (Dec. 1738), 629.

[39] Pope and the Bath inscription: *The Correspondence of Alexander Pope*, ed. George Sherburn, 5 vols. (Oxford: Clarendon Press, 1956), 4:170, 176.

[40] Reconsideration of his relations with Handel and motivation for sponsoring the Opera of the Nobility are given in McGeary, *Politics of Opera in Handel's Britain*, 155–65.

[41] On Frederick's arts patronage: See Kimerly Rorschach, "Frederick, Prince of Wales (1707–1751) as a Patron of the Visual Arts: Princely Patriotism and Political Propaganda," 2 vols. (Ph.D. dissertation, Yale University, 1985); Rorschach, "Frederick, Prince of Wales (1707–51) as Collector and Patron," *Walpole Society*, 55 (1989/1990), 1–76; and Rorschach, "Frederick, Prince of Wales: Taste, Politics and Power," *Apollo*, 134 (1991), 239–45; Gerrard, *Patriot Opposition*, 46–8, 58–67, 195–6; and Vivian, *Life of Frederick, Prince of Wales*, 149–69, 288–304, 314–17, 399–463.

See also Thomas McGeary, "Frederick, Prince of Wales, as Print Collector," *Print Quarterly*, 19 (2002), 254–60; Stephen Jones, "Frederick Prince of Wales: A Patron of

108   THE CULTURAL POLITICS OF OPERA, 1720–1742

the good will of the nation's artists. His patronage of the arts helped establish the prestige of his own court and created bonds with fellow aristocrats. In 1749, Frederick expressed interest in an academy for British painters, which was the occasion for a planned commemorative painting.[42] He collected painting and sculpture, and assisted in documenting the royal collections at Hampton Court.[43] He actively supervised the planting of his own gardens.[44]

Frederick had an avid interest in music and was an amateur cellist and composer.[45] He maintained a musical establishment at his court, hosted rehearsals of operas and oratorios,[46] and offered musical entertainments. Charles Burney would later repeat anecdotes about Handel at the Prince's concerts.[47] He was one of Farinelli's most lavish patrons and acquired manuscripts of four operas

---

the Rococo," pp. 106–12 in *The Rococo in England: A Symposium*, ed. Charles Hind (London: Victoria and Albert Museum, 1986); and Stephen Jones, *Frederick, Prince of Wales and His Circle*, exhib. cat., Gainsborough's House, 6 June–26 July 1981 (Sudbury, Suffolk: Gainsborough's House, 1981). Rorschach, contrary to Jones, minimizes both the importance of the rococo in Frederick's collection and his role in introducing the style into England.

[42] See the *modello* by Francis Hayman, "The Artists Presenting a Plan for an Academy to (?)Frederick, Prince of Wales, and Princess Augusta," *c.* 1750–1751 (Royal Albert Memorial Museum, Exeter); reproduced in *Manners and Morals*, no. 193; discussed further and reproduced in Brian Allen, *Francis Hayman* (New Haven, Conn.,: Yale University Press, 1987), 4–7, 65–6, 122, and Figure 6.

[43] Christopher White, *The Dutch Pictures in the Collection of Her Majesty the Queen* (Cambridge: Cambridge University Press, 1982), l–li.

[44] Ray Desmond, *Kew: The History of the Royal Botanic Gardens* (Kew: The Harvill Press with the Royal Botanic Gardens, 1995), 27–8.

[45] On Frederick and literary figures, Gerrard, *Patriot Opposition*, 46–67; and Thomas McGeary, "Pope and Frederick, Prince of Wales: Gifts and Memorials of Friendship," *Scriblerian*, 33 (2000), 40–7.

On Frederick's household musical establishment and other musical interests, see Peggy Daub, "Music at the Court of George II (*c.* 1727–1760)" (Ph.D. dissertation, Cornell University, 1985). Also, Derek McCulloch, "Royal Composers: The Composing Monarchs That Britain Nearly Had," *Musical Times*, 122 (1981), 525–9, with response by Peggy Daub, "Handel and Frederick," *Musical Times*, 122 (1981), 733.

On Frederick and Handel, Carole Taylor, "Handel and Frederick, Prince of Wales," *Musical Times*, 125 (1984), 89–92; Thomas McGeary, "Handel, Prince Frederick, and the Opera of the Nobility Reconsidered," *Göttinger Händel-Beiträge*, 7 (1998), 156–78; McGeary, "Handel and the Feuding Royals"; and McGeary, "Handel in the *Dunciad*: Pope, Handel, Frederick, Prince of Wales, and Cultural Politics," *Musical Quarterly*, 97 (2015), 542–74. Gerrard, *Patriot Opposition*, overlooks his long-standing relation with Handel.

[46] For example, "Last Night there was a Rehearsal of a new Opera before his Royal Highness the Prince of Wales at his House in Pall-Mall, in which Farinelli and Senesino each of them perform'd a part"; *London Daily Post, and General Advertiser*, no. 24 (30 Nov. 1734). The opera was likely the Nobility Opera's next new production, which was Handel's *Ottone*, produced on 10 December 1734.

[47] Anecdotes of Handel and Prince Frederick are collected in McGeary, "Handel and the Feuding Royals."

composed by Porpora for the Opera of the Nobility in which Farinelli sang.[48] As a patron of letters, Frederick was third only behind his son George III and the Earl of Chesterfield in receiving dedications of books in the eighteenth century.[49] An avid theatregoer, his attendance at a play would result in a bounty to the theatre.[50]

🦋 *Patriot Literature*

The political motives and ideology of writings – both literary and journalistic – that reflect or serve Patriot aims are unmistakable and coherent. The journalism in newspapers and pamphlets deals with topical partisan issues; high literary works in a range of genres contain allusions, subjects, allegories, and parallels that carry an oppositional sentiment.

Verse epics (Glover's *Leonidas*) and serious dramas by Thomson, Mallet, and Brooke (*Agamemnon, Sophonisba, Edward and Eleonora, Mustapha, Gustavus Vasa, Alfred*), although on distant historical subjects, have topical application. The plays derive their political effectiveness when characters on stage make speeches about past evil ministers, statesmen, or tyrants that could apply to a contemporary political figure (usually Walpole). The partisan nature of these plays was obvious and confirmed by comments in personal correspondence or the Opposition press; the Ministry reacted by banning or attacking the plays and their authors.[51]

Larded throughout many high literary forms, such as the formal verse satires of Pope, Johnson, Miller, and Gilbert (see Chapter 10), are laments over Britain's forlorn and fallen state, loss of liberty and virtue, and decline of the arts and sciences. Paeans to liberty, while part of long-standing Whig writing, now are implicit claims that Walpole's ministry is suppressing British liberties. Passing topical references to British shipping and sailors suffering from Spanish depredations in the West Indies will bring to mind long-standing claims that Walpole is unwilling or unable to protect British shipping and sailors from the Spanish *garda costas* (see Chapter 7). Patriot ideas that engage the cultural politics of opera are found in verse allegories by Thomson, Hill, and Miller (see Chapter 8).

It must be cautioned, though, that the mere presence of patriot themes (such as the Whig cry for liberty) need not mark a work as part of the Patriot movement; other contextual cues are needed. But the key to understanding the implicit oppositional nature of such literature is the answer to the question

---

[48] These are the manuscripts of *Arianna in Nasso* and *Enea nel Lazio* (1733–34 season) and *Polifemo* and *Iphigenia in Aulide* (1734–35 season); the scores are presently in the Royal Music Library, British Library: RM 22 m 29–31, RM 23a 1–3, RM 23a 7–9, and RMa 4–6, respectively.

[49] Pat Rogers, "Book Dedications in Britain, 1700–1799: A Preliminary Survey," *British Journal for Eighteenth-Century Studies,* 16 (1993), 222.

[50] Vivian, *Life of Frederick, Prince of Wales*, 452–62.

[51] On the politics of these plays, McGeary, *Politics of Opera in Handel's Britain*, 180–209.

110 THE CULTURAL POLITICS OF OPERA, 1720–1742

Cui bono? The innuendo, as in most Opposition propaganda, is clear: remove Walpole and Britain will be rescued – often with the arrival of the Patriot King.

Although the *Craftsman* continued to be published into the 1740s,[52] its importance was superseded by the fresh spirit and literary quality brought by two new newspapers: *Common Sense* with contributions by George Lyttelton and Lord Chesterfield,[53] and later Henry Fielding's *The Champion* (1739–43).

Unlike the earlier Scriblerian satire of Jonathan Swift, John Arbuthnot, and the early Alexander Pope, the tone of Patriot literature is more positive and has a hortatory tone. As counterbalance to the vices and corruption lashed by the satirist are paeans to liberty, virtue, Frederick, and Opposition statesmen. As a rebuke to the present ministry and Britain's forlorn condition, Patriot literature holds up Britain's once-great sea power and British Worthies (Elizabeth, Milton, Handel) as proof of Britain's native genius and faith that Britain's glory will be revived under a new king.

Often present in Patriot writings is the reversionary interest: now with an aging monarch on the throne, instead of just agitating against Walpole, Patriot writers – to balance their portrayals of corrupted Britain – hold up the vision of a regenerated Britain under Frederick, Prince of Wales.

The ideal of a messianic leader that was often applied to Frederick was articulated in Bolingbroke's *The Idea of a Patriot King*, written about 1738 and circulated in Patriot circles in manuscript and print.[54] Also prominent in Patriot works is the idea of a Britain at a Machiavellian moment.[55] At a crucial moment in history, Britain faces danger from external or internal corruption: Britain must challenge *fortuna* with revitalized virtue and Publick Spirit. Removing Walpole and placing hopes in a model of kingship that will be realized in the future is, of course, a rebuke of the reigning monarch.

The political intent and force of Patriot literature was obvious to Walpole's own propagandists. With his writers consolidated behind the *Daily Gazetteer*, the Ministry carried out systematic attacks on the writings and persons of Pope, Bolingbroke, Whitehead, Mallet, Thomson, and those whom they called

---

[52] Gerrard repeatedly refers to the demise of the *Craftsman* with the founding of *Common Sense* (see *Patriot Opposition*, pp. 39 and 42).

[53] *Common Sense* began on 5 February 1737. When *Fog's Weekly Journal* ceased publication, it transferred its subscribers and advertisers to *Common Sense*; see notice in the last issue of *Fog's*, no. 22, n.s. (29 Oct. 1737), 3.

Chesterfield's political writings are collected in Philip Dormer Stanhope (Lord Chesterfield), *Miscellaneous Works*, 3 vols. (1777–1778); and those of Lyttelton in *The Works of George Lord Lyttelton* (1776).

[54] On publication of the *Idea of the Patriot King*: Dickinson, *Bolingbroke*, 280–2, 290–4; and Giles Barber, "Bolingbroke, Pope and the Patriot King," *The Library: Transactions of the Bibliographical Society*, 19 (1964), 67–89. See also Chapter 3, n. 59.

[55] For application of the Machiavellian moment concept to opera, see McGeary, *Opera and Politics in Queen Anne's Britain* (Woodbridge: Boydell, 2022), 241–85.

EXCISE AND THE PATRIOT OPPOSITION   111

promoters of faction.[56] This ministerial reaction confirms the cultural politics of Patriot literature.

₰ Contested Use of Patriot

But the honorific of "patriot" was contested. The Ministry posed the question "Whether *Patriotism* lies on the Side of the *Ministry*, or of the *Opposition?*"[57] Walpole, as reported by Chesterfield, had nothing but contempt for the Opposition's claims of patriotism and virtue. He

> laughed at and ridiculed all notions of Publick virtue, and the love of one's Country, calling them the *Chimerical schoolboy flights of Classical learning*. ... He would frequently ask young fellows at their first appearance in the world ..., well are you to be an old Roman? a Patriot? You will soon come off of that, and grow wiser.[58]

The Ministry took great pains to argue that *its* members and adherents were the true patriots, for they had the best interest of the nation at heart: they protected liberties and kept peace abroad, which is the lifeblood of a trading nation.

Ministerial writers turned the Opposition's self-proclaimed patriotism against it.[59] The Opposition, they claimed, were in fact only "pretended Patri-

---

[56] For the ministerial literary attack on the Opposition, Tone S. Urstad, *Sir Robert Walpole's Poets: The Use of Literature as Pro-Government Propaganda* (Newark, N.J.: University of Delaware Press, 1999), esp. pp. 172–230; David H. Stevens, *Party Politics and English Journalism, 1702–1742* (Menasha, Wis.: Collegiate Press, 1961); and Goldgar, *Walpole and the Wits, passim.*

[57] *London Journal*, no. 730 (23 June 1733).

[58] Philip Dormer Stanhope (Lord Chesterfield), "Characters"; Indiana University, Lilly Library. Chesterfield MSS., II, p. 6.

[59] Ministerial tracts attacking false patriotism of the Opposition include: William Arnall, *Clodius and Cicero: With other Examples and Reasonings, in Defense of Just Measures Against Faction and Obloquy, Suited to the Present Conjuncture* (1727); Philomater, *Dr. South Still Speaking: or, A Lecture from the Dead, Concerning Modern Patriotism* (?1728); *Patriotism Delineated: With Advice How to Distinguish the True Patriot from the False One* (1731); N. J. R. K., *The Popularity of Modern Patriotism Examined* (1731); *Free Briton* (esp. nos. 57, 69, 160, 187, 275; 31 Dec. 1730, 25 March 1731, 21 Dec. 1732, 21 June 1733, 13 Feb. 1735); *Daily Courant* (esp. nos. 5345 and 5356; 25 May and 7 June 1733); *London Journal* (esp. nos. 164 and 730; 15 Sept. 1727 and June 23, 1733); *Corn-Cutter's Journal*, nos. 26 and 31 (26 March 1734, 30 April 1734); *Daily Gazetteer*, no. 137 (2 Dec. 1735), no. 654 (30 July 1737), no. 678 (25 Aug. 1737); *A Poetical Essay on Vulgar Praise and Hate; in Which Is Contain'd, the Character of a Modern Patriot* (1733); *Modern Patriotism. A Poem* (1734) [reissued as *Modern Patriotism, or Faction Display'd* (1734)]; John Lord Hervey, *The Conduct of the Opposition, and the Tendency of Modern Patriotism* (1734); Hervey, *The False Patriot's Confession; or, "B——k's Address to Ambition"* (1737); William Arnall, *Opposition No Proof of Patriotism: With Some Observations and Advice Concerning Party-Writings* (1735); *The Crafts of the Craftsmen; or, a Detection of the Designs of the Coalition: Containing Memoirs of the History of False Patriotism for the Year 1735* (1736); *An Apology for*

ots," "false Patriots," or "seeming Patriots." William Arnall, one of Walpole's most trusted writers, called Bolingbroke a "hungry and rapacious *Crocodile Patriot,* who, with *Tears* in his Eyes and *Sighs* from his Heart, … whilst, with *specious* and *insidious* Professions of *Love to Mankind,* he plots their Destruction and perpetrates their Ruin."[60]

The pretended Patriots, the Ministry claimed, opposed measures necessary for the safety and security of the state, and represented that the Ministry can do no good. They traduced a mild, tolerant government as if an arbitrary power, did everything to embarrass the Ministry as to foreign affairs, and recommended the greatest enemies of Great Britain (including Bolingbroke) as public spirited and patriotic men. Such faction only encouraged the Jacobites. Their writings were full of misrepresentations framed only to incense and frighten the people and to propagate strife for their own self-interest.[61] Despite their disavowals, they attacked men, not measures. Constant opposition to measures of the Court was a sign they are motivated by self-interest and resentment and will use any device to destroy Walpole.

The Patriots' proclaimed zeal for liberty, public welfare, and preservation of the constitution was "the old Stalking-Horse of *Faction*" – a pretense for ambitious men out of office who wanted to rule and to raise their own grandeur on the ruins of the nation.[62] The ministerial charge that the Patriots really only sought government places was proven true by the events of 1742. After Walpole fell from power, Pulteney accepted a peerage, and there was a scramble of Opposition Whigs for places.

* * *

After the defeat of the Excise, Lord Cobham organized an opposition largely of his extended family that rallied under the Patriot's banner and with Frederick, Prince of Wales as its figurehead. Frederick was looked to as a future Patriot King who would restore political virtue and British liberties, rise above political parties, and free Britain from Walpole's corrupt regime. These younger writers used a broad range of literature – from topical journalism to verse satire and plays – to carry on the campaign against Walpole. Unlike the bitter satire of the Scriblerians, these writings offer a more optimistic, hopeful vision of Britain under a future king. The following chapters will explore how opera was used in the realm of cultural politics in the campaign to bring down the Walpole ministry.

Ministers of State. Or, the Rudiments of Modern Patriotism (1736); and *The False Patriot: A Satire* (1739). See also Reed Browning, *Political and Constitutional Ideas of the Court Whigs* (Baton Rouge, La.: Louisiana State University Press, 1982), 192–5.

[60] William Arnall, *The Free Briton Extraordinary: or, a Short Review of the British Affairs* (1730), 30.

[61] For the Ministry's claim of the unprincipled, unreasonable nature of the Opposition's attacks: *Free Briton,* nos. 33 and 68 (16 July 1729, 18 March 1731).

[62] *An Apology for Ministers of State* (1738).

CHAPTER 6

Opera of the Nobility and the *Furor Farinellicus*

The year of the Excise was also an eventful for opera in London. Handel was known for his contentious relations with some of his singers,[1] and by the end of the 1732–33 season, he had fallen out irreconcilably with Senesino and decided not to re-hire him for the following season.

After his performance in *Griselda* on 9 June, the last night of the season, Senesino announced from the stage his dismissal by Handel. The *Daily Advertiser* carried a full report:

> Signor Senoseni [*sic*] took his Leave of the Audience in a short Speech, acquainting them, as he said with Regret, "That he had now perform'd his last Part on that Stage, and was henceforward discharg'd from any Engagement: He thank'd the Nobility for the Great Honours they had done him in an Applause of so many Years, and assured them, that whenever a Nation to whom he was so greatly obliged, should have any further Commands for him, he would endeavour to obey them."[2]

The following month, Handel took his troupe to Oxford without Senesino to produce a series of concerts and oratorios as part of the end-of-term Act of Convocation.[3]

Senesino's dismissal set in train the founding of a new opera company. Dissatisfied with Handel's management of the opera – now leading to the possible loss of London's star Italian singer – and to ensure opera continued in London, a group of operalovers took advantage of Senesino's offer to serve them and began planning an opera company that he would direct.[4] All Handel's singers

---

[1] David Hunter, *The Lives of George Friderick Handel* (Woodbridge: Boydell, 2015), 91–6, and especially his long-standing friction with Senesino.

[2] *Daily Advertiser*, no. 737 (11 June 1733).

[3] On Handel and the Act, Susan Wollenberg, "Music in 18th-Century Oxford," *Proceedings of the Royal Musical Association*, 108 (1981–82), 79–81; Wollenberg, "Music and Musicians," in *The History of the University of Oxford*. Vol. 5. *The Eighteenth Century*, ed. L. S. Sutherland and L. G. Mitchell (Oxford: Clarendon Press, 1986), 870–1; and H. Diack Johnstone, "Handel at Oxford in 1733," *Early Music*, 31 (2003), 248–60.

[4] For contemporary mentions of the opera being under Senesino's direction, see Thomas McGeary, *The Politics of Opera in Handel's Britain* (Cambridge: Cambridge University Press, 2013), 158–9.

114   THE CULTURAL POLITICS OF OPERA, 1720–1742

but the loyal soprano Anna Strada del Pò left him for the new company, conventionally known as the Opera of the Nobility.[5]

They acted quickly. A day after their first meeting on 15 June 1733, one of the organisers, John West, Lord De La Warr, wrote the Duke of Richmond:

> There is A Spirit got up against the Dominion of Mr Handel, A Subscription carry'd on, and Directors chosen, who have contracted with Senisino, and have sent for Cuzzoni, and Farrinelli, it is hoped he will come as soon as the Carneval of Venice is over, if not sooner.[6]

The directors engaged Nicola Porpora as composer but were unable to hire Farinelli. The subscription was to be for the usual twenty guineas,[7] presumably for about fifty performances. The directors used the old Lincoln's Inn Fields theatre for their first season. For the second season they moved to the traditional venue for opera, the Haymarket (or King's) theatre.

The directors chosen (see Table 6.1) had long been supporters of opera: ten had previously been shareholders or directors in the Royal Academy of Music; and several, Earl Cowper and Sir John Buckworth, had heard the rising star Farinelli in Italy.

In June, both opera companies announced calls for subscriptions for the 1733–34 season, and news of two companies offering opera excited the London society and the *beau monde*. The dowager Duchess of Leeds reported to the young Duke of Leeds, then traveling in Europe, "I am at Present in top spirits wth ye certainity [sic] of having a very good opera here next winter, in opposition to Handell."[8]

Handel started his season on 30 October with the royal family in attendance for the pasticcio *Semiramide*.[9] Only after Handel paused productions for the

---

[5] On the founding of the Opera of the Nobility: Carole Taylor, "Italian Operagoing in London, 1700–1745" (Ph.D. Diss., Syracuse University, 1991), 190–240; and McGeary, *Politics of Opera in Handel's Britain*, 155–68 (rejecting the idea of the political motives of the founding and relation to Prince Frederick). See also Thomas McGeary, "Handel, Prince Frederick, and the Opera of the Nobility Reconsidered," *Göttinger Händel-Beiträge*, 7 (1998), 156–78.

    Edmund Curll speculated on the response of opera's arch-foe John Dennis (d. 6 Jan. 1734) on the founding of the Opera of the Nobility: "How would this poor Gentleman's manly Spirit have been moved, if he had lived but a few Weeks longer than he did, to have seen two *Italian Operas*, established in *London* at once! and to have heard that grave Senators and Generals of the Army, have been ready to go to Logger-heads by siding with the different Parties of two squeaking Eunuchs, *Senesino* and *Carrastini*!"; [Edmund Curll], *The Life of Mr. John Dennis* (1734), 29–30. The *Life* also included a précis of his *Essay on the Opera's*. Curll's actual authorship is questionable.

[6] Letter from John West, Lord De La Warr, [?]London, 16 June 1733; West Sussex Record Office, Chichester, Goodwood MS 103, MF1177.

[7] *Daily Advertiser*, no. 743 (18 June 1733); repeated the following day.

[8] Letter from dowager Duchess of Leeds, 4 July 1733, to the Duke of Leeds; British Library, Add. MS 28,050, ff. 217-18, on 217r.

[9] See notices in the *Daily Advertiser*, nos. 857 and 859 (29 and 31 October 1733). The *Daily Courant*, no. 5481 (31 October 1733), explicitly states the Prince of Wales was among the royal family.

TABLE 6.1. Directors of the Opera of the Nobility, June 1733,
with Their Previous Opera Company Participation

John Manners, third Duke of Rutland
Royal Academy of Music: director (1727), subscriber (1723), pledged 1728

William Cowper, second Earl Cowper

Charles Cadogan, MP, second Baron Cadogan
Royal Academy of Music: shareholder, director (1727), subscriber (1723),
pledged 1728

John West, seventh baron De La Warr (later first Earl)
Royal Academy of Music: subscriber (1723)

Thomas Coke, MP, Baron Lovel (later first Viscount then Earl of Leicester)
Royal Academy of Music: shareholder, director (1719, 1720), pledged 1728

Charles Lennox, second Duke of Richmond and Lennox*
Royal Academy of Music: director (1727), subscriber (1723, 1726), pledged 1728

John Russell, fourth Duke of Bedford

John Dalrymple, second Earl of Stair [S]
Royal Academy of Music: director (1720), subscriber (1723)

James Hamilton, MP, first Viscount Limerick [I]
Royal Academy of Music: shareholder, director (1726, 1727), subscriber (1723)
pledged 1728

Allen Bathurst, first Baron Bathurst (later Earl)
Royal Academy of Music: shareholder, subscriber (1723)

Sir John Buckworth, MP, second baronet
Royal Academy of Music: director (1726, 1727), subscriber (1723)

Sir Michael Newton, MP, fourth baronet
Royal Academy of Music: director (1727)

Henry Furnese, MP
Royal Academy of Music: subscriber (1723), pledged 1728

Richard Boyle, third Earl of Burlington
Royal Academy of Music: shareholder, director (1719, 1720, 1726, 1727),
subscriber (1723)

---

* O. E. Deutsch, *Handel: A Documentary Biography* (New York, N.Y.: W. W. Norton,
1955), states he became a director, although he is only documented as being solicited
for a subscription; some participation may be that of his father, the first duke.

Used for identification of persons: Carole Taylor, *Italian Operagoing in London,
1700–1745* (Ph.D. Diss., Syracuse University, 1991); *History of Parliament: The House
of Commons, 1715–1754*, ed. Romney Sedgwick, 2 vols. (New York, N.Y.: Oxford
University Press, 1970) (also available online at the History of Parliament website).

Tenure of directors of the Royal Academy of Music: Elizabeth Gibson, "The Royal
Academy of Music (1719–28) and its Directors," pp. 138–64 in *Handel Tercentenary
Collection*, ed. Stanley Sadie and Anthony Hicks (Ann Arbor, Mich.: UMI Research
Press, 1987), 152.

For those pledging to the Royal Academy of Music, 1728–29, see Table 2.2.

116 THE CULTURAL POLITICS OF OPERA, 1720–1742

TABLE 6.2. Summary of 1733–34 to 1743–44 Opera Seasons

Season	Operas, Odes, and Oratorios	Number of Performances	Operas, Odes, and Oratorios	Number of Performances
	Handel		Opera of the Nobility	
1733–34	10	61	6	53?
1734–35	8	56	6	64
1735–36	6	19	7	56
1736–37	9	52	6*	50
1737–38	3	19	7	39?
	(As part of Nobility season)		(Includes 19 performances of three operas by Handel)	
	Handel		Middlesex Opera Companies	
1738–39	5	15	1**	4
1739–40	7	16	4	40
1740–41	7	15	–	–
1741–42***	–	–	6	56
1742–43	4	13	6	50
1743–44	4	12	6	55

Sources: Carole Taylor, "Italian Operagoing in London, 1700–1745" (Ph.D. dissertation, Syracuse University, 1991); and *George Frideric Handel, Collected Documents*, ed. Donald Burrows, Helen Coffey, John Greenacombe, and Anthony Hicks, 6 vols. (Cambridge: Cambridge University Press, 2013–), vols. 2–4.
*   Plus five buffa intermezzi
**   Plus one buffa opera
*** Handel in Dublin

holidays, did the Nobility Opera begin its season on 29 December with *Arianna in Nasso* by its principal composer Nicola Porpora. For this season, London's operagoers had the luxury of enjoying two opera companies competing for their attendance and patronage. Writing on 13 December, Handel's future librettist Charles Jennens was quite realistic: "How two Opera Houses will subsist after Christmas, I can't tell; but at present we are at some difficulty for the support of One; & Mr. Handel has been forc'd to drop his Opera three nights for want of company."[10]

[10] Letter from Charles Jennens, 13 December 1733, to John Ludford; transcribed and discussed by Anthony Hicks, "A New Letter of Charles Jennens," *Göttinger Händel-Beiträge*, 4 (1991), 254–7. Prior to Jennens's writing, Handel had skipped three of his usual Tuesday or Saturday performances (27 November and 1 and 11 December).

The competing seasons between Handel and the Nobility Opera are summarized in Table 6.2.

While the seasons of the Royal Academy of Music are popularly noted for the rivalry of Faustina and Cuzzoni and the rage for the *Beggar's Opera*, both which supposedly contributed to the demise of the Royal Academy, the Opera of the Nobility is celebrated for the presence in its cast of the singer Carlo Broschi (called "Farinelli"), who sang with the company for three seasons.[11] For two seasons, the Nobility Opera offered London two of Europe's most celebrated *castrati*, Farinelli and Senesino.

❧ Farinelli

What most filled London with excitement was the arrival of the star castrato Farinelli. Britain had known imported *castrati* since Siface's short visit from the Court of Modena in 1687, and beginning in 1707, Valentini and Nicolini were well enough known in general culture that they could be used for satire and political journalism.[12]

From its first meeting, the Nobility Opera had set its sights on Farinelli. The first report to England extolling him came from Owen Swiney in May 1726, but Britons had to wait almost eight and a half years to hear him on their stage. Swiney, former manager of the opera house (until he bankrupted it and fled to Italy in 1713), now in Italy and active in English operatic and artistic matters, wrote to the Duke of Richmond, then the Deputy Governor of the Royal Academy of Music, from Venice on 31 May 1726: "I am just returned from Parma where I heard yᵉ Divine Farinelli (another blazing star)."[13] In February 1729, Colonel Burges, the British minister in Venice, wrote back to London:

> yᵉ whole Town is so taken up with yᵉ diversions of yᵉ Carneval and yᵉ competition between Farinello and Faustina, that we think and talk of nothing else. … yᵉ Eunuch has allmost all yᵉ Italians of his side: a powerful Band! and esteem'd by much yᵉ best Judges of Musick.[14]

---

[11] On the protracted recruitment of Farinelli, Thomas McGeary, "Farinelli's Progress to Albion: The Recruitment and Reception of Opera's 'Blazing Star,'" *British Journal for Eighteenth-Century Studies*, 28 (2005), 339–61.

[12] For their early use in partisan political satire, see Thomas McGeary, *Opera and Politics in Queen Anne's Britain, 1705–1714* (Woodbridge: Boydell, 2022).

[13] Letter from Owen Swiney, Venice, 31 May 1726; West Sussex Record Office, Chichester, Goodwood MS 105/401, p. 3. On Swiney in Italy, see Elizabeth Gibson, "Owen Swiney and the Italian Opera in London," *Musical Times*, 126 (Feb. 1984), 82–6. For details on Farinelli's operatic performances in Italy, see Robert Freeman, "Farinello and His Repertory," pp. 301–30 in *Studies in Renaissance and Baroque Music in Honor of Arthur Mendel*, ed. Robert L. Marshall (Kassel: Bärenreiter, 1974).

[14] Letter from Colonel Elizeus Burges, Venice, 11 Feb. 1729, to Charles Delafaye; London, National Archives, SP 99/63, f.85v.

118   THE CULTURAL POLITICS OF OPERA, 1720–1742

For the Venetian Carnival of 1730, Burges wrote to the Duke of Newcastle, "Farinello draws hither a great many Strangers to hear him. The Virtuosi do all agree there never was such a Voice as his in ye World before."[15]

British Grand Tourists flocked to hear Farinelli, even following him from city to city, and wrote home extolling him. One of those who heard him was Earl Cowper, who wrote back to his sister on 31 December 1729: "You have yet one of ye best singers in all Italy yet to hear. Faranelli[.] He is ye most surprising Creature in ye World."[16] Charles Wyndham (later second Earl of Egremont) wrote his father on 6 January 1730: "Farinello is certainly the greatest prodigy in the world."[17]

Farinelli was reluctant to risk travel to England, and it took many years of tourists befriending him to lure him to England. The directors had agents working on their behalf. The Earl of Essex, ambassador at Turin, was given the commission for inviting him.[18] In Venice, Consul Joseph Smith, who acted as banker for many traveling Englishmen, executed the contract.[19] Early in May 1734, negotiations between the Nobility Opera and Farinelli were successful, and news of Farinelli's impending departure for London spread rapidly in Italy and on to London. In July 1734, London newspaper readers learned that "the famous Farinelli" was "on the Road from Italy, and is expected to land shortly at Dover, from whence he will repair to the Right Hon. the Earl Cowper's Seat in Kent, in order to pass some Time with his Lordship."[20] Cowper, whom Farinelli had met in Italy, was one of the original directors of the Opera of the Nobility.

Farinelli did not set out for England until September. His progress was monitored by his English friends, also on their way home and who assisted and possibly accompanied him.[21] He arrived in England shortly before 26 September, with promises of hospitality and introductions to aristocrats and persons of quality.[22] As was the custom with new opera singers, the following month he sang twice before the royal family.[23] The two appearances were reported in

15   Letter from Colonel Burges, Venice, 20 Jan. 1730; London, National Archives, SP 99/63, f.123r.
16   Letter from Earl Cowper, Venice, 31 Dec. 1729, to Sarah Cowper; Hertfordshire Archives and Local Studies, Panshanger Papers, D/EP/F237, f.18.
17   Petworth House Archives, Petworth, Sussex, 6320.
18   See letter from Joseph Smith, 14 May 1734, British Library, Add. MS 27,733, f.81, and Alexander Chalmers, *The General Biographical Dictionary*, new rev., enlarged ed., 45 vols. (1813), 7:65.
19   On Consul Smith's activities: Frances Vivian, *The Consul Smith Collection: Masterpieces of Italian Drawing from the Royal Library, Windsor Castle, Raphael to Canaletto* (Munich: Hirmer, 1989); Vivian, *Il console Smith: mercante e collezionista* (Venice: N. Pozza, 1971).
20   *London Evening Post*, no. 1037 (11 July 1734).
21   His route can be followed in McGeary, "Farinelli's Progress to Albion."
22   His arrival in Britain was announced, for example, in the *Daily Advertiser*, no. 1142 (26 Sept. 1734), and the *Bee Revived*, vol. 7, no. 83 (21–28 Sept. 1734), 195.
23   Farinelli singing at Court: Charles Burney, *The Present State of Music in France and Italy*, 2nd ed. (1773), 224; letter from Farinelli, London, 30 Nov. 1734 to Conte Pepoli,

OPERA OF THE NOBILITY AND THE *FUROR FARINELLICUS*   119

newspapers, which variously divulged to the public the terms of Farinelli's contract with the Nobility Opera. One stated "he has contracted with the Noblemen Subscribers to sing ... 50 Nights, for 1500 Guineas and a Benefit."[24]

Farinelli made his public debut on 29 October in the role of Arbace in the Nobility Opera's *Artaserse*. A newspaper reported "all the Royal Family were present," the theatre was "exceedingly crowded," and he was received "with prodigious Applause."[25] News of his reception spread throughout London society. Thomas Bowen, the Earl of Essex's London agent, reported to him, "Farinelli is allowed by everybody to be the best performer who has yet appeared from Italy."[26] John Perceval (later Earl of Egmont) proclaimed him "the finest voice that Europe affords."[27] The dowager Duchess of Leeds wrote her son, still in Italy, on 12 November 1734, "I dont know a word of news for nothing but Farinelli is talkd off, I think him handsome too." [28]

British adulation of Farinelli was summed up in the blasphemy uttered by one of his female admirers (often said to be Lady Rich): "One God! One Farinelli."[29] The phrase was taken up in many poems and epigrams, the most famous probably being the poem "On a Raptured Lady."[30] On the floor in

---

in *La solitudine amica: lettere al Conte Sicinio Pepoli*, ed. Carlo Vitali and Francesca Boris (Palermo: Sellerio 1999), letter no. 43, p. 132; *London Evening-Post*, no. 1076 (10–12 Oct. 1734); and *Daily Advertiser*, no. 1155 (11 Oct. 1734) and no. 1163 (21 Oct. 1734).

[24] *Fog's Weekly Journal*, no. 311 (19 Oct. 1734); *Weekly Register*, no. 243 (19 Oct. 1734)[quoted].

[25] *Daily Advertiser*, no. 1171 (30 Oct. 1734).

[26] Letter from Thomas Bowen, London, 30 Oct. 1734, to the Earl of Essex in Turin; London, British Library, Add. MS 27,738, f.122r.

[27] Historical Manuscripts Commission. Manuscripts of the Earl of Egmont. *Diary of Viscount Percival Afterward First Earl of Egmont*, 3 vols. (London: His Majesty's Stationery Office, 1920), 2:132.

[28] Letter from the Duchess of Leeds, London, 12 Nov. 1734; British Library, Add. MS 28,050, f.223r–24r.

[29] First reported in the *Prompter*, no. 37 (14 March 1735). The article in the *Prompter* is excerpted as "An Account of Farinelli" in the several editions of *A Trip Through the Town* (1735).

The female blasphemer was said by Horace Walpole to be Lady Rich (née Elizabeth Griffith, *c.* 1692–1773), who married in 1710 or 1714 Sir Robert Rich, 3rd baronet, MP (later Field Marshall); see *The Yale Edition of the Correspondence of Horace Walpole*, 48 vols. (New Haven, Conn.: Yale University Press, 1937–1983), 39:79 n. 7. Alternatively, she may be Mrs. Fox Lane, later Lady Bingley; see *Lichtenberg's Commentaries on Hogarth's Engravings*, intro. and trans. Innes and Gustav Herdan (London: Cresset Press, 1966), 122.

[30] "On a Raptur'd Lady" appeared in the *Daily Journal*, no. 4491 (6 June 1735). Other poems on Farinelli include "On Farinelli," *Grub-street Journal*, no. 285 (12 June 1735), and a reply in no. 286 (19 June 1735); and "Farinelli," *Grub-street Journal*, no. 284 (5 June 1735), and reprinted in *The Bee*, no. 117 (June 1735), 494. The first two poems were reprinted in *A Collection of Epigrams*, 2 vols. (1727, 1737), vol. 2, nos. 32 and 33. In *The Rake's Progress; or, the Humours of Drury Lane* (1735), a set of verses to accompany Hogarth's series of prints, it is the Rake who blasphemes "One God, one Songster,"

THE CULTURAL POLITICS OF OPERA, 1720–1742

Hogarth's print "The Rake's Levee" from the *A Rake's Progress* (Plate 9.7) is the title page of a poem that bears an illustration of women offering their hearts to an altar of Farinelli, with the legend "One God one Farinelli."

Farinelli so captivated the *beau monde*, that on 18 December 1734, one correspondent reported

> Faranelli employs every bodys thoughts & time, & our Ladys are stark mad in ye Country to hear him. what will be ye fate of ye few that will dare to stay in ye Country ye whole season, will be well off if they escape with a whole skin.[31]

The highpoint of Farinelli's London career was his benefit performance of *Artaserse* on 15 March 1735, quite possibly the most celebrated and spectacular single musical event of the century. The benefit was promoted by a series of advertisements in the London newspapers. Two days before the performance, a paper reported "'Tis expected that Signor Farinello will have the greatest Appearance on Saturday that has been known. We hear that a Contrivance will be made to accommodate 2000 people."[32] It went on to announce the gifts London's elite were showering upon him:

> His Royal Highness the Prince of Wales has been pleas'd to give him 200 Guineas, the Spanish Ambassador 100, the Emperor's Ambassador 50, his Grace the Duke of Leeds 50, the Countess of Portmore [Leeds's mother] 50, Lord Burlington 50, his Grace the Duke of Richmond 50, the Hon. Col. Paget 30, Lady Rich 20, and most of the other Nobility 50, 30 or 20 Guineas each; so that 'tis believ'd his Benefit will be worth to him upward of 2000l.

The list of presents was frequently reprinted as evidence of the sums lavished on Farinelli. Two days after the benefit, the *Daily Advertiser* reported:

> There was a very numerous and gay Appearance on Saturday Night at Signor Farinello's Benefit, the Pit was full soon after 4 o'Clock. There was no Scenes, the

---

p. 17; while in "'The Lady of Taste: or, F——'s Levee,'" in *A Collection of Miscellany Poems* (1737), it is the general *beau monde* who blaspheme (p. 152).

Other mentions of Farinelli charming audiences and the ladies' (often unseemly) adulation are found in Henry Fielding, *The Historical Register for the Year 1736* (1737), Act II; Joseph Peterson, *The Raree Show: or, the Fox Trap't* (1739), 25; *Woman Unmask'd, and Dissected* (1740), 78 [reissued as *Female Qualifications: or, Jilts and Hypocrites Portray'd* (1741)]; Joseph Dorman, "Some Memoirs of F——i," in *The Curiosity: or, Gentleman and Lady's Library* (1739), 138–45; Thomas Catesby Pagett, "Written in the Year 1735," *Miscellanies in Prose and Verse* (1741), 367–8; and Hercules Mac-Sturdy, *A Trip to Vaux-Hall* (1737), 10.

The *Gentleman's Magazine* for 6 February 1737 carried a news account of a woman who defended herself from a suit charging breach of a marriage promise on the grounds that her suitor had declared himself "no Admirer of Farinelli" and she didn't doubt "but the Court would think she had a fortunate Escape" ("Historical Chronicle, Saturday, 14," 64).

[31] Letter from Christopher Milles, 18 December 1734, to his sister, Mary (Mrs Lee Warner); Norfolk Record Office, Lee Warner, box 14. I thank David Hunter for providing his transcript of the letter.

[32] *Daily Advertiser*, no. 1286 (13 March 1734).

OPERA OF THE NOBILITY AND THE *FUROR FARINELLICUS*   121

stage being adorn'd as at a Ridotto, and curiously hung with gilt Leather. ... Many of the Songs in the Opera were new; that which preceded the Chorus [i.e., *coro*] was compos'd by himself, and so extremely applauded, that he sung it again, at the Request of the Audience.[33]

The splendor of Farinelli's first benefit and the riches it gained him made evident elite society's adulation of him. It is no exaggeration that London turned Farinelli into opera's first superstar. Even in its pre-industrial state, London had a celebrity-producing media industry that spread his fame by newspaper reports, concert advertisements, posted bills, celebratory poems, paintings, and statuary.[34] Jacopo Amigoni, Farinelli's friend and traveling companion, painted a large allegorical portrait, *Farinelli Crowned by Euterpe and Attended by Fame* (1735),[35] which became a "must see" for London society.[36] The painting was engraved for wider distribution.

The reaction to his benefit concert was immediate. With his presents and receipts widely reported, Farinelli and the benefit were condemned for their luxury and extravagant wastefulness to the economy. Essays, satires, and pamphlets vilified him as the greatest corruptor of English society and demonized him as the direct cause of all Britain's ills. These widespread indictments of Farinelli were repeated in the numerous satires that appear in following chapters.

The Prompter, a periodical concerned "to bring the *Taste* of the *Publick back again* to its *true Standard* of Tragedy and Comedy,"[37] sounded most of the themes on 14 March 1735, even before the performance. It complained of

[33] *Daily Advertiser,* no. 1289 (17 March 1734); a summary of the *Daily Advertiser* report appeared in *The Political State of Great Britain,* 49 (April 1735), 365–6.

[34] Many of the mentions of Farinelli in London are collected and discussed in, among other places: Judith Milhous and Robert D. Hume, "Construing and Misconstruing Farinelli in London," *British Journal for Eighteenth-century Studies,* 28 (2005), 361–86; Xavier Cervantes, "'Let 'em Deck their Verses with Farinelli's Name': Farinelli as a Satirical Trope in English Poetry and Verse in the 1730s," *British Journal for Eighteenth-century Studies,* 28 (2005), 421–36; Thomas McGeary, "Farinelli in Madrid: Opera, Politics, and the War of Jenkins' Ear," *Musical Quarterly,* 82 (1998), 383–421; McGeary, "Farinelli's Progress to Albion"; and Berta Joncus, "One God, So Many Farinellis: Mythologizing the Star Castrato," *British Journal for Eighteenth-century Studies,* 28 (2005), 437–96, which catalogues the graphic sources. McGeary, "Farinelli and the Duke of Leeds: 'tanto mio amico e patrone particolare,'" *Early Music,* 30 (2002), 202–13, publishes for the first time a portrait of Farinelli by Amigoni.

[35] Jacopo Amigoni's painting, *Farinelli Crowned by Euterpe and Attended by Fame,* is now at the National Museum of Art, Bucharest. Listed as nos. 27 (painting) and 28 (engraving) in Joncus, "One God, So Many Farinellis." See also Lorenzo Bianconi and Maria C. C. Pedrielli, "Corrado Giaquinto: Carlo Broschi detto il Farinelli," pp. 103–24 in *I ritratti del Museo della Musica di Bologna da Padre Martini al Liceo Musicale,* ed. Lorenzo Bianconi et al. (Florence: Leo S. Olschki, 2018).

[36] *Daily Advertiser,* no. 1382 (3 July 1735); reprinted in the *Grub-street Journal,* no. 289 (10 July 1735). See also McGeary, "Farinelli's Progress to Albion," 348.

[37] *Prompter,* no. 106 (14 Nov. 1735). The paper was generally pro-ministerial, but its primary goal was moral correction of the theatre. See also Chapter 8, note 30.

British women giving their largess to this "this Amphibious Animal," this "Poor Distressed Foreigner, whose Cries have a sort of a Magick Charm in them, that takes Possession, at once, of the Mov'd Listener's Soul ... [and] who is only fit to enervate the Youth of *Great Britain*, by the pernicious Influence of his Unnatural *Voice*." The writer asks,

> Is there is no Spirit left in the young Fellows of the Age? No Remains of Manhood? Will they suffer the *Eyes, Ears, Hearts*, and *Souls*, of their Mistresses, to follow an *Eccho of Virility*? ... Have they no Notion of this more Visible Prostitution, this Adultery of the Mind, ... when a Wife is alienated from her Husband, by any Pleasure whatsoever?[38]

That the vilification of Farinelli almost matched that of Walpole's ministry was not lost on a writer for the ministerial *Free Briton*, who ventured to say, "I have indeed wondered that none of the Lovers of Harmony have yet appeared in Vindication of their beloved *Farinelli*, who is treated with almost as much Asperity as the Present Ministry."[39]

A print (Plate 6.1) titled "The Opera House or the Italian Eunuch's Glory" (1735), ironically dedicated to "those Generous Encouragers of Foreigners and the Ruiners of England," recycles an earlier print mocking the *Beggar's Opera*.[40] By printing a list of Farinelli's gifts from the benefit in the right margin, the print deplores the effect of opera and Farinelli on the British stage. The six members of an *opera seria* cast are depicted with heads as squalling and braying animals assembled as if singing the *coro* (closing ensemble) of an opera, while the musicians below the platform play a cacophony-mélange of a bagpipe, salt box, jaw (jew's) harp, dulcimer, and bladder-and-string.[41] Above in a cloud, Harmony is shown fleeing the London stage.

London could not support two opera companies, especially given the enormous sums being paid to the leading singers. By the second half of the 1734–35 season it was clear to observers that both houses were suffering from poor attendance. Even Farinelli's success could not carry the Opera of the Nobility, so that Colley Cibber could smugly observe that after several years Farinelli was "singing to an Audience of five and thirty pounds."[42] Reduced houses for Farinelli's performances were probably due as much to suicidal competition

---

[38] *Prompter*, no. 37 (14 March 1735).

[39] *Free Briton*, no. 282 (3 April 1735).

[40] Frederick G. Stephens, *Catalogue of Prints and Drawings in the British Museum*. Division I. *Political and Personal Satires*, 3 vols. (London: British Museum, 1877), no. 2148; Joncus, "One God, So Many Farinellis," no. 25, Figure 9. On the original 1728 print about the *Beggar's Opera* and the 1735 adaptation, Jeremy Barlow, *The Enraged Musician: Hogarth's Musical Imagery* (Aldershot: Ashgate, 2005), 89–94. The engraving in turn is based on an ink and wash drawing; see A. P. Oppé, *The Drawings of William Hogarth* (London: Phaidon, 1948), cat. no. 12, Plate 3.

[41] On the cultural meaning of the musical instruments, Barlow, *The Enraged Musician*.

[42] *An Apology for the Life of Colley Cibber*, ed. B. R. S. Fone (Ann Arbor, Mich.: University of Michigan Press, 1968), 227.

PLATE 6.1. [After William Hogarth], *The Opera House or the Italian Eunuch's Glory* (1735). The plate reworks an earlier image that showed the stage of the *Beggar's Opera*, now showing the stage of the Italian opera. The banner to the right lists the gifts bestowed on Farinelli at his benefit.

between two opera companies for the same audience as to his novelty wearing off.

With the close of his first 1734–35 season, Farinelli set a pattern of leaving London for the summer. In the first summer of 1735, he traveled to Yorkshire with the Duke of Leeds, whom he befriended in Italy.[43] After the 1735–36 season, Farinelli spent the summer in Paris, where, as the London newspapers reported, he was fêted and received with raptures and gifts, including from the King "a fine Gold Snuff-Box, with his Picture set in Diamond in the Lid, and also a Purse of Louis d'Ors."[44]

---

[43] McGeary, "Farinelli and the Duke of Leeds," 205–7.
[44] *Old Whig*, no. 76 (19 Aug. 1736) and no. 84 (14 Oct. 1736). See also issue no. 80 (16 Sept. 1736). The *Daily Post*, no. 5305 (13 Sept. 1736) reported Farinelli received from the King "a Present of his Picture set in Diamonds." The *Journal de Paris* (24 Sept. 1736) reported, "Le grand Farinelly ... a chanté devant le roi, qui lui a fait présent d'une tabatière d'or"; reprinted in Norbert Dufourcq, "Nouvelles de la cour et de la ville," *Recherches sur la musique française classique*, 10 (1970), 105.

124   THE CULTURAL POLITICS OF OPERA, 1720-1742

The Earl of Essex was advised on 18 March 1736 of the declining fortunes of the Nobility Opera and the outlook for Farinelli's second benefit:

'Tis Generally thought the Operas will hardly last 'till the next Winter, the Spirit which supported them seems to flagg very much: Farinello has a Benefit next week [27 March], but I beleive he will find a vast difference between the Profits of this and his Benefit last year.[45]

As a concession to help the company for his upcoming third season Farinelli gave up his benefit concert, which cost him but saved the company money.[46]

Before the 1736-37 season was over, the Queen of Spain invited Farinelli to the Spanish Court.[47] Philip V was suffering from bouts of melancholia and depression. The nation was in effect being ruled by his Italian Queen, Elisabeth Farnese, who was looking for ways to divert and amuse him.[48] His stay in Madrid was widely known, yet his return for the following season was expected.

Farinelli's 11 June 1737 performance in *Sabrina* would be (unknown at the time) his last London performance and his last on the public opera stage. For this performance, Farinelli composed and performed a farewell aria, "Ah! che non sono le parole," to express his respect and gratitude to Britain.[49]

Farinelli's July arrival in Paris was greatly anticipated, and he again sang before the King and Queen before leaving on 15 July and traveling on to Madrid, where he arrived on 7 August. Benjamin Keene, the British minister to Madrid, reported home the anticipation at Farinelli's arrival and his reception.

The praise Farinelli received in Paris in 1736 is described by Luigi Riccoboni: "After he had sung in the most eminent Families, ... the King did him the Honour to hear him perform in the Queen's Chamber, and applauded him in a Manner that astonished the whole Court. ... It is on all Hands agreed *Italy* never did, and perhaps never will, produce so complete a Singer." *Réflexions historiques et critiques sur les différens théâtres de l'Europe*; translation from *An Historical and Critical Account of the Theatres in Europe* (1741), 81. For the 1737 visit, see also sources quoted in McGeary, "Farinelli in Madrid," notes 26 and 27.

45 Letter from Thomas Bowen, London, 18 March 1736, to the Earl of Essex in Turin; London, British Library, Add. MS 27,738, ff.186v and 187r.

46 Letter from Sir John Buckworth, London, 13 May 1736, to the Earl of Essex in Turin; London, British Library, Add. MS 27,735, f.177r.

47 McGeary, "Farinelli in Madrid," for documentation of Farinelli's recruitment to Spain.

48 Letter from Benjamin Keene, 18 February 1737 (n.s.), to the Duke of Newcastle, describing her plan: "The Queen is endeavouring to look out for diversion for the King, who has a natural aversion for music. If she can change his temper as far as to amuse him with it, it [music] may keep them both from thinking of more turbulent matter." British Library, Add. MS 37,794, f.137v.

49 Published in London as *Ossequioso ringraziamento le cortesissme grazie ricevute nella Britannica Gloriosa Nazione* [1737]; reprinted in Franz Haböck, *Die Gesangkunst der Kastraten. Erster Notenband: Die Kunst des Cavaliere Carlo Broschi Farinelli* (Vienna: Universal Edition, 1923), 126-31. A manuscript copy (with variants) is in the Edward Finch papers, Durham Cathedral Archive, MS 70. It is uncertain if Farinelli actually sang the aria from the stage.

How Farinelli charmed the Spanish Court has become music history mythology, as told by him to the music historian Charles Burney.[50] The Queen is said to have arranged for him to sing outside the King's chamber. Philip was so charmed by Farinelli's singing his disorder was cured. Farinelli became a royal favorite who sang privately to the King every evening and cured his melancholia.[51] Farinelli ended up spending twenty-two years in Spain, where, like eunuchs in eastern courts, he rose to hold important positions at court.[52]

Until recently, the decisive factor in Farinelli's not returning to London for the following season was not certain. It turns out the Nobility Opera directors still owed him £650 of his past season's salary, which they refused to pay unless he returned, despite their contract. Farinelli's friends convinced him it was to his advantage to forgo this debt for a lavish salary and pension from the Spanish King.

Farinelli's progress to Madrid, his decision to remain, and the honors and gifts bestowed on him by the Spanish King were widely reported in the London newspapers. The sorrow of his female admirers over his absence was represented in numerous lamentations, such as the widely printed song by James Miller, "England's Lamentation for the Loss of Farinelli" (1737), and Henry Carey's "The Beau's Lamentation for ye Loss of Farrinelli" (1740).[53] The poems probably do reflect the genuine sentiment of part of the public; but their

---

[50] The well-known narrative is given in Burney's *Present State of Music in France and Italy* (1771), *General History of Music* (1776–1789), and article on Farinelli in Abraham Rees, *Cyclopedia*, 45 vols. (1819).

[51] The story is always left off here, with the impression that Philip's disorder was cured. However, later in 1738 Keene described Philip's condition, which suggests that Farinelli's cure was far from complete (see Appendix II in McGeary, "Farinelli in Madrid").

[52] On Farinelli's later career in Spain, of the growing literature, see especially Daniel Martín Sáez, "La leyenda de Farinelli en España: historiografía, mitología y política," *Revista de musicología*, 41 (2018), 41–78; Nicolas Morales, "Farinelo à Madrid. Acte premier d'un séjour triomphant: 1737–1746," pp. 47–76 in *Il Farinelli e gli evirati cantori*. Atti del Convego Internazionale di Studi (Bologna – Biblioteca Universitaria, 5–6 April 2005), ed. Luigi verdi (Lucca: Libreria Musicale Italiana, 2007); Margarita Torrione, "Farinelli en la corte de Felipe V," *Revista de la Real Sociedad Económica Matritense de Amigos del País*, no. 38 (1999), 121–42; Lorenzo Bianconi, "Il Farinelli di Corrado Giaquinto. Il lusso disdegnato, l'intatta lealtà," *Atti della Accademia nazionale dei Lincei*, series 9, vol. 42 (2019–2020); Lorenzo Bianconi and Maria C. C. Pedrielli, "Corrado Giaquinto: Carlo Broschi detto il Farinelli," pp. 103–24 in *I ritratti del Museo della Musica di Bologna da Padre Martini al Liceo Musicale*, ed. Lorenzo Bianconi et al. (Florence: Leo S. Olschki, 2018).

[53] The song (without music) originally appeared (like Carey's, titled "The Beau's Lamentation for the Loss of *Farinello*") in James Miller's *The Coffee-House* (dated 1737; but advertised for publication in late January or early February 1738), 8–9, and was frequently printed separately with its music (as "England's Lamentation for the Loss of Farinello"); the text only was reprinted (as "The Loss of Faronello") in his *Miscellaneous Works* (1741), 109–10. Carey's song appeared in his *Musical Century*, vol. 2 (pub. 1740, though possibly composed earlier), 5, and his later collections of poems.

126   THE CULTURAL POLITICS OF OPERA, 1720–1742

exaggerated sentiment suggests they were also intended to satirize misplaced, unwarranted sorrow.

His departure at a time of increasing tension between Britain and Spain became grist for political exploitation. Spanish recruitment of Farinelli was compared to the Spanish detention of British shipping and sailors that set off the Depredations Crisis and the War of Jenkins' Ear in 1739 (see Chapter 7). Opposition propagandists used the comparison to draw attention to the Ministry's mishandling of the Crisis and to goad England into war. Even in his absence in Spain, Farinelli was such a potent figure in the public consciousness that he could be used in succeeding years in satires on False Taste (see Chapter 9) and in formal verse satires (see Chapter 10).

For their 1735–36 and 1736–37 seasons, Handel and the Nobility Opera struggled to survive in a town that could barely support one opera company. Senesino and Cuzzoni returned to Italy at the end of the 1735–36 season. In April of the 1736–37 season, Handel suffered a stroke ("rheumatic palsie") and left for Aix-la-Chapelle to spend the 1737 summer recovering his health. Now obese and suffering from gout and possibly lead poisoning, Handel abandoned producing full seasons of Italian opera under his own direction.[54] He agreed instead to write two new operas for the Nobility Opera's 1737–38 season.[55]

Heidegger, manager of the Haymarket theatre, decided to produce the 1738–39 opera season himself. After failing to raise the needed two hundred subscriptions that he deemed necessary to hire singers, he cancelled the season and refunded subscriptions.[56] *Common Sense* reported the news with mock sympathetic-serious reflections on "whether the Cessation of *Operas*, would prove a National Loss, or a National Advantage."[57] Handel took advantage of the empty Haymarket theatre to produce a short season (16 January to 5 May 1739) of oratorios, an ode, and an Italian opera, *Giove in Argo* (see Table 6.2).

---

[54] On the effects of Handel's health on his musical career, Hunter, *Lives of George Friderick Handel*, 234–5, 238–47.

[55] Letter from fourth Earl of Shaftesbury, 11 June 1737, to James Harris; in *Music and Theatre in Handel's World: The Family Papers of James Harris, 1732–1780*, ed. Donald Burrows and Rosemary Dunhill (Oxford: Oxford University Press, 2002), 31–2. On these seasons, the rival opera companies, and Handel's turn to oratorios: Carole Taylor, "Handel's Disengagement from the Italian Opera," *Handel Tercentenary Collection*, ed. Stanley Sadie and Anthony Hicks (Ann Arbor, Mich.: UMI Research Press, 1987), 165–81; Taylor, "Italian Operagoing in London," 245–308; Donald Burrows, "Handel and the London Opera Companies in the 1730s: Venues, Programmes, Patronage and Performers," *Göttinger Händel-Beiträge*, 10 (2004), 149–65; and Ilias Chrissochoidis, "Handel at a Crossroads: His 1737–1738 and 1738–1739 Seasons Re-examined," *Music and Letters*, 90 (2009), 599–635.

[56] *London Daily Post and General Advertiser*, no. 1113 (24 May 1738) and no. 1167 (26 July 1738).

[57] *Common Sense*, no. 89 (14 Oct. 1738). Excerpted in *Gentleman's Magazine*, 7 (1738), 533–6.

THE MIDDLESEX OPERA COMPANIES

A new opera impresario, Charles Sackville, Lord Middlesex (later second Earl of Dorset), now appeared in London. While on his second tour of Italy (1736–1738), he became an opera enthusiast. He joined other Englishmen in producing a masque in Florence and an opera in Lucca,[58] and became infatuated with the singer known as "La Muscovita."[59] Upon returning to London, he produced the serenata *Angelica e Medoro* (March–April 1739) at Covent Garden to showcase her.

With the Opera of the Nobility defunct, Handel disengaging from opera and producing short seasons of English odes and oratorios, and Heidegger (wisely) abandoning opera, Middlesex and other operalovers stepped up to fulfill London's desire for opera and undertook to produce full seasons of Italian opera. They managed to produce seasons for 1739–40, 1741–42, 1742–43, and 1743–44. For 1739–40, Middlesex gathered 78 subscriptions; for 1740–41, an insufficient number of 21; for 1741–42, 142 subscriptions; for 1742–43, probably fewer than 50 general subscriptions (plus the 30 who pledged £200); and for 1743–44, 131 subscriptions.

For the 1742–43 season, Middlesex replicated the pattern of the Royal Academy of Music and five directors were elected from subscribers. Most significantly, recognizing that the company was unlikely to be financially successful, thirty opera devotees each pledged £200 to underwrite any financial losses (see Table 6.3).

In total, Heidegger and Middlesex garnered 236 unique subscribers. Forty-five (20% of total) were peers; 91 (39%) were baronets or knights; and of the 100 (42%) untitled subscribers, almost half (50) were MPs (21%). With nobility being more than half of the subscribers, the exclusive and elite nature of the operagoing *beau monde* is maintained. Moreover, the 95 (40%) subscribers sitting in Parliament shows how much the opera audience was part of the life of Britain's political world.

Handel's 1740–41 season included among English-language productions his last two Italian operas *Imeneo* (Nov. 1740) and *Deidamia* (Jan. 1741). For the following season, Handel traveled to Dublin, where *Messiah* was premiered on 13 April 1742.

Handel and Middlesex were in competition for the 1739–40 and 1742–43 seasons. Since these two seasons of Handel's were devoted to dramatic works (odes, oratorios) in English, now the Handel-Middlesex competition should be seen as one of English dramatic music versus Italian opera. Handel alienated much of the Town by refusing to compose for Middlesex's company; the Town's displeasure with him increased when he offered his own subscription season

---

[58] Middlesex in Italy: John Ingamells, *A Dictionary of British and Irish Travellers in Italy, 1701–1800* (New Haven, Conn.: Yale University Press, 1997), 657–8.

[59] Middlesex's involvement in operatic matters is extensively documented in Taylor, "Italian Operagoing in London, 1700–1745"; and Taylor, "From Losses to Lawsuit: Patronage of the Italian Opera in London by Lord Middlesex," *Music and Letters*, 68 (1987), 1–25.

TABLE 6.3. Two-hundred-pound Subscribers to Middlesex's Opera
Company, 1742, with Their Previous Opera Company Participation

---

Charles Sackville, Lord Middlesex (later second Earl of Dorset, 1765)
  (none)

John Russell fourth Duke of Bedford
  Opera of Nobility director; Heidegger subscriber (1738); Middlesex subscriber (1741)

Scroop Egerton, first Duke of Bridgewater
  Middlesex subscriber (1741)

Charles FitzRoy, second Duke of Grafton
  Royal Academy of Music: shareholder, director (1719, 1726, 1727), pledged 1728;
  Heidegger subscriber (1738); Middlesex subscriber (1741), director (1741)

Charles Spencer, third Duke of Marlborough
  Royal Academy of Music: pledged 1728; Middlesex subscriber (1741)

John Montagu, second Duke of Montagu
  Royal Academy of Music: director (1719), subscriber (1723); Heidegger
  subscriber (1738); Middlesex subscriber (1740)

Thomas Pelham-Holles, first Duke of Newcastle
  Royal Academy of Music: shareholder, director (1719, 1720), subscriber (1723),
  pledged 1728; Heidegger subscriber (1738); Middlesex subscriber (1741)

John Manners, third Duke of Rutland
  Royal Academy of Music: director (1727), subscriber (1723), pledged 1728; Opera
  of Nobility director; Middlesex subscriber (1740), director (1742)

William van Keppel, second Earl of Albemarle
  Royal Academy of Music: director (1726, 1727), subscriber (1723), pledged 1728;
  Middlesex subscriber (1741)

Charles Bruce, third Earl of Aylesbury
  Middlesex subscriber (1740, 1741)

William Pulteney, first Earl of Bath (1742)
  Royal Academy of Music: shareholder, director (1719, 1720), subscriber (1723);
  Heidegger subscriber (1738); Middlesex subscriber (1741)

Philip Dormer Stanhope, fourth Earl of Chesterfield
  Royal Academy of Music: director (1720, 1726), subscriber (1723), pledged 1728;
  Heidegger subscriber (1738); Middlesex subscriber (1740, 1741)

Edward Bligh, second Earl of Darnley [I]
  Heidegger subscriber (1738); Middlesex subscriber (1741)

William Capel, second Earl of Essex
  Heidegger subscriber (1738); Middlesex subscriber (1741), director (1742)

William Fitzwilliam, third Earl Fitzwilliam [I]
  Middlesex subscriber (1741)

Francis Godolphin, second Earl of Godolphin
  Heidegger subscriber (1738)

Robert Darcy, fourth Earl of Holderness
  Middlesex subscriber (1740, 1741), director (1741, 1742)

Thomas Coke, Baron Lovel (later first Viscount and Earl of Leicester)
  Royal Academy of Music: shareholder, director (1719, 1720), pledged 1728; Opera
  of Nobility director; Heidegger subscriber (1738); Middlesex subscriber (1741)

OPERA OF THE NOBILITY AND THE *FUROR FARINELLICUS*   129

TABLE 6.3 *concluded*

Henry Pelham-Clinton, ninth Earl of Lincoln (later second Duke of Newcastle) (none)
Alan Brodrick, second Viscount Midleton Heidegger subscriber (1738); Middlesex subscriber (1741), director (1742)
Francis Greville, sixth Baron Brooke Middlesex subscriber (1741), director (1741)
Thomas Brand, esq., MP Middlesex subscriber (1741), director (1741)
George Lewis Coke Middlesex subscriber (1741)
John DePesters (none)
John Frederick, esq., MP Middlesex subscriber (1740, 1741), director (1741)
Charles Hanbury-Williams, MP (none)
Henry Pelham (younger brother of Thomas Pelham-Holles) Royal Academy of Music: subscriber (1723), pledged 1728; Heidegger subscriber (1738); Middlesex subscriber (1741)
(?)William Stanhope, MP, first Baron Harrington (later first Earl Harrington 1742) Heidegger subscriber (1738); Middlesex subscriber (1741)
(Hon.) Horace Walpole Middlesex subscriber (1741)

Sources: Carole Taylor, "From Losses to Lawsuit: Patronage of the Italian Opera in London by Lord Middlesex, 1739–45," *Music and Letters*, 68 (1987), 1–25 (Appendix 1); and Taylor, "Italian Operagoing in London, 1700–1745" (Ph.D. dissertation, Syracuse University, 1991).

that included the new oratorios *Semele* (10 February 1744) and *Joseph and His Brethren* (2 March 1744).[60] For season summaries, see Table 6.2.

Opera sung in Italian continued to be mounted at the Haymarket theatre through the rest of the century and beyond, even again offered by two competing companies in 1791.[61]

---

[60] See letter from John Christopher Smith, 28 July 1743, to the Earl of Shaftesbury; printed in Betty Matthews, "Unpublished Letters Concerning Handel," *Music and Letters*, 40 (1959), 261–8; and Donald Burrows, *Handel* (New York, N.Y.: Schirmer, 1994), 273–4; and *Handel: Collected Documents*, ed. Burrows et al., 4:100–1. For the opposition to Handel, see David Hunter, "Margaret Cecil, Lady Brown: 'Persevering Enemy to Handel' but 'Otherwise Unknown to History,'" *Women and Music*, 3 (1999), 43–58.

[61] See Curtis Price, Judith Milhous, and Robert D. Hume, *Italian Opera in Late Eighteenth-Century London: The Kings' Theatre, Haymarket, 1778–1791* (Oxford: Clarendon Press, 1995), 576–7.

* * *

At a time when London could not support even one opera company, for London's socio-political elite and *beau monde* to support two competing opera companies – each needing a cast of star-power Italian singers – was financial madness and mutual assured destruction.

Because of the extravagant sums he garnered and the widespread expressions of adulation, Farinelli's fame eclipsed that of any previous singer in England, and he became a metonym for the institution of opera. His role as symbol for the traditional evils of opera was emphasized by his foreign origins, sensuality of his singing, and ambiguous sexuality. The adulation of women for such a feminine creature made him appear a threat to traditional male notions of superiority in the prevailing gender hierarchy. The two conflicting responses to his benefit concert – material gifts and denunciation – exemplify how Farinelli became a bivalent figure in London's cultural world. But the *beau monde*'s great passion for Italian opera – confirming in no small way its role as a creator and marker of elite status – ensured its potential use for satire and verse.

CHAPTER 7

From Excise to the War of Jenkins' Ear

The nation exulted in the Opposition's success in forcing Walpole to abandon the Excise, and it still remained an incendiary issue after its defeat. The Opposition used it in subsequent electioneering propaganda; anti-Excise ballad operas reached the stage, and pamphlets and prints warned of the danger to liberty and property posed by Walpole's ministry. The Excise crisis revealed how mobilized out-of-doors public opinion from Country interests, defections of independent Whigs, and aroused merchants and traders could affect parliamentary legislation. Walpole thereafter took a more cautious approach to legislative proposals and never again advanced such a sweeping program.

Yet, the Opposition was unable to repeat the success on the Excise: it was still a minority in Parliament, and the united opposition of Tories and disaffected Whigs dissolved. Many of the efforts to topple Walpole were ill-conceived, failed, or backfired. For almost a decade, public opinion mattered little as long as Walpole still remained in the King's favor and controlled Parliament.[1]

The parliamentary sessions of 1734 to 1736 were relatively subdued, and domestic issues gave little opportunity for the Opposition. One of the most fateful parliamentary debates occurred on 13 March 1734 upon a motion to repeal the Septennial Act.[2] Repeal was an Opposition ploy to embarrass the Modern Whigs now in power, who otherwise should have supported a key principle in Whig ideology. The outcome of the motion revealed yet again the divisions in the Opposition.

Traditional Old Whiggism advocated Triennial Parliaments to force frequent elections, keep power with the electorate, and reduce the Crown's ability

---

[1] For sources covering domestic politics through the declaration of war: J. H. Plumb, *Sir Robert Walpole: The King's Minister* (London: Cresset, 1960); H. T. Dickinson, *Bolingbroke* (London: Constable); William Coxe, *Memoirs of the Life and Administration of Sir Robert Walpole, Earl of Orford,* 3 vols. (1798); Isaac Kramnick, *Bolingbroke and His Circle: The Politics of Nostalgia in the Age of Walpole* (Cambridge, Mass.: Harvard University Press, 1968); Brian H. Hill, *Sir Robert Walpole: "Sole and Prime Minister"* (London: Hamish Hamilton, 1989); Hill, *The Growth of Parliamentary Parties, 1689–1741* (Hamden, Conn.: Archon, 1976); Andrew C. Thompson, *George II: King and Elector* (New Haven, Conn.: Yale University Press, 2011). The parliamentary debates and other contemporary documents are given in William Cobbett, *Parliamentary History of England: From the Norman Conquest, in 1066, to the year, 1803* (London: T. C. Hansard, 1806–1820).

[2] Debate on the 1734 repeal, see Cobbett, *Parliamentary History of England*, 9 (1733–1737), 393–482. Coxe, *Memoirs of Robert Walpole*, 1: 411–26.

132 THE CULTURAL POLITICS OF OPERA, 1720–1742

to dominate Parliament by corruption. The government, now in the hands of Modern Whigs, argued that too-frequent elections kept the nation in continual ferment and exposed it to the evils arising from faction. With Septennial Parliaments, there were fewer opportunities to buy and corrupt elections. Bolingbroke prevailed on the Tory leaders to introduce the repeal. Dissident Whigs only reluctantly went along, for the repeal put them in the awkward position of opposing a bedrock Whig principle.

In his speech, William Wyndham made a tactical error by delivering an intemperate attack on Walpole and his followers and by making disrespectful remarks about the monarch. He asked the House to suppose

> a gentleman at the head of the administration, whose only safety depends upon corrupting the members of this House. ... A man abandoned to all notions of virtue or honour, ... ignorant of the true interest of his country, and consulting nothing but that of enriching and aggrandizing himself and his favourites. ... Let us suppose ... her trade insulted, her merchants plundered and her sailors murdered; and all these things overlooked, only for fear his administration should be endangered.[3]

Such a minister, Wyndham claimed, could corrupt Septennial Parliaments more easily than Triennial Parliaments.

Walpole replied in what many thought one of his finest speeches. In an equally violent but more accurate attack on Bolingbroke, he defended not himself but assailed instead a supposed "anti-Minister" (obviously Bolingbroke) and the self-proclaimed patriotism of Opposition Whigs. Instead of "wicked ministers," replied Walpole, others may

> speak of anti-ministers and mock patriots, who never had either virtue or honour, but in the whole course of their opposition are actuated only by motives of envy, and of resentment. ... Suppose this Anti-minister to be in a country where he really ought not to be, and where he could not have been but by an effect of too much goodness and mercy, yet endeavouring with all his might, and with all his art, to destroy the fountain from whence that mercy flowed. ... Let us farther suppose this Anti-minister ... making it his trade to betray the secrets of every court where he had before been; void of all faith or honour, and betraying every master he ever served. ... If we can suppose such a one, can there be imagined a greater disgrace to human nature than such a wretch as this?[4]

Reminding the Commons of Bolingbroke's intrigues with the Pretender and flight to France stigmatized him and the Opposition with the taint of Jacobitism.[5] Defeat of the motion by sixty-three votes revealed again the Opposition's disunity.

---

[3] Wyndham's speech: Cobbett, *Parliamentary History of England*, 9 (1733–1737), 454–66; Coxe, *Memoirs of Robert Walpole*, 1:413–20.

[4] Walpole's speech: Cobbett, *Parliamentary History of England*, 9 (1733–1737), 471–8; Coxe, *Memoirs of Robert Walpole*, 1:426–7.

[5] For an example of a gratuitous reminder, *Free Briton*, no. 256 (26 Sept. 1734).

FROM EXCISE TO THE WAR OF JENKINS' EAR   133

Humiliated by Walpole's speech, continuously attacked by Walpole's pamphleteers, and mistrusted by Pulteney and others, Bolingbroke realized he was a liability to the Opposition. In May 1735 he retired to France, bitter that despite his efforts on behalf of the Opposition, it was futile to hope of regaining his seat in the Lords while Walpole was in power.[6] As he wrote Wyndham from Paris, "My part is over, and he who remains on the stage after his part is over, deserved to be hissed off."[7] With Bolingbroke discredited and in exile, a dispirited and divided Opposition lost momentum, and a political calm settled as the Opposition reached its nadir in 1735. To curtail excesses from gin consumption, the government was able to pass in 1735 the resented Gin Act, which taxed gin and licensed dealers.[8]

1737 PARLIAMENT

The Parliament that sat on 1 February 1737 was unusually unruly and restless. The Opposition found several issues it used to challenge Walpole and the Ministry. One measure backfired.

As early as 1735, Bolingbroke had proposed that Frederick might apply to Parliament for the same portion of the Civil List that his father held as prince, but had refused him. Despite the opposition of Lyttelton, Frederick adopted the idea.[9] In February 1737, the Opposition took up the proposal in Parliament; the increased settlement was considered appropriate now that the Prince was married. Pulteney and Carteret moved address in both houses to the King to settle £100,000 on the Prince and a jointure on the Princess. The Ministry saw the motion as disrespectful and an affront to the King, in effect giving one-eighth of the government's funds to Frederick and the Opposition.[10] The measure failed, revealing again the lack of unity in the Opposition in the Commons: forty-five Tories absented themselves, refusing to vote for an interference with the royal prerogative. The Princess, though, received her jointure.[11]

---

[6] Bolingbroke's response, departure, and exile in France: Dickinson, *Bolingbroke*, 243–6.

[7] Bolingbroke, letter of 29 November 1735, to William Wyndam; in Coxe, *Memoirs of Robert Walpole*, 1:427.

[8] The unpopular act, passed in 1735, took effect in 1736 and provoked rioting and was poorly enforced; see Andrew A. Hanham, "The Gin Acts, 1729–51." Available at the History of Parliament online website, and Patrick Dillon, *The Much Lamented Death of Madam Geneva: The Eighteenth-Century Gin Craze* (London: Review, 2002).

[9] See Lyttelton's unheeded letter, *Memoirs and Correspondence of George, Lord Lyttelton, from 1734 to 1773*, ed. Robert Phillimore, 2 vols. (London, J. Ridgway, 1845), 1:74–8.

[10] Opposition pamphlets include *A Letter from a Member of Parliament to His Friend in the Country, upon the Motion to Address His Majesty to Settle 100,000 l. per Annum on His Royal Highness the Prince of Wales* [1737] and *Lords Protest on the Motion to Address His Majesty to Settle 100,000 l. per Annum on the Prince of Wales* [1737]. For the government, *An Examination of the Facts and Reasonings Contain'd in a Pamphlet intitled, A Letter from a Member of Parliament* [etc.] (1739).

[11] The Parliamentary debate is given in Cobbett, *Parliamentary History of England*, 9 (1733–1737), 1352–1454.

134   THE CULTURAL POLITICS OF OPERA, 1720–1742

One measure the Opposition failed to block had great consequences for British theatre. The Ministry had been enduring farces and comedies produced by Henry Fielding that reflected poorly on the Minister and royal family.[12] Walpole got hold of the manuscript of an obscene play, *The Festival of the Golden Rump* (probably not by Fielding), that attacked the King and Walpole. Walpole used the play as the pretext for the Licensing Act introduced in May. The Act allowed government censorship of plays and limited the number of theatres in London.[13] *Common Sense,* the *Craftsman,* and heated speeches by Lord Chesterfield argued the bill infringed British freedoms, but failed to prevent the bill's passing in June.

The Opposition had some success in June in weakening Walpole's bill for pains and penalties to punish the City of Edinburgh for the mob's lynching of Captain Porteous for his alleged role in ordering troops to fire on civilians during a public hanging. The measure was opposed in both houses, even by members of the government. The fine was reduced to £2,000 and yet passed by only six votes.[14]

🕭 Depredations Crisis

The Opposition had greater long-term success exploiting the Spanish seizures of British merchant shipping and seamen in the West Indies.[15] Trade between Britain and Spanish colonies in the West Indies had long been regulated by treaty. The Treaty of Utrecht (1713), ending Britain's role in the War of the Spanish Succession, granted Britain's South Sea Company the *asiento* (monopoly on slave trade to Spanish colonies) and the right to send an annual trading ship to Central America. The Treaty of Seville of 9 November 1729 affirmed these privileges.

Nonetheless, tensions between Britain and Spain flared up in 1737 as the Depredations Crisis, the run-up to the War of Jenkins' Ear in October 1739.[16]

---

[12] On the political, but not always partisan nature of Fielding's plays, the issues are summarized in Robert D. Hume, *Henry Fielding and the London Theatre, 1728–1737* (Oxford: Clarendon, 1988).

[13] For a detailed study, Vincent J. Liesenfeld, *The Licensing Act of 1737* (Madison, Wis.: University of Wisconsin Press, 1984. Summarized in relation to impacts on opera in McGeary, *Politics of Opera in Handel's Britain*, 186–9.

[14] Walpole allowed the bill to be modified; Coxe, *Memoirs of Robert Walpole*, 1:493–6.

[15] The Depredations Crisis is also discussed in McGeary, *Politics and Opera*, 173–8.

[16] On international politics leading to the war, the principal sources are: Philip Woodfine, *Britannia's Glories: The Walpole Ministry and the 1739 War with Spain* (London: Royal Historical Society, 1998), 75–101; Jean O. McLachlan, *Trade and Peace with Old Spain, 1667–1750* (Cambridge: Cambridge University Press, 1940), 78–121; and Richard Pares, *War and Trade in the West Indies, 1739–1763* (Oxford University Press, 1936), 14–43. H. W. Richmond, *The Navy in the War of 1739–48*, 3 vols. (Cambridge: Cambridge University Press, 1920). Coxe, *Memoirs of Robert Walpole*, 1:556–618, gives an account of the Crisis and outbreak of war that is sympathetic to Walpole. On the war in a wider cross-Atlantic context, Robert Gaudi, *The War of Jenkins' Ear: The*

FROM EXCISE TO THE WAR OF JENKINS' EAR   135

Disputes and legitimate grievances between the two nations had not been prevented by treaties. It was openly known that the British had been conducting illegal trade and smuggling with Spanish America,[17] which Spain to some extent tolerated all the while claiming Britain did nothing to prevent it. British merchants maintained the right of navigation without search in international waters. Spain insisted she owned the West Indies and surrounding seas, and foreign ships could only sail directly to and from foreign-owned ports; otherwise, they were subject to seizure. Such British trade undermined Spain's own commercial interests; the Spanish King moreover insisted the South Sea Company was not paying his rightful share of trading profits.[18]

The situation dragged on for years. In 1737 Spain increased efforts to control smuggling by licensing *guarda costas*. British merchants claimed these essentially legalized privateers seized ships and legally traded goods and imprisoned sailors. They demanded redress from Spain for unlawful seizures. To merchants and traders, the Ministry seemed powerless or unwilling to control Spanish captures of ships, crewmen, and cargoes.

Amid the Crisis, Farinelli left London at the end of 1736–37 season, with his initial destination Paris. He had accepted an invitation to the Spanish Court, but did not return to London from Madrid for the following season as he was contracted to do (see Chapter 6). The Opposition press quickly took up his decision to enter service to the Court and turned it to political use.[19] Beginning in September 1737, a series of satiric letters and essays in the Opposition newspaper *Common Sense* transformed his recruitment by the Spanish

---

Forgotten Struggle for North and South America: 1739-1742 (New York, N.Y.: Pegasus, 2021).

    See also Woodfine, "The Anglo-Spanish War of 1739," pp. 185–209 in Jeremy Black, ed., *The Origins of War in Early Modern Europe* (Edinburgh: John Donald, 1987); Woodfine, "'Suspicious Latitudes': Commerce, Colonies, and Patriotism in the 1730s," *Studies in Eighteenth-Century Culture*, 27 (1998), 25–46; Woodfine, "Ideas of Naval Power and the Conflict with Spain, 1737–1742," pp. 71–90 in *The British Navy and the Use of Naval Power in the Eighteenth Century*, ed. Jeremy Black and Philips Woodfine (Leicester: Leicester University Press, 1988).

[17] On the contraband trade, see Vera L. Brown, "The South Sea Company and Contraband Trade," *American Historical Review*, 31 (1926), 662–78; and George H. Nelson, "Contraband Trade under the Asiento, 1730–39," *American Historical Review*, 51 (1945–46), 55–67.

[18] On the role of the South Sea Company, John G. Sperling, *The South Sea Company: An Historical Essay and Bibliographic Finding List* (Cambridge, Mass.: Baker Library, Harvard Graduate School of Business Administration, 1962), 45–8; Ernest G. Hildner, Jr., "The Rôle of the South Sea Company in the Diplomacy Leading to the War of Jenkins' Ear, 1729–1739," *Hispanic American Historical Review*, 18 (1938), 321–41; and Harold W. V. Temperley, "The Causes of the War of Jenkins' Ear, 1739," *Transactions of the Royal Historical Society*, 3rd ser., vol. 3 (1909), 197–236.

[19] For political use of the episode, Thomas McGeary, "Farinelli in Madrid: Opera, Politics, and the War of Jenkins' Ear," *Musical Quarterly*, 82 (1998), 383–421 [reprinted in *Opera Remade, 1700–1750*, ed. Charles Dill (Farnham: Ashgate, 2010)]; and McGeary, *Politics of Opera in Handel's Britain*, 172–7.

136   THE CULTURAL POLITICS OF OPERA, 1720–1742

Court into a "capture" and compared it to Spain's seizing British merchant ships and seamen. The propaganda was intended to fuel public indignation at Walpole's failure to protect British shipping and his pacific policy of submitting to Spanish depredations – all to agitate for war.

In October and November 1737, merchants made their case known: they presented petitions to Parliament, the Privy Council, and the King; letters to newspapers protested the continued seizures of their ships and cruel treatment of their crews.[20] The public was outraged at insults to British honor and violation of liberty and rights. The *Craftsman* and *Common Sense* demanded satisfaction for the merchants, accusing the Ministry of failing to prevent "pyratical Depredations and cruel treatment of our Seamen."[21] Even the ministerial *Daily Gazetteer* had to concede the public anger and defended the Ministry in a series of papers in November and December.[22]

By early 1738 popular demand for outright war grew as relations between the nations grew even more strained. An agitated Commons demanded diplomatic correspondence to examine the Ministry's handling of Spanish depredations.

In March the Commons received a well-orchestrated series of petitions from ship owners and merchants from Bristol, Liverpool, and Glasgow trading in the West Indies.[23] They complained of their losses to *guarda costas*, asserted their treaty rights to trade, and pointed out depredations were continuing despite the King's assurances he would control them. The aggrieved merchants petitioned the Commons to put an end to all "Insults and Depredations on the *British Subjects*" and to grant "Relief for the unhappy Sufferers."

Public outrage at insults to British honor and liberty was further aroused in mid-March 1738 when letters reached London that thirty-one sailors captured in ships off Cuba had been robbed, forced to work their passage home, and were

[20] Letters from plundered ship captains and merchant petitions were widely reprinted: *London Evening-Post*, nos. 1517, 1544–45, 1548–49, 1552, 1560, 1566 (4–6 Aug.; 6–8, 8–11, 15–18, 18–20, 25–7 Oct.; 12–15, 26–9 Nov. 1737); *Daily Post*, nos. 5640, 5649 (8, 19 Oct. 1737); *Common Sense*, nos. 38, 42, 44 (22 Oct., 19 Nov., 3 Dec. 1737); *Old Whig*, no. 137 (20 Oct. 1737); and *Craftsman*, nos. 589, 591–3 (22 Oct. 1737, 5, 12, 19 Nov. 1737 [quoted]). On merchant opposition to Walpole, Nicholas Rogers, *Whigs and Cities: Politics in the Age of Walpole and Pitt* (Oxford: Clarendon, 1989), 56–67; and Rogers, "Resistance to Oligarchy: The City Opposition to Walpole and his Successors, 1725–47," pp. 1–29 in John Stevens, ed., *London in the Age of Reform* (Oxford: Blackwell, 1977).
[21] *Craftsman*, nos. 603, 605, 607–8, 610–11 (28 Jan., 11 and 25 Feb. 4 March, 18 and 25 March 1738).
[22] *Daily Gazetteer*, nos. 741, 743, 748, 759 (18, 21, and 26 Nov., 9 Dec. 1737). The paper asserted the Opposition was using the incidents "to sow Sedition and Discord amongst us." Incidences of depredations were rare, the *Gazetteer* argued, and smugglers had to accept the risks involved and realize that Spain had a right to seize contraband. Britain was unprepared for a hasty war, which would put a stop to all trade with Spain and do merchants more harm than good. The nation should be assured that the Ministry is taking proper measures that in due course will obtain justice and satisfaction.
[23] Cobbett, *Parliamentary History of England*, 10 (1737–1739), 561–643 (Commons), and 729–87 (Lords).

FROM EXCISE TO THE WAR OF JENKINS' EAR   137

now "groaning in the Fetters and Dungeons" in Cádiz.[24] This specter of mal-treated British seamen, slaves to the Spanish, "devouring by Vermin, and stifling with Filth," roused war fever. The *Gentleman's Magazine* for March inflamed the issue by printing a list of fifty-one British ships seized or plundered since 1728.

To dramatize Spanish depredations and cruelties, the Commons ordered Captain Robert Jenkins to appear on 28 March to tell how a Spanish privateer seized his brig in 1731, cut off his ear (among other cruelties), and told him to take it to King George.[25] It is uncertain if Jenkins actually did appear before the Commons.[26] His ear became the symbol of Spanish cruelty and gave its name to the ensuing war.

The session's climax came when the Commons met as a committee of the whole on 30 March 1738 and the following day voting an address to the King insisting on British rights of trade and navigation and beseeching him to obtain "effectual Relief for his injured Subjects."[27] The Lords passed an even stronger address on 2 May.[28] Despite the popular clamor, Walpole was desperate to avoid war, he said, "as long as there is any prospect of obtaining redress in a peaceable manner,"[29] by which he meant negotiating with Spain.

Sentiments for war were fanned by popular prints. "Slavery" (1738), for example, shows British merchants drawing a Spaniard's plow while Walpole in a Garter sash, drawing a sword, goads the British lion to follow behind. In the distance, Captain Jenkins is shown losing his ear, and a British naval ship fails to answer a volley fired by a Spanish ship.[30] The plate's caption beginning "This

---

[24] For news of the jailed sailors: *Daily Post*, nos. 5775, 5788, 5790, 5800 (15 and 30 March 1738, 1 and 13 April [quoted] 1738); and *London Evening-Post*, nos. 1618–19, 1621 (25–30 March [quoted], 30 March–1 April, 4–6 April 1738). See also McLachlan, *Trade and Peace*, 107; Woodfine, *Britannia's Glories*, 130–4. On 25 March, news reached London that the Spanish King had ordered the sailors released and returned home; *Daily Advertiser*, no. 2239 (29 March 1738).

[25] *Fog's Weekly Journal*, no. 164 (25 Dec. 1731), carried a poem on the incident, with a stanza:
> They cut off his Ear
> And said, Fellow, here
> Carry this to your Master, K— G—.

Accounts of the incident vary, as well as of its veracity. Sources citing Jenkins losing his ear are given in J. K. Laughton, "Jenkins' Ear," *English Historical Review*, 4 (1889), 741–9. For contemporary accounts, see also *Craftsman*, no. 259 (19 June 1731), and *Fog's Weekly Journal*, no. 137 (19 June 1731).

[26] Jenkins never appeared before the Commons; Woodfine, "Anglo-Spanish War," 196; and Cobbett, *Parliamentary History of England*, 10 (1737–1739), 638–40.

[27] Cobbett, *Parliamentary History of England*, 10 (1737–1739), 643.

[28] Debates and addresses: Cobbett, *Parliamentary History of England*, 10 (1737–1739), 729–87; *Journals of the House of Lords*, 25 (1736/7–1741), 237–8.

[29] Cobbett, *Parliamentary History of England*, 10 (1737–1739), 586.

[30] The print is reproduced in *Walpole and the Robinocracy. The English Satirical Print 1600–1832*, ed. Paul Langford (Cambridge: Chadwyck-Healey, 1986), no. 58 (see also nos. 53, 56, 57); and Herbert M. Atherton, *Political Prints in the Age of Hogarth: A*

PLATE 7.1. *Slavery* (1738), showing Britain suffering the humiliations of Spanish depredations.

fortress built by Nature for herself," from Shakespeare's *King Richard II* (II.i), is surely intended as an ironic comment on Walpole's Britain. Public opinion forced Walpole to send a squadron under Admiral Haddock to the Mediterranean on 9 May, which signaled to both sides that war was imminent.

Walpole tried to negotiate a settlement. In March 1738, the Ministry proposed that the £68,000 the Company owed the King of Spain be offset against the merchants' claims of £200,000 against Spain as compensation for lost goods. In July and August 1738, the minister to Spain, Benjamin Keene, negotiated reductions in claims until the amount Spain owed was £95,000. To avoid the indignity of the King making a direct payment, the Company was to make a payment of £68,000 on behalf of the King and loan the balance against future shares of profit.

CONVENTION OF THE PARDO

The settlement was incorporated in the Convention of the Pardo, signed in Madrid by Keene on 14 January 1739 (n.s.). The diplomats understood the Convention was a preliminary to future negotiations, and a treaty would settle the

---

Study of the Ideographic Representation of Politics (Oxford: Clarendon Press, 1974), 167–72 (esp. Plates 22 and 24).

FROM EXCISE TO THE WAR OF JENKINS' EAR   139

most pressing issues within eight months. Admiral Haddock's fleet was recalled; peace seemed at hand.

Laid before both houses on 8 February, the Convention's terms confirmed the Opposition's worst fears about Walpole's pacific policy toward Spain, for its terms settled none of the important matters such as British rights of navigation and freedom from search. The public was outraged, and the country was flooded with pamphlets, newspaper articles, and prints that furiously denounced the Convention as a national humiliation.[31] Pamphleteers recalled English triumphs against Spain in the days of Elizabeth and Cromwell; war was necessary to save British trade from Spanish pirates. In vain, the Ministry reminded that the Convention was merely a preliminary to a treaty that would settle outstanding issues, no British rights were given up, and a war disastrous to British merchants' interests had been avoided.

Now on the defensive against popular opinion and desiring peace, Walpole announced that if the Convention failed, he would assent to war. To excite public attention, William Wyndham led the Tories in a secession from the Commons vote on the Convention. The Secession proved a disastrous move: it discredited the MPs with their constituents and again revealed the lack of unity and leadership in the Opposition.[32] The Convention was narrowly approved by Parliament on 9 March 1739, although a Lord's Protest was entered.[33]

Distrusting the South Sea Company directors, the King of Spain had added the stipulation that he would withhold annual permission to conduct the *asiento* trade if the company did not pay the £68,000 owed him.[34] The £95,000 compensation to British merchants would be paid within four months of ratification. The Spanish King and the Company directors disagreed about making payments: each was unwilling to pay out of fear the other would not pay in return.[35] When both sides refused to make payments by the date due, the Convention was considered broken. Admiral Haddock's recall was withdrawn in March, and both sides realized war was inevitable. Britain would be outnumbered in a peninsular war with Spain; her only real military option was to

---

[31] Representative tracts surrounding the Convention are given in McGeary, *Opera and Politics in Handel's Britain*, p. 349: note 150 for Opposition attacks, and note 151 for defenses of Walpole and the Ministry.

[32] A defense of the Secession is given in *An Address to the Electors, and Other Free Subjects of Great Britain, Occasion'd by the Late Secession* (1739).

[33] For the debates, Cobbett, *Parliamentary History of England*, 10 (1737–1739), 1013–50, 1091–241 1243–6 (Lords), and 1050–90, 1246–319 (Commons). The protest is given in *The Lords Protest against the Convention Treaty* (1739), and in *A Complete Collection of the Protests of the Lords*, ed. James E. Thorold Rogers, 2 vols. (Oxford: Clarendon Press, 1875), 1:481–5.

[34] *The King of Spain's Protest, Relating to the South-Sea Company, not Printed with the Convention Treaty* (1739). Also appended to *The Convention. An Excellent New Ballad* (1739), a satire on the Convention.

[35] The Company's obstruction was a major cause of the collapse of negotiations; Hildner, "Rôle of the South Sea Company"; Sperling, *South Sea Company*, 45–8; and McLachlan, *Trade and Peace*, 78.

140   THE CULTURAL POLITICS OF OPERA, 1720–1742

attack Spain's overseas trade. In June and July British admirals were directed to begin reprisals against Spanish trade and seize fleets on their way to or from the West Indies.[36]

* * *

Reluctantly, and against his better judgment, Walpole declared war on 19 October 1739. The Ministry could cite the breach of the Convention as the cause for the war the public demanded.[37] With great ceremony, war was proclaimed on 23 October 1739.[38] With ringing of bells, bonfires, fireworks, and cheering of crowds, the country celebrated and looked forward to humbling Spain as in the days of Elizabeth and Cromwell. Walpole, long hoping to avoid war, bitterly uttered, "They now *ring* the bells, but they will soon *wring* their hands."[39]

---

[36] Richmond, *Navy in the War of 1739–48*, 1:14–38.

[37] Contrary to conventional wisdom, it was not public agitation that directly brought on the war, but the obstruction and obstinacy of the Company's directors, who pursued their own self-interest and tried to extract unreasonable payments from the King of Spain. By disregarding the Ministry, the Directors undermined the Convention; Sperling, *South Sea Company*, 45–6; Woodfine, "Anglo-Spanish War," 205.

[38] The proclamations are described in *Craftsman*, no. 694 (27 Oct. 1739).

[39] Coxe, *Memoirs of Robert Walpole*, 3:618 note.

CHAPTER 8

A Patriot Vision for Dramatic Music

Poets and dramatists in the Patriot circle embedded in their works themes that carry on the Opposition campaign.[1] Verse allegories by writers who drifted into the Patriot circle – James Thomson, Aaron Hill, and James Miller – present oppositional ideas to directly engage the cultural politics of opera. Their allegorical tableaux use the presence of opera in Britain as a contributor to the corruption, decay of culture, and loss of Publick Spirit under Walpole.

The allegories use the Whig mythology of the northward Progress of Liberty from Greece to Italy, through northern Europe to Britain, where she flourished, in contrast to the softer Mediterranean climate, where indolence and enslavement prevail.[2] The notion of the northern climes as especially hospitable to liberty goes back to Tacitus's description of the northern tribes in his *Germania*, where the primitive Germans under Arminius defeated the Roman legions at the Teutoburg Forest.

---

[1] A group of plays by James Thomson, David Mallet, Henry Brooke, and William Patterson from 1738 to 1740 on historical subjects carried clear Opposition application to the Ministry and Court; these Patriot dramas and their politics are discussed in Thomas McGeary, *Opera and Politics in Handel's Britain* (Cambridge: Cambridge University Press, 2013o), 180–209.

The ministerial paper *Hyp-Doctor*, no. 502 (10 June 1740) denounced these plays (and others):

The *Patriots act a Part on the Political Theatre*, more than the other Side: It is certain, they have endeavoured to make the *Theatre Political*, by *Edward and Eleonora, Pasquin, Gustavus Vasa, Arminius*, the *Golden Rump, Tom Thumb* the *Great*, and about a hundred Farces that might be mentioned.

The result, the paper continued, was to reduce debate in the two houses of Parliament to clapping and hissing, as in the theatre.

[2] For the Progress of Liberty topos: William Levine, "Collins, Thomson, and the Whig Progress of Liberty," *Studies in English Literature*, 34 (1994), 553–77; and Alan D. McKillop, *The Background of Thomson's "Liberty."* Rice Institute Pamphlet, vol. 38, no. 2 (July 1951), which provides essential background for this chapter, and explores topics in greater depth.

The notion that climate affected the physical and mental character of nations goes back to Aristotle, *Politics*, 7.7a, who attributed the spiritedness and freedom of those in Europe to the cold climate. A full study is Waldemar Zacharasiewicz, *Die Klimatheorie in der englische Literatur und Literaturkritik von der Mitte des 16. bis zum frühen 19. Jahrhundert* (Vienna: W. Braunmüller, 1877). See also Zera S. Fink, "Milton and the Theory of Climatic Influence," *Modern Language Quarterly*, 2 (1941), 67–80.

142   THE CULTURAL POLITICS OF OPERA, 1720–1742

In Thomson's *Liberty* (1735–1736), the goddess warns of the dangers of corruption, paints a prospect of Britain's future showing the fruits of liberty, and praises Frederick, Prince of Wales. Hill's *Tears of the Muses* (1737) presents the progress of Liberty as stalled in Britain, and in Miller's *The Year Forty-One* (1741) the Muses despair at what they see of Britain under Walpole. Hill and Miller portray the Muses as about to abandon Britain and seek a hardier, more favorable climate farther north. But the two poets hold out hope and present an optimistic vision of a Britain when virtue and Publick Spirit will flourish under a Patriot King. Thomson only laments the reigning taste for opera, but Hill and Miller imagine a dramatic music for Britain whose features they frame almost point by point as a contrast to those of opera. This dramatic music will be a social and moral force for the reformation and redemption of Britain.

The oppositional 'political work' of these allegories arises less from outright denunciations of Walpole than from offering a panegyric to Liberty as the source of all Britain's blessings and happiness, meanwhile deploring the present decayed state of the arts and public life (which is always a rebuke of the present national leadership), invoking the myth of the Gothic north (where the Saxons loved liberty and was the source of England's Ancient Constitution), and offering hopes for a revived Britain under a Patriot King.[3]

These allegories – grounded in classical republican, Old Whig, and Bolingbroke's ideas – position Britain at a Machiavellian moment: Britain must challenge *fortuna* with revitalized *virtù* and Publick Spirit.[4] Music (and this usually means the highest form of music, opera) plays an important role in diagnosing Britain's moral and civic state and (for Hill and Miller) a means of redemption.

Such poems using classical allegorical figures must have had a limited, sophisticated readership, as did the formal verse satires of Chapter 10. Their expected readership is reflected in their original published format as individual folio or quarto pamphlets, priced at one shilling (the upper end of single poems sold at book sellers), and in print runs probably no larger than 500.[5] Their audience was likely not the casual middling range of readers, but London's elite-status readers – those likely to attend, or be sympathetic to, opera.

These works are occasions for noting the culturally bivalent nature of opera: enjoyed and patronized by much of London's social-political elite, yet denounced by Opposition polemicists and social critics. Even *if* operagoers shared the oppositional politics expressed in the poems, we must assume they were able to bracket the indictment of opera from their own experience of the entertainment presented at the Haymarket theatre.

---

[3] C. A. Moore, "Whig Panegyric Verse, 1700–1760: A Phrase of Sentimentalism," *PMLA (Proceedings of the Modern Language Association)*, 41 (1926), 362–401.

[4] I have developed the idea of the Machiavellian moment in *Opera and Politics in Queen Anne's Britain, 1705–1714* (Woodbridge: Boydell, 2022), esp. Chapter 7, "Whigs Confront Opera: Britain at a Machiavellian Moment," 214–85.

[5] On the relative costs of such cultural productions, Robert D. Hume, "The Economics of Culture in London, 1660–1740," *Huntington Library Quarterly*, 69 (2006), 487–533 (for books, pp. 508–15).

℘ *James Thomson*: Liberty

James Thomson, the celebrated author of *The Seasons* (1726–1730), began his career as a writer of impeccable Whig credentials.[6] Of the separate parts of the *Seasons*, *Winter* (1726) was dedicated to the loyal Whig Sir Spencer Compton, speaker of the House of Commons, and *Summer* (1727) was dedicated to George "Bubb" Dodington, Whig MP and member of the Treasury board. When Isaac Newton, Britain's "Miracle of the Present Age" (as Addison celebrated him),[7] died on 20 March 1727, Thomson quickly published a *Poem to the Memory of Sir Isaac Newton* (8 May 1727), dedicating it to Sir Robert Walpole and praising him as Britain's "most illustrious *Patriot*" who is "balancing the Power of *Europe*, watching over our common Welfare."[8]

Two years later, Thomson anonymously published *Britannia* (21 January 1729), which shows him caught up in the fervor of current politics.[9] Published to coincide with the opening of Parliament, *Britannia* was part of the general public clamor against Walpole's humiliating course of peace and diplomacy toward Spain in the face of her continuing depredations on British shipping in the West Indies. A reminder of the nation's shame was the failure of Admiral Hosier's blockade of Porto Bello in 1726–1727.

Britannia is set as an allegorical tableau, a device to be used frequently again by Patriot writers. As it opens, Britannia is presented sitting in despair on a stormy, wind-beaten shore. The Muse records her lament and address to the nation. The cause of her despair is "the insulting *Spaniard*" who preys on British shipping while Britain remains at peace, in contrast to the glorious days of Elizabeth when the English navy defeated the Armada (lines 23–89).

The opening indictment of the Ministry's pacific policy toward Spain is balanced by a Whig paean to the benefits of peace, the course that Walpole was pursuing because it was more beneficial to trade. Britannia warns Britain that luxury and corruption destroy liberty and exhorts the need for virtue and

---

[6] On the publication history, see Introduction to James Thomson, *The Seasons*, ed. with intro. and commentary by James Sambrook (Oxford: Clarendon Press, 1981).

[7] Joseph Addison, *Spectator*, no. 543 (22 Nov. 1712).

[8] James Sambrook, *James Thomson (1700–1748): A Life* (Oxford: Oxford University Press, 1991), 59–60, points out that the dedication to Walpole need not have been a mercenary appeal for patronage (though he did receive £50 for the dedication). At this moment, with Spain besieging Gibraltar, for a Whig patriot like Thomson, Britain was certainly more secure under the guidance of Walpole than Bolingbroke or Pulteney. Further on Thomson's receipt of patronage, James Sambrook, "'A Just Balance between Patronage and the Press': The Case of James Thomson," *Studies in the Literary Imagination*, 34 (2002), 137–53.

[9] Commentary and edited texts of *Britannia* in James Thomson, *Liberty, the Castle of Indolence, and Other Poems*, ed. with intro. James Sambrook (Oxford: Clarendon Press, 1986), 15–30 (edition quoted); James Thomson, *The Castle of Indolence and Other Poems*, ed. Alan D. McKillop (Lawrence, Kans.: University of Kansas Press, 1961), 157–75. See also John W. Wells, "Thomson's *Britannia*: Issues, Attributions, Date, Variants," *Modern Philology*, 40 (1942), 43–56.

144   THE CULTURAL POLITICS OF OPERA, 1720–1742

Publick Spirit. Along with a panegyric to the royal throne, compliments are paid to Frederick, Prince of Wales, who recently had arrived in Britain on 3 December 1728. Finally, Britannia disappears in the gale.

Samuel Johnson later saw the poem as "a kind of poetical invective against the ministry, [by which] piece he declared himself an adherent to the opposition."[10] But both ministerial and oppositional newspapers selectively quoted from the poem to make it serve their own purposes.[11]

At the time, Thomson had not wholly abandoned his ministerial Whig allegiance (or at least hopes for patronage), judging by a subsequent dedication of his first play *Sophonisba* (1730) to Queen Caroline and the numerous courtiers and government members who subscribed for the complete *The Seasons* (1730), where *Autumn* (which closes the cycle) is dedicated to the new Whig speaker of the Commons, Arthur Onslow.

Thomson traveled in France and Italy with the eldest son of Lord Chancellor Charles Talbot from 1730 to 1733.[12] After his return, in November 1733 he accepted the post of secretary of briefs from Talbot, who at the time was a Walpole supporter, and so at this time Thomson could not be assumed to be allied with the Opposition circle. But in the following year, Talbot became disaffected over the court's accepting Bishop of London Edmund Gibson's objection to the appointment of Thomas Rundle to the see of Gloucester. Talbot's son William turned against Walpole and the following year voted against the ministry.[13] By 1733, Thomson's friend and patron Bubb Dodington was also in opposition. Most likely, then, following his patrons and friends, Thomson drifted into the Patriot circle and his works became vehicles for Opposition polemic.

Deeply affected by his contact with Italy, upon his return to Britain in March 1733, Thomson devoted two years to writing *Liberty*, published in installments from January 1735 to February 1736.[14] English travelers to Italy commonly

---

[10] Samuel Johnson, *Lives of the English Poets*, ed. George B. Hill, 3 vols. (Oxford: Clarendon Press, 1905), 3:286; see also Alan D. McKillop, "Thomson and the Licensers of the Stage," *Philological Quarterly*, 37 (1958), 448. The ministerial *Free Briton*, no. 37 (13 Aug. 1730), accused Thomson of ingratitude after receiving £50 for his ode on Newton.

[11] See the exchanges in the *Daily Journal*, no. 2514 (28 Jan. 1729); *Fog's Weekly Journal*, no. 19 (1 Feb. 1729); and the *Free Briton*, no. 37 (13 Aug.1730).

[12] On Thomson abroad, John Ingamells, *A Dictionary of British and Irish Travellers in Italy, 1701–1800* (New Haven, Conn.: Yale University Press, 1997), 937; and Sambrook, *James Thomson: A Life*, 108–19; and McKillop, *Background of Thomson's "Liberty,"* 12–25 (for the impact of Italy).

[13] For the Rundle controversy, Sambrook, *James Thomson: A Life*, 129–31.

[14] The five parts of *Liberty* are *Antient and Modern Italy Compared* (13 Jan. 1735), *Greece* (7 Feb. 1735), *Rome* (24 March 1735), *Britain* (16 Jan. 1736), and *The Prospect* (11 Feb. 1736). Commentary and edited text of *Liberty*: Thomson, *Liberty … and Other Poems*, ed. Sambrook, 31–147 (edition quoted).

See also Sambrook, *James Thomson: A Life*, 132–5, et seq.; McKillop, *Background of Thomson's "Liberty"*; McKillop, "Ethics and Political History in Thomson's *Liberty*," pp. 215–29 in *Pope and His Contemporaries: Essays Presented to George Sherburn*, ed.

A PATRIOT VISION FOR DRAMATIC MUSIC   145

contrasted the poverty of its inhabitants to the wealth of its churches and palaces, and noted the decayed state of learning and loss of liberty – all usually attributed to the effects of rule by the Catholic Church and arbitrary princely governance.[15]

In a clear Patriot gesture, Thomson dedicated the first book (as well as the complete poem) to Prince Frederick, in whom "the Cause and Concerns of Liberty have so zealous a Patron" and in whom "the noblest Dispositions of the Prince, and of the Patriot [are] united" (Dedication). Thomson's didactic restatements of the commonplaces that history is cyclic, that the arts and sciences rise and flourish under liberty and decline under tyranny, and that virtue is necessary to sustain the public good again demonstrate the persistence of classical republican thought and its perennial utility for any party in opposition. The rehearsal of these moral and political commonplaces apparently made the poem unreadable for Samuel Johnson.[16]

The five-part poem is an extended Whig panegyric to liberty. Amid the decay and ruins of modern Rome, Goddess Liberty will describe to the poet her rise and fall through Greece and Rome and her flight northward to Great Britain. In *Liberty*, Thomson forges a common bond between the Roman Republic and the way the British wishfully fashioned themselves as a nation that achieved and defended liberty; he reiterates the view that the enemy of liberty is not so much tyranny as it is luxury, commonly said a result of corruption and wealth. Luxury was the insidious inner force that undermined Rome; hence, wherever it occurs, it signals a threat to liberty.[17] Especially congenial to Opposition thought was *Liberty*'s use of the mythology of the Gothic or Saxon love of

---

James C. Clifford and Louis A. Landa (Oxford: Clarendon Press, 1949); and Dustin Griffin, *Patriotism and Poetry in Eighteenth-Century Britain* (Cambridge: Cambridge University Press, 2002), 74–97.

[15] For examples, Gilbert Burnet, *Some Letters Containing an Account of … Italy, &c.* (Rotterdam, 1686), widely reprinted under various titles; [George Lyttelton], *An Epistle to Mr Pope, from a Young Gentleman at Rome* (1730) (the poet would "Those hallow'd Ruins better pleas'd to see, / Than all the Pomp of modern Luxury" [p. 6]); Joseph Addison, *A Letter from Italy, … in the Year MDCCI* (1703), lines 111–12 ("Oppression in her vallies reigns, / And Tyranny usurps her happy plains").

On the origins of liberty in the Saxon or Gothic north, Gerrard, *Patriot Opposition*, 108–49; on the *translatio* topos: Levine, "Collins, Thomson, and the Whig Progress of Liberty"; Reginald H. Griffith, "The Progress Pieces of the Eighteenth Century," *The Texas Review*, 5 (1919–20), 218–33 [with list of progress pieces]; Mattie Swayne, "The Progress Piece in the Seventeenth Century," *The University of Texas Bulletin, Studies in English*, 16 (1936), 84–92; and McKillop, *Background of Thomson's "Liberty*," 74–85.

[16] Samuel Johnson wrote, "*Liberty*, when it first appeared, I tried to read, and soon desisted. I have never tried again." He objected that "The recurrence of the same images must tire in time; an enumeration of examples to prove a position which nobody denied, as it was from the beginning superfluous, must quickly grow disgusting"; *Lives of the English Poets*, ed. Hill, 3:289, 301.

[17] The importance of these historical and political commonplaces in *Liberty* are elaborated by McKillop, *Background of Thomson's "Liberty*," 86–7.

146   THE CULTURAL POLITICS OF OPERA, 1720–1742

liberty, government by assemblies, and elected monarchy. The idealization of hardy Saxons was embodied in numerous English writings.[18]

In Part I, *Antient and Modern Italy Compared*, the poet is musing in modern Rome, and a vision rises of the "majestic Power of Liberty." Liberty tells of her progress in the ancient world and offers the sweeping vista of the Roman Republic in her glory, when "every Virtue, Glory, Treasure, Art" shone. She claims all is now reversed in modern Italy, oppressed and sunk beneath Popery and rural poverty, without poets or heroes. In Rome today, even the architectural ruins shine greater than the pomp of modern oppression. Liberty even claims Michelangelo, Palladio, and Raphael are owed to her, since they are indebted to Greek models that were formed under Liberty. What, asks Liberty, would the ancient Romans say of modern Italy?

Liberty demands modern Britain know the lesson of the desolation of modern Italy: that her happiness arises from freedom and a limited monarch, where "King and People [are] equal bound / By guardian Laws." A paean to the royal family in the voice of the goddess includes a lengthy and prominent tribute to a prince, certainly to be taken for Frederick, who "burns sincere" for liberty and who aided by "the *Graces* and the *Muses*" will encourage the arts, and in whose breast "Britain's Glory swells" (I:359–79).

In Part II, *Greece*, the poet traces Liberty's progress from the pastoral ages, through the ancient empires, to Athens and Sparta. Liberty was the source of philosophy and "Nurse of Finer Arts": eloquence, epic poetry, music, sculpture, painting, and architecture were brought to their perfection under her protection. Liberty gave the Greek states their victory at Marathon. These "Wonders that illumin'd Greece" were lost – sunk by superstition, slavery, sloth, corruption, gold, and selfish passions. A peroration strikes home the lesson for Britain: freedom was never overcome by force, but sunk into slavery by vice and corruption.

In Part III, *Rome*, Liberty's progress continues to Rome, where her rise and fall is recalled. The cause of her decline in Rome is laid to "*Luxury, Dissension*, a mix'd *Rage* / Of boundless *Pleasure* and of boundless *Wealth*," which undermined virtue and public spirit (III:404–5). In revenge, Liberty then progresses to the northern nations, who – inspired by Liberty – wreak vengeance on the Roman Empire, plunging the magnificence of Rome into ruin. Then along with the arts and sciences, she quits the earth during the Dark Ages to retire to the celestial regions.

---

[18] See Samuel Kliger, *The Goths in England: A Study in Seventeenth and Eighteenth Century Thought* (Cambridge, Mass.: Harvard University Press, 1952), 7–9; and Howard D. Weinbrot, "Politics, Taste, and National Identity: Some Uses of Tacitism in Eighteenth-Century Britain," pp. 168–84 in *Tacitus and the Tacitean Tradition*, ed. T. J. Luce and A. J. Woodman (Princeton, N.J.: Princeton University Press, 1993), at 178–9. Sources for England include: Richard Verstegen, *A Restitution of Decayed Intelligence: In antiquities* (1605) (England and the Saxons share love of liberty, elected monarchs, and government by assemblies); Nicholas Bacon, *Historical Discourse of the Uniformity of the Government of England* (1647); and *An Answer to the Vindication of the Letter from a Person of Quality in the North* (1689).

A PATRIOT VISION FOR DRAMATIC MUSIC   147

Part IV, *Britain*, resumes the Progress of Liberty from "*Gothic* Darkness" with the rebirth of the arts and learning in Italy. Liberty traces her northward course to Britain; before her arrival, Neptune grants Britain dominion over the seas. Liberty is received and congratulated by Britannia, and her beneficent reign begins. The poet draws the progress of English history as the contest between liberty and the Constitution and corruption and luxury, as did Bolingbroke in his *Dissertation upon Parties* and *Remarks on the History of England*. The Worthies who preserved liberty are Alfred, Edward the Confessor, Henry III, Edward III, Henry V, Elizabeth, and Hampton. With the arrival of William, "Immortal Nassau," and the Glorious Revolution, Liberty's establishment is complete. Yet, she continually faces Machiavellian moments, for Liberty is always in danger from internal forces: "the felon undermining Hand / Of dark Corruption, can its Frame dissolve" (IV:118–91).

In the opening of Part V, *The Prospect*, Liberty proclaims "the Happiness and Grandeur of Great-Britain": "Thou Guardian of Mankind! Whence spring alone, / All human Grandeur, Happiness and Fame." But how shall this "mighty Kingdom" remain? Liberty proclaims the source of Britain's salvation: "*On* Virtue *can alone* my Kingdom *stand*, / On Public Virtue, Every Virtue join'd" (V:3–4, 93–4). The three public virtues necessary to maintain her establishment are the independent life of a country freeman, integrity in office, and a passion for the commonweal.

Liberty shows the consequences of those enslaved to wealth and desires, their wealth squandered on luxurious living and fashion. Such a "tasteless" one enslaved to "tyrant *Fashion*" exemplifies False Taste (see Chapter 9). She offers as an example those who flock to opera, identified by the "warbling" castrato singer:

> Then to adore some warbling Eunuch turn'd,
> With *Midas*' Ears they croud; or to the Buzz
> Of Masquerade unblushing: or, to show
> Their Scorn of *Nature*, at the Tragic Scene
> They mirthful sit, or prove the Comic true.   (V:178–82)

Those with False Taste respond inappropriately: like King Midas, who grew the ears of an ass when he made the wrong choice between Pan and Apollo, they make the wrong choice in music; they don't blush at the indecencies of masquerades; they laugh at a tragedy; or prove themselves rightful butts of comedies.

In Part II, Greece was hailed as the nursery of the finer arts, and Liberty's description of the arts and music there is important, for her description of music's noblest potential points to the non-corrupted, non-luxurious, classical republican-inspired music that will foster and sustain a virtuous republic. Liberty declares:

> The sweet Inforcer of the Poet's Strain,
> Thine [Greece's] was the meaning Music of the Heart.
> Not the vain Trill, that, void of Passion, runs
> In giddy Mazes, tickling idle Ears;
> But that deep-searching Voice, and artful Hand,
> To which respondent shakes the vary'd Soul.   (II:290–5)

148   THE CULTURAL POLITICS OF OPERA, 1720–1742

Desired by Liberty is song where music fortifies and is a handmaiden to the poet's verse. When poetry is supported by instrumental music, singing becomes a meaningful expression of the heart, not virtuosic display (such as elaborate Italianate arias that merely tickle the ear).

That the "vain Trill," "giddy Mazes," and "tickling idle Ears" are intended to stand for Italian music and opera is confirmed in a letter to his patroness Frances Thynne, Countess of Hertford (later Duchess of Somerset), to whom he dedicated *Spring* (1728) of the *Seasons*.[19] Written from Paris on 10 October 1732 during his return from Italy, the letter anticipates many of the ideas about contemporary Italy that would be developed in *Liberty*. To Lady Hertford, Thomson expresses his dismay at the "misery" and "destitute" state of the inhabitants of modern Italy, where almost all the "human arts and Industry" have been extinguished due to bad government and the Church. He carries his impression of what "ought to be considered rather as the land of the dead than of the living" to its music:

> The language and music in Italy are Inchanting. Being but an Infant in the language I ought not to pretend to judge of it, yet cannot I help thinking it not only very harmonious, and expressive, but even not at all incapable of manly graces. As for their Music, it is a sort of charming malady that quite dissolves them in softness, and greatly heightens in them that universal Indolence men naturally (I had almost said reasonably) fall into when they can receive little or no advantage from their Industry.[20]

In *Liberty*, Thomson does not further develop an idea for dramatic music; this will be left for Hill and Miller.

At the close of Part V, Liberty describes the prospect for Britain's future as it passes before the poet in a vision: science, arts, public works, and the fruits of commerce; kings who value only merit and virtue; a new race of noble and generous youth; justice that shines on all; arts and sciences that flourish; rising public works; and arts that pursue social ends and temper the passions.

The oppositional stance of *Liberty* arises not from overt denunciation of Walpole or his ministry. Liberty had long been the cry of Whigs, and so in itself was hardly controversial; but such an extended praise of liberty and her blessings, coupled with Liberty's warnings about the dangers of corruption, could not but be an innuendo that liberty was in danger in Britain under Walpole and scarcely differ from standard Opposition rhetoric. Praise of Frederick and

---

[19] Helen S. Hughes, "Thomson and the Countess of Hertford," *Modern Philology*, 25 (1928), 439–68. Further on Hertford, see Hughes, *The Gentle Hertford* (New York, N.Y.: Macmillan, 1940).

[20] Letter of 10 October 1732, from Paris, to Lady Hertford; Archives of the Duke of Northumberland, at Alnwick Castle, DNP, Ms 25 (p. 2 of letter). I am grateful to Christopher Hunwick for his generous assistance in accessing the Alnwick Castle archive and for permission to quote from the Archive. The letter is also printed in *James Thomson (1700-1748): Letters and Documents*, ed. Alan D. McKillop (Lawrence, Kans.: University of Kansas Press, 1958), 82.

A PATRIOT VISION FOR DRAMATIC MUSIC   149

prescription of virtue and Publick Spirit further tilt *Liberty* toward being sympathetic to the Opposition.

The harmony of ideas in *Liberty* with Opposition ideology is confirmed in the *Craftsman* for 16 August 1735.[21] The writer uses two lengthy passages as a springboard to assert that those who have sold their political independence to the ministry are "a Friend to *Slavery*" and cannot possess a true *Amor Patriæ* and passions for liberty and the public good; independent citizens without pensions or places are needed to preserve liberty. Newspaper advertisements for Part IV of *Liberty* also align the poem with the Patriot Opposition's view of the condition of contemporary Britain: "The Design of this Poem is to trace the Rise and Fall of Liberty, in the several States wherein she has flourish'd; and an Advice to Britons how to preserve it in this Island."[22]

While Thomson was abroad, Prince Frederick had seen a volume containing his *Seasons* and *Britannia* given him by Lady Hertford. Frederick's approbation, Thomson wrote her, gave him hope

> of seeing the fine arts flourish under a Prince of his so noble equal humane and generous dispositions; who knows how to unite the soveraignty of the prince with the liberty of the people, and to found his happiness and Glory on the publick Good.[23]

Thomson's subsequent revisions and additions to the *Seasons* cite Patriot statesmen,[24] and the complete poem's 1744 edition was dedicated to Frederick. When Lord Chancellor Talbot died in February 1737, Thomson lost his sinecure of secretary of briefs. Lyttelton, now secretary to Frederick, sent for Thomson and learning of his poverty, obtained for him in August a pension of £100.[25]

Further evidence of Thomson's allegiance to the Opposition appeared on 13 September 1737 with the publication of an ode to the Prince of Wales on the birth of the Princess Augusta on 31 July 1737.[26] The poem – with its tactless slighting of the reigning monarchs, while Thomson sings "the promis'd Glories" of the coming reign of Frederick, "Thou Friend of Liberty!," from whose blood

---

[21] *Craftsman*, no. 476 (16 Aug.1735); see McKillop, *Background of "Liberty*," 96–8; and Sambrook, *James Thomson*, 139.

[22] *Daily Advertiser*, no. 1551 (16 Jan. 1736).

[23] Thomson, 10 October 1732, Paris, to Lady Hertford; see note 20.

[24] See line numbers in *Seasons*, ed. Sambrook: *Autumn*, lines 1037–81 (Cobham, Stowe Gardens, and the Temple of Virtue), *Spring*, line 906 (George Lyttelton), *Autumn*, line 1048 (William Pitt), *Winter*, line 664 (Chesterfield).

[25] Thomson's *The Castle of Indolence* (begun or written 1733–1734; pub. 1748) contains two stanzas laudatory of Lyttelton: Canto I, stanzas 65 and 66. Gerrard argues (unpersuasively) that *Castle of Indolence* is a sustained allegory on the Walpole ministry; "*The Castle of Indolence* and the Opposition to Walpole," *Review of English Studies*, n.s., 41 (1990), 25–64.

[26] Text and commentary in Thomson, *Liberty ... and Other Poems*, ed. Sambrook, 301–2, 427–8 (edition quoted). The ode was published simultaneously in several newspapers.

150 THE CULTURAL POLITICS OF OPERA, 1720–1742

will rise new Edwards, Henrys, Annas, and Elizabeths – was attacked the following month in the ministerial *Daily Gazetteer*.[27]

His later plays, *Agamemnon* (1738) and *Edward and Eleonora* (1739) on historical subjects with application to current political figures, were vehicles for Opposition innuendo. *Edward and Eleonora* was seen by the Lord Chamberlain as such a formidable attack on Walpole that it was banned.[28]

Aaron Hill: Tears of the Muses

In two allegorical poems by Aaron Hill and James Miller, the Progress of Liberty is stalled: she is sunk in despair about Britain under Walpole and is about to seek more favorable climes in the north. But the poets counter with an optimistic vision of Britain redeemed by virtue, Publick Spirit, and Prince Frederick as the Patriot King. In these poems, Britain is at another Machiavellian moment: at a time of national shame and despair, sunk under internal corruption and an ineffectual war with Spain. Still alive are the classical republican ideals as a means for national transformation. Such creaking allegorical machinery can hardly be considered effective in the rough and tumble world of party politics, yet as high-literary expressions of Opposition beliefs, the poems illustrate yet again how closely connected were the realms of serious poetry and politics.

Another figure who drifted into the Patriot circle was the drama critic and aspiring playwright Aaron Hill. His *Tears of the Muses; in a Conference between Prince Germanicus, and a Male-content Party*, [29] published on the great Whig anniversary of 5 November 1737, unveils a vision of a meeting between Germanicus, who is likely intended to represent Prince Frederick, and the malcontent Muses. Like Thomson's *Britannia* and *Liberty*, Hill's *Tears of the Muses* uses an allegorical tableau to present a cautionary lesson about the arts in Britain and offer a vision of a redeemed Britain.

From the early 1730s, living outside London, Hill had been corresponding with literary figures in the Opposition circle: Pope, Bolingbroke, Thomson, and Mallet. In what must have seemed his wearying and pestering letters to them (especially to Pope), Hill advanced his own long-standing program of

---

[27] The *Daily Gazetteer*, no. 704 (6 Oct. 1737) devoted an entire lead essay to personal invective against the "impudent" poet and to exposing the insults, libels, and affronts of the poem. Why, the *Gazetteer* asks of Opposition writers, is it necessary that "to applaud his *Royal Highness*, they must reproach his Majesty?" If Britain really were in such a deplorable condition as Thomson presents, nothing could be a greater indignity to the Prince than to publish that fact and thereby affront the government of the King. But if Thomson has scandalously misrepresented the state of Britain, as the Gazetteer assures he has, then Thomson has committed the impudence of infamously libeling the King's government while under the Prince's patronage.

Noting that the ode had "occasioned some extraordinary political Reflections," the *Political State of Great Britain*, 54 (Oct. 1737), 361–2, 400–4, reprinted the ode and the *Daily Gazetteer* essay.

[28] See note 1.

[29] *Tears of the Muses* was reissued in 1738 and reprinted in Hill, *The Works of the Late Aaron Hill, Esq.*, 2nd ed., 4 vols. (1753), 4:163–89.

A PATRIOT VISION FOR DRAMATIC MUSIC   151

reforming the theatre, solicited comments on his own plays, critiqued others' plays, and angled to get his own plays staged.

Hill's ideas for reform of the theatre were expounded in the periodical *The Prompter* (1734–1736), written with William Popple;[30] his ideas on acting were later developed in the *Art of Acting* (1746) and *Essay on the Art of Acting* (1753). Numerous essays in the *Prompter* railed against Italian opera and especially the adulation of Farinelli.[31]

In 1731–1733 Hill was asking Pope and Bolingbroke for comments on his plays *Athelwold* (1731) and Voltaire translation *Zara* (1735; pub. 1736).[32] In August 1733 he described his ideas for a "tragic academy" that would improve the theatre by removing it from the hands of the actors and theatre managers, thus ensuring better choice of plays and teaching more expressive acting.[33] Throughout his concerns, Hill protests a decline in taste leading to public abandonment of theatre, and especially of ennobling tragedy. In many ways, Hill was in the vanguard of urging official control of the theatres, which the ministry obtained with the Licensing Act of 1737.

Twice Hill wrote to Thomson hoping he might engage Prince Frederick's patronage for the never-realized academy.[34] Frederick did command a performance of Hill's next Voltaire translation, *Alzira* (1736), and Hill dedicated it to him (as he had done *Zara*), renewing his wish

> that a Theatre entirely *new*, … professing only what is *serious*, and *manly*, and sacred to the Interests of *Wisdom*, and *Virtue*, might arise, under some powerful and popular Protection, such as That of Your Royal Highness's *distinguish'd Countenance!*[35]

---

[30] On Hill's ideas about theatre, drama, and acting, see the preface to *The Prompter: A Theatrical Paper (1734–1736) by Aaron Hill and William Popple*, ed. and sel. by William W. Appleton and Kalman A. Burnim (New York, N.Y.: Benjamin Blom, 1966); J. Merrill Knapp, "Aaron Hill and the London Theatre of His Time," *Händel-Jahrbuch*, 37 (1991), 177–85; Dorothy Brewster, *Aaron Hill, Poet, Dramatist, Projector* (New York, N.Y.: Columbia University Press, 1913), 122–39; Christine Gerrard, *Aaron Hill: The Muses' Projector, 1685–1750* (Oxford: Oxford University Press, 2003), 25–7, 145–71; and C. R. Kropf, "William Popple: Dramatist, Critic, and Diplomat," *Restoration and Eighteenth-Century Theatre Research*, 2nd series, vol. 1, no. 1 (July 1986), 1–17 (on Popple's role in the *Prompter*).

[31] Numerous items in the *Prompter* criticize or satirize Farinelli and Italian opera, especially nos. 7, 13, 37, 106, 116, and 155.

[32] Hill, *Works*, 1:145–7; 1:235–7. This posthumous edition is dedicated to the widowed Princess of Wales. Further on the correspondence with Pope and Bolingbroke, see Brewster, *Aaron Hill*, 201–38; and Gerrard, *Aaron Hill*, esp. 124–44.

[33] Hill, *Works*, 1:194–7. Hill's ideas on theatre reform are anticipated in an anonymous, *A Proposal for the Better Regulation of the Stage* (1732); Hill's possible authorship for this tract has not yet been suggested.

[34] Hill, *Works*, 1:285–6, 315–17. On Hill's earlier association with Thomson, see Robert Inglesfield, "James Thomson, Aaron Hill and the Poetic 'Sublime,'" *British Journal for Eighteenth-Century Studies*, 13 (1990), 215–21.

[35] Translator's Preface to Hill, *Alzira. A Tragedy* (1736), v–vi. Hill further congratulated the Prince "on the human Glories of your *future* Reign: and thank you for a thousand

152   THE CULTURAL POLITICS OF OPERA, 1720–1742

Hill's *Tears of the Muses* will also place hope in Frederick as a guardian of the arts.

In 1734–1735 Hill was offering Thomson suggestions for his *Liberty*, describing it as "the dying effort of despairing and indignant virtue, … the last *stretched blaze of our expiring genius*." Hill's letters to Thomson show him espousing Old Whig or Patriot rhetoric and lamenting this "devoted nation, irrecoverably lost in luxury" and seeing Britain's extended commerce and wealth as the "*sole root of every English evil*."[36]

In the summer of 1738, Hill was soliciting appraisals and improvements for his play *Caesar* (*The Roman Revenge*); he hoped Pope would use his influence to get it staged and that Bolingbroke would accept the dedication.[37] And in late 1741, Hill offered David Mallet corrections and suggestions for his masque *Alfred*, apparently in view of its theatrical production. Hill did note the topical application, recognizing there is a compliment to the "*living Alfred*, you design'd to glance at" – no doubt Frederick, Prince of Wales.[38]

Hill himself seems to have harbored no animus against Walpole: in 1734 he was writing to Lady Walpole with advice about rock grottos for her garden at Chelsea (one grotto being designed as a satire on false patriotism, probably that of her husband's opponents), and in 1740 he wrote to Sir Robert with advice on statecraft.[39]

Hill's motives in all these endeavors seem less overtly partisan than tied to advancing his own interests in producing his plays, managing a theatre, and reforming the stage and acting. He deliberately kept the *Prompter* free of politics, and its essays frequently comment on the evils of party spirit.[40] Nonetheless, it is to oppositional writers and Frederick that Hill looks for assistance in reforming the state of literature and drama.

In the allegorical conference presented in *Tears of the Muses*, Hill takes up the topos of the Progress of Liberty and the Arts.[41] In Hill's version, Liberty and the Arts are so despondent in Walpole's Britain, they intend to continue their northward progress. As the conference opens in a town grove, Germanicus is approached by the phantoms of the malcontent nine Muses, "thin Forms of shivering Woe, / … a wretched Sisterhood of Tears" (p. 11).[42] One of them laments that the "Arts, and polish'd Life" are now all in vain, where "Fool is Fashion, Ignorance is *Art*." In order to escape derision they have resolved on self-exile to "the bleak *North*'s new-rising Coasts," where they hope the beams

---

Blessings, *I expect not to partake of*." Hill also wrote a poem to Frederick on a blank leaf of *Alzira* when he presented a copy to him, where he is addressed as "thy *Country's* Hope"; see Hill, *Works*, 4:89. Frederick and his wife also attended a command performance on 1 July 1736.

[36] Hill, *Works*, 1:247–50, 277–82, 310–19.

[37] Hill, *Works*, 2:23–40 (Pope) and 1–22 (Bolingbroke). The play was ultimately passed over by the manager Fleetwood (2:65–6); it was printed as *The Roman Revenge* in *The Dramatic Works of Aaron Hill*, 2 vols. (1750), 2:257–327.

[38] Hill, *Works*, 2:147–56, 181–7.

[39] Hill, *Works*, 1:115–16.

[40] See *Prompter*, nos. 4, 12, 27, and 83.

[41] On the Progress poem, see note 15.

[42] *Tears of the Muses*, 11.

A PATRIOT VISION FOR DRAMATIC MUSIC   153

of glory will supply the absence of the sun. Germanicus asks the Muses why they would leave a land (presumably Britain)

> Where Freedom unrestrain'd her Empire holds,
> And Legal Monarchy new Bloom unfolds?   (p. 13)

Each Muse steps forth and indicts some appropriate vice or social neglect as a reason for departing to the North. Erato, Muse of erotic poetry, complains of venal love; Urania, Muse of astronomy, that Newton is neglected; Melpomene and Thalia, Muses of tragedy and comedy, how the "tasteless Town" has debased the stage. Terpsichore, Muse of choral dance and song, describes her anguish over opera:

> Near *Opera's* fribling *Fugues*, what Muse can stay?
> Where wordless Warblings winnow *Thought*, away!
> Music, when *Purpose* points her not the Road,
> Charms, to betray, and softens, to *corrode*.
> Empty of Sense, the Soul-seducing Art
> Thrills a slow Poison to the sick'ning Heart.
> Soft sinks *Idea*, dissolute in Ease,
> And all Life's feeble Lesson is, to *please*.
> Spirit, and Taste, and generous Toil, take Flight;
> And lazy Love, and indolent Delight,
> And low luxurious Weariness of Pain,
> Lull the lost Mind, —and all its Powers are vain.   (p. 24)

Terpsichore has succinctly reiterated the long-standing charge that without an intelligible text to provide purpose, ideas, and sense, music sinks to pleasure and merely charms, softens, and seduces the soul to indolent delight. All the great powers music had when sung by the ancient poets are in vain.

This vision of music is certainly a *volte-face* for the Aaron Hill of 1711, who as the manager of the Haymarket theatre prepared the scenario for Handel's first opera for England, *Rinaldo* (1711). Two decades after *Rinaldo*, a reformed Hill tried to enlist Handel in the cause of English musical dramatic works, in what seems a repudiation of their earlier collaboration. On 5 December 1732, he asked Handel to use his "inimitable genius" toward

> the establishment of *musick*, upon a foundation of good poetry; where the excellence of the *sound* should be no longer dishonour'd, by the poorness of the sense it is chain'd to.
>
> My meaning is, that you would be resolute enough, to deliver us from our Italian bondage; and demonstrate, that English is soft enough for Opera, when compos'd by poets, who know how to distinguish the sweetness of our tongue, from the strength of it, where the last is less necessary.
>
> I am of opinion, that … a species of dramatic Opera might be invented, that, by reconciling reason and dignity, with musick and fine machinery, would charm the ear, and hold fast the heart, together.[43]

---

[43] Hill, *Works*, 1:115–16; also in O. E. Deutsch, *Handel: A Documentary Biography* (New York, N.Y.: W. W. Norton, 1955), 299; and *George Frideric Handel: Collected Documents*, ed. Donald Burrows, Helen Coffey, John Greenacombe, and Anthony

154 THE CULTURAL POLITICS OF OPERA, 1720–1742

Since Handel had already produced the oratorio *Esther* earlier that year (but without staging), with the phrases "dramatic Opera" and "fine machinery," Hill seems to be calling for a form of staged, dramatic music sung in English. At some time, Hill's imagination turned to realizing his ideas for an English dramatic music and wrote a prose scenario for an opera to be called *Hengist and Horsa. Or, the Origin of England.* A dramatic work on ancient Britons would be congenial to the Patriot cause.[44]

Terpsichore's description of music in the North embodies a utopian vision of the true social function of music. By contrast to Italian opera ("expanded *Shakes,* / That wind wav'd Nothings"), music in the northern land can move all the noble passions. A manly "Martial" music, it increases the social affections, and quickens thought:

> There, to the Drum's big Beat, the Heart leaps high.
> There, sighing Flutes but temp'ring Martial Heat,
> Teach distant Pity and Revenge to *meet.*
> The manly Pipe, there, scorns th' expanded *Shakes,*
> That wind wav'd Nothings, till Attention *akes.*
> There *now,* concurring Keys and Chords increase
> The Heart's soft social Tyes, and cherish *Peace.*
> *Then,* Trumpets, answ'ring Trumpets, shrill, and far,
> Swell to the sounding Wind th' inspiring *War.*
> There, the rows'd Soul, in Exercise, grows strong:
> Nor *pools* to puddly Foulness, stopp'd, too long.
> Strength'ning, and strengthned by, the Poet's Fire,
> There, Music's meaning Voice *exalts* Desire.
> There, Harmony not drowns, but quickens, Thought;
> And Fools, unfeeling Words, by Notes are *caught.* (pp. 24–5)

Last to step forward is Calliope, Muse of epic poetry. She sings of an ideal prince who once was and before too long may be again. Her description of this prince who embodies every imaginable virtue, we may suppose, is a model for Germanicus/Frederick. Having spoken, she and her sisters rise to leave, but are stayed by Germanicus. He persuades the Muses to assume disguises, retire to "*Cornish* Boroughs" (the Prince of Wales is also the Duke of Cornwall), whence they can work their "unsuspected Influence" until the day they can quit their disguises and again be accepted by the wise. Hill tells us at the end that this scene was only a dream of a "Visionary Poet."

Tears of the Muses reflects the Aaron Hill of the *Plain-Dealer, Prompter,* and the reformer concerned with the integrity of the stage. As in other Patriot allegories, the desolate state of the arts in Britain, characterized by the presence of Italian opera, is a contrast to a utopia to be realized when Frederick ascends the throne.

Hicks, 6 vols. (Cambridge: Cambridge University Press, 2013–), 2:572–3. Handel subscribed to the first edition of Hill's *Works* (1754).

44 "Plan for an Opera, to be call'd Hengist and Horse. Or, the Origin of England"; in Hill, *Works,* 2:391–410.

A PATRIOT VISION FOR DRAMATIC MUSIC   155

❧ *James Miller:* The Year Forty-One

The themes from Thomson's and Hill's visions of a dramatic music for a Britain sunk in degeneracy and despair are taken up in James Miller's *The Year Forty-One. Carmen Seculare* (November 1741), published in time for the opening month of what would be the last Parliament of Walpole's rule as prime minister.[45] Miller presents a vision of the arts based on principles of classical republicanism and sketches the role of music and the arts in a Patriot's utopia of liberty. Miller does not invoke Italian opera directly, but his desiderata for a music under Frederick are framed in terms that suggest the usual criticisms of opera.

Miller's writings show an increasing commitment to the Opposition cause since his *Harlequin-Horace* of 1731 (see Chapter 9). Miller and Pope shared a publisher, Lawton Gilliver, and Pope commended *Harlequin-Horace* for its "good deal of humour."[46] Subsequent revisions of *Harlequin-Horace* increasingly include anti-ministerial passages. We will encounter his Opposition satire *Seasonable Reproof* of 1735 (see Chapter 10). His plays and poems proved a bar to his ecclesiastical preferment, and the Ministry apparently thought he could be bought out to write on its behalf. As his widow reported,

> He was so honest however in [his] principles, that upon a large offer being made him by the agents of the ministry in the time of a general opposition, he had virtue sufficient to withstand the temptation, though his circumstances at that time were far from being easy.[47]

In 1740, Miller engaged in overt, mean-spirited, vehement anti-Walpole pamphleteering. Reminiscent of Pope's 1738 *Dialogues*, Miller's *Are These Things So? The Previous Question, from an Englishman in His Grotto, to a Great Man at Court* (1740) represents Pope conversing with Walpole and set off a long series of exchanges and replies.[48] Walpole is asked, if it is true

> That You're the fatal Cause of *Britain*'s Shame,
> The *Spend-thrift* of her Freedom, and her Fame?   (p. 4)

---

[45] The poem is passed over in Gerrard, *Patriot Opposition*, 136, deferring to Goldgar, *Walpole and the Wits*, 211–13, who stresses how the poem puts "the decay of culture as the prime symptom of political infection" (p. 212). That is, False Taste is sign and result of political corruption.

[46] Letter from Pope, 6 February 1731, to John Caryll; *The Correspondence of Alexander Pope*, ed. George Sherburn, 5 vols. (Oxford: Clarendon Press, 1956), 3:172–3.

[47] Reported according to information provided by his widow, in Theophilis Cibber (Robert Shiells), *The Lives of the Poets of Great Britain and Ireland*, 5 vols. (1753), 5:332–4.

[48] On the pamphlet war set off by Miller, see Ian Gordon, Introduction to James Miller, *Are These Things So?* Augustan Reprint Series, no. 153 (1972); Goldgar, *Walpole and the Wits*, 210–11; and Maynard Mack, *The Garden and the City: Retirement and Politics in the Later Poetry of Pope, 1731–1743* (Toronto: University of Toronto Press, 1969), 194–200; and Paula O'Brien, "The Life and Works of James Miller, 1704–1744" (Ph.D. thesis, University of London, 1879), 66–72.

156   THE CULTURAL POLITICS OF OPERA, 1720–1742

Pope supposedly asks which group of dead will be among the British Worthies, but

> ... with the *Curs'd* your Tomb shall foremost stand,
> The Gaveston's and Wolsey's of the Land.
> Your Epitaph – *In this foul Grave lies He,*
> *Who dug the Grave of* British *Liberty.*[49]

In 1741, Miller included *Harlequin-Horace, Of Politeness,* and *Seasonable Reproof* in his *Miscellaneous Works in Verse and Prose*. In dedicating the collection to Prince Frederick, Miller especially recognizes the honor Frederick did him by attending Miller's comedies and acclaims the humane, beneficent, and princely qualities Frederick was exerting for the nation. Among the subscribers was Handel, who in 1737 had written a song for Kitty Clive in Miller's play *The Universal Passion*.[50]

The title *The Year Forty-One* carried complex allusions and resonances. The year 1741 hints a continuation of the topical annual satires begun by Pope's 1738 *Dialogues* and their reflections on the present state of Britain. Although called by Miller "an honest Satire on the Degeneracy of the Age," only a short central dialogue, in which a Court apologist and the poet disagree about the current state of Britain is satiric in form.

The subtitle recalls Horace's *Carmen Saeculare*, the ode written for the secular festival games revived by Augustus in 17 BC. The games were to initiate a new series of *saeculi*, each to last 110 years (the customary, previous *saeculum* was one hundred years).[51] Horace's ode contains prayers to Apollo and Diana for the continued prosperity of Rome and praise for the blessings Rome enjoys. Horace is confident the three-day festival will bring forth the gods' blessings and assure Rome's continued greatness. Miller's poem carries a wish for a *saeculum* to begin that parliamentary session, the removal of Walpole, and arrival of a Patriot King who will see Britain enter a golden age.

What ties *The Year Forty-One* to Bolingbroke's ideas is that 'forty-one' alludes to the famous parliamentary Grand Remonstrance of 22 November 1641, 100 years to the month before the publication of Miller's poem.[52] In that year,

---

[49] *Are These Things So?*, 11. The ministerial *Hyp-Doctor*, no. 482 (29 June 1740), included Miller among Opposition pamphleteers writing against the Convention of the Pardo, and ridicules him for preaching politics to ministers of state.

[50] *Handel: Collected Documents*, ed. Burrows et al., 3:243; premiered at Drury Lane on 28 February 1737. The song is "I like the am'rous youth that's free" in Act II.

[51] On Horace's *Carmen Saeculare*, following here Eduard Fraenkel, *Horace* (Oxford: Clarendon Press, 1957), 364–82.

[52] The Grand Remonstrance was presented to the King on 1 December 1641; abridged text in J. P. Kenyon, *The Stuart Constitution, 1603–1688* (Cambridge: Cambridge University Press, 1986), 207–17. On the Great Remonstrance and its relation to the Ancient Constitution, J. G. A. Pocock, *Virtue, Commerce and History* (Cambridge: Cambridge University Press, 1985), 233.

Several of the parliamentary grievances in 1641 could be seen as appropriate 100 years later: a request to remove those "as persist to favour and promote any of those

A PATRIOT VISION FOR DRAMATIC MUSIC   157

famously celebrated in English republican tracts, Parliament's "general remonstrance of the state of the kingdom, and the particular grievances it had sustained"[53] presented to Charles I was a prelude to the Civil War. In this sense, 1741 marks one *saeculum* from the Grand Remonstrance and is a call for a strong Parliament to act assertively against Walpole.[54] Further, the month of publication suggests the poem also marks the cycle of Septennial Parliaments, for over the summer, a new Parliament was elected that would sit on 1 December (the date the petition was presented to Charles). Horace Walpole, the prime minister's son, mocked the Opposition's hopes for the parliamentary session: "They talk loudly of the year forty-one, and promise themselves all the confusions, that began an hundred years ago from the same date."[55]

Miller's choice of title-page epigraph removes any doubt that Walpole motivates the poem. The epigraph, from Cicero's first Verrine oration, casts Walpole as a modern parallel of Gaius Verres,[56] whose three-year rule in 73–71 BC desolated the island of Sicily:

> Quas res luxuries in flagitiis, crudelitas in suppliciis, avaritias in rapinis, superbia in contumeliis efficere potuisset, eas omnes sese hoc uno praetore per Triennium (septenium) pertulisse aiebant.[57]

> During the three (seven) years in which this man has been their praetor, they have endured, they say, every outrage and torture, every spoliation and disgrace, that vice, cruelty, greed, and insolence could inflict.

Miller's note, a mock emendation of the type Pope used in the *Dunciad,* for the word *Triennium* ("Read it *now* Septennium, *meo Periculo,* Bentleius"), as if from Richard Bentley, suggests that the previous Septennial Parliament enabled Walpole's regime.

These allusions indicate a Britain poised at a Machiavellian moment: an invocation that the new Parliament will mark a new *saeculum,* a hope for parliamentary action that will see the downfall of Walpole. Moreover, Miller dedicated the poem to the dowager Duchess of Marlborough, whom he praises for her "firm Attachment to the Cause of Liberty." The Duchess had long been a

---

pressures and corruptions wherewith your people have been grieved" (209); and the claim that the root of all problems lies in "a malignant and pernicious design of subverting the fundamental laws and principles of government" (210).

[53] Edward Hyde, Earl of Clarendon, *The History of the Rebellion and Civil Wars in England,* ed. W. Dunn Macray, 6 vols. (Oxford: Clarendon Press, 1888), 4:32 (see also 4:49–74).

[54] In his Dedication, Miller mentions the *saeculum* as one hundred years long.

[55] Letter from Horace Walpole, 16 December 1741, to Horace Mann; *Yale Edition of the Correspondence of Horace Walpole,* ed. W. S. Lewis, 48 vols. (New Haven, Conn.: Yale University Press, 1937–1983), 17:245.

[56] Another use of the Verres-Walpole parallel is [Eustace Budgell], *Verres and His Scribblers* (1732), which predicts the triumph of political and moral corruption; see also *Craftsman,* no. 259 (19 June 1731), and Goldgar, *Walpole and the Wits,* 126.

[57] Cicero, "In Q. Caecilium, Orato Quae Divinato Dicitur," 1.3, in *The Verrine Orations,* 2 vols. Loeb Classical Library (London: Heinemann, 1928), 1:4.

158   THE CULTURAL POLITICS OF OPERA, 1720–1742

strong opponent of Walpole since the time of his break with Sunderland, her son-in-law. The Duchess had used her wealth and influence to put Opposition-minded family members and others into parliamentary seats, and she was a friend and supporter of Opposition politicians, including Carteret, Pulteney, Lord Polwarth (the Earl of Marchmont's son), Lyttelton, and Chesterfield.[58] Despite their life-long differences in politics, the Duchess cultivated a friendship with Pope, united in their opposition against Walpole.[59]

The dedication to the Duchess puts the poem in the obit of Patriot Opposition polemic:

> there [is] no one living to whom an honest Satire on the Degeneracy of the Age could be so properly address'd as to your Grace, who has at all times signalized yourself by a firm Attachment to the Cause of Liberty, and by bravely standing up to stem that Torrent of publick Enormities, which has of late bore in upon us with such Power and great Glory. (p. iii)

Miller paid the Duchess another compliment that year. In the 1741 version of *Harlequin-Horace*, the passage referring to Walpole is now altered to refer to the Duchess's late husband, the great Whig hero, the Duke of Marlborough:

> If mighty *Marlbro*'s Character you'd wield
> Describe Him rash, yet trembling in the Field;
> …
> False to his Queen, his Country, and his God;
> …
> The *Church*'s Downfall, and the *State*'s Disease.[60]

The tone is ironic, of course, reflecting the false standards of the political writer. Recalling Marlborough's victories at this time would invoke comparison to Britain's military successes under Queen Anne against the French and reproach Walpole's conduct of the war against Spain (see Chapter 11).

Miller opens *The Year Forty-One* voicing despair at the state of Britain and the arrival of the *saeculum*, "Lo Forty One's black *Cycle* reappear!":

> See ev'ry Vice in gay succession rise,
> That can pollute the Earth, or scale the Skies!   (p. 1)

---

[58] Frances Harris, *A Passion for Government: The Life of Sarah, Duchess of Marlborough* (Oxford: Clarendon Press, 1991), 294–300, 307, 309–10, 314, 316–19, 324–5, 329–33. The anonymous *The Life of Her Grace, Sarah, late Dowager Duchess of Marlborough* (1745), described "her hearty Detestation of the late Minister, whom she never nam'd without the most sovereign Contempt, and whose Measures she always oppos'd to the utmost of her Power" (p. 58).

[59] On the Duchess and Pope, Valerie Rumbold, *Women's Place in Pope's World* (Cambridge: Cambridge University Press, 1989), 199–207. Rumbold notes that the Duchess, like Pope in his *1740*, was not fully convinced of the effectiveness of the Opposition.

[60] The 1741 version of *Harlequin-Horace*, as included in Miller's *Miscellaneous Works in Verse and Prose* (1741), lines 217–18, 220, 223, 227–9. This version is printed by Anthony Coleman as Augustan Reprint Society Publication, no. 178 (1976).

A PATRIOT VISION FOR DRAMATIC MUSIC   159

Miller intones a usual Patriot Opposition litany against corruption in Walpole's government, unpunished crime, pensioned courtiers, absence of virtue and honesty at court, a venal clergy, lack of support for liberty and the arts, and decline in British trade, military valor, and patriotism – all offered as evidence of Britain's "political infection." The Poet begs, "O for a Muse of Fire!," not to sing Britain's glory as in the days of Henry V but to describe Britain's shame and degeneracy.

Like Thomson and Hill, Miller uses the allegorical figures of Liberty, the Muses, and Britannia to dramatize both his despair and hope for Britain. First invoked is Liberty, the Patriot's touchstone. Miller had traced her progress from Greece and Rome northward through Gothic climates to Britain; he now bids her farewell. A Britain willingly under Walpole's regime has in effect renounced her and her blessings:

> Now Liberty, thou heav'nly Guest, farewel,
> Source of all Blessings where thou deign'st to dwell:
> Adieu – no longer can we hope thy Stay,
> Since *Britain*'s abject Sons renounce thy Sway.   (p. 5)

Now having progressed as far as Britain, Liberty must search for another distant "barren Isle" to humanize and civilize. Lines that reverse the *Dunciad*'s image of the arrival of Dulness convey Miller's vision of Liberty's arrival at some unspecified northern region:

> Then plant the *finer Taste*, prepare the Way
> For Science's and Wisdom's lib'ral Sway;
> Bid Learning dawn, Art after Art arise,
> *Lights*, which alas! are *setting* in our [Britains'] Skies.   (p. 6)

As we have frequently seen, it was a commonplace of the classical republican tradition (and adopted by Whig writers) that only under Liberty do arts and sciences flourish. For Miller, Liberty humanizes and makes man a refined, social being. Miller takes up the *laus artium* tradition and extols the civilizing powers of the seven fine arts: poetry, painting, music, sculpture, architecture, logic, and eloquence.

In the praise of music, whose opening lines recall Thomson's lines in *Liberty*, it is apparent Miller has in mind the highest form of music, vocal music sung in English:

> Whilst, sweet Inforcer of the Poets Lays,
> Musick in meaning Sounds strong Sense conveys;
> Can each respondent Passion spur, or rein,
> And vary ev'ry Pulse with ev'ry Strain;
> Raise with a *Note* of Rapture the Depress'd,
> Or quell th' Outrageous with a dead'ning *Rest*;
> Plunge the struck Heart in sympathetick Woe;
> Or with imputed Ardors make it glow:
> In *Cytherea*'s silken Cordage bind,
> Or tune to *social* Harmony, the Mind.   (p. 7)

160 THE CULTURAL POLITICS OF OPERA, 1720–1742

This praise of music, especially the line "Musick in meaning Sounds strong Sense conveys," reverses the usual description of opera (with its unmeaning sounds) and is a deliberate indictment of Italian opera.

As did Thomson and Hill, Miller describes what we can call the music of classical republicanism – a music that is the servant of poetry, whose meaningful sounds are a vehicle for conveying sense. It is a music that has all the traditional powers claimed for it: to move or command the passions of men. Miller's list of the powers of music ends not with personal, individual passions, but with music's public, civic role: music instils virtue and leads the mind to a social harmony.

To crown her task, Liberty will bring a mixed constitutional government, planned for the public good and guided by independent councils, under which will arise new Miltons and Drydens, new Argylls and Pulteneys, and new Elizabeths. At her name, Miller is jolted back to present Britain under George, where the prophecy of Pope's *Dunciad* is being fulfilled:

> See *Dullness* lift her *consecrated* Head,
> And smile to view her dark Dominion spread;
> *Chaos* o'er all his leaden Sceptre rear,
> And not *one Beam* throughout the Gloom appear.   (p. 10)

Miller's poet is interrupted by a ministerial apologist:

> "Stay, Sir, says One, whence pray this groundless Cry?
> "*I do not find* the times so bad, not I"   (p. 12)

This brief section of satiric dialogue serves to introduce another allegorical scene. The Court spokesman defends the King's and army's conduct of the war against Spain and dismisses as "dreams" the satirist's abuse of the present golden age. The spokesman's weak defense does the Opposition service by reminding readers of the usual charges against the ministry's conduct of the war. The satirist, in turn, relates his dream-vision. Recalling the opening of Thomson's *Britannia*, on a bleak beach, Britannia wails in despair at her fate; she is the scoff of nations for the loss of her empire, freedom, and fame. Neptune replies with wrongs that match hers: the fallen state of Britain's naval might as Walpole has let the fleet lie idle and unsupplied in the West Indies. Britannia implores Liberty to bring again her blessings.

Upon Liberty's glorious appearance, she greets Britannia with the promise she will once again embrace her sons if they will prepare her way by deeds. Liberty's proposals read like the Patriot's program for removing Walpole (including a revival of The Motion (see p. 274) from the previous session of Parliament):

> To publick *Justice* publick *Plund'rers* bring,
> And *take the Wicked from before the King*;
> Purge the *distemper'd* Land of that dire Crew,
> The *low Corrupt* and *high Corruptors* too.   (p. 15)

When corruption ("thou eternal Bane, / To Virtue's, Liberty's, and Wisdom's Reign") is driven out, when there is public spirit in government, independence in Parliament, and courtiers are honest, then Liberty will be Britannia's again.

The tone and pessimistic view of *The Year Forty-One* anticipate Pope's *New Dunciad*, published three months later. But Miller, attuned to Patriot optimism, offers a vision of hope.

The passage on vocal music in English in *The Year Forty-One* may be brief but shows again how such a music that accords with classical republican ideas is the antithesis of Italian opera and has a central place in the Patriot vision for Britain. Three years later, Miller would contribute his mite to the program for an English dramatic music by providing Handel with the libretto for his oratorio *Joseph and His Brethren* (1744).

* * *

The allegories by Thomson, Hill, and Miller convey staples of a Patriot Opposition rhetoric about Britain under the Hanoverians and Walpole. Hopes for Britain are deferred to the accession of a Patriot King when virtue and public spirit reign instead of Walpolean corruption and faction. Also present is the importance the Opposition writers place on the arts in society.

For Opposition writers identifying what was morally wrong with Britain under the Hanoverians and Walpole, it was convenient to point to Italian opera as symptom and cause of the corruption in the body politic. As an alternative to Italian opera, these Patriot writers envision a dramatic musical entertainment that would serve moral and civic functions, restore virtue, and evade the supposed effects of Italian opera. The ideal English musical drama might be called the music of classical republicanism. As a powerful shaper of human passions and morals, music would be sung in English, grant primacy to the poetic text, and move the passions in accord with the sentiments of a text. Each feature of Italian opera usually objected to (sensuous music, effeminacy, and unintelligible text) has an opposite element, realized in their imagined dramatic music. These ideals were fulfilled in Handel's oratorios. It is not too far-fetched to suppose Handel's oratorios might have been welcomed as a sign of regeneration of Britain under a Patriot King.

CHAPTER 9

Opera and the Politics of Taste

Indictment of the fallen state of the arts has been a perennial theme in criticism. "There has never been a moment in the history of the arts and of literature," observes George Steiner, "in which practitioners and critics have not registered a perception of decay, of incipient vulgarization and dispersal."[1] No less so than in eighteenth-century Britain, where complaints about the fallen state of the arts as a symptom of the decline of culture at large was most commonly directed at the stage. Actors, authors, managers, and critics claimed that the popularity of certain theatrical forms – such as pantomimes, farces, harlequinades, and ballad operas – was destroying the public's taste and driving out good, solid British comedy and tragedy. Italian opera was often instinctively implicated in the decline of the stage.

The health of the stage was a serious public concern, for the theatre was one of the best signs of a republic's health. As the political paper *Common Sense* would affirm in 1737:

> The Stage is the Representation of the World, and certainly a Man may know the Humours and Inclinations of the People, by what is liked or disliked upon the Stage.[2]

The theatre was believed a strong shaper of public morals, for the lessons of vice punished and virtue rewarded were more vivid and effective when witnessed with the embellishment of theatrical spectacle and music, than when read privately or delivered as dry precept.[3]

It was often pointed out that Greek rulers and states had established the theatre for the public good. Since the days of Jeremy Collier, the English stage was under attack for its outright immorality, and reform of it was a continuing project of moralists, playwrights, and critics.

It was not so much that critics objected to popular theatre. In fact, some severe critics and reputable authors wrote their own share of comedies, pantomimes, and harlequinades. But when such popular forms dominate the stage, when England's taste is debased to the level of the footman and mechanic, and when the theatre manager produces farce and pantomime instead of serious drama and enlightening comedy, the very fabric of social order was threatened.

---

[1] George Steiner, "The Muses' Farewell," *Salmagundi*, no. 135/56 (Fall 2002), 148–56 (at p. 148).

[2] *Common Sense*, no. 19 (11 June 1737).

[3] For such a statement, see *Tatler*, no. 8. (28 April 1709).

Managers – it was claimed – debased the forms to appeal to larger audiences, emphasized sound and spectacle (as Horace had objected), and in the process sacrificed dramatic integrity. The attention paid to sound and spectacle meant that moral edification, the true aim of theatre, was neglected. For John Dennis, continued exposure to opera deformed one's taste:

> This general ill Taste [in theatre] is partly the Effect of the *Italian* Opera; that a People accustom'd for so many Years to that, are as ill-prepar'd to judge of a good Tragedy, as Children that are eating Sugar-plumbs are to taste *Champaign* [*sic*] and *Burgundy*.[4]

Especially susceptible to such debased forms were the newly monied *nouveaux riches* and *beau monde*. It was objected they patronized opera and the other arts not from a genuine love or connoisseurship but only out of affectation of taste, to follow what was fashionable, and to be seen in the places proper for elite society, such as the opera.[5] Their imposter status was shown by their outward manifestation of False Taste.

To combat the consequences of luxury and wealth upon the arts, correction of taste was a cultural imperative that crossed party lines. On the Whig side, the *Tatler* took as its mission "to expose the false Arts of Life, to pull off the Disguises of Cunning, Vanity, and Affectation, and to recommend a general Simplicity in our Dress, our Discourse, and our Behaviour."[6] In its sequel the *Spectator*, a correspondent asked Mr. Spectator to animadvert frequently upon the "false Taste of the Town."[7] Toward this end, both periodicals contained critical essays on painting, literature, the stage, and opera. While the principal goal of the Tory Scriblerus Club was to detect and ridicule pedantry, false

---

[4] John Dennis, *Remarks upon Cato, a Tragedy* (1713), 7.

[5] In a dream vision in *Fog's Weekly Journal*, no. 45 (2 Aug. 1729), a student is shown a sumptuous house with lavish interior furnishings. He comments:

> There is a vast Appearance of Wealth, answers the Student, but methinks in a very bad Taste; Yes, the master of that House knows that Pictures and Statues are counted fine Things, yet he has not Judgment enough himself to distinguish a Picture of *Apelles*, from one of him who paints the Sign-Posts; nor a Statue of *Apollodorius*, from one of the next Stone-cutter; but it is a Way of laying out Money, and all the Dollars in *Spain* are at his Command.

In *Pasquin*, no. 11 (6 Feb. 1723), pursuit of objects of False Taste (included are plays, balls, operas, masquerades, ridottos, and other polite diversions) is a result of the need to fill idle time. In Swift's *Intelligencer*, no. 3 (25 May 1729), was observed: "I am told there are as few good Judges in *Musick*, and that among those who crowd the *Opera's*, Nine in Ten go thither merely out of *Curiosity, Fashion*, or *Affectation*"; quoted from collected reprint ed. (1729), 17.

[6] Dedication to the collected edition of 1710; *The Tatler*, ed. Donald F. Bond, 3 vols. (Oxford: Clarendon Press, 1987), 1:8. On the *Tatler's* treatment of the arts, Richmond P. Bond, *The Tatler: The Making of a Literary Journal* (Cambridge, Mass.: Harvard University Press, 1971), 97–117.

[7] *Spectator*, no. 22 (26 March 1711); *The Spectator*, ed. Donald F. Bond, 5 vols. (Oxford: Clarendon Press, 1965), 1:94.

164 THE CULTURAL POLITICS OF OPERA, 1720–1742

scholarship, and follies in all branches of learning, the Scriblerians too did not neglect in their satire "the Polite Arts of Painting, Architecture, Musick, Poetry, &c."[8]

Taste

Taste, as a faculty for apprehending the arts, was typically defined metaphorically, compared to the pleasure derived from other senses such as taste, hearing, or sight:

> Taste is the peculiar Relish that we feel for any agreeable object; and is more or less perfect, according to the degree of judgment we employ in distinguishing its beauties. ... True taste is not to be acquir'd without infinite toil and study.[9]

A fine taste in writing Addison defined as "that Faculty of the Soul, which discerns the Beauty of an Author with Pleasure, and the Imperfections with Dislike."[10] Likewise, another writer stated "a *good Taste* in *Musick*" consists in knowing "how to esteem Things according to their real Value and Merit"; it requires both an ear and knowledge of music.[11]

In addition to immediate sensation of pleasure, true taste has a rational component. Natural sense was to be refined by the 'Rules,' the culmination of millennia of connoisseurship and practice. For Jonathan Richardson, the challenge for connoisseurship was to choose those pleasures "that are Worthy of Rational Beings, Such as are not only Innocent, but Noble and Excellent."[12] Alexander

---

[8] *Memoirs of the Extraordinary Life, Works, and Discoveries of Martinus Scriblerus*, ed. Charles Kerby-Miller (New Haven, Conn.: Yale University Press, 1950), 168. Pope said the design of the *Memoirs of Scriblerius* was to have "ridiculed all the false tastes in learning, under the character of a man of capacity enough that had dipped in every art and science, but injudiciously in each"; Joseph Spence, *Observations, Anecdotes, and Characters of Books and Men Collected from Conversation*, ed. James M. Osborn, 2 vols. (Oxford: Clarendon, 1966), no. 135, p. 56.

[9] [James Ralph], *A Critical Review of the Publick Buildings, Statues and Ornaments in, and about London and Westminster* (1734). The passage draws from "An Essay on *Taste* in General; With a View to the Elegancies of the *Grub-street Journal*," in the *Weekly Register*, no. 43 (6 Feb. 1731).

See also "Taste and Beauty. An Epistle to the Right Hon. the Earl of Chesterfield" in *The Weekly Register*, no. 216 (27 April 1734): "True Taste's the relish which the Mind receives / From Harmony, the Joy which Beauty gives!" A similar definition is given in a letter by "Crito" in *The Universal Spectator, and Weekly Journal*, no. 131 (10 April 1731). See also selections on Taste in *The Eighteenth Century: Art, Design and Society, 1689–1789*, ed. Bernard Denvir (London: Longman, 1983), 63–116. The *Universal Spectator* later printed a poem, "British Amusement: A Satire. In an Epistle to a Friend in the Country," censuring the follies, taste, and fashions of London (no. 313, 5 Oct. 1734).

[10] *Spectator*, no. 409 (19 June 1712), ed. Bond, 5:528.

[11] Review of M. Grandval, *Essai sur le bon gout en musique* in *The Bee: or, Universal Weekly Pamphlet*, no. 7 (24 March 1733), 297–9.

[12] Jonathan Richardson, *A Discourse on the Dignity, Certainty, Pleasure and Advantage of the Science of a Connoisseur* (1719), 44–5. Richardson expands on the benefits to the nation of cultivating connoisseurship, or good taste.

OPERA AND THE POLITICS OF TASTE   165

Pope had succinctly stated that "previous ev'n to Taste" is "Good Sense, which only is the gift of Heav'en."[13] Taste, properly formed, unites pleasure (sensation) and reason (judgment, sense).

As a guide to taste, critics and theorists had devised the rules, which for Dryden, "inform our Judgments, and … reform our Tast[e]s" and teach us when Nature was imitated justly.[14] True taste requires "infinite toil and study," but the "affectation of taste" prevails because men are too indolent to acquire "true understanding, and genuine politeness."[15] Those without taste, opined a critic, "prefer *Senesino* to *Shakespear*, as the highest Proof of modern Politeness."[16]

What abounded as False Taste Dryden succinctly defined as mistaking "what pleases most" for "what ought to please": "Our deprav'd Appetites, and ignorance of the Arts, mislead our Judgments, and cause us often to take that for true imitation of Nature, which has no resemblance of Nature in it."[17] The errant connoisseur values what easily pleases him above the consensus of the artistic and critical community, above Nature as embodied in the art works of the past two millennia.

While taste was an almost intuitive and immediate response when apprehending a work, it also denoted a person's long-term preference for (or aversion to) a singular style or genre of art, such as Italian or French opera.[18]

False Taste is not just an innocuous matter of misplaced aesthetic appreciation; it indicated deficiency in intellectual and moral standards as well. The near-identity of morality (ethics) and aesthetics was especially stressed in the Earl of Shaftesbury's influential writings, derived in part from the "moral sense" school of ethics identified with him. For Shaftesbury, both ethical action and aesthetic taste derived from this moral sense; hence, there was a unity of ethical truth and sense of beauty.[19] For Shaftesbury, False Taste would be a sign of inadequate moral development, since the same principles of harmony underlie truth, beauty, and virtue, and, hence, are apprehended by the moral sense.

---

[13] Pope, *An Epistle to the Right Honourable Richard Earl of Burlington* (1731), lines 42–3. Also known as the *Epistle to Burlington*, *Of False Taste*, or *Of the Use of Riches* (see below).

[14] John Dryden, "Preface with a Parallel, of Poetry and Painting"; in Charles Du Fresnoy, *De Arte Graphica. The Art of Painting*, trans. John Dryden (1695), xxxii.

[15] Preface to Ralph, *Critical Review of the Publick Buildings, Statues and Ornaments*, i–ii.

[16] *Weekly Register: or, Universal Journal*, no. 43 (6 Feb. 1731).

[17] Dryden, "Preface with a Parallel, of Poetry and Painting," xxxii. Similarly, a writer in the *Universal Spectator, and Weekly Journal* (no. 131, 10 April 1731), wrote: "The Signs of a good Taste, are our giving our Approbation to just and fine Sentiments; … as it is a certain Evidence of a bad one, our applauding vicious or improper Thoughts."

[18] On the several nuanced meanings of taste, James Noggle, "Taste and Temporality in *An Epistle to Burlington*," *Studies in the Literary Imagination*, 38 (2005), 120–35.

[19] See especially, Shaftesbury, *Characteristics of Men, Manners, Opinions, Times*, ed. Lawrence E. Klein (Cambridge: Cambridge University Press, 1999), 147–58 (esp. pp. 157–8) and 408–18 (esp. pp. 414–15); Shaftesbury describes how the development of taste goes wrong. Further on Shaftesbury, moral sense, and taste, see McGeary, *Opera and Politics in Queen Anne's Britain*, p. 289 n. 10.

166 THE CULTURAL POLITICS OF OPERA, 1720–1742

Aesthetic refinement indicated moral refinement. An outer refinement of manners and taste reflected inner moral virtue. Pope stressed the ethical dimension of False Taste in the *Epistle to Burlington*.[20]

Since good taste is the essence of the right judgment of truth and beauty, a properly cultivated taste is the basis of all domains of human accomplishment; wrote James Ralph:

> A good Taste is the heightner of every science, and the polish of every virtue; 'tis the friend of society, and the guide to knowledge: 'tis the improvement of pleasure, and the test of merit. By this, we enlarge the circle of enjoyment, and refine upon happiness. It enables us to distinguish beauty, wherever we find it, and detect error in all its disguises.[21]

William Gilpin claimed a connection between "an *improved* Taste for Pleasure, and a Taste for Virtue":

> When I sit ravished at an Oratorio, or stand astonished before the [Raphael] Cartoons, … I can feel my Mind expand itself, my Notions enlarge, and my Heart better disposed either for a religious Thought, or a benevolent Action: In a Word, I cannot help imagining a Taste for these exalted Pleasures contributes towards making me a better Man.[22]

False Taste could take two forms. Most obviously, it was excessive delight in unworthy and debased art forms: delight in what ought *not* to please. To some, Italian opera was a sensuous entertainment: singing in an unknown language (sound over sense), delight in spectacle over reason, and a feminizing experience. False Taste could also be the affected, pretentious, excessive, or ill-displayed enjoyment of otherwise worthy arts (what ought to please), as when the *beau monde* patronized what could be a worthy art, not out of connoisseurship but to follow what was fashionable, to ape the aristocrats, and to be seen in the places of elite society – only to respond in exaggerated or inappropriate ways.

Taste was, then, a matter of public concern. One "Crito" writing in 1731 cautioned that the state of the nation's taste was of real importance, for "a Decay of Taste, has been a constant Forerunner in most Nations, of a Decay of Empire." The decay of taste subverts the true end of the stage, he states, and the present age seems to have lost any care for how "despicable a Figure [it] must make to Posterity."[23]

---

[20] See Earl R. Wasserman, *Pope's Epistle to Bathurst: A Critical Reading with an Edition of the Manuscripts* (Baltimore, Md.: Johns Hopkins Press, 1960), 37–9. The *Epistle to Bathurst* stresses the right use of great riches.

[21] Ralph, from "An Essay on Taste," prefixed to *A Critical Review of the Public Buildings, Statues and Ornaments*, iii. The essay points out the causes of faulty taste and how to acquire a good taste.

[22] William Gilpin, *A Dialogue Upon the Gardens … at Stow* [*sic*], 2nd ed. (1749), 49. Gilpin thought it a national concern to regulate a nation's taste with regard to pleasure.

[23] *The Universal Spectator, and Weekly Journal*, no. 131 (10 April 1731).

The concern with true taste had nationalist and patriotic overtones; foreign artistic imports (such as opera, cooking, fashions, and dancing) not only displace native artists but destroy public spirit and virtue "as *Britannia's* Sons become / Dupes to each Vagabond from *France* and *Rome*."[24] Frequent are the patriotic exhortations to reject "the Taste of this fantastick Town":

> Now in the Name of Reason, where is fled
> The *British* Genius, whose triumphant Head,
> With native Majesty divinely bright,
> Thro' all the World transfus'd unrival'd Light?
> If foreign Tricks and Trumpery obtain,
> Whilst your once favoured Muses plead in vain.
> For Shame your *English* Energy resume,
> And scorn these Sorceries of *France* and *Rome*.[25]

Italian opera is instinctively included among the objects of False Taste and false connoisseurship, for opera had long been indicted for its foreign origin, expense, singing in an unknown language, feminizing qualities, and dominance of spectacle and sound over sense.

❧ *The Political Dimension of Taste*

On one level, there was the age-old disputing of personal taste. But there was a more serious level, in the sense of whose taste should prevail? What art should be valued in Britain? A campaign against False Taste in favor of high, serious literature was carried out vigorously in Alexander Pope's attacks on the Dunces in his *Dunciad* project spanning 1728 to 1743.[26] The Dunces, whom he is not afraid to identify, represented the low, mercenary literary culture of Grub Street's writers.

Combating False Taste had a crucial political dimension as well. It was a commonplace of the Roman historians, classical republicans, their modern English successors, and especially Whigs that the arts and sciences flourish during republics and liberty, and decline under conditions of tyranny, luxury, and corruption. Commonly, the loss of liberty and the decline in the arts and sciences went hand-in-hand and are laid to the rise of luxury and corruption, which also leads to the decline of public spirit and civic virtue. As succinctly claimed by Hildebrand Jacob:

> *Indolence*, and *Sloth*, the Effect of *Luxury*, and *Ease*, are equally prejudicial to these *Arts*, and have brought on a Neglect of *Study*, and all *Rules*, by which

---

[24] James Miller, *Man of Taste* (1735), Prologue.

[25] Prologue to *The Royal Convert* (20 Feb. 1724); printed in the *British Journal*, no. 76 (29 Feb. 1724).

[26] Valerie Rumbold (see her editions of the *Dunciad* cited below) rightly calls attention to the ongoing nature of Pope's revisions and expansions from the original *Dunciad* of 1728, hence, calling it a project. I follow her in discussing the *Dunciad* and *Dunciad Variorum* of 1728 and 1729 as distinct from the collected lifetime version (her term), the four-book *Dunciad* of 1743, whose last book appeared as the *New Dunciad* in 1742.

168   THE CULTURAL POLITICS OF OPERA, 1720–1742

Means so many *imperfect*, and *unfinish'd* Performances in every one of *Arts* are daily precipitated into the *World*.[27]

Consequently, debased arts and the prevalence of False Taste are symptoms of a republic in decline. This classical viewpoint can be found behind the critiques of Italian opera by John Dennis, Richard Steele, Shaftesbury, and Bolingbroke.[28] Writing at what could be called Machiavellian moments, they saw opera as an external threat or symptom of internal corruption.

The often-cited proof of the relation between corruption, luxury, liberty, the arts, and the fate of republics – and known to every school-boy reader of the classics – were the examples of Athens and Rome. For Rome, there were several key moments: the defeat of Carthage in the Second Punic War and the victories in the east that brought luxury, greed, and loss of liberty to Rome.

Recalling the connection between the rise and fall of liberty and the arts in Rome was a common theme of Whig writers.[29] One of the canonical Whig *Cato's Letters* from 1722 claimed:

> This prodigious progress of the Romans in learning [while they had leisure from their long and many wars] had no other cause than the freedom and equality of their government. The spirit of the people, like that of their state, breathed nothing but liberty. ... That liberty which made the Greeks and Romans masters of the world, made them masters of all the learning in it: And, when their liberties perished, so did their learning. ... This decay began in the time of Augustus, who began his reign with butchering Cicero [43 BC] ... [who was] the prodigy of Roman eloquence and learning.[30]

The Whig historian John Oldmixon, writing in 1728, also places the decline in the arts in the Age of Augustus, when show was preferred to true comedy, when

> Sound got the better of Sense, and solid Reason gave Way to Tales and Trifles; when Degeneracy reach'd their Morals as well as their Arts and Sciences, (as it will always do in all Countries) and the Loss of their Taste was follow'd with the Loss of their Liberty.[31]

Oldmixon claimed he had seen decay coming fast in all types of polite literature twenty to thirty years previously.

The classical republican tradition relating luxury and corruption to liberty and the arts and sciences readily lends itself to oppositional political rhetoric: such declines can easily be attributed to social conditions that are in the care of the leaders of government – in this case, as empirical evidence of the ruin caused by Walpole's ministry. The Opposition early on repeated the charge –

---

[27] Hildebrand Jacob, *Of the Sister Arts; An Essay* (1734), 32.

[28] For classical republican thought in Britain, see sources in McGeary, *Opera and Politics in Queen Anne's Britain*, 242–56.

[29] On Whig writers on liberty and the arts: McGeary, *Opera and Politics in Queen Anne's Britain*, 254–5.

[30] *Cato's Letters*, no. 71 (31 March 1722); quoting Hamowy edition, pp. 517, 523. Even the *True Briton*, no. 70 (31 Jan. 1724), could repeat the commonplace.

[31] John Oldmixon, Dedication to *The Arts of Logick and Rhetorick* (1728), ix–x.

well-founded or not – that the arts and sciences were in decline. Their decline was an early-warning sign that Britain was in danger.

In the common formulation of Opposition rhetoric, closely tied to the Old Whig and Country ideology, it was charged that the great wealth acquired by the new monied men of London through finance, stock-jobbing, speculation, and credit – joined to Walpole's infusion of money into society through granting places, pensions, and bribery – all bred greed, self-indulgence, and luxury, which found their outlet in debasements of the arts, taste, manners, and morals. Desire for wealth (to pursue luxury), it was claimed, led to men beholden to the ministry, lack of interest in public affairs, and unwillingness to pursue the national interests above one's own self-interest.

Explicitly charging that corruption was occurring simultaneously in politics and the arts and sciences is prevalent in Opposition polemic. Dedicating a collection of poetry to the Opposition politician William Pulteney in 1731, one writer claimed:

> That *Corruption*, which o'erspreads the Present Age, is not only visible in Transactions of State, or the Affairs of Human Life, but is equally remarkable at least, in the Republick of Letters. Nor is it any Wonder, the Loss of Virtue including the Loss of Taste; the *Greek* Spirit of Writing, and of Liberty, fell together; And the Elegancy of the *Latin* Stile, declined in exact Proportion with the [decline of the] *Roman* empire.[32]

Bolingbroke linked the aesthetic, moral, and political categories:

> the very idea of wit, and all that can be called taste, has been lost among the great; arts and sciences are scarce alive; luxury has been increased but not refined; corruption has been established, and is avowed. When governments are worn out, thus it is: the decay appears in every instance. Public and private virtue, public and private spirit, science and wit, decline all together.[33]

In the context of Opposition polemics, assertions of the decline of British taste – by satirizing Dulness and citing examples of False Taste – was sufficient proof that Walpole's corruption was at work, and a reason that he must be removed to reverse the process.

---

[32] Anonymous Dedication, *A Collection of Poems; Consisting of Odes, Tales, &c.* (1731), ii–iii. The collection is clearly an Opposition production: it includes an epistle in praise of Bolingbroke and "The Duel" (pp. 56–60), which praises Pulteney as the firmest champion of British liberties. The collection was reissued in the same year as *The Honysuckle. A Curious Collection of Poems upon Several Occasions.*

[33] "Letters on the Study and Use of History," letter no. 8, in *The Works of Lord Bolingbroke*, 4 vols. (Philadelphia, Pa.: Carey and Hart, 1843), 2:333; and Bolingbroke, *Lord Bolingbroke: Historical Writings*, ed. Isaac Kramnick (Chicago, Ill.: University of Chicago Press, 1972), 149.

170 THE CULTURAL POLITICS OF OPERA, 1720–1742

❧ False Taste at Court and the Ministry

It was convenient and politically effective to place blame for neglect of the arts and sciences on the lack of taste and patronage from the Ministry and Court, thus locating the cause of their decline at the very source of political power. As proof of the want of taste at Court, the Opposition pointed to the Ministry's supposed failure to support British arts and literature. By contrast, some writers looked back fondly to a time when peers – Harley, Somers, Dorset, Godolphin, and Halifax – were powerful in government and dispensed patronage in the form of positions for worthy writers.[34]

That Italian opera could be associated with the Court and Ministry had some basis in fact, given the widely known patronage of opera by the royal family, Walpole and his family, and other government and household office holders. Beginning with the 1719–20 season, the King gave a yearly £1,000 bounty to the opera company at the Haymarket. Royal attendance at the opera was frequently noted in the newspapers, and ministers and office holders took prominent roles in managing and underwriting the London opera companies (see Chapter 2). The patronage of Kings George I and II was important to the survival of the opera companies, though never enough to keep them afloat.[35]

In the *Dunciad*, Pope would hint that both Georges were Dunces. George I and II, indeed, are said to have taken little interest in art and literature,[36] although both were keen operagoers and the monarchs were frequent sitters for state portraits.[37] The choice of Colley Cibber as Poet Laureate in 1730, despite his image as a fop and fool, brought the Court little credit, nor did Queen Caroline's taste for the Thresher Poet Stephen Duck (who is consistently attacked in the *Grub-street Journal*).[38] The attacks on False Taste at Court may in part be an expression of anti-Hanoverian sentiment. About the monarchy perhaps little might be done, so it was more expedient to focus on the King's minister, who could more easily be embarrassed into retirement or discredited with the King and removed from office.

So it was to the prime minister that most of the blame for the decline in the arts was laid. He was assailed in the Opposition press for his patronage

---

[34] *Common Sense*, no. 36 (8 Oct. 1737).

[35] See Donald Burrows and Robert D. Hume, "George I, the Haymarket Opera Company and Handel's Water Music," *Early Music*, 19 (1991), 334–5; and Judith Milhous and Robert D. Hume, "Handel's Opera Finances in 1732–3," *Musical Times*, 125 (1984), 86–9 (at p. 88).

[36] "Neither George I nor George II manifested any serious interest in works of art – apart, in the case of the latter, from those with military associations"; Christopher White, *The Dutch Pictures in the Collection of Her Majesty the Queen* (Cambridge: Cambridge University Press, 1982), l.

[37] For fuller account of English monarchs and the arts, Jeremy Black, *A Subject for Taste: Culture in Eighteenth-Century England* (London: Hambledon, 2005), Chapter 2, "The Crown."

[38] On the choice of Cibber over Duck, Daniel J. Ennis, "The Making of the Poet Laureate, 1730," *Age of Johnson*, 11 (2000), 217–35.

OPERA AND THE POLITICS OF TASTE   171

of "hireling" political writers to the exclusion of genuine men of letters, and indicted, as well, for his own poor taste in poetry. His writers were immortalized among the Dunces of Pope's *Dunciad*, and his patronage of them earned him Swift's epithet "*Bob*, the Poet's Foe."[39] Swift decried that he "stoops to the vilest Offices of hiring Scoundrels to write *Billingsgate* of the lowest and most prostitute Kind, and has none but Beasts and Blockheads for his Pen-men, whom he pays in ready Guineas very liberally."[40]

William Pulteney sarcastically addressed Walpole: "I am told that you have lately taken the most eminent Authors of the *Dunciad* into your Pay, and employ them in your cause. … The *late Pieces*, utter'd in your Service, seem to put this Point beyond all Dispute."[41] He was contrasted to previous ministers who rewarded Congreve, Addison, Prior, and Swift; but Walpole, according to the *Grub-street Journal*, "Smil'd on Concanen, Cibber, Mitchell, Ralph."[42] In *The Candidates for the Bays … Written by Scriblerus Tertius* (1730), Thomas Cooke imputes the taste of the times (now sunk to the level of Fielding's *Tom Thumb*) to Walpole's failure to reward poets, as was done when Britain was a seat of the Muses and the bays crowned Ben Jonson. The laurels now crown Laurence Eusden, "whilst *P——*, *S——*, and *G——* [Pope, Swift, and Gay] / Are kept by Sir R—— [Robert] from Favour or Bay."[43]

Walpole's first knighthood (of the Bath) on 27 May 1725 set in train a pattern of panegyric epistles to him, which was the opening for *Mist's Weekly Journal* to use George Bubb Dodington's *An Epistle to the Right Honourable Sir Robert Walpole* (Dec. 1725) to impugn, under the guise of the task of criticism, Walpole's taste. Lamenting that

> We live at a Time when there is a kind of Barrenness spread over the land of the Muses, as if some unkind Blast had blighted all, and robb'd us even of the Expectation of a Harvest; … but so it will be, when the warm Sun of Favour and Encouragement withdraws its kind Influence, and shines no more upon it.

---

[39] Swift, "To Mr. Gay on his being Steward to the Duke of Queensbury," line 4; *Jonathan Swift: The Complete Poems*, ed. Pat Rogers (Harmondsworth: Penguin, 1983), 466.

[40] Swift, letter to Thomas Sheridan, 13 May 1727; *The Correspondence of Jonathan Swift*, ed. Harold H. Williams, 5 vols. (Oxford: Clarendon, 1963), 3:207. Also in *The Correspondence of Jonathan Swift, D.D.*, ed. David Woolley, 5 vols. (Frankfurt: Peter Lang, 1999–2014), 3:84, no. 750.

For a balanced view of Walpole's literary patronage, see J. A. Downie, "Walpole, 'the Poet's Foe,'" pp. 171–88 in *Britain in the Age of Walpole*, ed. Jeremy Black (London: Macmillan, 1984); and Dustin Griffin, *Literary Patronage in England, 1650–1800* (Cambridge: Cambridge University Press, 1996), 51–3.

[41] William Pulteney, *An Answer to One Part of a Late Libel* (1731), 8. See also the pointed attack on Walpole, Griffith Morgan D'Anvers, *Persius Scaramouch: or, a Critical and Moral Satire on the Orators, Scriblers, and Vices of the Present Times* (1734). The author is a pseudonym; likely by Nicholas Amhurst, dedicated to William Pulteney.

[42] A poem "On Wit," in *Grub-street Journal*, no. 247 (19 Sept. 1734).

[43] *The Candidates for the Bays … Written by Scriblerus Tertius* (1730), 2.

172   THE CULTURAL POLITICS OF OPERA, 1720–1742

The writer is resigned to the fact that nothing is offered to the public "except some Pieces of Flattery." His severe criticism of Dodington's epistle, exposing *doubles entendres* and turning clumsy verse into insults to Walpole, serves as evidence of the literary bareness of Britain and Walpole's taste.

An early essay in the *Craftsman* worked variations on this theme to the detriment of the Court and Walpole.[44] The writer notes it is "very melancholly to consider the great *Decay of Learning*, which is, at present, universally complain'd of," and further ironically denies that "the present Dearth of *Wit* and *Learning* [is caused] by the pretended want of *Patronage* and *Favour*," partly because to do so would reflect on "some men in Power" – but that, of course, is precisely the intended innuendo. He firmly believes, though, that having men of great ability and liberal understanding at the head of state who dispose offices and favor solely on merit is the best encouragement of useful learning. Men of merit and ability are justified in complaining when all the favors of a court are heaped on those in power and their relations. Then in a passage grinning with irony, he asserts,

> we have the particular Happiness to live under an *Administration*, which is not only compos'd of the *ablest Heads*, and most *uncorrupt Hearts* in the Kingdom, but hath also been constantly observ'd to shower down their Favours on those Persons only, who possess the same excellent Talents and Dispositions with themselves.

He challenges anyone "to instance any Period of Time, when *Wit* and *polite Literature* were more openly and amply encourag'd at present; not excepting even the two famous Reigns of *Augustus* and *Louis le Grand*."

As an illustration of the encouragement of literature, he ironically points to Walpole, who "does not disdain to Patronize the *Muses*," and to his "*own Immortal Poet*," the Court poet Edward Young, widely execrated for his panegyric verse that won him Court appointments (see p. 230). Given in identification of Young are his lines to Walpole from *The Instalment* (1726), celebrating his Garter:

> The streams of Royal bounty, turn'd by Thee,
> Refresh the dry Domains of Poesy.[45]

The present encouragement of wit and learning is also shown by the crowds who throng the theatres to see the antics of Harlequin and Scaramouch, tumblers, raree shows, rope dancers, and posture masters.

In August 1730, *Fog's Weekly Journal* and the *Craftsman* carried lengthy essays that – in the guise of ironically defending Walpole – assail his taste in the arts. *Fog's* recalls Augustus' encouragement of the arts and his own "fine understanding and delicate Taste." He concludes that

> Poets and Philosophers are the fit Ornaments of a Court, that is to say, of a polite and a sensible Court, such as was that of *Augustus*, but Fidlers, Singers, Buffoons, and Stock-jobbers, would best suit the Court of a *Tiberius* or a *Nero*, where

---

[44] *Craftsman*, no. 20 (10–13 Feb. 1727).
[45] Edward Young, *The Instalment* (1726), 5.

Stupidity, Lewdness and Rapine sat in Council, and exerted all their Strength, in Opposition to every Thing that was sensible and ingenuous.[46]

Since the Hanoverian court patronized the fiddlers and singers of Italian opera and stock-jobbers where overrunning London, the innuendo is that the court of George II resembles that of Tiberius or Nero, the latter especially known for his music-loving and decadence.

Great men and kingdoms make their reputations by how they favor the arts and men of genius, and hence the writer avers "we may know a Man by his Company," and Walpole's private company is also a sign of his taste. In his private hours, Maecenas would converse with Virgil, Horace, or Livy; but Walpole only admits nothing "into his Privacy but a *Sharper*, a *Pimp*, or a *Stock-jobber*, for these are the Tools of Corruption, the proper Instruments of Fraud."

Repeating gossip about "a certain great Man" heard around town, the writer asks, "Did he ever yet encourage or prefer one Man of Parts? What Man of Wit of Genius ever tasted of his Beneficence?" In mock disabuse of "the Disaffected [who] would represent him as a Barbarian in Wit, as one that has no Love for the *Belles Lettres*," the writer offers some contrary evidence: the Great Man subscribed for thirty copies of Samuel Johnson of Cheshire's *Hurlothrumbo*, and was seen three times at "that sublime *Drama* call'd the History of *Tom Thumb*."

Another ironic defense of Walpole, which allows the (supposed) ministerial writer fearlessly to air the usual charges against him, is offered in the *Craftsman* later that month. "Courtly Grub, *Esq.*" purports to answer a challenge from Caleb D'Anvers, who defies Walpole's advocates "*to produce a single Instance of* One Truely National Point *which hath been concerted, pursued and accomplished*" by him.[47] In his mock-defense of Walpole, Courtly Grub points to actions that usually were taken to be malfeasance by Walpole: his screening ministers and courtiers caught up in the South Sea Bubble scandal, expediting the Bank Contract, Wood's patent in Ireland, the Treaty of Hanover, and other financial affairs.

Courtly Grub turns to "the *Encouragement of Letters* and *learned Men*," which, he admits, is a "*truly National Point*." It does not count against Walpole that, unlike Godolphin, Harley, and Halifax, he has not provided places for "Men of *Letters* and *Wit*, by honourable Preferments in the *State*" because those ministers "proceeded upon *wrong Principles of Government*" and such men of learning or genius are not suited for court employment. But on Walpole's behalf, he ironically argues that if he

never affected to distinguish himself by conferring *Places* upon the *best Writers*, no *Minister* ever made Himself more remarkable by his Profusion of *Pensions* amongst the *worst*; which I think a much more generous and munificent Part; because *good Writers* may be able to support themselves by their *own Works*; whereas *bad Ones* must depend upon *his Protection*.

---

[46] *Fog's Weekly Journal*, no. 97 (1 Aug.1730).
[47] *Craftsman*, no. 216 (22 Aug.1730).

174   THE CULTURAL POLITICS OF OPERA, 1720–1742

And finally, as in *Fog's Weekly*, Courtly Grub mentions that even if Walpole patronized no poets, "he gave no small Encouragement to those sublime Productions, *Hurlothrumbo* and *Tom Thumb*." A year earlier, *Fog's Weekly* had ironically praised the "exalted Taste of the Age" for its favoring *Hurlothrumbo: or, the Super-Natural* (1729), which is damned by his fulsome praise. That the play is dedicated to Walpole proves him "so considerable a Person, and renown'd a Judge."[48] Since Walpole subscribed to the printed play, the dedication's address to Walpole, so long as you live, "fine Poetry will not want Encouragement," may not be meant seriously.

When Opposition journalism caught fresh wind with the founding of *Common Sense* in February 1737 after the closing of *Fog's Weekly Journal*, it resumed the attack on Walpole's arts patronage. In October, *Common Sense* and the ministerial *Daily Gazetteer* sparred over the literary quality of the ministerial writers and whether one side could lay claim to having a monopoly on wit. *Common Sense* led off, challenging

> the Ministerial Advocates to produce one Line of *Sense*, or *English*, written on their Side of the Question for these last Seven Years. — Has any one Person of distinguish'd Eminency, in any one Art or Science, shown the least Tendency to support or defend 'em?[49]

Whereas, the writer congratulates the Opposition:

> What Numbers of Dissertations, Essays, Treatises, Compositions of all Kinds, in Verse and Prose, have been written, with all that Strength of Reasoning, Quickness of Wit, and Elegance of Expression, which no former Period of Time can equal?

Lumping Walpole's writers among the sons of Dulness, the writer "cannot imagine why he will suffer, much less pay such Blockheads to write for him."

In previous reigns, the writer claims, Godolphin, Somers, Halifax, and Dorset engaged all the wits on the side of the ministry, and the best writers were proud to support it. "By what uncommon Fatality then, is this Administration destitute of all Literary Support?" The writer's answer carries an obvious innuendo:

> One would be apt to suppose, if one did not know the contrary, that there was something in the Measures so low, so corrupt, and so disgraceful, that common Decency would not suffer Wit, or good Sense, to appear on that Side; but made 'em, in this Case, withstand those Temptations [court places], to which, heretofore, they have too often yielded.

---

[48] *Fog's Weekly Journal*, nos. 37 and 41 (7 June and 5 July 1729). *Fog's* continued the innuendo in reference to the popularity of *Hurlothrumbo*: "Who will then say, that Arts and Sciences have no Patrons left amongst us?"; *Fog's Weekly Journal*, no. 64 (13 Dec. 1729).

[49] *Common Sense*, no. 36 (8 Oct. 1737). The point was repeated in the Dedication of the collected edition of *Common Sense* (1738): Britain is congratulated that "during the whole Course of our late political Controversies, all the Wit and good Sense should have appeared on the Side of Liberty, while the dull, the malicious, the dirty, and the ill-bred, have been listed under M——l [Ministerial] Colours" (vii).

OPERA AND THE POLITICS OF TASTE   175

By the phrase "if one did not know the contrary," *Common Sense* supplies the real reason in the guise of a rejected, false supposition.

In response, the *Daily Gazetteer* rather sensibly, it seems, reminds readers that all "*Controversial Writers*" treat their adversaries as "Fools and Blockheads" and assume "all the Reason, Good Sense, and Good Manners to themselves, and absolutely denying the least Glimmering of any one of these Qualities in those who may differ from them."[50] The folly of this method is obvious: "*both Sides* will mutually make Use of the Accusation of *Dullness*."

Yet by their "dull eternal Repetition" of republishing "worn-out Invectives" against the ministry when they can find no new ministerial scandal, the writers of the *Craftsman* and *Common Sense* demonstrate their lack of invention. The *Gazetteer's* writer ridicules *Common Sense* for introducing a new figure of modern rhetoric, "*Self Panegyrick*," when Opposition writers compliment each other in the pages of *Common Sense* for their literary efforts against the Ministry.

The *Gazetteer's* writer passes over examining "what Justice there is in Mr. *Common Sense's* claiming *all* the *Wit* to *his Party*, and fixing all the Dullness on the contrary [ministerial party]." He leaves the public to judge on the basis of a poem, "A *Familiar Epistle*," dedicated "To the no less *Politick* than *Witty*, G—e L—tl—n, *Esq*;" that can serve as a proper reply to numerous Opposition invectives against the Ministry.[51] For sake of argument, the poet asks what does it matter if all the flowers of rhetoric and wit are with the Opposition? Only "That a *Rymer* and *Wit* may be no *Politician*." Lyttelton's journalistic wit is of no avail in the Commons, where he is a "dull Dolt in Debate at *Committee*" and blunders "like some dull Blockhead at *Eton*" who for "his *Sense* and your *Wit* must still peep in [his] *Hat*." In contrast, "let *Walpole* but speak, and his Wit is confest"; in one hour, his replies and reason undo "the whole *Wit* of a *Year*."

Even as late as November 1740, the issue of the ministry's taste and could still be hauled out for partisan advantage. *Common Sense* observed (to disparage the current ministry) that "Arts and Sciences have constantly been the second Care [after manufacturing and commerce] of every Government, that made the Honour and Interest of the Nation its first [care]."[52] Louis XIV's patronage of the arts, the writer notes, brought both esteem and commercial advantage to France.

Although no nation was ever more inclined to encourage arts and sciences than present-day Britain, the writer is both surprised and concerned that "Arts and Sciences, as well as Trade and Manufactures, have been neglected or rebuked" by those in Government. This is all the more surprising since those in government – and here he condemns by excessive, unmerited praise – who are known for "their exquisite Judgment, their delicate Taste, their liberal

[50] *Daily Gazetteer*, no. 723 (28 Oct. 1737).
[51] The charge is leveled in *Common Sense*, 2 vols. (collected reprint edition, 1738), 1:vii.
[52] *Common Sense*, no. 196 (8 Nov. 1740). The point was continued in issue no. 201 (13 Dec. 1740), where Walpole is attacked in the guise of Colley Cibber, and in issue no. 211 (21 Feb. 1741), where it is claimed arts and sciences are out of favor under Walpole.

176   THE CULTURAL POLITICS OF OPERA, 1720–1742

Manner, their polite Address," would seem to promise "Arts and Sciences all the Encouragement and Perfection of the several Reigns of *Augustus Cæsar*, and *Lewis the XIVth*."

Despite all Walpole's paid political writers and the labors of the Laureate Colley Cibber, the writer prophesies:

> Posterity will not receive one Scrap of Paper in his Favour; whereas, on the other Hand, many of those Writings in which he is not very advantagiously [*sic*] delineated, will be preserved and read while Wit and Learning are tolerated or tasted in this Kingdom. In what a Light then must he inevitably, though unjustly, appear to Posterity? Innumerable Volumes remaining filled with the strongest Charges of Peculiar Oppression, Falshood, Nepotism, Ignorance, Pusillanimity, &c. and not five righteous Lines be found to save him, notwithstanding that a River of Ink hath been exhausted in Encomiums and Adulation upons him.

And with crocodile tears, the writer hopes Walpole would engage two or three able authors to produce some works that might outlive him, so that future historians may be able "to account for the greatest Part of his glorious Actions."

In December 1741, as Walpole's control of Parliament slipped away with the loss of the disputed Westminster election, *Common Sense* could portray "our Great Man" at the head of a legion of dunces, which shows "his excellent Judgment and fine Taste."[53] The nation and all the professions so abound in "Votaries of Dulness," that the journal hopes "the present excellent M——" will build a Temple to Dulness.

WALPOLE'S ARTS PATRONAGE

It must emphatically be stressed that the common impression of Robert Walpole as a crude, vulgar countryman more interested in weekend hunting parties in Norfolk than the fine arts is another example of the partisan polemics of the Scriblerians and Opposition surviving – even among scholars – as valid opinion, eclipsing the historical record.[54] The attack on Walpole's lack of patronage and connoisseurship must be seen as malicious, opportunistic political propaganda and, to some extent, the resentment of writers who failed to earn Court patronage.

Walpole came from a distinguished Norfolk family. He attended Eton and went on to King's College, Cambridge. As he amassed his considerable fortune in the 1720s, he filled his several London homes with painting, sculpture, and furniture and extended patronage to music and literature, in the process garnering his share of embarrassing verse panegyric.[55]

---

[53] *Common Sense*, no. 254 (26 Dec. 1741).

[54] Representative examples from Opposition polemic are given in Janet Wolf, "Political Allegory in the Later Plays of John Gay," pp. 275–93 in *Enlightening Allegory: Theory, Practice, and Contexts of Allegory in the Late Seventeenth and Eighteenth Centuries*, ed. Kevin L. Cope (New York, N.Y.: AMS Press, 1993).

[55] Tone S. Urstad, *Sir Robert Walpole's Poets: The Use of Literature as Pro-Government Propaganda, 1721–1742* (Newark, Del.: University of Delaware Press, 1999).

In 1722 he began constructing his magnificent country home Houghton Hall, in Norfolk, built by Thomas Ripley to plans by Colen Campbell; designs for the interior decoration were provided by Burlington's protégé William Kent.[56] Houghton was among the many great county homes begun in the great building boom of the 1720s.[57] The magnificence of Houghton was frequently remarked,[58] and it was supposed to be the model for Timon's Villa in Pope's *Epistle to Burlington* (see p. 207). Houghton came to house a large portion of his magnificent art collection.

Walpole used the Civil List and Secret Service funds to support a stable of political writers who would defend his policies and ministry. Regarding literary writers, it is demonstrably false that Walpole, the Ministry, or Court did not patronize writers or act to their advantage.[59] A poem in the *Grub-street Journal* in 1734 rightly notes Walpole's patronage of writers both ministerial and those who went into opposition:

> What tho' Concannen, Cibber, Mitchell, Ralph,
> Are smil'd on, by the Primier with the staff?
> So Pope, Young, Welsted, Thompson, Fielding, Frowde,
> Have, each by turns, to his [Walpole's] indulgence owed.[60]

Edward Young received a Court pension of £200 in 1726. Joseph Mitchell ("Walpole's poet") received £500 over ten years.[61] For his translation of the *Odyssey*, Alexander Pope received £200, and Walpole is said to have presented his *Dunciad* to the King and Queen on 12 March 1729.[62] James Thomson received a present from Walpole for his poem "To the Memory of Sir Isaac Newton," and money also went to Richard Savage, Henry Fielding, and Voltaire.[63] By the late 1730s, however, Pope, Thomson, and Fielding were in the Opposition camp. Whether their change of allegiance was due to genuine change in political

---

[56] The house was documented in Isaac Ware, *The Plans, Elevations, and Sections; Chimney-Pieces, and Ceilings of Houghton in Norfolk* (1735); Kent's decorative schemes are described in Charles Saumarez Smith, *Eighteenth-Century Decoration: Design and the Domestic Interior in England* (New York, N.Y.: Harry Adams, 1993), 66–9, and Plates 47–53.

[57] John Summerson, "The Classical Country House in 18th-Century England," *Journal of the Royal Society of Arts*, 107 (1959), 551–2.

[58] A writer to *Fog's Weekly Journal*, no. 156 (30 Oct. 1731), used the occasion of describing Houghton Hall to imply Walpole furnished it at the public expense and accuse him of vanity, and through three (probably) fictive allegorical paintings impugn his personal character (evil, avarice, and bribery).

[59] On Walpole's literary patronage, Griffin, *Literary Patronage*, 51–3.

[60] *Grub-street Journal*, no. 248 (26 Sept. 1734).

[61] Griffin, *Literary Patronage*, 53.

[62] The gift of £200 is noted in the *London Journal* for 16 July 1726. Walpole's presentation of the *Dunciad* to the King and Queen is widely reported, but no documentation has been presented. See Chapter 12, n. 18.

[63] Griffin, *Literary Patronage*, 52; W. A. Speck, "Politicians, Peers, and Publication by Subscription, 1700–1750," pp. 47–68 in *Books and Their Readers in the Eighteenth Century*, ed. Isabel Rivers (Leicester: Leicester University Press, 1982), 56.

178   THE CULTURAL POLITICS OF OPERA, 1720–1742

attitude, resentment at not gaining further Court positions, accepting any available patronage, or influence of friends and patrons is not always clear.

Another means of dispensing patronage was subscribing to books; and Walpole appears on sixty-four book subscription lists.[64] The numerous books and poems dedicated to Walpole might have earned the authors usually about £10, though larger amounts were possible.

Walpole amassed one of the nation's largest collections of art.[65] *Common Sense* could remark that he "hath laid out in the Article of *Italian* Pictures, three Times as much as the Estate he was born to is worth," asking readers to see this as a sign of the extent of his corruption.[66] Well represented in his collection were major works by Rembrandt, Rubens, Van Dyck, Rosa, Maratti, Poussin, Giordano, and Guido Reni. In 1739, the artist, engraver, and chronicler George Vertue called it "the most considerable now of any in England."[67] His son Horace Walpole, who described the collection in *Ædes Walpolianæ: or, A Description of the Collection of Pictures at Houghton-Hall in Norfolk* (1747), and the nation were outraged when Sir Robert's grandson, the third Earl of Orford, sold the collection in 1779 to Empress Catherine of Russia for £40,555. Before the sale, drawings were made of the most important paintings, and 162 of them were engraved and published by John Boydell as *A Set of Prints Engraved after the Most Capital Paintings ... Lately in the Possession of the Earl of Orford at Houghton Hall*, but more commonly known as Boydell's *Houghton Gallery* (1774–1788).[68] J. H. Plumb observes that had the collection not left the country, "Walpole would be recognized for what he was, one of the greatest connoisseurs of his time."[69]

---

[64] Speck, "Politicians, Peers, and Publication," 52.

[65] On Walpole's art collecting, J. H. Plumb, *Sir Robert Walpole: The King's Minister* (Boston, Mass.: Houghton Mifflin, 1961), 85–7. See the chapters by Andrew Moore, "Sir Robert Walpole: The Prime Minister as Collector," Andrew Moore, "The Sale to Catherine the Great," and Gregory Rubinstein, "The Genesis of John Boydell's *Houghton Gallery*," in *Houghton Hall: The Prime Minister, The Empress, and The Hermitage*, ed. Andrew Moore (London: Philip Wilson, 1996).

On Walpole's collection at Houghton, its sale, and the pictures now at the Hermitage, *A Capital Collection: Houghton Hall and the Hermitage, with a Modern Edition of Aedes Walpolianae*, ed. Larissa Dukelskaya and Andrew Moore (New Haven, Conn.: Yale University Press, 2002); *Houghton Revisited: The Walpole Masterpieces from Catherine the Great's Hermitage*, exhib. cat., Houghton Hall, King's Lynn, Norfolk, 17 May–29 Sept. 2013 (London: Royal Academy of Arts, 2013); and *Painting, Passion and Politics: Masterpieces from the Walpole Collection on Loan from the State Hermitage Museum, St. Petersburg*, exhib. cat., Somerset House, 28 Sept. 2002–23 Feb. 2003 (London: Hermitage Rooms, Somerset House, 2002).

[66] *Common Sense*, no. 244 (17 Oct. 1741).

[67] George Vertue, *Vertue Note Books*, The Walpole Society, 6 vols. (1930–1955), 1:6.

[68] See Moore, "The Sale to Catherine the Great," and Rubinstein, "The Genesis of John Boydell's *Houghton Gallery*," in Moore, ed., *Houghton Hall*.

[69] Plumb, *Walpole: The King's Minister*, 87.

OPERA AND THE POLITICS OF TASTE   179

In addition to collecting old masters and building a large library, Walpole patronized contemporary British artists. He kept the major portraitists of the day, including Charles Jervas, Michael Dahl, Thomas Hudson, Sir Godfrey Kneller, Jonathan Richardson, John Wootton, and Jean-Baptiste Van Loo, busy painting portraits of himself and his family. The prime minister's face must have been among the most recognizable of the day.[70]

Not least in importance was the Walpole family's extensive patronage of Italian opera and Italian musicians – illustrating the important role of opera for Britain's governing elite. When the Royal Academy of Music was founded in 1719, Walpole subscribed for a two-hundred-pound share. As a financial enterprise, the Academy was a failure, and Walpole ended up losing all his investment. Walpole's household account books record payments for the Haymarket theatre. All totaled, for the Royal Academy years 1719–1729, Walpole laid out £740 at the Haymarket.[71] Minus the subscription calls that consumed his two-hundred-pound investment, this leaves £540 spent for tickets (probably also including masquerades), librettos, and refreshments for himself, wife, and family members. And in the following seasons, eight members of the Walpole family subscribed to one or more seasons of opera.[72] Lady Walpole received the dedication of Veracini's *La clemenza di Tito* (1737).

Walpole and his family patronized music in other ways. Sir Robert and his eldest son, Robert, subscribed to Attilo Ariosti's *Six Cantatas and Six Lessons for the Viola d'Amore* (1724); Sir Robert, Lady Walpole, and their two elder sons subscribed to Carlo Arrigoni's *Cantate da camera* (1732); Walpole himself subscribed to *The Delightfull Musical Companion … Being a Choice Collection out of All the Latest Operas Composed by Mr: Handel, Sigr: Bononcini, Sigr: Attilio, &c.* (1724) and Mauro d'Alay's *Cantate a voce sola, e suonate a violino solo* (1728); and Lady Walpole received the dedication of John Christopher Smith the Younger's *Suites de pièces pour le clavecin* (1732).

His son Horace describes frequent concerts held at the family London home, at which Monticelli and Amorevoli, singers in Lord Middlesex's opera company, performed. Monticelli seems to have become a favorite of the Walpole household, for Horace wrote on 7 July 1742,

> Monticelli lives in a manner at our house … [and] dines frequently with Sir Robert which diverts me extremely; you know how low his ideas are of music and the virtuosi; he calls them all *fiddlers!*[73]

---

[70] Edward Bottoms, "Charles Jervas, Sir Robert Walpole, and the Norfolk Whigs," *Apollo*, vol. 145, no. 420 (1997), 44–8.

[71] See Thomas McGeary, "The Opera Accounts of Sir Robert Walpole," *Restoration and Eighteenth-Century Theatre Research*, 2nd ser., vol. 11, no. 1 (Summer 1996), 1–9.

[72] See Carole M. Taylor, "Italian Operagoing in London, 1700–45" (Ph.D. dissertation, Syracuse University, 1991), 331; and Judith Milhous and Robert D. Hume, "Handel's Opera Finances in 1732–3," *Musical Times*, 125 (1984), 86–9.

[73] Letters of 7 January and 7 July 1742, from Horace Walpole to Sir Horace Mann; *The Yale Edition of Horace Walpole's Correspondence*, ed. W. S. Lewis, 48 vols. (New Haven, Conn.: Yale University Press, 1937–1983), 17:274 and 487.

180 THE CULTURAL POLITICS OF OPERA, 1720–1742

The Opposition rightly identified operagoing as one of the perquisites of those in the Ministry or at Court, as is reflected by casual comments by political writers. In 1731, one Opposition writer rather wistfully confessed he too would like to become "a great Man" and "bask under the Shade of Power ... with a very large Salary ... that would furnish a Man *French* Wine, and Wenches, and Opera's, and Masquerades."[74] A decade later, one collection of satires against Walpole and the King contained a mock *libera nos*, a prayer to be freed from the ills associated with the Ministry:

> From *Ci—r's* [Cibber's] vile Odes, and *L—d C—n's* [Lord
>   Chamberlain's] Plays
> From *M—st—l* [ministerial] Shifts, Put-offs and Delays;
> From *Italian* Soft Operas and *Italian* Back-ways
>   [*Good Lord deliver us.*][75]

We know, of course, that arts and sciences of the 1720s and 1730s were not in such a state of "ignorance and barbarity," to use Johnson's words again,[76] as the Opposition claimed. The 1720s and 1730s, after all, produced literary works of Swift, Gay, Pope, Thomson, and Johnson; paintings and prints of Hogarth; decorative arts and gardens by Kent; posthumous scientific works by Newton; and the building of great country homes and palaces by Vanbrugh. The rhetoric does show, however, how widespread must have been tacit acceptance of the classical republican doctrine about the state of the arts as a proxy for the health of the state, for it to be invoked in political polemics.

The place of opera in the life of London's *beau monde* and social-political elite, the widespread concern with taste and its effect on the nation, coupled with Opposition charges that the spread of False Taste was due to Walpole, the Court, and Ministry are the backdrop for the prominent appearance of opera in the satires on False Taste discussed below.

🙙 *Opera and the Triumph of Dulness*

By the mid-1720s, opera was serving as a conspicuous example of the spread of False Taste throughout Britain – a symptom of all that was wrong under the new financial order and Walpole's rule.[77]

---

[74] *Fog's Weekly Journal*, no. 133 (22 May 1731); reprinted in *Select Letters Taken from Fog's Weekly Journal*, 2 vols. (1732), 2:204.

[75] M. B. S. E. M. M., *The Mi—st—l Light* (1741), 4–5. The mock *libera nos* was frequently put to political use in the late-seventeenth and early eighteenth century; see various volumes of *Poems on Affairs of State*.

[76] Samuel Johnson, "Life of Pope," in *Lives of the English Poets*, ed. George B. Hill, 3 vols. (Oxford: Clarendon, 1905), 3:212.

[77] Brief sketches of men and women of the Town foolishly pursuing opera are found in early plays, as well. See, for example: Thomas d'Urfey, *The Marriage-Hater Match'd* (1692), esp. p. 30; George Granville, *The She-Gallant* (1695/6), esp. pp. 18, 44; the character of Viscount Sans Terre in [Thomas Betterton], *The Amorous Widow: or, the Wanton Wife* (1704, pub. 1706); [Susanne Centlivre], *The Platonic Lady* (1706/7),

OPERA AND THE POLITICS OF TASTE   181

HOGARTH'S *MASQUERADES AND OPERAS*

Opera's contribution to the decline of the British stage is shown in William Hogarth's print *Masquerades and Operas: The Taste of the Town* (February 1724)[78] (Plate 9.1), advertised as "The Bad Taste of the Town." Hogarth described the print as showing "the Taste of the Town in which the then reigning follies were lashd."[79]

Second Epilogue and pp. 29–33; Colley Cibber, *The Double Gallant: or, the Sick Lady's Cure* (1707), esp. pp. 8–9, 12–13, 28; Colley Cibber, *The Rival Fools* (1709), pp. 66–8; Susanna Centlivre, *The Busie Body* (1709), Prologue; and Charles Shadwell, *The Humours of the Army* (1713), pp. 18–19.

Other instances of opera as an example of False Taste or the foolishness of a Man or Woman of Taste not discussed below include: (1) *A View of the Town* (1731), where the *beaux* are "better versed in the Performances of the Opera in the *Hay-Market* last Winter, than they are with any thing that has passed at *Westminster-Hall*," p. 33; (2) Hercules Mac-Sturdy, *A Trip to Vaux-Hall: or, A General Satyr on the Times* (1737), esp. p. 10; (3) Thomas Catesby, Baron Paget, "Written in the Year 1735," in *Miscellanies in Prose and Verse* (1741), pp. 367–8; (4) Thomas Newcomb, "Prologue to Henry the Fourth," in *A Miscellaneous Collection of Original Poems* (1740), pp. 66–8; (5) Tipping Silvestre, "The Beau and Academick," in *Original Poems and Translations* (1733), pp. 8–16; (6) Prologue to "The Royal Convert" in *British Journal*, no. 76 (29 Feb. 1724); (7) *The Connoisseur: or, Every Many in His Folly* (1736), pp. 37–8; (8) "An Epistle to Mr. Southerne, 1711," in Elijah Fenton, *Poems on Several occasions* (1717), pp. 67–83; (9) *The Connoisseur. A Satire on the Modern Men of Taste* [1735], p. 15; [Joseph Warton?], *Fashion: An Epistolary Satire to a Friend* (1742).

[78] Discussed here is the first state of the print; the second state has a different caption. On the print, see Ronald Paulson, *Hogarth's Graphic Works*, 2 vols. (New Haven, Conn.: Yale University Press, 1965), no. 34; Paulson, *Hogarth's Graphic Works*, 3rd rev. ed (London: Print Room, 1989), no. 44; Frederick G. Stephens, *Catalogue of Prints and Drawings in the British Museum. Division I. Political and Personal Satires*, 3 vols. (London: British Museum, 1877), no. 1742; Ronald Paulson, *Hogarth*. Vol. 1. *The "Modern Moral Subject," 1697–1732* (New Brunswick, N.J.: Rutgers University Press, 1991), 74–90; David Dabydeen, *Hogarth, Walpole and Commercial Britain* (London: Hansib Publishing, 1987), 42–8; and John Brewer, *The Pleasures of the Imagination: English Culture in the Eighteenth Century* (Chicago, Ill. University of Chicago Press, 1997), 369–71.

Dabydeen relates the print to Hogarth's larger attacks on stockjobbing and the financial corruption resulting from the South Sea Bubble. Elsewhere in his book, Dabydeen finds numerous allusions to politics and Walpole in Hogarth's works. However, David Bindman rightly points outs, "While Hogarth's satires of the 1730s and early 1740s make the implicit claim that the morals and manners of society were shameful and getting worse by the day, they do not contain any discernible rejection of Walpole's system of patronage, from which he had, as the son-in-law of the Serjeant Painter to the King, much to hope for"; David Bindman, *Hogarth and His Times: Serious Comedy* (Berkeley, Calif.: University of California Press, 1997), 45 (see the fuller discussion on pp. 41–5).

[79] Hogarth's "Autobiographical Notes," in William Hogarth, *The Analysis of Beauty*, ed. Joseph Burke (Oxford: Clarendon, 1955), 205. The print was approvingly described in *Pasquin*, no. 109 (18 Feb. 1724).

PLATE 9.1. William Hogarth, *Masquerades and Operas* (1724), showing crowd (at right) flocking to see Rich's pantomimes and (at left) crowd in costume rushing to Heidegger's masquerades at the Haymarket theatre, with banner showing lords imploring Cuzzoni to accept money.

The print, writes Joseph Burke, was Hogarth's "declaration of war on the connoisseurs."[80] As an artist, Hogarth was not opposed to the masterpieces of the classical tradition. But he did oppose what seemed to work against the development of a native English school: the theory of ideal beauty; authority and standards based on continental practice; the conception that imitation and precedence can prevail over an artist's interpretation of nature; and ignorant connoisseurs who were the dupes of picture dealers who deprecated English paintings in favor of "dismal Dark" foreign Old Masters.[81] In his own reaction against classical authority, Hogarth developed a narrative tradition of moral satires that he later developed in the series *A Harlot's Progress* (1732), *A Rake's Progress* (1735), *Marriage à la Mode* (1745), and *Industry and Idleness* (1747).

---

[80] Introduction, Hogarth, *Analysis of Beauty*, ed. Burke, xiv.
[81] Hogarth, *Analysis of Beauty*, ed. Burke, xiii–xvii, lxi.

OPERA AND THE POLITICS OF TASTE   183

In *Masquerades and Operas*, to the right, the town crowds to Lincoln's Inn Fields to attend John Rich's pantomimes and especially the harlequinades featuring Dr. Faustus, which were reviled for undermining legitimate drama.[82] At the left, a satyr and jester lead a crowd into Heidegger's Haymarket theatre, home of the Royal Academy of Music and the "Monsters" (*castrati*) of the caption, and where Heidegger (shown at the window) mounted his masquerades.

The caption in the first state of the print makes clear the contrast between the present "Debauch'd" English stage and its past glories:

> Could new dumb *Faustus*, to reform the Age,
> Conjure up *Shakespear's* or *Ben Johnson's* Ghost,
> They'd blush for shame, to see the *English Stage*
> Debauch'd by fool'ries, at so great a *cost*.
> What would their *Manes* say? should they behold
> *Monsters* and *Masquerades*, where usefull Plays
> Adorn'ed the fruitfull *Theatre* of old,
> And Rival Wits contended for the *Bays*.

The effect of this running after fooleries of the modern stage is symbolized by the barrow-woman who cries "Waste paper for Shops" and hauls away the works of Congreve, Dryden, Otway, Shakespeare, and Addison. The sheet labeled "Pasquin No. XCV" probably refers to that issue of the periodical *Pasquin* (27 December 1723), which carried an essay on good taste in architecture (in the later state of the print, this was replaced by "Ben Johnson").

The facade labeled "ACCADEMY OF ARTS" represents the gate to the Earl of Burlington's Palladian villa in Piccadilly. Burlington, an architect and patron, had traveled in Italy and was active as a director of the Royal Academy of Music. The crowd's indifference suggests how the arts of sculpture and painting (represented by Michelangelo and Raphael) are ignored. That Burlington's protégé William Kent stands above Michelangelo and Raphael may be Hogarth's jibe at Burlington's own taste, but especially at his patronage of foreign artists and schools above native English artists. Hogarth, though, had his own animus against Kent.[83]

In the print, opera is an instance of the veneration of foreign, continental taste, to the disadvantage of native theatre represented by those authors being hauled away by the barrow-woman. The banner labeled "Operas" hanging from the theatre depicts the monstrous appearance of the opera singers: in particular, the castrato Senesino's barrel-chest, elongated figure, knock-knees, and splay feet (features that identify Senesino in other prints). The banner also points up the foolish expense of opera. The design is adapted from the print

---

[82] The popularity of pantomime-harlequinades as afterpieces revives in 1723–24 when Drury Lane produced *Harlequin Doctor Faustus* and Lincoln's Inn Fields produced *The Necromancer or Harlequin Doctor Faustus* featuring John Rich (as "Lun"). On the harlequinades in British culture, John O'Brien, *Harlequin Britain: Pantomine and Entertainment, 1690–1760* (Baltimore, Md.: Johns Hopkins University Press, 2004).

[83] Paulson, *Hogarth: The Modern Moral Subject*, points out Hogarth's animosity toward Kent (82–90). Most vicious is his burlesque of Kent's altar piece at St. Clement Danes.

184 THE CULTURAL POLITICS OF OPERA, 1720–1742

often incorrectly attributed to Hogarth *Berenstadt, Cuzzoni, and Senesino* (Plate 9.2), which appeared in June 1723.[84] On the banner, Hogarth has reversed and regrouped Senesino and Berenstadt on the left of Cuzzoni. She turns to three kneeling noblemen, probably patrons of the Royal Academy of Music, and literally rakes in the money they are offering, while one of the noblemen implores, "Pray Accept 8000. *l.*"

POPE'S *DUNCIAD*

The triumph of Dulness and False Taste in Britain was epitomized and allegorized by Alexander Pope in *The Dunciad. An Heroic Poem*, which Pope described to Swift as "my Chef d'œuvre, the Poem of Dulness."[85] Begun about 1719, its publication on 18 May 1728 set off The War of the Dunces.[86]

The satire in three books first appeared as a sixty-page pamphlet; Pope disguised its author and publisher and used letters and dashes for the names of the Dunces intended. The writers Pope assails as Dunces are accused not so much of stupidity, but of misapplication of their learning; their learning represents not the humane letters (*litteræ humaniores*) but a perversion of the right use of reason and good taste.

The year after the appearance of the first edition, Pope published a full 180-page, apparently "authorized" critical edition of the poem. Replete with elaborate preface, notes, and appendices, this *Dunciad Variorum* (10 April 1729; cited as *DV*) is itself a parody of the Dulness in scholarship the poem itself satirizes.

---

[84] Stephens, *Catalogue of Prints and Drawings*, no. 1768; and Paulson, *Hogarth's Graphic Works* (1965), no. 266. There has been much guesswork about the date and the performers and opera depicted in the print. It is now accepted that the print was published in June 1723 and depicts Senesino (male alto), Francesca Cuzzoni (soprano), and Gaetano Berenstadt (bass) in Handel's *Flavio* (III.iv), which had its premiere on 14 May 1723; see Harry R. Beard, "An Etched Caricature of a Handelian Opera," *Burlington Magazine*, 92 (1950), 266. Gibson, *The Royal Academy of Music*, 180, cites an advertisement for the print on 14 June 1723.

[85] Letter to Jonathan Swift, ?January 1728; *The Correspondence of Alexander Pope*, ed. George Sherburn, 5 vols. (Oxford: Clarendon Press, 1956), 2:468.

[86] The most extensive discussion of the complete lifetime *Dunciad* project and its background is Aubrey L. Williams, *Pope's "Dunciad": A Study of Its Meaning* (London: Methuen, 1955). See also James Sutherland's Introduction to *The Dunciad. The Twickenham Edition of the Poems of Alexander Pope*, v. 5, 3rd ed. (New Haven, Conn.: Yale University Press, 1963); Robert W. Rogers, *The Major Satires of Alexander Pope* (Urbana, Ill.: University of Illinois, 1955), 9–31; Howard Erskine-Hill, *Pope: The Dunciad* (London: Edward Arnold, 1972); David Fairer, *The Poetry of Alexander Pope* (Harmondsworth: Penguin, 1989), 135–58; Robert K. Root, Introduction to *The Dunciad Variorum, with the Prolegomena of Scriberlus* [facs. ed.] (Princeton, N.J.: Princeton University Press, 1929), 1–42; and Valerie Rumbold, ed., *Alexander Pope: The Dunciad in Four Books* (Harlow, Essex: Longman, 1999). On the background of the 1728 edition itself, David L. Vander Meulen, *Pope's Dunciad of 1728: A History and Facsimile* (Charlottesville, Va.: Bibliographical Society of the University of Virginia/ University Press of Virginia, 1991).

PLATE 9.2 *Berenstadt, Cuzzoni, and Senesino* (1724), showing an opera stage with three singers (left to right) Senesino, Cuzzoni, and Berenstadt in scene from Handel's *Flavio*.

In the broadest sense, the action of the first three books of the *Dunciad* is a mock-epic of the coronation of the playwright and Shakespeare critic Lewis Theobald as the new monarch of Dulness in Britain, to replace Elkanah Settle.

Pope would revise and expand the *Dunciad*, publishing a fourth book in 1742 that relies on the Session of Poets genre. In this Session or Grand Levee scene, Dulness holds court and opera will appear as one of her votaries; the scene presents a vivid condemnation of opera as a major contributor to Dulness in Britain.

At the allegorical level, as Pope summarized in the Argument, "the Action of the Dunciad is the Removal of the Imperial Seat of Dulness from the City to the polite world."[87] The epic progress is east to west. The City was London's financial center, and, just as importantly, its outskirts housed the growing mob of aspiring authors and mercenary writers collectively living on "Grub Street," who in their scribbling for money were debasing literature – those "shoals of wretches who write for bread" who were infamously corrupting "the taste of England," as Swift put it.[88]

---

[87] *The Dunciad Variorum* (or *Dunciad* A), in *Dunciad*, ed. Sutherland, 51; citations in this chapter are to this edition (as *DV*).

[88] Jonathan Swift, letter to Charles Wogan, 2 Aug. 1732; in Swift, *Correspondence*, ed. Williams, 4:128. On the subculture of the writers collectively known as living on

186   THE CULTURAL POLITICS OF OPERA, 1720–1742

Dulness's goal is the seat of fashion and taste in the West End, where lie not only the theatres but Parliament and the Court. For Pope, the reign of Dulness approaches when the "Ear of Kings" and the Court – those whose background and education should be setting the standard of taste – stoop to the entertainments of the Smithfield Muses. Dulness's path takes the same westward direction as the progress of liberty and learning from Greece to Rome to Britain, but her progress instead mimics the westward migration of the Goths and Huns to Rome.

In Book I, after being introduced to Queen Dulness, "Daughter of Chaos and eternal Night" (*DV*, 1:10), we meet the hero-dunce Lewis Theobald in his library, despairing at the end of the Empire of Dulness, whose "good old Cause" he has served. The library holds the accumulated works of generations of dunces. Theobald lights a sacrificial altar built from these and his own works. Dulness appears, quenches the fire, and anoints him her new monarch of Dulness. Her empire is not to end but will be extended from the City to the Court.

Theobald was in Pope's eyes an apt choice for Dulness's favorite. Along with Elkanah Settle, he wrote many of the pantomimes and harlequinades produced by John Rich at Lincoln's Inn Fields in competition with Drury Lane. It was these dramatic pieces, with their monsters and spectacular stage effects and machinery, that so outraged serious critics, who claimed their popularity was debasing the London stage. More personally, Theobald had earned Pope's enmity for publishing *Shakespeare Restored: or, a Specimen of the Many Errors, as Well Committed, as Unamended, by Mr. Pope in His Late Edition of This Poet* (1726), which dared to point out legitimate deficiencies in Pope's Shakespeare edition.

The first hint of opera's role in the realm of Dulness appears when – as Theobald is being anointed with the sacred ointment opium – a bird descends to his head:

a monster of a fowl!
Something between a H*** and Owl.
(*DV*, I:243–4)

Pope's own note, "A strange Bird from *Switzerland*," makes clear the bird is a cross between an owl and John Jacob (or James) Heidegger, manager of the Haymarket theatre, that housed operas and masquerades, the twin-evils corrupting the taste and morals of London society.

Book II celebrates Theobald's coronation with entertainments of mock-heroic games, which begin the westward Progress of Dulness to her new temple in the fashionable West End of London (in fact, "The Progress of Dulness" was one of Pope's discarded titles for the poem).[89] To witness the games and sports in Theobald's honor, Queen Dulness summons the motley band of her sons

---

Grub Street, who allegedly produced debased writing, and who were the object of the *Dunciad*'s scorn, Pat Rogers, *Grub Street: Studies in a Subculture* (London: Methuen, 1972); on the *Grub-street Journal*, 353–63.

[89] A contemporary explanation of the *Dunciad* summarized it in its title: *The Progress of Dulness. By an Eminent Hand* (1728).

and their patrons, from ragged Grub-street hacks to peers in chariots. There are events in the games for booksellers, poets, and critics. The competitive games mimic aspects of the sub-literary world of publishing. Booksellers, including Bernard Lintot and Edmund Curll, run a footrace to seize the phantom of a fleeing poet; then William Chetwood and Curll engage in the infamous urinating contest. For poets, there are contests in "Tickling" (wooing a patron by writing a shamelessly flattering dedication) and "Vociferating" (noise and fustian). Finally, in a diving contest, poets (including Dennis, Eusden, Smedley, Concanen, and Welsted) dive into the Fleet Ditch, an open sewer that emptied into the Thames. In the final contest, critics compete to keep awake while listening to readings of "Orator" Henley and Sir Richard Blackmore. All those present, contestants and audience, succumb to boredom, and "Thus the soft gifts of Sleep conclude the day" (*DV*, II:387).

In Book III, set in Dulness's Temple, Theobald, exhausted after the day's celebrations, falls asleep on the goddess's lap. In his dream, he descends to the underworld, where Settle carries him to a Mount of Vision. There Settle shows Theobald the past, present, and future progress of the Reign of Dulness. Westward from the Orient through Egypt, Rome, Spain, and Gaul toward Britain, nations succumbed to her sway. Pope here perverts the usual progress from Athens to Latium to Britain of liberty and culture (a *translatio studii*) into a Progress of Dulness, darkness, and disorder (a *translatio stultitiae*).[90] Settle prophesies the unfolding Triumph of Dulness in Britain:

> And see! my son, the hour is on its way,
> That lifts our Goddess to imperial sway:
> This fav'rite Isle, long sever'd from her reign,
> Dove-like, she gathers to her wings again.
> (*DV*, III:115–18)

Then pass in review Dulness's progeny, "a hundred sons, and each a dunce," "blockheads" and "fools," who have been preparing Dulness's reign in Britain: Theophilus Cibber, Ward, Haywood, Centlivre, Jacob, Ralph, Welsted, Dennis, Gildon, Burnet and Duckett, "Orator" Henley, and Woolston. Passing before Theobald are the works that charm Dulness and her sons, works "Not touch'd by Nature, and not reach'd by Art" (*DV*, III:228). Whereupon, Theobald sees his own wondrous pantomines, harlequinades, and farces with all their monstrous absurdities and extravagancies. These productions

> Magistrates and Peers shall taste,[91]
> And from each show rise duller than the last:
> Till rais'd from Booths to Theatre, to Court,
> Her seat imperial, Dulness shall transport.
> (*DV*, III:299–302)

---

[90] On the significance of the westward progress in the *Dunciad*, Jonathan Pritchard, "Social Topography in the *Dunciad, Variorum*," *Huntington Library Quarterly*, 75 (2013), 527–60.

[91] Pope's manuscript shows he first had in mind "Peers and Potentates" for this line; *DV*, 3:299, p. 184 note.

THE CULTURAL POLITICS OF OPERA, 1720–1742

The westward Progress of Dulness will have its ultimate triumph at the Court of St. James's. Settle prophesies how at the commencement of Dulness's reign, "first the nation shall be overrun with farces, opera's, shows."[92] Finally, opera appears in Dulness's service to mark her farthest advance at the Haymarket theatre:

> Already, Opera prepares the way,
> The sure fore-runner of her gentle sway.
> (*DV*, III:303–4)

Opera represents not just the literal, geographic advance to the Haymarket. Its popularity at Court demonstrates that the highest ranks of polite society are already succumbing to Dulness and False Taste.

Settle's vision closes with a preview of the Triumph of Dulness and Theobald's reign:

> Lo! the great Anarch's ancient reign restor'd,
> Light dies before her uncreating word:
> …
> Thus at her felt approach, and secret might,
> Art after Art goes out, and all is Night.
> …
> They hand great Dulness! lets the curtain fall,
> And universal Darkness covers all.
> (*DV*, III:339–40, 345–6, 355–6)

Early in the *Dunciad* was introduced the innuendo that there is a second, shadow monarch of Dulness:

> Say from what cause, in vain decry'd and curst,
> Still Dunce the second reigns like Dunce the first?
> (*DV*, I:5–6)

Since George II had succeeded his father the previous year, the implication is hardly subtle: the Hanoverians are succeeding each other as monarchs of Dulness. A connection between Dulness and George II is also hinted, as Maynard Mack points out, because George patronized both operas and masquerades and shortly after his accession appointed as his Master of the Revels the Swiss Heidegger (who in the poem had appeared while Theobald was being anointed with opium).[93]

In the course of Pope's almost fifteen years of revisions of the first three-book *Dunciad*, the poem's true hero becomes Walpole himself at the head of the ministry. By portraying a London overrun by literary dunces, Pope obliquely attributes to Walpole and the court he served responsibility, writes Mack, "for a general moral and cultural decay which since the middle 30's even Whig

---

[92] Pope's argument to Book 3 (*DV*, 3:56).
[93] Maynard Mack, *Alexander Pope: A Life* (New York, N.Y.: W. W. Norton, 1985), 464.

OPERA AND THE POLITICS OF TASTE   189

observers had been deploring."[94] In general, though, the *Dunciad Variorum* deals little with the topical politics of the day. The most insistent point is the charge that Walpole's ministerial writers are chief among the Dunces: a point that will be exploited and elaborated by Opposition pamphleteers. Both politics and opera will be more prominent in the final four-book version of 1743 (see Chapter 12).

WHITEHEAD'S *STATE DUNCES*

Pope's attacks on contemporary writers and critics prompted his hapless victims to reply in kind, setting off in print a War of the Dunces. One follower of Pope is Paul Whitehead, whose *The State Dunces. Inscribed to Mr. Pope* (June 1733) explicitly develops at length the link between Dulness and Walpole's political writers, which we have already seen was a commonplace in much Opposition pamphleteering, newspapers, and satire. Whitehead may have been emboldened in his attack by Walpole's presumed weakness after the failure of the Excise Scheme in the previous April.

The satire's point of view is revealed quite clearly by the title-page epigraph adapted from Swift:

> I from my Soul sincerely hate
> Both —— [Kings] and M——rs [Ministers] of State.[95]

With its epigraph from Swift and dedication to Pope, Whitehead is throwing in his lot with the Scriblerians. *State Dunces* is, in a sense, a small-scale *Dunciad*, but less a *translatio stultitiae* than a Session of Poets-like audience between Dulness and her favorite, Robert Walpole. In the opening scene, Pope, the poem's hero ("chief to *Dulness* ever Foe decreed"), is shown peaceful in his Twickenham bower away from the corruptions of the Town and Court. Yet despite the sharpest rage of his satire, "Still starv'ling *Dunces* persecute the Age" (22).

Had the poet Pope's powers, he would praise Pulteney, who stands ready to save Britain as Brutus saved Rome from Tarquin; but "*Britannia* still laments a *W*——'s [Walpole's] Sway." While Walpole "stands amidst the *servile Crew*" and shamelessly spreads lawless corruption over England, Pope is urged not to trifle with the literary Dunces; he should sing of Virtue and the Patriots and inspire Britons to revenge their country's woeful state:

> Let dull *Parnassian* Sons of Rhime, no more
> Provoke thy [Pope's] Satire, and employ thy Power;

---

[94] Maynard Mack, *The Garden and the City: Retirement and Politics in the Later Poetry of Pope, 1731–1743* (Toronto: University of Toronto Press, 1969), 152; on Walpole's becoming the hero of the *Dunciad*, see pp. 150–62.

[95] Adapted from Jonathan Swift, "A Panegyric on the Reverend Dean Swift" (1729–30); Swift, *Complete Poems*, ed. Rogers, lines 154–6, p. 414:

> No less than reasons of such weight, ⎫
> Could make you so sincerely hate   ⎬
> Both kings and ministers of state.   ⎭

190 THE CULTURAL POLITICS OF OPERA, 1720–1742

> New Objects rise to share an equal Fate,
> The *big, rich, mighty, Dunces* of the *State.*   (p. 4)
> …
> *Dulness* no more roosts only near the Sky,
> But *Senates, Drawing-rooms*, with Garrets vye.   (p. 4)

Attention now turns to Walpole, "the *Tibbald* of the State." Pensive, mourning his lost Excise Scheme, he sits surrounded by loads of political pamphlets by Hoadley, Arnall, and Pitt, all inspired by his pay. Walpole drowses, but his sleep is disturbed by hideous visions of past executed and assassinated English politicians. Dulness comes to awaken her child and console him. He need despair no more as long as she extends her "universal Sway" over kings, prelates, peers, and rulers. Dulness anoints Walpole with opium and declares him her favorite son.

Walpole complains that Caleb D'Anvers is the "Rebel" to Dulness's power and betrays his plans to enslave Britain to the public. Shamelessly, Walpole calls his misdeeds and blunders as a statesmen "Works ever worth *Dulness's* fav'rite Son." He presents to Dulness her sons, upon whom alone Walpole showers his favors. The roster of Walpole's cabinet ministers and parliamentary supports includes Newcastle, Harrington, Argyll, Bishop Gibson, Horatio Walpole, Yonge, and Lord Hervey, as well as the writers Osborne and Walsingham. Dulness breaks off the train of State Dunces and assures Walpole that he will reign secure as long as "Grub-street hail Thee *Minister of State.*"

The satire's popularity called for five more editions that year; the number of ministerial replies appearing within the month attest that the satire hit home.[96] Whitehead added a second part to *State Dunces* in the same year, which portrays the ever-swelling "*hireling* Band" of the "*true Dunces* of the State."

Whitehead's wish to be associated with Pope was realized when "Britannicus," who styled himself friend to "the Cause of Liberty and *Britain*," attacked him and Pope for their satires in the ministerial *Daily Courant.*[97] In a poem addressed to Prejudice, Dulness toils to increase the votaries of Prejudice, who include Pulteney and Pope. Pope deserves censure for his friendship with

---

[96] Replies include *A Friendly Epistle to the Author of the State Dunces* (July 1733), *The Counterpart to the State-Dunces* (July 1733), Richard Verney (Lord Willoughby de Broke), *Dunces Out of State, Address'd to Mr. Pope* (1733), and "An Answer to the State Dunces" (in *Gentleman's Magazine* 3 [June 1733], 318). The *Friendly Epistle* recognizes the satire on the ministers and rebukes the author for using the satirist's rod on the "Allies of State." Verney had earlier defended the Ministry in *The Craftsman Answered Paper by Paper* (1727).

The poem was commended and excerpted in *The Bee: or, Universal Weekly Pamphlet*, no. 17 (6–23 June 1733), 758–61, and in "Characters from the State-Dunces," *Gentleman's Magazine*, 3 (June 1733), 317–18.

The previous year, Walpole had been shown at his levee surrounded by his "illiberal, servile, scribling Band" of journalists in *Verres and His Scribblers* (1732). At the implied levee of Walpole, the youth "dies away at a soft Eunuch's Voice" (line 234).

[97] *Daily Courant*, no. 5364 (16 June 1733). *A Friendly Epistle to the Author of the State Dunces* (1733) recognizes the satires on the ministers and groups the writers as imitators of Pope and members of the Opposition.

OPERA AND THE POLITICS OF TASTE   191

Bolingbroke and recommending him to the public as "Friend to Virtue."[98] Whitehead (though excused for his youth) is as "innocent of State Affairs as [of] Truth." He ridicules for him the "low Scandal" of thinking that calling ministers fools is wit and damns the Opposition with his praise.

HENRY FIELDING

Pope's war on Dulness was brought to the stage in Henry Fielding's comedies and farces of the 1730s, where he uses Opera's appearance at drawing rooms or on the stage to mock the Triumph of Dulness, Ignorance, or Nonsense, decrying the spread of popular forms of low culture and especially denying opera as a legitimate form of culture.[99] Fielding takes aim at many of the same targets as the Scriblerus Club of Swift, Pope, and Gay. But Ashley Marshall cautions that although Fielding early on signed himself "Scriblerus Secundus" and shares much of their cultural critique, he should not be seen as among the Scriblerian satirists, since there are significant differences in the tone, genre, and temperament of their satires.[100]

In *The Author's Farce; and the Pleasures of the Town* (30 March 1730), which ran for forty-one performances, the impoverished author Harry Luckless (a stand-in for Fielding himself) presents a puppet show called "The Pleasures of the Town" that ridicules London's literary, theatrical, and social world.[101] Attributing the play to Scriblerus Secundus, Fielding links his play with the Scriblerians.

In Luckless's play, at her "Court of Nonsense," Goddess Nonsense, "a lover of recitativo," assembles her suitors Don Tragedio, Sir Farcical Comic, Dr. Orator, and Monsieur Pantomime, as well as Mrs. Novel to celebrate "this joyful day." From among her suitors she declares, "Opera the Crown shall wear."[102]

The indictment of the risible entertainments of the Town in Luckless's puppet show has a counterpart in the play itself. A speech by Luckless's friend Witmore, whose ironic advice on how to succeed as an author, indicts the state

---

[98] See Pope's *First Epistle of the First Book of Horace Imitated* (*Epistle to Bolingbroke*).

[99] Xavier Cervantes points out that satiric mentions of opera, which are virtually a compendium of the criticisms of opera, seem to occur systematically in all of Fielding's plays; "Playwright Henry Fielding: Enemy or Connoisseur of Italian Opera?" *Theatre History Studies*, 16 (June 1996), 157–72.

[100] Ashley Marshall, *The Practice of Satire in England, 1658–1770* (Baltimore, Md.: Johns Hopkins Press, 2013), 226–9, 231–4, summarizing "Henry Fielding and the 'Scriblerians,'" *Modern Language Quarterly*, 72 (2008), 19–48. For Fielding's place in the 'culture wars' of the day, Marshall, *Practice of Satire*, 201–8.

Brean S. Hammond helps resolve the nature of Fielding's relation to the Scriblerians and his changing politics by arguing that his was "not a partisan but a cultural or aesthetic commitment ... a cultural politics more than a partisan politics"; "Politics and Cultural Politics: The Case of Henry Fielding," *Eighteenth-Century Life*, 16 (Feb. 1992), 76–93 (at p. 78).

[101] For introduction and edition of the two versions of *The Author's Farce*, Henry Fielding, *Plays*, ed. Thomas Lockwood, 3 vols. (Oxford: Clarendon Press, 2004–2011), 1:185–358.

[102] Fielding, *Plays*, ed. Lockwood, 1:352.

of the fine arts and carries innuendo about the arts patronage from the Ministry.[103] Witmore explains to Luckless why "scribbling" that employs wit is the sure path to poverty. Only pandering to False Taste will succeed:

> In an Age of Learning and true Politeness, where a Man might succeed by his Merit, it [writing] wou'd be an Encouragement. — But now, when Party and Prejudice carry all before them, when Learning is decried, Wit not understood, when the Theaters are Puppet-Shows, and the Comedians [are] Ballad-Singers: When Fools lead the Town, wou'd a Man think to thrive by his Wit? — If you must write, write Nonsense, write Opera's, write Entertainments, write *Hurlothrumbos*. — Set up an *Oratory* and preach Nonsense; and you may meet with Encouragement enough. (I.v)

Fielding's later plays rise from merely political to stridently partisan. They frequently exploit theatre-government parallels: the state of the stage reflects that of government. By this means, the indictment of False Taste becomes not merely cultural, but political. Author Medly explains the technique to the critic Sourwit prior to the rehearsal of his play in Fielding's *The Historical Register for the Year 1736 and Euridice Hiss'd* (1737).[104]

> You may remember I told you before my Rehearsal, that there was a strict Resemblance between the States Political and Theatrical; there is a Ministry in the latter as well as the former, and I believe as weak a Ministry as any poor Kingdom cou'd ever boast of; Parts are given in the latter to Actors, with much the same Regard to Capacity as Places in the former have sometimes been, in former Ages, I mean; … and if one considers the Plays that come from one Part, and the Writings from the other, one would be apt to think the same Authors were retain'd in both.[105]

Fielding has here worked the age-old stage-theatre parallel to Walpole's disadvantage: like a puppet-master, Walpole manages placemen MPs; the world of politics is as deceptive and illusory as the stage; and Walpole has reduced the dignity of government to the level of a farce or comedy. The corruption of the government is revealed in the widespread corruption of popular entertainment.

Pasquin
Fielding again allegorized opera's contribution to False Taste in the triumph of Ignorance over Common Sense in Fustian's tragedy in his popular *Pasquin. A Dramatick Satire on the Times: Being the Rehearsal of Two Plays, viz. A Comedy call'd The Election; and a Tragedy call'd, The Life and Death of Common-Sense* (5 March 1736), which played sixty times that season.[106] In Fustian's play-within-a-play, an officer informs Queen Common Sense that

---

[103] At this early date, the comedies may be political, but are not partisan party pieces. On the politics in *The Author's Farce*, see Sheridan Baker, "Political Allusion in Fielding's *Author's Farce, Mock Doctor*, and *Tumble-Down Dick*," *PMLA*, 77 (1962), 221–31.

[104] For introduction and edition cited of *The Historical Register, … to which Is Added … Eurydice Hiss'd*, see Fielding, *Plays*, ed. Lockwood, 3:353–460.

[105] Fielding, *Plays*, ed. Lockwood, 3:431–2.

[106] For introduction and edition cited of *Pasquin*, see Fielding, *Plays*, ed. Lockwood, 3:217–315.

OPERA AND THE POLITICS OF TASTE   193

> Queen *Ignorance* is landed in your Realm,
> With a vast Power from *Italy* and *France*
> Of Singers, Fidlers, Tumblers, and Rope-dancers.   (pp. 294–5)

All are the usual causes of the decline of the English stage. Representatives of Divinity, Law, and Physick (medicine) are ridiculed as opponents of Common Sense and join Queen Ignorance's invading forces. As they approach, a ghost calls out,

> Awake, great *Common Sense*, and sleep no more,
> …
> Thou wilt not suffer Men of Wit to starve,
> And Fools, for only being Fools, to thrive.
> Thou wilt not suffer Eunuchs to be hired,
> At a vast Price, to be impertinent.   (pp. 298–9)

In the final act of Fustian's play, Queen Ignorance and her attendants arrive at Covent Garden (where Handel's opera company then performed) and conquers the forces of Queen Common Sense. When mortally stabbed by Firebrand (a priest of the sun), Queen Common Sense laments,

> Henceforth all things shall topsy turvy turn;
> …
> Cits shall turn Beaus, and taste *Italian* Songs   (p. 310)

After her triumphal entry, Queen Ignorance proclaims:

> The powers of *Common-Sense* are all destroy'd;
> …
> To you, good *Harlequin*, and your Allies,
> And you, *Squeekaronelly*, I will be
> A most propitious Queen—   (pp. 310–11)

Squeekaronelly's name evokes the castrato Farinelli, whom Fielding had mocked in other farces.[107] To accompany the Queen's triumph, stage directions require "*Musick under the Stage*," at which Queen Ignorance exclaims,

> What hideous Musick, or what Yell is this?
> Sure 'tis the Ghost of some poor Opera Tune.   (p. 312)

Meanwhile, stage directions say the "*Ghost of* Common-Sense *rises to soft Musick*."

The *Grub-street Journal* commended the design and ingenuity of the farce. By showing the three professions opposed to Common Sense going over to Queen Ignorance and her army of "foreign *Singers*, Fidlers, Tumblers, and *Rope-dancers*," the allegory shows that these professions "have been the greatest encouragers of the late foreign senseless Entertainments which have been

---

[107] Cervantes, "Playwright Henry Fielding."

PLATE 9.3. *Pasquin, "Vivetur Stultitia"* (c. 1736). Scene from Fielding's play *Pasquin*, showing Queen Ignorance corrupting the British stage, with Pope to the right leaving a box.

exhibited in our Theatres."[108] Perhaps as a way of endorsing the play, the *Grub-street Journal* reported Pope's attendance.[109]

The farcical-chaotic scene of Queen Ignorance's triumph is portrayed in the print *Pasquin, "Vivetur Stultitia"* (Plate 9.3).[110] Shown filling a riotous, cacophonous stage below the legend MONSTRUM HORRENDUM are dancing dogs, fighting cats, a rope walker, Harlequin hanging from a rope, dancers, a strongman, and an acrobat. At center is Queen Ignorance, decked out in all the attributes of a fool. To her right are Law and Physick, while to her left Firebrand (representing divinity) stabs Queen Common Sense. The posture, costume,

---

[108] *Grub-street Journal*, nos. 330 and 332 (22 April and 6 May 1736).
[109] *Grub-street Journal*, nos. 328–9 (8 and 15 April 1736). See the poem "On seeing Mr. Pope at the *Dramatic Satire* call'd *Pasquin*," in the first issue.
[110] Although it appears to be signed by Hogarth, the print is no doubt a forgery; see Paulson, *Hogarth's Graphic Works* (1989), p. 317 and Plate 344; a reduced version was used as a ticket for the author's benefit (no. 343). See also Stephens, *Catalogue of Prints and Drawings*, no. 2466.

OPERA AND THE POLITICS OF TASTE   195

and knock-knees of Squeekaronelli recall the Senesino of the *Berenstadt, Cuzzoni, and Senesino and* print (Plate 9.2), though the name, of course, invokes Farinelli.

The text on the banner above the stage inverts the sense of that over the stage at Drury Lane: for *Vivetur Ingenio* (We live by our wits), it reads *Vivetur Stultitia* (We live by folly). A "Theatrical Barometer" at the back of the stage registers the taste of the stage. On the right, measuring "very low" are common sense, tragedy, and comedy; while on the left, operas register "very high." As in Hogarth's *Masquerades and Operas* (Plate 9.1), the print shows the effects of such dramatic entertainments on the British theatre. On the stage, Punch fans the flames of the burning pile of works of Ben Jonson, Shakespeare, Rowe, Congreve, and probably Fielding's own *Pasquin*. Of all this farrago on the stage, a short figure in the box at the right representing Pope exclaims as he turns to leave, "There is no whitewashing this stuff."

As Pope's presence at *Pasquin* suggests, the attack on Ignorance in Fielding's farces endorses Pope's program in the *Dunciad*. For the high-literary audience of the Scriblerians, the touchstone was the classical tradition of the *litteræ humaniores*, whose standards Italian opera violated. At Fielding's Little Theatre at the Haymarket, for an audience of middling ranks the touchstone was the more accessible Common Sense. For both, opera was a risible entertainment of London's cultural elite. Fielding's farcical royal drawing-room scenes served as models for the levee of Queen Dulness in the forthcoming final book of Pope's *Dunciad*.

Fielding's personal politics and those of the plays have been a source of controversy, but the political bite of his early comedies has long been recognized.[111] Of *Pasquin*, Robert Hume writes, "The play quite clearly says that England is politically corrupt and culturally degenerate, but the message is conveyed in a roundabout way and softened by theatrical high jinks."[112] The play's critique of False Taste and hits at Walpole are certainly oppositional, but it is not an outright party piece. Later, Fielding was allied with oppositional factions, and then would toss in his lot and write on the side of Walpole and the Ministry.

HARLEQUIN-HORACE

Another sequel to the *Dunciad*'s attack on Dulness that uses opera to condemn the taste of the Town and the general decay in British theatre is James Miller's elaborately worked out ironic Horatian imitation *Harlequin-Horace: or, The Art or Modern Poetry* (February 1731),[113] in which Miller turns Horace's guidelines

---

[111] Fielding's politics have been authoritatively surveyed in Robert D. Hume, *Henry Fielding and the London Theatre* (Oxford: Clarendon Press, 1988); for *Pasquin*, 209–15. There is no doubt that after his early political, then partisan plays, in the early 1740s, he went over and wrote for Walpole. See conclusively, Frederick G. Ribble, "Fielding's Rapproachement with Walpole in late 1741," *Philological Quarterly*, 80 (2001), 71–81.

[112] Hume, *Henry Fielding and the London Theatre*, 213.

[113] Along with James Bramston's *Art of Politicks* (1729) and Walter Harte's *An Essay on Satire, Particularly on the Dunciad* (1730). On the successors, see Anthony Coleman,

196   THE CULTURAL POLITICS OF OPERA, 1720–1742

for poetry into a satire on English taste, literature, and theatre. Judging from the number of reprints and editions, it was one of the most popular satires of the decade.

The choice of an Horatian imitation (the imitation in English of the satires, epistles, and odes of Horace) is itself suggestive. No doubt because it provided the cover that the subject and personages were actually Horace's and the time was Augustan Rome, the genre (even though in tone, often Juvenalian) became a favorite mode for both by oppositional and ministerial writers and was virtually synonymous with political satire.

In political writing, exposés of vice and corruption and portraits of past evil ministers were assumed by politically savvy contemporaries to be aimed at the Walpole regime. The notion that – despite its remove from contemporary Britain – Horatian satire was instinctively taken to have political application to the Court and Ministry is expressed in several verses of "An Excellent New Ballad, Call'd, A Bob for the C——t [Court]" that appeared in the *Craftsman* in 1728:

> Ye Poets, take Heed how you trust to the Muse, *fa, la*.
> What Words to make choice of, and what to refuse, *fa, la*.
> If she hint at a Vice of *political* Sort, *fa, la*,
> *Application* cries out, *That's* a Bob *for the C——t, fa la*.
> ...
> *Corruption, Ambition, Pomp, Vanity, Pride, fa, la*.
> Are Terms, that by Guess-work are often apply'd; *fa la*.
> To quote Horace is thought meer Derision and Sport; *fa, la*.
> *Application* cries out, *That's* a Bob *for the C——t, fa, la*.[114]

Harlequin-Horace resumes at full length the attack on John Rich already launched by Pope in the *Dunciad*.[115] Rich, dedicatee of *Harlequin-Horace*, was the manager of the theatre at Lincoln's Inn Fields. In 1714 he introduced the popular pantomimes and after 1717 appeared himself as Harlequin (under the name Lun). Such pantomimes, among other theatrical entertainments, were widely held to debase the British stage by supplanting legitimate drama.[116]

The satire has obvious connections to Pope, who seems to have been alert to enlist others in his battle against Dulness. It was first issued by Pope's printer

---

Introduction to James Miller, *Harlequin-Horace: or, the Art of Modern Poetry*. Augustan Reprint Society, no. 178 (1976), i. *Harlequin-Horace* appeared in numerous editions through 1785 (in *A Collection of Scarce, Curious, and Valuable Pieces* [1785]).

[114] *Craftsman*, no. 130 (28 Dec. 1728). Reprinted in *A Collection of Poems on Several Occasions; Published in the "Craftsman"* (1731), 57–60; and Milton Percival, *Political Ballads Illustrating the Administration of Sir Robert Walpole*. Oxford Historical and Literary Studies, vol. 8 (1916), no. ix.

[115] *Dunciad Variorum* (1729), 3:237–60.

[116] A print, ironically titled "The Stage's Glory," centers on Harlequin as emblem of the greatest corrupter of the theatre; Stephens, *Satiric Prints*, no. 1869; the print was approvingly explicated in the *Grub-street Journal*, no. 67 (15 April 1731). A common way to derogate Walpole's management of politics was to compare him to Harlequin; see *Robin's Game; or, Sevens the Main* (1731), 8.

and publisher Lawton Gilliver, who also included the poem in *A Collection of Pieces in Verse and Prose, Which Have Been Publish'd on Occasion of the Dunciad* (1732).[117] Pope recommended *Harlequin-Horace* to his friend John Caryll on 6 February 1731 as a piece "which has a good deal of humour."[118] Pope later echoed a couplet from it in his *Essay on Man* (1733–1734).[119]

Miller's vehicle is an ironic poetics, derived from Horace's *Ars Poetica*. Like its model, *Harlequin-Horace* offers advice on the writing of poetry, but this *ars poetica* is to be read Harlequin-style, up-side down. Miller makes certain the reader will not be misled by the device:

> [The poem] is a *System* of the Laws of *Modern Poetry*, establish'd amongst us by the Authority of the most *Successful* Writers of the present Age: by which it appears that the *Rules* now follow'd, are in all Respects exactly the *Reverse* of those which were observ'd by the Authors of *Antiquity*, and which were set forth of old by *Horace* in his Epistle *de Arte Poetica*. In a word, Sir, it is *Horace* turn'd *Harlequin*, with his Head where his Heels should be.[120]

By basing his system on the taste of the present age and recommending much that Rich is already doing, Miller condemns the pernicious effects of the Dunces and Rich on English taste.

Miller's more immediate model is Pope's *Peri Bathous: or the Art of Sinking in Poetry* (1728), especially the chapter "A Receipt to Make an Epic Poem." Modeled itself on Longinus's *Peri Hupsous* (On the Sublime), *Peri Bathous* ridicules bad writing by systematically presenting the precepts of modern writing – but inverted.[121] By doing so ironically, *Peri Bathous* and *Harlequin-Horace* do contain an implicit neoclassic poetics. However, the would-be writer (such as Rich) who follows the poems' literal advice does what is execrable and offends good taste.

As Miller systematically works his way through Horace, he updates him by citing modern British writers.[122] His tone shifts between offering false precepts

---

[117] On the relationships between Pope, Gilliver, and *The Grub-street Journal*, James McLaverty, "Lawton Gilliver: Pope's Bookseller," *Studies in Bibliography*, 32 (1979), 101–24. Most of the other authors published by Gilliver shared Pope's contempt of the Dunces and his social-political attitudes.

[118] *Correspondence of Pope*, ed. Sherburn, 3:173.

[119] Peter Dixon, "Pope and James Miller," *Notes and Queries*, n.s. 215, vol. 17 (1970), 91–2.

[120] Preface; citing 1741 edition, C2v–C3r.

[121] Bertrand Goldgar describes the process used in both: "By a simple process of reversing the ironic statements so that we equate poetic virtue with everything Martinus [the pedant writer of *Peri Bathous*] condemns and poetic vices with all that he recommends"; *Literary Criticism of Alexander Pope* (Lincoln, Nebr.: University of Nebraska Press, 1965), xviii. See also *The Art of Sinking in Poetry*, ed. Edna Leake Steeves (New York, N.Y.: Russell and Russell, 1952), xiii–lxix.

[122] For comparison of *Harlequin-Horace* and the *Ars Poetica*, and Miller's changes to the poem through the editions, Paula O'Brien, "The Life and Works of James Miller, 1704–1744, with Particular Reference to the Satiric Content of His Poetry and Plays" (Ph.D. thesis, University of London, 1979), 126–83. My readings of *Harlequin-Horace* tend to see passages as more ironic than does O'Brien.

198   THE CULTURAL POLITICS OF OPERA, 1720–1742

and occasionally offering literally sound, sensible poetic advice. For example, as the standard of taste, Miller holds up Pope for genuine praise:

> ... in *Pope's* harmonious Lays combine,
> All that is lovely, noble, and divine;
> Tho' every part with Wit, and Nature glows,
> And from each Line a sweet Instruction flows.   (p. 6)

In the context of providing a handbook for the theatrical success of Rich, such sensible precepts as Miller includes must be considered guides to literary failure at the hands of London's audiences.

Miller introduces opera in the section where Horace gives advice on dramatic poetry (beginning with line 153 in Horace). Whereas Horace prescribes five acts, rare use of the *deus ex machina*, and a real role for the chorus, Miller tells the poet to disregard the proper number of acts, to introduce at every opportunity ghosts, monsters, fiends, heaven, and hell, and to introduce frequent songs instead of choruses.

Like Horace, Miller contrasts earlier and present states of the arts. For Miller, at some idealized time in the past, both rural and urban Britons and their music were simple, grave, and manly:

> In Days of Old when *Englishmen* were *Men*,
> Their Musick like themselves, was grave, and plain;
> The manly Trumpet, and the simple Reed,
> Alike with *Citizen*, and *Swain* agreed,
> Whose Songs in lofty Sense, but humble Verse,
> Their Loves, and Wars alternately rehearse;
> Sung by themselves their homely Cheer to crown,
> In Tunes from Sire to Son deliver'd down.   (p. 28)

For Horace and Miller, wealth and luxury have corrupted and trivialized the present stage. For Horace, this meant loud, prominent, and elaborate *aulos* playing, additional notes (strings) on the lyre, and impetuous, rapturous diction. For Miller, the decline of the stage is represented by the cacophony of contending instruments and foreign singers, in which sense is sacrificed for sound and show, epitomized by Italian opera ruling over the nation's gentry:

> Since *South-Sea Schemes* have so inrich'd the Land,
> That *Footmen* 'gainst their *Lords* for *Boroughs* stand;
> Since *Masquerades* and *Opera's* made their Entry,
> And *Heydegger* and *Handell* rul'd our Gentry;[123]
> A hundred different Instruments combine,

---

[123] In the 1741 edition (to which Handel was a subscriber), this line reads: "And Heydegger reign'd Guardien of our Gentry." The dropping of the reference to Handel seems to reflect the fact that after 1734 Handel was no longer in partnership with Heidegger in producing operas and was receiving considerable patronage from the Prince of Wales (until the two-season lapse). In 1737 Handel had written an aria for one of Miller's plays, and Miller later wrote the text for the oratorio *Joseph and His Brethren* (1744). Further on Miller's activities in the pro-Handel James Harris circle,

> And foreign *Songsters* in the Concert join:
> The *Gallick* [French] *Horn*, whose winding Tube, in vain
> Pretends to emulate the *Trumpet*'s Strain;
> The *shrill-ton'd Fiddle*, and the *warbling Flute*,
> The *grave Bassoon, deep Base*, and *tinkling Lute*,
> The *jingling Spinet*, and the *full-mouth'd Drum*,
> A *Roman Weather* [*sic*] and *Venetian Strum*,[124]
> All league, melodious Nonsense to dispense,
> And give us Sound, and Show, instead of Sense;
> In unknown Tongues mysterious Dullness chant,
> Make Love in Tune, or thro' the Gamut rant.   (pp. 29–30)

The allusion to "mysterious Dullness" recalls the *Dunciad*, its attacks on Walpole's paid wits, and its image of Opera preparing the way for the Triumph of Dulness.

A special target here is the invasion of Britain by foreign musicians. The characterizations of the "foreign Songsters" are hardly complimentary: the male castrato is a wether (castrated ram) and the female singer, a strumpet. This contrast between sound and sense was a common topic in critique of Italian opera.

The allusion to the South-Sea schemes hints at the source of corruption. The South Sea Bubble of 1720 symbolized for Tories and Old Whigs the new economic order based on finance: the source of Walpole's strength, the basis for his supposed corruption, and a sign of the decline of Country values and way of life based on ownership of land.

Miller invokes opera once more in a passage of ironic advice on acting:

> But he that would in *Buskins* tread the Stage,
> With *Rant*, and *Fustian*, must divert the Age,
> And *Boschi* like, be always in a Rage.   (p. 33)

A note in the 1735 edition clarifies that the Italian bass Giuseppe Maria Boschi is here instanced with ironic praise:

> A useful Performer for several Years in the *Italian* Operas; for if any of the Audience chanc'd unhappily to be lull'd to sleep by these soothing Entertainments, he never fail'd of rouzing them up again, and by the extraordinary Fury both of his Voice and Action, made it manifest, that, tho' only a *Taylor* by Profession, he was *nine* times more a *Man* than any of his *Fellow-Warblers*. (p. 35)

Grub-street Journal on the Politics of *Harlequin-Horace*

Harlequin-Horace's inverted poetics was immediately endorsed by the *Grub-street Journal*, whose anti-ministerial stance is unmistakable despite its claims of political neutrality.[125] The *Journal* existed in part to take Pope's side in the

---

 see *Music and Theatre in Handel's Work: The Family Papers of James Harris, 1732–1780*, ed. Donald Burrows and Rosemary Dunhill (Oxford: Oxford University Press, 2002).

[124] Wether: a castrated ram (in later editions, a capon); Strum: strumpet.

[125] On the general anti-ministerial stance of the *Journal*, see Alexander Pettit, "The *Grub-street Journal* and the Politics of Anachronism," *Philological Quarterly*, 69 (1990), 435–51, and *Illusory Consensus: Bolingbroke and the Polemical Response to*

200 THE CULTURAL POLITICS OF OPERA, 1720–1742

War of the Dunces, although there is little evidence that Pope or the Scriblerians took any active part in it. The conceit underlying the *Journal* is that it is
the publication of the Society of Grubeans, who are defending themselves from
attacks by those on the heights of Parnassus – Pope being their chief enemy. The
Grubeans, living in the lowlands of Parnassus, represent Dulness; their enemies on the mountain, real literary merit. The Grubeans, as it were, are those
for whom the rules of art in *Peri Bathous* and *Harlequin-Horace* were written.

The *Journal* is aghast to note *Harlequin-Horace* was published by Lawton
Gilliver who "has been the author of much evil to our Society, by bringing to
light the works of our most inveterate enemies, Pope, Swift, &c.," and accuses
it of maliciously carrying on "the cause of Antigrubeanism, which was in such
an unchristian-like manner begun by the *Dunciad*."[126]

Harlequin-Horace is put to good use for material in three issues in February and April 1731. The *Journal* first introduces *Harlequin-Horace* in its news
column, "From the *Pegasus* in Grub-Street," in a report of its meeting:

> This afternoon was read before our Society the late published Poem called,
> *Harlequin Horace*; in which the Author proposes to set the dark and impracti-
> cable rules of that ancient *Anti-Grubean, Horace*, in a clear and proper light, to
> bring them down to the practice of the present age, and invert them for the use
> of our illustrious Body.[127]

The Grubeans squabble over whether to admit the author to their Society, and
Bavius is appointed to report further.

In the next issue, Bavius reports that the "invidious" publication "has, to
the grief of all true Grubeans, met with unmerited success" and undertakes to
vanquish it by "some proper Criticisms."[128] Of course, by this irony, the *Journal* endorses Miller's critique of modern False Taste. Many of the *Journal's*
criticisms Miller incorporated as footnotes and glosses in the expanded 1735
edition of the poem.

Interspersed with Bavius' mock-pedantic criticisms of *Harlequin-Horace*
are comments confirming the anti-ministerial politics of the *Journal* and its
own political application of *Harlequin-Horace*. Bavius reports that because on
the title page *Modern Poetry* was set in "old capitals" (black-letter font), many
Grubeans "imagined the performance was a political pamphlet, and that *Harlequin Horace* was little less than a squint on our Friend at Court." By stating the
Grubeans were mistaken in taking the work as political, the report denies the

---

    Walpole, 1730–1737 (Newark, Del.: University of Delaware Press, 1997), 140–1; Bertrand
    A. Goldgar, "Pope and the *Grub-street Journal*," *Modern Philology*, 74 (1977), 371,
    and Goldgar, *Walpole and the Wits: The Relation of Politics to Literature, 1722–1742*
    (Lincoln, Nebr.: University of Nebraska Press, 1976), 94. Pettit notes how the *Journal's*
    anachronistic religious views distinguish it from the more overtly political Opposition.

[126] *Grub-street Journal*, nos. 60 and 66 (25 Feb. and 8 April 1731).

[127] *Grub-street Journal*, no. 59 (18 Feb. 1731).

[128] *Grub-street Journal*, no. 60 (25 Feb. 1731). Bavius (along with Maevius) was a (probably
    fictitious) malicious poet who attacked Virgil and Horace.

OPERA AND THE POLITICS OF TASTE   201

very innuendo it suggests.[129] As to the friend at Court, the name *"Horace"* could refer to Robert Walpole's brother (Horatio), who served as a privy councilor, treasury secretary, cofferer of the Household, and frequent minister abroad.[130]

The friend at Court, however, could also be Robert Walpole, for at least since 1727, printmakers and satirists had been depicting him as Harlequin, a juggler, puppeteer, or Punch to reflect his trickery at manipulating government, much of it hidden from view through corruption of elections and placemen.

A letter to the *Craftsman* by "Philomimicus" in 1727 describes a play, "The Mock Minister; or, Harlequin turn'd Statesman," that relates Walpole's rise and fall as a corrupt statesman through the persona of Harlequin, the leader of a *commedia dell'arte* troupe, which he rules by virtue of a magic wand (a parallel to the minister of state's white staff).[131] In another essay, "Philomath" points out the lessons Walpole could draw from the conduct of Harlequin.[132] The frontispiece to the second volume of the 1731 collected edition of *The Craftsman* shows what the caption calls "a Harlequin of State."[133] A printed key states, "Its principal Figure is *Harlequin* with a *Blew String* about his Shoulder. By his Phiz ..., I could not help thinking it resembled an old Friend of mine, at *Chelsea.*" The blue string (sign of the Order of the Garter) and mention of Chelsea unmistakably identify Walpole. Later in 1737, "Philomath" writes to the *Craftsman* observing that "*Harlequin's* surprizing, and always-ready Expedients ... must be a very useful Lesson to a *Prime-Minister.*"[134]

With Robert Walpole as a Harlequin figure and the commonplace of theatre-state allegories, the *Grub-street Journal* seems to suggest Walpole is the true friend at Court of the Dunces and Grubeans, the Harlequin-Horace who turns the world of taste and culture up-side down. And as we have seen, this chimes with the innuendo that Walpole controls Parliaments as does a puppet-master and that his government is little different from a theatrical farce.

Bavius notes that *Harlequin-Horace's* title-page epigraph *Tempora mutantur, & nos mutamur in illis* (The times change and we change in them) would

---

[129] On avoiding libel, see C. R. Croft, "Libel and Satire in the Eighteenth Century," *Eighteenth-Century Studies*, 8 (1974–75), 153–68.

[130] For literary attacks on the brothers Horatio/Horace and Sir Robert, see Mack, *Garden and City*, 157. In *Fog's Weekly Journal*, no. 84 (2 May 1730), Harlequin as a Minister of State is clearly referring to Horatio/Horace.

[131] *Craftsman*, no. 74 (2 Dec. 1727).

[132] *Craftsman*, no. 588 (15 Oct. 1737).

[133] The description appears under several titles: *Robin's Game; or, Seven's the Main. Containing a Key to the State-Hieroglyphicks, and a Description of the Frontispieces to the Seven Volumes of the Craftsman* (1731), 8; and *State Hieroglyphicks: or, Caleb Decipher'd. Containing an Exact Account of the New Edition of the Craftsman* (1731), 8. The writer says Walpole is shown "making a Present of his Soul to the Devil, but [I] soon retracted that Opinion, when I discovered that that Burnt-Offering was indeed the Nation." The set of seven frontispieces (titled *Robin's Reign or Seven's the Main*) is reproduced in Herbert M. Atherton, *Political Prints in the Age of Hogarth* (Oxford: Clarendon Press, 1974), Plate 9.

[134] *Craftsman*, no. 588 (15 Oct. 1737).

confirm the members in their mistake, for the motto "is so peculiarly applicable to some famous Politicians." To an alert reader, the application is to MPs, placemen, and office-seekers who adapt their policies to their own advantages or sell their political loyalty for pensions and places.

Political Implications of *Harlequin-Horace*

Thus armed with the sanction of the *Grub-street Journal*, we can note the political innuendo or application of various passages in *Harlequin-Horace*. A common Old Whig and Opposition viewpoint is conveyed in the earlier passage quoted beginning "In Days of Old when *Englishmen* were *Men*." Nostalgia for the vague Saxon past had been central to the Old Whig and Opposition rejection of the social and moral consequences of modern, post-Revolution Britain in the throes of the Financial Revolution. Recently the *Craftsman* had carried Bolingbroke's series of letters (later collected as *Remarks on the History of England*)[135] that had espoused traditional Country principles and referred to that mythic pre-Norman past when the Ancient Constitution and Britain's immemorial free institutions supposedly originated. The origin of British liberties in fact had become a politically contested point in the 1730s. Walpole's ministerial writers countered that British liberties were fully achieved only with the Glorious Revolution and Settlement of 1688–1689 and continued by the Whig party. But to praise the "Days of Old when *Englishmen* were Men" and the virtues that then prevailed implied that the new financial and political order of Walpole's ministry and the Whig supremacy was corrupting and enslaving Britain and that freedom required a return to the Ancient Constitution.[136] Italian opera is certainly not to be found in these "Days of Old."

Where Horace had counseled "Either follow tradition or invent what is self-consistent" (line 119), the modern poet is advised:

> Take then no Pains resemblance to pursue,
> Give us but something very strange, and new,
> 'Twill entertain the more – that 'tis *not true*.   (p. 18)

If he takes the advice, the aspiring ministerial writer will end up producing (though it is claimed "'tis *not true*," and thus preempting charges of libel) a stock Opposition portrait of Walpole

> If great Sir *R——t*'s Character you'd feign,
> Describe him mean, revengeful, thoughtless, vain;
> A thousand monstrous Accusations bring,
> False to his *Friends*, his *Country*, and his *King*.

The following lines are a self-congratulatory sketch of Opposition journalism:

---

[135] *Remarks on the History of England* was first published in the *Craftsman* as twenty-four essays from 13 June 1730 to May 1731 (nos. 206–55); the letters were collected in 1735 and reprinted in 1743. See also Chapter 3.

[136] On the Ancient Constitution, see Chapter 3.

> Make *weekly Patriots* free from Envy seem,
> And publick Good their *Thought*, as well as *Theme*.[137]

In the *Journal*, Bavius commended as "incomparable" one of *Harlequin-Horace's* rules:

> In one scene make your Hero cant and whine,
> Then roar out *Liberty* in every line.[138]

His explication (later adopted by Miller as a footnote), though, is a gibe at corrupt ministerial MPs who call themselves patriots:

> The frequent exclamations of O *Liberty!* O *Freedom* O *my Country!* cannot but draw repeated claps from all true Patriots, especially those distinguished ones, who consult on the good of the nation in the Court of Requests.[139]

Consulting in the Court of Requests (an antechamber to the House of Commons) certainly was intended to describe MPs who vote on the basis of the minister's dictates (and purse) rather than the good of the country or their constituents.

🕮 *The Man of Taste*

False Taste is exemplified or personified in the figures of the Man and Woman of Taste. Satires on the Man or Woman of Taste hold up an implied standard of good taste by satirizing a person who is a victim of False Taste and false connoisseurship. If the pervasive ironic tone is recognized, the reader knows that the Man or Woman of Taste is pursuing unworthy objects, confusing mere possession of fine art or superficial acquaintance with it as true connoisseurship, or displaying an ill-informed enthusiasm for otherwise worthy art works. Frontispieces to these satiric poems or satiric prints show the victim of False Taste surrounded by acquisitions of his or her pursuits: music and musical instruments, paintings, architectural plans, statuary, books, antiquities, and natural curiosities (see Plate 9.4).[140]

English satires on the Man or Woman of Taste have a near model in Boileau's *Ninth Satire* (1668) where "un Sot de qualité" slights Malherbe and Virgil in favor of Tasso and Theophile.[141] When John Oldmixon published his translation

---

[137] Lines 209–12 and 217–18 in third edition (1735), and lines 209–12 and 223–4 in fourth edition (1735).

[138] *Grub-street Journal*, no. 60 (25 Feb. 1731).

[139] *Grub-street Journal*, no. 60 (25 Feb. 1731). See 1735 edition, p. 6.

[140] See the frontispieces to [Joseph Dorman], *The Rake of Taste* (1735); James Bramston, *The Man of Taste* (1733); James Miller, *The Man of Taste* (1735); and the engraved illustration to "Epistle IV, of the Use of Riches," in Alexander Pope, *Works*, ed. William Warburton (1751), vol. 3, opposite p. 262. For an example of the Woman of Taste, see [Josephy Dorman], *The Female Rake: or, Modern Fine Lady* [1735].

[141] For a distant example, see Lucian's diatribe, "The Ignorant Book Collector"; in *Lucian*, 8 vols. Loeb Classical Library, trans. A. M. Harmon (Cambridge, Mass.: Harvard University Press, 1960), 3:174–211 (at p. 209).

PLATE 9.4. Gerard van der Gucht, Frontispiece to James Bramston, *The Man of Taste* (1733), showing the Man of Taste, surrounded by objects of his False Taste.

in September 1707, he anglicizes Boileau's "sot" into "Dorimant." Both are types of the young man – usually with a newly acquired fortune – who becomes a Man of Taste: a connoisseur and critic. In proclaiming his artistic judgments, he ventures outside his competence and reveals instead his poor taste and ignorance of the arts. Dorimant, "great and rich in all things but his Mind, / Who for his lovely Ignorance was fame'd," has become "the first and fiercest Critick in the Town." Love of opera is one way Dorimant manifests his misguided connoisseurship, running to a stage work for the wrong reason:

> 'Tis for the Musick that he sees the Play,
> And visits for the Verse the Opera:
> He flies to *Tamerlane* to hear the Tunes,
> And for sound Reason to *Arsinoe* runs.
> Thus whether of a Scene or of a Song,
> He still will judge, and still is in the wrong.[142]

The English pattern for satires of the Man or Woman of Taste was set by Pope's *An Epistle to the Right Honourable Richard Earl of Burlington* (1731), more commonly known as *Of False Taste*,[143] which exposes "false Taste in *Books*, in *Music*, in *Painting*, even in *Preaching* and *Prayer*, and lastly in *Entertainments*."[144] Pope's *Epistle to Burlington* exposes False Taste through the figures of Sir Visto, Villario, Sabino, and Timon and his country house. As exemplars of those with taste, Pope mentions by name Lords Cobham, Bathurst, and Burlington himself. Pope's example of False Taste in music arises from Timon's chapel:

> And now the Chappel's silver bell you hear,
> That summons you to all the Pride of Pray'r:
> Light Quirks of Musick, broken and uneven,
> Make the Soul dance upon a Jig to Heaven.[145]

Although Pope did not adduce opera as an example of False Taste (perhaps because of Burlington's own involvement in the Royal Academy of Music), false appreciation of opera became common in numerous satires of false taste.

The *Epistle to Burlington* caused Pope some embarrassment and irritation, for many contemporaries took the portrait of Timon and his villa as an attack on Pope's friend James Brydges, the first Duke of Chandos – an attack made

---

[142] "The Ninth Epistle of Boileau … By J.O.," in the *Muses Mercury*, 1 (Sept. 1707), 198–205; quotation from p. 202. The translation in *The Works of Monsieur Boileau. Made English from the Last Paris Edition, by Several Hands*, 2 vols. (1712–1713), is completely different. This translation and its attribution to Oldmixon apparently have not hitherto been noted. The parallel passage in Boileau's ninth satire begins at line 173:

> Tous les jours à la Cour un Sot de qualité
> Peut juger de travers avec impunité:
> A Malherbe, à Racan, préfere Theophile,
> Et le clinquant du Tasse, à tout l'or de Virgile.

[143] "Of False Taste" was the half title of its second edition, and the full title of its third edition.

[144] Argument. See *Epistles to Several Persons (Moral Essays)*. The Twickenham Edition of the Poems of Alexander Pope, vol. 3/2, 2nd ed., ed. F. W. Bateson (New Haven, Conn.: Yale University Press, 1961), 131–3. On the poem: Julian Ferraro, "Taste and Use: Pope's *Epistle to Burlington*," *British Journal for Eighteenth-Century Studies*, 19 (1996), 141–59; T. G. A. Nelson, "Pope, Burlington, Architecture, and Politics: A Speculative Revisionist View," *Eighteenth-Century Life*, 21 (Feb. 1997), 45–61; and Noggle, "Taste and Temporality in *An Epistle to Burlington*."

[145] Alexander Pope, *Epistle to Burlington* (1st ed., 1731), p. 11 (cf. lines 141–4 in the Twickenham Edition).

206 THE CULTURAL POLITICS OF OPERA, 1720–1742

inexcusable because Chandos was a friend of Pope's own friends Dr. Arbuthnot, and Lords Bathurst, Bolingbroke, and Burlington. A well-known anonymous engraving, *Taste, or Burlington Gate* (Plate 9.5), captured the contemporary sense of indignation at Pope's supposed attack on Chandos.[146] Pope, with a brush and bucket of whitewash on scaffolding in front of the gate to Burlington House, bespatters with paint the Duke of Chandos's coach. Pope ultimately sent an apology to Chandos.[147] George Sherburn has affirmed that it is highly unlikely that Pope intended to ridicule Chandos, his country mansion, or the music of his chapel.[148] Timon, Sherburn suggests, was most likely a composite portrait of a number of wealthy sinners against good taste.

It has been plausibly argued, however, that Pope instead intended Timon and his villa to represent Walpole's vulgarity of taste in his building and furnishing Houghton Hall, and that the contemporary identifications with Chandos were spread by pro-Ministry writers to deflect the criticism of Walpole.[149] Ministerial writers would have avoided defending Walpole from Pope's attack because to do so would only call attention to and confirm the satiric portrait. Bertrand Goldgar does not find the parallels with Walpole completely convincing; but Pope and Bolingbroke both saw the Ministry behind the attacks on Pope, so there was what Goldgar calls "a political twist to the brouhaha over the *Epistle*."[150] If Walpole and Houghton are the targets, then the *Epistle to Burlington* is imputing False Taste to those at Court and the Ministry, as placing the source of False Taste with those in political power.

BRAMSTON'S *MAN OF TASTE*

James Bramston joined Pope in exposing False Taste in *The Man of Taste* (March 1733). Bramston's Man of Taste believes himself qualified "To give the laws of *Taste* to humane kind" (p. 19):

> True *Taste* to me is by this touchstone known,
> That's always best that's nearest to my own.   (p. 5)

---

[146] *Taste, or Burlington Gate*; Paulson, *Hogarth's Graphic Works* (1965), no. 277; and Stephens, *Catalogue of Prints and Drawings*, no. 1873. Paulson, *Hogarth's Graphic Works* (1989), considers it a forgery. The plate was re-engraved as the frontispiece to *A Miscellany on Taste* (1732), also an attack on Pope.

[147] See Pope's letter to Burlington (21 Dec. 1731) and from Chandos to Pope (27 Dec. 1731); *Correspondence of Pope*, ed. Sherburn, 3: 259, 262–3.

[148] George Sherburn, "'Timon's Villa' and Cannons," *Huntington Library Bulletin*, 8 (1935), 131–2; see also Appendix B, "Timon and the Duke of Chandos," in Pope, *Epistles to Several Persons (Moral Essays)*, ed. Bateson, 170–4.

[149] Kathleen Mahaffey, "Timon's Villa: Walpole's Houghton," *Texas Studies in Literature and Language*, 9 (1967): 193–222; and Mack, *Garden and the City*, 122–6; 172–3; 272–8.

[150] Goldgar, *Walpole and the Wits*, 124–6, suggests contemporaries missed recognition of the Timon-Walpole parallel because it may have been too literary and subtle to warrant attention. On occasion, Walpole's writers did not respond to Opposition attacks.

PLATE 9.5. *Taste, or Burlington Gate* (1732). Satire on Pope's *Epistle to Burlington*, showing Pope on a ladder at the gate of Burlington House spattering paint spilling on an earl's coach.

The satire is a recital of the Man of Taste's own accomplishments and opinions about literature (including his dislike of Swift, Milton, and Pope), learning, painting, sculpture, architecture, gardening, music, cooking, and fashion (see Plate 9.4). But the Man of Taste's touting of his connoisseurship is all to be taken ironically – as proof he is deceived by his own perverse or corrupt taste, and as an indictment of those contemporary fashions and fads he praises.

The Man of Taste admits that knowing no Italian and having no ear for music, he has no basis for his preference for Bononcini:

208   THE CULTURAL POLITICS OF OPERA, 1720–1742

> Without *Italian*, or without an ear,
> To *Bononcini*'s musick I adhere.   (p. 5)

His preference for Bononcini is an example of the Man of Taste's dubious taste. Giovanni Bononcini was prominent in Britain during the years of the Royal Academy of Music, when he was one of the principal composers along with Handel, with whom he seen as a rival. By 1733, Bononcini had slipped somewhat into disgrace for several misdeeds. In 1728 he was accused of submitting a plagiarized score of a madrigal to the Academy of Ancient Music; in 1731, Bononcini quarreled with his patroness, Henrietta, the young Duchess of Marlborough, and left her employ.[151]

The Man of Taste also freely admits his true pleasure is rural music of bagpipes and loud wind instruments:

> Musick has charms to sooth a savage beast,
> And therefore proper at a Sheriffs feast.
> My soul has oft a secret pleasure found,
> In the harmonious Bagpipes lofty sound.
> Bagpipes for men, shrill *German-flutes* for boys,
> I'm *English* born, and love a grumbling noise.   (p. 13)

In London, his taste runs toward the new oratorio.

> The Stage should yield the solemn Organ's note,
> And Scripture tremble in the Eunuch's throat.
> Let *Senesino* sing, what *David* writ,
> And *Hallelujahs* charm the pious pit.
> Eager in throngs the town to *Hester* came,
> And *Oratorio* was a lucky name.
> Thou, *Heeideggre!* [sic] the *English* taste has found,
> And rul'st the mob of quality with sound.   (p. 13)

Senesino sang "what David writ" in Handel's oratorio *The Sacred Story of Esther*, which had its first revised performance at the King's Theatre on 2 May 1732, in which he sang in Italian the role of Ahasuerus.

As Bramston confirms, Handel's earliest oratorios did not meet with universal approval; there were strong objections on religious grounds to the performing of sacred texts in theatres.[152] The Man of Taste's seeming approbation of *Esther* can thus ironically be taken to indicate disapproval of the work. The objection that Heidegger has now found a way to rule the quality with sound suggests *Esther* (with some roles sung in Italian) was seen as pleasing by its

---

[151] On these misdeeds, see Lowell Lindgren, "The Three Great Noises 'Fatal to the Interests of Bononcini,'" *Musical Quarterly*, 61 (1975), 60–83.

[152] For similar confusion about *Esther* (especially its only being staged) and objection about some roles being sung in Italian, see *See and Seem Blind: or, a Critical Dissertation on the Publick Diversions, &c.* (1732), 14–16, possibly by Aaron Hill; see attribution in the August Reprint Society, no. 235, ed. Robert D. Hume (1986).

OPERA AND THE POLITICS OF TASTE   209

musical sound, rather than instructing by its sense. Early oratorios were, in fact, occasionally called operas.[153]

Politics enters the *Man of Taste* where our connoisseur, almost as an afterthought, reveals he is a politician too:

> I'm for an *Act*, that he, who sev'n whole Years
> Has serv'd his *King* and *Country*, lose his ears.   (p. 19)

Alluded to here is the Septennial Act (1716), which allowed Parliament to sit for seven years before new elections and which helped consolidate the Whig supremacy. The Opposition frequently proposed the Act's repeal on the grounds that it subverted liberty and a responsive Parliament. His preference is a further example of the Man of Taste's foolishness – in this case ridiculing a foundation of Modern Whig politics by proposing disfigurement of those who serve full seven-year terms in Parliament – and perhaps showing him as an opposition partisan who endorses their objections to Septennial Parliaments.

MILLER'S *MAN OF TASTE*

James Miller's comedy *The Man of Taste* (6 March 1735) well illustrates opera's central role as an unworthy object of taste. In the Dedication, Miller makes certain the tactic of inversion of values in the play is clear:

> what is set up [in the play] for the Standard of Taste, is but just the Reverse of Truth and Common Sense; and that which is dignify'd with the Name of Politeness, is deficient in nothing – but Decency and Good Manners.

Miller identifies two consequences of the town's running after fashion. One is financial ruin: "Husbands are ruin'd, Children robb'd, and Tradesmen starv'd, in order to give Estates to a French Harlequin, and Italian Eunuch, for a Shrug or a Song." Second, when true standards of taste are upset, so is the social order: "all Distinctions of Station and Fortune are broke in upon, so that a Peer and a Mechanick are cloath'd in the same Habits, and indulge in the same Diversions and Luxuries" (Dedication).[154]

Miller sets out "to expose the several Vices and Follies that at present flourish in Vogue" (Dedication) by showing the pretentiousness of two young women who are trying to enter the *beau monde* in the West End by "setting up for People of Taste and Politeness." Their mindless adoring everything fashionable is exposed by their gullibility for Martin, a clever footman who assumed the name of Lord Apemode, a fashionable Man of Taste. The two women expect of their suitors (one of whom is Apemode) that "in Town they should attend us thro' all its Diversions; carry us to the Rehearsal of every new Opera, ... and

---

[153] In the Dublin 1733 edition of *The Man of Taste*, the word *Oratorio* carries this note: "A new Name that *Heeideggre* the Master of the Opera House gave to the Opera of *Hester*" (13).

[154] The idea that False Taste lies in one's self-deception of what is good in art is conveyed by the play's title-page epigraph: "Decipimur specie Recti——" (Horace, *Ars Poetica*, 25): "We deceive ourselves by the resemblance of truth" (Loeb trans.).

squeak with us [at] every *Masquerade*" (p. 7). Lord Apemode dutifully asks them, "Well, Ladies, ... what think you of a Taste of *Faronelli* to Night?"

> *Dorothea.* Oh! That charming Creature, *Faronelli!*
> *Maria.* Oh, Ravishing! Transporting! Killing!
> *Dorothea.* Admiration it self can't express it.
> *Maria.* Dying is too little. He does more than kill one—— (V:1)

THE MODERN POET

The politics of False Taste is revealed more directly the following month in *The Modern Poet. A Rapsody* (April 1735), an anonymous sequel to Bramston's *Man of Taste.* The Modern Poet expands on the Man of Taste's claim, "I was a Poet born."[155] He likewise proclaims himself a guide to perfection in poetry:

> On ev'ry Branch of Poetry I've writ,
> On ev'ry Branch display'd prodigious Wit. (p. 12)

Trusting his own inspiration, he writes without help from Phoebus or the Muses; excelling all other poets, his only rival is the Laureate Colley Cibber. With his self-acknowledged lack of reliance on standards, he aims to please every taste. An unabashed Walpole supporter, the Modern Poet would not agree with those opposition poets who claimed Walpole patronized only mediocre writers. His examples, however, only prove the Opposition's point: the two men he names are editors of ministerial newspapers.

> My Praises still Sir *R——t* shall attend;
> To Men of Wit he always was a Friend,
> And Men of Wit shall always sound his Fame;
> As grateful *Osborne* does, and *Walsingham.* (p. 8)

(Osborne and Walsingham were pseudonyms used by writers for the ministerial *Free Briton* and *Daily Gazetteer.*)

To please his patron and the Court, the Modern Poet himself tries his hand at writing *Free Briton's*, writes against the *Craftsman* and *Fog's Weekly Journal*, and satirizes Pope. His advice exemplifies the low opinion of Walpole's literary interest, and affirms Walpole's legendary disdain for London's merchants:

> To please Sir *R——t* be extreamly witty,
> And lash the richest Merchants of the City.
> I'd call them *Beggars*, and such Courtly Names,
> And wish their Ships might ne'er return to *Thames.*
> I'd curse them all who durst refuse *Excise*,
> And damn their *Craftsmen* under *Christmas* Pies. (pp. 7–8)

"Sturdy Beggars" was a term Walpole had hurled at the merchants who opposed his Excise Scheme. The Opposition and London's merchants would increasingly charge that Walpole was indifferent to their grievances and failed to take action

---

[155] A long passage from *The Man of Taste* is quoted on the title page of *The Modern Poet.*

against Spanish depredations on British merchant shipping. The proper use of the *Craftman* is for bakers to use in cooking pastry.[156]

The connection between False Taste and the politics of the ministerial Modern Poet is strengthened as he holds Italian opera superior to two recent anti-ministerial theatre productions. He asserts of the notoriously anti-ministerial *Beggar's Opera*:

> Its Want of Taste the Town did most display,
> When it receiv'd the Operas of *Gay*.   (p. 13)

He mocks Gay's "harsh Notes," drab scenery, native singers, and highwayman hero, compared with the "melting Sounds" of opera. What the Modern Poet describes onstage in opera enlarges on Addison's account of the lack of verisimilitude of opera, with several pointed insults to the castrati:

> Their [opera's] War-like Heroes are in Eunuchs shewn,
> And Gen'rals, without Manhood, fight in Tune.
> With melting Sounds the well-turn'd Periods chime,
> And *Roman* Senates sing the Laws in Rhime.
> Soft Tunes in female Breasts Delight inspire;
> Soft Eunuchs raise, but can't allay Desire;
> And pompous Scenes, at great Expence, are bought,
> Whilst *Gay*'s, alas! can only boast of Thought.   (pp. 13–14)

Gay's opera crowded the theatre for sixty-two nights,

> But, Heav'n be thank'd, our antient Taste returns,
> And with its former Fire each Bosom burns.
> *Italian* Strains again the Town delight,
> And Coaches croud the Streets each Op'ra Night.
> Ev'n Fustian Charms in smooth *Italian* Song,
> And Nonsense pleases from the Eunuch's Tongue.
> *Britain* in this its polish'd Taste does shew;
> The Tongue some few, but none the Meaning, know.   (pp. 14–15)

As well, the Modern Poet prefers Italian opera to William Duncombe's tragedy *Junius Brutus*, acted only five months earlier (25 November 1734; pub. 1735):

> With Liberty, tho' each Expression's fraught;
> Tho' great, yet just, and natural each Thought;
> Tho' lofty Words, and loftier Thoughts combine;
> Tho' Strength of Reason charms in ev'ry Line;
> And tho' the Words of *Brutus* might inspire,
> And *British* Bosoms warm with *Roman* Fire,
> *Italian Fustian sure has more Pretence*
> To please this polish'd Age, than *Roman* Sense.
> *Italian* Songsters all our Wealth deserve;
> Our dull, laborious, native Fools may starve.   (pp. 15–16)

---

[156] *The Art of Scribling, Address'd to All the Scriblers of the Age. By Scriblerus Maximus* (1733) contains cynical advice for writing either as an oppositional or ministerial writer (pp. 5–7).

212   THE CULTURAL POLITICS OF OPERA, 1720–1742

At one level, *Junius Brutus* is an example of tragedy being driven off the stage by debased theatrical entertainments.[157] But this is unlikely to have concerned the Modern Poet. More likely, he is responding to the clear topical political application of Duncombe's play. Lucius Junius Brutus is an example of the self-sacrificing patriot who led the Romans in overthrowing the cruel, tyrannical King Tarquinius Superbus, who subverted Roman law and whose son raped Lucretia, and returning Rome to a republican government. His sacrifice was to put to death his sons who attempted to restore Tarquinius. The play's prologue draws the parallel between the Roman hero and William III ("Who sav'd these Realms from double Tyranny" of church and absolute monarchy "And fixt her Liberties for Length of Years"). No doubt Tarquin was intended to be applied to Walpole.

It is especially in Brutus's speeches – with their sentiments declaring Romans as "Foes to Corruption [and] luxurious Pleasures," abjuring "servile Syco-phants," and asserting freedom, disdain of tyrants, and the imperative of yielding to the "Patriot's Claim" (pp. 25, 61, 94) – that we hear echoes of the contemporary political sloganeering that contemporaries would identify with the Opposition cause.

The Modern Poet's defense of Walpole, his pointed disparagement of the *Beggar's Opera* and *Junius Brutus*, and his partiality to Italian opera suggest that his False Taste and writing in service of Sir Robert and Dulness are evidence of how political and artistic corruption coincide in the Walpole regime.

❧ *The Woman of Taste*

Three months later, Bramston's *Man of Taste* inspired a companion, *The Woman of Taste. Occasioned by a Late Poem, Entitled, The Man of Taste ... In Two Epistles from Clelia in Town to Sapho in the Country* (1733), possibly by Thomas Newcomb.[158] Described is the rural Sapho's life in London had she been persuaded by Clelia to leave her "Ballads and bagpipes in a country hall" for the *à la mode* life in the town, with its luxurious fashions and manners, music and masquerades, balls and peers. In the city-country dichotomy that sets up the poem, the city is the haven of False Taste. The poem's title-page epigraph, "Sequimur, non passibus

---

[157] A translation from Voltaire by Duncombe, *Junius Brutus* was first acted at Drury Lane on 25 November 1734. On the political application of the play, see John Loftis, *Politics and Drama in Augustan England* (Oxford: Clarendon Press, 1963), 122–3, and James J. Lynch, *Box, Pit, and Gallery: Stage and Society in Johnson's London* (Berkeley, Calif.: University of California Press, 1953), 248.

   Although it likes the idea of a tragedy, the *Prompter* reported contemporary audiences did not appreciate the dull play; the essays made no mention of the politics; see issues nos. 10 and 29 (13 Dec. 1734 and 18 Feb. 1735).

[158] David F. Foxon, *English Verse, 1701–1750: A Catalogue of Separately Printed Poems with Notes on Contemporary Collected Editions,* 2 vols. (London: Cambridge University Press, 1975), N282, on no stated evidence, attributes the poem possibly to Thomas Newcomb.

æquis,"[159] hints that Women of Taste cannot keep up with their male counterparts in pursuit of the life of *beau monde*.

The satire arises as the author describes the trends Sapho would adopt in architecture, music, books, fashion, food, learning, and marriage. Clelia's advice would have Sapho violate standards of good taste or pretend to knowledge about the arts she affects to enjoy. Clelia assumes that Sapho will look to Italy for her taste in music, though she will "breathe *Italian musically* wrong" (p. 7). Even before she can pronounce or spell English, Sapho will affect to know Italian, whose vowels "ravish all, please much, and nothing mean!" At the opera, Sapho should disguise that she was born in England, yet she will feel bliss and be all raptures at Italian opera:

> The bliss much stronger than you ever felt,
> When in a *Latian* throat the numbers melt;
> No strain too high or low, too harsh or flat,
> Your self all rapture — *at you know not what*!
> …
> And while the music does such bliss dispense,
> Bid fools deride it for its want of sense.   (p. 7)

Clearly, Sapho's blissful, rapturous response to Italian opera is unseemly. And in ironic praise, opera is indicted as an irrational, sensuous luxury:

> Our joy the greater still the less we know;
> For the learn'd friends of softness, sound and ease,
> *Charo*'s [Caro sposo's] and *Tamo*'s [*Te amo*'s] sure must
>   ever please.   (p. 7)

The remainder of the passage on opera cautions Sapho that – because she does not know the language – she should watch a neighbor so she won't laugh or cry at the wrong place, mistake a wedding for a death and a jig for a dirge, or encore a bawdy scene.

Another of the town's joys she will indulge are Handel's new oratorios. The satire treats the oratorios with no more respect than operas, for it is directed as much against Sapho's excesses as the genre itself, from its violation of verisimilitude to breach of decorum. The False Taste of oratorio attendees is noted:

> Singing the bait, devotion the pretence,
> By music drawn, that modern foe to sense!   (p. 8)

Certainly recalling the outrage at Handel's raised prices for *Deborah* earlier that season, the expense of oratorio is indicted:

---

[159] ("We follow with steps that are not as great.") In Virgil (not Horace, as stated on title page), *Aeneid* 2:724, the child Iulus follows his father with steps that do not match his father's ("sequiturque patrem non passibus æquis").

214   THE CULTURAL POLITICS OF OPERA, 1720–1742

> Where lofty airs, and humble wit, are found,
> The charge quite small—five duets for a pound;
> As much each winter sunk, to please your ear,
> As wou'd your landlord pay, and semptress clear.   (p. 8)

As was opera in Addison's *Spectator*, Handel's *Esther* (recently revived at the opera theatre on 14 and 17 April 1733) is likewise criticized for its violation of verisimilitude:

> Here *Handell* kills fair *Hester*'s foes in metre;
> Flutes keep due measure with the victim's pangs,
> *Faustina quav'ring* just as *Haman* hangs.[160]
> …
> The beauteous *Hebrew* pensive for a time,
> Married by *Humphreys* to the king in rhime.   (p. 9)

Oratorio joins operas and masquerades as threats or substitutes for public religion. The theatre will replace the church as place of devotion, for now the stage and music will make people virtuous:

> Each pulpit scorn'd, the good reforming age
> More fond of morals taught 'em by the stage;
> …
> A vicious town and court not half so soon,
> Made vertuous by a sermon as a tune;
> Whose melting notes the souls of sinners sooth,
> Who fly from *Gibs—n* [Bishop Gibson] to be sav'd
>   by [Barton] Booth.   (p. 9)

Apparently, however, Sapho remained content in the country, for in the following month, in *The Woman of Taste. In a Second Epistle* (July 1733), also possibly by Thomas Newcomb,[161] Clelia scoffs again at Sapho's rural lifestyle and continues her instruction in "How to excel in taste, in parts to shine" (p. 9). She renews her entreaties to Sapho to abandon the country, where she imagines Sapho wasting her youth and beauty. Senesino and opera are preferable to any country delights:

> But ah! what arts can *Clelia* use, to call
> Her *Sappho* [sic] from her meadows to a ball;
> To draw her from her grotto's and her shades,
> Her bubbling fountains, and her cooling glades?
> The opera preferr'd to wakes and fairs,
> And *Senesino*'s songs to *William*'s airs.   (p. 5)

The tedium of the Town ladies in the country was described in 1709 by Susanna Centlivre early in the craze for opera: "Where wanting Opera's, Basset, and a Play, / They'll Sigh and stich a Gown, to pass the time away."[162]

---

[160] Faustina had actually returned to Italy in 1728.
[161] Foxon also attributes this poem to Newcomb (N 285).
[162] Susanna Centlivre, *The Busie Body* (1709), Prologue.

One of Clelia's sisters in London might have been the "gay Larilla" in *The Lady of Taste: or, F——'s [Farinelli's] Levee* (1737).[163] Larilla is shown pursuing her empty rounds of daily life in the town. Opera and Farinelli are among her ruling passions, which threaten her household with ruin:

> For Op'ra Tickets and her Debts of Play,
> Reduce her Houshold [*sic*] to one Meal a Day;
> Yet will she risque to starve the Twelvemonths round,
> To give her Fav'rite Songster *Fifty Pound*.   (p. 149)

Churches are empty, where "Clerks and Curates bawl," while she and

> ... the *Beau Monde* adore an Eunuch Shrine,
> Their Morning Pray'r, O *Far—i—llo*'s thine,
> One G—d, one Songster, they alike partake,
> But for the Songster, they'll their God forsake.   (p. 152)

Larilla attends Farinelli's levee with the other "unthinking dull Admirers of a Song" (p. 154) and adds to the gifts and adoration bestowed on him.

Such fashionable women and their taste for opera were frequent targets for satire. In Henry Carey's *Blunderella: or, the Impertinent* (1730) an opera enthusiast talks company to death with her opinions on singers and composers, whereas Blunderella is shown to be a false connoisseur when she cannot distinguish an opera aria from the tune of "Children Three" (p. 8). In *The Ladies of Pleasure* (1734), the ladies go to the opera or play, and pay half a crown to have the highest place. In "The Town Lady's Answer to— What tho' I am a Country Lass," the Town Lady goes to the opera only to be seen:

> What tho' I to Assemblies go,
>   And at the Operas shine, a?
> It is a thing all Girls must do,
>   That will be Ladies fine, a:
> And while I hear *Faustina* sing
>   Before the King and Queen, a,
> My Eyes they are upon the Wing,
>   To see, if I am seen, a.[164]

In "The Ancient Gentry and Moderns Compar'd," the Ladies announce:

> Each Day and Night we Ladies have a Call
> To grace th' Opera, Masquerade, or Ball.[165]

James Miller presents a model of taste in *Of Politeness. An Epistle to the Right Honourable William Stanhope, Lord Harrington* (1738). But in contrast to true politeness, Miller holds up opera among the pursuits of those who pursue false

---

[163] In *A Collection of Miscellany Poems* (1737), 145–57. The poem includes a passage exploiting the *double entendre* of Farinelli's vocal-sexual ravishment of his female devotees (p. 148).

[164] *The Bee: or, Universal Weekly Pamphlet*, no. 2 (Feb. 1733), 85.

[165] In *Miscellany Poems. By a Gentleman of Oxford* (1737), 20.

216   THE CULTURAL POLITICS OF OPERA, 1720-1742

notions of politeness and taste. One character "less delights to hold his Tongue, / Yet sits four Hours to hear an Op'ra sung" (lines 90–1). While another,

> My-Lady dubb'd, she needs polite must turn,
>
> …
>
> At each Assembly she's the first to play,
> At ev'ry Masque the last to go away;
> All Ear at Opera, and at Church all Tongue,
> How came she here? —How! Why an Anthem's sung.
>
> (lines 289, 295–8)

THE COUNTESS'S LEVEE

Among the Women of Taste must also be counted the Countess, as shown in "The Countess's Levee" (Plate 9.6) from William Hogarth's series *Marriage à la Mode* (1745).[166] She represents all the fine ladies of the day who indulge all the tastes of the newly rich. Aesthetic vice is inseparable from moral vice, for in Hogarth's narrative, the Countess, her husband, and her lover the lawyer Silvertongue meet suitably sordid ends, as the Countess dies from a laudanum overdose after Silvertongue is hanged for murdering her husband in a duel after he discovered them during a post-masquerade assignation in a bagnio.

A contemporary commentary describes the levee of the "modern Countess grown compleat":

> At such a Scene what can we say,
> But that *Taste* dwindles quite away;
> That Women of the present Age,
> In Trifles all their Time engage;
> And that the Subjects of their Life,
> Are *Lust* and *Folly*, *Noise* and *Strife*.[167]

Saturating the Countess's dressing room are signs of False Taste and its moral corruption. To one side, she is having her hair dressed by a French *valet de chambre* and accepts from Silvertongue a ticket to a masquerade, which will

---

[166] See Paulson, *Hogarth's Graphic Works* (1965), no. 231; Paulson, *Hogarth's Graphic Works* (1989), 161; and Stephens, *Catalogue of Prints and Drawings in the British Museum*, no. 2731.

[167] *Marriage à la Mode: An Humorous Tale, in Six Canto's in Hudibrastic Verse; Being an Explanation of the Six Prints Lately Published by the Ingenious Mr. Hogarth* (Feb. 1746), 36. See also the commentary by Georg Lichtenberg in *Lichtenberg's Commentaries on Hogarth's Engravings*, intro. and trans. Innes and Gustav Herdan (London: Cresset Press, 1966), 114–28; and *Hogarth on High Life: The "Marriage à la Mode" Series from Georg Christoph Lichtenberg's "Commentaries,"* trans. and ed. Arthur S. Wensinger with W. B. Coley (Middletown, Conn.; Wesleyan University Press, 1970), 63–81; and John Trusler, *Hogarth Moralized. Being a Complete Edition of Hogarth's Works* [1768], 64–6. On the series, Judy Egerton, *Hogarth's "Marriage à la Mode"* (London: National Gallery Publications, 1997); Robert L. S. Cowley, *Hogarth's "Marriage à la Mode"* (Ithaca, N.Y.: Cornell University Press, 1983); and Mark Hallett, *Hogarth* (London: Phaidon, 2000), 167–84.

PLATE 9.6. William Hogarth, "The Countess's Levee," Plate 4 from *Marriage à la Mode* (1745), showing the Woman of Taste at her morning levee, surrounded by evidence of her False Taste, including a castrato singer.

218   THE CULTURAL POLITICS OF OPERA, 1720–1742

culminate afterwards at a bagnio. In the foreground, a black servant unpacks a basket of second-hand toys and trinkets bought from the auctioneer Cock. The statuette of the horned Actaeon alludes to the future cuckolding of the Countess's husband.

On her walls are lavishly framed, sexually suggestive paintings: Correggio's *Jupiter Embracing Io*, Michelangelo's *Jupiter and Ganymede (The Rape of Ganymede)*, and Caravaggio's *Job and His Daughters*.[168] Rather than truly appreciating them, the Countess more likely bought them at the urging of a picture dealer and is oblivious of their quality and unaware they were probably copies sold by duplicitous dealers as originals – exemplifying one form of False Taste, as described by Pope:

> Is it less strange, the Prodigal should *waste*
> His Wealth to purchase what he ne'er can *taste?*
> Not for himself he sees, or hears, or eats;
> Artists must chuse his Pictures, Music, Meats.[169]

The Countess's paintings are no doubt examples of what Hogarth decried, "dismal Dark Subjects" passed off on the English by "Picture-Jobbers from abroad" to the detriment of native English painters.[170]

Almost dominating the scene is her morning concert of a castrato, usually identified as Senesino (less often Carestini), "That Capon grown too fat and jolly / At *England*'s sad Expense and Folly,"[171] singing with the accompaniment of a flutist, usually identified as Charles Weidemann. The singer, of course, represents Italian opera, and his conspicuous jewelry shows the lavishness of his admirers and "what Dupes the *English* be, / To *France* and *chiming* Italy."[172] For the Countess, the castrato's arias are mere background to

[168] Significantly, the subject of the strategically placed *Jupiter and Ganymede* reflects on the sexual relations between the castrato (they were often imputed to be catamites) and the flute player; the other two paintings reflect on Silvertongue's seduction of the Countess. Cowley, p. 115, states Job and His Daughters, then attributed to Caravaggio, is now known to be by Bernard Cavallino. On the sexuality in the print, see also David Dabydeen, *Hogarth's Blacks: Images of Blacks in Eighteenth Century English Art* (Athens, Ga.: University of Georgia, 1987), 74–81.

[169] Pope, *Epistle to Burlington* (1st ed., 1731), lines 3–5. A discussion of the English being duped by "picture-jobbers" in contained in the "Britophil" essay cited in the following note. Instances of the Countess's False Taste are noted in David Bindman, *Hogarth* (London: Thames and Hudson, 1981), 111–15.

[170] See the essay by "Britophil" (likely by Hogarth) in the *St. James's Evening Post* (7–9 June 1732); reprinted in Ronald Paulson, *Hogarth: His Life, Art, and Times,* 2 vols. (New Haven, Conn.: Yale University Press, 1971), Appendix F, 2:490–3.
  The point of this essay coincides with Hogarth's long efforts to encourage a native British school of painting and to wean collectors from Italian masterworks; see Ronald Paulson, *Hogarth.* Vol. 2. *High Art and Low, 1732–1750* (New Brunswick, N.J.: Rutgers University Press, 1992), 136–8.

[171] "That Capon grown too fat and jolly / At *England*'s sad Expense and Folly"; *Marriage à la Mode,* 33.

[172] *Marriage à la Mode,* 33.

OPERA AND THE POLITICS OF TASTE   219

her seduction, but a female visitor swoons in rapture (while the black servant looks on reproachfully).

❧ *The Rake of Taste*

A worst-case scenario arises when False Taste is combined with the profligacy of the rake, an incarnation of the corrupting effect of wealth and luxury.[173] Opera is among the luxuries of the rake in "The Rake's Levee," (Plate 9.7) the second plate of Hogarth's *A Rake's Progress* (25 June 1735),[174] where opera is associated with both moral and aesthetic corruption.[175]

Hogarth shows us Tom Rakewell, recently arrived in London, a newly rich man-about-town, where at his morning levee "Fools, Fops, and Knaves of every Kind, / Assemble all t'improve his Mind,"[176] where "He Sets up for a fine Gentleman; directs the Opera's; an Encomium on the *Immortal F——lli.*" Vying for Tom's attention are the professors and purveyors of the fashion and follies that

---

[173] For the antecedents of the Rake, see Harold W. Webber, *The Restoration Rake-Hero: Transformation in Sexual Understanding in Seventeenth-Century England* (Madison, Wis., University of Wisconsin Press, 1986).

[174] Shown is the third state of the plate. See Paulson, *Hogarth's Graphic Works* (1965), no. 133; Paulson, *Hogarth's Graphic Works* (1989), no. 133b; and Stephens, *Catalogue of Prints and Drawings*, no. 2173.

On the print, see Jeremy Howard, "Hogarth, Amigoni and 'The Rake's Levee': New Light on *A Rake's Progress,*" *Apollo*, no. 429, n.s. (Nov. 1997), 31–3; and Daniel Heartz, "Farinelli Revisited," *Early Music*, 18 (1990), 430–43.

Dabydeen sees Tom Rakewell as "Walpolian in manner, aspects of his life and action exemplifying the moral decadence of Walpole's Britain"; *Hogarth, Walpole and Commercial Britain*, 132–5 (citing p. 135). Richard Pound interprets the *Rake's Progress* series in light of eighteenth-century concerns with the danger of social mobility, emulation of foreign taste and manners, and denial of one's place in the natural order; "'Fury after Licentious Pleasures'; A 'Rake's Progress' and Concerns about Luxury in Eighteenth-Century England," *Apollo*, no. 438 (1998), 17–21.

[175] In Mary Davys, *The Accomplish'd Rake: or, Modern Fine Gentleman* (1727), the Knight sets out in his new coach to make his appearance at all the public places, including the opera, where he had hopes of being seen (p. 111). In many other accounts, the Rake is rather a low-life whose ambitions do not aspire to the opera house; as in, for example, *The Rake Reform'd* (1718); "The Batchelor-Keeper: or, Modern Rake," in *Atterburyana. Being Miscellanies, by the Late Bishop of Rochester* (1727), 101–46; *The Rake's Adventures: or a Trip Through the Bills of Mortality* (?1731); *The Finish'd Rake; Or, Gallantry in Perfection* [1733]; and *The Progress of a Rake* (1732).

[176] [John Brevel], *The Rake's Progress; or, the Humours of Drury-Lane. ... Which Is a Compleat Key to the Eight Prints, Published by the Celebrated Mr. Hogarth*, 3rd ed. (1742), 17. A passage exploiting the *double entendre* of Farinelli's vocal-sexual ravishment of his female devotees appears on pp. 18–19. See also the contemporary descriptions of the plate in *The Rake's Progress; or, the humours of St. St. James's being the Life of the Celebrated Squire Rakewell*, new ed. (?1750), 19–20; Trusler, *Hogarth Moralized*, 21–3; Lichtenberg in *Lichtenberg's Commentaries on Hogarth's Engravings*, 114–28; and Jean-André Rouguet, *Lettres de Monsieur [Rouquet] à un de ses amis à Paris, pour lui expliquer les estampes de Monsieur Hogarth* (1746), Plate 2 and pp. 16–19.

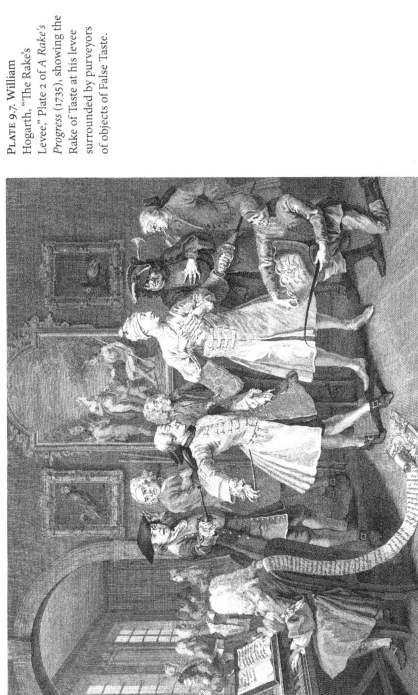

PLATE 9.7. William Hogarth, "The Rake's Levee," Plate 2 of *A Rake's Progress* (1735), showing the Rake of Taste at his levee surrounded by purveyors of objects of False Taste.

OPERA AND THE POLITICS OF TASTE   221

he indulges: dancing, fencing, gardening, horse racing, and hunting. The paintings on the wall show he has become an art collector and fan of cock fighting. On the floor, a poem dedicated to him shows Tom has become a patron of literature. Through the archway we see a milliner, tailor, and poet – all lining up and begging for their bills to be paid.[177]

In Hogarthian fashion, opera is represented by allusive elements throughout the room and especially by allusions to Farinelli, who represents the extravagancy of opera and Tom's taste in patronizing it. The long scroll and the poem on the floor signify the most objectionable abuses of opera: the great sums expended upon it and women's misplaced and inappropriate enthusiasm for his singing.

The scroll hanging over the harpsichordist's chair records the fabulous sums the aristocracy and gentry expended upon Farinelli at his March 1735 benefit:

> A List of the rich Presents Signor Farinelli the Italian Singer Condescended to Accept of ye English Nobility & Gentry for one Nights Performance in the Opera Artaxerses — A pair of Diamond Knee Buckles Presented by — A Diamond Ring by — A Bank Note enclosed in a Rich Gold Case by — A Gold Snuff box Chac'd with the Story of Orpheus charming ye Brutes by T: Rakewell Esq: 100l 20[ol] 100[l]

Farinelli made his London debut in the Opera of the Nobility's production of *Artaserse* on 29 October 1734. But it was his benefit concert the following March that was the season's highlight. Lists of presents bestowed him on the occasion were widely reported in newspapers and magazines (see Chapter 6). The harpsichordist (who is a generalized figure, unlikely to be specifically Handel or Porpora) has opened the score of an opera of Hogarth's invention, *The Rape of the Sabines. A New Opera*, with the following cast (composed of singers of both Handel's and the Nobility Opera's companies):

Romulos	Sen: Fari – li	[Farinelli]
1 Ravisher	Sen: Sen – no	[Senesino]
2 Ravisher	Sen: Car – ne	[Carestini]
3 Ravisher	Sen: Coz – n	[Cuzzoni]
Sabine Women		
	Sen.ra Str – dr	[Strada]
	Sen.ra Ne – gr	[Negri]
	Sen.ra Ber – le	[Bertolli]

---

[177] There are other instances of tradesmen going unpaid while the *beau* spends on opera: (1) In Edward Phillips's ballad opera *The Livery Rake, and Country Lass* (1733), Tom describes the fashionable taste of his master: "He loves Balls, Masquerades, subscribes to the *Italian* Operas; whilst his Tradesmen go unpaid, and his Servants without Wages" (p. 26). (2) In Hercules Mac-Sturdy, *A Trip to Vaux-Hall: or, A General Satyr on the Times* (1737), a rich lord allows his tailor and butcher to go unpaid and to jail because he "Had lost six hundred pounds at th' Masquerade. / Had given *Farinelli* fifty more" (p. 4). (3) Also in *The Woman of Taste* (1733) is recommended: "To be compleatly modern, ne'er forget / With half your tradesmen to be deep in debt" (p. 7).

222 THE CULTURAL POLITICS OF OPERA, 1720–1742

Satire here arises on one level from the irony of confusing the operatic roles the *castrati* Farinelli, Senesino, and Carestini play as ravishers with their real-life sexual incapacity. The notion of the eunuch as ravisher is carried over to the poem that lies on the floor. All that we see of "A Poem Dedicated to T. Rakewell Esq." is what must be a title-page vignette, in which Farinelli, seated on top of a pedestal, looks down on an altar with a burning sacrificial offering, while a crowd of women approach, offering their hearts in their outstretched hands. One of them blasphemes, "One God, one Farinelli."[178] The woman who uttered this is identified by Horace Walpole as Lady Rich (wife of Sir Robert Rich, fourth baronet, née Elizabeth Griffith).[179] On one level, the ladies are ravished by Farinelli's singing. But the obvious *double entendre* implies the women's adulation may be due to their ravishment from illicit sexual favors offered by Farinelli.

A set of poetic commentaries to Hogarth's set of prints clearly points out the foolishness of Tom Rakewell's taste:

> To hear a favorite Eunuch squall,
> Without dispute must please us all:
> With long *Stoccato's* song or trio
> 'Tis ravishing, none can deny-O,
> And, who would grudge a thousand pounds,
> To hear such sweet enchanting sounds?
> Such trilling, killing, shivering, quaking,
> O, la! O what delightful shaking![180]

Poetic justice to Tom for his aesthetic and moral failures is achieved in the last plate of the series, where we see a half-naked, insane Tom, shackled and tearing at his flesh in Bethlehem Hospital (Bedlam).

---

[178] The blasphemy is first recorded in the *Prompter*, no. 37 (14 March 1735).

[179] Identified by a manuscript note of Horace Walpole; *Correspondence of Horace Walpole*, 35:79 n. 7; see also Paulson, *Hogarth's Graphic Works* (1965), 1:163. A Lady Rich received the dedication of Paolo Rolli's *Six Italian Cantatas* (1733); see Gibson, *Royal Academy of Music*, p. 273. Elsewhere, Paulson identifies the blaspheming lady as Mrs. Fox Lane (later Lady Bingley); *Hogarth's Graphic Works* (1965), 1:273.

[180] *The Rake's Progress; or, the Humours of St. James's being the Life of the Celebrated Squire Rakewell in Six Hudibrastic Cantos*, new ed. [?1750], 19–20. *The Rake's Progress; or, the Humours of Drury Lane*, 2nd ed. (1735), 17, similarly writes,

> But Music most his Bosom warms,
> And heav'nly *Farinelli* charms.
> One God, one Songster he'll confess,
> But of the two thinks the first less.
> He scorns to be by ought outdone,
> And pays the tributary Loan.
> On all Things foreign much he doats,
> And hums each Morning o'er his Notes.

DORMAN'S *RAKE OF TASTE*

The rake's morals and taste are joined with political corruption in Joseph Dorman's *The Rake of Taste* (8 November 1735). The poem certainly issues from, or is sympathetic to, the Opposition camp: it was dedicated to Pope and first published by Pope's own publisher Lawton Gilliver. The engraved frontispiece, "The Beau Monde in St. James's Park," carries an epigram from Pope's *Epistle to Bathurst (Of the Use of Riches)* (1733):

> The ruling Passion, be it what it will,
> The ruling Passion conquers Reason still.   (lines 155–6)

The rake's ruling passion is the pursuit of pleasure.

The Rake of Taste, not unexpectedly, is a proselyte of False Taste, who urges a certain Jack to abandon his futile studies at "the muddy College" and to seek in the Town the true knowledge to be found among "the Men of Pleasure" (unlike the falsehood of everything taught in college):

> Here, the soft Sex, here, the enlivening Bottle
> Will teach you more than can old *Aristotle*.   (p. 1)

In London, Jack's cicerone shows him the *beau monde* in the pursuit of pleasures, chief among them being opera. The man of pleasure is excused for failing to pay tradesmen's bills:

> My Lord has Money; — well; — we grant it true,
> It is for *FARINELLI*, — not for you:
> …
> The Op'ra too, will ready Money take,
> His Lordship must Subscribe, his Rep's at Stake.   (p. 7)

Tom Rakewell and Larilla, as we saw, were others who kept creditors lining up in their hallways. In town, the Rake of Taste will also see "the gay Coquette":

> At Plays, at Op'ras, and at Masquerade,
> She eagerly pursues a flying Shade.   (p. 5)

The satire takes a political turn as the Rake takes his charge to Parliament and shows Jack an MP, one of Walpole's placemen who – while another pleads for liberty – sells his country's freedom:

> Now to the Senate, let us turn our Sight,
> And while *Agrippa* pleads the People's Right,
> See *him*, with Ballances, intently weigh,
> His Country's Freedom, 'gainst his Patron's pay.   (p. 7)

The ironic mask is momentarily dropped as the author delivers the political commonplace that repeats the stock Opposition claim that, as in ancient Rome, political corruption and luxury threaten to rob Britain of her freedom:

> Thus, when the World obey'd all conqu'ring *Rome*,
> She was, herself, by Luxury o'ercome:
> Her boasted Freedom publickly was sold,
> And the World's Lords, became the Slaves of Gold.   (p. 8)

224 THE CULTURAL POLITICS OF OPERA, 1720–1742

The man of pleasure and the coquette, both sharing a passion for opera, as well as the other persons Jack has encountered, are a colorful parade of Londoners pursuing False Taste promoted by the luxury and corruption of the Walpole regime.

The Rake of Taste has a counterpart in Libertina, represented in the ballad-comedy afterpiece *The Female Rake: or, Modern Fine Lady* (26 April 1736), attributed to Joseph Dorman. Libertina has parted from her old master's country seat to live in London; she lives for pleasure and frequents balls, plays, opera, and masquerades. According to her maid, she goes nowhere but in the company of "a Crew of Coxcombs, and to hear *Farranelli* sing." Sings her maid:

> Of a rural Life she's tir'd,
>   Which sweet Contentment brings,
> But ravish'd and inspir'd,
>   When *Faranelli* sings. (Act II, Air 2)

Another of the *beau monde*, Lord Fashion arises unusually early in the morning in the interest of Farinelli and encourages his friend Townly to take an interest in him too. In his opinion of Farinelli, the servant Tim represents the moral center of the piece: "But as for *Farranelli's* Singing, I can compare it to nothing better, than to *Chloe's* [a lap dog] Howling when my Lady's not within to play with her."

Although satires of False Taste, the Man and Woman of Taste, and the Rake of Taste often have no specific political or partisan allusions, given the commonplace of the interconnection among arts, liberty, and luxury, their portrayals of a society permeated by corrupt taste and fashion serve to validate the premise of moral, social, and political corruption spreading throughout British culture, portending tyranny and loss of liberty and adding their mite as evidence for the need to remove Walpole, their supposed prime cause.

⁊ *The Independent Patriot*

The foregoing examples have shown how Italian opera was used to identify False Taste and was implicated in social-moral corruption. The alignment of political virtue that would correspond to good taste in music is shown in Francis Lynch's comedy *The Independent Patriot: or Musical Folly* (12 Feb. 1737), produced at Lincoln's Inn Fields, a theatre of oppositional sympathies.[181] In the conflict of taste, the moral center of proper taste is embodied in Medium, a Man of Taste and an Independent Patriot – that is, a man independent of a court place, pension, or ministerial appointment. Lynch dedicated the play to Richard Boyle, Earl of Burlington, who in the play is the model for Medium, described as

> an Enemy to Corruption, and the false Taste of the Age; ... Impartial in his Legislative Capacity, Zealous in the genuine Interest of his Country, and a Despiser of the Covetous of all Party Denominations. (Dedication)

---

[181] Loftis, *Politics of Drama*, 107–8.

In his architecture, Burlington, according to Lynch, avoids "the Defects of the *Italians*" and preserves "their Excellencies." If British youth followed Burlington's example and studied abroad to improve their own and their country's taste, "there would have been no Foundation for satyrizing that affected, false, modern, musical Taste, which partly gave rise to /the following Scenes." Burlington's actions distinguish his "noble Thirst of improving the Taste of your Cotemporaries, and of embellishing your Country, in Imitation of those fam'd Patriots of Ancient *Rome*."[182]

Medium's creed of political independence forbids him from accepting either a pension or employment that required obedience; he stands clear of the impetuosity of intemperate Opposition members; and he votes his judgment without prejudice or partiality. This description fairly well describes Burlington politically by 1737.[183] Burlington had been Captain of the Band of Gentleman Pensioners and a member of the court Whig party in the Lords; he resigned all his offices in May 1733 when the King apparently broke a promise and did not offer him the next vacant cabinet post. The Countess, though, continued her place as Lady of the Bedchamber "Extraordinary" in Queen Caroline's household, an important and prestigious office she had held since 1727.[184] Afterwards, Burlington seems to have taken active interest only in occasional matters in the Lords that directly affected him, friends, or his interests in Ireland or the Yorkshire area; he was not part of the active political opposition, though he often voted with it. No evidence convincingly supports the notion that he was a Jacobite sympathizer.[185]

In the play, the avid devotees of False Taste are Lady Warble, "infected with the Musical Contagion of the Age" (p. 17), and her coterie, including Dulcissa, who display an excessive enthusiasm for Italian music and opera. Lady Warble reveals the superior attitude and self-deception of those with False Taste: "To see the gaping Ignorants of this Town croud to an Opera," she proclaims, "is

---

[182] See also Pope's characterization of him in the *Epistle to Burlington* (1731).

[183] Jacques Carré, "Lord Burlington's Book Subscriptions," pp. 129–30 in *Lord Burlington – The Man and His Politics: Questions of Loyalty*, ed. Edward Corp. (Lewiston, N.Y.: Edwin Mellen Press, 1998); Eveline Cruickshanks, "The Political Career of the Third Earl of Burlington," pp. 201–15 in *Lord Burlington: Architecture, Art and Life*, ed. Toby Barnard and Jane Clark (London: Hambledon Press, 1995).

[184] Susan Jenkins, "Lady Burlington at Court," pp. 149–79 in *Lord Burlington*, ed. Corp.

[185] The case for Burlington as a Jacobite: Jane Clark, "The Mysterious Mr Buck: Patronage and Politics, 1688–1745," *Apollo*, 129 (May 1989), 317–22, 371; Clark, "Palladianism and the Divine Right of Kings: Jacobite Iconography," *Apollo*, 135 (April 1992), 224–9; Clark, "For Kings and Senates Fit," *Georgian Group Journal*, (1989), 55–63; Clark, "Lord Burlington Is Here," pp. 251–310 in *Lord Burlington*, ed. Barnard and Clark; and Clark, "'His Zeal Is Too Furious': Lord Burlington's Agents," pp. 181–97 in *Lord Burlington*, ed. Corp.

More convincing is the case against Burlington's Jacobitism: Clyve Jones (review of Barnard and Clark, eds., *Lord Burlington*), *Parliamentary History*, 18 (1999), 217–19; Edward Gregg (review of *Lord Burlington – The Man and His Politics*, ed. Corp), *British Journal for Eighteenth-Century Studies*, 24 (2001), 95–7.

226   THE CULTURAL POLITICS OF OPERA, 1720–1742

enough to give a Connoisseur the Vapours" (p. 25). When a new composer from Italy is mentioned, Dulcissa exclaims, "What! Excel Mr. *Handel*?" To which Lady Warble responds, "Did you know the Merit of the *Italians*, you wou'd not name a frozen, northern Composer" (p. 45).

Lady Warble cites with condescension the tastes of another – presumably from her point view, less of a connoisseur – Lady Braun, a patroness of Farinelli, as one who has neither ear nor taste. She never misses a night of an opera and pretends to die at one of Farinelli's songs, but her ecstasies are ill-timed, for she laughs when others are in raptures. Worse, her husband will not advance £200 of her pin money for a benefit concert ticket for her favorite Italian (pp. 25–6)

Dulcissa, according to Medium, "dotes on Musick, and knows not one Note in the Gamut; the *Italians* have charm'd her without [her] ever having known any but a few of their warbling Strolers; and [she] is in Rapture with their Language tho' she understands that and *Hebrew* alike— ... Musick's her Idol, and *Italy* her Paradise" (pp. 3, 34). Moreover, Dulcissa, we learn, hates English music and singing, especially *The Beggar's Opera*. Equally a victim of False Taste is Addle, a fop besotted of Italian music, who appropriately anticipates marrying Dulcissa.

The action of the comedy involves Medium's vain courtship of Dulcissa, who is destined for Addle. He plans to expose her affected taste by introducing a new musician from Italy, "*Signior Sonata*," who will deceive her into thinking an Irish song is an Italian aria – to reason her out of her follies.

It is Lady Warble and her coterie who are presumably the objects of the printed play's title-page epigram from Juvenal:

—— Quis iniquæ
Tam patiens Urbis, tam ferreus, ut teneat se?)

Who can be so tolerant of this monstrous city,
who so iron of soul, as to contain himself?[186]

By contrast to the Women of False Taste, is Julia, the moral center of female virtue, a complement to Medium, and a severe critic of the chasing after music and fashion by her own sex. Deplores Dulcissa, Julia has "no Taste for Musick; Divine, ravishing Musick" (p. 42), which – coming from Dulcissa – is rather a commendation. The ladies' insults at Medium's want of taste only endear him to Julia. Julia's (supposed) want of taste is expressed by her preference for poetry (sense) over music (sound). She admits, "I'm unhappy in a want of Taste, and have no Relish for Operas. I've seen one this Season already, which abundantly satiates my Curiosity" (p. 42). She is not averse to music, only that which gratifies only the least useful of the five senses (p. 44).

Paralleling Medium's creed of political "independent virtue" is his sense of taste. He rails that "the reigning Taste's all *Italian*. Musick has ingross'd the Attention of the whole People" (p. 2). His preference is for "Wit, Humour and

[186] Juvenal, *Satires*, I.30–1; *Juvenal and Persius*, trans. G. G. Ramsay. Loeb Classical Library (Cambridge, Mass.: Harvard University Press, 1950), 4–5.

Instruction" above the "Sound and Nonsense" of opera. Medium, the Man of Sense, is dropped by the ladies because he is "an utter Stranger to Politeness" (p. 43) and is accused by Dulcissa of preferring "odious Tragedies and Comedies to dear Operas."

Poised against Medium is the politically duplicitous Sanguine with his vociferous Patriot pretensions. In the guise of an opponent, he exaggerates his complaints against the Ministry and inveighs against his degenerate, corrupt countrymen. Nothing, he says, would sway him from his genuine love of his country. Sanguine utters the usual civic humanist critique of opera, "'twas rather the Offspring of cool Villany, imported and propagated, like our other Luxuries, for Purposes injurious to Liberty—," and the commonplace gibe at eunuchs: "a *Farinelli* may charm the Ear; but … Women expect the Gratification of more Senses than one" (pp. 1, 2). Sanguine's Patriot pretensions are ultimately exposed, for he is silent in Commons debates and has a secret "Interest with the Ministers" (p. 31); he is revealed as a villain, libertine, and seducer.

With a dose of irony, the Epilogue points the moral for the Ladies of False Taste:

> Musick may charm the strict attentive Ear,
> But ne'er affect the Sense we hold most dear.
> Ah Ladies! —cou'd in that, *Italians* please[,]
> Cuckolds, and *Warblers* wou'd alike increase,
> And Gifts to *Farinelli* never cease.

The lesson of taste and politics is confirmed by the denouement: Julia and Medium are to be married. Good taste and rejection of Italian opera are thus equated with political independence and triumph of true love.

❧ *False Taste from Within the Walpole Circle*

Indictment of luxury, False Taste, and opera in early eighteenth-century Britain came from many quarters. Donald Greene points out that "satire is a *genre*, and if you are going to write satire, you must find something to satirize. Since satire was fashionable in the eighteenth century, every budding poet, whatever his politics, wrote satire and found the state of England deplorable."[187] The satires of opera and False Taste just examined have cues that spin the critique to go beyond just mild, Horatian rebuke of personal follies and – perhaps intentionally – carry an oppositional political burden. To suggest this oppositional burden is not just a function of generic satire of the times, it is instructive to look at several satires that touch on opera coming from friends of the Court and ministerial sympathizers.

Edward Young, Thomas Newcomb, and Francis Manning are writers who show how satire of opera can be managed without offending the Court or ministerial patrons. While many satires of the period (such as the formal verse

---

[187] Donald Greene, *The Politics of Samuel Johnson*, 2nd ed. (Athens, Ga.: University of Georgia Press, 1990), 306 n. 16.

228   THE CULTURAL POLITICS OF OPERA, 1720–1742

satires in the next chapter) were, or claimed to be, Horatian imitations, many in fact belied their model and took on a Juvenalian tone: that of the righteous outsider vigorously decrying vices of the Court. Those of Young, Newcomb, and Manning, however, are genuinely Horatian: the tone of a moralist and friend of the court mildly admonishing or smiling to shame the follies and petty vices of the *beau monde*.

YOUNG'S *LOVE OF FAME*

The century's most famous satire (at least before Pope's *Moral Essays*) was *Love of Fame: The Universal Passion: In Seven Characteristical Satires* (1728) by Edward Young.[188] Young, as Howard Weinbrot observes, "hoped to offend no one and to please the powers-that-be."[189] Joseph Warton found the satires "without a single mark of spleen and ill-nature."[190] Swift found them too insipid to be acceptable as satire.[191]

The first five satires published (nos. 1–4, 7) were so inoffensive and pleasing they won for Young, already chaplain-in-ordinary to the Princess of Wales (and to the King in 1728), a pension of £200. In gratitude, Young wrote *The Instalment* (5 July 1726) upon the occasion of Walpole's installation as a Knight of the Garter on 26 June. Young proclaimed that "The streams of Royal bounty, turn'd by Thee, / Refresh the dry domains of Poesy," now that the arts are under Walpole's care.

The satires are dedicated with the usual fulsome panegyric to the Duke of Dorset, George Bubb Dodington, Spencer Compton (courtier and Speaker of the House of Commons from 1715 to 1727), and Robert Walpole. Young's flattery of Whigs in power and their rewards for his poetry earned him the disdain of many in the Opposition, although he remained friendly with Pope. Within a month, the Tory (?Jacobite) William Shippen declared Young's inappropriately sordid flattery and adulation of Walpole were such that Walpole's "Name and Character [are] debased by the worst of Sycophants, and the most ridiculous Encomiums" – in effect, illustrating Shippen's title-page epigraph,

---

[188] The seven satires were published individually from 1725 to 1728, each titled *The Universal Passion*, and collected in 1728 with the title *Love of Fame: The Universal Passion* (edition cited).

[189] *The Formal Strain: Studies in Augustan Imitation and Satire* (Chicago, Ill.: University of Chicago Press, 1969), 97. Further on the satires and Young's establishment sympathies, see Weinbrot, *Formal Strain*, 95–128, and Harold Forster, *Edward Young: The Poet of the Night Thoughts, 1683–1765* (Alburgh Harleston, Norfolk: Erskine Press, 1986), 86–100, 111–18.

[190] Joseph Warton, *An Essay on the Writings and Genius of Pope*, 2 vols. (1756, 1782), 2:203. Warton saw them as the "first *characteristical* satires" in English, 76. Further on characteristic satire, see Charlotte E. Crawford, "What Was Pope's Debt to Edward Young?" *English Literary History*, 13 (1946), 157–67.

[191] Swift remarked on the inoffensive nature of Young's satires in a letter to Pope: "The Doctor is not merry enough nor angry enough for the present age to relish as he deserves"; Letter of 1 May 1733; Pope, *Correspondence*, ed. Sherburn, 1:153.

> Some Venal Pens so prostitute the Bays,
> Their Panegyricks *lash*, their Satires *praise*.[192]

Shippen mischievously wondered whether the author had in fact a malicious design of traducing Walpole under the pretext of extolling him.[193] Young's pension, Shippen ironically observes, is "a full Confutation of those dissatisfy'd Spirits, which complain that *Arts* and *Sciences* are totally neglected in this Age" (p. 6).

Jonathan Swift mocked the sincerity of Young's satire. If such great men deserved his panegyric, Swift asked, "What land was ever half so blessed?" But if the age indeed deserved his satire, "What land was ever half so cursed?"[194] Swift would later use the example of Young to describe a Court

> Where Young must torture his invention,
> To flatter knaves, or lose his pension.[195]

Young's lack of further patronage, despite his ministerial allegiance, made him a butt of yet more Opposition satire. When in February 1727 the *Craftsman* issued an ironic challenge to its critics "to instance any Period of Time, when *Wit* and *polite Literature* were more openly and amply encourag'd than at present," as evidence of poetry's flourishing state, its writer ironically adduces Young, Walpole's "*own immortal Poet*, who is Himself a Witness and Partaker of his [Walpole's] *Munificence.*"[196]

In the Preface to the collected satires, now titled *Love of Fame* (1728), Young rejected the Juvenalian and embraced the delicate "laughing Satire" of Horace; he avows there is no personal malevolence in any of his satires and minimizes the seriousness of his satires. This is, as Weinbrot wrily observes, an "unlikely, and, Young to the contrary, un-Horatian, role for a satirist."[197] Young writes that the follies he describes "are of a private kind, / Their sphere is small, their mischief is confined" (Satire 7, p. 163).

Young is writing "characteristical" satire: he creates a gallery of general portraits of those who pursue "the love of fame," vanity, or ambition in various activities.[198] But they fall instead into fashionable follies and petty vices. A pru-

---

[192] The title-page epigraph is falsely attributed to Pope.

[193] William Shippen, *Remarks Critical and Political, Upon a Late Poem, Intitled, The Instalment* (22 July 1726), 4 and 6.

[194] Jonathan Swift, *On Reading Dr. Young's Satires, Called the Universal Passion* (1726); in Swift, *Complete Poems*, ed. Rogers, lines 12 and 48, pp. 318–19. Probably written in 1726, although first published in 1733; the poem was reprinted in the 1738 installment of the Opposition anthology *A New Miscellany for the Year 1737, [1738, 1739]*, 8–9.

[195] "On Poetry: A Rhapsody" (Jan. 1733), in Swift, *Complete Poems*, ed. Rogers, lines 325–6, p. 530; also reprinted in the Huntington Library copy of the 1738 installment of *A New Miscellany for the Year 1737, [1738, 1739]*, 10–21. Young is also vilified in Swift's "A Copy of Verses upon Two Celebrated Modern Poets," in Swift, *Complete Poems*, ed. Rogers, 317.

[196] *Craftsman*, no. 20 (13 Feb. 1727).

[197] Weinbrot, *Formal Strain*, 97.

[198] Title-page epigraph for *Love of Fame*.

dent ministerial poet who certainly knew that both the King and Walpole were patrons of the Royal Academy of Music, Young makes only passing and rather gentle mention of Italian opera. Satirized are the naïve, overly enthusiastic, yet uninformed devotees of opera.

Some nymphs fancy any taste that is expensive. To be well known, they buy reputations

> And love a market, where the rates run high.
> *Italian* musick's sweet, because 'tis dear;
> Their *vanity* is tickled, not their *ear*;
> Their tastes wou'd lessen, if the prices fell,
> And *Shakespeare's* wretched stuff do quite as well.
>
> (Satire 3, p. 55)

In what seems an authorial comment, Young introduces a couplet that took on life as an independent epigram:

> An Opera, like a Pillory, may be said
> To nail our *ears* down, but expose our *head*.[199]
>
> (Satire 3, p. 56)

Punishment at the pillory occasionally had included nailing the victim's ears to the horizontal beams. In this case, the couplet presumably means that opera captivates the rapt listener and exposes her reason to nonsense.

The fifth satire, "On Women," is a gallery of women who are fond of admiration and run after vanity; their fancy and pride seek things at vast expense, which they neither relish by reason or sense. Such seekers of fame are vain to be seen at the opera. One fashionable woman, Lemira, is sick, but when the doctor arrives, he is informed the patient is at the ball. Reports her maid:

> "Diversions put her maladies to flight;
> …
> "I've known my lady (for she loves a Tune)
> "For *fevers* take an Opera in *June.*
>
> (Satire 5, p. 94)

Walpole, writes Young, deserves the honor of the dedication of the last poem, which is a satire on those who seek false glory by destroying nations by warfare or intrigue. Young is aware of how blame for the supposed vice and corruption of the age has been heaped onto Walpole, but he dismisses the charge by asking

> How all mankind will be surpris'd, to see
> This flood of *British* folly charg'd on thee?
>
> (Satire 7, p. 162)

Walpole is the Palinurus of the state, whose counsels brighten the reign of George II and under whose guidance the arts and commerce of Britain

---

[199] Reprinted as an independent epigram in *A Collection of Epigrams*, 2 vols. (1727, 1737), vol. 2, no. 10.

OPERA AND THE POLITICS OF TASTE   231

flourish.[200] This satire bears an epigraph from Virgil that succinctly reveals Young's self-conscious role as a true Augustan court poet and suggests Walpole as the new Maecenas: "Carmina tum melius, cum venerit *Ipse*, canemus."[201] Further panegyric of King George, Queen Caroline, and Walpole concludes the satire.

NEWCOMB'S *MANNERS OF THE AGE*

The intent of the clergyman Thomas Newcomb is clear from his title, *The Manners of the Age: In Thirteen Moral Satires. Written with a Design to Expose the Vicious and Irregular Conduct of Both Sexes, in the Various Pursuits of Life* (1733). Newcomb's sympathy with the Court is scarcely concealed.[202] Each satire bears a dedication, and most dedicatees are supporters or friends of Walpole and the Court: Edward Young (the pensioned author of *Love of Fame*), the Duke of Newcastle (member of Walpole's ministry), Walpole himself, Arthur Onslow (now Speaker of the House of Commons), and Henry Pelham (Newcastle's brother, placeholder, and Walpole supporter in the Commons). Moreover, the satires are larded with rebukes of Opposition figures (Bolingbroke and Caleb D'Anvers) and poets (including Pope and Swift) and favorable mentions of Walpole, the dedicatees, the Dukes of Argyll and Richmond, and the House of Brunswick.

In 1740, Newcomb was identified as a writer for the ministerial *Daily Gazetteer*.[203] When he published *A Miscellaneous Collection of Original Poems* in that year, Newcomb added a group of letters and essays "in Defence of the Present Government and Administration." The subscription list is a veritable roll call of government MPs and officeholders, including Walpole and three members of his family, Newcastle and his brother Henry Pelham, Speaker Onslow, Montague, Richmond, Nicholas Paxton, and William Yonge.

In his moral satires, Newcomb dutifully flails all the usual subjects: False Taste in art and learning, fops and fashionable young ladies, inconstancy of taste and love, and pursuit of the latest follies and entertainments of the town. A true Horatian court satirist, Newcomb's passing references to opera are made with the tone of a moralist gently admonishing the follies of the town's fashionable young so as to recommend their opposite virtues. His ultimate purpose is reforming the *status quo*, not overturning it, not taking the next step of urging

---

[200] In Pope's *Dunciad*, IV:614, Walpole would be the Palinurus who nods at the helm of the Ship of State as Dulness settles over the land.

[201] ("Our songs we shall sing the better, when the master himself is come"); Virgil, *Eclogues*, 9.67.

[202] On Newcomb's ministerial sympathies, see Weinbrot, *Alexander Pope*, 135–6, 161. See, for example, his *Vindicta Britannica: An Ode, to the Real Patriot. Occasioned by the Declaration of War Against Spain* (1740); Britain has "One Scepter, made so strong by Thee" (12).

[203] *An Historical View of the Principles, Characters, Persons, &c. of the Political Writers in Great Britain* (1740), 53.

232   THE CULTURAL POLITICS OF OPERA, 1720–1742

the political program of the Opposition. This timid Horatian tone ultimately vitiates Newcomb's satire, just as it did Young's.

Opera is frequently invoked as one of the follies of the town, and in this sense, *Manners* continues the themes of satires on False Taste. Newcomb introduces opera in several general portraits of young men and women who run after the fashions of the town. Even the most ardent opera patron could object to those whose appreciation is uninformed and excessive. One of the portraits in Satire 12 is of the fop Boyet, who frequents the playhouse and opera. Boyet's exquisite responses to opera arias in a language he does not understand and his need to ask for guidance in responding satirize one not capable of properly appreciating opera:

> Dying each *Duett* at *Catzoni*'s [Cuzzoni] feet;
> Too gentle, to survive a dirge so sweet.
> What raptures does her sense and musick breed,
> Pleas'd with soft phrases, which he cannot read?
> Assur'd of something great in every note,
> So smoothly warbled through so soft a throat;
> Expiring as she sings — then begs to know
> If 'tis a strain she breathes of mirth or woe;
> What passion in his breast he shou'd prepare,
> To mourn, or else be merry with the fair;
> Till well instructed, very much perplext
> To know, if he shou'd smile or sorrow next.
>
> (Satire 12, p. 540)

Here the fault lies in Boyet, whose naïveté would embarrass any opera lover. Boyet has often been mistaken in his responses:

> How oft deluded by the various tune,
> In smiles, or in despair, too late or soon:
> Entring the stage, he knows not his design,
> If *Porus* is that act to die, or dine;
> A stranger, as he sings, to what he wants,
> If for his night-gown, or his sword he pants;
> Nor knows, when first he enters in the ring,
> If **Handel*'s lion is to fight, or sing.
>
> (Satire 12, p. 540)

[Newcomb's note:] * Opera of *Hydaspes.*

Satirized is not a confusing opera plot, but Boyet's lack of knowledge of the libretto.

Newcomb echoes Addison's remarks in the *Spectator* about the lack of verisimilitude in opera:

> Whose [Handel's] Heroes, as they now ascend the sky,
> Just like sweet swans, are merriest when they die.
> Each stage, the sad *Caisters* banks — which hears
> Monarchs so oft in musick mount the spheres;
> Who hurried from their throne, by death, too soon,
> Lament their fates, and make their wills — in tune:

> Each heart, no doubt, affected with their case,
> Sung to the box — in treble and in base:
> Soft warbling victims, who for pity call,
> Gay in despair, and tuneful, as they fall.
>> (Satire 12, p. 541)

But the satire finally turns on Boyet's lack of connoisseurship: finally "no longer guided by his friends," Boyet is exposed and shamed:

> He smiles at murder, and he sighs at jokes;
> And cheated by his warbling warriors, cries
> When *Ammon* courts — and laughs when *Clitus* dies.
>> (Satire 12, p. 541)

Satirized, again, is Boyet's not understanding the libretto.

The thirst of fame captivates the fair, as seen in the tenth satire's portrait of Mirtilla, a young woman whose deathbed thoughts are more on the town entertainments and social events she is missing than on the state of her soul:

> "Ah, Doctor! must I die, — so near a ball!
> "Whose heart with patience can submit to fate,
> "When the gay chariot's ready at the gate?
> "What saint in prayer, or penitence delight,
> "When dear *Faustina* sings this very night?
>> (Satire 10, p. 473)

And similarly, in Satire 2, Flora, a nymph of delicate health is

> … oblig'd at home to stay,
> And miss a sermon; dearer yet —— a play!
> At home —— what sadness the reflection brings,
> When *Herr—ng* preaches, or *Cutzoni* sings!
>> (Satire 2, p. 53)

Walpole was the dedicatee of Satire 4, whose first part satirizes those who fear to offend and, consequently, judge by following the prevailing taste. Society's ideas of truth, virtue, and vice are unreliable because inconstant:

> Tho' truth is one, as sages all confess,
> We change our notions, like our wine and dress.
>> (Satire 4, p. 89)

Most people suspend judgment and take guidance from others:

> The realm in doubt, till sages shall ordain,
> If *Paul* henceforth, or *H—deg—r* [Heidegger], shall reign.
> …
> If sacred opera's [oratorios] shall instruct us still,
> And churches empty, as *ridotto's* fill;
> The *Hebrew* or the *German* leave the field,
> And *David's* lyre to *Handel's* spinnet yield.
>> (Satire 4, p. 90)

234   THE CULTURAL POLITICS OF OPERA, 1720–1742

Here sacred opera (probably meaning oratorio), ridottos, and Handel's music hang in the balance with sacred texts and the church. By calling oratorios "sacred opera's," Newcomb is reflecting the confusion about the genre of oratorio and carrying over from opera to oratorio the imputation that its sensuous sound will be emptying the churches.

The second part of Satire 4 takes up a topic pertinent to Walpole the politician: the right use of learning acquired while traveling on the continent. British coxcombs look or journey abroad for instruction in taste and fashion. Instead, Britons should learn about warfare, politics, and history to enable them to restore domestic and political peace to Britain. Nowdays, the Town follows fashions from abroad more eagerly than news of war or peace. When the navy returns,

> What pious *Britain* more than peace adores;
> Two *Gallick* tumblers, and two *Parma* whores.
> See! her good patriots rob themselves of rest
> To judge which warbling *Syren* squeaks the best;
> To rail at *Rome* in gratitude who cease;
> For tho' her faith is bad, her singers please.
>
> (Satire 4, p. 115)

Britons no longer discuss peace and war but are "charm'd to hear each nymph her dirges thrill," and soldiers only dispute which nation "can fiddle best."

The final verses show a Britain abandoning her days of military conquest and virtue:

> 'Twas once fair *Britain's* glory and her praise
> To bind her heroes brows with foreign bayes;
> Victorious wreaths from vanquish'd realms to bring,
> She cannot conquer now — but she can sing;
> And while her warriors on the stage look gay,
> Gentle or eager, just as fiddlers play;
> Made soft or fierce by *Handel's* potent lyre;
> Their rage and love both weakened by the wire [strings];
> Of *Latian* eunuchs, and sweet tunes possest,
> The opera is safe — and *England* blest.
>
> (Satire 4, pp. 115–16)

The irony is that the *beaux* and soldiers care more for opera than the national welfare. Implicit in the satire is that the dedicatee, Walpole, does use foreign news properly in care of Britain's welfare, unlike those just portrayed.

Newcomb has taken up many of the usual satirical and moralistic *topoi* about opera; but opera is never charged with being evidence of luxury, corruption, or a reason to take up opposition to the ministry. The intent of his satire is not to impugn the government but to correct and reform members of society.

MANNING'S *OF BUSINESS AND RETIREMENT*

Another satire from the Court circle that keeps operatic references clear of indicting the Court or Ministry is Francis Manning's ode *Of Business and Retirement* (1735). The poem is addressed to "the British Atticus," Viscount

OPERA AND THE POLITICS OF TASTE   235

Charles Townshend of Raynham, Walpole's brother-in-law.[204] In the late 1720s, and especially after the Treaty of Seville in 1729, Townshend's relations with Walpole cooled; he lost influence with the King and resigned in disgrace from all politics in 1730, with "a most unsullied character for integrity, honour, and disinterestedness," according to William Coxe, Walpole's biographer.[205] He retired to his Norfolk estate at Raynham and devoted himself to the improvement of agriculture.

An extended poem in the Horatian vein of praise of rural retirement, Manning's ode offers examples of those who – having pursued fame and power or, even more nobly, public service – find that renown is transient, that success does not bring the sought-for happiness and contentment, and that no amount of virtue or merit can shield them from malice and blame. Other examples of modern rulers (and even possibly Bolingbroke) show "What fatal Ills from mad Ambition grow" (p. 15).

Even Walpole, "The Strength and Ornament of *George*'s Reign" (p. 5), though he is "sway'd by nobler Motives" (p. 15) and shuns repose, is none the happier, for he is surrounded by foes and must endure being torn by faction as he tries to sustain liberty. Courtiers and soldiers learn that fate and favoritism rule their chances of promotion. Of members of life's "less dazling Stations" – physicians, clergy, misers, merchants, and diplomats – even a "bright Genius" devoted to the Muse,

> Seduc'd by Love of Fame and flattering Hope
> To prove a *Swift*, a *Granville*, or a *Pope*?
> …
> Or when provok'd to lash a Vicious Age,
> He flame, like *Young*, with bold *Lucilian* Rage.   (p. 27)

will remain unrewarded and unrecognized.

After remarking how even Pope's poetry (excepting the translations) brought him little gain and noting the current absence of patrons such as Halifax, Dorset, and Somers to protect wit and poetry, Manning considers the theatre, where

> The manly Labours of *Dramatick* Rage
> Unheeded grace no more the sinking Stage.   (p. 29)

---

[204] Manning's obsequious *An Essay on the Vicious Bent and Taste of the Times* (1737), dedicated to Walpole, contains a routine, passing mention of opera among the luxuries and follies of the day (p. 10), which Walpole will redress (p. 19).

[205] For a sympathetic account of his retirement, Coxe, *Walpole* (1798), 1:337–8. The flattering comparison of Townshend with Atticus is apt. Pomponianus Atticus (109–32 BC) was born into a wealthy Roman family. He remained uninvolved during the civil tumults, although on amicable and intimate terms with all members; he was long a friend of Cicero. In 85 BC he took his wealth to Athens where he immersed himself in study of Greek literature and philosophy (hence his name), becoming an Epicurian. Returning to Rome in 65 BC, he purchased an estate in Epirus, where he spent most of his time and devoted himself to literature and commercial projects, remaining uninvolved in politics.

236   THE CULTURAL POLITICS OF OPERA, 1720–1742

Like Fielding, Hogarth, Miller, and others, Manning includes opera ("empty Sound, without Pretence / To Art or Wit") with Harlequin pantomimes and farce among the entertainments that have driven tragedy off the stage:

> Low Farce, and empty Sound, without Pretence
> To Art or Wit, have left no room for Sense.
> An antick *Harlequin*, or *Eunuch*'s Voice,
> Against our Judgment over-rules our Choice.
> Fond of what charms the Ear, or strikes the Sight,
> The solid Pleasures of the Mind we slight.
> An Apish Mimick, or a *French* Buffoon
> Now please beyond a *Booth* or *Betterton*.
> Soft *Roman* Airs o'er Sterling Wit prevail,
> And Sense than Sound proves lighter in the Scale.
> Yet dares even *Farinelli*'s Artful Song,
> The Theme and Wonder of each raptur'd Tongue,
> And every Ear's Delight, presume to vye
> With *Philomela*'s Native Melody. (p. 29)

The permanent eclipse of the stage may be averted:

> Your Fall, O *Muses*, Ages shall deplore,
> Unless good *Caroline* your Wings restore.
>
> …
>
> Her Self too vers'd in polish'd Arts, will deign
> To hear your Just complaints, and ease your Pain.
> Her Aid obtain'd your righteous claim secures,
> For well She knows true Harmony is Yours. (p. 30)

The Muses, in turn, will "tune each Verse to *Carolina*'s Praise" and of her (Queen Caroline's) children. Manning's moral is pointed by the closing salute:

> Hail sweet Retirement, uncorrupted Good,
> By most how prais'd, yet by how few pursu'd! (p. 44)

And Townshend, a second Atticus and

> … *Raynham*'s Lord, in Wise Retirement blest,
> Renouncing publick Cares for private Rest, (p. 45)

joins those, like Scipio, Timoleon, Diocletian, and Atticus, whose lives are crowned by rural retreat.

The passages on opera, which might have been turned by an Opposition satirist to an indictment of luxury and corruption of taste under the Walpole regime, serve in this ode to retirement as a caution to ambitious poets against seeking fame on a stage that has "left no room for Sense [and] the solid Pleasures of the Mind."

* * *

Critiques of False Taste show a preoccupation with the unstated question, What art should prevail as a standard of taste in Great Britain? In addition to direct denunciation of John Rich, the denizens of Grub Street, or Walpole's poets, the question was also answered by negative examples.

OPERA AND THE POLITICS OF TASTE   237

Writers of high culture and custodians of taste, such as Swift, Pope, Johnson, and the Patriot dramatists, would valorize art that preserves the classical tradition, that honors what Aubrey Williams, in reference to Pope's *Dunciad*, calls "'humane wisdom' – that wisdom which ministered to the needs of the whole man, his political social, moral, and religious, as well as economic requirements."[206] On the stage, this would mean tragedy that does not descend into bathos or fustian; comedy that does not degrade into farce, pantomime, and harlequinades; or the Bartholomew Fair shows at Smithfield (which Pope asserts in the *Dunciad* had invaded the Court) – all examples of theatre that succumbed to commercial popularization. Above all, most would agree, common sense must rule all. And of course, for many vocal critics, Italian opera – an art sung in a foreign language by sexually ambiguous singers that pleases easily because it is all sensuous sounds – is beyond the pale.

From our modern perspective, we see that the *litterae humaniores* of the vaunted classical traditional and liberal arts is not a universal taste, but one reflecting the values and interests of European, upper-status, educated males.

Critiques of False Taste by means of satiric sketches of Men and Women of Taste reveal what their authors saw as the follies and foolishness in artistic taste of the *beau monde* and those aspiring to it. Newly acquired wealth created by the Financial Revolution gave men and women of the Town the means to accumulate objects of fine art and to cultivate music and opera for what were often seen as inappropriate motives – to keep up with fashion, to assume a place in elite society. Opera was claimed a fashionable entertainment that the Men and Women of False Taste praise without real pleasure or understanding, "suffer[ing] with Impatience the Musick they pretend to hear with Rapture."[207] Indeed, Jonathan Swift had opined that "few have a *Taste* or *Judgment* of poetry and eloquence," and added he was told that "among those who crowd the *Opera's*, Nine in Ten go tither merely out of *Curiosity, Fashion*, or *Affectation*."[208]

Satires on False Taste can be seen as protests against the misuse of wealth, against attempting to buy marks of social and cultural prestige without the requisite cultural capital, and the invasion of *hoi polloi* into the aristocratic preserve of the fine arts. Their taste in art is but a symptom of corruption and debasement of standards in wit, learning, and manners.

Any indictment of the decayed taste of one's time carries an implicit oppositional, delegitimizing undertone: it questions the standards, judgment, capability of the nation's governors. As we saw, writers often harkened back to the days of Halifax, Godolphin, and Harley (as well as those of Augustus) as a golden age when politicians supported men of letters – an example Walpole supposedly was not carrying on. As we have seen, Bolingbroke and writers for *Mist's, Fog's*, the *Craftsman*, and *Common Sense* relentlessly charged that

---

[206] Aubrey L. Williams, *Pope's "Dunciad": A Study of its Meaning* (London: Methuen, 1955), 108. The chapter well contrasts wisdom and Dulness.

[207] From an essay on taste in *Common Sense*, no. 54 (11 Feb. 1738).

[208] *Intelligencer*, no. 3 (25 May 1728); collected ed. (1729), 17. See also his *Correspondence*, ed. Williams, 4: 307–8.

238   THE CULTURAL POLITICS OF OPERA, 1720–1742

Robert Walpole's corruption of politics and the new commercial order of the Modern Whigs were the direct, proximate cause of the decline in the nation's arts and sciences.

Polemic against False Taste gains force when joined with deep-seated classical republican views that the state of the arts and sciences mirrored the health of the republic. Their decline was due to luxury, effeminacy, and loss of liberty and were a sure sign and symptom of decay in the nation's public spirit. From the classical republican standpoint, the Men and Women of Taste are pursuing their own private self-satisfaction at the expense of Publick Spirit and civic responsibility.

For operagoers and patrons, the sketches of Men and Women of False Taste show there are those without the taste (cultural capital) to appreciate a worthy art form or respond to it inappropriately.

The politics of False Taste, then, maps well with the critique of luxury. Both are socially corrosive, excessive indulgences arising from the fruits of a thriving modern commercial society. But there is an inherent paradox, for it was commonly recognized that rise and cultivation of the arts and sciences required such wealth and riches of a commercial society, and often occurred under tyrannical rulers (such as Augustus or Louis XIV). The conditions that led to luxury also grounded the genuine connoisseurship to acquire, collect, and patronize the fine arts and the leisure and education to form good taste. The success of Pope's subscriptions for his translations of Homer, to cite only one convenient example, depended on a capitalistic publishing industry and a social elite who could buy the volumes as much for the prestige of appearing on the subscription list and owning the finely printed volumes, as for reading Homer in polite English verse.

The resolution of the paradox at the heart of both luxury and taste, was what Pope called "the true use of Riches":

> The Sense to value Riches, with the Art
> T'enjoy them, …
> To balance Fortune by a just expense.[209]
>
> 'Tis Use alone that sanctifies Expence,
> And Splendor borrows all her rays from Sense.[210]

---

[209] Pope, *Epistle to Bathurst*, Argument, lines 219–20, 223.
[210] Pope, *Epistle to Burlington*, lines 179–80.

CHAPTER 10

Opera in Formal Verse Satire

Despite the Opposition's success in forcing Walpole to withdraw his Excise proposal and a constant flood of pamphlets, prints, newspaper essays, and parliamentary obstruction, Walpole retained the King's favor; and by rewarding men with places and pensions, his control of Parliament and the Ministry seemed secure. With a fragmented Opposition unable to shake Walpole from power and continuing humiliations by Spanish depredations on merchant shipping and seamen, despair over a forlorn and dejected Britain, now spiritually sunk under Walpole's rule, was now a prominent theme of oppositional verse from the late 1730s. Louis Bredvold's classic phrase "the Gloom of the Tory satirists" – describing "the declining moral tone of England under Walpole [in which] they now professed to see the extinction of the best elements of English life" – would be an apt expression of the mood of some Britons – except that the gloom was shared by many across the political spectrum, not only Tories but also many dissident Whigs.[1]

From the mid-1730s, the most sophisticated and subtle cultural vehicle for challenging British cultural and civic life under Walpole and the Hanoverians was formal verse satire.[2] Often Horatian and Juvenalian imitations, they are typically erudite and learned, citing classical sources or printing the Latin original and English on facing pages. Best known are works by Alexander Pope

[1] Louis I. Bredvold, "The Gloom of the Tory Satirists," pp. 1–19 in *Pope and His Contemporaries: Essays Presented to George Sherburn*, ed. James L. Clifford and Louis A. Landa (Oxford: Clarendon Press, 1949), quoting p. 11. This chapter expands greatly on sources previous discussed in my "Opera, Satire, and Politics in the Walpole Era," pp. 347–72 in *The Past As Prologue: Essays to Celebrate the Twenty-Fifth Anniversary of ASECS*, ed. Carla H. Hays with Syndy M. Conger (New York, N.Y.: AMS Press, 1995).

[2] On the political use of literature and satire against Walpole, the major studies are: Maynard Mack, *The Garden and the City: Retirement and Politics in Later Poetry of Pope, 1731–1743* (Toronto: University of Toronto Press, 1969); Bertrand A. Goldgar, *Walpole and the Wits: The Relation of Politics to Literature, 1722–1742* (Lincoln, Nebr.: University of Nebraska Press, 1976); and Christine Gerrard, *The Patriot Opposition to Walpole: Politics, Poetry, and National Myth, 1725–1742* (Oxford: Clarendon, 1994). See also Vincent Carretta, *The Snarling Muse: Verbal and Visual Satire from Pope to Churchill* (Philadelphia, Pa.: University of Pennsylvania Press, 1983); William C. Dowling, *The Epistolary Moment: The Poetics of the Eighteenth-Century Verse Epistle* (Princeton, N.J.: Princeton University Press, 1991); and J. A. Downie, *To Settle the Succession of the State: Literature and Politics, 1678–1750* (New York, N.Y.: St. Martin's Press, 1994), 111–45.

240   THE CULTURAL POLITICS OF OPERA, 1720–1742

and Samuel Johnson; but the genre was cultivated by other lesser pens who also turned it to partisan ends. Explicit topical references to current events and statesmen, Spanish depredations on British merchant shipping, indictments of luxury and corruption, appeals to patriotism and public spirit, and praise of Prince Frederick and Opposition politicians show how the ideas and agenda of Opposition politics infiltrated high literary culture. In the midst of the usual litany of political complaints, Italian opera – and its most celebrated singer Farinelli – figure prominently as evidence of the declining state of Britain. As the careers of some authors reveal, throwing in one's lot with the Opposition seemed necessary for an aspiring writer.

With the epic no longer suitable for the times,[3] the formal verse satire was the dominant verse genre of the first half of the eighteenth century.[4] The most common models were Horace, Juvenal, and Persius, and more recently Boileau. In the poetic imitation, as Samuel Johnson describes it, "the ancients are familiarised by adapting their sentiments to modern topicks. ... It is a kind of middle composition between translation and original design, which pleases when the thoughts are unexpectedly applicable, and the parallels lucky."[5]

Despite their often explicitly declared models in Horace, Juvenal was highly valued, and his characteristic *sæva indignatio* often breaks through, making the

---

[3] Howard Weinbrot, *Britannia's Issue: The Rise of British Literature from Dryden to Ossian* (Cambridge: Cambridge University Press, 1993), 204–56.

[4] On the many aspects of eighteenth-century formal verse satire touched on in this chapter, see the exemplary studies of Howard D. Weinbrot, *The Formal Strain: Studies in Augustan Imitation and Satire* (Chicago, Ill.: University of Chicago Press, 1969); Weinbrot, *Alexander Pope and the Traditions of Formal Verse Satire* (Princeton, N.J.: Princeton University Press, 1982); and the collection of his essays, *Eighteenth-Century Satire: Essays on Text and Context from Dryden to Peter Pindar* (Cambridge: Cambridge University Press, 1988). See also George Southern, "The Satire of Dissent," pp. 56–73 in *The Oxford Handbook of Eighteenth-Century Satire*, ed. Paddy Bullard (Oxford: Oxford University Press, 2019).

Unlike earlier satire, which is often just malicious vituperation (see Ashley Marshall, *The Practice of Satire in England, 1658–1770* [Baltimore, Md.: Johns Hopkins Press, 2013]), these formal satires tend to follow the pattern of the two-part *laus et vituperatio*, by which the attack on vice or folly is balanced by praise of, or an example of, the *vir bonus*; see Maynard Mack, "The Muse of Satire," *Yale Review*, 41 (1951), 80–92; reprinted on pp. 55–65 in *Collected in Himself: Essays, Critical, Biographical, and Bibliographical on Pope and Some of His Contemporaries* (Newark, Del.: University of Delaware Press, 1982), and elsewhere.

[5] Samuel Johnson, "Life of Pope"; in *Lives of the English Poets*, ed. George B. Hill, 3 vols. (Oxford: Clarendon Press, 1905), 3:176. On the imitation in Britain, Weinbrot, *Formal Strain*, 1–30; Leonard A. Moskovit, "Pope and the Tradition of the Neoclassical Imitation," *Studies in English Literature*, 8 (1968), 445–62; Frank Stack, *Pope and Horace: Studies in Imitation* (Cambridge: Cambridge University Press, 1985) (esp. Introduction); Harold F. Brooks, "The 'Imitation' in English Poetry, Especially in Formal Satire, Before the Age of Pope," *Review of English Studies*, 25 (1949), 129–40; and William Kupersmith, *English Versions of Roman Satire in the Earlier Eighteenth Century* (Newark, Del.: University of Delaware Press, 2007). Dowling, *Epistolary Moment*, explores the sociopoetic of the verse epistle.

tone of many satires bitterly Juvenalian.[6] The Horatian satirist is a reasonable man in respectful conversation with the great. Using gentle ridicule and irony, he exposes human folly and upholds shared family or civic values to affirm right conduct in life; he turns his elegant and muted irony to private, biographical, or moral concerns. In contrast, the Juvenalian satirist is the indignant outsider harshly confronting corruption, decay, and vice. Darkly ironic rather than gentle or witty, the Juvenalian satirist invokes by-gone classical republican and country values to indict violators of decency and law in a collapsing world. Juvenalian satire often works to obliquely indict those at the helm of the ship of state: the King or Ministry. As John Dryden put the contrast: "*Horace* was a Mild Admonisher, a Court Satirist," who "confin'd himself to the ridiculing of Petty Vices, and common Follies" in order to "give the Rules of a Happy and Virtuous Life"; whereas, Juvenal "wholly employ'd in lashing Vices, … treats Tyranny, and all the Vices attending it, as they deserve, with the utmost rigour … [and] always intends to move your Indignation."[7] As a tool for political opposition and social critique, Juvenalian satire is by far the more effective. From him, Dryden said, "all the moderns have notoriously stolen their sharpest Railleries."[8]

Horatian satire admonishes general vices and characters; but in the British political climate of the day, it was instinctively taken to have particular current application, as we saw in several verses of "An Excellent New Ballad, Call'd, A Bob for the C——t [Court]," to be sung to the tune "In the Days of My Youth" (from *The Beggar's Opera*) that appeared in the *Craftsman* in 1728:

> Ye Poets take Heed how you trust to the Muse, *fa, la*.
> What Words to make choice of, and what to refuse, *fa, la*.
> If she hint at a Vice of *political* Sort, *fa, la*,
> *Application* cries out, *That's* a Bob *for the C——t, fa la*.
>
> *Corruption, Ambition, Pomp, Vanity, Pride fa, la*,
> Are Terms, that by Guess-work are often apply'd; *fa la*.
> To quote Horace is thought meer Derision and Sport; *fa, la*.
> *Application* cries out, *That's* a Bob *for the C——t. fa, la*.[9]

---

[6] On the contrasting types of satire, Weinbrot, *Pope and Formal Verse Satire*, xiii–xv; 40, 343; Ian Jack, *Augustan Satire: Intention and Idiom in English Poetry, 1660–1750* (Oxford: Clarendon Press, 1952), 102–4, 136–8; and P. K. Elkin, *The Augustan Defence of Satire* (Oxford: Clarendon Press, 1973), 146–66. On Dryden's distinction, Weinbrot, *Eighteenth-Century Satire*, 2–7, 133–6, who notes that characteristic of Pope is the mingling of Horatian, Juvenalian, and Persian satire. See also John Dennis, *Original Letters, Familiar, Moral and Critical*, 2 vols. (1721), 2:432.

[7] "Discourse Concerning the Original and Progress of Satire"; in *The Works of John Dryden*. Vol. 4. *Poems 1693–1696*, general editor H. T. Swedenberg, Jr. (Berkeley, Calif.: University of California Press, 1974), 59, 62, 65, 68, 69, 72.

[8] Dryden, "Discourse Concerning the Original and Progress of Satire"; in *Works of John Dryden*, 4:72.

[9] *Craftsman*, no. 130 (28 Dec. 1728). Reprinted in *A Collection of Poems … in the Craftsman* (1731), 57–60, and in Milton Percival, *Political Ballads Illustrating the*

242   THE CULTURAL POLITICS OF OPERA, 1720–1742

Donald Greene has cautioned against uncritically using satire as a guide to the political or social climate of Britain. As he had pointed out, "Satire is a *genre*, and if you are going to write satire, you must find something to satirize. Since satire was fashionable in the eighteenth century, every budding poet, whatever his politics, wrote satire and found the state of England deplorable."[10] Given opera's prominent place in the life of the *beau monde*, we can expect satiric mentions of it and its star singers coming from social critics; we cannot therefore uncritically take all satire on opera to be oppositional. (As we have seen, satire of False Taste coming from members of court and ministerial circles did not over-reach to suggest Walpole and the Court were the cause of False Taste.) To show that some uses of opera in formal verse satires did go on to engage cultural politics and have significant partisan implication, we need also show how such satires also did work as oppositional propaganda, did some 'political work.' The following will show how some verse satires are directly accusatory of the Walpole ministry: the charge was often directly carried out by citing opera as evidence of the corruption, luxury, and softening of moral tone brought on by the Robinocracy. One advantage of using the imitation was that if the persons or vices struck too close to current figures, the ancient originals provided defense against a charge of libel or slander.

The key to understanding the implicit oppositional nature of such literary satire is to pose the question *Cui bono*? These formal verse satires address the high-literary readers in Britain and attempt to confront the reader with the (supposed) social and cultural decline of Britain, as part of the 'culture wars' of Walpoleian Britain. In the classic pattern, the satires lash social or personal vices and fashions, while as a positive counter to the vices condemned they extoll Patriot ideals or statesmen. The innuendo, as in most Opposition propaganda, is clear: remove Walpole and Britain will be rescued – often with the arrival of the Patriot King.

POPE'S SATIRES OF THE 1730S

Gloom and despair about a forlorn and sunken Britain under the Hanoverians is the ruling theme of Alexander Pope's poetry of the 1730s and culminating in the life-time revised *Dunciad in Four Books* (1743). Pope was the era's foremost, though not the only, exponent of formal verse satire, and especially the Horatian imitation. Such was his dominance of the genre, that some satirists tried to trade on his reputation – and a few in turn were vilified because Walpole's writers mistakenly thought their anonymous works were written by Pope.

At his Thames-side retreat, Pope assumed, as Maynard Mack put it, "the posture of the honest satirist" conducting an intensely personal campaign against

---

Administration of Sir Robert Walpole. Oxford Historical and Literary Studies, 8 (1916), no. 10, pp. 20–1.

[10] Donald Greene, *The Politics of Samuel Johnson*, 2nd ed. (Athens, Ga.: University of Georgia Press, 1990), 81.

the corruption of the Walpole ministry and the Court of George II.[11] Around his villa, garden, and grotto at Twickenham, Pope created a mythology of rural Horatian retirement and set the moral tone of virtue for the Opposition.[12] Here he entertained Swift, Bolingbroke, Lyttelton, and other members of the Opposition circle, and even received a highly publicized visit from Frederick, Prince of Wales.[13]

In his poems, continues Mack, Pope created the "type-hero of a highly traditional confrontation between virtuous simplicity and sophisticated corruption, … [and an] imagined counter-kingdom to the kingdom represented by St. James's."[14] Since as a Catholic, Pope had no hopes of holding office or place in the event the Opposition assumed power, his indictments have been seen as all the more disinterested, sincere, and principled.[15]

Pope's satires of the 1730s embody a stark contrast of vice and virtue that align with the Court and Opposition. Luxury, moral and financial corruption, greed and avarice, and debasement of national honor all reside with those at the center of government. The classical republican, Country, and Old Whig virtues of rural retirement reside with Pope's friends and those who had gone, or been forced, into retirement or opposition: Atterbury, Bolingbroke, Pulteney,

---

[11] The fullest treatment of the political nature of Pope's satire in the 1730s is Mack, *Garden and the City*, esp. Chapter 4. A full account of Pope's lifelong relation to politics is given in Pat Rogers, *A Political Biography of Alexander Pope* (London: Pickering and Chatto, 2010). See also Goldgar, *Walpole and the Wits*; Carretta, *The Snarling Muse*; Howard Erskine-Hill, "Alexander Pope: The Political Poet in His Time," *Eighteenth-Century Studies*, 15 (1981–82), 123–48 [reprinted in *Modern Essays on Eighteenth-Century Literature*, ed. Leopold Damrosch, Jr. (New York, N.Y.: Oxford University Press, 1988), 123–40, without appendix]; John Butt, "Pope and the Opposition to Walpole's Government," pp. 111–26 in *Pope, Dickens, and Others: Essays and Addresses* (Edinburgh: Edinburgh University Press, 1969); Robert W. Rogers, *The Major Satires of Alexander Pope* (Urbana, Ill.: University of Illinois Press, 1955), 71–7; and Dowling, *The Epistolary Moment*. Weinbrot's surveys of Pope's satire are always attentive to the political topics and uses of his satire, as well as the politically motivated attacks on Pope himself.

[12] On this theme, in addition to Mack, *Garden and the City*, see Peter Dixon, *The World of Pope's Satires: An Introduction to the "Epistles" and "Imitations of Horace"* (London: Methuen, 1968), 90–107. A reconsideration of Pope's changing attitude to rural retirement is given by Claudia Thomas Kairoff, "Living on the Margin: Alexander Pope and the Rural Ideal," *Studies in the Literary Imagination*, 38 (2005), 15–38.

[13] Further on Frederick and Pope, see Chapter 12 and Thomas McGeary, "Pope and Frederick, Prince of Wales: Gifts and Memorials of Their Friendship," *Scriblerian*, 23 (Autumn 2000), 40–7, and McGeary, "Handel in the *Dunciad*: Pope, Handel, Frederick, Prince of Wales, and Cultural Politics," *Musical Quarterly*, 97 (2015), 542–74.

[14] Maynard Mack, "A Poet in His Landscape: Pope at Twickenham," pp. 3–29 in *From Sensibility to Romanticism: Essays Presented to Frederick A. Pottle*, ed. Frederick W. Hilles and Harold Bloom (Oxford: Oxford University Press, 1965), 3.

[15] Butt, "Pope and the Opposition to Walpole's Government," 111. On limitations on Pope as a Catholic, Peter Davidson, "Pope's Recusancy," *Studies in the Literary Imagination*, 38 (2005), 64–76.

244   THE CULTURAL POLITICS OF OPERA, 1720–1742

Chesterfield, Marchmont, Peterborough, Argyll, Wyndham, Shippen, Cornbury, Lyttelton, Cobham, and Prince Frederick.[16]

Pope generally stayed free of partisan politics before 1733. The *Dunciad* is certainly a piece of cultural politics but not yet an Opposition tract. Previously, he and Walpole apparently had relaxed, cordial relations: they exchanged visits and Pope attended Walpole's Sunday dinners.[17] He received £200 from the Treasury to encourage his translation of the *Odyssey*, and Walpole (perhaps unwittingly) presented Pope's *Dunciad* to the King and Queen in 1728.[18]

The turning point in Pope's relationship with the Ministry was marked by the satire *Fortescue* (*The First Satire of the Second Book of Horace Imitated*) (February 1733). Thereafter, many reasons drove Pope to make politics central to his satires. Attacks on Pope himself, dating from even before the *Dunciad*, and many of them from Walpole's literary hacks, certainly set the ever-vengeful Pope against the Ministry and its writers.[19] By 1733 his friends and their sympathies had likely influenced his own opinion of Walpole. Foremost of these friends was Viscount Bolingbroke, co-founder of the *Craftsman* and principal theorist of the Opposition.[20] Finally, the extent of Walpole's wealth and power, combined with the supposed threat he posed to British virtues, arts, and liberty made it impossible for a high-minded satirist not to attack the supposed source of social evil at Court and Ministry.[21]

Pope's favored medium for his political satires was the Horatian imitation, a genre that came to invite political application to the Court.[22] Despite the Horatian form, Pope's tone is more often Juvenalian: the outsider decrying the vices of the Court.[23] Like much Opposition propaganda, Pope's satire works by

[16] Butt, "Pope and the Opposition to Walpole's Government," 117–24.

[17] Rogers, *Major Satires*, 71; Tone S. Urstad, *Sir Robert Walpole's Poets: The Use of Literature as Pro-Government Propaganda, 1721-1742* (Newark, Del.: University of Delaware Press, 1999), 220–1. Their affable relationship was at best what Mack calls "a wary armed truce" (*Garden and the City*, 121). Pope wrote to Swift that at the time (1729) "I am civilly treated by Sir R. Walpole"; letter of 28 November 1729 to Jonathan Swift in Pope, *Correspondence*, ed. Sherburn, 3:81; see also 2:323, 368, 441, 530; 3:11–12, 53, 81, 112, 139. Pope's changing relationship with Walpole is examined in Howard Erskin-Hill, "Pope and the Poetry of Opposition," pp. 134–49 in *The Cambridge Companion to Alexander Pope*, ed. Pat Rogers (Cambridge: Cambridge University Press, 2007).

[18] The episode is often mentioned, but no documentation has yet been found; Erskin-Hill, "Pope and the Poetry of Opposition," writes it was a "very unlikely event which may, nevertheless, have actually occurred" (pp. 142–3).

[19] On attacks against Pope, J. V. Guerinot, *Pamphlet Attacks on Alexander Pope, 1711–1744: A Descriptive Bibliography* (New York, N.Y.: New York University Press, 1969). Attacks on Pope in Opposition newspapers are found below.

[20] Their relationship is explored in Brean S. Hammond, *Pope and Bolingbroke: A Study of Friendship and Influence* (Columbia, Mo.: University of Missouri Press, 1984).

[21] Mack, *Garden and the City*, 117–28.

[22] On how Horace served Pope's oppositional aims, Weinbrot, *Eighteenth-Century Satire*, 187–8.

[23] On Pope's mingling of satiric modes, Weinbrot, *Eighteenth-Century Satire*, 128–43.

innuendo and irony, and the intended applications were not difficult for those who knew the times to find. Pope often abandons general satire, what Edward Young had called characteristic satire, for particular satire directed at specific persons, a use he defended in a letter of 1734 to John Arbuthnot:

> That disdain and indignation against Vice, is (I thank God) the only disdain and indignation I have: It is sincere, and it will be a lasting one. But sure it is as impossible to have a just abhorrence of Vice, without hating the Vicious. ... To reform and not to chastise, I am afraid is impossible, and that the best Precepts, as well as the best Laws, would prove of small use, if there were no Examples to inforce them. To Attack Vices in the abstract, without touching Persons, may be safe fighting indeed, but it is fighting with Shadows.[24]

In his formal satires with their clear political targets, Pope need only mention opera to transfer its opprobrium as foreign, sensuous, effeminate, and luxurious onto Walpole and the Court. In the *Dunciad*, Pope had already introduced opera as the forerunner that prepares the way for the Triumph of Dulness.

The Impertinent
In 1733 Pope took the politically ambiguous *Fourth Satire* of John Donne and fashioned a topical, anti-court poem rife with oppositional sentiment in *The Impertinent, or a Visit to the Court. A Satyr* (5 November 1733).[25] Donne not only provides Pope's model, but evokes Elizabeth, one of the Opposition's worthies. She indulged the liberty and freedom of her people and was victorious over Spain – both achievements implicit reproaches of Walpole.[26]

---

[24] *Letters of Mr. Alexander Pope* (1737), 293. The letter (dated 26 July 1734) that Pope printed in 1737 is fictitious. The authentic letter to Arbuthnot read in part:

> General Satire in Times of General Vice has no force, & is no Punishment: People have ceas'd to be ashamed of it when so many are joined with then; and tis only by hunting One or two from the Herd that any Examples can be made. If a man writ all his Life against the Collective Body of the Banditti, or against Lawyers, would it do the least Good, or lessen the Body? But if some are hung, or pilloryed, it may prevent others.

In Pope, *Correspondence*, ed. Sherburn, letter of 2 Aug. 1734, 3:423. On the difference between Swift and Pope, James McLaverty, "Naming and Shaming in the Poetry of Pope and Swift, 1726–1745," pp. 160–75 in *Swift's Travels: Eighteenth-Century British Satire and Its Legacy*, ed. Nicholas Hudson and Aaron Santesso (Cambridge: Cambridge University Press, 2008).

[25] The poem was later titled *The Fourth Satire of Dr. John Donne*. On Pope's satire and its relations to Donne, see Howard Erskine-Hill, "Courtiers out of Horace: Donne's *Satyre IV*; and Pope's *Fourth Satire of Dr John Donne, Dean of St Paul's Versifyed*," pp. 273–307 in *John Donne: Essays in Celebration*, ed. A. J. Smith (London: Methuen, 1972). See also Weinbrot, *Pope and Verse Satire*, 302–7; and Erskine-Hill, *Augustan Idea*, 88–98. Donne's poem is in turn based on Horace's *Satire* I:9.

[26] Elizabeth was so praised in the *Craftsman*, no. 377 (22 Sept. 1733), and elsewhere in other Opposition literature.

246   THE CULTURAL POLITICS OF OPERA, 1720–1742

In *The Impertinent*, the Poet grudgingly goes to a vicious court as if sentenced to purgatory; there he encounters an impertinent, outlandish, talkative, sycophantic courtier eager for court news. The two are Country/Opposition and Court/Ministry spokesmen.[27] The Poet need only tell of "new Plays, / New Eunuchs, Harlequins, and Operas"[28] as a short-hand indictment of the vice, luxury, and decadence at Court. When the Courtier shares his own news, he becomes a veritable speaking *Craftsman*, repeating all the stock Opposition charges against Walpole: his use of bribery, subservience to France, and refusal to defend British merchants against Spanish depredations.[29] The delicious irony in the Courtier's report is that he seems not to realize how his news indicts the Court and ministers.

Epistle to Augustus

By straight-faced panegyric, Pope's *Epistle to Augustus* (*The First Epistle of the Second Book of Horace Imitated*) (25 May 1737) transforms Horace's poem into an indictment of George II as an unworthy monarch whose Court is corrupting the taste of Britain.[30]

The satire can work for the Opposition in two ways because of the age's ambivalent attitude toward the Roman emperor.[31] On the one hand, George Augustus can be seen as directly compared with Caesar Augustus, the tyrant and butcher who was the father of Rome's decline, debased poetry by demands

---

[27] The political positions are delineated by Carretta, *Snarling Muse*, 110–15.

[28] *Imitations of Horace*, ed. John Butt. The Twickenham Edition of the Poems of Alexander Pope, vol. 4, 2nd ed. (New Haven, Conn.: Yale University Press, 1953), p. 35, lines 124–5.

[29] *Imitations of Horace*, ed. Butt, lines 160–5.

[30] *Epistle to Augustus*: Stack, *Pope and Horace: Studies in Imitation*, 150–97; Malcolm Kelsall, "Augustus and Pope," *Huntington Library Quarterly*, 39 (1976), 117–31; Rogers, *Major Satires*, 89–91; Jay A. Levine, "Pope's *Epistle to Augustus*, Lines 1–30," *Studies in English Literature, 1500–1900*, 7 (1967), 427–51; Erskine-Hill, *Augustan Idea*, 324–34; Weinbrot, *Augustus Caesar*, 182–217; Kupersmith, *English Versions of Roman Satire*, 108–17; Jacob Fuchs, "Horace's Good Augustus and Pope's Imitation of *Epist*. 2.1," *Classical and Modern Literature: A Quarterly*, 3 (1983), 75–87.

[31] The controversy is whether the comparison is to be seen as ironic (positive view of Augustus as literary patron) or not (Augustus as emperor who suppressed liberty). See Weinbrot, *Augustus Caesar*; Weinbrot, *Eighteenth-Century Satire*, 21–33; Erskine-Hill, *Augustan Idea*; and Thomas Kaminski, "Rehabilitating 'Augustanism'": On the Roots of 'Polite Letters' in England," *Eighteenth-Century Life*, 20 (Nov. 1996), 49–65. Manuel Schonhorn, "The Audacious Contemporaneity of Pope's *Epistle to Augustus*," *Studies in English Literature, 1500–1900*, 8 (1968), 431–43, highlights the satire's topical polemic against George II.

Kaminski, "'Oppositional Augustanism' and Pope's *Epistle to Augustus*," *Studies in Eighteenth-Century Culture*, 26 (1998), 57–72, provides a resolution of the equivocal nature of the poem by validating the view of Augustus as fulfilling the ideal of the benevolent arts patron, while at the same time poets can criticize the Court and Ministry for neglecting or betraying that ideal. An application to George Augustus was invited by an advertisement in *Common Sense*, no. 28 (11 Aug. 1737), which ended with "Translated and apply'd to the present Times. By Mr. Pope."

for flattery, and ruined theatre by making it a distraction for the people. On the other, an ironic comparison to the Augustus, an ideal patron of the poets, who brought peace, stability, and refinement of style to the arts becomes mockery of George Augustus and his lack of taste and patronage, and his mean spirit and weak conduct of foreign affairs. Whatever way the poem is taken, the *Epistle to Augustus* epitomizes the theme of neglect of genius and literary merit by the Ministry and Court as a symptom of moral and public corruption.

With praise of the British Worthies Dryden, Addison, and Swift, Pope defends the merit and dignity of literature against the debased taste of the Court. As did Horace for Greece and then Rome in the *Ars Poetica*, Pope wrote a history of the letters and taste in Britain in his satire. At the Restoration of Charles II,

> In Days of Ease, when now the weary Sword
> Was sheathed, and *Luxury* with *Charles* restored;
> …
> No wonder then, when all was Love and Sport,
> The willing Muses were debauch'd at Court;
> On each enervate string they taught the Note
> To pant, or tremble thro' an Eunuch's throat.[32]

Pope's note to the penultimate line cites "The Siege of Rhodes [1656] by Sir William Davenant, the first Opera sung in England." But it is unlikely any castrati sang in these productions at this time, though castrati sang in London later in the Restoration.

Like James Miller, Pope contrasts some mythic, virtuous, rural English existence –

> Time was, a sober Englishman wou'd knock
> His servants up, and rise by five a clock,
> Instruct his Family in ev'ry rule,
> And send his Wife to Church, his Son to school.
> To worship like his Fathers was his care;
> To teach their frugal Virtues to his Heir.[33]

– to present city life, where the men fancy themselves poets and women while their time reading and at the theatres:

> Now Times are chang'd, and one Poetick Itch
> Has seiz'd the Court and City, Poor and Rich:
> Sons, Sires, and Grandsires, all will wear the Bays,
> Our Wives read Milton, and our Daughters Plays,
> To Op'ra's, Theatres, Rehearsals throng,
> And all our Grace at Table is a Song.[34]

Opera characterizes the luxury of the court of Charles and the foolishness of modern London.

---

[32] *Imitations of Horace*, ed. Butt, pp. 207, 209, lines 139–40, 151–4.

[33] *Imitations of Horace*, ed. Butt, lines 161–6.

[34] *Imitations of Horace*, ed. Butt, lines 169–74; citing here variant of line 173.

248   THE CULTURAL POLITICS OF OPERA, 1720–1742

Epistle to Bolingbroke

In his last Horatian imitation, the *Epistle to Bolingbroke* (*The First Epistle of the First Book of Horace Imitated*) (7 March 1738),[35] Pope, following Horace, writes to his patron to explain why he is abandoning poetry and such trifles for rural retirement, and is turning to meditate on virtue and wisdom. For Horace's Maecenas, Pope substituted Bolingbroke, whom he addressed as an exemplar of virtue, his "Guide, Philosopher, and Friend."[36]

Despite its opening nod to rural retirement and Horatian contemplation, the *Epistle* is a very public poem, a daring avowal of friendship and admiration for Walpole's most implacable foe. In its second part, the epistle vigorously attacks corruption and evil at Court. The core of the poem articulates the contrast between the voice of Wisdom, which calls, "Seek Virtue first! be bold!," and the voice of London and the Court, which cries, "Get Mony, Mony still!"[37] Pope reports the prevailing morality and wisdom at Court, where at the center is George II:

> Who counsels best? who whispers, "Be but Great,
> "With Praise or Infamy, leave that to fate;
> "Get Place and Wealth, if possible, with Grace;
> "If not, by any means get Wealth and Place."   (lines 101–4)

By a chain of association, this might be Walpole's advice, for Jonathan Wild, model for Macheath (and hence analogue to Walpole), commended the advice of a dying man to his son: "Get Money Son, honestly, if you can; but, however, get Money."[38]

Pope, the Voice of Wisdom, scorns the results of Avarice:

> For what? to have a Box where Eunuchs sing,
> And foremost in the Circle eye a King.   (lines 105–6)

The end of wealth is a box at the opera, a spectacle dominated by castrato singers – themselves reminders of the tyranny of Catholic Italy and emblems of the luxury spawned by corruption and wealth.

Pope Attacked

The *Epistle* includes common topical hits at the Court and Ministry – from Walpole's brazen screening of corrupt politicians to the King's domination first by Queen Caroline and then by his German mistress Madame de Walmoden.

---

[35] *Epistle to Bolingbroke*: Frank Stack, "*Pope's Epistle to Bolingbroke* and *Epistle I.i*," pp. 169–91 in *The Art of Alexander Pope*, ed. Howard Erskine-Hill and Anne Smith (New York, N.Y.: Barnes & Noble, 1979); *Stack, Pope and Horace*, 245–74; Weinbrot, *Pope and Verse Satire*, 292–5; and Erskine-Hill, *Augustan Ideal*, 339–44. Thomas E. Maresca, *Pope's Horatian Poems* (Columbus, Ohio: Ohio State University Press, 1966), 151–93, stresses Pope's inversion of Christian values in the poem.

[36] *Imitations of Horace*, ed. Butt, line 177; the compliment also appeared in the *Essay on Man*, IV:390. Pope was earlier reproached for his friendship with Bolingbroke by the *Daily Courant*, no. 5364 (16 June 1733) and in *The False Patriot* (1734).

[37] *Imitations of Horace*, ed. Butt, lines 77, 79.

[38] Reported in *Mist's Weekly Journal*, no. 7 (12 June 1725).

OPERA IN FORMAL VERSE SATIRE   249

But it was the compliments to Walpole's foe Bolingbroke that aroused ministerial writers, who would finally attack Pope by name. The *Epistle to Bolingbroke* was followed several months later by Pope's last published satires, a pair
of *Dialogues* for 1738 collected as the *Epilogue to the Satires*[39] (see Chapter 12).

The effectiveness – or at least the Ministry's sensitivity to them – of Pope's
satires, with their carefully placed mentions of opera as evidence of the social
and moral decay of the day, can be gauged by the prompt and *ad hominem* ministerial counterattacks. One way of deflecting the satiric lashes was to charge
that Pope, Miller, and others had mistaken the proper role of satire. Instead of
ridiculing folly, painting the horror of vice, or showing the charms of virtue,
Pope and others are charged with descending to malice, slander, libel, and
invective: demeaning themselves rather than their targets and casting disrespect on the King, government, and men of honor.[40] These satirists, the ministerial writers claimed, are the false patriots, who – motivated by envy, ambition,
or disappointment in seeking office – libel statesmen and nourish faction.

Previously, the Ministry seems to have tolerated Pope's attacks on the Court
and its writers, probably because to respond to them too strongly (as the Opposition may have hoped) would call attention to and validate the accusations.
His subsequent attacks were now too public and vicious for the Ministry to
ignore. It seems to have been Pope's compliments to Bolingbroke that provoked
attacks on him and Bolingbroke.[41] Barely three weeks after the *Epistle* appeared,
the ministerial *Daily Gazetteer*[42] reprinted Pope's earlier lines on Bolingbroke,
where Pope had urged

> Come then, my Friend, my Genius, come along,
> Oh master of the poet, and the song!

Everyone knew, responded the *Gazetteer*, ridiculing his flattery of Bolingbroke,
that the facts of Bolingbroke's political career so contradicted Pope's portrait
of him as a virtuous, patriotic, and great man that Pope's lines must be ironic,
not panegyric.

Two issues of the *Gazetteer* in April 1738 turn Horace against Pope, Bolingbroke, and friends by printing original Horatian imitations.[43] In the first, "A.Z."
observes that in Pope's recent Horatian imitations, "the Friends to the present

---

[39] *One Thousand Seven Hundred and Thirty Eight. A Dialogue Something like Horace* (16
May 1738) and *One Thousand Seven Hundred and Thirty Eight. Dialogue II* (18 July
1738). The *Dialogues* were collectively renamed in 1740 as the *Epilogue to the Satires*.
On the *Epilogue to the Satires*, see Rogers, *Major Satires*, 91–3; Erskine-Hill, *Augustan
Ideal*, 344–9; Weinbrot, *Augustus Caesar*, 137–41.

[40] On debates at the time of the true (proper) nature of satire, Weinbrot, *Formal Strain*,
59–75; the issue is a constant theme in Marshall, *Practice of Satire*.

[41] On attacks on Pope from ministerial writers, Weinbrot, *Eighteenth-Century Satire*,
44–7; Weinbrot, *Augustus Caesar*, Appendix; and Urstad, *Walpole's Poets*, 216–30.

[42] *Daily Gazetteer*, no. 851 (27 March 1738); the lines were from the *Essay on Man*
(1733–34), IV:373–90. Later the *Daily Gazetteer*, no. 1261 (6 July 1739) delights in the
(supposed) decline of Pope's reputation in "Some Thoughts on Humility. To Mr. Pope."

[43] *Daily Gazetteer*, nos. 860 and 865 (6 and 11 April 1738).

250 THE CULTURAL POLITICS OF OPERA, 1720–1742

Government are continually the Subject of his *Satire*, as they who are avowed Enemies to their Country are thought worthy of his Panegyricks." A.Z. asserts Bolingbroke in reality is "the homebred Traitor and the foreign Spy" and urges him to retire to Twickenham where he can be the harmless hero of Pope's poetry. Lyttelton is ridiculed as a "*Would be*" statesman and ambitious, pretentious "young, mock Patriot." The second issue prints "The Fourth Epistle of the First Book of *Horace*'s Epistles" as if "by A. P. of Twickenham, Esq." Here, Pope supposedly invites Bolingbroke to retire to Twickenham, where, if Bolingbroke still must rail and write "Schemes of Politics," the two will "ridicule both Church and State."

The 1738 *Dialogues* were quickly turned against Pope in the *Daily Gazetteer* in August.[44] In a prose dialogue about Pope, "A." urges his friend not to write about Pope for fear of becoming an object of his spleen and being "marked out for a Dunce." A.'s respectful commendations of Pope's patriotism, virtue, regard for truth, and great integrity and justice, as well as his claim that "wicked *Placemen* and *Courtiers*" are terrified of Pope's pen, are, of course, ironic. But the skeptical "B." (the ministerial voice) is little in awe of Pope, and mocks Pope's praise of Bolingbroke and questions the Patriots' principles.

Two days later, "Rusticus" sent the *Daily Gazetteer* a poem occasioned by reading Pope's *Essay on Man* (1733–1734). If what this "malevolent Satyrist" says be true, he writes, that "whatever is, is best,"[45] there must then be in the world such a man as Pope, "a hodgepodge Sound of Bad and Good" who "can the Best in foulest Colours paint" and would "make B—l—broke a Saint." [46]

JAMES MILLER'S *SEASONABLE REPROOF*

We have already encountered James Miller as the oppositional poet of *Harlequin-Horace*. The poem became more topically political and anti-Walpolean in later editions, a trend continued in his *Seasonable Reproof, a Satire, in the Manner of Horace* (November 1735).[47] Miller announces the poem as a "poetical *Pillory*,

---

[44] *Daily Gazetteer*, no. 980 (24 Aug.1738).

[45] *Daily Gazetteer*, no. 982 (26 Aug.1738). Pope, though, actually wrote, "Whatever is, is Right" (I:294). The *Daily Gazetteer*, no. 1035 [*recte*: 1043], 27 Oct. 1738) will accuse the *Craftsman* and *Common Sense* in mistaking the nature of true Horatian satire and mistaking libel for satire.

[46] One continuation supposedly by Pope, is, in fact, a pro-Walpole poem that attacks Pope and the Patriots (see Guerinot, *Pamphlet Attacks*, 278–9). Two other imitation verse-dialogues are *A Dialogue on One Thousand Seven Hundred and Thirty-Eight* (Aug. 1738; Guerinot, *Pamphlet Attacks*, 269–70); and the ministerial writer Thomas Newcomb's *A Supplement to One Thousand Seven Hundred Thirty-Eight. Not written by Mr. Pope* (Oct. 24, 1738; Guerinot, *Pamphlet Attacks*, 270–3). These charge Pope is a venal, false patriot who writes ill-natured satire that praises anyone of the Opposition.

[47] The poem was reprinted in 1736 and revised in Miller's *Miscellaneous Works* (1741). *Seasonable Reproof* is dedicated to the military hero, the Duke of Argyll, who managed Walpole's Scottish MPs; Argyll seemed to be amicable with the Court until publicly opposing the Ministry in 1736 over its efforts to punish the city of Edinburgh in the wake of the Porteous affair; see Robert Campbell, *The Life of the Most Illustrious Prince*

OPERA IN FORMAL VERSE SATIRE   251

to execute Justice upon such *Vices* and *Follies,* as are either above the Reach, or without the Verge of the *Laws.*"[48] These are far more severe goals than the Horatian satirist's usual gentle ridicule of vice and folly, and they announce Miller's aim goes well beyond the private to the political realm.[49]

Featured in the satire is the recently arrived Farinelli. He was about to begin his second season as London's most stellar opera singer, and his recurring appearance in Miller's cultural critique of Britain is testament to Farinelli's fame and Miller's indignation at the adulation of him. It was in the previous 1734–35 season that contemporary sources estimated Farinelli received up to £4,000, including possibly as much as £1,500 for a single benefit concert on 15 March 1735.[50] Such gifts to Farinelli, we saw, were inscribed on the unrolled scroll prominent in the "The Rake's Levee" plate in Hogarth's *A Rake's Progress* and widely reported in the press.

Miller opens *Seasonable Reproof* by printing (on a left-facing page) the beginning of Horace's *Satire* I.3, with its well-known indictment of the fickle singer Tigellius:

> Omnibus hoc Vitium est *Cantoribus,* inter Amicos,
> Ut nunquam inducant Animum *cantare rogati.*
>   ... *Sardus* habebat
> Ille *Tigellius* hoc. *Cæsar* qui cogere posset
> Si peteret per Amicitiam patris atque suam, non
> Quidquam proficeret.

> All singers have this fault: if asked to sing among
> their friends they are never so inclined; [omitted by
> Miller: if unasked, they never leave off.] That son of
> Sardinia, Tigellius, was of this sort. If Caesar, who
> might have forced him to comply, should beg him
> by his father's friendship and his own, he could make
> no headway. [51]

In his own imitation of Horace (printed on the right-facing page), Miller separates the inconstant traits of Tigellius and out of them creates several modern

---

   John, Duke of Argyle and Greenwich (1745), 301–4. The dedication seems to anticipate Argyll's turn to the Opposition. On the poem, Kupersmith, *English Versions of Roman Satire,* 96–101.

[48] Title page. See also the Preface to the collected edition of *Common Sense,* 2 vols. (1738–1739), on punishing those beyond laws.

[49] The topicality of the poem is suggested by fact that these lines were omitted when the poem was reprinted in 1741 in Miller's *Miscellaneous Works.*

[50] For example, *The Political State of Great-Britain,* 49 (Jan.–June 1735), 365–6. For an evaluation of the claims, see Judith Milhous and Robert D. Hume, "Opera Salaries in Eighteenth-Century London," *Journal of the American Musicological Society,* 46 (1993), 26–83 (at p. 38), and Milhous and Hume, "Construing and Misconstruing Farinelli in London," *British Journal for Eighteenth-Century Studies,* 28 (2005), 361–85.

[51] Horace, *Satires, Epistles, Ars Poetica,* trans. H. Rushton Fairclough. Loeb Classical Library (London: William Heineman, 1926), *Satire* I.3, lines 1–6, pp. 32–3.

252   THE CULTURAL POLITICS OF OPERA, 1720–1742

characters who each have a single fault. The most fully developed example is Farinelli, who supposedly is never inclined to sing. Miller attacks the impudence of "such a low Creature as an *Opera Songster*" (Dedication) and expands it into an indictment of False Taste and corrupt fashion with an image of a London so deserted by its populace running to the opera that Excisemen could conquer the city, and Walpole can safely make a narrow escape with his plunder ("save his Bacon"):[52]

> Ask *Fa—ro—li* [Farinelli], please your Grace, to sing.
> No, the cram'd Capon answers — no such Thing.
> Shall I, who, being *less* than Man, am *more*;
> Whom Beaux, Belles, Peers, and Senators adore;
> For whose sweet Pipe the City's so forsaken,   ⎫
> That, by *Excisemen*, it might now be taken,   ⎬
> And great Sir *Bob* [Walpole] ride thro', and save his Bacon; ⎭
> What! shall I sing when *ask'd?* — I'm no such Elf:
> Not I, by *Jove*, tho' ask'd by *G——e* [George] himself.   (p. 1)

The castrato's impudence even before the King is reinforced by the speaker's comment,

> Yet, for that single End [singing] the Worm was bred;
> Yet, by that single Means, both cloath'd and fed.   (p. 3)

Miller gives a sharper political edge to the satire in the following verse paragraph (lacking a counterpart in Horace), which indicts Walpole's conduct of British foreign policy and his pacific attitude toward Spain. Britain's political decline and subservience to foreign powers seems almost minor by comparison to British women expiring over the singing of Farinelli ("a warbling Ass") and the French dancers and Italian castrati ("Gelt for a Song") who carry off the nation's riches:

> Sleep, *Britain*, in thy State of Reprobation,
> Thou mere *Milch-cow* to ev'ry foreign Nation.
> *Heaps* upon *Heaps* thy Fair expire, alas!
> Slain by the *Jaw-bone* of a warbling *Ass*;
> Whilst Shoals of Locusts, spawn'd in *Rome* or *France*,
> *Gelt* for a Song, or *shrivel'd* for a Dance,
> O'er thy dup'd Sons usurp supreme Command,
> And carry off the *Fat* of half the Land.   (p. 3)

Vignettes of the songwriter Henry Carey and poet Aaron Hill illustrate the opposite form of Tigellius's inconstancy: those who "Oblige you cruelly *against* your *Will*" and will not cease singing their songs or reciting their fustian verse (p. 6).

---

[52] See *A New Canting Dictionary* (1725), s.v. *bacon*: "Bacon, in the Canting Sense, is the Prize, of whatever kind, which Robbers make in their Enterprizes. *He has sav'd his Bacon; i.e.*, he has himself escap'd the Hue-and-Cry, and carry'd off his Prize to boot: Whence it is commonly us'd for any narrow Escape."

Miller breaks off from his Horatian model with an extended attack (taking up almost one-quarter of the poem) on the hypocrisy, selfishness, and rigid orthodoxy of the Bishop of London, Edmund Gibson, who managed the ecclesiastical interest for Walpole.[53] The reason for the attack seems to be that Gibson objected to Miller's continuing to write for the stage as unbecoming a clergyman. Upon Miller's refusal to abandon the stage without assurance of financial security, Gibson withdrew his patronage – inciting Miller's retaliation.[54] The attack on Gibson coupled with Miller's frequent satires on Walpole surely blocked his further preferment and encouraged his allegiance to the Opposition.

Despite *Seasonable Reproof*'s models in Horace's *Satires* I.3 and 4,[55] Miller's tone and stance are quite Juvenalian: the outsider decrying the vices of the court. It was this tone that no doubt caused at least one reader to believe the anonymous satire was written by Pope,[56] an inference made plausible by its being printed for Pope's bookseller at the time, Lawton Gilliver.[57]

THOMAS GILBERT

In Thomas Gilbert, we find a young satirist whose inspiration and models in Pope and Juvenal are everywhere obvious and who repeatedly honors Pope as the poet of virtue. Gilbert's major satires – *A View of the Town* (1735), *The World Unmask'd* (1738), *A Panegyric on a Court* (1739), *The First Satire of Juvenal* (1740), and *The Second Epistle of the First Book of Horace* (1741) – relentlessly condemn the vices and corruptions of an age in decline. Although the scant biographical information about Gilbert reveals no personal links with Opposition circles, his persistent and sharp attacks on Walpole and the Court and his steady rehearsal of stock Opposition polemic clearly mark him as "a foot soldier in the opposition's army," as Howard Weinbrot calls him.[58]

---

[53] On this section of the poem, Powell Stewart, "A Bibliographical Contribution to Biography: James Miller's *Seasonable Reproof*," *The Library*, ser. 5, vol. 3 (1949), 293–9.

[54] Furthermore, *Seasonable Reproof* returns to the Rundle controversy of 1733–1735 by extolling the virtue of Thomas Rundle, whom Gibson had opposed for the see of Gloucester. On Miller's concern in the Rundle controversy, Paula O'Brien, "The Life and Works of James Miller, 1704–1744, with Particular Reference to the Satiric Content of His Poetry and Plays" (Ph.D. thesis, University of London, 1979), 36–7. On his advancement in the clergy and his apologia for dramatic writing, see Preface to Miller, *Miscellaneous Works* (1741).

[55] Miller takes up only briefly Horace's fourth satire. Like Horace, he defends himself against the charge of writing unfair, personal libel. He avows his contempt of such satire: "None, but the *Vicious*, in my Verses *bleed*: / ... / Not at the *Man*, but at the *Vice* I strike" (p. 23). Rhetorically asking Argyll if he is to blame for writing just satire, Miller answers, "No, 'tis a *British* Right I still shall claim."

[56] *Prompter*, no. 120 (2 Jan. 1736).

[57] James McLaverty, "Lawton Gilliver: Pope's Bookseller," *Studies in Bibliography*, 32 (1979), 101–24.

[58] Weinbrot, *Eighteenth-Century Satire*, 43. There are several hints that Gilbert suffered a personal injury from someone in the church; note the anti-clerical tone of *A View of the Town* and a comment addressed to a cleric in *A Panegyric on a Court*, 21.

254 THE CULTURAL POLITICS OF OPERA, 1720–1742

Writing in 1747, some five years after Walpole's fall, when he collected his poems, Gilbert's choice of title-page epigraph shows him looking back at his early highly political poems and realizing he has, like Horace, opened his whole life to view:

Votivâ
Veluti descript Tabellâ
Vita patet —— Juvenis.   Horace

The old poet's whole life is open to view,
as if painted on a votive tablet.[59]

But Gilbert evinced no regret for the topical satire of his youth:

> I have freely declared my Sentiments of some great Men, whose Measures were in my Opinion destructive to the Interest of the Kingdom. ... [I] could not help expressing indignation against him [Walpole], in such a manner, as his conduct appeared to deserve.[60]

Gilbert's *A View of the Town* censures the "flagrant Vices committed by the corrupt Part of the Clergy" and lashes at the fashionable ambitions, follies, and vices (avarice, adultery, sodomy) in town. Exploiting Pope's principle that "Praise undeserv'd is scandal in disguise,"[61] with exaggerated and unwarranted praise, *A Panegyric on a Court* indicts those at Court, primarily the King and Walpole, for Britain's submissive posture toward France and Spain. According to the ironic panegyrist, George II reigns "In Peace, the Dread of *France* and Scourge of *Spain*." While "Each Merchant Ship secure from Plunder sails" because Walpole has made Great Britain "the Scourge of foreign Foes" for causing Spain to dread Britain as a naval power and quickly dispatch tribute for plundered ships (p. 8). At the moral center of the satire are its non-ironic general portraits of statesmen and patriots who labor for their country's welfare, guard liberty, and inveigh against corruption (pp. 14–15).

The World Unmask'd

In two of Gilbert's satires, opera is situated in the politically charged atmosphere of the Depredations Crisis with Spain, which was the run-up to the War of Jenkins' Ear. The oppositional stance of *The World Unmask'd* is unmistakable. Gilbert's title alludes to the traditional purpose of satire, to tear off the mask of hypocrisy and vice. The poem's gallery of satiric portraits personally indicts the Court poet and Queen Caroline's favorite Stephen Duck, the Laureate Colley

---

[59] Horace, *Satires, Epistles, Ars Poetica*, trans. Rushton. Gilbert has adapted Horace's original:

ut omnis
votiva pateat veluti descripta tabella
vita senis. (*Satires*, II.32–4)

[60] Thomas Gilbert, *Poems on Several Occasions* (1747), Dedication and p. 123. The collected *Poems* reprints all the satires discussed here except *A Panegyric on a Court*; *The World Unmask'd* is retitled *A Satire*.

[61] *The First Epistle of the Second Book of Horace Imitated* (*Epistle to Augustus*) line 413; in *Imitations of Horace*, ed. John Butt. The Twickenham Edition of the Poems of Alexander Pope, vol. 4, 2nd ed. (New Haven, Conn.: Yale University Press, 1953), 229.

OPERA IN FORMAL VERSE SATIRE   255

Cibber, and pensioned poets, while Walpole is the object of an ironic panegyric portrait.

The dialogue of *The World Unmask'd* is set off by the poet's friend-adversary, who counsels him to leave off writing satire and to forgo venting his spleen at the *beaux* of the fashionable world: "Forbear to rail, 'tis safer to commend!" The *adversarius* concedes that although vices may abound –

> Tho' Fools and Coxcombs every where abound,
> And Friends, or honest Men are seldom found;
> Tho' to an *Eunuch*'s Voice such Charms belong,
> That Families are ruined for a Song,
> And, without Benefit of Propagation,
> Gay F——*i* [Farinelli] Cuckolds half the Nation.[62]

– to "treat those harmless Things, / As if they libelled Ministers or Kings," only enrages readers and makes the satirist an enemy of half the world. The *adversarius* here functions as an apologist for the social order, who tries to moderate his friend's indignation. Yet, in effect, the friend-adversary unwittingly concedes all the vices and follies the satirist is straining to lash.

At first, it seems that the ruin produced by Farinelli's charming singing is financial, for Gilbert here echoes satiric accounts of women and *beaux* of the *beau monde* ruining their families and fortunes by the fabulous sums they lavished on the singer. Now with Farinelli explicitly designated a eunuch and not even the benefit of propagation when he cuckolds half the nation, the passage recalls the sexual services the eunuch singers supposedly provided their English admirers; the ruin caused by Farinelli's singing is also one of sexual and moral aberration.[63]

Partisan polemic comes to the fore as the *adversarius* tries to minimize the consequences of Farinelli's departure from England. Despite lamenting admirers and the vast sums squandered on Farinelli, the *adversarius* claims some good may now come from Farinelli's having left Britain for Spain the previous June:

> Tho' tender Virgins of the *British* Isle
> Mourn *Farinelli*'s Absence from our Soil,
> Perhaps our Trade some Benefit may boast,
> To recompence the Loss of such a Toast.
> For now the *Syren* is the Taste of *Spain*,
> No more will *Spaniards* plunder o'er the Main,
> But ravished with his Song, enchanted lie,
> While our rich Merchants sail unheeded by;
> No more shall Lust of Gold their Sons entice,
> But *Farinelli* be the reigning Vice.
> Such the great Pow'r of Kings his Notes delight,
> He kneels an Eunuch, rises up a Knight.   (p. 6)

[62] Page 5. Punctuation of the first edition is revised following the 1747 edition, whose punctuation clarifies the meaning.

[63] On castrati and how contemporaries perceived them as fostering sexual aberration, see Introduction, note 3.

256 THE CULTURAL POLITICS OF OPERA, 1720–1742

Here Gilbert turns Farinelli's decamping to Spain into a reminder of Spanish depredations on British shipping, an issue the Opposition had inflamed and used to force Britain into war. Farinelli's enchanting, ravishing, and enervating singing will now affect the Spanish, and British shipping and gold will supposedly be safe from Spanish greed. The last line alludes to the mistaken British belief that the King of Spain had granted Farinelli a knighthood; he was granted instead several household appointments and pensions. He did later receive the Order of Calatrava in 1750.[64]

If the poet is still resolved to write verse in the vain effort to achieve wealth and fame, his friend urges him to abandon his oppositional Juvenalian satire, become a Court poet, and "To Great *Augustus* Praises tune your Lyre" (p. 6). By "Augustus" we are to think of Britain's monarch, yet the comparison to the Roman emperor by the *adversarius* inadvertently raises the charge that Britain's George Augustus was insensitive to art and literature and a cause of the prevailing False Taste.[65]

Wanting only friends who are virtuous and rejecting for himself as unfitting the role of Court poet, the poet will not write panegyrics to Walpole, who (he affirms ironically)

> Preserves our Commerce safe from Shore to Shore,
> While *Europe* trembles at our Cannons roar.   (p. 9)

In the remainder of the poem, Gilbert takes his cue from Pope to show the sources of False Taste at the center of the Court. On the poet's mind are a moralist's themes of the corruptions of wealth, the woes of avarice and penury, and the sorrows of vain fools who seek fame. One Titus, who is beset by "Thirst of universal Fame," resembles the Man of Taste who must declare his opinion

> Alike on Trifles, or important Things,
> On Plays, Religion, Opera's, or Kings.   (p. 14)

We certainly know to take operas and plays as trifles; but not religion and kings. Titus, a Man of Taste, does not.

If the satirist's parade of fools who seek fame and renown has not sufficiently chastened one who strives "to catch at universal Praise," we are reminded that merit is not always rewarded,

> That *Pope* in Poetry has suffer'd Scandal,
> In Physic *Nichols*, and in Music, *Handell.*[66]   (p. 15)

---

[64] On British response to Farinelli's departure from Britain to Spain, Thomas McGeary, "Farinelli in Madrid: Opera, Politics, and the War of Jenkins' Ear," *Musical Quarterly*, 82 (1998), 383–421.

[65] Gilbert associates the Hanoverian reign with the decadence of Rome when, to clinch his case, the *adversarius* asks the poet, if his goal is to achieve fame,

> Why then's your blotted Page with Satire stain'd
> As if a *Nero* or *Domitian* reign'd? (p. 6)

[66] Francis (Frank) Nicholls (1699–1778), son of a barrister, obtained a medical degree from Oxford and became skilled in anatomy; while still a student he was appointed

First Satire of Juvenal

In his final major satire, *The First Satire of Juvenal Imitated*, Gilbert justifies his writing verse by asking, as did Juvenal, if "such a swarm of Scribblers plague this age," why shouldn't he too write? Yet it is disgust at the topics chosen by the "youthful Poetasters" that ultimately drives him to satire, "To warn corrupted Statesmen of their Fate" (p. 5).

In adapting Juvenal to contemporary Britain, Gilbert admits that some lines are "inserted that glance at the reigning Vices of the Age, without any Authority from Juvenal" (Preface). Some poets choose to write about

> What Ladies an *Italian* Favour boast,
> (For him the Fair Sex innocently toast)
> When the shrill Eunuch warbles out his Charms,
> What Rapture, Gods! to pant within his Arms!
> His thrilling Notes their ravish'd Souls employ,
> Tho' drudging Husbands scarce can give them Joy.   (p. 4)

By associating castrato singers with the sexual vices of the age (as did Juvenal in *Satire* VI.368ff.), Gilbert further emphasizes the moral corruption caused by Italian opera.[67]

Following his model, Gilbert engages an imaginary opponent in banter that reveals the satirist's anti-ministerial position. The ministerial advocate asks rhetorically if there is no subject worthy of being spared the satirist's wit. His proposal that "Sir *Robert*'s Virtues claim a just Applause" is curtly rebuffed with the wish, "*I leave Sir* Robert—— *to his Country's Laws.*" Likewise, the suggestion that the mighty squadrons of the British fleet that make Spain tremble deserve encomia arouses the Opposition rebuke: Walpole refused to let the British navy fight to protect shipping, and all he gained by the Convention of the Pardo was the Spanish King's signature on a treaty.

Gilbert follows Juvenal in painting the corruptions of wealth, sex, rank, and money that incite him to satire. Walpole, the Court, and ministers receive

---

professor of anatomy. In the early 1730s, he moved to London and was the leading anatomical teacher in England and had a successful medical practice, becoming a fellow of the Royal College of Physicians in 1732. The nature of Nicholls's scandal is unclear, although he was headstrong and erratic. Scandal may have been arisen due to his notoriety as a militant deist (if not agnostic); see George Clark, *A History of the Royal College of Physicians of London*, 2 vols. (Oxford: Clarendon Press, 1966), 2:503–5; and H. M. Sinclair and A. H. T. Robb-Smith, *A Short History of Anatomical Teaching in Oxford* (Oxford: Oxford University Press, 1950), 26–30.

On the calumny against Pope, Guerinot, *Pamphlet Attacks on Pope*. The scandal against Pope and Handel could refer to the Author's Bill, passed in 1737, which some observers believed was motivated by pique against them; see correspondence between the fourth Earl of Shaftesbury and James Harris, in *Music and Theatre in Handel's World*, ed. Donald Burrows and Rosemary Dunhill (Oxford: Oxford University Press, 2002), 26, 28, 29, and 57; and *Handel: Collected Documents*, ed. Burrows et al., 3:263.

[67] On the Italian castrati as sources of sexual corruption and immorality in Britain, see Introduction, note 3.

258 THE CULTURAL POLITICS OF OPERA, 1720–1742

due mention. His reference to eunuchs does parallel Juvenal's original (line 22, where wealthy eunuchs who were former slaves take wives for the sake of respectability); but in London we recognize again British women showering favors on Italian castrati:

> Eunuchs by the Ladies Favour thrive,
> And in the Sunshine of a Palace live.   (p. 7)

Gilbert closes by perhaps optimistically asserting the utility of satire. Whereas Juvenal held up the example of the satirist Lucilius, Gilbert substitutes Pope, whose satire the fools flee, reforms the atheist's life, and the villain dreads more than the law.

FOUR SATIRES

Opera is given prominence in the panorama of vices and corruptions displayed by the anonymous *Four Satires* (1737). The title-page epigraph from Persius ironically invites the reader:

> Aspice & hæc, si fortè aliquid decoctius audis.

> Look here too, if you have an ear for anything
> of the finer sort.[68]

Apologizing for the alarm the term *satire* often arouses, the anonymous author assures his reader that the following satires reflect on no private person's scandal "any further than he may be a public Nuisance, or the Cause of some Vice or Folly which affects the Nation in general" (pp. iii–iv). Notwithstanding, Britain teems with numerous "particular Persons" whose nuisance, vices, and follies warrant their public exposure. The four satires go on to expose religious disputants (no. IV), quacks (no. III), political writers (no. II), and a swarm of national vices (no. I).

Juvenal is the point of departure for the first satire, "On National Vices. Inscrib'd to K—t, S—, H—d—egg—er, F—rn—lli, &c." The epigraphs from Juvenal's first and sixth Satires set the tone and themes for the satire:

> Quandoquidem inter nos sanctissima Divitiarum
> Majestas.——

> For no deity is held in such reverence amongst
> us as Wealth.

> Prima peregrinos obscæna Pecunia Mores
> Intulit, & turpi fregerunt sæcula luxu
> Divitiæ Molles.

> Filthy lucre first brought in amongst us foreign ways;
> wealth enervated and corrupted the ages with foul
> indulgences.[69]

---

[68] Persius, *Satires* I.125; *Juvenal and Persius*, trans. G. G. Ramsay. Loeb Classical Library (Cambridge, Mass.: Harvard University Press, 1950).

[69] Juvenal, *Satires* I.112–13, and VI.298–300; *Juvenal and Persius*, ed. Ramsay.

OPERA IN FORMAL VERSE SATIRE   259

Like Juvenal's first Satire (lines 87–146), "On National Vices" elaborates the twin, complementary corruptions associated with wealth: greed/avarice and extravagance, the vices of getting and spending money. The names hinted in the title exemplify the two vices. Robert Knight was treasurer of the South Sea Company, and Sir Robert Sutton, MP and Privy Counsellor, more recently was the Charitable Corporation director held most responsible for the frauds and expelled from the Commons in 1732. The South Sea Company and the Charitable Corporation are examples of the companies that had enriched their directors ("Great Thieves," the author calls them), impoverished their investors, and stood for the corruption bred by the modern financial system.

After describing avarice, the source of "our public Woes," the satirist turns to the corruptions arising from the misuse of wealth. Here Heidegger and Farinelli (alluded to in the title) represent the luxury and extravagance of the opera and masquerades spawned by profligate spending of money. The second epigraph (above) from Juvenal reveals it is the effects on Britain's character of expensive foreign vices and effeminate follies that most alarm the satirist. Here again we have reminders of Britain at a Machiavellian moment. Not far in the satire's background looms the Depredations Crisis, against which is juxtaposed the domestic threat from opera, which distracts from the higher civic concern for national self-defense:

> Do ye not Sums immense subscribe
> To benefit a squeaking Tribe?
> Deaf to impendent War's Alarms,
> Your Ears are caught with minstrel Charms.   (p. 13)

Italian opera's "emasculated Crew" will accomplish what France, Spain, and Papists failed to do:

> What *France* ambitious, leagu'd with *Spain*,
> Cou'd ne'er affect on open Plain;
> Nor *Jesuits* by secret Wile,
> Who hank'ring haunt this fav'rite Isle;
> Lo! an emasculated Crew
> The Sons of Liberty subdue.
> Lull'd by the soothing Pow'rs of Sound,
> Our Lyon couches on the Ground.   (p. 13)

The author is fixated on opera as the cause of the national malaise:

> … warbling Eunuchs on our Stage,
> Vocal Corruptors of this Age!   (p. 13)

For Britain to escape her fate, Britons must adopt "*Rome's* more warlike Shews" and let "inbred Roughness … cruel Sports, and bloody Sights, / Be still our national Delights." An unnamed Genius is charged to break the enchantment of the eunuchs' songs and to rouse the land from lethargy before "ev'ry martial Soul's unman'd" (p. 14). Recalling Britain's great European victories under Queen Anne, the satirist fears that if the spell of opera's enchanting lethargy is not broken, France will avenge Marlborough's victories at Blenheim and Ramillies.

260   THE CULTURAL POLITICS OF OPERA, 1720–1742

THE MODERN ENGLISHMAN

The expanding sway of opera and foreign taste as corruptors of the age is further censured in the anonymous *The Modern Englishman* (1738),[70] whose indictment is far more pointed and vicious than the gentler Horatian satires of False Taste we have already seen in Chapter 9.

With little irony or subtlety of tone, the poetic monologue addressed to the Muse of Satire denounces the invasion of foreign taste from Italy and France and again shows the political dimension of False Taste. An extended passage on Farinelli brings the satire into the orbit of propaganda against Walpole's pacific policy toward the Spanish depredations.

A line from the title-page epigraph –

> Good Sense *is scorn'd* —— what *Rivals all is* Taste.

– characterizes the Town's taste in a satiric inversion of the moral of Pope's *Epistle to Burlington*:

> Something there is more needful than Expence,
> And something previous ev'n to Taste —'tis Sense.[71]

The Town's "Fine Taste" is denounced in opposition to "Virtue, Sense, and Truth" (p. 7). That corruption and enslavement are a consequence of luxury and the past fifteen years of Walpole's rule are suggested by the satirist's opening rehearsal of that commonplace of Whig history, the decline of Rome and the Progress of Liberty to Great Britain. When "Luxury and Lust" enslaved Rome, science and art expired, the bards were neglected, vice ran free, and Minerva left Rome for "ancient Albion," where Britons were virtuous, brave, and just.

The poet would prefer to "speak my Country's loud Applause," but truth requires he must write of "A Nation fill'd with Folly, Fraud, and Vice." After doing so for three pages, he asks Satire to "scourge a guilty Land" of the follies transplanted from abroad,

> The reigning Foible of the Times explode,
> This Thing call'd Taste, this new fam'd Alamode!
> This Term for something that was never found,
> Which leaves our Sense and Reason lost in Sound.   (p. 6)

Opera ("Sound") proves the corruption of the present times, and the satirist shows the consequences of the empty sound of Italian opera. Imagine, he asks, how past Englishmen would regret to see their venerable estates and fortunes now squandered and mortgaged:

---

[70] Also published in 1743 with the title *The Characters of the Age; or the Modern Englishman*.

[71] *Epistle to Burlington; in Epistles to Several Persons (Moral Essays)*, ed. F. W. Bateson. The Twickenham Edition of the Poems of Alexander Pope, vol. 3, pt. 2, 2nd ed. (New Haven, Conn.: Yale University Press, 1961), p. 140, lines 41–2. A Dublin reprint of the poem in 1739 as "By A. P. Esq;" was certainly meant to suggest Pope as the author.

OPERA IN FORMAL VERSE SATIRE   261

> For Baubles, Toys, and all the foreign Trades
> Of Operas, Balls, Ridottos, Masquerades;
> Cooks, Tumblers, Dancers, Taylors, Politicians,
> Hair-frizzers, Eunuchs, *Frenchmen* and Musicians.   (p. 8)

He describes the effects of luxury in the way wives and matrons spend their time in town:

> … in soft lethargic Pleasures drown'd,
> Gently move on in one eternal Round!
> From Day to Day, but just repeat the same,
> Rise, Eat and Drink, undress and Sleep again;
> Except an *Opera*, or a *Masquerade*,
> Or else a Sunday's Visit's to be paid:
> …
> Next Home to Dress and Paint, and then away
> To hear some sweet *Italian* Music play.   (p. 14)

The spread of Folly in Britain is suggested by the metaphor of a crescendo of music and exemplified by the growing crowds of women leading the admiring crowds raving after Farinelli:

> In swelling Sounds extensive Folly grows,
> Who now the Value of a *Quaverer* knows?
> (*Tho it's the same, say but he comes from* Rome,
> *Were he an Idiot with a whistle Spoon.*)
> Lo! throngs of Females, big with Eunuchs Song,
> Leading Mankind like tattling Babes along.   (p. 10)

But Farinelli's departure for the Spanish court is a catastrophe for Great Britain:

> See *F——li* from the Stage retire!
> Bright Splendors fade, and dying Nymphs expire!
> "*Lov'd* Far——li! *quickly him restore,*
> "*Come chanting Angel whom we all adore;*
> "*Sweet* Senesino *is already gone,*
> "*If thou art lost three Kingdoms are undone!*"   (p. 10)

In despair, adorers of Farinelli would pay anything for the return of "*The pretty harmless soft melodious Thing!*"

The satirist here breaks in and urges the cruel Farinelli to return to England and his fair admirers:

> Fly! Warbler, fly the torrid Climes of Spain,
> And let the Fair [British women] enjoy their own again;
> The hated Kingdom [Spain] leave that forc'd thee hence: (p. 11)

But he realizes,

> Vain Thought——! Redress can Mer——ts [Merchants] hope to see,
> *When that proud Court durst make a Prize of thee!*   (p. 11)

The futility of expecting redress for merchants as long as Spain retains Farinelli indicts Walpole's policy toward Spain. If Britain can't enforce its opera

262 THE CULTURAL POLITICS OF OPERA, 1720–1742

company's contractual rights with a mere opera singer, it is unlikely merchants can expect the government will obtain reparations for their greater losses.

JOHNSON'S *LONDON*

Samuel Johnson takes as his model for *London* (1738) Juvenal's third Satire, where Umbricius describes to the poet in livid detail all the vices and corruption of city life that lead him to leave Rome; by contrast, the country emerges as a positive norm.[72] Johnson transports the setting to the banks of the Thames at Greenwich. He adds topical political attacks that have no parallels in Juvenal, including opera as among the ills of London.

While awaiting a wherry, Thales (the rechristened Umbricius) – who is a 'true Briton' and moral center of the poem – and the poet kneel to kiss the consecrated ground where Elizabeth was born and to

> … call Britannia's glories back to view;
> Behold her cross triumphant on the main,
> The guard of commerce, and the dread of Spain,
> Ere masquerades debauch'd, excise oppress'd,
> Or English honour grew a standing jest.[73]

The evocation of the glories of Elizabeth's reign is a common Patriot Opposition theme and a rebuke of Britain under Walpole's rule.

Thales then vigorously denounces all that disgusts him about London and recites Walpole's crimes. In London, Thales says,

> Here let those reign, whom pensions can incite
> To vote a patriot black, a courtier white;
> Explain their country's dear-bought rights away,
> And plead for pirates in the face of day;
> …
> Let such raise palaces, and manors buy,
> Collect a tax, or farm a lottery,
> With warbling eunuchs fill our silenc'd stage,[74]
> And lull to servitude a thoughtless Age.
> (lines 51–4, 57–60)

In this brief passage, Johnson deftly touches on most of the usual themes of Opposition propaganda: Walpole's use of pensions and appointments to create dependent politicians, the loss of British liberty, the servile appeasement of

---

[72] Weinbrot, "Johnson's *London* and Juvenal's Third Satire: The Country as 'Ironic Norm,'" pp. 164–71 in *Eighteenth-Century Satire*, defends the usual reading of the poem wherein the country is a positive norm.

[73] Samuel Johnson, *London: A Poem in Imitation of the Third Satire of Juvenal*, pp. 45–61 in *The Yale Edition of the Works of Samuel Johnson*. Vol. 6. *Poems*, ed. E. L. McAdam, Jr. (New Haven, Conn.: Yale University Press, 1964), p. 49, lines 26–30.

[74] Citing here the first edition. Johnson later altered the phrase to "fill a licens'd stage."

OPERA IN FORMAL VERSE SATIRE   263

Spain in the face of its depredations on British merchant shipping, and Walpole's wealth acquired by corruption.[75]

Whatever wit or thought London may have had, has fled from the stage that has been silenced of Opposition drama by the recent Licensing Act and supplanted by the "warbling eunuchs" of Italian opera. The immediate inclusion of opera with political measures of taxation, bribery, and running lotteries imputes it to be a deliberate part of the government's plan to subjugate Britain by diverting or lulling it with Italian music – as Augustus distracted Rome with spectacles and games.[76] Suggesting comparisons between Rome and Britain suggests that under Walpole and the Hanoverians, Britain may share Rome's fate.

The suggestion of deliberate subjugation of Britain by the monarch is not completely far-fetched, for, since the founding of the Royal Academy of Music, George I and II had awarded £1,000 yearly to the opera company at the Haymarket theatre (see Chapter 2) and Walpole and other ministers were subscribers and directors of the opera.

London became a popular Opposition tract, calling for four more editions within two months. George Lyttelton, secretary to Prince Frederick, is said to have "carried a copy of the poem in high glee to Pope"[77] – validating Donald Greene's observation the poem was "a stridently political versification of the polemic stock-in-trade of the 'patriot' opposition to Walpole."[78]

The image of the young Johnson espousing anti-ministerial, opposition-minded Whig polemic conflicts with the more common impression of the mature Johnson as a deeply committed Tory, defending absolute governments and bulwark of establishment and monarchy. But F. R. Lock has shown *London*

---

[75] The political context and references are pointed out in John Hardy, "Johnson's *London*: The Country Versus the City," *Studies in the Eighteenth Century*. Papers presented at the David Nichol Smith Memorial Seminar, Canberra 1966, ed. R. F. Brissenden (Toronto: University of Toronto Press, 1968), 251–68; John Cannon, *Samuel Johnson and the Politics of Hanoverian England* (Oxford: Clarendon Press, 1994); Thomas Kaminski, *The Early Career of Samuel Johnson* (New York, N.Y.: Oxford University Press, 1987), 14–23, 98–100; and Greene, *The Politics of Samuel Johnson*, 81–92 (the poem "rehearses all the commonplaces of contemporary Opposition propaganda against the Walpole regime," p. 88). On Johnson's response to the fall of Walpole, Robert Giddings, "The Fall of Orgilio: Samual Johnson as Parliamentary Reporter," pp. 86–106 in *Samuel Johnson: New Critical Essays*, ed. Isobel Grundy (London: Vision Press, 1984).

[76] On the evidence of Augustus distracting Rome with spectacles and circuses, Richard C. Beacham, *Spectacle Entertainments of Early Imperial Rome* (New Haven, Conn.: Yale University Press, 1999). Thomas Blackwell identified Augustus's intentions: "[His] Motive for multiplying them [shows and entertainments] was of a more serious Nature. They fed the Curiosity of a restless People, engrossed their Thoughts, and made them forget all Affairs of State, in which they had formerly so great a share"; *Memoirs of the Court of Augustus*, 3 vols. (1753–1763), 3:379.

[77] Hardy, "Johnson's *London*: The Country Versus the City," 268.

[78] *The Yale Edition of the Works of Samuel Johnson*. Vol. 10, *Political Writings*, ed. Donald Green (New Haven, Conn.: Yale University Press, 1977), xxvi.

264   THE CULTURAL POLITICS OF OPERA, 1720–1742

and other works of 1738 and 1739 were products of a young, struggling writer trying to make his way in literary London.[79]

RIVAL WIVES

Whereas George II had his German mistresses and infidelities to Queen Caroline, Walpole's domestic life was no less reproachable, though hardly beyond acceptable bounds. Since 1724 he had kept Maria (Molly) Skerrett, a stay maker's daughter, and annually drew £1,000 of public funds for her upkeep, all the while tolerating his own wife Catherine's infidelities.[80] In *The Beggar's Opera*, the name of Polly Peachum was probably meant to recall Molly Skerrett, and Peachum's remark that Robin "spends his life among women" (I.iv) likely alludes to Walpole's personal life.

Molly bore Walpole two children while his wife was yet alive. Catherine died on August 20, 1737, and Walpole outraged a good deal of the country when he announced his marriage to Molly on 3 March 1738.[81] She died of a miscar-

---

[79]   F. P. Lock, "'To preserve order and support Monarchy': Johnson's Political Writings," pp. 175–194 in *Samuel Johnson: New Contexts for a New Century*, ed. Howard D. Weinbrot (San Marino, Calif.: Huntington Library, 2014). Lock cogently argues it is misguided to attempt to find consistency of political thought across a writer's career. Political opposition to Walpole is also conveyed in Johnson's *Marmor Norfolciense* (1739) and *A Compleat Vindication of the Licensers of the Stage* (1739). See also Kaminski, *Early Career of Samuel Johnson*, 100–4; and Weinbrot, *Formal Strain*, 165–91.

  London has been read as revealing Johnson's Jacobitism by Howard Erskine-Hill, "The Political Character of Samuel Johnson," pp. 107–36 in *Samuel Johnson: New Critical Essays*, ed. Isobel Grundy (London: Vision Press, 1984), 125–6; Erskine-Hill, *Poetry of Opposition and Revolution: Dryden to Wordsworth* (Oxford: Clarendon Press, 1996), 119–26; and J. C. D. Clark, *Samuel Johnson: Literature, Religion and English Cultural Politics from the Restoration to Romanticism* (Cambridge: Cambridge University Press, 1994), 41, 145–6). This Jacobite reading of *London* has been effectively challenged by Cannon, *Johnson and the Politics of Hanoverian England*, 46–8; Greene, *Politics of Samuel Johnson*, xxix–lvii; and Howard D. Weinbrot, "Johnson and Jacobitism Redux: Evidence, Interpretation, and Intellectual History," *Age of Johnson*, 8 (1997), 99–100. Kaminski suggests that although Johnson may have had Jacobite sympathies, he acquiesced in the *de facto* Hanoverian kingship; *Early Career of Samuel Johnson*, 105. William Kupersmith, though, argues the poem would appeal to a reader of any politics: "Johnson's *London* in Context: Imitations of Roman Satire in the Later 1730s," *Age of Johnson*, 10 (1999), 1–28.

[80]   For Walpole's relations with Catherine and Molly, J. H. Plumb, *Sir Robert Walpole: The King's Minister* (London: Cresset, 1960), 78, 112–13, 114, 114 n. 2.

[81]   For examples of the disdain for Molly and ridicule of Walpole for marrying her, see the Earl of Egmont's diary, Historical Manuscripts Commission. *Manuscripts of the Earl of Egmont. Diary of the First Earl of Egmont* (Viscount Perceval), 3 vols. (London: His Majesty's Stationery Office, 1920–1923), 2:250, 469, and 471. Egmont writes about "Sir Robert marrying his whore," and copied out a poem that charges that Walpole took Molly as his wife "That he may rob the public, one way more, / The only way he never rob'd before." *The Secret History of an Old Shoe* (1734) viciously attacks Molly

OPERA IN FORMAL VERSE SATIRE   265

riage followed by a fever on 4 June, an event which deeply affected him. Public indignation was aroused later in February 1742, when, after his own ennoblement, his securing a patent of precedent as an earl's daughter for his and Molly's daughter Maria was seen as an insult to British honor.[82] While Molly was alive, Pope had alluded to her as Phryne, a notorious Athenian courtesan, in the *Epistle to Bathurst* (1732); and in *One Thousand Seven Hundred and Thirty Eight* (1738), he portrayed her as Vice Triumphant, the Whore of Babylon, the prostitute Theodora who became Emperor Justinian's wife, and a symbol of corruption at the highest level of government.[83]

Molly's death provided an Opposition satirist the opportunity for a vicious attack on ministerial corruption and Britain's political decline, for which opera again serves as evidence. *The Rival Wives. Or, the Greeting of Clarissa to Skirra in the Elysian Shades* (August 1738) is set in the underworld as Clarissa (Catherine Walpole) greets the recently deceased Molly Skerrett (Skirra).[84] The wronged Clarissa will now have revenge on her low-born rival. In fact, she is a mouthpiece for stock Patriot Opposition propaganda against Walpole. Clarissa charges Molly kept Walpole distracted in dalliance and so shifts onto Molly much of the blame for a Britain sunk in sloth, luxury, and corruption, a nation the scorn and dupe of France and Spain. Like Anthony, Walpole abandoned statecraft:

> Debas'd, he [Walpole] cry'd, let who will *rule the Main*,
> I for this Kiss would give up all for *S——n*.   (p. 12)

Britain's sons, eager to revenge the insults of her foes, are now grown degenerate, one sign of which is their love of opera:

> From martial Camps and Fields their Youth retire
> To lulling Sounds, and female soft Desire;
> From the shrill Trumpet's Clang, the Drum's loud Note,
> They fly enraptur'd, to an *Eunuch's* Throat.   (p. 15)

---

and accuses her father of procuring her to be Walpole's mistress.

Walpole and Molly also appear in Henry Fielding's *The Welsh Opera* (1731) [revised as *The Grub-street Opera* (1731)]; David Morgan, *The Country Bard: or, the Modern Courtiers* (1739), compared Walpole to Macheath for trying to legitimate Molly. See also *The Constant Lovers: or, the Pleasures of Matrimony* (1738) and *The Greatest Statesman and the Happiest Fair, a Pastoral* (1738).

[82] See *Modern Quality. An Epistle to Miss M—— W—— on Her Late Acquired Honour. From a Lady of Real Quality* (1742) and a letter to the *Westminster Journal*, no. 13 (20 Feb. 1742), reprinted in *Letters from the Westminster Journal* (collected ed., 1747), 77–83.

[83] *Epistle to Bathurst*, lines 121–2; *One Thousand Seven Hundred and Thirty Eight. A Dialogue Something like Horace*, lines 141–61; see James M. Osborn, "Pope, the Byzantine Empress, and Walpole's Whore," *Review of English Studies*, n.s., 6 (1955), 372–82; and Weinbrot, *Alexander Pope*, 317–18.

[84] Osborne, "Pope and Walpole's Whore," points out parallels in the description of Molly in Pope's poem and *Rival Wives*. *Rival Wives* was reprinted in the Opposition anthology *A New Miscellany for the Year 1738* (1738), 50–8.

266 THE CULTURAL POLITICS OF OPERA, 1720-1742

A reply appearing the same month, *The Rival Wives Answer'd: or, Skirra to Clarissa*, praises Walpole and asserts the crimes of both wives are equal. The reply is among many poems that used the marriage as an occasion for panegyric.[85]

WHITEHEAD'S *MANNERS*

One satire, Paul Whitehead's *Manners* (1739), attacked those at Court and in the Ministry so sharply that the Lords voted the poem "a wicked, malicious and infamous Libel, containing divers scandalous Matters, and highly reflecting on several Lords of this House."[86]

Whitehead and his publisher, Robert Dodsley, were called before the Lords to face the charges. Whitehead fled; but Dodsley appeared, and remaining copies of the poem were seized. Fined £70 and sentenced to three weeks' imprisonment, Dodsley become a martyr to freedom of the press and a symbol of British liberty. Chesterfield and Lyttelton offered to make his bail, and other Opposition peers, including Lords Marchmont, Granville, and Bathurst, offered their services; Dodsley was released upon his own petition after a week.[87] Although Dodsley had published the second of Pope's two 1738 *Dialogues* without government response, Pope took the prosecution of *Manners* as a warning to moderate the severity of his own attacks on George II and the Court.[88]

Whitehead's biographer Edward Thompson makes clear his affiliation with the Patriot Opposition: "As the party of the Prince of *Wales's* Court began to embody, he sided with his Royal Highness's partisans, and became the Champion and Bard of *Leicester-House*." Stressing how his satires declare his strong patriotism and zeal for liberty, Thompson praised Whitehead's enthusiasm for

---

[85] The marriage was also celebrated in *The Greatest Statesman and the Happiest Fair* (1738) and the ballad *The Constant Lovers: or, the Pleasures of Matrimony* (1738).

[86] Resolution of 12 February 1739; *Journals of the House of Lords*, 25 (1736–41), 290. On the Lords debate, Cobbett, *The Parliamentary History of England*, 10 (1737–1739), 1325–33. *Manners*, its author, and other Opposition writers are denounced at length in *Observations on the Present Taste for Poetry; With Remarks, in Particular, on a Piece Lately Published by Mr. Whitehead, called Manners* (1739), 26–37, 42–53.

[87] Ralph Straus, *Robert Dodsley: Poet, Publisher and Playwright* (London: John Lane, 1910), 49–54; Harry M. Solomon, *The Rise of Robert Dodsley: Creating the New Age of Print* (Carbondale, Ill.: Southern Illinois University Press, 1996), 74–6. James Tierney notes Dodsley's early sympathies with the Opposition, *The Correspondence of Robert Dodsley, 1733–1764*, ed. James E. Tierney (Cambridge: Cambridge University Press, 1988), 21.

[88] The usual report of Pope's reaction is by Johnson, "Life of Pope"; in *Lives of the Poets*, ed. Hill, 3:181. The report is confirmed in a letter from Thomas Edwards to Lewis Crusius (8 June 1739), Oxford, Bodleian Library, MS Bodl. 1009, f.36: "Mr Pope has published nothing new this winter, some people say he had a piece or two ready, but was deterred by the Lords ordering one Paul Whitehead into custody for publishing an impudent poem called Manners, in which there were many scandalous & barefaced reflections upon several of the Peers"; as quoted in Clark, *Samuel Johnson*, 150.

OPERA IN FORMAL VERSE SATIRE   267

public virtue, his hatred of kings and arbitrary power, and the severity of his lashing private vices and public crimes.[89]

Manners is modeled on Pope's 1738 *Dialogues*. Its speaker, Philemon, content "in his calm Retreat, / Too wise for Pow'r, too virtuous to be great," converses with "his Grace," a court apologist. Despite the Horatian pose of the satirist, the tone is quite Juvenalian, as Philemon unrelentingly rails at False Taste, vice, corruption, and luxury as a consequence of the political corruption of church and state. While a place may claim one's reverence, only manners, virtue, and merit grant dignity to the officeholder.

One peer's love of opera is the subject for what must have been perceived as a libelous attack:

> Who blushes not to see a C—— Heir
> Turn Slave to Sound, and languish for a Play'r?
> What piping, fidling, squeaking, quav'ring, bawling,
> What sing-song Riot, and what Eunuch-squawling:
> C——, thy Worth all *Italy* shall own,
> A Statesman fit, where *Nero* fill'd the Throne.   (p. 8)

This dissolute, music-loving peer is certainly William Cowper, second Earl Cowper.[90] He met Farinelli while on his Grand Tour in Italy and hosted him at his home outside Canterbury upon his arrival in Britain in September 1734. Cowper introduced Farinelli at Court the following month in London. An amateur violinist, he was one of the directors of the Opera of the Nobility. Pope identified him as one of the opera-loving sons returned from the Grand Tour in the final book of the *Dunciad* (see Chapter 12). It was, in fact, Cowper's fellow opera director, Lord De La Warr, who complained to the House of Lords about *Manners*.[91]

Beyond the characterization of Cowper languishing enslaved to Farinelli's singing, the passage certainly could be a libel on the peer: praise from Italians that he would be a statesman suitable to serve the despotic Nero (whom

---

[89] "Life of Paul Whitehead," in Edward Thompson, *The Poems and Miscellaneous Compositions of Paul Whitehead* (1777), xiii, xv, xvii. *Observations on the Present Taste for Poetry* calls Whitehead "a Parasite" to the Prince of Wales (p. 36).

[90] The identification of Earl Cowper is confirmed in *Observations on the Present Taste for Poetry*: "A noble Earl is also abused, for being fond of Music; and very politely told, that he is fit to rule in a Court that belong'd to one of the greatest Monsters that ever disgraced human Nature" (p. 31). Manuscript additions to the Huntington Library copy (106574) of *Satires Written by Mr. Whitehead* (1739) and the British Library copy (1490.f.20) of *Manners* (1739) also identify "Earl Cooper."

On Cowper and Farinelli, and Farinelli's arrival in England, see Thomas McGeary, "Farinelli's Progress to Albion: The Recruitment and Reception of Opera's 'Blazing Star,'" *British Journal for Eighteenth-Century Studies*, 28 (2005), 339–61.

[91] Letter from Lord De La Warr to Earl Cowper, 10 February 1939; Hertfordshire Archives and Local Studies, Panshanger Papers, D/EP/249: "I complained Yesterday to the House of a Pamphlet call'd Manners, and the Author is order'd to attend on Monday, and I am most exceedingly mistaken if he is not very severely handled."

Whitehead described in a note as "A *Roman* Emperor remarkable for his foolish Passion for Music") is certainly an attack on him and opera-loving George II. Whitehead's note identifies the "Eunuch-squawling" player: "That living Witness of the Folly, Extravagance and Depravity of the *English*; *Farinello*, who is now at the Court of *Spain* triumphing in the Spoils of our Nobility, as their Pyrates are in those of our injur'd Merchants." Again, the image of Farinelli gloating at the Spanish Court serves as a vehicle for an Opposition hit at Walpole for appeasing the Spanish and tolerating their depredations on British shipping.

Elsewhere in *Manners*, Philemon paints recognizable portraits of those unworthy their places in the church or at court, including Lord Hervey and Colley Cibber. In contrast, he cites as paragons of virtue Lords Cobham and Chesterfield, Sir John Barnard (Lord Mayor of London), William Pulteney, and William Pitt. *Manners* closes with a prophecy anticipating British triumphs over Spain and a time when Peace, Plenty, and Freedom will flourish under the reign of Frederick, Prince of Wales.

The political import of *Manners* was recognized by the Ministry, and Walpole's stable of writers took up pens to vilify Whitehead and his *Manners*. Within two weeks of its publication, the *Daily Gazetteer* devoted two essays by "A Satirist" to Whitehead's satire. He charged Whitehead himself showed great want of manners in his own licentious verse, which could easily be mistaken for Pope's. His general reflections on courts are not satire but commonplace abuse that destroys proper respect for honor and eminence. After all, Satirist shrewdly notes, even the very Patriots themselves have titles and stars and seek posts of profit and honor at the court of the Prince of Wales.[92]

Although his subsequent reputation has not benefited, at the time, the Ministry took Whitehead the satirist as seriously as it took Pope, and the two were often bracketed in denunciations.[93] The month following *Manners*'s publication, in *Characters: An Epistle to Alexander Pope Esq; and Mr. Whitehead* (13 March 1739), a ministerial writer assails Pope and Whitehead, whose "Stew of Satire on the State ... favours more of Malice, Spleen, and Ill-nature, than good Sense, Wit, Learning, and Judgment" (14). Except for eulogies to the "implacable Enemies" of the present Ministry, their satire is "little else but personal Abuse and Slander." Pope and Whitehead are trying to scribble kings into disgrace only

---

[92] *Daily Gazetteer*, nos. 1140 and 1143 (15 and 19 Feb. 1739). *Manners Decypher'd. A Reply to Mr. Whitehead, on His Satire Call'd Manners* (March 1739), by James Meredith, charged that satire such as Whitehead's, written against reason, truth, and manners, was "The Rust and Canker of malignant Thought. / Th'ungovernable Frenzy of the Brain; / The Spawn of Envy, and of truth the Stain" (p. 2). *Manners* and Whitehead were also attacked in *Observations on the Present Taste for Poetry*.

An anonymous manuscript "Answer" to *Manners* lashed Whitehead and Pope as "sower & snarling Curs" who invent specious lies; that Whitehead lashed only the vices at court suggested that were a place offered, he himself would be "a mercenary Knave / A Fool of Power and of State the Slave" (London. British Library, Add. MS 25,277, f. 121).

[93] An early instance is the *Daily Courant*, no. 5364 (16 June 1733).

because the poets and their friends have no friends or favor at Court. In closing, Prince Frederick is warned against trusting such Patriots (p. 15).

An omnibus attack on anti-ministerial satirists is mounted in *The Satirists: A Satire* (December 1739), whose author invokes Satire "On Satirists selves thy Vengeance pour!" (p. 4). Among the poem's targets are Pope, Whitehead, and Miller, each of whom is graced with an abusive character sketch; for good measure, the playwright James Thomson is included. Satirists rage against whatever the ministry proposes and are "Eternal Teasers of a Court and King." Instead of writing general satire that delicately reproves, these satirists fill their pages with personal abuse and scandal. When there is panegyric (such as of Prince Frederick), it is at the expense of his father, the King (p. 12).[94]

Included is a charge that Pope's satiric attacks on opera are hypocritical and misplaced:

> ... he [Pope] lashes with small Grace
> Members or Ministers, or Lords in Place,
> Who for *Italian* Song shall shake the Rod,
> Yet make it trifling to deny a God.   (p. 6)

That is, Pope attacks ministers or peers over such a trifle as opera yet overlooks Bolingbroke, who flirts with atheism.

Although none of these ministerial essays and attacks against Pope, Miller, and Whitehead go so far as to defend Italian opera, their swiftness and severity do show how politically sensitive were the satires in which opera appeared.

* * *

The cultural politics of opera in these formal verse satires arises from its utility as an index of the state of a Britain supposedly sunk in moral and spiritual decay caused by luxury and corruption, humiliated by continued Spanish depredations, and enslaved by the tyranny of Walpole's ministry. If we ask of these satires *Cui bono?*, the answer is clear: the increasingly broad array of disaffected Whigs, Tories, merchants, and traders opposed to Walpole's rule. The satires discredit and delegitimize a favorite entertainment of the Ministry and Court and erode their authority. Implicit is a call to action: remove Walpole and Britain will be free from the evils symbolized by opera and its most celebrated singer Farinelli.

There is here a seeming contradiction to be confronted: these satires demonized and vilified an art form favored and patronized by Prince Frederick, William Pulteney, the Earl of Chesterfield, and other members of the Opposition.[95] We can evade this contradiction by recognizing the inherent bivalent nature of cultural productions. In one way, opera as a cultural product esteemed by London's political-social elite (of both oppositional and ministerial disposition) was

---

[94] This point recalls the *Daily Gazetteer*'s charge made against Thomson's verses on Prince Frederick in 1737.

[95] See Appendix 3 in McGeary, *The Politics of Opera in Handel's Britain*, for opera patrons associated with the Opposition.

dissociated from its role in Opposition polemic. We can suppose that opera-going readers who were sympathetic to the Opposition bracketed off and tolerated the rhetorical and partisan vitriol against opera for the greater good of turning out the Walpole ministry.

CHAPTER 11

War of Jenkins' Ear and the Fall of Walpole

War with Spain was imminent in the summer of 1739, but due to Walpole's disagreements with Newcastle and Hardwicke in the cabinet, serious military preparations had begun only until after war was declared. The high cost of a land war on the Spanish peninsula meant the War of Jenkins' Ear would be fought in the West Indies. Having been dragged into a war, the Ministry largely mis-managed it.

The British naval expedition that set out for the West Indies in summer 1739 had an initial success. On 22 November 1739 and "with six ships only," Admiral Vernon, captured and demolished the fortifications at Porto Bello, Panama. The port's loss prevented return of the Spanish galleons with their gold necessary for financing Spain's war.[1] Vernon's victory was in sharp contrast to Admiral Hosier's failed six-month blockade of the port in 1726 with twenty ships: Hosier lost 4,000 men, his ships were ruined by worms, and he himself died in the expedition. Vernon's victory fulfilled his earlier boast as an outspoken Opposition MP that he could do with six ships what Hoiser failed to do with twenty. When news of Vernon's victory arrived on 13 March 1740,[2] the nation erupted in expressions of patriotic pride and celebrated Vernon as a national hero. Bonfires burned throughout London and the country, and Vernon became the most popular and beloved man in Britain.[3]

Vernon's victory became a party issue. The Ministry used it to vindicate its war conduct. The Opposition, furious that Walpole would try to take credit

---

[1] On Vernon's campaign against Porto Bello and Chagre, see H. W. Richmond, *The Navy in the War of 1739–48*, 3 vols. (Cambridge: Cambridge University Press, 1920), 1:45–52; and W. Laird Clowes, *The Royal Navy: A History from the Earliest Times to the Present*, 7 vols. (London: Sampson Low, Marston and Co., 1897–1903), 3:43–5, 52–62.

   Contemporary poems include *A Poem on the Glorious Atchievements* [sic] *of Admiral Vernon in the Spanish West-Indies* (1740), and Thomas Martin, *A Poem on the War in the West-Indies under Admiral Vernon* (1742).

[2] *The Correspondence of the Dukes of Richmond and Newcastle, 1724–1750.* Sussex Record Society, 73 (1982–3), 32.

[3] On Vernon's popular reception and elevation to national hero, see Kathleen Wilson, "Empire, Trade and Popular Politics in Mid-Hanoverian Britain: The Case of Admiral Vernon," *Past and Present*, 121 (Nov. 1988), 74–109; Wilson, *The Sense of the People: Politics, Culture and Imperialism in England, 1715–1785* (Cambridge: Cambridge University Press, 1995), 142–53; and Gerald Jordan and Nicholas Rogers, "Admirals as Heroes: Patriotism and Liberty in Hanoverian England," *Journal of British Studies*, 28 (1989), 201–24.

272 THE CULTURAL POLITICS OF OPERA, 1720–1742

for Vernon's victory, claimed he triumphed *despite* the Ministry. His victory demonstrated that Britain had needlessly suffered indignations from a weak enemy while Walpole had permitted merchant trade to be harassed by Spain.[4] On 24 March 1740, Vernon took the fort at Chagres, west of Porto Bello, the headquarters of the *guarda costas* and a port of embarkation of treasure. The dispatches to London included news of £100,000 of plunder.[5] Euphoria over Vernon's initial successes turned to discontent with the Ministry's conduct of the war.

Admiral Haddock's fleet was sent to Gibraltar on 1 October 1739, but with insufficient ships to both protect Minorca and blockade Cadiz. More failures followed next summer. Due to confusing ministerial orders, Haddock sailing from the Mediterranean and Admiral Norris from Britain failed to intercept the French and Spanish squadrons, allowing them to escape an attempted blockade and sail to the West Indies.

During the new Parliament that sat in November, Opposition motions calling for Vernon's and Haddock's instructions to be laid before Parliament to shed light on mismanagement of the navy developed into a full-scale parliamentary attack on ministerial conduct of the war.[6]

For the campaign in the West Indies, an expedition was at last ordered to Jamaica on 5 December 1739; transports for 8,000 marines were ordered on 31 December, but the troops had yet to be raised, nor was the fleet ready. Six thousand troops under General Wentworth were embarked on transports in early August 1740 but did not sail until late October and only joined Vernon

---

[4] On Porto Bello as an occasion to criticize the Ministry's war program, see *Common Sense*, 165 (29 March 1740). The Ministry was charged with not following up the advantage gained by Vernon's victory.

The Opposition's point was expressed in Richard Glover's popular ballad "Admiral Hosier's Ghost" (21 May 1740), in which the ghosts of Hosier and his crew appear before Vernon's crew off Porto Bello and recall the shameful fate of Hosier, who died of a broken heart. Hosier's ghost asks Vernon to temper the joy of his triumph by recalling the sailors lost because his orders forbade him to fight the Spanish. Hosier and his ghosts will not rest unless Vernon and England recall his shame and seek vengeance for his ruin. The ballad is reprinted in *Political Ballads Illustrating the Administration of Sir Robert Walpole*, ed. Milton Percival. Oxford Historical and Literary Studies, 8 (1916), no. 57. For a print illustrating the ballad, see Frederick Stephens, *Catalogue of Prints and Drawings in the British Museum*. Division I. *Political and Personal Satires*, 3 vols. (London: Trustees of the British Museum, 1873), no. 2422; illustrated in Paul Langford, *Walpole and the Robinocracy. The English Satirical Print, 1600–1832* (Cambridge: Chadwyck-Healy, 1986), no. 74.

[5] *Daily Gazetteer*, no. 1570 (1 July 1740).

[6] *Journals of the House of Commons*, 23 (1737/8–1741), 616; *Journals of the House of Lords*, 25 (1736/7–1741), 551. For the debates, see William Cobbett, *The Parliamentary History of England*, 11 (1739–1741), 699–768, 768–845 (Lords), 1001–1010 (Commons). A resolution demanded that any peace must affirm Britain's "natural and indubitable Right to navigate in the American Seas" without any searches or seizures; see *A Resolution of the ... Lords Spiritual and Temporal and the Commons. ... On Friday, the Twenty Third Day of November, 1739* (1739).

WAR OF JENKINS' EAR AND THE FALL OF WALPOLE   273

in the Indies just before Christmas. Decisions for operations were left to the commanders.

The expedition's first objective was the port of Cartagena, which it reached on 4 March 1741. Forces quickly took the outworks, seized fortifications, and gained possession of the harbor. The Spanish scuttled five of their own ships, and Vernon captured Don Blas's flagship. Vernon's first dispatches reporting these initial successes reached London on 17 May[7] and raised hopes of a quick capture of Cartagena and dominance of the West Indies trade. But an army attack on the fortifications was repulsed. With 4,500 men lost, mostly from fever, and more dying every day, the force returned to Jamaica in early May, leaving the Spanish still in possession of Cartagena.[8]

The next plan was to capture Cuba. The operation against Santiago began in July 1741 and was hindered by delays on the part of the army. With some 2,260 men down with fever, this expedition was also abandoned in November. An expedition against a Spanish squadron at Porto Bello in March 1742 was likewise abandoned. With some 7,000 solders lost and nothing gained, Vernon and Wentworth were recalled at the end of the year, ending offensive operations in the West Indies.

The traditional explanation for the failure of the army-naval campaigns in the West Indies, as summarized by the naval historian H. W. Richmond, was "the incompetent Administration at home," which broke every canon of the art of war. In addition to delays in ordering troop transports, the Ministry failed to supply Vernon needed stores, sent raw soldiers instead of seasoned marines, and tolerated Wentworth's indecision and lack of initiative.[9] Richard Harding, though, has recently argued that the failure of the campaign lay in the significant operational problems involved in executing such long-distance combined army-navy campaigns at short notice.[10]

Having gotten the war it wanted, the Opposition continued its clamour, berating Walpole for not vigorously prosecuting a war that could easily have been won: he neglected to provide convoys to protect trade from the *guarda costas*, failed to equip and provision the fleet and land forces, and failed to follow up military victories.[11] The sense of national dishonor and shame at

---

[7] *Correspondence of Richmond and Newcastle*, 60–1; Richmond, *Navy in the War of 1739–48*, 1:144.

[8] On the expeditions against Cartagena, Santiago, and Porto Bello, see Richmond, *Navy in the War of 1739–48*, 1:110–33; and Clowes, *The Royal Navy*, 3:68–78.

[9] Richmond, *Navy in the War of 1739–48*, 1:133–7.

[10] Richard Harding, *Amphibious Warfare in the Eighteenth Century: The British Expedition to the West Indies, 1740-1742* (Woodbridge: The Boydell Press, 1991).

[11] Attacks on Walpole's conduct of the war include: *Britain's Mistakes in the Commencement and Conduct of the Present War* (1740); *Britannia in Mourning: or, A Review of the Politicks and Conduct of the Court of Great Britain* (1742); *England's Triumph; or, Spanish Cowardice Expos'd* (1739); *An Essay on the Management of the Present War with Spain* (1740); *Hireling Artifice Detected: or the Profit and Loss of Great Britain* (1742) [a reply to *The Profit and Loss of Great Britain*]; *A Letter from a Member of the Last Parliament ... Concerning the Conduct of the War with Spain* (1742); and *A Supplement to Britain's*

274   THE CULTURAL POLITICS OF OPERA, 1720–1742

the course of the war found wide-spread expression in newspapers, pamphlets, ballads, satirical poems, and popular prints.

The Opposition's parliamentary successes in December 1740–January 1741 on motions for Haddock's instructions were offset by its later defeat on a daring personal attack on the prime minister. On 13 February 1741, Samuel Sandys and Lord Carteret offered motions in both houses requesting that the King "will be graciously pleased to remove the Right honourable Sir *Robert Walpole* … from his Majesty's Presence and Councils for ever."[12] The debate and pamphleteering over what was called The Motion was an opportunity for an examen of recent political history and a critique of Walpole's career as minister: all the reverses and supposed failures of recent diplomacy were laid at his feet (although he was not one of the secretaries of state).[13] The Motion was defeated in the Commons by 184 votes, and by 49 in the Lords, largely due to poor management and disunity among the Tories and Opposition Whigs. Suspicious Tories opposed The Motion as an infringement upon the King's prerogative. Some Tories withdrew from the House, and others voted against The Motion. A daring challenge to Walpole, its defeat was a victory for Walpole but lulled him into a sense of false security.

Mistakes in the Commencement and Conduct of the Present War (1740).

Prints against the conduct of the war: Langford, *Walpole and the Robinocracy*, nos. 64, 66, 73–5, 78, 93–5.

Defenses of the Ministry's conduct of the war include: *The Conduct of the Late Administration* (1742); *The False Accusers Accused* (1741); John Lord Hervey, *Miscellaneous Thoughts on the Present Posture Both of Our Foreign and Domestic Affairs* (1742); Honestus, *The Profit and Loss of Great Britain in the Present War with Spain* (1741); *A Letter to a Member of Parliament. Concerning the Present State of Affairs* (1740); Philalethes, *The Profit and Loss of Great-Britain and Spain* (1742); *A Second Letter to a Member of Parliament Concerning the Present State of Affairs* (1741); and *Vindicta Britannica* (1740). See also *An Apology for the Minister* (1739); and *To Arms; or, The British Lyon Rouz'd. Occasion'd by the Present Armaments against the Spaniards* (1739).

[12] *Journals of the House of Commons*, 23 (1737/8–1741), 648; *Journals of the House of Lords*, 25 (1736/7–1741), 596–7. For the debates, see Cobbett, *The Parliamentary History of England*, 11 (1739–1741), 1047–1223 (Lords), 1223–1387 (Commons). A Lords Protest was entered on the loss of Carteret's motion; James E. T. Rogers, *A Complete Collection of the Protests of the Lords*, 2 vols. (Oxford: Clarendon, 1875), 1:10–13, no. 319. See also I. G. Doolittle, "A First-hand Account of the Commons Debate on the Removal of Sir Robert Walpole, 13 February 1741," *Bulletin of the Institute of Historical Research*, 53 (1980), 125–40; and Coxe, *Memoirs of Walpole*, 1:644–73.

[13] Pamphlets justifying The Motion include: *Reasons Founded on Facts for a Late Motion* (1741); *The Sense of the Nation: In Regard to the Late Motion in Parliament* (1741); *A Review of the Late Motion for an Address to His Majesty Against a Certain Great Minister, and the Reasons for It* (1741). *The Grand Defeat: or, the Downfall of the S——d——an Party* (1741) exults in the failure of The Motion, as does the poem *The Funeral of Faction* (1741).

See also Langford, *Walpole and the Robinocracy*, nos. 82–7; Herbert M. Atherton, *Political Prints in the Age of Hogarth: A Study of the Ideographic Representation of Politics* (Oxford: Clarendon, 1974), no. 34; and Percival, ed., *Political Ballads*, no. 66.

♨ *The Fall of Walpole*

The Spanish depredations on shipping continued through the war. The failed campaigns in the West Indies and constant Opposition pamphleteering did not yet drive Walpole from office. So far, though, he had been safe from a fragmented Opposition and securely in the King's favor. The parliamentary elections in the summer of 1741 were fiercely contested, primarily due to dissatisfaction over the Ministry's handling of the war. The dowager Duchess of Marlborough, William Pulteney, and the Prince of Wales spent great sums on the election; the Prince himself was said to have spent £12,000.[14]

The new Parliament met on 1 December 1741. Signs were that Walpole's hold on the Commons was waning; one estimate has his majority reduced to approximately eighteen votes.[15] The war's late start and slow progress were now eroding his support. Moreover, it was widely known Walpole was at odds with Newcastle and Harwicke, who had been supporting a more aggressive policy toward Spain.[16]

When the Opposition objected to including in its Address of Thanks to the King the phrase "returning his majesty the thanks of this house, for his royal care in prosecuting the war with Spain," Walpole – instead of defending the Ministry's conduct of the war – agreed to the omission. This uncharacteristic concession signaled his vulnerability. His biographer William Coxe cites the declining state of Walpole's health as preventing him from exerting himself sufficiently to prevail in the Commons.[17]

At first, the session generally went to Walpole's advantage. But the elections produced a larger than the usual number of contested outcomes. Customarily resolved by the Commons along party lines, these contested returns usually

---

[14] Frederick's expenses are reported in Richard Glover's *Memoirs by a Celebrated Literary and Political Character*, new ed. (London: John Murray, 1814), 1.

[15] For events leading to the fall of Walpole and aftermath, John B. Owen, *The Rise of the Pelhams* (London: Methuen, 1957), 1–40; R. Harris, "A Leicester House Political Diary, 1742–43," *Camden Miscellany*, 4th ser., vol. 44, and vol. 31 (1992), 373–411; W. A. Speck, "'The Most Corrupt Council in Christendom': Decisions on Controverted Elections, 1702–42," pp. 107–21 in *Party and Management in Parliament, 1660–1784*, ed. Clyve Jones (Leicester: Leicester University Press, 1984); Basil Williams, *The Life of William Pitt, Earl of Chatham*, 2 vols. (London: Longmans, Green, and Co, 1914), 1:81–93; Jeremy Black, *Walpole in Power* (Stroud: Sutton Publishing, 2001), 168–79; John Perceval, Earl of Egmont, *Manuscripts of the Earl of Egmont. Diary of Viscount Percival, afterwards First Earl of Egmont*, 3 vols. (London: His Majesty's Stationery Office, 1930), 3:232–50; Cobbett, *Parliamentary History of England*, 12 (1741–1743), 188–404; and Coxe, *Memoirs of Robert Walpole*, 1:682–97.

[16] On dissention in the Cabinet: George L. Lam, "Walpole and the Duke of Newcastle," pp. 57–84 in *Horace Walpole: Writer, Politician, and Connoisseur*, ed. Warren H. Smith (New Haven, Conn.: Yale University Press, 1967), Philip Woodfine, *Britannia's Glories: The Walpole Ministry and the 1739 War with Spain* (London: Royal Historical Society, 1998), 213–28.

[17] Coxe, *Memoirs of Robert Walpole*, 1:689–90, 692.

offered the Ministry the opportunity to gain some seats. The danger to Walpole was deliberate abstentions by his own supporters and placemen, who in more favorable circumstances would have voted with him. In this session, the outcomes revealed his weakness. Walpole and the Opposition split the first two petitions, but the Opposition then carried selection of the chairman of the Committee of Elections and Privileges by four votes. The first great shock to Walpole's command of the Commons was the disputed Westminster election, which had been won by two Ministry candidates. The petition was heard on 22 December. Due primarily to defections by the Ministry's supporters, the government lost all four divisions by two to six votes.[18]

Over the holiday recess, an optimistic Walpole dismissed ideas of resignation; he still had the King's support, but popular opinion expected his fall.[19] Opposition figures secretly negotiated his safe retirement from office in turn for their favor at Court. One Walpole sympathizer urged him – "Crown'd with Success, the shining Course is run!" – to retire.[20]

On 5 January 1742, Walpole made a last, desperate effort to retain his position by trying to detach Frederick from the Opposition: if the Prince would go to Court and beg pardon, the King would grant the Prince an increase of £50,000 in his allowance, pay off his debts, and provide for his servants as vacancies occurred.[21] Frederick refused such an offer while Walpole remained in power. His rejection of the offer stiffened the resolve of the Opposition. Walpole's resignation was now considered certain.

Walpole fought off by three votes a motion by Pulteney for a committee to examine papers relating to the conduct of the war. On 28 January, the Opposition carried a division on the Chippenham election by one vote. Facing the fact that he no longer had control of the Commons and could no longer carry on the King's business, Walpole accepted the necessity of his retirement. On 2 February, the Opposition carried the Chippenham petition by sixteen votes. The following day, Walpole announced his resignation and left the Commons for the last time.

Parliament was recessed for two weeks for the formation of a new Whig Ministry. On 9 February Walpole was created Earl of Orford; he resigned all his places on 11 February and assumed his place in the Lords with a promised pension of £4,000. The *Craftsman* rejoiced with his countrymen "for their

---

[18] In the polling on 9 May 1741 at Westminster, it was claimed the books had been closed early to allow Lord Sundon and Admiral Sir Charles Wager to win; the intervention of troops to handle rioting was considered unconstitutional; Owen, *Rise of the Pelhams*, 26n.

[19] On the role of the press in the fall of Walpole, Robert Harris, *A Patriot Press: National Politics and the London Press in the 1740s* (Oxford: Clarendon Press, 1993), 95–113; and for the Lords' role, Clyve Jones, "The House of Lords and the Fall of Walpole," pp. 102–36 in *Hanoverian Britain and Empire: Essays in Memory of Philip Lawson*, ed. Stephen Taylor, Richard Connors, and Clyve Jones (Woodbridge: Boydell, 1998).

[20] *The Statesman's Mirrour: or, Friendly Advice to a Certain Great Minister* (Dec. 1741), 8.

[21] Coxe, *Memoirs of Walpole*, 1:692–3. Walpole's offer and rejection are noted by, for example, the Countess of Hertford, *The Gentle Herford: Her Life and Letters*, ed. Helen S. Hughes [New York, N.Y.: Macmillan Co., 1940], 185); and Egmont, *Diary*, 3:238–41.

happy Deliverance from a most oppressive Bondage of, at least, twenty Years Duration."[22]

As the new government was being formed, many leaders of the Opposition sullied their reputations as they shamelessly scrambled for places and peerages: Pulteney entered the Lords as Earl of Bath, and Carteret, Sandys, and Wilmington accepted cabinet posts. Their readiness to accept such places fulfilled long-standing ministerial claims that the Opposition's appeals to virtue and public spirit were just opportunistic ruses by ambitious men to gain power. Lord Hervey observed that the people's "Hopes and Expectations" turned to "Derision and Odium" as the masks of the Patriots were thrown off, and they fulfilled every prophecy of the *Daily Gazetteer*.[23] Carteret and Pulteney now found themselves subjects of brutal satire.[24] Because of their role in forcing Walpole's removal and the King's disdain for Frederick and his allies, Chesterfield and Pitt were excluded from places. Walpole's influence and friends in the Ministry were still so strong that – despite demands for inquiry into his past conduct – parliamentary investigation into his ministry was abandoned when Parliament was prorogued.

After Walpole's fall, Frederick reconciled with the King.[25] His allowance was increased by £50,000, he went to Court on 17 February 1742, and places were promised for several of his followers. Despite the public reconciliation, the spiteful King continued to inflict indignities on the Prince.[26]

* * *

Historians have offered more favorable, balanced assessments of the Walpole ministry than have literary historians and critics, most of whom seem to have uncritically accepted the charges by the satirists Pope, Swift, Fielding, and Gay, and the propaganda of Bolingbroke and the *Craftsman*. Instead of corruption as charged by the Opposition, Walpole, historians point out, was effectively using the traditional means of patronage, places, and pensions to build a loyal government and Parliament that could carry out the King's business.[27]

---

[22] Reports of celebration in the Opposition press: *Craftsman*, no. 816 (20 Feb. 1741); *Common Sense*, nos. 262 and 263 (20 and 27 Feb. 1742).

[23] John Lord Hervey, *Miscellaneous Thoughts on the Present Posture both of our Foreign and Domestic Affairs* (1742), 26–7 (citing 80-page edition). He attributed the makeup of the new Parliament to "the Weight and Industry of the P. of W."

[24] Anti-Carteret and Pulteney satire: see *The False Patriot: A Satyrical Epistle to W——P——y, Esq; on his being created E——l of B——th* (1742); *The New Ministry*, 3 vols. (1742) is a collection of poems on the new ministry, cynical about the members and their integrity.

[25] The reconciliation at Court is described by Lady Hertford; *Gentle Herford*, 187–8; Egmont, *Diary*, 3:253–4; and *Common Sense*, no. 260 (6 Feb. 1742). In 1747, Frederick went into active opposition to the Whig ministry and his father with a Leicester House opposition (named after his London residence).

[26] Indignities of the King to the Prince are noted by Egmont, *Diary*, 3:253–4.

[27] J. H. Plumb, "Sir Robert Walpole," *History Today* (Oct. 1951), 9–16; Plumb *The Growth of Political Stability in England, 1675–1725* (Harmondsworth: Penguin Books, 1969),

By dint of prodigious amounts of hard work, exhaustive knowledge of finance, control of Crown patronage, attention to detail, and mastery of men and government, he established a political system that preserved the Hanoverian Succession and kept the Whig oligarchy in power. Importantly, by remaining in the Commons, he was able to maintain control of Parliament. Domestically, he moderated the ferocity of party and religious strife that roiled the reign of Anne; he established the Sinking Fund to finance the national debt and reduced the land tax to the benefit of the landed gentlemen. He tried to keep Britain out of costly wars, which would have increased taxes and harmed commerce, and his system of tariffs and taxation improved trade and manufacturing.[28] Through his command of government, finances, and Parliament, he established the modern role of prime minister.

Walpole, Plumb summarizes, created

> what has eluded king and ministers since the days of Elizabeth I – a government and policy acceptable to the Court, to the Commons, and to the majority of the political establishment in the nation at large. Indeed, he made the world so safe for Whigs that they stayed in power for a hundred years.[29]

By all measures and contrary to Opposition propaganda, under his ministry, Britain experienced expansion of trade and commerce, peace on the Continent, and flourishing arts and sciences.

160, 187–8; Plumb, *Sir Robert Walpole: The King's Minister* (London: Cresset Press, 1960), 325–33 (for first twelve years of his ministry); Plumb, *England in the Eighteenth Century* (Harmondsworth: Penguin Books, 1950), 72–3; W. A. Speck, "Britain's First Prime Minister," pp. 12–19 in Andrew Moore, ed., *Houghton Hall: The Prime Minister, The Empress, and The Hermitage* (London: Philip Wilson, 1996); Jeremy Black, *Walpole in Power* (Stroud: Sutton Publishing, 2001), 180–2; H. T. Dickinson, *Walpole and the Whig Supremacy* (London: English University Press, 1973), 191–2; Stephen Taylor, "Robert Walpole (1676-1745)," *Oxford Dictionary of National Biography*, Oxford University Press, online edition, January 2008; and B. W. Hill, *Sir Robert Walpole* (London: Hamish Hamilton, 1989), 217–20.

[28] David Hume could only credit Walpole with flourishing trade: "During his time trade has flourished, liberty declined, and learning gone to ruin"; "A Character of Sir Robert Walpole," pp. 203–5 in *Essays, Moral and Political*, 2 vols. (1742); 2:203; on the character, R. C. Elliott, "Hume's 'Character of Sir Robert Walpole': Some Unnoticed Additions," *Journal of English and Germanic Philology*, 48 (1949), 367–78. He later softened his harsh opinion.

[29] Plumb, *Growth of Political Stability*, 160.

CHAPTER 12

The New Dunciad: Opera and the Triumph of Dulness

The national euphoria over Vernon's initial success at Porto Bello in November 1739 in the long-sought war against Spain quickly turned to public clamour against the Ministry's mismanagement of the war, and Britain continued to suffer the humiliation of Spanish depredations on shipping in the West Indies. The failure of later campaigns in the West Indies, harassment of the Ministry in Parliament, and the ceaseless domestic pamphlet warfare did little to weaken Walpole's hold on power. So far, he was still in favor with the King and safe from a fragmented Opposition whose only program was to remove the prime minister.

Members of the Opposition were becoming disillusioned. Privately there was growing suspicion among the younger ones of the motives of Pulteney and Carteret, believing they were motivated only by their own ambition for power and establishing influence over Prince Frederick. Or, it was thought, they were tempering their attacks on Walpole and secretly communicating with Newcastle and Hardwicke in the possibility of being invited to join the Ministry.[1]

To his friends, Alexander Pope expressed his despair about Hanoverian Britain. In July 1738, he wrote to Ralph Allen, "I can but Skirmish, & maintain a flying Fight with Vice; its Forces augment, & will drive me off the Stage. ... The Condition of Morality is so desperate, as to be above all Human Hands."[2] In this

---

[1] Suspicion of Pulteney and Carteret: John B. Owen, *The Rise of the Pelhams* (London: Methuen, 1957), 15–17; Basil Williams, *The Life of William Pitt, Earl of Chatham*, 2 vols. (London: Longmans, Green, and Co., 1914), 1:81–6 (especially Pitt's letter to Chesterfield, Aug.1741 [p. 86]); *A Selection from the Papers of the Earls of Marchmont*, ed. George H. Rose, 3 vols. (London: John Murray, 1831), 2:107–8, 114, 129–36, 204; letter from Pope to Lyttleton, November 1738, *The Correspondence of Alexander Pope*, ed. George Sherburn, 5 vols. (Oxford: Clarendon Press, 1956), 4:142–4; letter from Lord Chesterfield to Dodington, *The Letters of Philip Dormer Stanhope*, ed. with intro. by Bonamy Dobrée, 6 vols. (London: Eyre & Spottiswood, 1932), 2: 467–8; Philip C. Yorke, *The Life and Correspondence of Philip York, Earl of Hardwicke*, 3 vols. (Cambridge: Cambridge University Press, 1913), 1:190–4; *Horace Walpole: Writer, Politician, and Connoisseur*, ed. Warren H. Smith (New Haven, Conn.: Yale University Press, 1967), 63–4.

On Opposition dis-unity, W. B. Coley, "Henry Fielding and the Two Walpoles," *Philological Quarterly*, 45 (1966), 157–76 (on 162–5).

[2] Pope to Ralph Allen, 6 July 1738; Pope, *Correspondence*, ed. Sherburn, 4:109. Further on Pope's disillusion and despair: Paul Gabriner, "Pope's 'Virtue' and the Events of

280 THE CULTURAL POLITICS OF OPERA, 1720–1742

mood of pessimism, Pope published his two final satires, *One Thousand Seven Hundred and Thirty Eight. A Dialogue Something like Horace* (16 May 1738) and *One Thousand Seven Hundred and Thirty Eight. Dialogue II* (18 July 1738).[3] The first satire went through three issues,[4] and the ministerial *Daily Gazetteer*, aware of its impact, published three attacks on its poet.[5]

Joseph Warton called them

> some of the strongest Satires ever written in any age or any country. Every species of sarcasm and mode of style are here alternately employed; … Many persons in power were highly provoked, but the name of Pope prevented a prosecution, for what Paxton [Solicitor to the Treasury] wished to have called a libel.[6]

Pope would later describe this pair of satires as "a sort of Protest against that insuperable corruption and depravity of manners, which he [the poet] had been so unhappy as to live to see," as well his reason for leaving them off: "Could he have hoped to have amended any, he had continued those attacks; but bad men were grown so shameless and so powerful, that Ridicule was become as unsafe as it was ineffectual."[7]

Adding to the sense of futility, the Opposition suffered leadership losses. The Earl of Marchmont died on 27 February 1740. His son, Lord Polwarth, highly regarded by Pope and the Duchess of Marlborough, assumed his father's title and was thereby advanced out of the Commons and was thus lost to the parliamentary Opposition; he was not elected a Scottish Peer to the Lords until 1750. William Wyndham's death on 17 June 1740 dissolved the alliance between the Hanoverian Tories and Opposition Whigs, and Tory resentment at being led

---

1738," *Scripta Hierosolymitana*, 25 (1973), 96–110 (esp. 115–19); and Christine Gerrard, "Pope and the Patriots," pp. 25–43 in *Pope: New Contexts*, ed. David Fairer (London: Harvester Wheatsheaf, 1990).

3 The *Dialogues* were collectively published and renamed in 1740 as the *Epilogue to the Satires*. On the *Dialogues/Epilogue*, see Robert W. Rogers, *The Major Satires of Alexander Pope*. Illinois Studies in Language and Literature 40 (Urbana, Ill.: University of Illinois Press, 1955), 91–3; Howard Erskine-Hill, *The Augustan Idea in English Literature* (London: E. Arnold, 1983), 344–9; Howard Weinbrot, *Augustus Caesar*, 137–41; Gerrard, "Pope and the Patriots"; and Maynard Mack, *The Garden and the City: Retirement and Politics in the Later Poetry of Pope, 1731–1743* (Toronto: University of Toronto Press, 1969), *passim*.

4 Reginald H. Griffith, *Alexander Pope: A Bibliography*, 2 vols. (Austin. Tex.: University of Texas, 1927), 2:383, estimates 4,000 copies were printed.

5 See *Daily Gazetteer* for 26 and 30 May and 24 August 1738 (no. 980). Pope was again attacked in the issue for 26 August 1738 (no. 982).

6 "The Life of Alexander Pope"; in *The Works of Alexander Pope*, 9 vols. (1797), 1:lx.

7 Pope's note in 1744 to the last line of *One Thousand Seven Hundred and Thirty Eight. Dialogue II*; in Alexander Pope, *Imitations of Horace*, ed. John Butt. The Twickenham Edition of the Poems of Alexander Pope, vol. 4, 2nd ed. (New Haven, Conn.: Yale University Press, 1953), 327. The mention of the danger of writing satire is usually taken to refer to the action taken against Paul Whitehead's *Manners*.

by Whigs increased. Bolingbroke could marvel at Walpole's tenacity in office: "What a Star has our Minister? Wyndham dead, Marchmont disabled!"[8]

William Pitt, one of Cobham's "cubs," lamented to Lord Chesterfield in August 1741,

> The scene abroad is most gloomy; whether day is ever to break forth again or destruction and darkness is finally to cover all — impiaque æternam meruerunt sæula noctem — must soon be determined. ... I only wish, in this great crisis, every, man in England may awake.[9]

Amid this climate of despair, after almost thirteen years Pope returned to his *Dunciad* project and on 20 March 1742 published *The New Dunciad: As It Was Found in the Year 1741*,[10] which became the final book of the lifetime *The Dunciad, in Four Books* (29 October 1743). In *The New Dunciad*, the prophecies of Book III of the *Dunciad* are fulfilled.[11] The book presents a vivid portrayal of opera as the agent of Dulness, chaos, and darkness. Yet the passage paradoxically contains the famous image of the Briareus-like Handel as the last bulwark against the reign of Dulness, itself symbolized by Italian opera, the form to which Handel had devoted most of his first thirty years in London.

By the time *The New Dunciad* was published, Walpole, who now appears as the High Priest or Wizard of Dulness, had been driven from office. It is possible Pope already had the poem printed, but cautioned by the reaction to Paul Whitehead's *Manners* felt that only after Walpole fell from power was it safe to publish it. Although thus slightly anachronistic when finally published, *The New Dunciad* is Pope's most dispirited and dismal image of Britain under Walpole and the Hanoverians.[12]

---

[8] Reported by Pope in a letter to the Earl of Marchmont, October 1740; Pope, *Correspondence*, ed. Sherburn, 4:272.

[9] Letter from William Pitt, August 1741, to the Earl of Chesterfield; in Basil Williams, *The Life of William Pitt, Earl of Chatham*, 2 vols. (London: Longmans, Green, and Co., 1914), 1:86. The Latin tag is from Virgil, *Georgics*, 1: 468 (substituting for 'timuerunt'). Virgil's poet describes the ills that followed the death of Caesar.

[10] *George Frideric Handel, Collected Documents*, ed., Donald Burrows, Helen Coffey, John Greenacombe, and Anthony Hicks, 6 vols. (Cambridge: Cambridge University Press, 2013–), 3:796–7, gives the erroneous publication date of 29 April 1742 and prints an unauthorized text published by J. H. Hubbard.

[11] On revisions of the *Dunciad Variorum* and genesis of Book IV of the *Dunciad*: Rogers, *Major Satires of Alexander Pope*, 106–13; George Sherburn, "The *Dunciad*, Book IV," *University of Texas Studies in English*, 24 (1944), 174–90; Aubrey L. Williams, *Pope's "Dunciad": A Study of its Meaning* (London: Methuen, 1955), 87–158; Williams, "Literary Backgrounds to Book Four of the *Dunciad*," *Publications of the Modern Language Association*, 68 (1953), 806–13; Maynard Mack, *Alexander Pope: A Life* (New York, N.Y.: W. W. Norton, 1985); Alexander Pope, *The Dunciad*, ed. James Sutherland. The Twickenham Edition of the Poems of Alexander Pope. Vol. 5, 3rd ed. (London: Methuen, 1963); and Alexander Pope, *The Dunciad in Four Books*, ed. Valerie Rumbold (Harlow: Longman, 1999).

[12] On the politics (and especially the anti-Hanoverianism) of the *Dunciad*: Howard Erskine-Hill, *Pope: The Dunciad* (London: Edward Arnold, 1972), 48–60; Mack, *The*

282   THE CULTURAL POLITICS OF OPERA, 1720–1742

In *The New Dunciad* (hereafter *Dunciad* IV), the reign of Dulness begins at last. The central scene is a levee in a grand drawing room at which Queen Dulness will present awards to those who have advanced her cause. The poet's invocation describes Dulness mounting her throne in majesty "to destroy *Order* and *Science*, and to substitute the *Kingdom of the Dull* upon earth" (Argument). To emphasize the Hanoverian Court's responsibility for the Triumph of Dulness, in the final version, Pope installs as the *Dunciad*'s hero the Poet Laureate Colley Cibber, replacing Lewis Theobald. Pope now shows that bad writing arises less from ignorant and mercenary Grub Street dunces than from the corrupt taste at Court that patronized them. The source of Dulness is the nation's polite, fashionable elite and the "great Patricians."

Pope's image of Dulness as patroness of False Taste holding sway at the Ministry and Court so chimed with Opposition polemic about the failure of Walpole to support men of letters that in the previous December, just as Walpole's command of Parliament was slipping away, *Commons Sense* would ironically point to "That Legion of Dunces which our Great Man, to shew his excellent Judgment and fine Taste, hath listed into his Service."[13]

As the levee begins, Laureate Cibber is asleep on Dulness's lap.[14] At her feet, prostrate and bound in chains, are those the goddess leads in captivity: Science, Wit, Logic, and Rhetoric. In "ten-fold bonds" lie the Muses. At this sight, the poet addresses Lord Chesterfield, who could not "a tear refuse" at the sight of the Muses enchained at Dulness's feet. Pope's note cites the misfortunes of the 1737 Licensing Act that subjected plays to the judgment of the envious and recalls Chesterfield's well-known speech against the Act. Pope thus allies the actions of the Ministry as agents of Dulness.

🐌 *Opera in* The New Dunciad

As prophesied, first to appear at Dulness's Grand Session is Opera, "The sure fore-runner of her gentle sway," as she was described at the end of Book III. Pope's portrait is the most notorious poetic image of opera:

Garden and the City, 150–62; Valerie Rumbold, "'The Reason of this Preference': Sleeping, Flowing and Freezing in Pope's *Dunciad*," *Proceedings of the British Academy*, 167 (2010), 423–51 (on George II as King of Dulness); Richard Braverman, "'Dunce the Second Reigns Like Dunce the First': The Gothic Bequest in the *Dunciad*," *ELH* (*English Literary History*), 62 (1995), 863–82; and Brean S. Hammond, *Pope and Bolingbroke: A Study of Friendship and Influence* (Columbia, Mo.: University of Missouri Press, 1984), 51–4. Vincent Carretta, *The Snarling Muse: Verbal and Visual Satire from Pope to Churchill* (Philadelphia, Penn.: University of Pennsylvania Press, 1983), 140–72 touches on politics and treatment of opera.

13 *Common Sense*, no. 254 (26 Dec. 1741; not in collected reprint edition). The lead essay continues with "A Panegyrick upon Dulness," recommending Dulness to all those who wish to succeed and urging the minister to erect to her a temple.

14 In the final lifetime form (as Rumbold terms it) of *The Dunciad in Four Books* (1743), Colley Cibber replaces Lewis Theobald (Tibbald), who had (rightly) criticized Pope's edition of Shakespeare, as the hero of the *Dunciad*.

THE NEW DUNCIAD: OPERA AND THE TRIUMPH OF DULNESS 283

> When lo! a Harlot form soft sliding by,
> With mincing step, small voice, and languid eye;
> Foreign her air, her robe's discordant pride
> In patch-work flutt'ring, and her head aside:
> By singing Peers up-held on either hand,
> She tripp'd and laugh'd, too pretty much to stand;
> Cast on the prostrate Nine a scornful look,
> Then thus in quaint Recitativo spoke.
>   O *Cara! Cara!* silence all that train:
> Joy to great Chaos! let Division reign:
> Chromatic tortures soon shall drive them hence,
> Break all their nerves, and fritter all their sense:
> One Trill shall harmonize joy, grief, and rage,
> Wake the dull Church, and lull the ranting Stage;
> To the same notes thy sons shall hum, or snore,
> And all thy yawning daughters cry, *encore.*[15]

This vivid personification of Italian opera deftly alludes to its risible features long charged against it: its degraded form that elevates music over poetry (harlot form); its effeminate nature (soft form, mincing step, small voice); foreign origin; compilations of arias from various composers (fluttering patch-work of the *pasticci*); aristocratic and royal patronage (upheld by singing peers); drawing patronage away from other arts (scorned Muses); and the singers' virtuoso vocal embellishments (divisions and chromatic tortures).[16]

The action of the Grand Session, which to critics has often seemed confused, draws on several models that would have been familiar to Pope's readers. The primary one is the Session of Poets poem, in which Apollo calls an assembly of

---

[15] *Dunciad*, IV:45–60; all quotations from *The Dunciad in Four Books* are to the Rumbold edition.

[16] On Pope's treatment of opera in the *Dunciad*, see Robert Ness, "*The Dunciad* and Italian Opera in England," *Eighteenth-Century Studies*, 20 (1986–87), 173–94; Pat Rogers, "The Critique of Opera in Pope's *Dunciad*," *Musical Quarterly*, 59 (1973), 15–30; Rogers, *Grub Street Literature and Popular Culture in Eighteenth Century England* (Brighton: Harvester Press, 1985), 102–19; Morris R. Brownell, "Ears of an Untoward Make: Pope and Handel," *Musical Quarterly*, 62 (1976), 554–70; Deborah J. Knuth, "Pope, Handel and the *Dunciad*," *Modern Language Studies*, vol. 10, no. 3 (Fall 1980), 22–8; and Valerie Rumbold, "Ideology and Opportunism: The Role of Handel in Pope's *The Dunciad in Four Books*," pp. 62–80 in *"More Solid Learning": New Perspectives on Alexander Pope's "Dunciad*," ed. Catherine Ingrassia and Claudia N. Thomas (Cranbury, N.J.: Associated University Presses, 2000).

Pope provided this note to the passage: "The Attitude given to this Phantom represents the nature and genius of the *Italian* Opera; its affected airs, its effeminate sounds, and the practice of patching up these Operas with favourite Songs, incoherently put together. These things were supported by the subscriptions of the Nobility"; note to *Dunciad*, IV:45; on Pope's note, see *Dunciad in Four Books*, ed. Rumbold, 279–80. On the feminization of opera, see Thomas McGeary, "'Warbling Eunuchs': Opera, Gender, and Sexuality on the London Stage," *Restoration and Eighteenth-Century Theatre Research*, 2nd ser., 7 (1992), 1–22.

284   THE CULTURAL POLITICS OF OPERA, 1720–1742

poets, dramatists, or writers to compete for the bays. One after another, they parade their unworthy claims and are dismissed for some personal or literary failing, earning instead of the laurels only ridicule for their foolish pretensions.

Opera had a central place in the *Dunciad* as early as Pope's early notes and sketches for the poem. What at the time was an unused outline for Book II became the basis for the Grand Session scene of Book IV.[17] In the first sketch, the "Sons of Dullness" march in a procession to present addresses and pay homage to the new King Tibbalds. Among the train are figures that did appear at Dulness's levee: "Governors to Travelling Noblemen / Academy of Musick, Virtuosos (ye Corruptions of Each)." The virtuosos are collectors of "Editions, Statues, Paintings, silly Affecta- / tion of Taste."

Pope notes to himself:

Then introduce ye Directors of Musick with all
their Set of fine Gentlemen of Taste. All telling Dullness
& their King Tibbalds what they will perform with yr [their]
Lives & Fortunes for her, & what they have done in
bringing up ye Youth to such Ends for ye Next Age.

Opera was, then, from the very inception of the *Dunciad* among those perversions of taste and education that divert Dulness's votaries from the proper goal of humane learning.[18]

What may have been a model for Opera appearing at a session presided over by Folly (a Dulness surrogate) occurs in Thomas Fitzgerald's *Folly* (February 1727), a poem likely known to Pope.[19] Folly assembles a court of her followers "to know / How far the Limits of her Empire go" (p. 1).[20] To receive Folly's rewards, by virtue of their patronage of opera, appear

---

[17] The drafts (called the First and Second Broglio Manuscripts) were transcribed by Jonathan Richardson, Jr. Transcriptions and commentary given here as in Maynard Mack, *The Last and Greatest Art: Some Unpublished Poetical Manuscripts of Alexander Pope* (Newark, Del.: University of Delaware Press, 1984), 97–155 (on p. 127); also given in slightly different transcription in Mack, "'The Last and Greatest Art': Pope's Poetical Manuscripts," in Mack, *Collected in Himself: Essays Critical, Biographical, and Bibliographical on Pope and Some of His Contemporaries* (Newark, Del.: University of Delaware Press [1982]), 341–2.

[18] Pope's notion that opera was essential to Dulness was later developed in *The Temple of Dullness* (1745), whose Preface observes that "Mr. *Pope*, in his last *Dunciad*, makes the Goddess of *Dullness* preside over *Italian* Operas, from whence her Character is taken." The comic opera, possibly by Colley Cibber, with music by Thomas Arne, develops the idea that Dullness, in love with Merit, invites him to a rehearsal of scenes from an opera, which Merit scorns. The Chorus proclaims, "Adieu to Merit; Dullness hail!"

[19] On the poem's attribution to Thomas Fitzgerald and its relation to Pope's *Dunciad*, see Valerie Rumbold and Thomas McGeary, "*Folly*, Session Poems, and the Preparations for Pope's *Dunciads*," *Review of English Studies*, n.s., 56 (2005), 577–610, which also contains a brief history of the Sessions tradition.

[20] Fitzgerald, *Folly*, 1.

THE NEW DUNCIAD: OPERA AND THE TRIUMPH OF DULNESS   285

> ... a Throng
> Of Lords and Beaux, that tripping it along
> To some new Op'ra Tune, designed to prove
> They had the best Pretence to claim her Love;
> Since their Subscriptions had the Pow'r to bring
> The dear *Italians* o'er to act and sing.   (pp. 16–17)

Royal levees crowded with bizarre characters would also have been familiar to many of Pope's readers from the farcical scenes in several of Henry Fielding's politically charged plays and farces that anticipate the one in *The New Dunciad*. *The Author's Farce* (1730), ridiculing London's irrational theatrical entertainments, features in the drawing room of Queen Nonsense (a lover of recitativo) a contest for the bays, which are won by Opera. In *Pasquin* (1736), a play inspired by the *Dunciad* and attended by Pope,[21] Queen Common Sense was stabbed by her priest Firebrand, while in her drawing room, Queen Ignorance settles in to rule with a vast number of "singers, fiddlers, tumblers, and rope-dancers" from Italy and France (see Chapter 9).[22]

Appearing at the Grand Session to vie for Dulness's honors is "a vast involuntary throng" (IV:82) of her votaries, who had abandoned good sense to pursue the follies and False Taste of the day: scholars and editors, teachers and divines, foppish travelers returned from the Grand Tour,[23] indolent virtuosi (antiquarian coin collectors, flower growers, and butterfly collectors), philosophers, and free-thinkers. Of note is that none of these tourists' follies included collecting painting, prints, and sculpture – arts to which Pope was devoted.

The devotees of Dulness lack learning and social responsibility: their study of nature and the arts is perverted by pedantic attention to factual detail, not the true goals of virtue and humane learning. They all ignore the higher goal of learning and study,

> How parts relate to part, or they to whole,
> The body's harmony, the beaming soul.   (IV:235–6)

Among the follies indulged by the votaries of Dulness is opera. A tutor introduces his charge, "thy accomplish'd Son," to Dulness (IV:282). During their Grand Tour, opera was one of their preoccupations. On the Continent, they

> Saw ev'ry Court, heard ev'ry King Declare
> His royal Sense, of Op'ra's or the Fair.   (IV:313–14)

The "glorious Youth" so emptied his head of all classical learning that

---

[21] See *Grub-street Journal*, no. 328 (8 April 1736), which reprints a poem "On Seeing Mr. Pope at the *Dramatic Satire* call'd *Pasquin*." The following issue corrects the date of attendance.

[22] On Fielding's later change in attitudes toward Handel, Charles Trainor, "Fielding, Opera, and Oratorio: The Case of Handel," *Eighteenth-Century Life*, 46, no. 3 (2022), 83–100.

[23] The Grand Tour passage is *Dunciad* IV:297–334. On betrayal of the ideals of the Grand Tour in the levee scene: Williams, *Pope's "Dunciad,"* 121–3, and Mack, *Alexander Pope*, 791–3.

286 THE CULTURAL POLITICS OF OPERA, 1720–1742

> And last [he] turn'd *Air*, the Echo of a Sound!
> See now, half-cur'd, and perfectly well-bred,
> With nothing but a Solo in his head. (IV:322–4)

The opera-besotted youth has returned from Italy not with the verbal word that embodies wisdom and classical learning enriched by contact with the persons and places of antiquity, but the empty sound of Dulness. Pope drives home the point in his note. Since "nothing but a *Solo*" is a tautology, he supposes the classical scholar Richard Bentley (an exemplar of Dulness) would emend the line pedantically, "Read boldly an *Opera*, which is enough of conscience for such a head as has lost all its Latin." Dulness accepts the youth and frees him from "sense of Shame" (IV:336).

When the aspirants have proven their rights to Dulness's favor, the celebration of her mysteries begins with libations offered by the Magus (the High Priest) of Dulness:

> With that, a Wizard Old his *Cup* extends;
> Which whoso tastes, forgets his former friends,
> Sire, Ancestors, Himself. (IV:517–19)

The Wizard is certainly meant to recall Walpole offering bribes and places,[24] and Pope here describes the compromising effects of his venal corruption on a susceptible politician's responsibilities to his friend, family, and himself.

Dulness's initiates are each assigned a hierophant – Impudence, Stupefaction, Self-conceit, or Interest – to lead them through the mysteries. The Muses of Opera are assigned to one group of "empty heads," sons of peers who are devotees of opera:

> … the Syren Sisters warble round,
> And empty heads console with empty sound.
> No more, alas! the voice of Fame they hear,
> The balm of Dulness trickling in their ear.
> Great C * *, H * *, P * *, R * *, K *.
> Why all your Toils? your Sons have learn'd to sing.
> How quick Ambition hastes to ridicule!
> The Sire is made a Peer, the Son a Fool. (IV:541–8)

Several of Pope's near-contemporaries supplied names for the initials of the late peers whose sons were opera-crazy. The consensus is that the sires are William Cowper (*c*. 1665–1723), first Earl Cowper and Lord Chancellor; Simon Harcourt (1661–1727), first Viscount Harcourt and Lord Chancellor; Thomas

---

[24] Walpole had appeared as the chief magician in the print "The Festival of the Golden Rump" (1737); Frederic G. Stephens and M. Dorothy George, *Catalogue of Prints and Drawings in the British Museum*, 11 vols. (London: British Museum Publications, 1870–1919), no. 2327. See also Paul Langford, *Walpole and the Robinocracy. The English Satirical Print, 1600–1832* (Cambridge: Chadwyck-Healy, 1986), no. 48; and Herbert M. Atherton, *Political Prints in the Age of Hogarth: A Study of the Ideographic Representation of Politics* (Oxford: Clarendon, 1974), no. 19. Illustrated in Mack, *Garden and the City*, Plate 37.

THE NEW DUNCIAD: OPERA AND THE TRIUMPH OF DULNESS   287

Parker (1667–1732), first Earl of Macclesfield and Lord Chancellor; Sir Robert Raymond (1673–1733), first Baron Raymond and Lord Chief Justice; and Peter King (1669–1734), first Baron King of Ockham and Lord Chancellor.[25]

The involvement of each of the sons (or Harcourt's grandson) is documented or likely.[26] While on his Grand Tour in Italy in 1729–1730, William Cowper (1709–1764), second Earl Cowper, wrote home in raptures about hearing Farinelli perform during Carnival in Venice in 1729–1730 and befriended him. He received the dedication of Johann Hasse's opera *Artaserse* produced there in 1730, in which Farinelli sang.[27] Upon his arrival in Britain in September 1734, Farinelli visited Cowper at this country seat near Canterbury; Cowper presented Farinelli at Court and was one of the principal managers of the Opera of the Nobility, for which Farinelli starred along with Senesino.[28] He is likely the peer cited in Paul Whitehead's *Manners* (1738).

Simon Harcourt (1714–1777), second Viscount (later first Earl) Harcourt, was in Italy on his Grand Tour in 1730–1734. His letters and those of his tutor to his mother and sister record their plans to see opera in Milan and probably Rome and Venice.[29]

George Parker, (*c.* 1697–1764), second Earl of Macclesfield, was in Italy on his Grand Tour 1719–1722. He received the dedication of the opera *Griselda*, which was produced in Venice in 1720.[30]

---

[25] Identifications are given in *The Dunciad*, ed. Sutherland, 395–6, note to line IV:545 (the Biographical Appendix provides documentation of some of the sons' operatic activities); *The Works of Alexander Pope. New Edition,* ed. Whitwell Elwin and William J. Courthope, 10 vols. (London: John Murray, 1882), 4:365; and *Dunciad in Four Books*, ed. Rumbold, 343n.

[26] On the operatic activities of the sons/grandsons, Thomas McGeary, "Opera-Loving Sons of Peers in *The Dunciad*," *Notes and Queries*, vol. 62, no. 2 (June 2015), 279–85, from which the following is adapted or elaborated.

[27] The manuscript copy of Hasse's Artaserse, which Cowper obtained in Venice, is at the British Library, Add. MS 22,107, with bookplate with his family arms. I thank Graham Cummings for drawing this manuscript to my attention.

[28] Thomas McGeary, "Farinelli's Progress to Albion: The Recruitment and Reception of Opera's 'Blazing Star,'" *British Journal for Eighteenth-Century Studies*, 28 (2005), 339–61; and John Ingamells, *A Dictionary of British and Irish Travellers in Italy, 1701–1800* (New Haven, Conn.: Yale University Press, 1997). Xavier Cervantes, "History and Sociology of the Italian Opera in London (1705–45): The Evidence of the Dedications of the Printed Librettos," *Studi musicali*, 27 (1998), 339–82 (at 381) records the opera dedication (but mis-identified as the third Earl).

Cowper's travels and acquaintance with opera on his Grand Tour can be followed in his and his tutor Joseph Atwell's letters at Hertford Archives and Local Studies, Panshanger Papers: D/EP F 234.

[29] Harcourt: His Italian trip is described in letters from him and his tutor Walter Bowman, now at the Bodleian Library. Harcourt Papers. MS Eng. D. 3829. Excepts in *The Harcourt Papers*, ed. Edward W. Harcourt, 14 vols. (Oxford: James Parker, 1880–1905), 3:11, 26–7; see also, Ingamells, *A Dictionary of British and Irish Travellers*, 463–4.

[30] Parker: His own letters home do not mention opera, possibly because his father disapproved; but opera is mentioned or implied in other letters to his father; British

288   THE CULTURAL POLITICS OF OPERA, 1720–1742

Sir Robert Raymond (*c.* 1717–1756), second Baron Raymond, was in Italy in 1736–1738, and reports spread to England of his theatrical activities there. Horace Mann wrote Horace Walpole that Lords Middlesex and Raymond had been cheated by the present London opera manager Vanneschi "in their opera at Lucca."[31] William Bristow wrote how at Florence during Carnival 1737, Lords Barrington, Middlesex, and Raymond had produced "une masque superbe, reppresantant un Général ou Consul Romain revenant d'une Victoire en triomphe á cheval, le premier etoit le Consul & les deux autres les Tribuns du peuple suivis d'un grand train, le tout reussissoit fort bien & a fait parler toute l'Italie."[32] In June 1737, Barrington wrote to David Mallet that "Lord Raymond plays much the same game with the —— at Venice, that he played with the singing women at Florence."[33] He received the dedications of operas in Venice and Florence.[34]

John King (1706–1740), second Baron King, was in Italy in 1728 on his Grand Tour, when he likely saw opera.[35]

Pope charges that the sires' accomplishments earned them first peerages and then ridicule when their foolish descendants became opera patrons ("have learned to sing"). The contrasts between sire and son are, as Valerie Rumbold observed, "a striking instance of Pope's sense of opera as a touchstone of aristocratic degeneracy."[36]

At last, Dulness confers her titles and degrees and sends her opera-loving sons out to make "one Mighty Dunciad of the Land!" (IV:604). Her mighty, unmeaning yawn causes all Nature to nod, and her "long solemn Unison" (recalling Opera's "one long Trill") spreads far out over all the realm, overcoming even the chief ministers of state:

Library Stowe 750, ff.327–42. His travels and mentions of opera can also be found in his tutor Edward Wright's *Some Observations Made in Travelling Through France, Italy, &c. in the Years 1720, 1721, and 1722* (1730; 2nd ed., 1764); and Ingamells, *Dictionary of Travellers*, 737–8. Cervantes, "History and Sociology of the Italian Opera," 380, records the opera dedication. See also T. P. Connor, "The Fruits of a Grand Tour: Edward Wright and Lord Parker in Italy, 1720–22," *Apollo*, vol. 148, no. 437 (July 1998), 23–30.

[31] Raymond: Letter from Horace Mann, Florence, 10 December 1741 n.s., to Horace Walpole; *Yale Edition of the Correspondence of Horace Walpole*, ed. W. S. Lewis, 48 vols. (New Haven, Conn.: Yale University Press, 1937–1983), 17:216; Ingamells, *Dictionary of British and Irish Travellers*, 657–8 and 804; Cervantes, "History and Sociology of the Italian Opera," 382, records the opera dedication.

[32] Letter from William Bristow, Rome, 10 March 1737, to the Countess of Denbigh; Warwickshire Record Office, Denbigh Papers, CR 2017 / C241, no. 20. Also transcribed in Historical Manuscripts Commission. *Report on the Manuscripts of the Earl of Denbigh. Pt. V* (London: His Majesty's Stationery Office, 1911), 212.

[33] Letter from Lord Barrington, 7 June, to [David] Mallet; quoted in *Works of Alexander Pope*, ed. Elwin and Courthope, 4:365.

[34] Cervantes, "History and Sociology of the Italian Opera," 382, records the opera dedication.

[35] King: Ingamells, *Dictionary of British and Irish Travellers*, 576.

[36] *Dunciad in Four Books*, ed. Rumbold, 343n.

THE NEW DUNCIAD: OPERA AND THE TRIUMPH OF DULNESS   289

> More she had spoke, but yawn'd—All Nature nods:
> What Mortal can resist the Yawn of Gods?
> …
> Lost was the Nation's Sense, nor could be found,
> While the long solemn Unison went round:
> Wide, and more wide, it spread o'er all the realm;
> Ev'n Palinurus nodded at the Helm:
> The Vapour mild o'er each Committee crept;
> Unfinish'd Treaties in each Office slept;
> And Chiefless Armies doz'd out the Campaign;
> And Navies yawn'd for Orders on the Main.   (IV:605–18)

The image of Palinurus inverts Edward Young's image of Walpole from *Love of Fame*, where "Walpole, pilot of the realm! / Our Palinurus slept not at the helm."[37] As in the earlier *State Dunces* of Paul Whitehead, Dulness extends her rule to the realm of politics and the Ministry, and Pope here indicts the Ministry's delays and mismanagement of the recent campaigns in the West Indies.[38] With Handel – that last bulwark against her – exiled to Ireland, Dulness expands her sway over the entire world of learning, culminating in Pope's apocalyptic vision of the restoration of the empire of Chaos:

> Lo! thy dread Empire, Chaos! is restor'd;
> Light dies before thy uncreating word:
> Thy hand, great Anarch! lets the curtain fall;
> And Universal Darkness buries All.   (IV:653–6)

Pope published revisions of *The Dunciad Variorum* in the 1730s, and the succeeding revisions, though often minor, sharpened its political partisanship.[39] With *The New Dunciad*, Pope had produced, writes Maynard Mack,

> a satire of 600-odd lines of unparalleled specificity and boldness, attributing to the Hanoverian court and its former first minister primary responsibility for a general moral and cultural decay which since the middle 30's even Whig observers had been deploring.[40]

The confirmation of Walpole as the true agent of Dulness was made in a print titled "The late P—m—r M—n—r." (Plate 12.1) that appeared in the year

---

[37] Edward Young, *Love of Fame* (1728), Satire 7.
[38] Here Pope is adapting lines from the poem "On Orpheus and Margarita," where Nottingham sleeps, lulled by the singing of Margarita, in reference to naval action against France in the War of the Spanish Succession; see McGeary, *Opera and Politics in Queen Anne's Britain*, 108–9.
[39] The evolving political animus against the royal family and Ministry are traced in Mack, *Garden and the City*, 150–62; Pat Rogers, "Ermine, Gold and Lawn, *The Dunciad* and the Coronation of George II," pp. 102–19 in *Literature and Popular Culture in Eighteenth Century England* (Sussex: Harvester Press, 1985); Erskine-Hill, *Pope: The Dunciad*, 48–60; and Richard Braverman, "Dunce the Second Reigns Like Dunce the First."
[40] Mack, *Garden and the City*, 152.

PLATE 12.1. George Bickham, *The Late Premier Minister* (1743), showing Robert Walpole as the hero of the *Dunciad* yawning the great yawn of Dulness.

following his downfall.[41] The portrait shows a gaping-mouthed Walpole yawning. To the printed question, "Lo! What are all your Schemes come to?" the caption provides the answer, quoting fourteen lines from the *Dunciad* (IV:605–618), beginning (with the pronoun altered to "he"):

> More he had said, but yawn'd — All Nature nods:
> What Mortal can resist the Yawn of Gods?

The effects of Dulness's yawn are the same as the consequences of Walpole's rule over Britain. Ultimately, Walpole, not Cibber, is the real hero of the *Dunciad*.[42]

---

[41] "The late P—m—r M—n—r": published on 3 December 1743. Stephens and George, *Catalogue of Prints and Drawings in the British Museum*, 2607; reproduced in Langford, *Walpole and the Robinocracy*, no. 109; Atherton, *Political Prints in the Age of Hogarth*, no. 54; and Mack, *Garden and the City*, 161.

[42] Mack, *Garden and the City*, 150–62. The central place of Walpole is stressed in Erskine-Hill, "The Politics of 'The Dunciad,'" in *Pope: The Dunciad*, 48–60.

THE NEW DUNCIAD: OPERA AND THE TRIUMPH OF DULNESS   291

❧ *Handel in* The New Dunciad

The celebrated image of Handel – what George Sherburn calls "the most famous and most timely compliment ever paid to Handel" – had occurred early in the levee scene.[43] Handel – his music stirring, rousing, and shaking the soul – poses a threat to the coming reign of Dulness, and Opera urges her to exile him to Ireland, where politicians out of favor were often sent:

> Another Phœbus, thy own Phoebus, reigns,
> Joys in my jiggs, and dances in my chains.
> But soon, ah soon Rebellion will commence,
> If Music meanly borrows aid from Sense:
> Strong in new Arms, lo! Giant Handel stands,
> Like bold Briareus, with a hundred hands;
> To stir, to rouze, to shake the Soul he comes,
> And Jove's own Thunders follow Mars's Drums.
> Arrest him, Empress; or you sleep no more —
> She heard, and drove him to th' Hibernian shore.   (IV:61–70)

Handel was in fact not 'driven' to Ireland; his 'exile' was a well-planned trip to Dublin from November 1741 to August 1742 for a subscription concert series and first performance of *Messiah*.[44]

Commentators on the passage have noted that this panegyric to Handel seems inconsistent with Pope's previous vilification of opera in the *Dunciad* of 1728, satires of the 1730s, and elsewhere in *The New Dunciad*. Why would Pope now hold up Handel as a threat to Dulness when, as Pope certainly knew, Handel was by then the most prominent composer of opera living in London, and hence one of the followers of Dulness?

Political context and Pope's circle of friends, though, certainly suggests that Pope is celebrating not Handel as the opera composer, but Handel the oratorios composer. Handel had achieved an increasingly dominant position as Britain's national composer with his gradual turn from producing Italian opera to producing oratorios.

Pope's lines –

> To stir, to rouze, to shake the Soul he comes,
> And Jove's own Thunders follow Mars's Drums.

---

[43] Sherburn, "The *Dunciad*, Book IV," 179." I have expanded on this section in McGeary, "Handel in the Dunciad: Pope, Handel, Frederick, Prince of Wales, and Cultural Politics," *Musical Quarterly*, 97 (2015), 542–74.

[44] On Handel's advance planning for the trip to Dublin, see David Hunter, "Dublin," in *The Cambridge Handel Encyclopedia*, ed. Annette Landgraf and David Vickers (Cambridge: Cambridge University Press, 2009), 198–9; Hunter, "Inviting Handel to Ireland: Laurence Whyte and the Challenge of Poetic Evidence," *Eighteenth-Century Ireland*, 20 (2005), 156–68; Hunter, *The Lives of George Frederic Handel* (Woodbridge: Boydell Press, 2015), 360–8; Donald Burrows, "Handel's Dublin Performances," *Irish Musical Studies*, 4 (1996), 46–70; and Burrows, *Handel*, 2nd ed. (New York, N.Y.: Oxford University Press, 2012), 339–52.

292   THE CULTURAL POLITICS OF OPERA, 1720–1742

– evoke the mighty choruses and drums of *Saul* and *Israel in Egypt* recently produced in January and April 1739 and revived in following seasons.

Various explanations have been offered for Pope's panegyric to Handel. Supposedly being insensitive to music, Pope was deferring to the musical opinions of Dr. Arbuthnot and others. Or, Pope was motivated by his friendship with Handel going back to their meetings at Lord Burlington's in the years *c*. 1715–1717, and their collaboration on the two masques Handel wrote (or first produced) for the Duke of Chandos at Cannons in 1718, *Acis and Galatea* and *Haman and Mordecai* (later rewritten as the oratorio *Esther*).[45] Or, it is suggested their friendship is shown by the appearance of lines by Pope in the texts of Handel's *Semele* (1744) and *Jephtha* (1752), which reciprocate Pope's tribute in *The New Dunciad*. There is, though, little or no evidence of sustained contact or collaboration between them.[46]

In one sense, Pope is joining many others in endorsing English-language oratorio on biblical themes as a dramatic music superior to opera.[47] Despite the still-prevailing animosity of some toward Italian opera and the Hanoverians, Handel's foreign origins are overlooked and his English oratorios begin to be seen to embody those national virtues opposed to those commonly ascribed to Italian opera.[48]

But other motives can be found in the political context of the poem: Prince Frederick's own friendship with and patronage of Handel; Pope's friendship with Frederick; Pope's own sympathy with Opposition politics; and the Patriot Opposition's appropriation of Handel as a National Worthy.

FREDERICK AND HANDEL

The impressions given by Lord Hervey's biased *Memoirs* that Prince Frederick was an opponent of Handel and was involved in the founding of the Opera of the Nobility in 1733 to oppose Handel's company in order to spite his sister and the royal family, and that the Nobility Opera was specifically associated with the political opposition, have been shown to be largely fictions.[49]

Handel and Frederick generally had amiable contact at Court following Frederick's arrival in December 1728, Handel being music teacher to two of

---

[45] See sources cited in note 16 above. Ness concentrates more than the others on explaining the paradox of Pope's attitude toward Handel.

[46] These explanations are set forth and considered in more detail in McGeary, "Handel in the Dunciad: Pope, Handel, Frederick, Prince of Wales, and Cultural Politics."

[47] On how oratorio would have met many of Pope's ideals for setting of texts, see Rumbold, "Ideology and Opportunism," esp. 65–70. For a change in attitudes for Handel, focusing on oratorio, see Trainor, "Fielding, Opera, and Oratorio: The Case of Handel."

[48] On how Handel's oratorios carry patriotic themes and positive values associated with English dramatic music, Ruth Smith, *Handel's Oratorios and Eighteenth-Century Thought* (Cambridge: Cambridge University Press, 1995).

[49] On the founding of the Opera of Nobility, the support by both the King and Prince Frederick, correction of the many fictions about Frederick's participation, and Handel's turn to opera, see McGeary, *Opera and Politics in Handel's Britain*, 150–68; and Chapter 6 above.

his sisters. Handel provided occasional music for Frederick. For his wedding to Augusta, Princess of Saxe-Gotha, on 27 April 1736 at St. James's Palace, he composed the wedding anthem, *Sing unto God*.[50] For Frederick's wedding, he presented "for the Entertainment of her Royal Highness the future Princess of Wales" performances of *Ariodante* and *Atalanta* in May 1736. Later that year at the request of the Prince and Princess, Handel began his new opera season early on 6 November 1736, and later that month, revived *Atalanta* on 20 November for the Prince's birthday. Except for the period after September 1737, when the King expelled Frederick and his family from St. James's and forbade him and his supporters from Court, commanding those with appointments in both households to quit one of them,[51] Handel was a frequent visitor at the Prince's residences, where he held rehearsals and participated in concerts.

To his credit, Frederick apparently bore Handel no ill-will for his obeying the King's command. In March 1738 his name headed the list of subscribers to the publication of Handel's *Alexander's Feast*.[52] The following 1738–39 season, Frederick would attend Handel's oratorios (see Table 12.1). Attendance by Frederick and Augusta at Handel's oratorios or their commanding performances of them are announced in the press and are mentioned in contemporary diaries and correspondence as well.[53] Sometime before 1742, Frederick acquired a portrait of Handel painted by Joseph Goupy.[54] After the Prince and his father reconciled after the fall of Walpole in February 1742, Handel resumed socializing with the Prince, holding rehearsals and attending his private concerts (Frederick was a keen amateur cellist and composer).

Although Handel once passed severe judgment on his compositions,[55] Frederick paid tribute to Handel in a Temple of Mount Parnassus he planned for Kew about the year 1751.[56] The temple would have had the paired busts of ancient and modern Worthies. For example, Lycurgus, Socrates, Archimedes, Homer, Aeschylus, and Horace were to be paired with Alfred, Locke, Newton, Milton, Shakespeare, and Pope, respectively. Among artists, Frederick paired Handel with the ancient Greek musician Timotheus, whose musical powers

---

[50] On the ceremonies and two anthems, Burrows, *Handel and the English Chapel Royal*, 309–38, 339–54.

[51] The episode is given in more detail in Thomas McGeary, "Handel and the Feuding Royals," *The Handel Institute Newsletter*, 17 (Autumn 2006), 5–8 (reprinted in *Handel: The Baroque Composers*, ed. David Vickers [Farnham: Ashgate, 2010]).

[52] Deutsch, *Handel*, 453; *Handel: Collected Documents*, ed. Burrows et al., 3:364–7.

[53] Mentions of Prince and Princess at oratorios: Carole Taylor, "Handel and Frederick, Prince of Wales," *Musical Times*, 125 (1984), 89–92, and *Handel: Collected Documents*, ed. Burrows et al., vols. 3–4.

[54] Listed in Kimerly Rorschach, "Frederick, Prince of Wales (1707–51) as Collector and Patron," *Walpole Society*, 55 (1989–1990), p. 73, no. 152; also in Rorschach, "Frederick, Prince of Wales (1707–1751) As a Patron of the Visual Arts: Princely Patriotism and Political Propaganda," 2 vols. (Ph.D. dissertation, Yale University, 1985), no. 122, 1:370.

[55] The anecdote is reported in McGeary, "Handel and the Feuding Royals," 7–8.

[56] The project is described in Rorschach, "Frederick, Prince of Wales, As a Patron of the Visual Arts," 1:164–74.

294 THE CULTURAL POLITICS OF OPERA, 1720–1742

TABLE 12.1. Prince Frederick's Patronage of Handel's Operas,
Odes, and Oratorios

| Season | Payment to Handel* | Handel Performances* | |
		Number Given	Attendance by Frederick
1733–34	£250	61	12
1734–35	0	56	0
1735–36	0	19	0
1736–37	£250	52	14
1737–38	£250	19*	1**
1738–39	£73 10s	15	7
1739–40	£94 10s	14	9
1740–41	£52 10s	15	5
1741–42***	0	0	0
1742–43	£73 10s	12	7
1743–44	0	12	0
1744–45	£94 10s	16	9

* Three operas as part of Opera of the Nobility season, plus Handel benefit
** Only Frederick's attendance at Handel's benefit is documented; but
   attendance at operas presumed (since bounty was paid)
*** Handel in Dublin
Sources: Handel: Collected Documents, ed. Burrows et al., vols. 3 and 4;
Carole Taylor, "Handel and Frederick, Prince of Wales," *Musical Times*, 125
(1984), 89–92; and Taylor, "Italian Operagoing in London," 348–60.

Handel himself had celebrated in *Alexander's Feast* (1736). The temple project,
though not carried out due to Frederick's early death in 1751, must have been
meant to demonstrate the Prince's commitment to encouraging the arts and
sciences and British Worthies.[57]

POPE AND FREDERICK

Pope's panegyric to Handel in *The New Dunciad* may have arisen from Pope's
friendship with Frederick, who, as we have seen, was a friend and patron of
Handel. Pope's befriending Frederick may have been encouraged by his involvement and sympathies with the new Patriot Opposition, his friendship with its
leaders, and their taking Frederick as their figurehead.

Pope and Frederick likely met through one of their friends in common,
among them William Kent, George Lyttelton, Lord Bathurst, Viscount Boling-

---

[57] In about 1749, Frederick became involved in planning for an academy for drawing and
painting, commemorated in an oil sketch by Francis Hayman; see Brian Allen, *Francis
Hayman* (New Haven, Conn.: Yale University Press, 1987), cat. no. 48, fig. 36.

THE NEW DUNCIAD: OPERA AND THE TRIUMPH OF DULNESS   295

broke, and Lord Cobham. Pope shared their antipathy toward the Walpole ministry. Pope and Frederick also shared interests in art and gardening.[58]

Frederick was informed about Pope as an eminent English writer while he was still in Hanover[59] before coming to Britain in 1728. It is not known when Pope and Frederick first met, but Frederick's first known visit to Pope on 4 October 1735 was widely reported in the press and contemporary correspondence.[60]

The warmth of their friendship is revealed in a series of reciprocal gifts, favors, and gestures.[61] Between April 1735 and 1739, Pope presented to Frederick a set of elaborately bound quarto and octavo sets of his complete works. Frederick presented Pope a set of four small marble busts of Spencer, Shakespeare, Milton, and Dryden, and in April 1739, Frederick was arranging to present Pope with his choice of a set of urns for his garden.[62] Frederick paid a tribute to Pope in a portrait he commissioned from Jacopo Amigoni in 1735. There, a seated Frederick holds a book titled "Pope's Homer."[63] The iconography presents Frederick as a patron of British arts and traces a poetic lineage from Pope back to Homer. In 1738, one of the young Patriots George Lyttelton, Frederick's secretary and friend of Pope, was encouraging Pope to take on the role of Frederick's mentor and animate the Prince along the path of Virtue.[64]

---

[58] Morris R. Brownell, *Alexander Pope and the Arts of Georgian England* (Oxford: Clarendon Press, 1978), 175–6, 194.

[59] The diplomat Ludwig von Schrader wrote to Pope's friends the Blount sisters from Hanover, sometime between 1725 and December 1728, that he read "Mr Pope's Preface to Shakespear with him; that he might see how Men of Great Sense do Judge of Books and Learning"; quoted in Valerie Rumbold, *Women's Place in Pope's World* (Cambridge: Cambridge University Press, 1989), 258.

[60] Letter from Pope, 8 October 1735, to Bathurst, in Pope, *Correspondence*, ed. Sherburn, 3:500; letter from Lyttelton, 12 October 1735, to Frederick in *Memoirs and Correspondence of George, Lord Lyttelton*, ed. Robert Phillimore, 2 vols. (London: James Ridgway, 1845), 1:77; *Old Whig*, no. 3 (9 Oct. 1735); *London Evening Post*, no. 1230 (4–7 Oct. 1735); and letter from Lyttelton, 25 October [1738], to Pope, Pope, *Correspondence*, ed. Sherburn, 4:139.

[61] See Thomas McGeary, "Pope and Frederick, Prince of Wales: Gifts and Memorials of Their Friendship," *Scriblerian*, 23 (Autumn 2000), 40–4, for details of the gifts.

[62] Letter from Lyttelton, April 1739, to Pope; Pope, *Correspondence*, ed., Sherburn, 4:170 (also mentioned on 4:178 and 181).

[63] Amigoni painting: Rorschach, "Frederick as Collector and Patron," p. 73, no. 152; and Rorschach, "Frederick, Prince of Wales, as a Patron of the Visual Arts," p. 310, no. 3. Illustrated in Oliver Millar, *The Queen's Pictures* (New York, N.Y.: Macmillan, 1977), no. 106, p. 97; and the cover of Frances Vivian, *A Life of Frederick, Prince of Wales: A Connoisseur of the Arts*, ed. Roger White (Lewiston, N.Y.: Edwin Mellen Press, 2006). In the painting, Frederick gestures toward two hovering putti: one wearing a laurel wreath holds a lyre (sign of the lyric poet), while the other holds a snake (symbol of wisdom or attribute of Apollo).

[64] Letter from Lyttelton, 25 October 1738, to Pope, in Pope, *Correspondence*, ed. Sherburn, 4:138–9; letter from Pope to Lyttelton, *ca.* 1 November 1738, in Pope, *Correspondence*, ed. Sherburn, 4:142–4.

296 THE CULTURAL POLITICS OF OPERA, 1720–1742

While Pope's satires of the 1730s reveal his increasing disdain for the Hanoverians and their prime minister, they also reveal by contrast his respect and friendship with many persons in the Opposition circle, including Frederick. The hope he places in Frederick's future reign is shown in the second of the 1738 *Dialogues* (July 1738), where Pope lists those politicians who have won his love: Somers, Halifax, Pulteney, and Chesterfield (all at one time had lost their places at Court). Pope alludes to his friendship with Frederick:

> And if yet higher the proud List should end,
> Still let me say! No Follower, but a Friend.[65]

Pope's unfinished poem *One Thousand Seven Hundred and Forty* (begun in 1740, unpublished until 1797), continues the tone of the early 1738 *Dialogues*, but prominently casts Frederick in the role of Patriot King. After its opening cry of despair –

> O wretched B—— [Britain], jealous now of all,
> What God, what mortal, shall prevent thy fall?[66]

– the poem forsakes any nuance for straightforward denunciation of the ineffectual Opposition.

The poem's peroration, though, abandons disenchantment and looks to the future when Frederick will be the nation's sole savior (the gaps in the text are filled in italics):

> Alas! on one alone our all relies,
> Let him be honest, and he must be wise,
> Let him no trifler from his [?] school,
> Nor like his *father* still a *fool*
> Be but a man! unministered, alone,
> And free at once the Senate and the Throne.[67]

Here, as in other poems of the Patriot and oppositional circle, despair at Britain's sunken state has a complementary hope for redemption in the person of Frederick as Patriot King.[68]

HANDEL AS OPPOSITION WORTHY

In the late 1730s, as he was disengaging from opera and producing seasons containing an increasing variety of musical-dramatic works in English, Handel came to be acclaimed a British Worthy and source of national pride. The defining moment of his canonization was in the summer of 1738, when a life-sized marble statue of him by François Roubiliac was erected in the Spring-Gardens

---

[65] Pope, *Imitations of Horace*, ed. Butt, 318, lines 92–3.

[66] Pope, *Imitations of Horace*, ed. Butt, 332, lines 1–2.

[67] Pope, *Imitations of Horace*, ed. Butt, 337, lines 85–98; gaps in the text are supplied in italics as suggested in the Butt edition; see also *Works of Alexander Pope*, ed. Elwin and Courthope, 3:500–1.

[68] My account here paints Pope as more sympathetic and sincere in his attitude toward Frederick than in Gerrard, "Pope and the Patriots."

at Vauxhall.[69] A public statue to a living artist was unprecedented in Europe and testifies to the central place Handel had assumed in Britain's musical life. The statue was celebrated with poems and illustrations that were popular in the engraved vignettes of song sheets.

In satires and plays with oppositional thrust, we find Handel enlisted as a paradigm of a national, patriotic, redemptive music in accord with the Patriot's vision of Britain under a Patriot King (see Chapter 8). Paradoxically, both the nationalized court composer and the disenfranchised Catholic poet appear in Opposition literature as national Worthies. It was perhaps natural that Patriot poets – rising above faction and laying claims for a unifying British patriotism – would try to legitimate themselves by enlisting both Pope and Handel their Worthies.

There is no evidence that Handel was in any way sympathetic to the Opposition to Walpole and his ministry. At one point, he was drawing (before deductions) £600 annually as holder of two royal pensions and music teacher to the royal princesses, and he held an unofficial post as composer to the Chapel Royal.[70]

While Handel the opera composer had been complicit in an institution used by Opposition writers to exemplify the consequences of corruption, luxury, and False Taste, the Handel who presented seasons of exclusively English dramatic music could be enlisted with Pope on the side of virtue and other values opposed to the Ministry and government – as well as to opera.

---

[69] On the statue, its location, and subsequent history before arriving at its present home in the Victoria and Albert Museum, see Terence Hodgkinson, *Handel at Vauxhall.* Victoria and Albert Museum Bulletin Reprints no. 1 (1969) [expanded reprint from the *Bulletin of the Victoria and Albert Museum*, vol. 1. no. 4 (Oct. 1965), 1–13]; and Hunter, *George Frideric Handel*, 368–76.

From the extensive literature on Vauxhall and the statue, the principal discussions are D. Coke and A. Borg, *Vauxhall Gardens: A History* (New Haven, Conn.: Yale University Press, 2011), 89–96; Terence Hodgkinson, *Handel at Vauxhall.* Victoria and Albert Museum Bulletin Reprints 1 (London: Victoria and Albert Museum, 1969); David Bindman, "Roubiliac's Statue of Handel and the Keeping of Order in Vauxhall Gardens in the Early Eighteenth Century," *Sculpture Journal*, 1 (1997), 22–31; Suzanne Aspden, "'Fam'd Handel Breathing, tho' Transformed to Stone': The Composer as Monument," *Journal of the American Musicological Society*, 55 (2002), 39–90; David Coke, "Roubiliac's Handel for *Vauxhall* Gardens: A Sculpture in Context," *Sculpture Journal*, 16 (2007), 5–22; Thomas McGeary, "*Handel as Orpheus*: The Vauxhall statue re-examined," *Early Music*, 43 (2015), 291–308; and Malcolm Baker, *The Marble Index: Roubiliac and Sculptural Portraiture in Eighteenth-Century Britain* (New Haven, Conn.: Yale University Press, 2015).

Frederick, as Duke of Cornwall, was the ground landlord of Vauxhall Gardens, as well as its most prominent patron; Brian Allen, *Francis Hayman* (New Haven, Conn.: Yale University Press, 1987), 64.

[70] On royal pensions and teacher of princesses: Hunter, *Lives of George Frideric Handel*, 168–9, 175–90. On Handel's unofficial appointment as composer to the Chapel Royal in 1723: Donald Burrows, *Handel and the English Chapel Royal* (Oxford: Oxford University Press, 2005), 175–82.

298   THE CULTURAL POLITICS OF OPERA, 1720–1742

An early sign of this gradual oppositional appropriation of Handel occurs in James Miller's revision of his *Harlequin-Horace* for its third edition of 1735. One line from the 1731 edition is conspicuously altered. There, in reference to masquerades and Italian opera, Miller had charged "And *Heydegger* and *Handell* now rul'd our Gentry." In 1735, the disparaging comment is softened to "And Heydegger reign'd Guardian of our Gentry."[71]

Handel becomes an oppositional British Worthy in Thomas Beach's poem *Eugenio: or, Virtuous and Happy Life. Inscrib'd to Mr. Pope* (1737). John Dryden had introduced a Eugenius character in the dialogue *Essay of Dramatic Poetry* (1668) as a patriot who is proud of English drama.[72] In the *Tatler*, Richard Steele introduced Eugenio as "a Gentleman of a just Tast[e]," who is indignant at the fallen taste of theatre audiences.[73]

Early in 1735, Beach sent the manuscript to Swift, who approved his method "of describing a person who possesseth every virtue."[74] Although the poem in manuscript was intended as a panegyric to Sir William Fownes, who though died on 3 April 1735, the poem as published appears to be about Pope.

The Pope-Eugenio identification is confirmed in the woodcut vignette of a hill-side grotto on the poem's first page, which no doubt was intended to suggest Pope's own Thames-side grotto.[75] The figures standing on the lawn and the running hound (Pope's Bounce?) recall motifs found in other early views of Pope's villa.[76] In the poem, Eugenio is transparently Pope himself:

> See in Eugenio all the wond'rous Man!
> Whose Life was form'd, and rose on Virtue's Plan.   (p. 9)

Eugenio/Pope is a model for Virtue: he seeks and obeys truth and reason and draws on universal knowledge, history, and heroes. To provide Eugenio beauty and art, Beach proposes Raphael, Michael Rysbrack, and the two great Whig Lords Burlington and Cobham will provide Eugenio models for painting, sculpture, architecture, and a landscape garden (Stowe), respectively.

The music Beach provides Eugenio is composed and led by Handel:

---

[71] In 1731 edition (p. 29) and 1735 edition (p. 27) of Miller's *Harlequin-Horace*.

[72] See Howard Weinbrot, *Britannia's Issue: The Rise of British Literature from Dryden to Ossian* (Cambridge: Cambridge University Press, 1993), 167.

[73] *Tatler*, no. 8 (28 April 1709).

[74] Letter from Swift, 12 April 1735, to Beach, in Jonathan Swift, *Correspondence*, ed. Harold Williams, 5 vols. (Oxford: Clarendon Press, 1965), 4:320–2; and *The Correspondence of Jonathan Swift, D.D.*, ed. David Woolley, 4 vols. (Frankfurt am Main: Peter Lang, 1999–2007), 4:87–90, no. 1147.

[75] The source of the woodcut is an engraving of Queen Caroline's Hermitage by Claude Du Bosc after Hubert Gravelot, "View of the Hermitage in the Royal Garden at Richmond" (1735); illustrated in John Dixon Hunt, *William Kent: Landscape Garden Designer* (London: A. Zwemmer, 1987), 63.

[76] See illustrations nos. 4–5 in Morris R. Brownell, *Alexander Pope's Villa: Views of Pope's Villa, Grotto and Garden: A Microcosm of English Landscape* (London: Greater London Council, 1980).

THE NEW DUNCIAD: OPERA AND THE TRIUMPH OF DULNESS   299

> If *Handel*'s Fingers strike the tuneful Strings;
> *Cuzzoni* soft, or *Farinelli* sings;
> …
> The melting Music, and melodious Note
> From the sweet Concert, or warbling Throat,
> Regale Eugenio's Taste, and raise his Heart
> To the great Source of Beauty, and of Art! (pp. 19–20)

Burlington and Cobham were friends of Pope, as well as statesmen who had withdrawn from the Court (Burlington) or lost their appointments due to opposition to Walpole's policies (Cobham). The Fleming John Michael Rysbrack was the leading sculptor in Britain between 1720 and 1740.[77] For Burlington's Palladian Chiswick villa he provided both statues and busts of Andrea Palladio and Inigo Jones. He executed Pope's bust for Robert Harley, Earl of Oxford, and with Peter Scheemakers executed the busts for Lord Cobham's Temple of British Worthies at Stowe, both of which carried oppositional political meaning.[78] He possibly collaborated with Pope on monuments in Westminster Abbey,[79] and like Kent, Rysbrack had an official household appointment to Frederick.[80] We have seen in Chapter 10 that in *The World Unmask'd* Thomas Gilbert had cited both Pope and Handel as artists who had suffered the scandal of unrewarded virtue.

Handel and Pope again receive homage in James Miller's *The Art of Life. In Imitation of Horace's Art of Poetry* (1739). Miller was a member of the James Harris circle,[81] a group of Handel enthusiasts, and later wrote the libretto for *Joseph and His Brethren* set by Handel in 1744.[82] In the poem, modeled after the *Ars Poetica*, Miller gives rules for the conduct of life to a rich youth setting out in the world. Following the Golden Mean he can achieve grace and refined

---

[77] M. I. Webb, *Michael Rysbrack: Sculptor* (London: Country Life, 1954).

[78] On garden statuary and politics, in addition to Chapter 5, note 15, see Judith Colton, "Kent's Hermitage for Queen Caroline at Richmond," *Architectura*, 4 (1974), 181–91; Colton, "Merlin's Cave and Queen Caroline: Garden Art as Political Propaganda," *Eighteenth-Century Studies*, 10 (1976–77), 1–20; Ronald Paulson, *Emblem and Expression: Meaning in English Art of the Eighteenth Century* (Cambridge: Harvard University Press, 1975), 19–34; and John Dixon Hunt, "Emblem and Expression in the Eighteenth-Century Landscape Garden," *Eighteenth-Century Studies*, 4 (1970–71), 294–317.

[79] See Morris R. Brownell, *Alexander Pope and the Arts of Georgian England* (Oxford: Clarendon Press, 1978), 330–1.

[80] He was appointed "carver in stone"; see "Tradesmen and others, without salaries," British Library Add. MS 24,399, f. 19v (date: 8 Nov. 1732). Kent was appointed architect to Frederick on August 30 of the same year (f. 16r).

[81] On Miller in the Harris circle: *Music and Theatre in Handel's World: The Family Papers of James Harris, 1732–1780*, ed. Donald Burrows and Rosemary Dunhill (Oxford: Oxford University Press, 2002), 13–15, 20, 41, 50, 52–3, 57, 77, and 1108.

[82] On Miller as Handel's librettist, Ruth Smith, "Handel's English Librettists," pp. 92–108 in *The Cambridge Companion to Handel*, ed. Donald Burrows (Cambridge: Cambridge University Press, 1997), 9–94, 105–8.

300   THE CULTURAL POLITICS OF OPERA, 1720–1742

pleasures. He is advised to avoid "those false Tastes which opulent Youth is so generally Heir to" and to follow a "universal Simplicity and Decorum in Manners, Conversation and Dress" (Dedication). For the fine arts, Miller advises

> Let *Pope* and *Handel* then, with Sister Arts,
> At once improve your Joys, and mend your Hearts;
> When such Delights your leisure Moments know,
> Virtue and Wisdom from Amusement flow.   (p. 16)

Pope the satirist is praised for railing against vice:

> A righteous Rage at our degen'rate Days,
> Arm'd *Pope* with his *own* keen *Iambick* Lays,
> To scourge th' enormous Folly o' the Times,
> And make the Vicious tremble at his Rhimes.[83]

Miller the clergyman makes a point of celebrating Handel the composer recently turned to sacred oratorios:

> Hark! *Handel* strikes the Lyre — He whom the *Nine*
> Have crown'd sole Prince of Harmony Divine:
> Now sacred Themes his sacred Strains employ,
> And pour upon the Soul Seraphick Joy.[84]

Miller provides the equivalent of a musical *ekphrasis* of the highlights of *Saul* (premiered earlier that year on 16 January 1739):

> Hear *David* sooth the Phrensy of the King,
> In Sounds as sweet as *David's* Self could sing;
> When *Samuel's* boding Notes his Heart appall,
> We stand aghast, and tremble too with *Saul*;
> And when the solemn Fun'ral March moves on
> To plaintive Chords, whilst *David* joins his Moan
> Lamenting *Saul* and *Jonathan* his Son,
> *How are the Mighty fall'n!* we sighing cry,
> And Tears spontaneous gush from ev'ry Eye.
> Now gayer Subjects animate his Strings,
> The Lover's Fires, and Victor's Wreaths he sings;
> Hark, how the Joy-inspiring Concords roll!
> Exalt our Mirth, and all our cares controul.   (pp. 14, 16)

In his setting of *Alexander's Feast* (revived earlier that year), Handel rivals Orpheus himself:

> Whilst in his Royal *Macedonian's* Feast
> Th'almighty Pow'r of Harmony's exprest,
> Our Joy and Grief, and Transport and Despair,

---

[83] Page 14. The passage parallels Horace's description of Archilochus (*Ars Poetica*, lines 79–82).

[84] This and the following passage parallel Horace's mentions of lyric poetry as encompassing tales of gods and their children, odes commemorating victors in sports, the loves of swains, and drinking songs (*Ars Poetica*, lines 83–5).

THE NEW DUNCIAD: OPERA AND THE TRIUMPH OF DULNESS 301

Wait on each Touch, and change with ev'ry Air.
Stupendous Master! now, amaz'd, we see
All that was *feign'd* of *Orpheus true* of Thee.   (p. 16)

Although *The Art of Life* is only occasionally political, the praise of Pope the satirist for scourging the folly and vices of the day, plus Miller's own known sympathies, give the poem an oppositional cast.

Miller pays Handel another compliment in his one-act comic afterpiece *An Hospital for Fools. A Dramatic Fable* (1739), adapted from William Walsh's *Hospital of Fools* of 1714.[85] Jupiter, hearing complaints of the follies of mankind, sent Æsculapius the physician to earth to cure anyone troubled with folly. At first, no one appears (since no one knows himself to be a fool), so Æsculapius invites people to bring forth friends or relations to be cured, whereupon he discovers all men have their sufficient share of folly, the most universal of which is being too severe on others' follies.

To the characters of Walsh's original, Miller introduces a father and his daughter (played by Catherine "Kitty" Clive), who is mad over music and oratorio. Mercury, present as Æscalapius's assistant, remarks as an aside, "This is an *English* Fool, I suppose" – a recognition that Handel's oratorios were becoming a characteristic national form, and another object of False Taste.[86]

The father says the object of his daughter's folly is nothing but "Piping and Fiddling," and her raptures over oratorio recall the women's ecstasies over Farinelli:

O charming *Oratorio!* O dear, *dear Saul!* I expire at that
Duetto, and the *Dead March* brings me to life again.   (Act I)

When her father wishes she really would expire for good so he could save the crowns in his pocket, the daughter retorts that her frugal father can subscribe £5 to support a sick hospital, "and yet grudge a few Crowns to a ravishing Foreigner." Now Mercury cannot tell who is the greater fool.

The daughter continues to Æsculapius:

Come, come, Signior Doctor, you must love Musick; you know
Alexander's Feast, to be sure; I'll sing you a Song out of it.

SONG.
The Prince, unable to conceal his Pain,
Gaz'd on the Fair
Who caus'd his Care,
And sigh'd, and look'd, and sigh'd again, &c.

---

[85] The afterpiece played at Drury Lane on 15 and 17 Nov. 1739. It was adapted from William Walsh's "Æsculapius, or the Hospital of Fools," appended to *Poems and Translations by Several Hands. To which Is Added, The Hospital of Fools; a Dialogue* (1714).

[86] See *Craftsman*, no. 680 (21 July 1739); *A Satirical Epistle to Mr. Pope* (1740), 7; and *The Comedian, or Philosophical Enquirer*, no. 3 (June 1732). On the last, see Ilias Chrissochoidis, "Oratorio *à la Mode*," *Newsletter of the American Handel Society*, vol. 23, nos. 1–12 (Spring/Summer 2008), 7–9.

302   THE CULTURAL POLITICS OF OPERA, 1720–1742

The upshot of Mercury's interrogation of the father and daughter as he tries to find the source of the daughter's oratorio-folly is that, as the daughter explains, her father's jealous temper allowed her to attend only oratorios and not so much an innocent opera, "Not so much as to see poor, dear, harmless *Faronelli* act—poor dear Creature!" (p.18). Æsculapius finally accuses the father of the folly of condemning his daughter's passion for oratorios, the only entertainment he allowed her to enjoy.

In this episode, added by Miller to his model in Walsh, the daughter is clearly a fool passionate for music. The tone of the episode is comic, and there is no indictment of music or oratorio per se. The daughter's fixation on oratorio (by ironic inversion) is certainly a compliment to Handel, since Miller could have chosen any number of fixations (tea, chocolate, cards, plays) for the daughter.

The favorable Handel connections are strengthened because previously Kitty Clive, who played the daughter, had sung the song "I like the am'rous youth that's free" that Handel wrote for her in Miller's play *The Universal Passion* (28 February 1737).[87] Later, in March 1738 she and John Beard were advertised as singing several Handel songs in a benefit concert; and for Clive's benefit performance of a revival of Congreve's *The Way of the World* (17 March 1740), Handel wrote her a new setting of "Love's but the Frailty of the Mind." She sang in Handel's 1743 oratorio season.[88]

* * *

The New Dunciad, published little more than a month after the fall of Walpole, is the culmination of Pope's portrayal of the Walpolean-Hanoverian Britain that created the conditions for the Triumph of Dulness. Opera will thrive in the realm of Dulness, so Handel, now the composer of oratorio, must be rusticated to Ireland.

The New Dunciad with its portrayal of opera and Handel are, as suggested, immersed in current cultural politics. Given Frederick's long-standing patronage and personal relations with Handel, as well as Pope's friendship with the Prince, it would certainly have been tactless for Pope to disparage Handel by presenting him as an opera composer in *The New Dunciad*. Hence, its panegyric of Handel may be understood as Pope's recognition of his friend Prince Frederick's own friendship and respect for Handel, and to Handel's place as an Opposition Worthy. Similarly, because other oppositional poets were enlisting and appropriating Handel, it was only natural that Pope too celebrate Handel the oratorio composer as the foe of Dulness.

---

[87] *Handel: Collected Documents*, ed. Burrows et al., 3:243.

[88] The songs are printed in G. F. Handel, *Songs and Cantatas for Soprano and Continuo*, ed. Donald Burrows (Oxford: Oxford University Press, 1988). On Clive and Handel, see Bertha Joncus, "Handel at Drury Lane: Ballad Opera and the Production of Kitty Clive," *Journal of the Royal Musical Association*, 131 (2006), 179–226.

Coda: The Cultural Work of Opera

Three events bring this study to a close. Sir Robert Walpole fell from power in 1742, bringing to an end the Robinocracy against which many of the best writers of the period railed. With Walpole gone from the political stage, British writers and artists lost a target that motived some of the century's most vivid satire. Second, in March 1742 came the culmination of the cultural war against False Taste and Italian opera. After almost thirteen years, Pope returned to his *Dunciad* project and published *The New Dunciad*, which would become Book IV of the *Dunciad*, the book that contains the most notorious denunciation of opera as the agent of Dulness.

By now, Handel had produced his last opera, *Deidamia* in 1741 for the London stage. Although implicated in Pope's attacks on opera and the Hanoverian royal family, his celebrity emerged unscathed. In 1742 he had completed his disengagement from opera and was devoting his energies, as much as his health allowed, to shorter spring seasons of exclusively music-dramatic works in English – coming to rank with Milton and Shakespeare as one of Britain's Worthies.[1] Italian opera continued to be produced in London well into following century, at times supporting two companies. But with Handel gone from the scene, the history of Italian opera in London entered a new period.

* * *

As the most spectacular public theatre entertainment in London, opera was a cultural product with great symbolic power that occupied what Ian Hacking calls a "bivalent" position in eighteenth-century Britain,[2] hovering between poles of approval or disdain.

Opera was patronized and supported by a narrow social-political elite, the *beau monde* or *bon ton*, whose members rarely, if ever it seems, felt the need to defend or advocate it in print; but they manifested its value to them by the economic capital they devoted to it.

Yet from its introduction, opera was continuously attacked as a danger to British political, social, moral, and theatrical welfare. Opera's antagonists reviled it in a broad swathe of satires, verse, polemic tracts, and prints, such as many of those used by oppositional polemicists encountered in this book. In the same way as opera itself, Farinelli held a bivalent position: famed and

---

[1] Handel's declining health as a major factor in his turning to short Lenten seasons of oratorio has been argued in David Hunter, *The Lives of George Friderick Handel* (Woodbridge: Boydell, 2015), 233–47.

[2] I borrow the concepts of bivalent and cultural polarity from Ian Hacking, *Mad Travelers: Reflections on the Reality of Transient Mental Illness* (Charlottesville. Va.: University Press of Virginia, 1998).

praised for his stellar vocal artistry yet denounced and reviled for his supposed role in corrupting society morally, sexually, and financially.

In the Introduction, I discussed how, in Pierre Bourdieu's sense, Italian opera occupied a dominant, prestigious position in the cultural field of Britain, at least certainly in the theatrical domain. Its prestige, its symbolic capital, derived from its restricted audience and repeated inability to survive as a viable commercial-financial enterprise, even with substantial royal and noble patronage. The economic, social, and cultural capital required to participate in the elite world of opera confer prestige upon opera; patronizing opera was expected of the *bon ton*, and marked one as a member it.

It was this dominant position as a cultural product – created by the nation's political-social elite for itself, to reproduce itself, and to affirm its own status – that enabled opera to be a ready target in the domains of cultural and political politics.

We can further understand (and theorize) this equivocal status of Italian opera. The idea from Ian Hacking of a bivalent opera that is placed on an axis of positive and negative value can be refined by using Bourdieu's concept of hierarchic fields (or planes).[3] Although Bourdieu often uses the phrases "field of cultural production" or "cultural field," he actually makes use of numerous hierarchic fields: power, literary, religious, intellectual, scientific, etc., each with its own relational logic of positions.[4]

For Bourdieu, at its simplest, a field will have a dominant (prestigious) end opposite to the dominated (less prestigious) end. In the field of cultural production (as seen in Chapter 2), the cultural field has an inverse hierarchy: the more prestigious (dominant) the position of a product (opera or verse satire), the more limited the audience and hence commercial potential it has; whereas, less prestigious (dominated) forms have greater commercial value or profitability. A field may be chiastic, with two oppositions, with many positions that can be distributed over the field.[5] Such a more complexly constructed field may

[3] Principal expositions of Bourdieu's ideas about cultural fields: *"The Field of Cultural Production, or the Economic World Reversed,"* in *The Field of Cultural Production: Essays on Art and Literature,* ed. and trans. Randal Johnston (New York, N.Y.: Columbia University Press, 1993), 29–73; *The Rules of Art: Genesis and Structure of the Literary Field,* trans. Susan Emanuel (Stanford, Calif.: Stanford University Press, 1996), 113–25, 181–3, 199–200, 202–6, 215–52 (esp. p. 205 on the merits of the approach); "The Market of Symbolic Goods," first published in French in 1971, abbreviated trans. by Rupert Swyer, in *Poetics,* 14 (1985), 13–44, and reprinted in *The Field of Cultural Production,* 112–41; "Principles for a Sociology of Cultural Works," in *The Field of Cultural Production,* 176–91; and *Distinction: A Social Critique of the Judgement of Taste* (originally published in 1979) trans. Richard Nice (Cambridge, Mass.: Harvard University Press, 1984), 226–32.

[4] The cultural product, its creators, and its consumers occupy positions within a field. The positions are determined by both objective (empirical) criteria, and subjectively as the consumers of each cultural product perceive themselves and other consumers.

[5] For examples of complex hierarchic fields with multiple poles, see Bourdieu, *The Rules of Art,* 121–5; and *Field of Cultural Production,* 16–17, 46–50, 183–4.

CODA: THE CULTURAL WORK OF OPERA   305

have subfields based on audience size, degree of consecration by connoisseurs and critics, profitability, length and cost of production, and a work's lifespan. The field of cultural production itself will have a position within the larger field of political power.

Opera can have differently valued positions in different fields. In (what I call) the field of public, theatre entertainment, the institution of Italian opera at the Haymarket theatre occupies the dominant (positive) position of greatest prestige and least commercial potential, as opposed to the undemanding farces, pantomimes, harlequinades, puppet shows, and Bartholomew Fair entertainments at the negative end. Drama and comedy, neither so profitable or exclusive, could occupy a middle positions.

In (what I call) the moral field are the religious and charitable activities devoted to one's spiritual welfare and that furthered religion, sociability, and charity. In this field, the positive position would be held by a cluster of devotional literature, sermons, and hymns and religious observation, moral decency, piety, chastity, and charity. At the negative position of this moral field would be Italian opera and especially Farinelli. In fact, the effects of the newly introduced Italian-style music and operas were specifically denounced in spiritually oriented texts representing values of the positive position – works such as Jeremy Collier's *A Short View of the Immorality and Profaneness of the English Stage* (1698), Arthur Bedford's *The Evil and Danger of Stage-Plays; Shewing their Natural Tendency to Destroy Religion* (Bristol, 1706)[6] and *The Great Abuse of Musick* (1711),[7] William Law's *The Absolute Unlawfulness of the Stage-Entertainment Fully Demonstrated* (1726),[8] and Erasmus Jones's *Luxury, Pride, and Vanity, the Bane of the British Nation* (1736).[9]

There are other fields in which opera could be considered. For example, in the field of literary production, the opera librettos, due to poor verse quality, and contrived plots, could lie somewhere between Milton, Virgil, and Homer and verse doggerel.

It can only be the fact that opera's power was purely symbolic – and not based on real economic utility or political power – that made it capable of

[6] Bedford extensively quotes pages and lines from *Arsinoe* (1705), *The British Enchanters* (1706), and *The Temple of Love* (1706). He presumably had not seen the text of *Camilla*, premiered on 30 March 1706.

[7] *The Great Abuse of Musick* (1711), carries on the campaign against the "Immodesty and profeness [sic] of our English Operas" and cites examples from all the recent operas and dramatic operas from *Arsinoe* (except *Li Amori d'Ergasto*) to *Hydaspes* (23 March 1710), 104–34.

[8] William Law railed against the immorality and lasciviousness of *Apollo and Daphne* (1726).

[9] From a moralist's point of view, Jones challenges John Jacob Heidegger, leaseholder of the Haymarket theatre, to deny that "*Balls, Assemblies* and *Musick Entertainments* &c. are generally so vitiated and corrupted, and the Pleasure that they pretend to, is so interwoven with Danger as well as Vexation of Spirit … that there is … more Pain and Disappointment, than there is real Pleasure or Satisfaction attending upon the best of 'em" (3rd ed., 32).

306 THE CULTURAL POLITICS OF OPERA, 1720–1742

occupying a dominant position in the cultural field at large, and yet negative positions in other fields – and suitable for use in the culture wars of the Walpole era.

Eclipsed by the monitory and often lively and amusing literary and print campaign against opera is the inescapable fact that opera must have been a valued cultural production for many Britons. In Bianconi and Walker's sense, the addressee of the Royal Academy of Music and later opera companies was the *beau monde* and social-political elite itself: those who established and funded the opera, not the royal family and the court in their boxes (as in many continental court-sponsored productions), nor the general populace. The elite, prestigious cultural product reviled by oppositional journalists and moralist writers must have done some significant, advantageous 'cultural work' aside from, or in addition to, aesthetic enjoyment; it must have served the personal interests of Britain's political-social elite and justified it in the face of (or despite) constant ridicule and financial setbacks.

Not only did Britain's elite and *beau monde* create opera for its own personal pleasure, but in Bourdieu's sense, it both created and reproduced itself by its opera patronage.[10] Possession of the scarce combination of cultural, social, and financial capital required for participation in the world of opera created the status of its attendees by exclusion of the general populace. Participation in the world of opera validated and naturalized one's membership in London's elite. Those who did not properly belong to the social elite (by virtue of birth, family, and landed wealth) revealed their *parvenu* status by demonstrating their False Taste.

The necessity of attending opera to mark one as a member of the *beau monde* was noted by a contemporary journalist in December 1725:

> Musick is so generally approv'd of in *England*, that it is look'd upon a want of Breeding not to be affected by it, insomuch that every Member of the *Beau Monde* at this Time either do, or, at least, think it necessary to appear as if they did understand it; and, in order to carry on this Deceit, it is requisite every one, who has the Pleasure of thinking himself a fine Gentleman, should, being first laden with a Competency of Powder and Essence, make his personal Appearance every Opera Night at the Haymarket, tho' not less ignorant of the Performance than of the Language it is perform'd in.[11]

The nobility and gentry spent lifetimes and fortunes building great country houses and London mansions, managing far-flung holdings, developing agricultural and mineral resources on their lands, engaging in financial and real

---

[10] On how choice of art works helps reproduce distinction and status, Pierre Bourdieu and Jean-Claude Passeron, *Reproduction in Education, Society and Culture*, 2nd ed., trans. Richard Nice, foreword Pierre Bourdieu (1970; London: Sage Publications, 1990). See also Bourdieu, *Distinction*, 4–7, 125–32 135–43, 147–50; and Bourdieu, *Field of Cultural Production*, 7–8.

[11] *Mist's Weekly Journal*, no. 34 (18 Dec. 1725); also printed in Elizabeth Gibson, *The Royal Academy of Music, 1719–1728: The Institution and Its Directors* (New York, N.Y.: Garland Publishing, 1989), 388.

CODA: THE CULTURAL WORK OF OPERA   307

estate enterprises, attending Parliament or Privy Council, or serving at Court or in the Ministry.

The values of the ancient world represented by the operatic spectacles was out of step with the modern Britain of commerce, leisure, and politeness.[12] The lives of modern Britons offered few opportunities for the displays of heroic virtue, glory, sacrifice, and magnanimity along the examples of the great Roman heroes Cato of Utica, Mutius Scaevola, Martius Curtius, Scipio Africanus, Lucius Brutus, the Horatii, and others.[13]

Bolingbroke simultaneously laments Britain's lack of heroes and decries the modern opera in a political catechism:

> Q. What is become of the *Scipio's* and *Cato's* of *Rome*?
> A. They sing now on the *English* stage.[14]

Yet the world of opera may have resonated with the classically tutored aristocrats and gentry because it recalled the lessons and examples from their schoolboy readings in the classics. Heroic opera offered the opportunity to live such lives vicariously. The "Heroick Virtue" that was celebrated in classical history and opera was, according to Sir William Temple, the preserve of the aristocrat: "It must be ennobled by Birth, to give it more Lustre, Esteem and Authority."[15] One writer in the *London Magazine* (1762) explained why history was especially the preserve of the men of wealth and privilege:

> [In] the contents of the historick page, … men of quality and fortune are deeply interested, as their conduct must necessarily have great influence in promoting the grandeur and happiness, or preventing the fall and misery of their country.[16]

Opera in London must also have served the civic interests of those for whom it was produced in ways suggested by Linda Colley. In *Britons: Forging the*

---

[12] Charles de Saint-Evremond had noted the ancient heroes could not be appropriate models for modern behavior; see Timothy Hampton, *Writing from History: The Rhetoric of Exemplarity in Renaissance Literature* (Ithaca, N.Y.: Cornell University Press, 1990), 298–304.

[13] Later in the century, the classical scholar Samuel Butler could lament, "No Age ever abounded with more Heroical Poetry than the present, and yet there was never any wherein fewer Heroical Actions were performed"; Samuel Butler, *Characters and Passages from Note-Books*, ed. A. R. Waller (Cambridge: Cambridge University Press, 1908), 442.

[14] *Craftsman*, no. 377 (22 Sept. 1733); reprinted from *The Freeholder's Political Catechism* (1733), 15.

[15] William Temple, "Upon Heroick Vertue," in *Miscellanea. The Second Part,* 2nd ed. (1690), 146. Previously, he wrote,

> it may be said to arise, from some great and native Excellency of Temper or Genius transcending the common race of Mankind, in Wisdom, Goodness and Fortitude. These ingredients advantaged by Birth, improved by Education, and assisted by Fortune, seem to make that noble composition, which gives such a lustre to those who have possest it, as made them appear to common eyes, something more than Mortals. (p. 144)

[16] "Letters to a Young Nobleman," *London Magazine*, 31 (1762), 76.

308   THE CULTURAL POLITICS OF OPERA, 1720–1742

Nation, Colley has shown how the heroic episodes in classical histories, such as those presented in Italian operas, were congenial to eighteenth-century Britons.[17] First, the patriotic achievement celebrated was highly specific: the heroic acts were those of men of superior rank and title; they reminded the British elites of their duty to country, virtue, and liberty, but also affirmed that it was men of rank, education, and lineage who were qualified to do so. The world shown in operas represented a hierarchical society based on status and rank.

Second, the societies represented were not threatening: they could inspire without challenging the present. The operas could celebrate an image of male virtue and glory, suitable for male elites – without being threatening because the settings are distant in time and place. Operas (unlike the popular theatre) do not acknowledge the modern commercial world of the middling orders nor challenge the ruling oligarchy. By contrast to the ancient, pagan courts ruled by the absolute princes who inhabit operas, Britain – as a Protestant nation with a constitutional monarchy – was a modern Christian nation and bastion of liberty and property; the emerging British aristocracy and elites could still surpass the Roman and near-eastern heroes and contribute to national greatness. Needless to say, even plots that celebrate liberty, resistance to despots, or show tyrannicide offered no versions of a social order to challenge that of Britain.

How, after the Glorious Revolution, the British cultural and political elites (both Tories and Whigs) imagined themselves as virtuous Romans has been explored by Philip Ayres.[18] In *Classical Culture and the Idea of Rome in Eighteenth-Century England*, he examines how Britons identified with the Roman Republic, and proclaimed their allegiance to, and gave form to, Roman ideals of liberty and civic virtue. Appealing to this classical heritage of civic virtue was a form of cultural politics: another way of the elite (re)creating itself.

The arts collaborated to allow Britons to fashion themselves as embodiments or representatives of Roman ideals and virtue. In all manner of works – literature, drama, sculpture, portraiture, architecture, and even gardening – Britain's elites expressed a frame of mind based on the classical foundations of liberty and civic virtue. Britons planned gardens on Roman models and filled their landscapes with Roman temples and monuments. British architecture imitated Roman models as transmitted through Palladio. In their formal verse satire, writers assumed the personae of Horace and Juvenal, now writing on British themes and characters. Their adoption of a virtuous Roman self-image went as far as aristocrats portraying themselves in statuary as Romans dressed in togas and military armor. Being represented as Romans was visual evidence the sitters were spiritual Romans of the republican past. Poets extolled, and

---

[17] Linda Colley, *Britons: Forging the Nation 1707–1837* (New Haven, Conn.: Yale University Press, 1992), 168, 180. The harmony of the contents of operas and the values of the operagoing class is suggested in J. C. D. Clark's *English Society, 1688–1832: Ideology, Social Structure and Political Practice During the Ancien Regime* (Cambridge: Cambridge University Press, 1985), 102–5.

[18] Philip Ayres, *Classical Culture and the Idea of Rome in Eighteenth-Century England* (Cambridge: Cambridge University Press, 1997), 1–47.

CODA: THE CULTURAL WORK OF OPERA 309

painters portrayed the Thames valley as equivalent – if not superior – to the Roman Campagna.

Horace, Cicero, and Quintilian were taken as guides for poetry and oratory. Contemporaries drew connection from plays, such as Nathaniel Lee's *Lucius Junius Brutus* (1681) and Addison's *Cato* (1713), drew parallels with contemporary political events and ancient Rome – often identifying republican Romans as Whigs. Modern politicians were celebrated or vilified under the names of Roman types: Atticus, Caesar, Cato, Catiline, Cicero, Clodius, Nero, Sejanus, Verres. One Briton, the Earl of Shaftesbury, came to share more cultural ground with Cicero and classical virtue than with Christianity.

The importance of the Roman examples for Britons was made explicit by Lord Chesterfield to his son in 1738:

> De toutes les histoires anciennes, la plus intéressante, et la plus instructive, c'est l'histoire Romaine. Elle est la plus fertile en grands hommes, et en grands événements. Elle nous anime, plus que toute autre, à la vertue.[19]

In seeing on the opera stage ancient and Roman figures sacrificing for freedom and liberty, striving for virtue and honor, and restoring rightful princes to their thrones, Britons could recall and celebrate what they saw as their nation's own constant struggles against Stuart monarchs and Louis XIV – struggles undertaken in both opera and Britain by ruling elites and the aristocracy. Endorsing operas with their classical plots could be a form of political self-justification; Britons could imagine themselves embodying Roman ideals and sharing civic values,[20] a process in which, Italian opera could participate. What was learned from classical history and opera was the necessity of having virtuous, public-spirited men and women participate in public life to preserve liberty.

Some operagoers found the opera librettos themselves of value enough to keep and bind up in volumes for their family libraries, including those of the Duke Portland, Earl Cowper, and George Baillie, one of the lords of the Treasury.[21]

---

[19] *The Letters of Philip Dormer Stanhope, 4th Earl of Chesterfield*, ed. with intro. Bonamy Dobrée, 6 vols. (London: Eyre and Spottiswoode, 1932), 2:340.

[20] Ayres, *Classical Culture and the Idea of Rome*, does not specifically deal with Italian opera; the extrapolation is mine.

[21] Groups of bound librettos with identifying arms or bookplates are those of the Duke of Portland at the Newberry Library, Chicago, for the years 1720–1721, 1723–1730: CASE V/4609.56 (in 4 vols.)

Those of the Earl Cowper are at the University of California at Los Angeles Performing Arts Special Collections, for the years 1733-1759: ML 48.O615 (v. 1); ML 50.2.F272A77/1734 (vol. 2); ML 50.2.A36V47/1735 (vol. 3); ML 50.2.V25P76/1736 (vol. 4); ML 50.2.P589O74/1737 (vol. 5); ML 50.2.R72V47/1744 (vol. 6); ML 50.2.M68T47/1746 (vol. 7); ML 50.2.R88/1747 (vol. 8); ML 50.2.F434L46/1754 (vol. 9); ML 50.2.P325G2/1754 (vol. 10); ML 50.2.P325G2/1754 (vol. 11); and ML 50.2.B37C/1755 (vol. 11).

Those of George Baillie are at the Folger Shakespeare Library, Washington, D.C., for the years 1712–1729: PR 1259/O6/B3/Cage (in 6 vols.). A companion volume of

THE CULTURAL POLITICS OF OPERA, 1720–1742

Many of Italian opera's fiercest opponents could not acknowledge it might make any contribution to civil society. Such critics seem to attend only to the surface, aesthetic qualities of the music and singing – disregarding completely the verbal content of the narrative and history enacted on stage. In fact, the plots and instructive morals proclaimed at the *lieto fine* of the opera satisfy the traditional demands of history, drama, comedy, and satire, to delight and instruct: to show vice vanquished, virtue triumphant – and especially the rewards of virtuous love.[22] Many contemporaries did believe that opera could fulfill the traditional goals of a history and drama: to teach by showing exemplars of great men.[23]

Unsurprisingly, a writer for *Fog's Weekly Journal* in 1735 claimed that whatever might be said in defense of drama and comedy "cannot be urged to justify those more effeminate and expensive Amusements which the present Age has introduced." He asked rhetorically,

> I would fain to know whether a Man ever returned wiser from an Opera than he was before he went to it, except he repented, and laugh'd at his own Folly, for having given so much Money for a song. —— Has *Faronelli*, with that sweet Pipe of his, inspired any of our Mercenaries, who are the People that flock most to hear him, with more vertuous or honourable Sentiments in respect to their Country?[24]

Historians taught that the actions of individual men and women made states great. Hence, it is precisely those ancient heroes (of both Rome and Greece) who demonstrate these civic virtues who appear in seventeenth- and eighteenth-century opera librettos. Many famous exemplars of Roman virtue are the basis for opera libreti: Cato of Utica (who chose suicide over life under a dictator), Scipio Africanus Major (who practiced self-mastery and gave freedom to a favored conquered female slave), Mucius Scaevola (who burned his hand to demonstrate the fortitude of the Romans), and Titus Vespasianus (who extended clemency to plotters against him).

---

miscellaneous librettos from Italy, France, and London is at the Newberry Library: Case PQ/4688 F 17 GV 47.

[22] On how opera librettos could present ideas of virtue: Michael F. Robinson, "How to Demonstrate Virtue: The Case of Porpora's Two Settings of Mitridate," *Studies in Music from the University of Western Ontario*, vol. 7, no. 1 (1982), 47–64; Don Neville, "Moral Philosophy in the Metastasian Drama," *Studies in Music from the University of Western Ontario*, vol. 7, no. 1 (1982), 28–46; Neville, "Metastasio: Poet and Preacher in Vienna," pp. 47–61 in *Pietro Metastasio: uomo universal (1698–1782)*, ed. Andrea Sommer-Mathis and Elisabeth T. Hilscher (Vienna: Österreichische Akademie der Wissenschaften, 2000).

[23] I have expanded the notion of opera as a teacher of history by means of example in *The Politics of Opera in Handel's Britain*, Chapter 8, "The Opera Stage as Political History."

[24] *Fog's Weekly Journal*, no. 338 (26 April 1735). This is a sequel to a previous article denouncing opera as a luxury (no. 335, 5 April 1735).

CODA: THE CULTURAL WORK OF OPERA   311

That opera's audience members might indeed identify with characters on the stage is suggested by Alexander Pope in his Prologue to Addison's play *Cato* (1713), which presents one of the great exemplars of Roman Stoic self-sacrifice in the cause of liberty. The audience would be absorbed into the spectacle and emulate worthy protagonists, he believed; Addison's achievement was, Pope claimed,

> To make mankind, in conscious virtue bold,
> Live o'er each scene, and be what they behold:
> …
> He bids your breasts with ancient ardour rise,
> And calls forth Roman drops [tears] from British eyes.[25]

Some opera librettos with Roman subjects quite explicitly connected Britain with ancient Rome. Paolo Rolli developed the conceit of the parallel between Britain and the Roman Republic in the dedication of *Il Muzio Scevola* (1721) to George I. Rolli compares George I with Alexander Severus and concludes that George is "one worthy the obedience of this glorious people who so resemble ancient Rome" (cui degni d'ubidire quest' Inclito Popolo che tanto all' Antico Romano Somiglia).[26] In dedicating the libretto of *Scipione* (1726) to Charles Lennox, Duke of Richmond and Lennox, Rolli stated:

> Gli antichi Romani sono il Modello di questa in Armi e in Lettere floridissima Nazione: e non può trovarsi Soggetto più Nobile delle loro gran Geste, per un Teatro ove la Medesima vegga rappresentati i Personaggi a' quali i suoi più gloriosi Figli somigliano.

> The ancient Romans are the model for this nation, flourishing in arms and letters: there is not to be found a more noble subject than their grand deeds, for a theatre where this nation may see represented the characters resembling her [the nation's] most glorious children.[27]

With their classical plots, placing examples of ancient heroes before London's aristocratic and political elite – making Roman virtue visible on stage, adorned with music and all the adornments of theatrical spectacle – Italian operas could have done some cultural and political work, to help Britons self-fashion themselves as what Ayers called an "oligarchy of virtue."

* * *

---

[25] Pope, Preface to Joseph Addison, *Cato* (1713), lines 3–4, 15–16.

[26] Rolli, Dedication to *Muzio Scevola*: printed and trans. in full in *George Frideric Handel: Collected Documents*, ed. Donald Burrows, Helen Coffey, John Greenacombe, and Anthony Hicks, 6 vols. (Cambridge: Cambridge University Press, 2013–), 1:538–40. On the opera's politics, see McGeary, *Politics of Opera in Handel's Britain*, 79–81. John Shebbeare would later state that "No compliment … can impart a more flattering idea to an Englishman, than that which compares him to an old Roman"; *Letters from England* (1756), 1. He lists the attributes "which he receives with most delight."

[27] Rolli, Dedication of *Scipione*: printed and trans. in full in *Handel: Collected Documents*, ed. Donald Burrows et al., 2:40–2.

To step back and make a sweeping summary of the cultural politics of opera: The preceding sketch of the possible cultural work that Italian opera might have done for its elite Whiggish socio-political audience may balance the previous chapters that presented the view of opera by oppositional writers as an instance of False Taste or a sign of the luxury and corruption said to be caused by the Walpole regime.

The two attitudes toward opera can be seen as expressions of two contrasting views of the nation as it is completing a social-economic transformation at the turn of the eighteenth century. The hallowed Augustan worldview of Pope, Swift, and Bolingbroke was (in Kramnick's phrase) "nostalgic." It valorized a passing, Tory England grounded on landed wealth, patriarchy, church, and family pedigree.[28] The political face of this fading England was the Country tradition or Old ("True") Whiggism, and expressed in the writings of the Commonwealthmen, the followers of James Harrington and Machiavelli, the English Republican tradition, Bolingbroke, the *Craftsman*, and verse of Pope. Their polemic bugbears were the corruption caused by commerce and new forms of finance and wealth that destroyed liberty and traditional virtue and values. In this view, going back to ancient Roman sources, luxury destroyed liberty, which depended on a stern, frugal lifestyle that put public good above self-interest. Liberty was protected by militias of freemen.

The Whig tradition was born during the Exclusion Crisis and was initially an oppositional program: one opposed to the Court and Ministry. Its principles were a low land tax; mixed (or balanced) constitution; avoidance of land wars; limits on placemen and pensioners in the Commons; frequent and independent parliaments; and support of the Church of England against both Catholicism and dissent. This tradition later became the Tory political worldview.

The Financial Revolution of the 1690s – the creation of the Bank of England and East India Company, the national debt (needed to finance the continental wars of William), the enlarged size and power of the administrative executive (needed to conduct the wars), and new forms of intangible money (in the form of stocks, credit, bonds, annuities) – ushered in a new Britain. The Revolution created forms of instant and intangible wealth not based on the stability of land. Commerce did not destroy virtue, but was essential for polite society. Those who benefited from the new financial order were the "monied" men of the City and those who held positions in the Ministry and at Court.

The advocates for this new financial world were the Modern (or Court) Whigs writers of the Walpole Ministry. For the Modern Whigs, and famously expressed by Mandeville's paradox, commerce and luxury, the self-indulgent desire for consumer goods, were not corruption but the engines that drove commerce, the basis of the new economy. What was condemned as corruption was but the way a ministry assembled an administration that would carry out

---

[28] This is the view of England as an ancien regime is elaborated in Clark's controversial *English Society, 1688–1832*. It must be emphasized that notwithstanding the rhetoric of his writings and his relations with Pope and Bolingbroke, throughout his life Swift considered himself a Whig.

the King's business. Preservation of liberty was left to the army and a strong central government.

It is not too great a generalization to see that attitudes toward Italian opera largely align with these two ideological points of view: for the old England of John Dennis, Alexander Pope, Bolingbroke, the *Craftsman*, the *Grub-street Journal*, and *Mist's* and *Fog's* journals, opera and its castrato singers were a product and symbol of the new financial order. As such, opera was claimed to have insidious, pernicious effects on personal morals, public virtue, and the sexual-gender order. It was a convenient target for the rhetoric of social critics and those opposed to the Walpole regime.

For the Modern Whig of transformed Britain, opera was a benign, polite entertainment; a product of wealth and evidence of the advances in the arts and sciences made possible by England's economic prosperity; and a sign that England had emerged as a powerful nation in Europe. The opera at the Haymarket was an economic benefit to the merchants and tradesmen of London. The viewpoint of the Modern Whigs was rarely expressed explicitly; it can be seen in the founding documents of the Royal Academy of Music, the several *London Journal* essays, and most emphatically by the actual patronage and attendance of London's *beau monde* and opera patrons.

Difficult to answer, though, are two questions. How effective was the campaign against opera in effecting the fall of Robert Walpole? The campaign may have been powerful social critique, but it is doubtful it was an effective tool for turning Britons against Walpole. He survived almost two decades of abuse in the press and harassment in Parliament for the supposed effects of his Ministry on the morals and arts of England, all the while retaining the King's favor as long as he could control Parliament to carry out the King's business. It was only when he realized that he had lost control of Parliament did he accept that he had to resign.

Were the attacks on opera in the Opposition's propaganda campaign against Walpole taken seriously, and did they affect operagoing? W. H. Auden proclaimed that "poetry makes nothing happen."[29] Perhaps oppositional satirists and dramatists did think they were adding their mite to undermining the Walpole regime. Nonetheless, there were members of the political Opposition (and especially its later figurehead Prince Frederick) who were committed and devoted opera patrons and supporters. Most likely, like other opera patrons, they bracketed out and disregarded the political polemic against opera.

A greater portion of London's populace did not have the financial, cultural, or social capital nor interest in attending opera. They may have found the polemic against opera sympathetic and a rationale for not attending it. Others, perhaps of the middling sorts, such as the audiences for Fielding's comedies and farces, may have enjoyed the fun of ridiculing opera and Farinelli as an expression of resentment against Britain's powerful elite and confirmation of their own common sense taste. A small portion of London may have had

---

[29] *In Memory of W. B. Yeats*, II.5.

314   THE CULTURAL POLITICS OF OPERA, 1720–1742

deeply felt moral objection to entertainments such as opera and endorsed the invective against opera.

* * *

Critique and polemic about opera continued as a background chorus through the century, yet the institution of opera at the Haymarket theatre prevailed as London's most prestigious theatrical entertainment – at times the city was hosting two competing opera companies. But with Walpole driven from power, satirists and political writers lost a target, and Italian opera never again played such a role in the cultural politics of Britain.

Bibliography

Addison, Joseph. *The Freeholder*, ed. James Leheny. Oxford: Oxford University Press, 1980.

Allen, Brian. *Francis Hayman*. New Haven, Conn.: Yale University Press, 1987.

Arbuthnot, John. *The Correspondence of Dr. John Arbuthnot*, ed. Angus Ross. Munich: Wilhelm Fink, 2006.

Aristocratic Government and Society in Eighteenth-Century England: The Foundations of Stability, ed. and intro., Daniel A. Baugh. New York, N.Y: Franklin Watts, 1975.

Armitage, David. "A Patriot for Whom? The Afterlives of Bolingbroke's Patriot King." *Journal of British Studies*, 36 (1997), 397–418.

Armitage, David, ed. Bolingbroke, *Political Writings*. Cambridge: Cambridge University Press, 1997.

Arnall, William. *The Case of Opposition Stated, Between the Craftsman and the People*, ed. Simon Varey. Lewisburg, Penn.: Bucknell University Press, 2003.

Aspden, Suzanne. "'Fam'd Handel Breathing, tho' Transformed to Stone': The Composer as Monument." *Journal of the American Musicological Society*, 55 (2002), 39–90.

——. *The Rival Sirens: Performance and Identity on Handel's Opera Stage*. Cambridge: Cambridge University Press, 2013.

Atherton, Herbert M. *Political Prints in the Age of Hogarth: A Study of the Ideographic Representation of Politics*. Oxford: Clarendon, 1974.

Ayres, Philip. *Classical Culture and the Idea of Rome in Eighteenth-Century England*. Cambridge: Cambridge University Press, 1997.

Bailyn, Bernard. *The Ideological Origins of the American Revolution*. Cambridge, Mass.: Harvard University Press, 1967.

Baker, Malcolm. *The Marble Index: Roubiliac and Sculptural Portraiture in Eighteenth-Century Britain*. New Haven, Conn.: Yale University Press, 2015.

Baker, Sheridan. "Political Allusion in Fielding's *Author's Farce, Mock Doctor*, and *Tumble-Down Dick*." *PMLA*, 77 (1962), 221–31.

Barber, Giles. "Bolingbroke, Pope and the Patriot King." *The Library: Transactions of the Bibliographical Society*, 19 (1964), 67–89.

——. "Some Uncollected Authors XLI: Henry Saint John, Viscount Bolingbroke, 1678–1751." *The Book Collector*, 14 (1965), 528–37.

Barbon, Nicholas. *A Discourse of Trade*, ed. and intro. Jacob H. Hollander. Baltimore, Md.: Johns Hopkins Press, 1905.

Barlow, Graham. *The Enraged Musician: Hogarth's Musical Imagery*. Aldershot: Ashgate, 2005.

Beacham, Richard C. *Spectacle Entertainments of Early Imperial Rome*. New Haven, Conn.: Yale University Press, 1999.

Beard, Harry R. "An Etched Caricature of a Handelian Opera." *Burlington Magazine*, 92 (1950), 266.

Beattie, John M. *The English Court in the Reign of George I*. Cambridge: Cambridge University Press, 1967.

Beckett, J. V. "The English Aristocracy." *Parliamentary History*, 5 (1986), 133–42.

—. *The Rise and Fall of the Grenvilles, Duke of Buckingham and Chandos, 1710 to 1921*. Manchester: Manchester University Press, 1994.

Bennett, G. V. "Jacobitism and the Rise of Walpole." In *Historical Perspectives: Studies in English Thought and Society in Honour of J. H. Plumb*, ed. Neil McKendrick, pp. 70–92. London: Europa Publications, 1974.

—. *The Tory Crisis in Church and State, 1688-1730: The Career of Francis Atterbury, Bishop of Rochester*. Oxford: Clarendon Press, 1975.

Berg, Maxine, and Elizabeth Eger. "The Rise and Fall of the Luxury Debate." In Berg and Eger, eds., *Luxury in the Eighteenth Century: Debate, Desire and Delectable Goods*, pp. 78–27. Houndmills, Basingstoke: Palgrave Macmillan, 2003.

Berry, Christopher J. *The Idea of Luxury: A Conceptual and Historical Investigation*. Cambridge: Cambridge University Press, 1994.

Bianconi, Lorenzo. "Il Farinelli di Corrado Giaquinto. Il lusso disdegnato, l'intatta lealtà." *Atti della Accademia Nazionale dei Lincei*, series 9, vol. 42 (2019–2020).

—. *Music in the Seventeenth Century*, trans. David Bryant. Cambridge: Cambridge University Press, 1987.

Bianconi, Lorenzo, and Maria C. C. Pedrielli. "Corrado Giaquinto: Carlo Broschi detto il Farinelli." In *I ritratti del Museo della Musica di Bologna da Padre Martini al Liceo Musicale*, ed. Lorenzo Bianconi et al., pp. 103–24. Florence, Leo S. Olschki, 2018.

Bianconi, Lorenzo, and Thomas Walker. "Production, Consumption and Political Function of Seventeenth-Century Italian Opera." *Early Music History*, 4 (1985), 209–96.

Bindman, David. *Hogarth*. London: Thames and Hudson, 1981.

—. *Hogarth and His Times: Serious Comedy*. Berkeley, Calif.: University of California Press, 1997.

—. "Roubiliac's Statue of Handel and the Keeping of Order in Vauxhall Gardens in the Early Eighteenth Century." *Sculpture Journal*, 1 (1997), 22–31.

Black, Jeremy. "The Anglo-French Alliance, 1716–1731: A Study in Eighteenth-Century International Relations." *Francia: Forschungen zur westeuropäischen Geschichte*, 13 (1985), 295–310.

—. *British Foreign Policy in the Age of Walpole*. Edinburgh: John Donald, 1985.

—. *The Collapse of the Anglo-French Alliance, 1727–1731*. Gloucester: Alan Sutton, 1987.

—. *The English Press in the Eighteenth Century*. London: Croom Helm, 1987.

—. "Giving Life to the Honest Part of the City: The Opposition Woo the City in 1721." *Historical Research*, 60 (1987), 116–17.

—. "Parliament and the Political and Diplomatic Crisis of 1717–18." *Parliamentary History*, 3 (1984), 77–101.

—. *Pitt the Elder*. Cambridge: Cambridge University Press, 1992.

—. "Press and Politics in the 1730s." *Durham University Journal*, 77 (1984), 87–93.

—. *A Subject for Taste: Culture in Eighteenth-Century England*. London: Hambledon, 2005.

—. "An Underrated Journalist: Nathaniel Mist and the Opposition Press during the Whig Ascendancy." *British Journal for Eighteenth-Century Studies*, 10 (1987), 27–42.

—. *Walpole in Power*. Stroud: Sutton Publishing, 2001.

Black, Jeremy, ed. *Britain in the Age of Walpole*. London: Macmillan, 1984.

Bond, Richmond P. *The Tatler: The Making of a Literary Journal*. Cambridge, Mass.: Harvard University Press, 1971.

Bottoms, Edward. "Charles Jervas, Sir Robert Walpole, and the Norfolk Whigs." *Apollo*, vol. 145, no. 420 (1997), 44–8.

Bourdieu, Pierre. *Distinction: A Social Critique of the Judgement of Taste*, trans. Richard Nice. Cambridge, Mass.: Harvard University Press, 1984.

—. *The Field of Cultural Production: Essays on Art and Literature*, ed. and intro. Randal Johnson. New York, N.Y.: Columbia University Press 1993.

—. "The Forms of Capital," trans. Richard Nice. In John G. Richardson, *Handbook of Theory and Research for the Sociology of Education*, pp. 241–58. New York, N.Y.: Greenwood Press, 1986.

—. "The Market of Symbolic Goods." *Poetics*, 14 (1985), 13–44.

—. *The Rules of Art: Genesis and Structure of the Literary Field*, trans. Susan Emanuel. Stanford, Calif.: Stanford University Press, 1996.

Bourdieu, Pierre, and Jean-Claude Passeron. *Reproduction in Education, Society and Culture*, trans. Richard Nice. London: Sage, 1977.

Braverman, Richard. "'Dunce the Second Reigns Like Dunce the First': The Gothic Bequest in the *Dunciad*." *ELH* (*English Literary History*), 62 (1995), 863–82.

Bredvold, Louis I. "The Gloom of the Tory Satirists." In *Pope and His Contemporaries: Essays Presented to George Sherburn*, ed. James L. Clifford and Louis A. Landa, pp. 1–19. Oxford: Clarendon Press, 1949.

Brewer, John. *The Pleasures of the Imagination: English Culture in the Eighteenth Century*. Chicago, Ill. University of Chicago Press, 1997.

Brewster, Dorothy. *Aaron Hill, Poet, Dramatist, Projector*. New York, N.Y.: Columbia University Press, 1913.

Brooks, Harold F. "The 'Imitation' in English Poetry, Especially in Formal Satire, Before the Age of Pope." *Review of English Studies*, 25 (1949), 129–40.

Brown, Vera L. "The South Sea Company and Contraband Trade." *American Historical Review*, 31 (1926), 662–78.

Brown, Peter Douglas. *William Pitt, Earl of Chatham: The Great Commoner*. London: George Allen and Unwin, 1978.

Brownell, Morris R. *Alexander Pope and the Arts of Georgian England*. Oxford: Clarendon Press, 1978.

—. "Ears of an Untoward Make: Pope and Handel." *Musical Quarterly*, 62 (1976), 554–70.

—. *Alexander Pope's Villa: Views of Pope's Villa, Grotto and Garden: A Microcosm of English Landscape*. London: Greater London Council, 1980.

Browning, Reed. *Political and Constitutional Ideas of the Court Whigs*. Baton Rouge, La.: Louisiana State University Press, 1982.

Bullion, John L. "'To Play What Game She Pleased without Observation': Princess Augusta and the Political Drama of Succession, 1736–56." In *Queenship in Britain*, ed. Orr, pp. 207–35.

Burden, Michael "Opera, Excess, and the Discourse of Luxury in Eighteenth-Century England." *Revue de la Société d'études anglo-américaines des XVIIe et XVIIIe siècles*, 71 (2014), 232–48.

318   BIBLIOGRAPHY

Burgess, Glenn. *The Politics of the Ancient Constitution: An Introduction to English Political Thought, 1603–1642*. University Park, Penn.: Pennsylvania State University Press, 1993.

Burrows, Donald. *Handel*. New York, N.Y.: Schirmer, 1994.

——. *Handel and the English Chapel Royal*. Oxford: Oxford University Press, 2005.

——. "Handel and the Foundling Hospital." *Music and Letters*, 58 (1977), 270.

——. "Handel and the London Opera Companies in the 1730s: Venues, Programmes, Patronage and Performers." *Göttinger Händel-Beiträge*, 10 (2004), 149–65.

——. "Handel as a Court Musician." *Court Historian*, vol. 3, no. 2 (July 1998) 3–9.

Burrows, Donald, and Robert D. Hume. "George I, the Haymarket Opera Company and Handel's Water Music." *Early Music*, 19 (1991), 323–44.

Burrows, Donald, and Rosemary Dunhill, eds. *Music and Theatre in Handel's World: The Family Papers of James Harris, 1732–1780*. Oxford: Oxford University Press, 2002.

Burrows, Donald, Helen Coffey, John Greenacombe, and Anthony Hicks, comps. and eds. *George Frideric Handel: Collected Documents*, 6 vols. Cambridge: Cambridge University Press, 2013– .

Burtt, Shelley. *Virtue Transformed: Political Argument in England, 1688–1740*. Cambridge: Cambridge University Press, 1992.

Bush, M. L. *The English Aristocracy: A Comparative Synthesis*. Manchester: Manchester University Press, 1984.

Butler, Samuel. *Characters and Passages from Note-Books*, ed. A. R. Waller. Cambridge: Cambridge University Press, 1908.

Butt, John. "Pope and the Opposition to Walpole's Government." In John Butt, ed., *Pope, Dickens, and Others: Essays and Addresses*, pp. 111–26. Edinburgh: Edinburgh University Press, 1969.

Butt, John, ed. Alexander Pope, *Imitations of Horace. The Twickenham Edition of the Poems of Alexander Pope*. Vol. 4, 2nd edn. New Haven, Conn.: Yale University Press, 1953.

Cable, Mabel H. "The Idea of a Patriot King in the Propaganda of the Opposition to Walpole, 1735–1739." *Philological Quarterly*, 18 (1939), 119–30.

Cannon, John. *Samuel Johnson and the Politics of Hanoverian England*. Oxford: Clarendon Press, 1994.

Carretta, Vincent. *The Snarling Muse: Verbal and Visual Satire from Pope to Churchill*. Philadelphia, Penn.: University of Pennsylvania Press, 1983.

Carswell, John. *The South Sea Bubble*, rev. ed. London: Alan Sutton, 1993.

Cervantes, Xavier. "Henry Fielding: Enemy or Connoisseur of Italian Opera?" *Theatre History Studies*, 16 (June 1996), 157–72.

——. "History and Sociology of the Italian Opera in London (1705–45): The Evidence of the Dedications of the Printed Editions." *Studi musicali*, 37 (1998), 339–82.

——. "'Let 'em Deck their Verses with Farinelli's Name': Farinelli as a Satirical Trope in English Poetry and Verse in the 1730s." *British Journal for Eighteenth-Century Studies*, 28 (2005), 421–36.

——. "'Tuneful Monsters': The Castrati and the London Operatic Public, 1667–1737." *Restoration and Eighteenth-Century Theatre Research*, 2nd ser., 13 (1998), 1–24.

Chambers, Douglas. *The Planters of the English Landscape Garden: Botany, Trees, and the "Georgics."* New Haven, Conn.: Yale University Press, 1993.

Chance, James F. *The Alliance of Hanover: A Study of British Foreign Policy in the Last Years of George I.* London: John Murray, 1923.

Chrissochoidis, Ilias. "Handel at a Crossroads: His 1737–1738 and 1738–1739 Seasons Re-examined." *Music and Letters*, 90 (2009), 599–635.

——. "Oratorio *à la Mode*," *Newsletter of the American Handel Society*, vol. 23, nos. 1–12 (Spring/Summer 2008), 7–9.

Cibber, Colley. *An Apology for the Life of Colley Cibber*, ed. B. R. S. Fone. Ann Arbor, Mich.: University of Michigan Press, 1968.

Clark, George. *A History of the Royal College of Physicians of London*, 2 vols. Oxford: Clarendon Press, 1966.

Clark, J. C. D. *English Society, 1688–1832: Ideology, Social Structure and Political Practice During the Ancien Regime.* Cambridge: Cambridge University Press, 1985.

——. *Samuel Johnson: Literature, Religion and English Cultural Politics from the Restoration to Romanticism.* Cambridge: Cambridge University Press, 1994.

Clark, Jane. "For Kings and Senates Fit." *Georgian Group Journal* (1989), 55–63.

——. "Lord Burlington Is Here." In *Lord Burlington*, ed. Barnard and Clark, pp. 251–310.

——. "The Mysterious Mr Buck: Patronage and Politics, 1688–1745." *Apollo*, 129 (May 1989), 317–22, 371.

——. "Palladianism and the Divine Right of Kings: Jacobite Iconography." *Apollo*, 135 (April 1992), 224–9.

Clarke, George. "Grecian Taste and Gothic Virtue: Lord Cobham's Gardening Programme and Its Iconography." *Apollo*, 97 (June 1973), 566–71.

Clowes, W. Laird. *The Royal Navy: A History from the Earliest Times to the Present*, 7 vols. London: Sampson Low, Marston and Co., 1897–1903.

Cobbett, William. *The Parliamentary History of England*, 36 vols. (1806–1820).

Cohen, Mitchell. *The Politics of Opera: A History from Monteverdi to Mozart.* Princeton, N.J.: Princeton University Press, 2017.

Coke, David. "Roubiliac's Handel for *Vauxhall* Gardens: A Sculpture in Context." *Sculpture Journal*, 16 (2007), 5–22.

Coke, D., and A. Borg. *Vauxhall Gardens: A History.* New Haven, Conn.: Yale University Press, 2011.

Colbourn, Trevor. *The Lamp of Experience: Whig History and the Intellectual Origins of the American Revolution.* Indianapolis, Ind.: Liberty Fund, 1998.

Coleman, Anthony. Introduction to James Miller, *Harlequin-Horace: or, the Art of Modern Poetry.* Augustan Reprint Society, no. 178 (1976).

Coley, W. B. "Henry Fielding and the Two Walpoles." *Philological Quarterly*, 45 (1966), 157–76.

Colley, Linda. *Britons: Forging the Nation, 1707–1837.* New Haven, Conn.: Yale University Press, 1992.

——. *In Defiance of Oligarchy: The Tory Party, 1714–60.* Cambridge: Cambridge University Press, 1982.

Colton, Judith. "Kent's Hermitage for Queen Caroline at Richmond." *Architectura*, 4 (1974), 181–91.

——. "Merlin's Cave and Queen Caroline: Garden Art as Political Propaganda." *Eighteenth-Century Studies*, 10 (1976–77), 1–20.

320 BIBLIOGRAPHY

A Complete Collection of the Protests of the Lords, ed. James E. T. Rogers, 2 vols. Oxford: Clarendon Press, 1875.

Conn, Stetson. *Gibraltar in British Diplomacy in the Eighteenth Century*. New Haven, Conn.: Yale University Press, 1942.

Connor, T. P. "The Fruits of a Grand Tour: Edward Wright and Lord Parker in Italy, 1720–22." *Apollo*, vol. 148, no. 437 (July 1998), 23–30.

Cooper, Anthony Ashley (Earl of Shaftesbury). *Characteristics of Men, Manners, Opinions, Times*, ed. Lawrence E. Klein. Cambridge: Cambridge University Press, 1999.

——. *Shaftesbury's Characteristics, of Men, Manners, Opinion, Times*, ed. John M. Robertson, 2 vols. London: Grant Richards, 1900.

The Correspondence of the Dukes of Richmond and Newcastle, 1724–1750. Sussex Record Society, 73 (1982–3).

Cottret, Bernard, ed. *Bolingbroke's Political Writings: The Conservative Enlightenment*. London: Macmillan, 1997.

Cowley, Robert L. S. *Hogarth's "Marriage à la Mode."* Ithaca, N.Y.: Cornell University Press, 1983.

Coxe, William. *Memoirs of Horatio, Lord Walpole* (1802).

Crawford, Charlotte E. "What Was Pope's Debt to Edward Young?" *English Literary History*, 13 (1946), 157–67.

Croft, C. R. "Libel and Satire in the Eighteenth Century." *Eighteenth-Century Studies*, 8 (1974–75), 153–68.

Cruickshanks, Eveline. "Lord Cowper, Lord Orrery, the Duke of Wharton, and Jacobitism." *Albion*, 26 [1994], 27–40.

——. "Lord North, Christopher Layer and the Atterbury Plot: 1720–23." In *The Jacobite Challenge*, ed. Eveline Cruickshanks and Jeremy Black, pp. 92–106. Edinburgh: John Donald, 1988.

——. "The Political Career of the Third Earl of Burlington." In *Lord Burlington: Architecture, Art and Life*, ed. Toby Barnard and Jane Clark, pp. 201–15. London: Hambledon Press, 1995.

Cruickshanks, Eveline, and Howard Erskine-Hill. *The Atterbury Plot*. Basingstoke: Palgrave Macmillan, 2004.

Dabydeen, David. *Hogarth, Walpole and Commercial Britain*. London: Hansib Publishing, 1987.

——. *Hogarth's Blacks: Images of Blacks in Eighteenth Century English Art*. Athens, Ga.: University of Georgia Press, 1987.

Daub, Peggy. "Handel and Frederick." *Musical Times*, 122 (1981), 733.

——. "Music at the Court of George II (ca. 1727–1760)." Ph.D. dissertation, Cornell University, 1985.

Davidson, Peter. "Pope's Recusancy." *Studies in the Literary Imagination*, 38 (2005), 64–76.

Davis, Rose Mary. *The Good Lord Lyttelton: A Study in Eighteenth Century Politics and Culture*. Bethlehem, Pa.: Times Publishing Co., 1939.

Dean, Winton, and Merrill Knapp. *Handel's Operas, 1704–1726*, rev. ed. Oxford: Clarendon Press, 1995.

Desmond, Ray. *Kew: The History of the Royal Botanic Gardens*. Kew: The Harvill Press with the Royal Botanic Gardens, 1995.

Deutsch, O. E. *Handel: A Documentary Biography*. New York, N.Y.: W. W. Norton, 1955.

Diary of Mary Countess Cowper, Lady of the Bedchamber to the Princess of Wales, ed. Spencer Cowper, 2nd ed. London: John Murray, 1865.

Dickinson, H. T. *Bolingbroke*. London: Constable, 1970.

——. "Bolingbroke: 'The Idea of a Patriot King.'" *History Today*, 20 (1970), 13–19.

——. "The Eighteenth-Century Debate on the 'Glorious Revolution.'" *History*, 61 (1976), 28–45.

——. *Liberty and Property: Political Ideology in Eighteenth-Century Britain*. New York, N.Y.: Holmes and Meier, 1977.

——. *The Politics of the People in Eighteenth-Century Britain*. New York, N.Y.: St. Martin's Press, 1995.

——. *Walpole and the Whig Supremacy*. London: English Universities Press, 1973.

Dickinson, H. T., ed. John Lord Hervey, *Ancient and Modern Liberty Stated and Compar'd*. Augustan Reprint Society, no. 255–6 (1989).

Dickson, P. G. M. *The Financial Revolution in England: A Study in the Development of Public Credit, 1688–1756*. London: Macmillan, 1967.

Dillon, Patrick. *The Much Lamented Death of Madam Geneva: The Eighteenth-Century Gin Craze*. London: Review, 2002.

Dixon, Peter. "Pope and James Miller." *Notes and Queries*, 215, new series, vol. 17 (1970), 91–2.

——. *The World of Pope's Satires: An Introduction to the "Epistles" and "Imitations of Horace."* London: Methuen, 1968.

Doolittle, I. G. "A First-hand Account of the Commons Debate on the Removal of Sir Robert Walpole, 13 February 1741." *Bulletin of the Institute of Historical Research*, 53 (1980), 125–40.

Dorris, George E. *Paolo Rolli and the Italian Circle in London, 1715–1744*. The Hague: Mouton, 1967.

Dowling, William C. *The Epistolary Moment: The Poetics of the Eighteenth-Century Verse Epistle*. Princeton, N.J.: Princeton University Press, 1991.

Downie, J. A. "The Development of the Political Press." In *Britain in the First Age of Party, 1680–1750: Essays Presented to Geoffrey Holmes*, ed. Clyve Jones, pp. 111–27. London: Hambledon Press, 1987.

——. *Robert Harley and the Press: Propaganda and Public Opinion in the Age of Swift and Defoe*. Cambridge: Cambridge University Press, 1979.

——. *To Settle the Succession of the State: Literature and Politics, 1678–1750*. New York, N.Y.: St. Martin's Press, 1994.

——. "Walpole, 'the Poet's Foe.'" In *Britain in the Age of Walpole*, ed. Jeremy Black, pp. 171–88. London: Macmillan, 1984.

Dufourcq, Norbert. "Nouvelles de la cour et de la ville." *Recherches sur la musique française classique*, 10 (1970), 105.

A Duke and His Friends: The Life and Letters of the Second Duke of Richmond, ed. Charles March, Earl of March, 2 vols. London: Hutchinson, 1911.

Edwards, Averyl. *Frederick Louis, Prince of Wales, 1707–1751*. London: Staples Press, 1947.

Education, Culture, Economy, and Society, ed. A. H. Halsey et al. Oxford: Oxford University Press, 1997.

Egerton, Judy. *Hogarth's "Marriage à la Mode."* London: National Gallery Publications, 1997.

The Eighteenth Century: Art, Design and Society, 1689–1789, ed. Bernard Denvir. London: Longman, 1983.

322   BIBLIOGRAPHY

Elias, Norbert. *The Court Society*, trans. Edmund Jephcott. New York, N.Y.: Pantheon Books, 1983.

Elkin, P. K. *The Augustan Defence of Satire*. Oxford: Clarendon Press, 1973.

Elliott, R. C. "Hume's 'Character of Sir Robert Walpole': Some Unnoticed Additions." *Journal of English and Germanic Philology*, 48 (1949), 367–78.

Ennis, Daniel J. "The Making of the Poet Laureate, 1730." *Age of Johnson*, 11 (2000), 217–35.

Erskine-Hill, Howard. "Alexander Pope: The Political Poet in His Time." *Eighteenth-Century Studies*, 15 (1981–82), 123–48.

——. *The Augustan Idea in English Literature*. London: E. Arnold, 1983.

——. "Courtiers Out of Horace: Donne's *Satyre IV*; and Pope's *Fourth Satire of Dr John Donne, Dean of St Paul's Versifyed*." In *John Donne: Essays in Celebration*, ed. A. J. Smith, pp. 273–307. London: Methuen, 1972.

——. *Poetry of Opposition and Revolution: Dryden to Wordsworth*. Oxford: Clarendon Press, 1996.

——. "The Political Character of Samuel Johnson." In *Samuel Johnson: New Critical Essays*, ed. Isobel Grundy, pp. 107–36. London: Vision Press, 1984.

——. *Pope: The Dunciad*. London: Edward Arnold, 1972.

——. "Pope and the Poetry of Opposition." In *The Cambridge Companion to Alexander Pope*, ed. Pat. Rogers, pp. 134–49. Cambridge: Cambridge University Press, 2007.

Fairer, David. *The Poetry of Alexander Pope*. Harmondsworth: Penguin, 1989.

Ferraro, Julian. "Taste and Use: Pope's *Epistle to Burlington*." *British Journal for Eighteenth-Century Studies*, 19 (1996), 141–59.

Fielding, Henry. *The Author's Farce (Original Version)*, ed. Charles B. Woods. Lincoln, Nebr.: University of Nebraska Press, 1966.

——. *The Historical Register for the Year 1736 and Eurydice Hissed*, ed. by William W. Appleton. Lincoln, Nebr.: University of Nebraska Press, 1967.

——. *New Essays by Henry Fielding: His Contributions to the "Craftsman (1734–1739)" and Other Early Journalism*, ed. Martin C. Battestin. Charlottesville, Va.: University Press of Virginia, 1989.

Fink, Zera S. "Milton and the Theory of Climatic Influence." *Modern Language Quarterly*, 2 (1941), 67–80.

Foord, Archibald S. *His Majesty's Opposition, 1714–1830*. Oxford: Clarendon Press, 1964.

Forster, Harold. *Edward Young: The Poet of the Night Thoughts, 1683–1765*. Alburgh Harleston, Norfolk: Erskine Press, 1986.

Foxon, David F. *English Verse, 1701–1750: A Catalogue of Separately Printed Poems with Notes on Contemporary Collected Editions*, 2 vols. London: Cambridge University Press, 1975.

Fraenkel, Eduard. *Horace*. Oxford: Clarendon Press, 1957.

Freeman, Robert. "Farinello and His Repertory." In *Studies in Renaissance and Baroque Music in Honor of Arthur Mendel*, ed. Robert L. Marshall, pp. 301–30. Kassell: Bärenreiter, 1974.

Fritz, Paul S. *The English Ministers and Jacobitism between the Rebellions of 1715 and 1745*. Toronto, Canada: University of Toronto Press, 1975.

Fuchs, Jacob. "Horace's Good Augustus and Pope's Imitation of *Epist.* 2.1." *Classical and Modern Literature: A Quarterly*, 3 (1983), 75–87.

Gabriner, Paul. "Pope's 'Virtue' and the Events of 1738." *Scripta Hierosolymitana*, 25 (1973), 96–110.

BIBLIOGRAPHY   323

Gaudi, Robert. *The War of Jenkins' Ear: The Forgotten Struggle for North and South America: 1739-1742*. New York, N.Y.: Pegasus, 2021.

George, M. Dorothy. *English Political Caricature to 1792: A Study of Opinion and Propaganda*, 2 vols. Oxford: Clarendon Press, 1959.

Gerrard, Christine. *Aaron Hill: The Muses' Projector, 1685-1750*. Oxford: Oxford University Press, 2003.

——. "*The Castle of Indolence* and the Opposition to Walpole." *Review of English Studies*, n.s., 41 (1990), 25-64.

——. *The Patriot Opposition to Walpole: Politics, Poetry, and National Myth, 1725-1742*. Oxford: Clarendon, 1994.

——. "Pope and the Patriots." In *Pope: New Contexts*, ed. David Fairer, pp. 25-43. London: Harvester Wheatsheaf, 1990.

——. "Queens-in-waiting: Caroline of Anspach and Augusta of Saxe-Gotha as Princesses of Wales." In *Queenship in Britain, 1660-1837*, ed. Clarissa Campbell Orr, pp. 143-61. Manchester: Manchester University Press, 2002.

Gibson, Elizabeth. "Owen Swiney and the Italian Opera in London." *Musical Times*, 126 (Feb. 1984), 82-6.

——. *The Royal Academy of Music, 1719-1728: The Institution and Its Directors*. New York, N.Y.: Garland Publishing, 1989.

——. "The Royal Academy of Music (1719-28) and its Directors." In *Handel Tercentenary Collection*, ed. Stanley Sadie and Anthony Hicks, pp. 138-64. Ann Arbor, Mich.: UMI Research Press, 1987.

Giddings, Robert. "The Fall of Orgilio: Samual Johnson as Parliamentary Reporter. In *Samuel Johnson: New Critical Essays*, ed. Isobel Grundy, pp. 86-106. London: Vision Press, 1984.

Gilman, Todd. "The Italian (Castrato) in London." In *The Work of Opera: Genre, Nationhood, and Sexual Difference*, ed. Richard Dellamora and Daniel Fischlin, pp. 49-70. New York, N.Y.: Columbia University Press, 1997.

Gilpin, William. *A Dialogue upon the Gardens ... at Stow [sic]*, ed. with intro. John Dixon Hunt. Augustan Reprint Society, no. 176 (1976).

Glover, Richard. *Memoirs by a Celebrated Literary and Political Character*, new ed. London: John Murray, 1814.

Goldgar, Bertrand A. *Literary Criticism of Alexander Pope*. Lincoln, Nebr.: University of Nebraska Press, 1965.

——. "Pope and the *Grub-street Journal*." *Modern Philology*, 74 (1977), 371.

——. [Review of Gerrard, *Patriot Opposition*.] In *Modern Philology*, 94 (1997), 393-6.

——. *Walpole and the Wits: The Relation of Politics to Literature, 1722-1742*. Lincoln, Nebr.: University of Nebraska Press, 1976.

Goldgar, Bertrand A. ed. *The Grub Street Journal, 1730-33*, 4 vols. London: Pickering and Chatto, 2002.

Goldie, Mark. "The Roots of True Whiggism, 1688-94." *History of Political Thought*, 1 (1980), 195-236.

Goldsmith, M. M. "Faction Detected: Ideological Consequences of Robert Walpole's Decline and Fall." *History*, 64 (1979), 1-19.

——. "Liberty, Luxury and the Pursuit of Happiness." In *Languages of Political Theory in Early Modern Europe*, ed. A. Pagden, pp. 225-51.

——. "Liberty, Virtue, and the Rule of Law, 1689-1770." In *Republicanism, Liberty, and Commercial Society, 1649-1716*, ed. David Wootton, pp. 197-232. Stanford, Calif.: Stanford University Press, 1994.

324 BIBLIOGRAPHY

——. Mandeville and the Spirit of Capitalism." *Journal of British Studies*, 17 (Fall 1977), 63–81.

——. "The Principles of True Liberty: Political Ideology in Eighteenth-Century Britain." *Political Studies*, 27 (1979), 141–6.

——. *Private Vices, Public Benefits: Bernard Mandeville's Social and Political Thought*. Cambridge: Cambridge University Press, 1985.

Greene, Donald. *The Politics of Samuel Johnson*, 2nd ed. Athens, Ga.: University of Georgia Press, 1990.

Gregg, Edward. *The Protestant Succession in International Politics, 1710–1716*. New York, N.Y.: Garland Publishing, 1986.

——. [Review of *Lord Burlington – The Man and His Politics*, ed. Corp.] *British Journal for Eighteenth-Century Studies*, 24 (2001), 95–7.

Greig, Hannah. *The Beau Monde: Fashionable Society in Georgian London*. New Haven, Conn.: Yale University Press, 2013.

Griffin, Dustin. *Literary Patronage in England, 1650–1800*. Cambridge: Cambridge University Press, 1996.

——. *Patriotism and Poetry in Eighteenth-Century Britain*. Cambridge: Cambridge University Press, 2002.

Griffith, Reginald H. *Alexander Pope: A Bibliography*, 2 vols. Austin, Tex.: University of Texas, 1927.

——. "The Progress Pieces of the Eighteenth Century." *The Texas Review*, 5 (1919–20), 218–33.

Guerinot, J. V. *Pamphlet Attacks on Alexander Pope, 1711–1744: A Descriptive Bibliography*. New York, N.Y.: New York University Press, 1969.

Gunn, J. A. W. *Beyond Liberty and Property: The Process of Self-Recognition in Eighteenth-Century Political Thought*. Kingston and Montreal: McGill-Queen's University Press, 1983.

——. "Court Whiggery – Justifying Innovation." In *Politics, Politeness, and Patriotism*, ed. Gordon J. Schochet, pp. 125–56. Washington, D.C.: The Folger Shakespeare Library, 1993.

——. *Factions No More: Attitudes to Party in Government and Opposition in Eighteenth-Century England*. London: Frank Cass, 1972.

——. "Mandeville: Poverty, Luxury and the Whig Theory of Government." In *Political Theory and Political Economy: Papers from the Annual Meeting of the Conference for the Study of Political Thought, 1974*, ed. Crawford M. Macpherson, pp. 12–17. Toronto: n.p., [1975].

Habermas, Jürgen. *Structural Transformation of the Public Sphere: An Inquiry into a Category of Bourgeois Society*, trans. Thomas Burger. Cambridge, Mass.: MIT Press, 1991.

Haböck, Franz. *Die Gesangkunst der Kastraten. Erster Notenband: Die Kunst des Cavaliere Carlo Broschi Farinelli*. Vienna: Universal Edition, 1923.

Habakkuk, H. J. "England's Nobility." In *Aristocratic Government and Society in Eighteenth-Century England: The Foundations of Stability*, ed. Daniel A. Baugh, pp. 97–115. New York, N.Y., New Viewpoints, 1975.

Hacking, Ian. *Mad Travelers: Reflections on the Reality of Transient Mental Illness*. Charlottesville, Va.: University Press of Virginia, 1998.

Haig, Robert L. *The Gazetteer, 1735–1797: A Study in the Eighteenth-Century English Newspaper*. Carbondale, Ill.: Southern Illinois University Press, 1960.

Hallett, Mark. *Hogarth*. London: Phaidon, 2000.

——. *The Spectacle of Difference: Graphic Satire in the Age of Hogarth.* New Haven, Conn.: Yale University Press, 1999.

Hammond, Brean S. "Politics and Cultural Politics: The Case of Henry Fielding." *Eighteenth-Century Life,* 16 (February 1992), 76–93.

——. *Pope and Bolingbroke: A Study of Friendship and Influence.* Columbia, Mo.: University of Missouri Press, 1984.

Hamowy, Ronald, ed. John Trenchard and Thomas Gordon, *Cato's Letters: Or, Essays on Liberty, Civil and Religious, and Other Important Subjects,* 2 vols. Indianapolis, Ind.: Liberty Fund, 1995.

Hampton, Timothy. *Writing from History: The Rhetoric of Exemplarity in Renaissance Literature.* Ithaca, N.Y.: Cornell University Press, 1990.

Handel, George Frideric. *Songs and Cantatas for Soprano and Continuo,* ed. Donald Burrows. Oxford: Oxford University Press, 1988.

Hanham, Andrew. "Early Whig Opposition to the Walpole Administration: The Evidence of Francis Gwyn's Division List on the Wells Election Case, 1723." *Parliamentary History,* 15 (1996), 333–60.

——. "The Gin Acts, 1729–51." Available at the History of Parliament Online website.

——. "Whig Opposition to Sir Robert Walpole, 1727–1734 in the House of Commons." Ph.D. dissertation, University of Leicester, 1992.

Hanson, Laurence. *Government and the Press, 1695–1763.* London: Oxford University Press, 1936.

The Harcourt Papers, ed. Edward W. Harcourt, 14 vols. Oxford: James Parker, 1880–1905.

Harding, Richard. *Amphibious Warfare in the Eighteenth Century: The British Expedition to the West Indies, 1740–1742.* Woodbridge: Boydell Press, 1991.

Hardy, John. "Johnson's *London*: The Country Versus the City." *Studies in the Eighteenth Century.* Papers Presented at the David Nichol Smith Memorial Seminar, Canberra 1966, ed. R. F. Brissenden. Toronto: University of Toronto Press, 1968.

Hargreaves-Mawdsley, W. N. *Eighteenth-Century Spain, 1700–1788: A Political, Diplomatic and Institutional History.* London: Macmillan, 1979.

Harris, Ellen. "'Master of the Orchester with a Salary': Handel at the Bank of England." *Music and Letters,* 101 (2020), 1–29.

Harris, Frances. *A Passion for Government: The Life of Sarah, Duchess of Marlborough.* Oxford: Clarendon Press, 1991.

Harris, Michael. *London Newspapers in the Age of Walpole: A Study of the Origins of the Modern English Press.* Cranbury, N.J.: Associated University Presses, 1987.

——. "Print and Politics in the Age of Walpole." In *Britain in the Age of Walpole,* ed. Jeremy Black, pp. 189–210. London: Macmillan, 1984.

Harris, R., ed. "A Leicester House Political Diary, 1742–43." *Camden Miscellany,* 31, 4th ser. (1992), 373–411.

Harris, Robert. *Patriot Press: National Politics and the London Press.* Oxford: Clarendon, 1993.

Hatton, Ragnhild. *George I: Elector and King.* Cambridge, Mass.: Harvard University Press, 1978.

Heartz, Daniel. "Farinelli Revisited." *Early Music,* 18 (1990), 430–43.

Hervey, John Lord. *Memoirs of the Reign of George the Second,* ed. John W. Croker, 3 vols. London: Bickers and Son, 1884.

326 BIBLIOGRAPHY

——. *Some Materials Towards Memoirs of the Reign of King George II*, ed. Romney Sedgwick, 3 vols. London: Eyre and Spottiswoode, 1931.

Hicks, Philip. "Bolingbroke, Clarendon and the Role of the Classical Historian," *Eighteenth-Century Studies*, 20 (1987), 445–71.

Hildner, Ernest G., Jr. "The Rôle of the South Sea Company in the Diplomacy Leading to the War of Jenkins' Ear, 1729–1739." *Hispanic American Historical Review*, 18 (1938), 321–41.

Hill, Aaron, and William Popple. *The Prompter: A Theatrical Paper (1734–1736)*, ed. and sel. William W. Appleton and Kalman A. Burnim. New York, N.Y.: Benjamin Blom, 1966.

Hill, Brian W. *The Growth of Parliamentary Parties, 1689–1741*. Hamden, Conn.: Archon, 1976.

——. *Sir Robert Walpole: "Sole and Prime Minister."* London: Hamish Hamilton, 1989.

Hill, Christopher. "The Norman Yoke." In *Puritanism and Revolution: Studies in Interpretation of the English Revolution of the 17th Century*, pp. 50–122. New York, N.Y.: Schocken, 1964.

Hillhouse, James T. *The Grub-street Journal*. Durham, N.C.: Duke University Press, 1928.

Hirsch, E. D. "The Politics of Theories of Interpretation." *Critical Inquiry*, 9 (1982), 321–33.

Historical Manuscripts Commission. *15th Report, Appendix*, Pt. II, *The Manuscripts of J. Eliot Hodgkin*. London: Her Majesty's Stationery Office, 1897.

——. *The Manuscripts of the Earl of Buckinghamshire* [etc.]. London: Her Majesty's Stationery Office, 1895.

——. *The Manuscripts of the Earl of Carlisle*. London: His Majesty's Stationery Office, 1911.

——. *The Manuscripts of the Earl of Egmont. Diary of Viscount Percival afterwards First Earl of Egmont*, 3 vols. London: His Majesty's Stationery Office, 1920–1923.

——. *Reports of Manuscripts in Various Collections*. Vol. 8. *Manuscripts of M. L. S. Clements*. London: His Majesty's Stationery Office, 1913.

——. *Report on the Manuscripts of the Earl of Denbigh*. Pt. V. London: His Majesty's Stationery Office, 1911.

The History of Parliament: The House of Commons, 1715–1754, ed. Romney Sedgwick, 2 vols. New York. N.Y.: Oxford University Press, 1970.

Hodgkinson, Terence. *Handel at Vauxhall*. Victoria and Albert Museum Bulletin Reprints, no. 1 (1969).

Hogarth, William. *The Analysis of Beauty*, ed. with intro. Joseph Burke. Oxford: Clarendon, 1955.

Holmes, William C. *Opera Observed: Views of a Florentine Impresario in the Early Eighteenth Century*. Chicago, Ill.: University of Chicago Press, 1993.

Horace. *Satires, Epistles, Ars Poetica*, trans. H. Rushton Fairclough. Loeb Classical Library. London: William Heineman, 1926.

Horace Walpole: Writer, Politician, and Connoisseur, ed. Warren H. Smith. New Haven, Conn.: Yale University Press, 1967.

Horne, Thomas A. "Politics in a Corrupt Society: William Arnall's Defence of Robert Walpole." *Journal of the History of Ideas*, 41 (1980), 601–14.

——. *The Social Thought of Bernard Mandeville: Virtue and Commerce in Early Eighteenth-Century England*. New York, N.Y.: Columbia University Press, 1978.

Houghton Revisited: The Walpole Masterpieces from Catherine the Great's Hermitage, exhib. cat., Houghton Hall, King's Lynn, Norfolk, 17 May–29 September 2013. London: Royal Academy of Arts, 2013.

Howard, Jeremy. "Hogarth, Amigoni and 'The Rake's Levee': New Light on *A Rake's Progress*." *Apollo*, vol. 146, no. 429 (November 1997), 31–7.

Hughes, Helen S. *The Gentle Hertford: Her Life and Letters*. New York, N.Y.: Macmillan, 1940.

——. "Thomson and the Countess of Hertford." *Modern Philology*, 25 (1928), 439–68.

Hume, Robert D. "The Economics of Culture in London, 1660–1740." *Huntington Library Quarterly*, 69 (2006), 487–533.

——. "Handel and Opera Management in London in the 1730s." *Music and Letters*, 67 (1986), 347–62.

——. *Henry Fielding and the London Theatre, 1728–1737*. Oxford: Clarendon, 1988.

——. "The Value of Money in Eighteenth-Century England: Incomes, Prices, Buying Power – and Some Problems in Cultural Economics." *Huntington Library Quarterly*, 77 (2015), 373–416.

Hundert, E. J. *The Enlightenment's "Fable": Bernard Mandeville and the Discovery of Society*. Cambridge: Cambridge University Press, 1994.

Hunt, John Dixon. "Emblem and Expression in the Eighteenth-Century Landscape Garden." *Eighteenth-Century Studies*, 4 (1970–71), 294–317.

——. *William Kent: Landscape Garden Designer*. London: A. Zwemmer, 1987.

Hunter, David. "Bragging on *Rinaldo*: Ten Ways Writers have Trumpeted Handel's Coming to Britain." *Göttinger Händel-Beiträge*, 10 (2004), 113–31.

——. "Dublin." In *The Cambridge Handel Encyclopedia*, ed. Annette Landgraf and David Vickers, pp. 198–9. Cambridge: Cambridge University Press, 2009.

——. "Inviting Handel to Ireland: Laurence Whyte and the Challenge of Poetic Evidence." *Eighteenth-Century Ireland*, 20 (2005), 156–68.

——. *The Lives of George Frideric Handel*. Woodbridge: Boydell, 2015.

——. "Margaret Cecil, Lady Brown: 'Persevering Enemy to Handel' but 'Otherwise Unknown to History,'" *Women and Music*, 3 (1999) 43–58.

——. "Patronizing Handel, Inventing Audiences: The Intersection of Class, Money, Music and History." *Early Music*, 28 (2000), 32–49.

Hyde, Edward (Earl of Clarendon). *The History of the Rebellion and Civil Wars in England*, ed. W. Dunn Macray, 6 vols. Oxford: Clarendon Press, 1888.

Ingamells, John, comp. *A Dictionary of British and Irish Travellers in Italy, 1701–1800*. New Haven, Conn.: Yale University Press, 1997.

Inglesfield, Robert. "James Thomson, Aaron Hill and the Poetic 'Sublime.'" *British Journal for Eighteenth-Century Studies*, 13 (1990), 215–21.

Irwin, W. R. "Prince Frederick's Mask of Patriotism." *Philological Quarterly*, 27 (1958), 368–84.

Jack, Ian. *Augustan Satire: Intention and Idiom in English Poetry, 1660–1750*. Oxford: Clarendon Press, 1952.

Jack, Malcolm. *Corruption and Progress: The Eighteenth-Century Debate*. New York, N.Y.: AMS Press, 1989.

328 BIBLIOGRAPHY

Jacobson, David L. *The English Libertarian Heritage from the Writings of John Trenchard and Thomas Gordon in "The Independent Whig" and "Cato's Letters,"* ed. with intro. David L. Jacobson. Indianapolis, Ind.: Bobbs-Merrill, 1965.

Johnson, Samuel. *Lives of the English Poets*, ed. George B. Hill, 3 vols. Oxford: Clarendon Press, 1905.

——. *Poems*, ed. E. L. McAdam, Jr. *The Yale Edition of the Works of Samuel Johnson*. New Haven, Conn.: Yale University Press, 1964.

Johnstone, H. Diack. "Handel at Oxford in 1733." *Early Music*, 31 (2003), 248–60.

Joncus, Bertha. "Handel at Drury Lane: Ballad Opera and the Production of Kitty Clive." *Journal of the Royal Musical Association*, 131 (2006), 179–226.

——. "One God, So Many Farinellis: Mythologizing the Star Castrato." *British Journal for Eighteenth-Century Studies*, 28 (2005), 437–96.

Jones, Clyve. "The House of Lords and the Fall of Walpole." In *Hanoverian Britain and Empire: Essays in Memory of Philip Lawson*, ed. Stephen Taylor, Richard Connors and Clyve Jones, pp. 102–36. Woodbridge: Boydell, 1998.

——. "The Impeachment of the Earl of Oxford and the Whig Schism of 1717: Four New Lists." *Bulletin of the Institute of Historical Research*, 55 (1982), 66–87.

——. "Jacobitism and the Historian: The Case of William, 1st Earl Cowper." *Albion*, 23 (1991), 681–96.

——. "The New Opposition in the House of Lords, 1720–3." *Historical Journal*, 36 (1993), 309–29.

——. "Opposition in the House of Lords, Public Opinion, Newspapers and Periodicals." *Journal of Newspaper and Periodical History*, vol. 8, no. 1 (1992), 51–5.

——. [Review of Barnard and Clark, eds. *Lord Burlington*.] *Parliamentary History*, 18 (1999), 217–19.

——. "1720–23 and All That: A Reply to Eveline Cruickshanks." *Albion*, 26 (1994), 41–53.

——. "'Venice Preserv'd; Or a Plot Discover'd': The Political and Social Context of the Peerage Bill of 1719." In Clyve Jones, ed., *A Pillar of the Constitution*, pp. 79–112. London: Hambledon, 1989.

——. "William, First Earl Cowper, Country Whiggery, and the Leadership of the Opposition in the House of Lords, 1720–1723." In *Lords of Parliament: Studies, 1714–1914*, ed. R. W. Davis, pp. 29–43. Stanford, Calif.: Stanford University Press, 1995.

Jones, Stephen. *Frederick, Prince of Wales and His Circle*, exhib. cat., Gainsborough's House, 6 June–26 July 1981. Sudbury: Gainsborough's House, 1981.

Jordan, Gerald, and Nicholas Rogers. "Admirals as Heroes: Patriotism and Liberty in Hanoverian England." *Journal of British Studies*, 28 (1989), 201–24.

Juvenal and Persius, ed. and trans. G. G. Ramsay. Loeb Classical Library. Cambridge, Mass.: Harvard University Press, 1950.

Kairoff, Claudia Thomas. "Living on the Margin: Alexander Pope and the Rural Ideal." *Studies in the Literary Imagination*, 38 (2005), 15–38.

Kaminski, Thomas. *The Early Career of Samuel Johnson*. New York, N.Y.: Oxford University Press, 1987.

——. "'Oppositional Augustanism' and Pope's *Epistle to Augustus*." *Studies in Eighteenth-Century Culture*, 26 (1998), 57–72.

—. "Rehabilitating 'Augustanism': On the Roots of 'Polite Letters' in England." *Eighteenth-Century Life*, 20 (November 1996), 49–65.

Kaye, F. B., ed. Bernard Mandeville, *The Fable of the Bees: or Private Vices, Publick Benefits*, 2 vols. Indianapolis, Ind.: Liberty Fund, 1988.

Kelsall, Malcolm. "Augustus and Pope." *Huntington Library Quarterly*, 39 (1976), 117–31.

Kenyon, J. P. *The Stuart Constitution, 1603–1688*. Cambridge: Cambridge University Press, 1986.

Kilburn, Matthew. "Cobham's Cubs." *Oxford Dictionary of National Biography*. Online ed., October 2016.

King, Richard G. "Two New Letters from Princess Amelia." *Händel-Jahrbuch*, 40/41 (1994/1995), 169.

Kliger, Samuel. *The Goths in England: A Study in Seventeenth and Eighteenth Century Thought*. Cambridge, Mass.: Harvard University Press, 1952.

Knapp, J. Merrill. "Aaron Hill and the London Theatre of His Time." *Händel-Jahrbuch*, 37 (1991), 177–85.

—. "Handel, the Royal Academy of Music, and Its First Opera Season in London (1720)." *Musical Quarterly*, 45 (1959), 145–67.

Knowledge and Social Capital: Foundations and Applications, ed. Eric L. Lesser. Woburn, Mass:, Butterworth-Heinemann, 2000.

Knuth, Deborah J. "Pope, Handel and the *Dunciad*." *Modern Language Studies*, vol. 10, no. 3 (Fall 1980), 22–8.

Kramnick, Isaac. "Augustan Politics and English Historiography: The Debate on the English Past, 1730–35." *History and Theory*, 6 (1967), 35–56.

—. *Bolingbroke and His Circle: The Politics of Nostalgia in the Age of Walpole*. Cambridge, Mass.: Harvard University Press, 1968.

Kramnick, Isaac, ed. *Lord Bolingbroke: Historical Writings*. Chicago, Ill.: University of Chicago Press, 1972.

—. *Viscount Bolingbroke: Political Writings*. New York, N.Y.: Appleton-Century-Crofts, 1970.

Kropf, C. R. "William Popple: Dramatist, Critic, and Diplomat." *Restoration and Eighteenth-Century Theatre Research*, 2nd ser., vol. 1, no. 1 (July 1986), 1–17.

Kupersmith, William. *English Versions of Roman Satire in the Earlier Eighteenth Century*. Newark, Del.: University of Delaware Press, 2007.

—. "Johnson's *London* in Context: Imitations of Roman Satire in the Later 1730s." *Age of Johnson*, 10 (1999), 1–28.

Lam, George L. "Walpole and the Duke of Newcastle." In *Horace Walpole: Writer, Politician, and Connoisseur*, ed. Warren H. Smith. New Haven, Conn.: Yale University Press, 1967.

Lamb, Jonathan. "The Medium of Publicity and the Garden at Stowe," *Huntington Library Quarterly*, 50 (1987), 374–93.

Langford, Paul. *A Polite and Commercial People: England, 1727–1783*. Oxford: Oxford University Press, 1989.

—. *The Excise Crisis: Society and Politics in the Age of Walpole*. Oxford: Clarendon Press, 1975.

Langford, Paul, ed. *Walpole and the Robinocracy. The English Satirical Print, 1600–1832*. Cambridge: Chadwyck-Healy, 1986.

Laughton, J. K. "Jenkins' Ear." *English Historical Review*, 4 (1889), 741–9.

Lawson, Philip. *George Grenville: A Political Life*. Oxford: Clarendon Press, 1984.

330 BIBLIOGRAPHY

Lenman, Bruce. *The Jacobite Risings in Britain, 1689–1746*. London: Eyre Methuen, 1980.

Leppert, Richard. "Imagery, Musical Confrontation and Cultural Difference in Early 18th-Century London." *Early Music*, 14 (1986), 323–45.

Lesser, Eric L., ed. *Knowledge and Social Capital: Foundations and Applications*. Woburn, Mass.: Butterworth-Heinemann.

Levine, Jay A. "Pope's *Epistle to Augustus*, Lines 1–30." *Studies in English Literature, 1500–1900*, 7 (1967), 427–51.

Levine, William. "Collins, Thomson, and the Whig Progress of Liberty." *Studies in English Literature*, 34 (1994), 553–77.

Lewis, Peter. *John Gay: The Beggar's Opera*. London: Edward Arnold, 1976.

Lewis, W. S., ed. *The Yale Edition of the Correspondence of Horace Walpole*, 48 vols. New Haven, Conn.: Yale University Press, 1937–1983.

Lichtenberg, George. *Hogarth on High Life: The "Marriage à la Mode" Series from Georg Christoph Lichtenberg's "Commentaries,"* trans. and ed. Arthur S. Wensinger with W. B. Coley. Middletown, Conn.: Wesleyan University Press, 1970.

——. *Lichtenberg's Commentaries on Hogarth's Engravings*, intro. and trans. Innes and Gustav Herdan. London: Cresset Press, 1966.

Liesenfeld, Vincent J. *The Licensing Act of 1737*. Madison, Wis.: University of Wisconsin Press, 1984.

Lindgren, Lowell. "La carriera di Gaetano Berenstadt, contralto evirato (ca. 1690–1735)." *Rivista italiana di musicologia*, 19 (1984), 36–112.

——. "Critiques of Opera in London, 1705–1719." In *Il melodramma italiano in Italia e in Germania nell' età barocca. Contributi musicologici del Centro Ricerche dell' A.M.I.S.-Como*, 9, pp. 145–65. Como, 1995.

——. "Musicians and Librettists in the Correspondence of Gio. Giacomo Zamboni (Oxford Bodleian Library, MSS Rawlison Letters 116–38)." *Royal Musical Association Research Chronicle*, 24 (1991).

——. "Parisan Patronage of Performers from the Royal Academy of Music (1719–29)." *Music and Letters*, 58 (1977), 4–28.

——. "The Three Great Noises 'Fatal to the Interests of Bononcini.'" *Musical Quarterly*, 61 (1975), 60–83.

Lock, E. P. "'To preserve order and support Monarchy': Johnson's Political Writings." In *Samuel Johnson: New Contexts for a New Century*, ed. Howard D. Weinbrot, pp. 175–94. San Marino, Calif.: Huntington Library, 2014.

Lockwood, Thomas. "The Life and Death of *Common Sense*." *Prose Studies: History, Theory, Criticism*, 16 (1993), 78–93.

Lodge, Richard. "The Treaty of Seville (1729)." *Transactions of the Royal Historical Society*, 4th ser., 16 (1933), 1–43.

Loftis, John. *The Politics of Drama in Augustan England*. Oxford: Oxford University Press, 1963.

Lord Burlington: Architecture, Art and Life, ed. Toby Barnard and Jane Clark, pp. 201–15. London: Hambledon Press, 1995.

Lord Burlington – The Man and His Politics: Questions of Loyalty, ed. Edward Corp. Lewiston, N.Y.: Edwin Mellen Press, 1998.

Lord Hervey and His Friends, 1726–38, ed. Earl of Ilchester. London: John Murray, 1950.

Lynch, James J. *Box, Pit, and Gallery: Stage and Society in Johnson's London*. Berkeley, Calif.: University of California Press, 1953.

Lyttelton, George Lord. *Memoirs and Correspondence of George, Lord Lyttelton*, ed. Robert Phillimore, 2 vols. London: James Ridgway, 1845.

Mack, Maynard. *Alexander Pope: A Life*. New York, N.Y.: W. W. Norton, 1985.

——. *Collected in Himself: Essays Critical, Biographical, and Bibliographical on Pope and Some of His Contemporaries*. Newark, Del.: University of Delaware Press, [1982].

——. *The Garden and the City: Retirement and Politics in the Later Poetry of Pope, 1731-1743*. Toronto: University of Toronto Press, 1969.

——. "'The Last and Greatest Art': Pope's Poetical Manuscripts." In Mack, *Collected in Himself: Essays Critical, Biographical, and Bibliographical on Pope and Some of His Contemporaries*, pp. 341-2. Newark, Del: University of Delaware Press, [1982].

——. *The Last and Greatest Art: Some Unpublished Poetical Manuscripts of Alexander Pope*. Newark, Del.: University of Delaware Press, 1984.

——. "The Muse of Satire." *The Yale Review*, 41 (1951), 80-92.

——. "A Poet in His Landscape: Pope at Twickenham." In *From Sensibility to Romanticism: Essays Presented to Frederick A. Pottle*, ed. Frederick W. Hilles and Harold Bloom, pp. 3-29. Oxford: Oxford University Press, 1965.

Mahaffey, Kathleen. "Timon's Villa: Walpole's Houghton." *Texas Studies in Literature and Language*, 9 (1967), 193-222.

Mandeville and Augustan Ideas: New Essays, ed. Charles W. A. Prior. Victoria, British Columbia: University of Victoria, 2000.

Manners and Morals: Hogarth and British Painting, 1700-1760, exhib. cat. London: Tate Gallery, 1987.

Maresca, Thomas E. *Pope's Horatian Poems*. Columbus, Ohio: Ohio State University Press, 1966.

Marshall, Ashley. "Henry Fielding and the 'Scriblerians.'" *Modern Language Quarterly*, 72 (2008), 19-48.

——. *The Practice of Satire in England, 1658-1770*. Baltimore, Md.: Johns Hopkins Press, 2013.

Matthews, Betty. "Unpublished Letters Concerning Handel." *Music and Letters*, 40 (1959), 261-68.

McCulloch, Derek. "Royal Composers: The Composing Monarchs That Britain Nearly Had." *Musical Times*, 122 (1981), 525-9.

McGeary, Thomas. "Farinelli and the Duke of Leeds: 'tanto mio amico e patrone particolare.'" *Early Music*, 30 (2002), 202-13.

——. "Farinelli in Madrid: Opera, Politics, and the War of Jenkins' Ear." *Musical Quarterly*, 82 (1998), 383-421.

——. "Farinelli's Progress to Albion: The Recruitment and Reception of Opera's 'Blazing Star.'" *British Journal for Eighteenth-Century Studies*, 28 (2005), 339-61.

——. "Gendering Opera: Italian Opera as the Feminine 'Other' in England, 1700-42." *Journal of Musicological Research*, 14 (1994), 17-34.

——. "Handel and the Feuding Royals." *The Handel Institute Newsletter*, 17 (Autumn 2006), 5-8; reprinted in *Handel: The Baroque Composers*, ed. David Vickers. Farnham: Ashgate, 2010.

——. "*Handel as Orpheus*: The Vauxhall Statue Re-examined," *Early Music*, 43 (2015), 291-308.

——. "Handel in the *Dunciad*: Pope, Handel, Frederick, Prince of Wales, and Cultural Politics." *Musical Quarterly*, 97 (2015), 542-74.

332 BIBLIOGRAPHY

——. "Handel, Prince Frederick, and the Opera of the Nobility Reconsidered." *Göttinger Händel-Beiträge*, 7 (1998), 156–78.

——. "More Light (and Some Speculation) on Vanbrugh's Haymarket Theatre Project." *Early Music*, 48 (2020), 91–104.

——. "The Opera Accounts of Sir Robert Walpole." *Restoration and Eighteenth-Century Theatre Research*, 2nd ser., vol. 11, no. 1 (Summer 1996), 1–9.

——. *Opera and Politics in Queen Anne's Britain, 1705–1714*. Woodbridge: Boydell, 2022.

——. "Opera-Loving Sons of Peers in *The Dunciad*." *Notes and Queries*, vol. 62, no. 2 (June 2015), 279–85.

——. "Pope and Frederick, Prince of Wales: Gifts and Memorials of Their Friendship." *Scriblerian*, 23 (Autumn 2000), 40–7.

——. "Repressing Female Desire on the London Opera Stage, 1724–1727." *Women and Music: A Journal of Gender and Culture*, 4 (2000), 40–58.

——. *The Politics of Opera in Handel's Britain*. Cambridge: Cambridge University Press, 2013.

——. "Verse Epistles on Italian Opera Singers, 1724–1736." *Royal Musical Association. Research Chronicle*, 33 (2000), 29–88.

——. "'Warbling Eunuchs': Opera, Gender, and Sexuality on the London Stage." *Restoration and Eighteenth-Century Theatre Research*, 2nd ser., 7 (1992), 1–22.

McKay, Derek. "The Struggle for Control of George I's Northern Policy, 1718–19." *Journal of Modern History*, 45 (1973), 367–86.

McKillop, Alan D. "Ethics and Political History in Thomson's *Liberty*." In *Pope and His Contemporaries: Essays Presented to George Sherburn*, ed. James C. Clifford and Louis A. Landa, pp. 215–9. Oxford: Clarendon Press, 1949.

——. *The Background of Thomson's "Liberty."* Rice Institute Pamphlet, vol. 38, no. 2 (July 1951).

——. "Thomson and the Licensers of the Stage." *Philological Quarterly*, 37 (1958), 448.

McLachlan, Jean O. *Trade and Peace with Old Spain, 1667–1750*. Cambridge: Cambridge University Press, 1940.

McLaverty, James. "Lawton Gilliver: Pope's Bookseller." *Studies in Bibliography*, 32 (1979), 101–24.

——. "Naming and Shaming in the Poetry of Pope and Swift, 1726–1745." In *Swift's Travels: Eighteenth-Century British Satire and Its Legacy*, ed. Nicholas Hudson and Aaron Santesso, pp. 160–75. Cambridge: Cambridge University Press, 2008.

McLynn, Frank. *The Jacobites*. London: Routledge and Kegan Paul, 1985.

McMahon, Marie P. *The Radical Whigs, John Trenchard and Thomas Gordon: Libertarian Loyalists to the New House of Hanover*. Lanham, Md.: University Press of America, 1990.

McMinn, Joseph. "'Was Swift a Philistine?': The Evidence of Music," *Swift Studies*, 17 (2002), 59–74.

Memoirs of the Extraordinary Life, Works, and Discoveries of Martinus Scriblerus, ed. Charles Kerby-Miller. New Haven, Conn.: Yale University Press, 1950.

Michael, Wolfgang. *England Under George I: The Beginning of the Hanoverian Dynasty*, trans. and adapted L. B. Namier. London: Macmillan, 1936.

——. *England Under George I: The Quadruple Alliance*, trans. and adapted Annemarie MacGregor and George E. MacGregor. London: Macmillan, 1939.

Milhous, Judith. "The Capacity of Vanbrugh's Theatre at the Haymarket." *Theatre History Studies*, 4 (1984), 38–46.

——. "Opera Finances in London." *Journal of the American Musicological Society*, 37 (1984), 567–92.

Milhous, Judith, and Robert D. Hume. "Box Office Reports for Five Operas Mounted by Handel in London, 1732–1734." *Harvard Library Bulletin*, 26 (1978), 245–66.

——. "The Charter for the Royal Academy of Music." *Music and Letters*, 67 (1986), 50–8.

——. "Construing and Misconstruing Farinelli in London." *British Journal for Eighteenth-Century Studies*, 28 (2005), 361–85.

——. "Handel's Opera Finances in 1732–3." *Musical Times*, 125 (1984), 86–9.

——. "The Haymarket Opera in 1711." *Early Music*, 17 (1989), 543–57.

——. "Heidegger and the Management of the Haymarket Opera, 1713–17." *Early Music*, 27 (1999), 65–84.

——. "New Light on Handel and The Royal Academy of Music in 1720." *Theatre Journal*, 35 (1983), 149–67.

——. "Opera Salaries in Eighteenth-Century London." *Journal of the American Musicological Society*, 46 (1993), 26–83.

Millar, Oliver. *The Queen's Pictures*. New York, N.Y.: Macmillan, 1977.

Moore, Andrew, ed. *Houghton Hall: The Prime Minister, The Empress, and The Hermitage*. London: Philip Wilson, 1996.

Moore, Andrew, and Larissa Dukelskaya, eds. *A Capital Collection: Houghton Hall and the Hermitage, with a Modern Edition of Aedes Walpolianae*. New Haven, Conn.: Yale University Press, 2002.

Moore, C. A. "Whig Panegyric Verse, 1700–1760: A Phrase of Sentimentalism." *PMLA (Proceedings of the Modern Language Association)*, 41 (1926), 362–401.

Morales, Nicolas. "Farinelo à Madrid. Acte premier d'un séjour triomphant: 1737–1746." In *Il Farinelli e gli evirati cantori*. Atti del Convengo Internazionale di Studi (Bologna – Biblioteca Universitaria, 5–6 April 2005), ed. Luigi Verdi, pp. 47–76. Lucca: Libreria Musicale Italiana, 2007.

Moskovit, Leonard A. "Pope and the Tradition of the Neoclassical Imitation." *Studies in English Literature*, 8 (1968), 445–62.

Mulcaire, Terry. "Public Credit; or, the Feminization of Virtue in the Marketplace." *PMLA*, 114 (1999), 1029–42.

Murray, John J. *George I, the Baltic, and the Whig Split of 1717: A Study in Diplomacy and Propaganda*. London: Routledge and Kegan Paul, 1969.

Music and Theatre in Handel's World: The Family Papers of James Harris, 1732–1780, ed. Donald Burrows and Rosemary Dunhill. Oxford: Oxford University Press, 2002.

Nadel, George H. "Philosophy of History before Historicism." *History and Theory*, 3 (1964), 291–315.

Namier, Lewis. *The Structure of Politics at the Accession of George III*, 2nd ed. London: Macmillan, 1957.

Nelson, T. G. A. "Pope, Burlington, Architecture, and Politics: A Speculative Revisionist View." *Eighteenth-Century Life*, 21 (Feb. 1997), 45–61.

Nelson, George H. "Contraband Trade under the Asiento, 1730–39." *American Historical Review*, 51 (1945–46), 55–67.

Ness, Robert. "*The Dunciad* and Italian Opera in England." *Eighteenth-Century Studies*, 20 (1986–87), 173–94.

334 BIBLIOGRAPHY

Neville, Don. "Metastasio: Poet and Preacher in Vienna." In *Pietro Metastasio - uomo universal (1698–1782)*, ed. Andrea Sommer-Mathis and Elisabeth T. Hilscher, pp. 47–61. Vienna: Österreichische Akademie der Wissenschaften, 2000.

———. "Moral Philosophy in the Metastasian Drama." *Studies in Music from the University of Western Ontario*, vol. 7, no. 1 (1982), 28–46.

Newman, A. N., ed. *The Parliamentary Diary of Sir Edward Knatchbull, 1722–1730. Camden Third Series*, 94 (1963).

Noggle, James. "Taste and Temporality in *An Epistle to Burlington*." *Studies in the Literary Imagination*, 38 (2005), 120–35.

North, Sir Dudley. *Discourses upon Trade*, ed. with intro. Jacob H. Hollander. Baltimore, Md.: Johns Hopkins Press, 1907.

O'Brien, John. *Harlequin Britain: Pantomine and Entertainment, 1690–1760*. Baltimore, Md.: Johns Hopkins University Press, 2004.

O'Brien, Paula. "The Life and Works of James Miller, 1704–1744, with Particular Reference to the Satiric Content of His Poetry and Plays." Ph.D. thesis, University of London, 1979.

Oppé, A. P. *The Drawings of William Hogarth*. London: Phaidon, 1948.

Orestano, Francesca. "Bust Story: Pope at Stowe, or the Politics and Myths of Landscape Gardening." *Studies in the Literary Imagination*, 38 (2005), 39–61.

Orr, Clarissa Campbell, ed. *Queenship in Britain, 1660–1837*. Manchester: Manchester University Press, 2002.

Osborn, James M. "Pope, the Byzantine Empress, and Walpole's Whore." *Review of English Studies*, n.s., 6 (1955), 372–82.

Owen, John B. *The Rise of the Pelhams*. London: Methuen, 1957.

Pares, Richard. *War and Trade in the West Indies, 1739–1763*. Oxford: Oxford University Press, 1936.

Paulson, Ronald. *Emblem and Expression: Meaning in English Art of the Eighteenth Century*. Cambridge, Mass.: Harvard University Press, 1975.

———. *Hogarth*. Vol. 1. *The "Modern Moral Subject," 1697–1732*. New Brunswick, N.J.: Rutgers University Press, 1991.

———. *Hogarth*. Vol. 2. *High Art and Low, 1732–1750*. New Brunswick, N.J.: Rutgers University Press, 1992.

———. *Hogarth: His Life, Art, and Times*, 2 vols. New Haven, Conn.: Yale University Press, 1971.

———. *Hogarth's Graphic Works*, 2 vols. New Haven, Conn.: Yale University Press, 1965.

———. *Hogarth's Graphic Works*, rev. ed. New Haven, Conn.: Yale University Press, 1970.

———. *Hogarth's Graphic Works*. New Haven, Conn.: Yale University Press, 1989.

Perceval, John (Earl of Egmont). *Manuscripts of the Earl of Egmont. Diary of Viscount Percival, afterwards First Earl of Egmont*, 3 vols. London: His Majesty's Stationery Office, 1930.

Percival, Milton. *Political Ballads Illustrating the Administration of Sir Robert Walpole*. Oxford Historical and Literary Studies, 8 (1916).

Pettit, Alexander. *Illusory Consensus: Bolingbroke and the Polemical Response to Walpole, 1730–1737*. Newark, Del.: University of Delaware Press, 1997.

———. "Lord Bolingbroke's *Remarks on the History of England* and the Rhetoric of Political Controversy." *Age of Johnson*, 7 (1996), 365–95.

——. "Propaganda, Public Relations, and the *Remarks on the Craftsman's Vindication of His Two Honble Patrons, in His Paper of May 22, 1731.*" *Huntington Library Quarterly*, 57 (1994), 45–59.

——. "*The Grub-street Journal* and the Politics of Anachronism." *Philological Quarterly*, 69 (1990), 435–51.

Phillipson, Nicholas. "Politics and Politeness in the Reigns of Anne and the Early Hanoverians." In *The Varieties of British Political Thought, 1500–1800*, ed. J. G. A. Pocock, Gordon J. Schochet, and Lois Schwoerer, pp. 211–45. Cambridge: Cambridge University Press, 1993.

Plumb, J. H. *England in the Eighteenth Century*. Harmondsworth: Penguin Books, 1950.

——. *The Growth of Political Stability in England, 1675–1725*. Harmondsworth: Penguin Books, 1969.

——. "Sir Robert Walpole." *History Today* (October 1951), 9–16.

——. *Sir Robert Walpole: The King's Minister*. London: Cresset, 1960.

——. *Sir Robert Walpole: The Making of a Statesman*. London: Cresset, 1956.

Pocock, J. G. A. *The Ancient Constitution and the Feudal Law: A Study of English Historical Thought in the Seventeenth Century. A Reissue with a Retrospect*. Cambridge: Cambridge University Press, 1987.

——. "Machiavelli, Harrington and English Political Ideologies in the Eighteenth Century." In Pocock, *Politics, Language and Time: Essays on Political Thought and History*, pp. 104–147. New York, N.Y.: Atheneum, 1971.

——. *The Machiavellian Moment: Florentine Political Thought and the Atlantic Republican Tradition*. Princeton, N.J.: Princeton University Press, 1975.

——. *Politics, Language and Time: Essays on Political Thought and History*. New York, N.Y.: Atheneum, 1971.

——. *Virtue, Commerce, and History: Essays on Political Thought and History, Chiefly in the Eighteenth Century*. Cambridge: Cambridge University Press, 1985.

Pope, Alexander. *The Art of Sinking in Poetry*, ed. Edna Leake Steeves. New York, N.Y.: Russell and Russell, 1952.

——. *The Correspondence of Alexander Pope*, ed. George Sherburn, 5 vols. Oxford: Clarendon Press, 1956.

——. *The Dunciad*, ed. James Sutherland. *The Twickenham Edition of the Poems of Alexander Pope*. Vol. 5, 3rd ed. London: Methuen, 1963.

——. *The Dunciad in Four Books*, ed. Valerie Rumbold. Harlow: Longman, 1999.

——. *The Dunciad Variorum, with the Prolegomena of Scriberlus* [facs. ed.] with Introduction by Robert K. Root. Princeton, N.J.: Princeton University Press, 1929.

——. *Epistles to Several Persons (Moral Essays)*, ed. F. W. Bateson. *The Twickenham Edition of the Poems of Alexander Pope*. Vol. 3, pt. 2, 2nd ed. New Haven, Conn.: Yale University Press, 1961.

——. *Imitations of Horace*, ed. John Butt. *The Twickenham Edition of the Poems of Alexander Pope*. Vol. 4, 2nd ed. New Haven, Conn.: Yale University Press.

——. *The Poems of Alexander Pope*. Vol. 3. *The Dunciad (1728) and The Dunciad Variorum (1729)*, ed. Valerie Rumbold. Harlow: Pearson, 2007.

——. *The Works of Alexander Pope. New Edition*, ed. Whitwell Elwin and William J. Courthope, 10 vols. London: John Murray, 1882.

Porter, Roy. *English Society in the Eighteenth Century*, rev. ed. London: Penguin, 1991.

BIBLIOGRAPHY

Pound, David F. "'Fury after Licentious Pleasures'; A *'Rake's Progress'* and Concerns about Luxury in Eighteenth-Century England," *Apollo*, no. 438 (1998), 17–21.

Price, Curtis, Judith Milhous, and Robert D. Hume. *Italian Opera in Late Eighteenth-Century London: The Kings' Theatre, Haymarket, 1778–1791.* Oxford: Clarendon Press, 1995.

Pritchard, Jonathan. "Social Topography in the *Dunciad, Variorum,*" *Huntington Library Quarterly*, 75 (2013), 527–60.

Queenship in Britain, 1660–1837, ed. Clarissa Campbell Orr. Manchester: Manchester University Press, 2002.

Ratchford, Fannie E. "Pope and the *Patriot King.*" *Texas Studies in English*, 6 (1926), 157–77.

Realey, Charles B. *The Early Opposition to Sir Robert Walpole.* Lawrence, Kans., University of Kansas Press, 1931.

Rees, Abraham, ed. *The Cyclopædia; or, Universal Dictionary of Arts, Sciences, and Literature*, 39 vols (1819).

Ribble, Frederick G. "Fielding's Rapproachement with Walpole in late 1741." *Philological Quarterly*, 80 (2001), 71–81.

Richmond, Herbert. *The Navy as an Instrument of Policy, 1558–1727.* Cambridge: Cambridge University Press, 1953.

——. *The Navy in the War of 1739–48*, 3 vols. Cambridge: Cambridge University Press, 1920.

Riepe, Juliane. *Händel vor dem Fernrohr: Die Italienreise.* Beeskow: Ortus Musikverlag, 2013.

Robbins, Caroline. *The Eighteenth-Century Commonwealthman.* Cambridge, Mass.: Harvard University Press, 1959.

Robinson, Michael F. "How to Demonstrate Virtue: The Case of Porpora's Two Settings of Mitridate." *Studies in Music from the University of Western Ontario*, vol. 7, no. 1 (1982), 47–64.

Rogers, James E. T. *A Complete Collection of the Protests of the Lords*, 2 vols. Oxford: Clarendon, 1875.

Rogers, Nicholas. "Resistance to Oligarchy: The City Opposition to Walpole and His Successors, 1725–47." In John Stevens, ed., *London in the Age of Reform*, pp. 1–29. Oxford: Blackwell, 1977.

——. *Whigs and Cities: Politics in the Age of Walpole and Pitt.* Oxford: Clarendon, 1989.

Rogers, Pat. "Book Dedications in Britain, 1700–1799: A Preliminary Survey." *British Journal for Eighteenth-Century Studies*, 16 (1993), 222.

——. "The Critique of Opera in Pope's *Dunciad.*" *Musical Quarterly*, 59 (1973), 15–30.

——. "Ermine, Gold and Lawn, *The Dunciad* and the Coronation of George II." In *Literature and Popular Culture in Eighteenth Century England*, pp. 102–19. Brighton: Harvester Press, 1985.

——. "Gay and the World of Opera." In *John Gay and the Scriblerians*, ed. Peter Lewis and Nigel Wood, pp. 147–62. New York, N.Y.: St. Martin's Press, 1988.

——. *Grub Street: Studies in a Subculture.* London: Methuen, 1972.

——. *Grub Street Literature and Popular Culture in Eighteenth Century England.* Brighton: Harvester Press, 1985.

——. *A Political Biography of Alexander Pope.* London: Pickering and Chatto, 2010.

——. "Swift and Bolingbroke on Faction." *Journal of British Studies*, vol. 9, no. 2 (1970), 71–101.

Rogers, Robert W. *The Major Satires of Alexander Pope*. Urbana, Ill.: University of Illinois Press, 1955.

Rorschach, Kimerly. "Frederick, Prince of Wales (1707–1751) as a Patron of the Visual Arts: Princely Patriotism and Political Propaganda," 2 vols. Ph.D. dissertation, Yale University, 1985.

——. "Frederick, Prince of Wales (1707–51) as Collector and Patron." *Walpole Society*, 55 (1989–1990).

Rose, George H., ed. *A Selection from the Papers of the Earls of Marchmont*, 3 vols. London: John Murray, 1831.

Rossiter, Clinton. *The First American Revolution: The American Colonies on the Eve of Independence*. New York, N.Y.: Harcourt, Brace, and World 1956.

Rumbold, Valerie. "Ideology and Opportunism: The Role of Handel in Pope's *The Dunciad in Four Books*." In *"More Solid Learning": New Perspectives on Alexander Pope's "Dunciad,"* ed. Catherine Ingrassia and Claudia N. Thomas, pp. 62–80. Cranbury, N.J.: Associated University Presses, 2000.

——. "'The Reason of this Preference': Sleeping, Flowing and Freezing in Pope's *Dunciad*." *Proceedings of the British Academy*, 167 (2010), 423–51.

——. *Women's Place in Pope's World*. Cambridge: Cambridge University Press, 1989.

Rumbold, Valerie, and Thomas McGeary. "*Folly*, Session Poems, and the Preparations for Pope's *Dunciads*." *Review of English Studies*, n.s., 56 (2005), 577–610.

Sáez, Daniel Martin. "La leyenda de Farinelli en España: Historiografía, mitología y política." *Revista de Musicología*, 41 (2018), 41–78.

St. John, Henry (Viscount Bolingbroke). *Bolingbroke: Political Writings*, ed. David Armitage. Cambridge: Cambridge University Press, 1997.

——. *The Works of Lord Bolingbroke*, 4 vols. Philadelphia, Pa.: Carey and Hart, 1843.

Sambrook, James. *James Thomson, 1700–1748: A Life*. Oxford: Clarendon, 1991.

——. "'A Just Balance between Patronage and the Press': The Case of James Thomson." *Studies in the Literary Imagination*, 34 (2002), 137–53.

Saumarez Smith, Charles. *Eighteenth-Century Decoration: Design and the Domestic Interior in England*. New York, N.Y.: Harry Adams, 1993.

Schonhorn, Manuel, "The Audacious Contemporaneity of Pope's *Epistle to Augustus*." *Studies in English Literature, 1500–1900*, 8 (1968), 431–43.

Schultz, William E. *Gay's Beggar's Opera: Its Content, History and Influence*. New Haven, Conn.: Yale University Press, 1923.

See and Seem Blind: or, a Critical Dissertation on the Publick Diversions, &c. 1732, ed. Robert D. Hume. Augustan Reprint Society, no. 235 (1986).

Sekora, John. *Luxury: The Concept in Western Thought, Eden to Smollett*. Baltimore, Md.: Johns Hopkins University Press, 1977.

A Selection from the Papers of the Earls of Marchmont, ed. George H. Rose, 3 vols. London: John Murray, 1831.

Sherburn, George. "The *Dunciad*, Book IV." *University of Texas Studies in English*, 24 (1944), 174–90.

——. [Review of Hillhouse edition of the *Grub-street Journal*.] *Modern Philology*, 26 (1928–29), 361–7.

Sherburn, George, and H. S. John, "'Timon's Villa' and Cannons." *Huntington Library Bulletin*, 8 (1935), 131–52.

338 BIBLIOGRAPHY

Sinclair, H. M., and A. H. T. Robb-Smith. *A Short History of Anatomical Teaching in Oxford.* Oxford: Oxford University Press, 1950.

Skinner, Quentin. "History and Ideology in the English Revolution." *Historical Journal*, 8 (1965), 151–78.

——. "The Principles and Practice of Opposition: The Case of Bolingbroke versus Walpole." In *Historical Perspectives: Studies in English Thought and Society in Honour of J. H. Plumb*, ed. Neil McKendrick, pp. 93–128. London: Europa Publications, 1974.

Smith, Hannah, and Stephen Taylor, "Hephaestion and Alexander: Lord Hervey, Frederick, Prince of Wales, and the Royal Favourite in England in the 1730s." *English Historical Review*, 124, no. 507 (2009), 283–312.

Smith, R. J. *The Gothic Bequest: Medieval Institutions in British Modern Thought, 1688–1863.* Cambridge: Cambridge University Press, 1987.

Smith, Ruth. "Handel's English Librettists." In *The Cambridge Companion to Handel*, ed. Donald Burrows, pp. 92–108. Cambridge: Cambridge University Press, 1997.

——. *Handel's Oratorios and Eighteenth-Century Thought.* Cambridge: Cambridge University Press, 1995.

Snyder, Henry L. "The Pardon of Lord Bolingbroke," *Historical Journal*, 14 (1971), 227–40.

Solomon, Harry M. *The Rise of Robert Dodsley: Creating the New Age of Print.* Carbondale, Ill.: Southern Illinois University Press, 1996.

Southern, George. "The Satire of Dissent." In *The Oxford Handbook of Eighteenth-Century Satire*, ed. Paddy Bullard, pp. 56–73. Oxford: Oxford University Press, 2019.

Speck, W. A. "Britain's First Prime Minister." In *Houghton Hall: The Prime Minister, The Empress, and The Hermitage*, ed. Andrew Moore, pp. 12–19. London: Philip Wilson, 1996.

——. "Politicians, Peers, and Publication by Subscription, 1700–1750." In *Books and Their Readers in the Eighteenth Century*, ed. Isabel Rivers, pp. 47–68. Leicester: Leicester University Press, 1982.

——. *Stability and Strife: England, 1714–1760.* Cambridge, Mass.: Harvard University Press, 1977.

——. "The General Election of 1715." *English Historical Review*, 90 (1975), 507–22.

——. "'The Most Corrupt Council in Christendom': Decisions on Controverted Elections, 1702–42." In *Party and Management in Parliament, 1660–1784*, ed. Clyve Jones, pp. 107–21. Leicester: Leicester University Press, 1984.

——. "The Whig Schism Under George I." *Huntington Library Quarterly*, 40 (1977), 171–9.

Spence, Joseph. *Observations, Anecdotes, and Characters of Books and Men Collected from Conversation*, ed. James M. Osborn, 2 vols. Oxford: Clarendon Press, 1966.

Sperling, John G. *The South Sea Company: An Historical Essay and Bibliographic Finding List.* Cambridge, Mass.: Baker Library, Harvard Graduate School of Business Administration, 1962.

Stack, Frank. *Pope and Horace: Studies in Imitation.* Cambridge, Mass.: Cambridge University Press, 1985.

——. "Pope's *Epistle to Bolingbroke* and *Epistle I.i.*" In *The Art of Alexander Pope*, ed. Howard Erskine-Hill and Anne Smith, pp. 169–91. New York, N.Y.: Barnes & Noble, 1979.

Stafford, J. Martin. "Mandeville's Contemporary Critics," *1650–1850: Ideas, Aesthetics, and Inquiries in the Early Modern Era*, 7 (2002), 387–401.

Stafford, J. Martin, ed. *Private Vices, Publick Benefits? The Contemporary Reception of Bernard Mandeville*. Solihull: Ismeron, 1997.

Stanhope, Philip Dormer (Earl of Chesterfield). *The Letters of Philip Dormer Stanhope, 4th Earl of Chesterfield*, ed. with intro. Bonamy Dobrée, 6 vols. London: Eyre and Spottiswoode, 1932.

Steiner, George. "The Muses' Farewell." *Salmagundi*, no. 135/56 (Fall 2002), 148–56.

Stephens, Frederic G. *Catalogue of Prints and Drawings in the British Museum*. Division I. Political and Personal Satires. 3 vols. London: British Museum, 1877.

Stephens, Frederic G., and M. Dorothy George. *Catalogue of Prints and Drawings in the British Museum*, 11 vols. London: British Museum Publications, 1870–1919.

Stevens, David H. *Party Politics and English Journalism, 1702–1742*. Menasha, Wis.: Collegiate Press, 1961.

Stewart, J. Douglas. *Sir Godfrey Kneller*. Oxford: Clarendon Press, 1983.

Stewart, Powell. "A Bibliographical Contribution to Biography: James Miller's *Seasonable Reproof*." *The Library*, ser. 5, vol. 3 (1949), 293–9.

Stone, Lawrence, and Jeanne C. F. Stone. *An Open Elite? England, 1540–1880*. Oxford: Clarendon Press, 1984.

Straus, Ralph. *Robert Dodsley: Poet, Publisher and Playwright*. London: John Lane, 1910.

Strohm, Reinhard. *Essays on Handel and Italian Opera*. Cambridge: Cambridge University Press, 1985.

Sullivan, Alvin, ed. *British Literary Periodicals*, 4 vols. Westport, Conn.: Greenwood, 1983–1986.

Summerson, John. "The Classical Country House in 18th-Century England." *Journal of the Royal Society of Arts*, vol. 107, no. 5036 (1959), 539–87.

Swayne, Mattie. "The Progress Piece in the Seventeenth Century." *The University of Texas Bulletin, Studies in English*, 16 (1936), 84–92.

Swift, Jonathan. *The Complete Poems*, ed. Pat Rogers. New Haven, Conn.: Yale University Press, 1983.

——. *The Correspondence of Jonathan Swift*, ed. Harold H. Williams, 5 vols. Oxford: Clarendon Press, 1963.

——. *The Correspondence of Jonathan Swift, D.D.*, ed. David Woolley, 5 vols. Frankfurt: Peter Lang, 1999–2014.

Swift, Jonathan, and Thomas Sheridan. *The Intelligencer*, ed. James Woolley. Oxford: Clarendon Press, 1992.

Szechi, David. *1715: The Great Jacobite Rebellion*. New Haven, Conn.: Yale University Press, 2006.

Targett, Simon. "Government and Ideology During the Age of Whig Supremacy: The Political Argument of Sir Robert Walpole's Newspaper Propagandists." *Historical Journal*, 37 (1994), 289–317.

340 BIBLIOGRAPHY

——. "'The Premier Scribbler Himself': Sir Robert Walpole and the Management of Political Opinion." *Studies in Newspaper and Periodical History: 1994 Annual*, (1996), 19–33.

Taylor, Carole M. "From Losses to Lawsuit: Patronage of the Italian Opera in London by Lord Middlesex." *Music and Letters*, 68 (1987), 1–25.

——. "Handel and Frederick, Prince of Wales." *Musical Times*, 125 (1984), 89–92.

——. "Handel's Disengagement from the Italian Opera." In *Handel Tercentenary Collection*, ed. Stanley Sadie and Anthony Hicks, pp. 165–81. Ann Arbor, Mich.: UMI Research Press, 1987.

——. "Italian Operagoing in London, 1700–45." Ph.D. dissertation, Syracuse University, 1991.

Taylor, Edward Raymond. "The Peerage Bill of 1719." *English Historical Review*, 28 (1913), 243–59.

Taylor, Stephen. "Robert Walpole (1676–1745)." *Oxford Dictionary of National Biography*. Oxford University Press, online edition, January 2008.

Temperley, Harold W. V. "The Causes of the War of Jenkins' Ear, 1739." *Transactions of the Royal Historical Society*, 3rd ser., 3 (1909), 197–236.

Thompson, Andrew C. *George II: King and Elector*. New Haven, Conn.: Yale University Press, 2011.

Thomson, James. *The Castle of Indolence and Other Poems*, ed. Alan D. McKillop. Lawrence, Kans.: University of Kansas Press, 1961.

——. *James Thomson (1700–1748), Letters and Documents*, ed. Alan D. McKillop. Lawrence, Kans.: University of Kansas Press, 1958.

——. *Liberty, the Castle of Indolence, and Other Poems*, ed. James Sambrook. Oxford: Clarendon Press, 1986.

——. *The Seasons*, ed. James Sambrook. Oxford: Clarendon Press, 1981.

Thompson, E. P. "Patrician Society, Plebeian Culture." *Journal of Social History*, 7 (1974), 382–405.

Tierney, James, ed. *The Correspondence of Robert Dodsley, 1733–1764*. Cambridge: Cambridge University Press, 1988.

Timms, Colin. "George I's Venetian Palace and Theatre Boxes in the 1720s." In *Music and Theatre: Essays in Honour of Winton Dean*, ed. Nigel Fortune, pp. 95–130. Cambridge: Cambridge University Press, 1987.

Torrione, Margarita. "Farinelli en la corte de Felipe V." *Revista de la Real Sociedad Económica Matritense de Amigos del País*, no. 38 (1999), 121–42.

Trainor, Charles. "Fielding, Opera, and Oratorio: The Case of Handel." *Eighteenth-Century Life*, vol. 46, no. 3 (2022), 83–100.

Turberville, A. S. *The House of Lords in the XVIIIth Century*. Oxford: Clarendon Press, 1927.

Turner, E. Raymond. "The Excise Scheme of 1733." *English Historical Review*, 42 (1927), 34–57.

Urstad, Tone S. *Sir Robert Walpole's Poets: The Use of Literature as Pro-Government Propaganda, 1721–1742*. Newark, Del.: University of Delaware Press, 1999.

Vander Meulen, David L. *Pope's Dunciad of 1728: A History and Facsimile*. Charlottesville, Va: Bibliographical Society of the University of Virginia/ University Press of Virginia, 1991.

Varey, Simon. "Hanover, Stuart, and the Patriot King." *British Journal for Eighteenth-Century Studies*, 6 (1983), 163–72.

——. *Henry St. John, Viscount Bolingbroke*. Boston, Mass.: Twayne, 1984.

Varey, Simon, ed. and intro. *Lord Bolingbroke: Contributions to the "Craftsman."* Oxford: Clarendon Press, 1982.

Veblen, Thorstein. *The Theory of the Leisure Class.* New York, N.Y.: Macmillan, 1899.

Vertue, George. *Vertue Note Books,* 6 vols. London: The Walpole Society, 1930–1955.

Vivian, Frances. *Il console Smith: mercante e collezionista.* Venice: Neri Pozza, 1971.

——. *The Consul Smith Collection: Masterpieces of Italian Drawing from the Royal Library, Windsor Castle, Raphael to Canaletto.* Munich: Hirmer, 1989.

——. *A Life of Frederick, Prince of Wales, 1707–1751: A Connoisseur of the Arts.* Lewiston, N.Y.: Edwin Mellen Press, 2006.

Walkling, Andrew. *English Dramatick Opera, 1661–1706.* London: Routledge, 2019.

——. *Masque and Opera in England, 1656–1688.* Abingdon: Routledge, 2017.

Walpole, Horace. *Writer, Politician, and Connoisseur,* ed. Warren H. Smith. New Haven, Conn.: Yale University Press, 1967.

——. *Yale Edition of the Correspondence of Horace Walpole,* ed. W. S. Lewis, 48 vols. New Haven, Conn.: Yale University Press, 1937–1983.

Wasserman, Earl R. *Pope's Epistle to Bathurst: A Critical Reading with an Edition of the Manuscripts.* Baltimore, Md.: Johns Hopkins Press, 1960.

Webb, M. I. *Michael Rysbrack: Sculptor.* London: Country Life, 1954.

Webber, Harold W. *The Restoration Rake-Hero: Transformation in Sexual Understanding in Seventeenth-Century England.* Madison, Wis., University of Wisconsin Press, 1986.

Weber, Max. *Economy and Society: A New Translation,* ed. and trans. Keith Tribe. Cambridge, Mass:. Harvard University Press, 2019.

Weber, William. "Musical Culture and the Capital City: The Epoch of the *beau monde* in London, 1700–1870." In *Concert Life in Eighteenth-Century Britain,* ed. Susan Wollenberg and Simon McVeigh, pp. 71–89. Aldershot: Ashgate, 2004.

Weinbrot, Howard D. *Alexander Pope and the Traditions of Formal Verse Satire.* Princeton, N.J.: Princeton University Press, 1982.

——. *Britannia's Issue: The Rise of British Literature from Dryden to Ossian.* Cambridge: Cambridge University Press, 1993.

——. *Eighteenth-Century Satire: Essays on Text and Context from Dryden to Peter Pindar.* Cambridge: Cambridge University Press, 1988.

——. *The Formal Strain: Studies in Augustan Imitation and Satire.* Chicago, Ill.: University of Chicago Press, 1969.

——. "The Historiography of Nostalgia." *Age of Johnson,* 7 (1996), 183–7.

——. "Johnson and Jacobitism Redux: Evidence, Interpretation, and Intellectual History." *Age of Johnson,* 8 (1997), 99–100.

——. "Politics, Taste, and National Identity: Some Uses of Tacitism in Eighteenth-Century Britain." In *Tacitus and the Tacitean Tradition,* ed. T. J. Luce and A. J. Woodman, pp. 168–84. Princeton, N.J.: Princeton University Press, 1993.

Wells, John W. "Thomson's *Britannia*: Issues, Attributions, Date, Variants." *Modern Philology,* 40 (1942), 43–56.

White, Christopher. *The Dutch Pictures in the Collection of Her Majesty the Queen.* Cambridge: Cambridge University Press, 1982.

BIBLIOGRAPHY

Wiggin, Lewis M. *The Faction of Cousins: A Political Account of the Grenvilles, 1733–1763*. New Haven, Conn.: Yale University Press, 1958.

Williams, Aubrey L. "Literary Backgrounds to Book Four of the *Dunciad*." *PMLA*. (Publications of the Modern Language Association), 68 (1953), 806–13.

——. *Pope's "Dunciad": A Study of Its Meaning*. London: Methuen, 1955.

Williams, Basil. "The Foreign Policy of England under Walpole." *English Historical Review*, 15 (1900), 251–76, 479–94, 665–98; 16 (1901) 67–83, 308–27, 439–51.

——. *The Life of William Pitt, Earl of Chatham*, 2 vols. London: Longmans, Green, and Co., 1914.

——. *Stanhope: A Study in Eighteenth-Century War and Diplomacy*. Oxford: Clarendon Press, 1932.

Wilson, Gladys. "'One God! One Farinelli!' Amigoni's Portraits of a Famous *Castrato*." *Apollo*, 140 (Sept. 1994), 45–51.

Wilson, Kathleen. "Empire, Trade and Popular Politics in Mid-Hanoverian Britain: The Case of Admiral Vernon." *Past and Present*, 121 (Nov. 1988), 74–109.

——. *The Sense of the People: Politics, Culture and Imperialism in England, 1715–1785*. Cambridge: Cambridge University Press, 1995.

Wolf, Janet. "Political Allegory in the Later Plays of John Gay." In *Enlightening Allegory: Theory, Practice, and Contexts of Allegory in the Late Seventeenth and Eighteenth Centuries*, ed. Kevin L. Cope, pp. 275–93. New York: AMS Press, 1993.

Wollenberg, Susan. "Music and Musicians." In *The History of the University of Oxford*. Vol. 5. *The Eighteenth Century*, ed. L. S. Sutherland and L. G. Mitchell. Oxford: Clarendon Press, 1986.

——. "Music in 18th-Century Oxford." *Proceedings of the Royal Musical Association*, 108 (1981–82), 79–81.

Woodfine, Philip. "The Anglo-Spanish War of 1739." In Jeremy Black, ed., *The Origins of War in Early Modern Europe*, pp. 185–209. Edinburgh: John Donald, 1987.

——. *Britannia's Glories: The Walpole Ministry and the 1739 War with Spain*. London: Royal Historical Society, 1998.

——. "Ideas of Naval Power and the Conflict with Spain, 1737–1742." In *The British Navy and the Use of Naval Power in the Eighteenth Century*, ed. Jeremy Black and Philips Woodfine, pp. 71–90. Leicester: Leicester University Press, 1988.

——. "'Suspicious Latitudes': Commerce, Colonies, and Patriotism in the 1730s." *Studies in Eighteenth-Century Culture*, 27 (1998), 25–46.

Wright, Thomas. *Caricature History of the Georges; or, Annals of the House of Hanover*. London: Chatto and Windus, 1868.

Yorke, Philip C. *The Life and Correspondence of Philip Yorke, Lord High Chancellor of Great Britain*, 3 vols. Cambridge: Cambridge University Press, 1913.

Zacharasiewicz, Waldemar. *Die Klimatheorie in der englische Literatur und Literaturkritik von der Mitte des 16. bis zum frühen 19. Jahrhundert*. Vienna: W. Braunmüller, 1877.

Index

Page numbers in **bold** indicate quotations from newspaper.

Addison, Joseph   xiv, 14, 16, 143, 164, 211, 214, 232, 247, 232, 309, 311
Aislabie, John   18
Akenside, Mark   103
Albemarle, Countess of (Anne Lennox)   41
Alexander Severus   311
Alfred, King   62, 147
Alliance of Hanover   88
Amhurst, Nicolas   50
Amigoni, Jacopo   121, 295
Amorevoli   179
Ancient Constitution   51, 57, 60, 61, 68–9, 142, 202
Angelica e Medoro (Pescetti)   127
Anne, Princess Royal   43, 93, 105
Anne, Queen   48, 93, 158
Arbuthnot, Dr. John   50, 110, 206, 245, 292
Archytus of Tarentum   81
Argyll, Duke of (John Campbell)   12, 13, 101, 160, 190, 231, 244
aristocracy   34
Arnall, William (Francis Walsingham)   65, 66, 112
asiento   134, 139
Atterbury, Bishop Francis   11, 17, 19–21, 47
   English Advice, to the Freeholders of England   11
Auden, W. H.   313
Augusta, Princess of Saxe–Gotha (Princess of Wales)   105, 133, 149, 293
Augustine, St   96
Augustus, Emperor   156, 168, 172, 176, 196, 237, 238, 246–7, 256, 263
Ayres, Philip, *Classical Culture and the Idea of Rome*   308, 311

Baillie, George   309
Barbon, Nicholas, *A Discourse of Trade*   78
Barnard, Sir John   268
Bathurst, Allen (Lord)   205, 206, 266, 294
Beach, Thomas, *Eugenio: or, Virtuous and Happy Life*   298
beau monde   3, 16, 25, 31, 34–5, 36, 70, 77–8, 90, 114, 120, 127, 130, 163, 166, 180, 209, 228–31, 255, 256, 303, 306

Bedford, Arthur
   The Evil and Danger of Stage–Plays   305
   The Great Abuse of Musick   305
Bentley, Richard   157, 286
Berenstadt, Cuzzoni, and Senesino   184–5, 195
Bernacchi, Antonio   43
Bernardi, Francesco. *See* Senesino
Bertolli, Francesca   221
Bianconi, Lorenzo   36, 306
Bickham, George, "The Late Premier Minister"   290
Bingley, Lord (Thomas Benson)   74
bivalency (concept)   xiii, 2, 9, 130, 142, 269, 303, 304
Boileau-Despréaux, Nicolas   203–4, 240
Bolingbroke, Viscount (Henry St. John)   7, 10, 11, 75, 84, 93, 103, 112, 132, 133, 134, 150, 156, 168, 169, 231, 244, 249, 269, 281, 294, 307
   Dawley Farm   49
   early political career   49
   exile to France   11, 49, 50, 133
   ideas about English History   58–62
   organizes opposition   49–50
   political ideas   51–2, 55–8, 68, 312–13
      See also Bolingbroke, *Dissertation upon Parties, Idea of a Patriot King, Observations on Publick Affairs*, and *Remarks on the History of England*
   Dissertation upon Parties   58, 147
   Idea of a Patriot King   59–60, 110
   Observations on Publick Affairs   94
   Remarks on the History of England   57, 147, 202
Bononcini, Giovanni   27, 38, 207–8
   Griselda   113
   Il Muzio Scevola   311
Bordoni, Faustina. *See* Faustina
Boschi, Giuseppe Maria   199
Boswell, James   82
Bourdieu, Pierre   3–4, 27, 43, 304–5, 306
   See also capital and fields of production
Bowen, Thomas   119
Boydell, John, *Houghton Gallery*   178
Bramston, James, *The Man of Taste*   206–9

343

344   INDEX

Bredvold, Louis   62, 239
Britannia (allegorical figure)   143–4, 159, 160
British Journal   45, **89–90, 95–6**
Brooke, Henry   109
Browning, Reed   69
Brutus, Lucius Junius   189, 211, 212, 307
Buckingham, Duchess of (Catherine Sheffield)   5
Buckworth, Sir John   114
Burges, Colonel Elizeus   117–18
Burke, Joseph   182
Burlington, Countess of (Dorothy Boyle)   225
Burlington, Earl of (Richard Boyle)   5, 26, 74, 120, 183, 205, 206, 207, 224–5, 292, 298–9
Burney, Charles   24, 26, 82, 108, 125
Burney, Fanny, *Evelina*   6

Campbell, Colen   177
capital (cultural, social, economic)   4, 6
Caravaggio, *Job and His Daughters*   218
Carestini, Giovanni   22–21, 218
Carey, Henry   83, 125, 252
  Faustina: or the Roman Songstress   83
  Blunderella: or the Impertinent   215
Caroline, Queen   63–4, 104–6, 106, 144, 170, 225, 231, 236, 248, 254, 264
Carteret, James Lord   18–19, 21, 48, 49, 64, 104, 133, 158, 274, 277, 279
Catherine, Empress of Russia   178
Cato of Utica   45, 69–70, 309, 310
Cato the Censor   69
Cato's Letters   45–6, 57, 69, 168
Catonic (Old Whig) viewpoint   69–70, 81, 89, 93–4, 98, 313
The Censor Censur'd   46
The Champion (Henry Fielding)   53, 110
Chandos, Duke of (James Brydges)   205–6, 292
characteristic satire   229–30, 245
Characters: An Epistle to Alexander Pope Esq; and Mr. Whitehead   268
Charles I, King   57, 157
Charles II, King   36, 94, 247
Chesterfield, Earl of (Philip Dormer Stanhope)   49, 74, 101, 104, 109, 110, 111, 134, 158, 244, 266, 268, 269, 277, 281, 282, 296, 309
Cibber, Colley   71, 122, 170, 176, 180, 210, 254–5, 268, 282, 290
Cicero   69–70, 91, 92, 157, 309
  De Legibus   91

Ciceronian (Modern Whig) viewpoint   69–70, 89, 98, 313
Clive, Catherine ("Kitty")   156, 301, 302
Cobham, Lord (Sir Richard Temple, later Earl)   8, 49, 50, 104, 112, 205, 244, 268, 295, 298, 299
  organizes Patriot Opposition   101–3
Cobham's Cubs   102, 281
Cohen, Mitchell, *The Politics of Opera*   2
Coke, Thomas   11
Colley, Linda   33
  Britons: Forging the Nation   307–8
Collier, Jeremy   162
  A Short View of the ... English Stage   305
commerce, attitudes toward   75–8
Common Sense   47, 50, 53, 54, 110, **126**, 134, 135–6, **162, 174–5, 175–6**, 176, 178, 237, 282
Compton, Sir Spencer   63, 143, 228
Congreve, William, *The Way of the World*   302
Convention of the Pardo   138–9, 257
Cooke, Thomas, *The Candidates for the Bays*   171
Correggio, *Jupiter Embracing Io*   218
corruption
  charged against Walpole   169
  effects   168–9
  source of   75–7
Country Journal. See The Craftsman
Courteville, Ralph (Ralph Freeman)   65
Cowper, first Earl (William Cowper)   15, 44–5, 47, 286
  organizes opposition   44–5
Cowper, second Earl (William Cowper)   114, 118, 267, 287, 309
Coxe, William   235, 275
The Craftsman: or the Country Journal   47, **50–2**, 53–4, **54**, 58, **61, 71**, 71, **72**, 75, **82–3, 83, 89, 90**, 93–95, **94, 95**, 101, 110, 134, 136, 149, **172, 173–4**, 175, **196**, 201, 229, **241**, 244, **276**
  See also Viscount Bolingbroke
Craggs, Sir James (the elder)   18
Craggs, James (the younger)   14, 16, 18
Cromwell, Oliver   139, 140
Cuzzoni, Francesca   27, 37, 38, 41, 72, 73, 83, 97, 114, 117, 126, 182, 184, 185, 221, 232, 233, 299
Cyrus (of Persia)   91–2

Daily Advertiser   113, **120–1**
Daily Courant   190
Daily Gazetteer   64, **69, 86**, 110, 136, 150, 174, **175**, 210, 231, 249–50, 268, 277, 280

D'Anvers, Caleb 51, 90, 173, 190, 231
   See also The Craftsman
Davenant, William, *The Siege of Rhodes* 247
Davis, Mary, *The Accomplished Rake* 92
De La Warr, Lord (John West) 114, 267
de Walmoden, Amalie Sophie Marianne 248
del Pò, Anna Strada 114, 221
Delany, Mary 43
Dennis, John xiv, 75, 81–2, 93, 163, 168,
   187, 313
   Vice and Luxury Publick Mischiefs 81–2
Depredations Crisis 8, 9, 126, 134–8, 254, 259
Dickinson, H. T. 56
dissent (dissenters) 15, 44, 70, 312
Dodington, George "Bubb" 143, 144,
   171–2, 228
Dodsley, Robert 266
Donne, John 245
Dorman, Joseph
   *The Female Rake: or a Modern Fine
      Lady* 224
   The Rake of Taste 223–4
Dryden, John 160, 165, 241, 247, 295, 298
Duck, Stephen 170, 254
Dulness xvii, 8, 9, 159, 169, 174, 176, 180,
   184–91, 195, 199, 200, 212, 245, 281–2,
   284–6, 288, 289–91, 302, 303
   westward progress 186–8
Duncombe, William, *Junius Brutus* 211–12

Edward I, King 62
Edward III, King 62, 147
Edward the Confessor 147
Elizabeth I, Queen 57, 59, 62, 110, 139, 140,
   143, 147, 160, 245, 262, 278
Ernst August, elector 22
Essex, Earl of (William Capel) 118, 124
Excise taxation scheme 8, 63, 75, 99, 99–
   101, 112, 131, 189, 190, 210, 239, 252, 262

False Taste 8, 147, 165–7
Farinelli (Carlo Broschi) 8, 27, 42, 54, 86,
   96–7, 97–8, 108–9, 114, 117–26, 130, 135,
   151, 193, 195, 210, 215, 219–22, 221–2,
   223, 224, 226–7, 240, 251–2, 255–6,
   258–9, 267–8, 269, 287, 301–2, 303–4,
   305, 310
   benefit concert 120, 122, 221, 251
   departure and residence in Madrid 54,
      124–6, 135–6, 255–6, 261, 268
   recruitment and arrival in England 118
   sings before royal family 118–19
   visits to Paris 123, 124, 135
Farnese, Elisabeth, Queen of Spain 124–5

Faustina (Faustina Bordoni) 27, 37, 38, 41,
   72, 73, 83, 97, 117, 233
The Festival of the Golden Rump 134
Fielding, Henry 134, 177, 191–5, 285
   personal politics 195
   The Author's Farce 191–2, 285
   The Champion 53, 110
   *The Historical Register . . . and Euridice
      Hiss'd* 192
   Pasquin 192–4, 285
   Tom Thumb 171, 173, 174
fields of production 3, 304–5
Financial Revolution 7, 46, 56, 75–6, 81,
   95, 202, 312
   consequences of 59, 95, 168
Fitzgerald, Thomas, *Folly* 284
Fog's Weekly Journal 47, 54, **83, 96–7,
   97–8, 119, 137 n.25, 172–3,** 174, 210, 237,
   310, 313
Four Satires 258–9
Frederick (Prince of Wales) 8, 60, 74,
   102–9, 110–12, 133, 142, 144, 145, 146,
   148, 149, 150, 151–2, 154, 155–6, 240,
   243, 244, 263, 268, 269, 275, 277, 276,
   279, 292–6, 299, 302, 313
   arts and music patronage 107–10, 295
   as figurehead of Patriot Opposition 60,
      103, 105–6
   as Patriot King 112, 296
   courts public opinion 106–7
   relations with father 104–6, 276, 277, 293
   relations with Handel 107–8
   Temple of Parnassus project 293–4
Free Briton 101, **122,** 210
Freeholders Journal 47, 57
Free-Thinker **32–3**

Gaius Verres 157
Gay, John 50
   The Beggar's Opera 38, 41, 62, 71–4, 117,
      122, 123, 211, 212, 226, 241, 264
Gentleman's Magazine 137
George I, King 10, 13–14, 16, 19, 22, 24, 25,
   27, 49, 63, 66, 87, 93, 170, 263, 311
George II (as King) 11, 16, 58, 63–4, 103,
   104–5, 109, 170, 173, 188, 230–1, 243, 246–7,
   248, 254, 256, 263, 268, 269, 277, 293
George II (as Prince of Wales), relations
   with father 13–16, 24, 24, 33
Gibraltar, Britain and Spain dispute over
   86–89
Gibson, Bishop Edmund 144, 190, 214, 253
Gilbert, Thomas 103, 109, 253–8, 299
   The First Satire of Juvenal Imitated 253,
      257–8

346 INDEX

Gilbert, Thomas (*cont.*)
  A Panegyric on a Court 253, 254
  A View of the Town 253, 254
  The World Unmask'd 253, 254–6, 299
Gilliver, Lawton 155, 197, 200, 223, 253
Gilpin, William 166
Gin Act 133
Glorious Revolution 58, 62, 66, 67–8, 69,
  76, 147, 202, 308
Glover, Richard 103, 109
Goldgar, Bertrand 206
Goldsmith, M. M. 77
Gordon, Thomas, *The Character of an
  Independent Whig* 70
Gothic north, myth of the 60–1, 141–2,
  145–6, 147, 159, 202
Goupy, Joseph 293
The Grand Remonstrance 156–7
Greene, Donald 227, 242, 263
Greig, Hannah, *The Beau Monde* 34–35
Grenville, George 102
Grenville, James 102
Grenville, Richard (later second Earl
  Temple) 102
Griselda (Bononcini) 113
Grub-street Journal 52–3, **53 n.32,** 54, 170,
  171, **177,** 193–4, **199–203,** 313
Gunn, J. A. W. 66

Habermas, Jürgen, *Structural Transformation of the Public Sphere* 6
Hacking, Ian 2, 303–4
Haddock, Admiral Nicholas 138–9, 272–4
Hammond, James 103
Handel, George Frideric (principal
  mentions) 5, 9, 26, 32, 35–36, 38, 42,
  73, 96, 101, 105, 108–9, 110, 113–14, 126,
  127, 153–4, 156, 161, 197, 208, 213, 221–2,
  226, 232, 233, 256, 289, 291–4, 296–302
  and Frederick, Prince of Wales 107–8
  and Ministry 297
  as British Worthy 292, 293–4, 296–302
  Ireland, trip to 127, 291
  Acis and Galatea 292
  Alexander's Feast 293, 300
  Ariodante 293
  Atalanta 293
  Deborah 99, 213
  Deidamia 127, 303
  Esther 154, 208–9, 214, 292
  Flavio 185
  Giove in Argo 126
  Imeneo 127
  Israel in Egypt 292
  Jephtha 292

Joseph and His Brothers 129, 161, 299
  See also under Miller, James
  Lothario 43
  Messiah 127, 291
  Il Muzio Scevola 311
  Radamisto 16
  Rinaldo 25, 153
  Saul 292, 300–1
  Scipione 311
  Semele 129, 292
  Semiramide 114
  Sing unto God 293
  Utrecht *Te Deum* and *Jubilate* 10
  Water Music 15
Handel–Heidegger partnership 5, 37, 41–3
Hanoverian Succession 10, 22, 33, 49, 57, 278
Harcourt, Simon (Viscount) 286
Harcourt, Simon (second Viscount) 287
Harding, Richard 273
Hardwicke 271, 275, 279
harlequinades 3, 162, 183, 186, 187, 237, 305
Harley, Robert (Earl of Oxford) 64, 299
Harris, James 299
Hasse, Johann, *Artaserse* 119, 120, 221, 281
Haymarket theatre, capacity 32
Heidegger, John Jacob (James) 5, 22, 24,
  26, 41, 42, 126, 183, 186, 197, 208, 233,
  258–9, 298
  See also Handel–Heidegger partnership
Henry III, King 147
Henry V, King 47, 62, 159
Hertford, Countess of (Frances Thynne)
  148, 149
Hervey, John Lord 65, 69, 71, 84, 101, 190,
  268, 277
  Memoirs 104, 105 n.26, 107, 292
Hill, Aaron 109, 141, 252
  Handel, writes to 153
  ideas on drama 151
  literary activities 150–2
  Alzira 151
  Athelwold 151
  Caesar 152
  Hengist and Horsa 154
  The Prompter **121–2,** 151, 152, 154
  Tears of the Muses 142, 152–4
  music in 153–4
  Zara 151
Hirsch, E. D. 7
Hoadly, Bishop Benjamin 65
Hogarth, William 123, 180, 181–5, 216–22
  "The Countess's Levee" (from Hogarth,
    Marriage à la Mode) 216–19
  Masquerades and Operas 181–3, 195
  A Rake's Progress 219, 251

INDEX   347

"The Rake's Levee" (from *A Rake's Progress*)   119–20, 218–22
Horace (and Horatian satire)   8, 163, 173, 195–8, 228, 229, 239–41, 246,–7, 248, 249, 250, 251–4, 308–9
   Ars Poetica   197, 247, 299
   Carmen Saeculare   156
Hosier, Admiral Francis   88, 143, 271–3
Houghton Hall   177, 206
Hume, David   82
Hume, Robert D.   8, 23, 31, 195
Hunter, David   6–7

Jacob, Hildebrand   167
Jacobites (Jacobitism)   11, 12, 15, 19, 20, 23, 44, 46, 47, 49, 52, 57, 63, 65, 103, 112, 132, 228
James II, King   62, 69
Jenkins, Captain Robert   137
Jennens, Charles   116
Johnson, Samuel   52, 62–3, 82, 109, 180, 237, 240, 263–4
   on Thomson, *Britannia*   144
   on Thomson, *Liberty*   145
   London   52, 262–3
Johnson, Samuel, of Cheshire, *Hurlothrumbo*   173, 174
Jones, Inigo   299
Jones, Erasmus, *Luxury, Pride, and Vanity*   305
Julius Caesar   45
Juvenal (and Juvenalian satire)   8, 51, 96, 97, 196, 226, 228, 229, 239–41, 244, 253, 256, 257–9, 262, 267, 308

Keene, Benjamin   124, 138
Kelly, George   20
Kent, William   177, 180, 183, 294, 299
King, John (second Baron King)   288
King, Peter (Baron King)   287
Knight, Robert   258–9
Kramnick, Isaac   76, 312

The Ladies of Pleasure   215
The Lady of Taste: or, F[arinelli]'s Levee   215
Langford, Paul   77
Law, William, *The Absolute Unlawfulness of the Stage-Entertainment*   305
Layer, Christopher   20
Lee, Nathaniel, *Lucius Junius Brutus*   309
Leeds, dowager Duchess of (Juliana Osborne)   114, 119, 120
Leeds, Duke of (Thomas Osborne)   114, 120, 123
liberty
   and the arts   167–9
   northward progress of   61, 145–9, 152

Liberty (goddess, allegoric figure)   142, 145, 146, 147, 148, 159
   progress of   141–2, 145–7, 149, 150, 152, 159
Licensing Act   134, 151, 263, 282
Livy   173
Lock, F. R.   263–4
Locke, John   46
London Journal   45, **69, 72–3, 85**
London Magazine   307
Longinus   84, 197
Louis XIV   36, 86, 88, 172, 175, 176, 238, 309
Lynch, Francis, *The Independent Patriot: or Musical Folly*   224–7
Lyttelton, George   102–3, 105, 110, 133, 149, 158, 175, 243, 244, 250, 263, 266, 294, 295

Machiavelli, Nicolo   46, 57, 60, 62, 75, 78, 81, 96, 312
Machiavellian moment   xiv, 60, 90–1, 92, 110, 142, 147, 150, 157–8, 168, 259
Mack, Maynard   188–9, 242–3, 289
Maecenas   173, 231, 248
Magna Carta   62
Mallet, David   103, 109, 110, 150
   Alfred   152
Manchester, Earl of (Charles Montagu)   26
Mandeville, Bernard   79–82, 85, 93, 312
   paradox of vice and virtue   79–80, 85, 312
   The Fable of the Bees   79–81
   The Grumbling Hive   79
Manning, Francis   227, 234
   Of Business and Retirement   234
Mar, Earl of (John Mar)   12
Marchmont, Earl of (Alexander Hume-Campbell)   101, 158, 280–1, 244, 266
Marlborough, Duchess of (Sarah Churchill)   157–8, 275, 280
Marlborough, Duke of (John Churchill)   10, 13, 158, 259
Marlborough, younger Duchess of (Henrietta Godolphin)   208
Marshall, Ashley   191
Marxism   34
Mattheson, Johann, *Der musikalische Patriot*   7, 33
Michelangelo   146, 183
   Jupiter and Ganymede   218
Middlesex, Lord (Charles Sackville, later Earl of Dorset), establishes opera company   127–9
Milhous, Judith   23, 31, 32, 38
Miller, James   103, 109, 125, 141, 142–50, 155, 195–203, 269
   Are These Things So?   155
   The Art of Life   299–301

348   INDEX

Miller, James (*cont.*)
  Harlequin-Horace   155, 156, 158, 195–203,
    250, 298
  An Hospital for Fools   301
  Joseph and His Brethren   129, 161, 299
  Man of Taste   167, 209–10
  Of Politeness   156, 215–16
  Seasonable Reproof   155, 250–3
  The Universal Passion   156, 302
  The Year Forty-one   142, 155–61
    music in   159–60
Milton, John   110, 160
Mist's Weekly Journal   52–3, 54, **171–2**, 237,
  306, 313
Mitchell, Joseph   177
The Modern Englishman   260
The Modern Poet   210–12
Monticelli, Angelo Maria   179
The Motion   160, 274–5
Mucius Scaevola   310
"La Muscovita"   127
Muses   152–4
music in Hill, *Tears of the Muses*   153–4
music in Miller, *The Year Forty-One*   159–60
music in Thomson, *Liberty*   147–7
Il Muzio Scevola (Amadei, Bononcini,
  Handel)   311

Namier, Sir Lewis   73
Nash, Beau   105
Negri, Maria   221
Nero, Emperor   173, 267–8, 309
Newcastle, Duchess of (Henrietta
  Godolphin)   5
Newcastle, Duke of (Thomas Pelham-
  Hollis)   15, 27, 48, 118, 190, 231, 271, 275,
  279
Newcomb, Thomas   212–15, 227, 231–4
  Manners of the Age   231–4
  *A Miscellaneous Collection of Original
    Poems*   231
  The Woman of Taste   212–15
  The Woman of Taste. In a Second Epistle
    214
Newton, Isaac   13, 17, 153, 180
Nicolini (Nicola Grimaldi)   22, 117
Norman Conquest   57, 68
Norman Yoke   62, 68–9
Norris, Admiral John   272
North and Grey, Lord (William North)   19, 20
North, Sir Dudley, *Discourses of Trade*   78
Nottingham, Earl of (Daniel Finch)   11

Occasional Conformity and Schism Acts   15
Old Whig   **123**

Oldmixon, John   168, 203–4
Onslow, Arthur   19, 20–21, 144, 231
opera
  as cultural product   2–4, 9, 43
  as *instrumentum regni*   36
  attendance, conditions for   4–6
  audience   3–4, 31–3, 142, 304, 313–14
  audience, social class of (analyzed)   34–5
  criticism and charges against   1, 2–3,
    168, 303
  financing of   24–5, 27, 43
  resumption of   16, 24
  royal patronage of   170, 263
  subscribers   127
Opera of the Nobility (Nobility Opera)   8,
  96, 109, 114–19, 124, 122, 125, 126, 127,
  221, 267, 287, 292
  directors   114–15
  founding   113–19
"The Opera House or the Italian Eunuch's
  Glory" (after Hogarth)   122–3
oppositions, political
  effectiveness   63
  losses and disillusionment of   279–81
  polemics and tactics   51–2, 54–5
  See also Bolingbroke, political ideas of;
    Patriot opposition; *The Craftsman*;
    Walpole, charges against
Ormonde, Duke of (James Butler)   11, 19
Orrery, Earl of (Charles Boyle)   20
Oxford, Earl of (Robert Harley)   10, 11–12,
  299
  See also Robert Harley

Paget, Colonel Thomas   120
Palinurus   230, 289
Palladio, Andrea   146, 299, 308
Parker, George (second Earl of
  Macclesfield)   287
Parker, Thomas (Earl of Macclesfield)   287
Pasquin "Vivetur Stultitia"   194–5
pasticcio   42, 114, 283
Patriot King   8, 57, 59, 60, 110, 112, 142, 150,
  156, 161, 242, 296, 297
Patriot Opposition (Patriots)   8, 101–2,
  104, 109, 112
  formation of   101–3
  Ministry's charges against   111–12
Peachum, Polly   72, 73, 264
Peerage Bill   15–16, 44
Pelham, Henry   231
Perceval, Sir John (later Earl of Egmont)
  100, 119
Pericles   91
Persius   258

Philip V, King of Spain   88, 124–5, 135–8, 139
Pitt, James (Francis Osborne)   65
Pitt, Thomas   102
Pitt, William (later Earl of Chatham)   102, 105, 268, 277, 281
Plato   91, 92
Plumb, J. H.   11, 101, 178
  on Bolingbroke   60
  on *Craftsman*   54
  on Walpole   19, 21, 278
Plunkett, John   20
Pocock, J. G .A.   67
Polwarth, Lord (Hugh-Hume Campbell   158, 280
Polybius   62
Pompey   93
Pope, Alexander (principal mentions)   50, 53, 97, 102–3, 105, 109, 110, 150, 155, 165, 189, 190–1, 195, 198, 231, 235, 242–50, 254, 256, 263, 266, 268, 298–300, 300
  and Patriot Opposition   295
  attacked by Ministry   248–50
  disillusion with Opposition   279–80
  turns to Opposition, 244
  villa at Twickenham   243
  Dialogues (*Epilogues to the Satires*)   155, 249–50, 266–7, 280, 296
  The Dunciad (all versions)   8, 9, 53, 62, 157, 159, 160, 161, 167, 170–1, 177, 184–9, 195, 237, 242, 267, 281, 281, 289, 294, 302, 303
  The Dunciad. An Heroic Poem   184
  The Dunciad in Four Books   242
  The Dunciad Variorum   184, 189, 289
  The New Dunciad   9, 161, 281–302, 303
  Epistle to Augustus   246–7
  Epistle to Bathurst   76, 223, 238, 265
  Epistle to Bolingbroke   248
  Epistle to Burlington (*Of False Taste*)   166, 177, 205, 238, 261
  Essay on Man   197, 250
  Fortescue   244
  The Impertinent   245–6
  Odyssey   177, 244
  One Thousand Seven Hundred and Forty   296
  One Thousand Seven Hundred and Thirty Eight   265
  Peri Bathous; or the Art of Sinking in Poetry   197
  Preface to Addison, Cato   311
Popple, William   151
Porpora, Nicola   109, 114, 116, 221
  Arianna in Nasso   116

Porteus, Captain John   134
Portland, Duke of (Henry Bentinck)   309
Porto Bello   88, 143, 271–2, 279
The Pretender (James Edward Stuart, the "Old Pretender")   12, 19, 47, 49, 132
The Prompter (Aaron Hill)   **121–2**, 151, 152, 154
Publick Spirit   1, 47, 52, 57, 59, 75, 68, 69, 77, 81, 82, 91, 92, 94, 110, 141, 142, 149, 150, 238, 277
Pulteney, Daniel   49–50
Pulteney, William (later Earl of Bath)   10, 14, 16, 48–50, 64, 74, 104, 112, 133, 158, 160, 169, 171, 189, 190, 243, 268, 269, 275, 276, 277, 279, 296

Quadruple Alliance   14, 87–8
Quintilian   309

Ralph, James   166
Raphael   146, 183, 299
Raymond, Sir Robert (Baron Raymond)   287
Raymond, Sir Robert (second Baron Raymond)   288
Rich, John   183, 186, 196, 236
Rich, Lady (Elizabeth Griffith or Lady Bingley)   119, 120, 222
Richardson, Jonathan   164
Richmond, Duke of (Charles Lennox)   114, 117, 120, 231, 311
Richmond, H. W.   273
Ripley, Thomas   177
The Rival Wives   264
The Rival Wives Answer'd   265
Rolli, Paolo   42, 311
Roman Republic   45, 46, 53, 76, 84, 95, 145–6, 168, 308, 311
Roubiliac, François   296
Royal Academy of Music   4–5, 7–8, 16, 22–43, 70, 73, 90, 93, 114, 127, 179, 183, 184, 205, 208, 230, 263, 313
  audience   31–33, 35–7, 306
  chartering of   24–7
  continuation of   38–41
  decline and collapse   38, 41, 72, 117
  governance   27
  organization   35–7
  patrons   35–7
  politics in   23–4, 33
  shareholders and subscribers   27–32
The Royal Convert   167
Rumbold, Valerie   288
Rundle, Thomas   144
Rysbrack, John Michael   299

350   INDEX

Sabrina (Pescetti)   124
Sandys Samuel   49, 55, 274, 277
satire
   characteristical   229–30, 245
   Horatian   229, 249
      See also Horace
   Juvenalian   229, 249
      See also Juvenal
   proper nature of   249
The Satirist. A Satire   269
Savage, Richard   177
Saxon past, mythic   60–1, 68, 142, 145, 202
Scheemakers, Peter   299
Scipio Africanus Major   310
Scipione (Handel)   311
Scriblerus Club (Scriblerians)   50, 76, 110,
   112, 163–4, 176, 189, 191, 195
The Secession   139
Second Royal Academy. *See* Handel–
   Heidegger partnership
Senesino (Francesco Bernardi)   27, 38, 41,
   42, 43, 72, 73, 101, 113, 117, 126, 127, 183,
   184, 185, 195, 208, 214, 218, 221–2, 261, 287
Septennial Act   12, 44, 131
Septennial Parliaments   131–2, 157, 209
session poems   283–4
Settle, Elkanah   185–8
Shaftesbury, fourth Earl of (Anthony
   Ashley Cooper)   42
Shaftesbury, third Earl of (Anthony Ashley
   Cooper)   165–6, 168, 309
Shakespeare, William, *Richard III*   138
Sherburn, George   206, 291
Shippen, William   49
   Remarks Critical and Political   228–9
Sidney, Algernon   46, 81
Siface (Giovanni Francesco Grossi)   117
Skerrett, Maria (Molly)   264–5
"Slavery"   137–8
Smith, Adam   82
Smith, Consul Joseph   118
South Sea Company
   and King of Spain   138–9
   South Sea Bubble and scandal   17–19,
      25, 45–6, 55, 84, 173, 174, 199, 259
   trade in West Indies   134–40, 258–9
Spanish depredations   8, 109, 126, 134–5,
   135–7, 143, 210–11, 254, 256, 261–2, 263,
   268, 279
Sparta   92
The Spectator   163, 214, 232
Stair, Earl of (John Dalrymple)   101
Stanhope, James (Viscount then Earl)
   10–11, 13–15, 16, 17–19, 87

Stanhope–Sunderland ministry   14, 17–19,
   21, 44–5
Steele, Richard   xiv, 16, 168, 298
Steffani, Agostino   22
Steiner, George   162
Stowe   102, 299
Strafford, Earl of (Thomas Wentworth)   11, 19
Sunderland, Earl of (Charles Spencer)   13–
   19, 158
Sunderland–Stanhope ministry. *See*
   Stanhope–Sunderland ministry.
Sutton, Sir Robert   258
Swift, Jonathan   11, 50, 56, 62, 64, 76, 110,
   171, 180, 184, 185, 189, 228, 229, 231, 237,
   243, 247, 277, 298
   The Intelligencer   72
Swiney, Owen   117
Sybaris   92

Tacitus   96
   Germania   141
Talbot, Charles (Lord Chancellor)   101,
   144, 149
Talbot, William   144
Tarquinius Superbus, Roman king   212
taste (general faculty)   8, 164–7
Taste, or Burlington Gate   206–7
The Tatler   163, 298
Temple, William   307
Theobald (Tibbald), Lewis   185–8, 189,
   190, 282, 284
   Shakespeare Restored   186
Thompson, Edward   266
Thomson, James   103, 109, 110, 143–50, 269
   Agamemnon   150
   Britannia   143–4, 149, 150, 160
   Edward and Eleonora   150
   Liberty   142, 144–50, 152, 159
      music in   147–8
      oppositional stance of   149–50
   To the Memory of Sir Isaac Newton   143, 177
   The Seasons   143, 144, 148, 149
   Sophonisba   144
Tiberius, Emperor   91, 173
Timotheus   92
Titus Vespasianus   310
Tories (Tory party)   10–12, 14, 15, 19, 20,
   21, 33, 44, 49, 58, 59, 63, 66, 67, 76, 131, 133,
   139, 199, 233, 239, 269, 274, 280–1, 300
Townshend, Charles (Viscount
   Townshend)   10, 13–16, 19, 20, 21, 33,
   64, 234–6
Townshend–Walpole ministry. *See*
   Walpole-Townshend ministry

INDEX 351

Treaties of Vienna 88
Treaty of Seville 134
Triennial Act 12
Triennial Parliaments 55, 57, 131–2
Triple Alliance 14, 87–8
True Briton (Philip Wharton) 47, 57

Utrecht, Treaty of 13, 86, 134

Valentini (Valentino Urbani) 117
van der Gucht, Gerard
    frontispiece to James Bramston, *The
        Man of Taste* 204
Vanbrugh, Sir John 26, 27, 180
Varey, Simon 56, 63
Vernon, Admiral Edward 271–4, 279
Vertue, George 178
Virgil 173, 203, 205, 231, 305

Walker, Thomas 36, 306
Walpole, Lady Catherine 5, 152, 264
Walpole, Horace 157, 179, 222
    Ædes Walpolianæ 178
Walpole, Horatio (Horace) 65, 201
Walpole, Sir Robert
    and Alexander Pope 244
    art collection, sale of 178
    as art collector 178
    as book collector 178
    as Harlequin 201
    as hero of *Dunciad* 188, 281, 286, 289–90
    as music and opera patron 179, 230
    as Palinurus 230–1
    Atterbury plot, resolution of 20–1
    charges against 51–2, 57, 75–6, 82–4,
        84, 93, 109, **170–6,** 189–90, 201, 210–11,
        212, 244, 246, 257, 262–3
    created Earl of Orford 276
    early life 176–7
    historians' assessment of 19, 21, 277–8
    knighthoods 48, 171, 172, 201, 228
    literary patronage 177–8
    loses control of Commons 275–7
    ministry, defended 64–7, 84–6
    motion for his removal 274–5
    on declaration of war with Spain 140
    opera patronage 5
    questions patriotism 111

resignation 276
rise to power 7, 63–4
ruler of the Dunces 189–90
satirized 55, 201
secures power 48
South Sea Scandal, resolution of 18–19
Walpole-Townshend ministry 19, 21, 45–6
Walsh, William, *Hospital of Fools* 301
War of Jenkins' Ear 8, 9, 126
    army-navy campaigns 271–4
    causes 109, 135–8
War of the Dunces 184, 189, 200
War of the Spanish Succession 10, 22, 86
Warton, Joseph 228, 280
Weekly Journal, or British Gazette 33, 52, **73**
Weidemann, Charles 218
Weinbrot, Howard 228, 229, 253
Wentworth, General Thomas 272–3
Westminster Journal 53
Wharton, Duke of (Philip Wharton) 15, 47
    True Briton 47, 57
Whig Schism 12–17, 33
Whigs (Whig party) xiv, xvii, 8, 10–12,
    13, 14, 15–16, 20, 26, 33, 45, 49, 58, 59,
    63, 66–8
    party prinicples 12–13, 15, 45–7, 66–8,
        75, 81, 84–5, 95–6, 98, 103, 131–2, 202,
        312–13
Whitehead, Paul 103, 110, 189–91, 266–8, 269
    Manners 266–8, 281, 287
    State Dunces 189–90, 289
Wild, Jonathan 248
William III, King 147, 212
William the Conqueror 62
Williams, Aubrey 237
Wilmington, Earl of (Spencer Compton) 101
Wilson, Richard 105
Wyndham, Charles (later second Earl of
    Egremont) 118
Wyndham, Sir William 49, 104, 132, 133,
    139, 280

Yonge, Sir William 65, 84
Young, Edward 172, 177, 227, 228, 231, 245,
    289
    The Instalment 172, 228
    Love of Fame: The Universal Passion
        228–31, 289

Titles listed here were originally published
under the series title *Music in Britain, 1600–1900*
ISSN 1752-1904

Lectures on Musical Life: William Sterndale Bennett
edited by Nicholas Temperley, with Yunchung Yang

John Stainer: A Life in Music
Jeremy Dibble

*The Pursuit of High Culture: John Ella and
Chamber Music in Victorian London*
Christina Bashford

Thomas Tallis and his Music in Victorian England
Suzanne Cole

The Consort Music of William Lawes, 1602–1645
John Cunningham

Life After Death: The Viola da Gamba in Britain from Purcell to Dolmetsch
Peter Holman

*The Musical Salvationist: The World of Richard Slater (1854–1939)
'Father of Salvation Army Music'*
Gordon Cox

*British Music and Literary Context
Artistic Connections in the Long Nineteenth Century*
Michael Allis

New titles published under the series title *Music in Britain, 1600–2000*
ISSN 2053-3217

Hamilton Harty: Musical Polymath
Jeremy Dibble

Thomas Morley: Elizabethan Music Publisher
Tessa Murray

*The Advancement of Music in Enlightenment England:
Benjamin Cooke and the Academy of Ancient Music*
Tim Eggington

George Smart and Nineteenth-Century London Concert Life
John Carnelley

The Lives of George Frideric Handel
David Hunter

Musicians of Bath and Beyond: Edward Loder (1809–1865) and his Family
edited by Nicholas Temperley

Conductors in Britain, 1870–1914: Wielding the Baton at the Height of Empire
Fiona M. Palmer

Ernest Newman: A Critical Biography
Paul Watt

The Well-Travelled Musician:
John Sigismond Cousser and Musical Exchange in Baroque Europe
Samantha Owens

Music in the West Country: Social and Cultural History Across an English Region
Stephen Banfield

British Musical Criticism and Intellectual Thought, 1850–1950
edited by Jeremy Dibble and Julian Horton

Composing History: National Identities
and the English Masque Revival, 1860–1920
Deborah Heckert

With Mornefull Musique: Funeral Elegies in Early Modern England
K. Dawn Grapes

Music for St Cecilia's Day: From Purcell to Handel
Bryan White

Before the Baton: Musical Direction and
Conducting in Stuart and Georgian Britain
Peter Holman

Organ-building in Georgian and Victorian England:
The Work of Gray & Davison, 1772–1890
Nicholas Thistlethwaite

Musical Exchange between Britain and Europe, 1500–1800:
Essays in Honour of Peter Holman
edited by John Cunningham and Bryan White

The Symphonic Poem in Britain, 1850–1950
edited by Michael Allis and Paul Watt

Music in North-East England, 1500–1800
edited by Stephanie Carter, Kirsten Gibson, Roz Southey

British Music, Musicians and Institutions, c. 1630–1800:
Essays in Honour of Harry Diack Johnstone
Edited by Peter Lynan and Julian Rushton

John Gunn: Musician Scholar in Enlightenment Britain
George Kennaway

Exhibitions, Music and the British Empire
Sarah Kirby

Opera and Politics in Queen Anne's Britain, 1705–1714
Thomas McGeary

The Life and Music of Elizabeth Maconchy
Erica Siegel

Music in Edwardian London
Simon McVeigh

Printed and bound by CPI Group (UK) Ltd, Croydon, CR0 4YY
19/11/2024

14595408-0005